To *Tarewin Robinson*

Dear friend, as you know, I am dedicated to you not only **residing**
you can be and **reaching your full potential in this life**. I want you
Thank you for your decision to seek God with all your heart and sou
practicing one of His character traits for 21 days. II Peter 1:4-11 giv
for this truly enjoyable pursuit. The calendar below will help you keep on this schedule even with all the press
of business and life. I am thrilled about what I know God will do with your life and service. He will surely
bless you for your diligent dedication (Hebrews 11:6) to seek first the Kingdom and His righteousness.
(Matthew 6:33) and you will, in deed, become a vessel of honor for Him. For this to happen, we can't overlook
the importance of being faithful to a local church and being in covenant with your finances. Malachi 3:8-12

It would be a great blessing if you would write once a year and let me know your progress as a testimony to
Him. In His name,   Your servant,

Winston Menzies

2018	2019	2020	2021
2022	2023	2024	2025
2026	2027	2028	2029

The
CHARACTER TRAIT
Journal

BY WINSTON MENZIES

Xulon
ELITE

What others are saying about
The Character Trait Journal

I recently read a book entitled *The Noticer Returns* in which the author discussed the need for a gold standard for raising our youth. He was teaching a group of young couples who, like so many today, were trying to juggle their efforts between raising their children and pursuing the American dream. He never identifies the gold standard but makes it known that we definitely need to find it because of the encroachment of worldly values into the lives of our children. Statistics show that of all the young people of high school age presently engaged in church, 70% will be gone by age 22[1] and 80% by the time they are 29.[2] These figures are alarming to say the least. In my mind, this gold standard should encompass a vehicle that would enable parents to engraft the godly character and ideals of our Founding Fathers into the hearts and minds of their children. Shortly after I finished this book, I was given a copy of a writing which I believe could be the "Silver Bullet" to answer this great need. It is a book by my longtime friend, Winston Menzies, which teaches the principals and ideals of which I speak. The other part of the equation is parents who will take this tool and use it to teach their children a higher and more noble standard than they would know otherwise. The book I speak and feel so strongly about is *The Character Trait Journal.* It contains over twelve years of material that will enrich the hearts and minds of our youth and do the same for the parents who teach it. I sincerely believe this journal is a "Godsend" for such a time as this.

Herbert A. Peavy, Jr., President
The Horizon Foundation

––––––––––––––

Winston Menzies, is a master teacher, who has provided us with a life-changing manual filled with the practical, foundational building-blocks of character. Each Character quality is a conversation with "life coach" Winston Menzies, whereupon you can construct your life's foundation. Arrange the traits in the priority you want to first apply. Do you want a life of adventure, true success and fulfilled dreams without regret or sorrow? Take a few minutes each day to study *The Character Trait Journal,* then practice the application as he instructs and your life will be transformed into the life you've always dreamed of. But don't stop with yourself! When read together as a family, perhaps at the dinner table, *The Character Trait Journal* will anchor your children in the practical applications of character. It will reward you with a generation who can grow into mighty oak trees! Thank you, Brother Winston for this timeless, priceless gift of character training!

Bob Bird
The Lighthouse of Hope Church, Pastor
Bird Family Insulation, President

––––––––––––––

[1] *Theology in the Raw,* Ranier Research9/2015 The Horizon Foundation

[2] Ibid, Barna

Winston Menzies' new book, *The Character Trait Journal*, helps parents do something really special for their children by giving them a bite sized, practical way to build biblical character into their lives. It does so in easy to read chapters that help you teach your kids not the "what" to be: cute, funny or popular but the "who" to be: grateful, brave, persistent. It teaches them who they can be in Christ. If character counts, and it does, *The Character Trait Journal* is not only a must read but it is also a must have tool for every parent who wants to gain character personally, as well as raise the next generation of faithful, successful, God honoring Americans.

Brant Frost IV, President
First Liberty Building & Loan

———————————————

The Character Trait Journal, written by my friend and fellow minister in the Gospel of God's grace, Winston Menzies, is both timely and much needed. It seems we find ourselves ministering to a generation that has moved far, far away from the Biblical moorings that have, in the past, produced men and women of great character. It is not that there are none today who have pinned their worth to the moorings of Biblical character, but far less. There are surely not as many as are needed to stem the tide of the ever-encroaching characterlessness that has besieged our nation, yea, even our world.
It is for this reason *The Character Trait Journal* is so needed. For those who read, contemplate and strive to put these character traits to practical use in their daily living, I am persuaded that they will be of immeasurable help. Each trait is written from personal knowledge and the deep experience of having seen the blessings of God upon their application. To this end, all who will read and heed them will likewise be blessed!
It is my prayer that this work will be widely used of God to challenge everyone who comes in contact with it to live a life of true character. I pray that they may attain to that which was said about our Lord in Luke 2:52: "And Jesus increased in wisdom and stature, and in favor with God and man." Surely this is the best measure of the results of Biblical character, and where properly applied, it would rescue the present generation and save the next.

Richard A Stucke, Pastor
Gethsemane Baptist Church

The CHARACTER TRAIT Journal

Other Books and CD Series by the Author

The ABC's of
Winning Phone Etiquette
You Can Master

Being God's Man
Booklet and Five Audio Presentations

Called To Lead
Three Audio Presentations

How To Build A Debt-Free Home
Booklet and Three Audio Presentations

How to Buy A Used Car

Prudence
Ten Audio Presentations

Secrets of Prayer That Avails Much
Booklet and four Audio Presentations

The Fulfilled Life In Christ
Book and Four Audio Presentations

The Spirit of Texas

The Success Secret of the Ages

Total Victory
Four Audio Presentations

Walking in Divine Favor
Five Audio Presentations

All can be found at:
WinstonMenzies.com

The
CHARACTER TRAIT
Journal

BY WINSTON MENZIES

Published by Creative Publishing Co.
P.O. Drawer 90 Conyers, GA 30012
WinstonMenzies.com
CreativePublishing.us
Thecharactertraitjournal.com

Published with assistance from Xulon Press

Copyright © 2016 by Winston Menzies

The Character Trait Journal
by Winston Menzies

Printed in the United States of America.

ISBN 9781498476232

All rights reserved solely by the author. The author guarantees all contents are original and do not infringe upon the legal rights of any other person or work. All artwork herein was either drawn by or commissioned by the author and is copyrighted by him. No part of this book may be reproduced or transmitted in any form or by any means, electronic or mechanical, including photocopying and recording, or by any information storage and retrieval system, without permission in writing from the publisher, except for brief quotations in critical reviews and articles. The views expressed in this book are not necessarily those of the publisher.

Unless otherwise indicated, Scripture quotations taken from the New King James Version (NKJV). Copyright © 1996 by Holeman Bible Publishers Used by permission. All rights reserved.

Scripture quotations taken from the Holy Bible, New International Version (NIV). Copyright © 1973, 1978, 1984, 2011 by Biblica, Inc.™. Used by permission. All rights reserved.

Cover design by author and typesetting by Mike Gibson of M-Print USA, Conyers, GA 30013. Knight: Sir Jack Seymour and Sir Dennis Bennett knighting with sword. Back cover design by author with typesetting by Xulon Press.

Dropcap fonts used by permission of the owner. © Tyypographer MEDIENGESTAITUNG, 2000.

Library of Congress Catalogue-in-Publication Data

www.xulonpress.com

To my darling, faithful wife, Donna.
A mate more beautiful inside and out, no one could find.
I am indebted to her more ways than I can number.

Acknowledgements

As the author, I am deeply indebted to my wife, Donna, and my cousin, Mrs. Tyra Bevers, for all their edits and proof reading. This entailed an enormous amount of work. I am also indebted to the fantastic leaders I have worked for over a lifetime who have taught me so many things, leading by example. What great leaders I have been blessed with! Not the least of which, I want to thank my own parents for their patience and the tremendous example they set, not just in my early years, but over my entire life. I came into this life with so little and so little talent. Others have given me so very much.

Contents

Acknowledgements xiii

Chapter One – Introduction. 17

Chapter Two – How to best use this Journal 25

Chapter Three–Character Traits. 29

Chapter Four–Epilogue 546

Bibliography 549

Index. 551

Chapter One

Introduction

Life on this planet is truly a gift—bursting with opportunities, challenges, possibilities and pleasures. Even the trials are a gift because we learn that through faith they can be overcome, learned from and turned into blessings. But, the greatest gift of one human life is not just the benefits it can bring to us but also to our family, friends and, in many cases, even the whole world. Tragically, however, for the most part we live in a world full of unrealized potential. So few ever become all God would have them to be or find true happiness when the Bible tells us this whole life is all about just that: production and fulfilling our God given potential. Success in this life and the one to follow, according to the Parable of the Talents, will be determined by what each of us do with the gifts and talents we were given. (Matthew 25:14) Success can be had by virtually anyone but, contrary to popular belief, it is not something we seek. It is something we attract as a byproduct of gaining character and becoming attractive as an individual and a leader. When we equip ourselves with an attractive, positive personality, the ability to work with different people, wisdom about life and a knowledge of the markets, etc., success will naturally come to us. These are things that can be acquired with study, focus and application.

My desire is to help as many people as possible find both happiness and success so they can enjoy life, be mightily blessed and, hopefully, spread it around. What makes me more excited than anything else is, hopefully, either through ministry or the use of this book to hear the Lord tell as many of the people as possible when they get to Heaven, "Well done, thou good and faithful servant."

Today many people are so discouraged. Not only are they not working, but they aren't even looking for a job, choosing rather to sit it out in life on the sidelines, taking the government dole. This means, of course, that all their talents, skills and education are going to waste, and they are missing all the opportunities life has for them besides. To say nothing about the consequences in Heaven for not using their talents. Eternity, by the way, is reality. In addition to all this, they are making no effort to improve themselves. Realizing now that no matter where any of us may find ourselves today, we all have so much room for improvement and tremendous opportunities awaiting us. The more we learn, the better we can accomplish our tasks in life as well as contribute to the lives of others. Working hard at your job, and you should, will get you a good living. But, if you will work harder at personal development than you do at work, it will earn you a life of high achievement, freedom and unlimited rewards.

Hopefully, this book will disprove the widely held notion that only the well-favored and greatly gifted can succeed in life and see their dreams fulfilled. Believe me, character makes the difference. And know this, none of us were born with even a modicum of it. . We were all "shaped in iniquity" (Psalm 51:5) and born with a fallen nature. On our own, this very nature causes us to think we know what was right— but our thoughts are always leading us to death. (Proverbs 14:12) Fact is, if we don't make a study of character and try to apply it to our lives, we will have precious little and are doomed to failure in one of its many forms.

Every person has a purpose. No one is here by accident. It would be such a waste to run the race of life, approach our natural end and then discover at that late date that we had missed an incredible assist of which we were unaware. Yes, we might have acquired some knowledge and possibly exercised and buffeted our bodies. We might have even acquired an education but found there was something critically important we missed which could have assisted us greatly. The thing we needed so badly but missed was readily available had we just known about it and made the effort to acquire it. It was something that could have helped us immensely to succeed in every area of life: to build businesses, ministries, thriving families, find happiness and form life-long friendships in this our one, short stay here on earth. What if there was one simple but powerful weapon we could have had in our personal arsenal that would have made us a success and—sadly, we missed it?

Many today think that once they have gotten a high school or college education and a job, all that is necessary is to show up for work on time. No. Not only is it essential to show up for work on time, but we need to come in early and bring a whole lot of positive character to the table. Such things as a positive attitude, loyalty, enthusiasm, honesty, diligence, sincerity, a teachable spirit and a number of other positive traits are indispensable. To succeed at any job, the employer's plan for new hires is always the same. New employees are granted a reasonable but limited period of time to learn the trade, company policies and generally get up to speed with the company's technology, systems and industry to become proficient. No matter where one is employed, the law of the survival of the fittest is still invisibly very much at work. God built it into all of nature. Like it or not, hindered as it may be by political correctness from time-to-time, it continues on among nations, companies and individual employees every day. Besides, God, in His infinite wisdom, has designed life to be structured so as to allow families, businesses and individuals to be confronted with enormous obstacles at various times to test men's souls. These things happen so that success in every field will depend on the one thing so many have missed: character—not talent, knowledge, ability, networking, education or personal privilege. These tests soon reveal one's character and it also happens to be, we will find from recent scientific research, the very thing that also brings a person lasting success and happiness. Its presence will either cause one to be victorious and distinguish as a winner in life or a lack of it will soon crush and defeat them. Character decides our destiny.

HEAT TEMPERS STEEL

Character not only consists of one's inner sense to know right from wrong but, of the accompanying conviction to do what is right regardless. It will, when learned, also include the invisible set of positive traits and winsome attitudes a person can have resident within. Success is actually an attitude. It is something any of us can attain by becoming attractive people. Others will certainly be able to see some of them from the outside but, more importantly, these traits will manifest themselves on a daily basis, especially when confronted with the trials, troubles and temptations of life. Squeeze a lemon or an orange and you will soon find out what you have in your hand. Trials, the book of James tells us, are good because they actually strengthen people just like heat tempers and hardens steel. (James 1:2,3) If we were not challenged, we would never find the motivation to improve. As human beings we have always learned more in the valleys than on the mountaintops of life. In addition, unchallenged, we would never increase in another area which is vitally necessary, that of our faith. Why? Because there would be no need of it. Trials are a blessing because of the character they form in people. Thank God, character causes those who have it to overcome. It is so very valuable because, once acquired, it is not consumed with the using and doesn't fade with time. It is actually strengthened with use and will continue to grow and benefit a person again and again throughout life. Truth is, we all have considerable room for improvement. We all can improve by acquiring positive character traits that will bless our entire life, improve our performance for God as well as increase our worth to those we serve in this present generation. Character, we will soon find also determines to a large extent how happy one will be in life.

CHARACTER v. HUMAN NATURE

It is important to note that a man's reputation is only what others might perceive it to be at some point in time. It usually has little to do with reality, can change like the weather and is all about one thing: perception. Forget about your reputation. Character is the real thing. It will determine both who you are, what you become, how far you go and whether or not you will stay there in life.

Psychologists tell us that anything a person practices for twenty-one days will become a habit and an integral part of their personality. The most effective way we have found to date to build character and make it a lasting part of our lives is to study and practice one character trait at a time for three weeks. This only takes a few minutes a day. The extent to which we make the effort to build character on the inside, will eventually determine how big our world will be on the outside. On the contrary, if our world becomes too large on the outside, not met by an increase in the level of character and discipline on the inside, it will soon begin to shrink and our life will likely crumble to the ground around us. Gaining character is important because it saves us from what we all are by nature: selfish introverts. In the area of personal character, no one starts out in life any better or worse than another. We are all born flawed vessels, having many quirks, bents, negative attitudes and rough edges. Every child starts out in the default position of being a totally lazy, fearful, self-centered creature. Remember, we all wanted our bottles and we wanted them right away. Having what we call character is totally foreign to the base nature we were born with. Some may become a little better off in some areas, character-wise, because of the positive examples and instructions of parents, teachers and the church but—all of us have tremendous room for improvement.

Character has unbelievable value in that it gives us the ability to respond to life's challenges, pressures and temptations in a manner totally different from how we would have responded by nature. All of the character traits taught in this book are, in fact, contrary to human nature. Certainly, we can all agree that the course of our individual lives is determined by the choices we make. We can take the easy way out: drop out of school, become a video game pro and get hooked on drugs and alcohol to escape our problems—and then complain about having to live off the public dole or in prison. No one will challenge the notion of where these lame decisions will lead us. However, with a study of character and diligent application we can discipline ourselves not to act according to the dictates of our base nature. Instead, we can respond to life, its challenges and the people around us in a very plausible, courageous and winsome manner. Character is actually what gives a person value—to God, employers, family, friends and associates.

You needn't think that, as the writer, I was born with any special gifting in this area. As a matter of fact my dad told me as a kid, "If you don't change your ways you will never see sixteen." That's pretty bad but it only got worse! He later said, "The way you are going, you will be so far back in a prison cell one day they will have to air mail your lunch to you." I was an excellent candidate to be the poster child of abysmal failures. Sad to say, nothing changed in this regard until I began to see the extremely high cost poor character was costing me personally. It took failing and feeling the pain for me to open my eyes and see that it was me, not the world around me, that needed to change. Amazingly, absent some kind of external motivation like this, most people refuse to pay the price to incorporate principles of success and character in their daily practice, life and personality. That is just the stubbornness and laziness of the flesh we were all born with. Gems of character and self-improvement are immediately brushed aside and forgotten, either because of apathy, a lack of discipline or a refusal to see ourselves as we truly are. Everyone is in need of improvement. No one has "arrived." It takes work, time and motivation to gain character. Having experienced it myself, I can tell you that it takes more courage to see ourselves as we really are, flaws, warts, freckles and all, than it does to face an enemy on the battlefield. But, because I was such a pitiful failure early-on in life that it caused me to make a determined effort to acquire the principles of success. This quickly led me to the study of character. Reading the biographies of great generals and studying leadership in the military college I attended, ignited and continued to fuel my life-long study of character. The 13th century jurist, poet and theologian, J. A. Rumi once said, "Yesterday I was clever and wanted to change the world. Today I am wise and want to change myself." I found the key to being a leader is learning to manage ourselves. When we change, the whole world begins to change around us. Simply applying these positive character traits in my life turned things around completely. If they could do what they did for someone like me, I am sure will do the same for you. The whole world is in need of leaders and the key to being a leader, said a little different way, is learning to discipline our self.

CHARACTER IS ALWAYS THE ARBITER

Ever wonder what makes the difference between a general and a major in the United States Army? Was it the luck of the draw, who they knew, how they parted their hair? No. In a word, it is character. Character is always the arbiter. A major can be counted on to do an average job most of the time but a general, on the contrary, can be trusted to do an excellent job all the time. Time and again, in job after job, generals demonstrate the ability to accomplish, build consensus, solve difficult problems and do it all with excellence. Their work, year after year, establishes for them a "manner of performance." Early in my service in the Army I was blessed to be chosen to serve as aide de camp to a Major General, commander of the 82nd Airborne Division, a unit of 16,000 men. In that position, as a very young officer, I was able to see, first hand, the importance of character. Later I commanded a couple rifle companies in Vietnam and my final tour of duty in the Army was to serve as a brigade adjutant. Although I had numerous faults, the small amount of character I had acquired by that time paid dividends beyond my greatest expectation in every job I held in the military. However, I also had an interest in entering business and hoped to have my own company someday. Although I loved the Army, when my commitment was fulfilled I resigned my commission and entered the real estate business. Through all the trials, success and failures life sent my way, I continued on in my mission of acquiring character. It helped me at seemingly every turn. It was incredible. If it did it all for someone like me, you can be assured it will do that much and more for you.

Along the way I was honored to work with several other 'generals,' not just in the military but in the civilian world as well. The first real estate company I worked for was owned by a man who was a former Air Force captain who initially served our country as a pilot. He then built a vertically integrated company from the ground up that consisted of not only a large real estate brokerage firm but also a builder's supply, a cabinet shop, a manufactured housing plant, five major subdivisions, two mobile home parks, five field construction crews and a mortgage company. Later, I was blessed to serve as an elder in a church that the pastor had grown to ten thousand members and also worked for a number of other employers, who were, likewise not only gifted as generals in business life, you might say, but were most assuredly men of character as well. Needless to say, they taught me many things for which I will be forever grateful. Through it all, I found that God needs generals in the military, ministry, marketing, industry, commerce, banking, politics, agriculture, education and the home. He needs His generals everywhere and still has a number of job openings today should anyone want to apply.

OUR GOAL IN LIFE

I believe it is important in life to stop at some point to see where we came from, where we are, and where we are going as well as to contemplate, of course, how we might well get there. First, where we came from. It is said that if scientists could take all the minerals and compounds out of our bodies and sell them on the open market with no deduction for the cost of extraction, we would each be worth about two dollars and seventy-five cents. Realizing also that each of us is just a sack of protoplasm that is about 75% water and the rest made completely of dirt, we should hope rather to be the sum total of our character. What is the content of your character? Don't worry, we all have room for improvement and should be trying to improve daily. Remember this, the effort expended to improve your character won't pay you back one for one. It will pay you back in a multiplied fashion day after day and year after year, making you more valuable to God and your present generation. And, as we know, character decides your destiny.

Amazingly, parents spend great sums of money providing their children with an education but rarely spend even a few paltry pennies on helping them gain character. They don't realize it is character that will determine who and what their children actually become in life—not education. Too much knowledge, without the accompanying character to handle it, can cause a person to puff up with pride. (I Corinthians 8:1) It can actually set a person up for a fall and, sometimes, even total destruction (Proverbs 16:18) I have heard parents telling their kids, "Get yourself an education because nobody can steal it from you." Not so. Every state and federal prison in the country is filled with highly educated doctors, lawyers, stock brokers, historians, physicists, philosophers and mathematicians. Many are either on death row awaiting execution or serving a life sentence. Something stole not only their educations but their lives as well. What was it? The trials, pressures and temptations of life. All these people had head knowledge but little or no character in their hearts to face the temptations, aggravations and attacks by the enemy of their souls.

It is no secret that character and the principles of success they spawn really do work. The problem is, first of all, acquiring them and, secondly, incorporating them into our heart of hearts so we can put them into practice automatically in the course of our lives. Assuredly, there is competition out in the world not only getting jobs but keeping them, selling products and services and getting promoted in every field of endeavor. Sooner or later, the employer will have to make decisions about whom to promote, whom to give a pay raise, whom they will tap to lead various projects, solve problems, manage the satellite office in another city and, sometimes, who gets the pink slip. Our goal should be to become the best person we possibly can and this will only happen by acquiring character. If we will, success will surely come—in due time of course. Some people, notwithstanding, will always be "hearers only" and not "doers." They will choose rather to remain the same, unwilling to accept the fact that this will likely, sooner or later, result in their being an abysmal failure.

THE STATE OF SOCIETY

Today we see systemic moral failure in nearly every professional field in life. We have recently witnessed scandals in all the branches of the military services, the service academies, the State Department, the Secret Service, the White House and the Justice Department. The wholesale loss of ethics by many in the Atlanta Public School System was also recently exposed. Many but certainly not all teachers, principals and even the Superintendent, participated in and encouraged the changing of answers on tests to meet scoring quotas and proficiencies. Such elevated scores temporarily brought them bonuses and promotions. This was not, of course, an indictment against all teachers. There are still excellent people in all fields of endeavor, not withstanding, but the point is we have recently seen moral failure on a scale like never before. A recent Inspector General's (I.G.) reported systemic moral failure in high level Veteran's Administration hospital personnel according to the September 10, 2014 issue of the Atlanta-Journal Constitution. The I.G. said in this article and others that 112 VA hospitals needed to be investigated further and that 450 high level executives should be fired. Nearly 1,000 of the hospitals in the agency's network were keeping a computer list of appointments and a fraudulent paper list on the side for two reasons: so the average time it took for the vets to see doctors would look better and the staff could qualify for bonuses. This scandal has been reported in the Atlanta Journal-Constitution almost daily now for a couple years. On June 11, 2014 it was front page news that 500 policemen here in Georgia may have claimed credit for taking the state's required training online last year. Many of them are being fired now as the facts surrounding their false reporting has been verified.

Scandals are everywhere. The next day more front page news about 88 officials who were indicted by the U.S. Justice Department in a massive WIC (Women, Infants and Children) scheme to defraud the poor of $18 million in food benefits. The Nov. 11, 2014 Atlanta Journal-Constitution cited that stock market traders from five major banks colluded to rig the market to boost their profits and bilk the system. They were fined 3.4 billion dollars. The headline of the November 17, 2014 Atlanta paper was the "Military Fraud's Scale Troubles Prosecutors." It has become so pervasive and abundant in recent years, that the U.S. Justice Department says they can't provide "sufficient oversight and monitoring." They estimated the fraud in just the Iraq and Afghanistan wartime contracting at $31 to $60 billion. Of course this geometric increase in wickedness in the Last Days was prophesied in the Bible more than two thousand years ago.

Regrettably, it is also true that more generals and admirals have been fired in the last few years than ever before in our nation's history. Most, but certainly not all, for cause. Did all these outstanding officers lack character? In some areas yes but certainly not generally. What we need to remember is that there are actually two kinds of character traits, both of which are extremely important. One set are the performance traits and the others have to do with morals. Performance traits would include traits like courage, diligence, perseverance, audacity and decisiveness, all of which most can agree, generals must possess. Moral character, on the other hand, would include such traits as integrity, honesty, morality, humility and selflessness. While being closely supervised by others coming up the ranks, an officer may possess the performance character sufficient for promotion to general. However, when there is less supervision and an increase in freedom suddenly afforded them in a high position, a lack of moral character can quickly sink their ship. Sadly, a lifetime of hard work, long hours, excellent performance, sweat, tears and devotion to duty can be destroyed by a few minutes of foolishness. Their careers come to naught in a moment because of one bad decision precipitated by a lack moral character.

Without character, our entire society will collapse because all social interaction, employment and contracts are based on trust and trust is founded on truthfulness and character. A contract is nothing more than a written list of promises between the parties to an agreement. Without trust, there is no reason to enter into a contract to expend time and resources if the other party can't be expected to uphold their end of the transaction as well. No marriage, friendship, contract or society can long exist without the integrity and truth which makes trust possible. Today we are seeing the devastation a lack of honesty is causing our country, especially in high positions of government. In addition, a society devoid of trust will soon enter a spiral of decadence that will only end in anarchy—an every man for himself, "anything goes" mentality and total destruction. People will be running in the streets, stealing, raping, maiming, burning and pillaging. We can do better and, by obtaining character, I believe we will.

HAPPINESS AND SUCCESS

If you ask people what they really want in life, the majority would likely tell you happiness and success. After all, what would success in any field be worth if it didn't make a person happy? Contrary to popular opinion, climbing to the top of the various professional ladders of success in life, will not make you happy. Many have reached the top in their field of endeavor only to find that there was nothing there; just a lonely, empty space. Using short-sighted tactics such as taking advantage of folk, lying, cheating and stealing to get there simply makes it all the more lonely at the top. What scientists are finding today and psychiatrists and psychologists are confirming, is that gaining character is actually what makes people happy. Aristotle once said, "Happiness is the reward for virtue." At the end of life, if we see that we have helped no one but ourselves and can't respect the person we see in the mirror every morning, what is there to enjoy in that and with whom?

Years ago, as I mentioned, I was blessed to have served in the United States Army. I was also favored to attend several of the Army's best schools, graduating from the Army's Ranger, Airborne, Pathfinder and Jumpmaster Schools. My first assignment and first real job after graduating from college was to lead an airborne rifle platoon, in the 82nd Airborne Division. What a great job. What a challenge! Commanding thirty men tasked from time-to-time with jumping out of airplanes in full battle gear in the middle of the night to assist our Division to take over a foreign country—at the direction of the President of the United States, of course. It was quite an exciting calling but it wasn't just a job to me. No one became wealthy on lieutenants' pay back then but, thankfully, it had little to do with receiving a pay check. Extrinsic motivations won't give a person the power in life to blow the fuzz off of a peach. The important thing to me was, after years in a military college and Army training, I was finally able to work in a job that actually served all the ideals I cherished. Being from a long line of military men in our family, it was my turn to defend our country, our flag, the family, our next door neighbors, our freedoms, our way of life and to do it with a commitment unto death. What a challenge! A man is at his best when challenged. Here though, just an obscure, 2nd lieutenant at the bottom of a 16,000 man division, I had an intrinsic desire to serve and give it my very best. I got at it early and had no problem staying late helping my men and my company be the best it could be. Providence had it that I was also blessed to serve under a man I greatly admired—who was likewise more than thrilled to serve in the Army as well. My commander was Capt. John Alex Hottell, an Airborne Ranger, Rhodes Scholar and tenth in his class at West Point. He was an incredible man and certainly a joy and honor to work for. Had he lived through his two tours in Vietnam, I am certain he would have achieved star rank.

Later, after being selected as the aide to the Commanding General of the Division, I was privileged, once again, to work for another incredible leader. The job and the things learned were immense. Again, I had an intrinsic desire to serve him, the Division and all my ideals giving 110%, all the time. Just being allowed to serve was pay enough but I was pleasantly surprised the day I left the Division in route to my assignment in Vietnam to be rewarded, certainly, far more than I deserved. The general, like my company commander, gave me an incredible efficiency report, presented me with a bronze airborne soldier statue for my service to the Division and an Army Commendation Medal. This was unheard of for a lieutenant. He even wrote a letter to the Commanding General of the new unit I was headed to in Vietnam and recommended me to command a company as a lieutenant. All company commanders were captains. Now I only said all that to say this. As I left the Post in my car that day headed for Vietnam, I thought back over the time I served there. All the awards were great and the attainments were wonderful but they weren't what really meant the most to me. It was certainly a happy occasion and I don't want to diminish in the least my gratitude for the thoughtfulness and kindness of my leaders. However, something surprised me at the time and I really didn't understand until years later. All the awards, although I was more than appreciative, seemed a bit empty. Far more meaningful to me was the trust my two commanders had placed in me to do important and sometimes difficult tasks. I also valued the love and respect we shared while serving the Division and each other. The character they displayed and the growth they inspired in me were what really mattered. Believe me, I made a lot of mistakes. Happiness, I now realize, was the result of my growth in character and the joy of serving them, the Division, my Country and all the ideals I believed in.

Yes, life is such that we will always have goals and ladders to climb. Goals will always be necessary in an ordered society for people to advance and serve together in community. Attaining those goals, though needful and important in life, do not, however, contribute that much to our long-term happiness. Amazingly, our happiness in life is found in being our best and respecting the type of person the rigors of the climb have made us. It is also the closeness of the friendships we make and enjoy along the way. Gaining competence in our chosen field, along with character, effectiveness and the security it brings, contribute greatly to our happiness in life. Without a doubt, genuine happiness is also derived from the opportunities we have taken to contribute to and enhance the lives of others around us.

Recently, as I mentioned, many scientists, physiologists and psychiatrists have made amazing new discoveries about the origins of true happiness. Jim Loehr, in his excellent book, *The Only Way to Win*, delves into much of this research. In the book, he draws from a career of helping Fortune 500 executives, military officers, governmental officials and world-class athletes find happiness in his seminars at the Human Performance Institute. His studies found "that the blind pursuit of external achievement often results in emptiness, addiction, and, ironically, poor performance." He goes on to note that "It's not really about what you achieve.... It's about who you become as a consequence of the chase."[1] In a word, it's about character.

Neuroscientists like Norman Doidge, John Medina, Michael Merzenich and Joseph LeDoux, have recently done studies on "the prefrontal cortex—the brain region thought to be involved in, among other functions, personality expression and behavior moderation—and of the limbic system—whose structures are involved in functions including emotion and behavior." They discovered how our brains actually work. They found, among other things, "especially notable are the *amygdala,* which is active in monitoring stimuli that 'reward,' and the *dentante gyrus,* implicated in the regulation of happiness. These scientists have made great advances in understanding how the brain is stimulated and how it regulates emotion, behavior, and, yes, even happiness."[2] Happiness, they have determined, has a great deal to do with gaining character.

There are many others like Roy Baumeister, Robert Biswas-Diener, Ed Diener, Carol Dweck, Robert Emmons and Barbara Fredrickson who have also contributed greatly in their recent studies about the origin of happiness, self-esteem and human gratitude. [3]

Extrinsic rewards in life will never really satisfy, so it is important to know how all this actually works in our brain. Both short and long-term activities required to excel, eat, learn new skills, improve our education, etc. do give the mental sense of pleasure and happiness. In each of these cases, the beneficial activity practiced increases the dopamine which is our neurotransmitter that actually activates the *nucleus accumbens,* the receptors in a certain part of our brains. This is the area that sends out the signal of what people today call a "rush" or a really good feeling. Daniel Pink writes in his book, *Drive,* "The mechanism of most addictive drugs is to send a fusillade of dopamine to the nucleus accumbens." These surges raise the dopamine levels three to fivefold normal and thereby provide feelings of relief or pleasure. Dopamine, accompanied by a couple of other brain hormones, noradrenaline and serotonin, are referred to by scientists as "happy messengers." In this way, dopamine acts as a naturally formed drug that contributes to our happiness.[4] It also does many other things but, for our purposes here, it is important to note that gaining character definitely triggers these happy messengers as well. If we want to be truly happy, gaining character will not only do this for us but will pay us many other dividends besides.

Chapter Two
How To Best Use This Journal

Life is too important to all of us not to give it our best shot. God loves all of us as much as His own Son and wants us to have the greatest success and the most fulfilling life possible. For this to happen, we need to make use of every legal assist that has been given us through education and gaining character as well as acquiring all the skill we can. We only have one life to live and it is my desire to see these character traits do what we know they will: add value to your life, bring you happiness and make you all you can be. The benefits of success in terms of security, peace of mind, personally rewarding relationships and increased finances to help our families and others, are too important, not to take advantage of every means of improvement available. Possibly the most important thing we can do is to make a study of character since it is, in fact, God's desire to reveal His nature in His created beings. This can be accomplished by allowing us to acquire as much of His character, goodness and glory as each of us is able to receive. No, we are never to take or even touch God's glory. That is His alone. However, His loving-kindness and generosity are so great, He not only allows us to become like His Son, Jesus, but He also wants us to be partakers of His own blessedness and divine nature. His plan has already been laid out, knowing that "as He is so are we (to be) in the world." (I John 4:17) He is the example we should strive for but, certainly, none of us will reach perfection this side of Heaven. Ultimately, once some degree of character is acquired, it is God's desire for His children to show forth the glory of His love, wisdom, grace, and power to a lost and dying world. If this is of interest to you, He made you a solemn promise: It is yours for the seeking. We have His word on it, "… I say to you, ask, and it will be given to you; seek, and you will find; knock, and it will be opened to you" Luke 11:9

ENGRAFTING CHARACTER

There have always been books about character but a couple very important things have recently surfaced. First, we now know how critically important it is in terms of a person's ability to obtain success and happiness in life. Secondly, what has always been, however, was a way to engraft these traits in our own hearts and make them operable in our lives as well as part of our own personality. Reading about character is fine but just reading about character traits will not be remembered? We have a little short-term excitement about a trait or two and then in a few days, poof it is gone. We have forgotten about it. The exciting thing here is that this book offers us a proven way to engraft these traits permanently into a person's life and heart. Psychologists tell us anything we practice for twenty-one days becomes a habit and will, in fact, be an integral part of our personality.

For engrafting character traits, the most effective method we have found to date is to read *The Character Trait Journal* like a regular book to become familiar with all the individual character traits. It is most important for us to understand a trait before it can ever be a benefit to us. Only when we truly understand a trait and know its benefit can we then add our faith to it. What we don't understand and believe in, we know, will be quickly stolen by the enemy of our soul. The Book of Hebrews tells us in Chapter 4 verse 2 that even the Word spoken to many did not profit them because it was not mixed with faith by those who heard it. It just won't do for us to be a "hearer only" and not a "doer" of the Word, moved and energized by faith.

Once you have reviewed all of the traits, mark the character traits you are most interested in developing or feel you have the most urgent need to incorporate into your life in the Index of Character Trait. It is in the back of the book. Mark them in numerical order from one to 185 so you can study them in order of your own personal needs.

First, of course, take them one at a time and read the narrative about the trait you are most interested in. Then review just the definition section (bullet points) of the character trait you have chosen to work on as your first order of business during your prayer and Bible study time each morning. **Do this every day for three weeks. The three week concept is critical to the prospect of having time to practice the trait in your daily living. Please don't try to cut this short.** Work on them all this way, one at a time—reading only the definition section of the trait daily. Some of us like to put the definition section on our mirror in the bathroom so we can redeem the time and focus on it the first thing of every day. It will only take a minute or two each day but this will allow the Holy Spirit to develop it, quicken it to your heart and fit it into your personality and practice. Remember, the Spirit hovered over the waters of the earth in the beginning. The earth was void, without form and dark. Soon the Spirit gave it definition. (Gen 1:2) You will then be able to practice it in your daily living as it is placed permanently in the workings of your subconscious mind and heart. Indeed, it will soon become part of your character and will be yours by nature without even thinking about it. Then start on the second. Just as muscles grow with energy investments from the exercise of lifting weights, character building likewise requires investments in the areas of study, meditation and practice. It is very important here to keep a calendar showing your start and ending dates for each trait. This keeps you from letting it slide to initiate a new trait every twenty-one days because of the press of other things. Be faithful to this part of your personality development. You will enjoy it and will soon be able to see your progress

Fathers and single-mom's will want to sit down at the kitchen table with their children (six years and up) once every three weeks for about 30 minutes. Read the narrative on each trait and then tell the family how the Lord has helped you with the trait and then give each of them a copy of just the definition section (bullet points) as mentioned above. Then ask them to take the bullet points to their place of prayer and ask the Holy Spirit to quicken it to them and help them be a test pilot for God out in the world each day for the next twenty-one days. Then ask them to tell you what they have learned out on the mission field practicing the trait at the dinner table each night. This gives the family purpose and a reason to have dinner together at the table once again,. For this book to have the proper impact, this three week, daily prayer and practice system must be followed. Time can get away from you and other things can easily crowd this out so be sure to keep the aforementioned calendar and purpose to stay on a twenty-one day schedule. If you will do this, you will be surprised at the phenomenal results. The family will grow and prosper greatly and it will become character oriented rather than seeking the world's goal of "more and bigger."

Single adults must follow the same twenty-one day schedule of learning and practicing the traits as well. There is no shortcut. It will be worth far, far more than the time and effort as it will pay you back in a multiplied form over a lifetime.

What follows here are a number of character traits listed in alphabetical order. Each trait described in the front of the book has a place to the side of it to record the day you start your twenty-one day study and practice of it and the day you expect to have your study of it completed. A systematic study may take several years but will, I believe, be very enjoyable and more helpful to you than even a college education. Although it won't take much time each day, it will be well worth the effort.

The Character Trait Journal can also be used very effectively by husbands and wives as a daily devotional. This study will knit your hearts together and make you more valuable to each other, to God and your current generation—for life.

THE NEXT GENERATION

John Ankerberg mentioned a startling statistic on his Sunday TV program in April of 2015. He said recent studies indicate that "seventy-eight percent of all children raised in Christian homes will lose their faith by the time they either graduate from high school or college." Many of these parents are trying so hard to do what other families have been doing for years and it is simply not working today. You may be wondering how such a cataclysmic, pervasive, wholesale loss of faith could ever occur. The Bible actually prophecies clearly about the very things that will cause this falling away of young people in the End Times. Because of:

- The terrible example and depraved nature of most people around them in today's society. II Timothy 3:1–4
- The general, steady "increase of wickedness" in the world in the Last Days. Matthew 24:12
- The "coming of the lawless one with … all power, signs and lying wonders." II Thessalonians 2:10
- The ungodly influence of radically liberal high school teachers and college professors
- Social media, M-TV, pornography, sexual perversion and the pervasiveness of drugs to include the legalization of marijuana, etc.
- Peer Pressure
- The horrible things available on personal cell phones today (which most young people have).
- The promise that those who are deceived, who compromise and do not receive the love of the Truth, "God will send them strong delusion." II Timothy 2:11

The world system and spiritual darkness will be too powerful, easily overwhelming our children. But, the good news is that a strong foundation of truth and character can now be laid in the hearts of the hearts. As important as our pastors and evangelists are and we certainly can't make it without their valuable input, God's Word says the ability to lay this foundation and successfully raising children lies with someone else. Psalm 78 says God's plan is for the fathers to teach the children in the home so the generations to come would not only have the knowledge of God but would actually set their hope in Him. His character is truly the standard and is what we need to be teaching them. This can be done so easily, enjoyably and effectively by the father taking fifteen to thirty minutes every three weeks to sit at the kitchen table and introduce them to a new character trait as mentioned above. Then he can share his own insights on the trait, give them a copy of the definition section and ask them to pray over it every morning in their individual prayer time. At that time it is also important for each person to ask God to quicken it to their hearts and help them practice it out in the world every day for the next three weeks as test pilots for God. In so doing, it will then become a permanent part of their personalities.

In addition, building character will joyfully become the focal point of family life and energize the discussions at dinnertime. Each member of the family will naturally begin to share how these character traits have worked positively in their lives and how they might have noticed a lack of them adversely affecting the lives of those around them in everyday life. Remember, the key to this is a three week process on each trait. Reading about these character traits may be interesting but a momentary glance at them won't engraft them in your heart. It takes a little work on our part every day for three weeks and the Holy Spirit working along with us. Companies, churches, Sunday school classes, businesses, ministries, men's and women's groups can all benefit from this systematic method of character study. The enemy may have been able to steal faith from some of our kids in times past. However, this method of character study in the home, where it is practiced effectively for several years, I don't believe can be stolen unless a person just wants to let it. As the family members walk these traits out in their daily lives in the home, at school and work and reap the benefits of these traits daily, they will never cast them away.

Amazing as it sounds, the next generation can truly be saved if fathers will practice this easy, enjoyable and efficient method of character study in the home. Another benefit of this character trait study is that it restores the fathers to their proper place as the high priest, spiritual leaders and teachers within the home. For those in one-parent homes, the fathers or the single moms are the spiritual leaders and have the authority to teach the children. The prayers of mothers and grandmothers have brought many well-known people not only to the saving grace but power and prominence.

Chapter Three

Individual Character Traits

CCEPTANCE, SELF-   **Study start date** _____ **Finish date**_____

We could all agree that there are some things in life that are not perfect and never will be. Just one of which is the people here—they are just like you and me. I am certain that we are all imperfect and all of us have done some things wrong because the Bible tells us, " … all have sinned and fall short of the glory of God." (Romans 3:23) We have all done things we ought to be ashamed of even if we are not. So many people can't accept themselves because they have made some big mistake in their lives. The problem is, we men want to remember things God has forgotten and forget things He remembers. He has already hurled out sins into the sea of forgetfulness never to remember them again. We would do well to do the same. We won't make any progress trying to live in the past, bemoaning our forgiven sins. For some reason we want to forget that we are weak, that we came from dust and are in desperate need of all of the grace we can get.

I well remember as a seven year old boy a hot summer's day growing up in Savannah, Georgia. I was out in our front yard with my trusty BB gun looking for a target. A dry cleaner van drove by momentarily and I thought the back window looked like a pretty good moving target. I quickly took aim as it drove by and shot it out. The driver threw on the brakes and backed up to the front of our house. I, being alert and well experienced at detecting when big trouble was imminent, quickly dove behind the shrubs in front of the house with my BB gun. Thought I was invisible or something. The dry cleaner man exited his vehicle, walked up to the house and rang the doorbell. When my mom came to the door he gave her the low down on what I had done and, my mom, not being the type that would put up with Tom-foolery (that's what they called what I was doing back then) said, "And have you seen him?" He said, "Yes ma'am, he is right over there in the shrubs." She called me to the front door and asked if I shot his window out. I promptly said, "No ma'am." Of course you know that she didn't believe me for a minute with all the evidence right there: a broken window, an eye witness, me hiding in the bushes and the smoking BB gun in my grubby little hands. Man I got a whipping for that when my dad came home from work! But I still remember very clearly, the thought occurred to me right then and there when I told that lie to my mom that I would never be a George Washington. He answered up for his failing, chopping down the cherry tree and I didn't. No matter what I could never change what I had done. Good thing our God is the God of the second chance!

My dad told me as a child "If you don't change your ways, you will soon be so far back in a prison that they would have to air mail your lunch to you" and he wasn't trying to be funny. I got so many whippings as a kid, thinking he might feel he had been a little too strict, I felt compelled to tell him on his death bed, "Dad, I deserved every one of those whippings you gave me and probably needed a few more." But, for any of us to make any headway in life at all, we must accept the fact that we have made mistakes and name them one-by-one. This is very important. Write them all down on a sheet of paper. Ask God to forgive us and then burn that sheet of paper. That's right, burn up the whole mess. Then, just as importantly, you need to forgive yourself and forget all about it. God already has. We know "He has not dealt with us according to our sins, nor punished us according to our iniquities. For as the heavens are high above the earth, so great is His mercy toward those who fear Him; as far as the east is from the west, so far has He removed our transgressions from us." (Psalm 103:10–13) Now that is great mercy and we are to be like Him! Admit your faults and sins. Make restitution if possible but then forgive yourself and forget it. Paul, who was chief of sinners, said, " … this one thing I do, forgetting those things which are behind and reaching forward to those things which are ahead, I press toward the goal for the prize of the upward call of God in Christ Jesus." (Philippians 3:13) What is he saying? Two things here. We must forget the past with all its mistakes and all of its glory. You can't live in yesterday. No one ever has. Let it all go—the good, the bad and the ugly. Then, go and sin no more.

Now that we have dealt with the past, it is critically important that we accept ourselves. So many people go the full distance of their short life and find they never liked themselves or accepted the way God made them. What a huge mistake! Certainly there are things about our size, shape and appearance that we might like to change if we could—but we can't. The Bible poses this question, "Which of you by worrying (or wishing) could add one cubit to your stature?" (Matthew 6:27) Answer: no one. Why wrestle with it any longer? It is said that ninety percent of the Hollywood stars would change something materially about their physical appearance yet the world worships these people. Movie stars don't like the way they look either. Sure we are all a little peculiar looking. Some of us are too tall and others are too short. Some of us don't have enough hair and others have too much. Some of us have long noses and some have short. Just accept the fact that you were made in "the secret place" according to the counsel of God and God makes no mistakes. Oh, it's fine to go to the gym and try losing a little weight or to eat-up if you need to gain a bit but go on ahead and give the devil a very bad day. Accept yourself just as you are.

Remember, the human race got in all the trouble we are currently in here because someone wasn't willing to accept themselves the way God made them. The devil told Eve, " . the day you eat of (the forbidden fruit) your eyes will be opened, and you will be like God." (Genesis 3:5) He aroused in her a serious discontent with her present state. She was created, with Adam, to dress and have dominion over the Garden of Eden. They had a perfect World if anyone ever has. But she took the forbidden fruit, ate of it and you know the result. We have never recovered to this very day! Do yourself a favor. Accept yourself just the way God made you. Realize that you have a ministry to others and a sphere of influence because of the way you were made and are where God has placed you. Be thankful and rejoice. We were each made to have influence with a certain circle of people to fulfill our own divine purpose. Stop, right now. Thank God and accept the way you were made.

I heard a true story about a journalist who was studying success principles among several prominent preachers of the day. One preacher he went to see lived in North Carolina and had a church that seated more people than those who lived in the entire city. For some reason people came for miles around to hear him preach. When the writer went to interview him, he couldn't believe what he was seeing. This preacher was about the homeliest looking person he had ever seen in his entire life. During the interview, he couldn't help himself; he just had to ask the question. "Sir, with all due respect, you are not the most handsome person ever to be called a preacher. How do you command crowds like these who come to hear you?" He replied, "I just accept myself just like I am and other people have no choice but to do the same." That, to be sure, is great advice. Accept yourself. Get in sync with God. Yes, thank God for the way He made you. Agree with God and the way you were created. There is power in being in agreement with God. You can't move forward and no one else can accept you if you don't accept yourself. Remember, we are to love others as we love ourselves. Loving yourself and liking yourself is where it all begins. You were created in the image of God!

Now, after having accepted and forgiven yourself, you are in a position, for the first time, to accept others in your life. Like you, none of them are perfect either. Accept others just like they are. Don't make mental demands so as to force them to be good enough to be your friend. We are commanded to not only "Associate with the humble (men of low estate)" (Romans 12:16) but also, "in lowliness of mind let each esteem others better than himself." (Philippians 2:3) There should never be a person who is not good enough to be our friend unless they are a terrorist or someone trying to do you harm. Life is a joy when you are friendly but "To have friends, you must show yourself to be friendly." (Proverbs 18:24) Having true, life-long friends is a major blessing. It can be pretty lonely out there in the world without friends.

It is the enemy's job to do everything he can to condemn you, your past or the way God made you, anything and everything. He will do everything he can to cause you not to accept yourself as a viable candidate for success in life. This is so important, because the law of reciprocity dictates that no one else can accept you if you don't accept yourself. Further, people will only accept you to the extent and to the degree, as we have seen here, that you accept yourself in life. Even according to the law of faith, God can and will meet you only at the level of your expectations. It is also comforting to know that God has always used imperfect people.

Adam couldn't accept responsibility for his sins, being one to pass the buck.

Noah was a drunk.

Abraham listened to his wife instead of waiting on God for the child of promise.

Jacob was so crooked he wouldn't hang straight if you hung him.

Moses tried to take part of the credit for God causing the water to flow out from a rock.

Aaron started making golden calves and leading the people to worship idols.

Gideon didn't think he could do what God told him to and, time and again, had to have all kinds of super-natural assurances.

Samson was a womanizer who never did do what God told him to.

Saul thought ninety-nine and a half would do with God.

David was a womanizer and a murderer.

Solomon was told not to multiply his gold, horses or his wives and disobeyed God on all three.

Ahaziah entered in to a forbidden partnership with another king to build ships and worshipped Baal.

Jehu had a zeal for God but not according to knowledge.

Hezekiah was a show-off.

Uzziah failed to remove the high places of idol worship in the land, offered strange fire and trusted in his riches, fortifications, war machines, armies and his own wisdom instead of God's.

Zerubbabel was told to build the temple but succumbed to the opposition, allowing construction to stop temporarily.

Job accused God of the works of satan. (Cut him a little slack though because none of us have had to face what he did.)

Simon Peter took his eyes off the Master while walking on the water, denied Christ three times and stopped eating with the Gentiles in order to gain the approval of men, specifically the Jews.

John was plagued with trying to be the greatest, selfish ambition and wanted to call fire down from Heaven on all those who didn't receive Christ or assist in the ministry

Thomas was slow to comprehend the Kingdom mysteries, failed to wait with the other disciples for Christ's return and required visual proof of the Lord's scars from the cross before he would believe. **Matthew** was a cheat just like all the other government tax collectors (we still have some of his descendants at the I.R.S. today).

So, you see, God can still use you.

What it means to have the character trait of **SELF-ACCEPTANCE:**

- Accepting yourself just as you are, warts and all, being thankful to God
- Realizing God made you to be a perfect fit in His world and universe like a hand in a glove, just as you are
- Accepting the fact that we have all failed at many things, sinned and fallen short but going on to *forgive ourselves* and put it all behind us
- Accepting that we all, as human beings, have both assets and liabilities, gifts and talents as well as strong points and limitations
- Believing that nothing is impossible with you and God
- Knowing it makes the devil mad for you to accept yourself

ACCURACY (See also: Attention to Detail) Study start date: _____ Finish date: _____

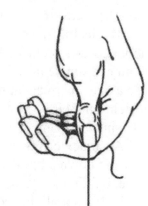

The goal of character is to prepare us for leadership and increase our ability to function effectively serving others. Today's world is increasingly technical and filled with numbers, reports, emails, messages and phone calls. Accuracy in all these things is imperative if we are to avoid mistakes and misunderstandings that will, in fact, result in lost time, materiel and, sometimes, even the loss of life. This is an important topic to focus on because God knows we have all made our share of mistakes.

To reach any degree of accuracy in life, one must first be dedicated to the truth. We must stop somewhere along the path of life and make a conscious effort to dedicate ourselves to it. We must declare to ourselves that we are not going to color the truth grey, bend it, trifle with it, twist it or tell half of it at any time—any more—for any reason whatsoever. A half-truth is a lie because it doesn't include enough information to be an accurate representation of the situation. It leaves room for misinterpretation, manipulation and deceit. No wonder the court system requires those who give testimony to affirm that they will "tell the truth, the whole truth and nothing but the truth so help me God." This time of decision, when a person stops and makes a commitment to accuracy and honesty, is the time we start living by the truth. From that moment on we will be building our life on the rock-solid foundation of the truth. From that moment on, we never have to remember or to keep a record of what we said because the truth is the truth. Reports made will have to stand as they are; an accurate representation of the facts on the ground. Telling the truth is the basis for noble leadership. Without it, there will be no respect and one will have vacated their moral authority to lead. A leader who can't be counted on to tell the truth is a leader who simply can't be trusted and trust is the basis of all human relationships. This certainly includes keeping one's promises.

Being accurate also means being explicit. It is making the effort to include all the pertinent facts and data for the recipient to form the correct conclusions and opinions. Writing legibly is also important in life. Sloppy handwriting has caused train wrecks and airplane accidents over time. Those who have been in the military must be especially attentive to details and accuracy. Getting just one number confused on one's grid coordinate describing your location to the artillery battery on the supporting fire base can sometimes cause a round to land on your own troops. This has happened more times than people would like to admit. In fact, it would be important to note that more people get killed by accident in war than do on purpose. Just being in the vicinity of so many vehicles, explosives, tanks, aircraft and weapons lends itself to mistakes, accidents, human error and trouble. Accuracy and attention to detail helps us avoid a great deal of trouble.

I still remember very clearly one fateful afternoon in Tampa, Florida coming home from school on the bus in the second grade. Bouncing off that bus, I came

into the house only to find my dad lying unconscious on the living room floor. His face, arms and hands had turned purple. Mom called an ambulance which took him immediately to the hospital. We all feared that he was going to die. I really don't know what the doctor did for him but I do remember it was determined that the pharmacy had given him the wrong medication. The name of the wrong medicine sounded and actually was spelled similarly to what he should have had. That mistake almost killed him but thank God, he recovered. God spared us the loss of a great dad.

Medical mistakes, many times due to poor hand writing, are all too common today. We often hear about doctors accidentally amputating the wrong leg or removing the wrong eye. Many times, people die from just simple mistakes and human error. Today in an effort to stop some of these costly errors, doctors use a black permanent marker to note the proper leg, foot or hand to amputate and have the patient sign it right on their body. It still happens though. This week, the Atlanta Journal-Constitution reported that a hospital had amputated the wrong finger.

Accuracy can be achieved many times just by making a conscientious effort to do things right and slowing down a bit. For example, almost anyone can build a house but not everybody can be a builder. True, building, putting sticks and bricks together, simply has to do with common sense and basic arithmetic. It's not all that complicated. However, the only people who can stay in the building business are those who can make beauty. They must show careful attention to detail. Nobody wants to buy a sloppily built house or office building. They want craftsmanship, quality, style, durability and the finer touches. When the builder has been paid, the buyer is left with the product for the rest of his life. The doors must be hung correctly. The corners of the interior trim must be mitered precisely. The mantle above the fireplace must look like it was built for a home and not a barn, etc. A builder's product yet remains and is his calling card for future referrals which are the heart and soul of his business.

Accuracy must include taking the time to stop and double check our own work. If time and organization permits, have an assistant proof your work as well. Accuracy is also bolstered tremendously by follow through, neatness and organization. For example, work and storage areas maintained in an orderly fashion will contribute to beauty, service and people being able to work together conveniently as a team. Things that are organized accurately by type, size, etc., have an added beauty all their own. Accuracy will be noticed and appreciated by your coworkers immediately and will pay dividends for the rest of your life.

What it means to have the character trait of **ACCURACY**:

- To be free from error
- Showing attention to detail
- An absence of sloppiness
- Building to perfection
- Conforming completely to the truth
- Conforming to a certain, high standard
- Having no mistakes

ADVENTUROUS—   **Study start date:** _____ **Finish date:** _____

Life on this planet is dull, dusty and quite dreary for so many. That's really sad because God meant it to be one tremendously exciting adventure. But, for this to happen, we must be willing to launch out into the deep, take a few risks and try things we have never done before. You must dare to do new things, go to new places, take in new territory and gain new qualifications. If you stand still, you will go stale. Obviously there are some areas we definitely need to avoid but there are so many other things in life we need to try just to see if we like them. You benefit several ways when you try something new: You will either decide that you like the new concept or product better than the old or you will confirm that the old is better and be able to completely dismiss the new with conviction, certainty and finality. Trying the new might cause you to appreciate the old, all the more. Most importantly, you will also be opening the door to new and unforeseen opportunities, allow the hand of God to move and the tremendous forces of serendipity to take effect.

Why are people reticent to adventure out in life? Primarily because of one thing: fear of failure. Fear of public opinion if we don't do well for a minute. Failure should be what we eat for breakfast instead of Wheaties. We must fail in order to succeed in this life. It might be well to note that most entrepreneurs fail in business at least once before they succeed. Failure is the pathway, yea even the ticket to accomplishment.

The opportunities and challenges of life don't assail us all at once. They usually reveal themselves in a sequence of events but seizing new opportunities requires a certain mixture of courage, audacity and humility. Since the fearful never venture out to try anything new, they never get anywhere in life. This is because, most opportunities usually require us to have enough humility to take one step backwards to make two forward. We might have to leave the success we had in a previously, perfectly good job or take a pay cut or both. All of life is pretty much one audacious gamble and even with all of the best planning, things rarely turn out the way we imagined. Notwithstanding a few bumps on the road, it is usually much better that we thought.

Being the son of an Air Force pilot and a man I always looked up to and admired, I, as most other kids, wanted to either consciously or subconsciously be like him, follow in his footsteps and fly planes. However, the college I attended my first year only had Army R.O.T.C so flying airplanes had to be put on hold for a while. At the very beginning of that year, the commander of the Wainwright Rifle Drill Team visited each of the companies in the Corps and asked for volunteers to try out for the team. The drill team members had a reputation for being quite a wild and crazy bunch anyway so that all sounded pretty interesting—even a bit adventurous. So I shot my biscuit hook up in the air and, along with several others, got to try out for the team. Three of us made the cut but they did say all of us would need a whole lot of work. Don't know about or even remember the other two, but it was certainly true about me. We practiced close order drill for hours and hours several times a week. They also had a bunch of cool cadence calls designed, I think, to take your mind off of how much work all this was. Just one of which we echoed as we double-timed from one place to another in formation was: "I want to be an Airborne Ranger; I want to live a life of danger. Air—borne! Ran- ger! Arruh!" Well, that was not at all in my plans in those tender, younger years but we repeated that cadence call so many times, I started thinking that this kind of a life would be pretty adventurous. This was before they even had documentaries on TV and I had never even heard of an Army Ranger. I certainly didn't intend for this to happen but over time this thing about being a Ranger got down in my heart and that was it. It was what I wanted to do—no matter if I didn't ever do anything else in life. I was going to, God helping me, be an Airborne Ranger and live a life of danger. I didn't know it at the time, but that one fortuitous decision to join the drill team would markedly change my whole life forever.

Later in college, the Army had a program where those who had Regular Commissions could obtain a pilot's license at the government's expense. So I did that too. However, flying a plane never set me on fire like being an Army Ranger. Looking back, that one decision to try out for the drill team and pursue a little adventure led me to pilot training, Airborne School, of course Ranger School, Jumpmaster School and Pathfinder School. It led to the opportunities of leading men in battle which very few officers ever have in life. Vietnam was the last time in recent history a war was fought with men in company formations (four platoons of men under one commander). In Iraq, for instance, the war was mostly won by our superior air power with the Army sweeping up behind it doing squad size, door-to-door, urban clearing operations. Very little contact was made with the enemy while in large unit formations (companies and larger). Afghanistan was quite similar but a lot of squad-size units doing recons and some larger unit surgical attacks. All these schools and experiences in the Army prepared me for other ventures, challenges and opportunities later in life. Learning to take risks, solve problems and make plans quickly while under fire on the battle field was transferable to so many other difficult situations.

This deal about jumping off of things seems to have been with me from an early age. At about six, while living in Savannah, Georgia, I remember that I just had to jump off the high diving board at the Oglethorpe Hotel pool. At the ripe old age of eight we lived in a subdivision right outside of Hunter Air Field there in Savannah. For a while I had a little gang called the 13th Street Tigers. Keep in mind now that we were just little termites in the second grade. To be in our gang you had to run and dive straight over a carpenter's saw horse without touching it and jump off of a one-story garage as well. In those days, builders would saw the trees on the vacant building lots into lumber of various sizes and stack those long boards, one on top of another, in a triangle. This was done to air-dry the wood so it wouldn't warp when they built houses with it. We'd pull a 2 X 12 out of the stack about five feet, half-way up the stack. Then stand on top of the stack and jump down on the end of that plank like a diving board. This would shoot you up in the air to catch a tree limb so you could climb up to the top of the tree. One day this plan was working perfectly for me. I jumped off on that board, bounced up and grabbed just the limb I wanted—perfectly. Success!!! Eureka!!! However, the limb cracked and I hit the ground like a sack of potatoes breaking my arm. But remember—it wasn't easy for the Wright Brothers learning to fly either. Then in the 82nd Airborne Division I got to jump out of their prop-planes, jets and helicopters forty times one year. What a joy and they even paid you for doing it!

Being a bit adventurous might get you in a little trouble from time-to-time though. One summer during college some friends and I were swimming at our favorite place, an old, abandoned grist mill dam on the Guadalupe River in New Braunfels, Texas. It was a wonderful, secluded spot with a huge limestone dam that had been built across this beautiful river over a hundred years ago (back then) that was fed by thousands of crystal clear springs. There was and still is a huge tower on one side of the dam that looked a lot like the parapet of an old castle with a pond of water in the river bed below. We would go there time and again, spending the whole day going over the dam in our inner tubes and swimming through the caverns under it. On one particular occasion, I challenged my friends to jump off of the tower with me but, of course, nobody would. So, you guessed it, I did it myself. High dives and towers don't look real high from the ground you know. They look high when you get on top of them. Regardless, I jumped and hit the bottom of that pond, which I expected, but it also felt like someone had stuck an ice pick in my little toe. Not to be bothered by a little pain, I swam to the other side of the river and jumped up on the bank. Then, looking down at my feet, I found that I had nine toes pointing straight ahead of me and one little toe bent at about 90 degree angle to the left. I went by the doctor's office on the way home that day and he said, "You have two choices: I can put your foot in a cast and you won't be able to go back to your construction job for the rest of the summer. Or, I can tape the broken toe to the one next to it. It is going to be extremely painful but you can shove it in your boot and still keep your job if you can stand the pain. I opted for the latter because I was—not—even- going—to—lose—my—summertime job. However, every time I jumped in a ditch (laying a pipe line) or stuck my foot on a shovel to dig, it stung like fire. Such is the price sometimes of adventure.

Certainly everyone doesn't have to go this way, i.e.: the Army Rangers, but that experience certainly has been helpful in civilian life. Each time a new opportunity came along, I had to leave the success and security of my current job to venture out into something new. My first job in the civilian world was to run a roof truss plant, which was in line with my college degree, Industrial Technology. However, I could see pretty quickly that doing the same things over and over was not for me. I soon opted for sales, selling house packages to builders (and I had never sold anything in my life). Then the real estate business and later started a building business and a home design plan service for builders along with it. Finally I started a commercial real estate company. Most of those moves required taking a rather big risk, leaving the security of the old, as I said, to accept the challenges of adventure. Finally, after twelve years as a real estate broker, when I actually loved the business and thought I would be doing it for the rest of my life, God called me into full-time ministry. With no promise, no pay and only one service a month in a prison and a whole lot of "calling," I left my civilian interests behind and started living by faith. Now that was an adventure! I have always told people, I'm still in the Army—just got a branch transfer to the Army of the Lord. It sure is exciting, taking in new ground for God! We build buildings with no money, simply trusting the Master to come along and be the banker and superintendent of the work! It is quite an adventure and I wouldn't trade it for anything in the world. The opportunity to see literally hundreds and sometimes thousands come to the Lord each year is unfathomable—and these people will live forever! The Lord does all the work. He just needs an empty vessel to work with.

Did I ever intend to go where I've been and be where I am today? No, not at all. Somebody was just looking for a few warm bodies to whip into shape for a drill team and I just happened to be a naïve college freshman, looking for a little adventure. When they called for some volunteers to try out for the drill team, I shot my little biscuit hook up in the air and that was it. One risky, fortuitous decision. That day my life went from plain vanilla to off-the-charts exciting. Who knew? From then on, it has either been directed by some kind of cataclysmic, cosmic roulette or the hand of God—and I have to believe it was the latter.

What it means to have the character trait of being **ADVENTUROUS:**

- Willing, inclined and adept at encountering the various new risks, tasks and challenges of life
- Willing to enter into and deal with the new and unknown
- Venturesome
- Being excited about the tests and opportunities of life
- Refusing to be deterred by the difficulty of the task
- Able to venture out beyond the call of duty
- Never being afraid to fail, knowing that failure leads to success
- A willingness to face risks and dangers because you see the possibilities of raw opportunity
- Remembering, "I can do all things through Christ who strengthens me." Philippians 4:13

ADVERSITY, ABLE TO OVERCOME   Study start date: _____ Finish date: _____

Thank God life has its blessings, rewards and positive, sunshiny days. However, to live and prepare for the day of trouble is wisdom. We know there are certainly going to be some calamities down the road. There are going to be some misfortunate events, troubles and accidents in everyone's lives. Some crumble in face of tough problems and unfair odds but we have to decide that, with God's help, we are not going to be one of them. Solomon spoke to this saying, "If you faint in the day of adversity, your strength is small." (Proverbs 21:10) For those who are in covenant with Him, God says, "In time of trouble He shall hide (you) in His pavilion; in the secret place of His tabernacle. He shall hide (you); He shall set (you) high upon a rock." (Psalm 27:5) He goes on to say in Psalm 50:15 that you can "call upon Me in the day of trouble; I will deliver you, and you shall glorify Me." What incredible promises!

Life is a battle for all of us. There are, thankfully, a whole lot more sunshiny days than dark ones but it is the dark days that have the power to devastate. It is the dark days that cause the weak to despair and give up. Adversity and conflict are simply unavoidable in life. For this reason and to encourage us to be prepared, the Master counsels us to count the cost before we ever step out on the field of battle. Before we even begin a battle, we need to decide if we have the gear to go all the way and obtain the victory. In order to get the true picture of what we are facing He poses this question: "What king, going to make war against another king, does not sit down first and consider whether he is able with ten thousand to meet him who comes against him with twenty thousand? Or else, while the other is still a great way off, he sends a delegation and asks conditions of peace." (Luke 14:31, 32) In other words, if we are looking for a fair fight in this life, we are going to be sadly disappointed. Don't. Our adversary is the devil will be working in and through people and circumstances right in our very neighborhood, the community we live in. the company and ministry we are working for. The question is can you still keep the faith and believe you have the victory even when we are outnumbered two to one? Even two against one would be a blessing compared to what we might have to face on occasion. If we handle these conflicts success-fully, positive results will strengthening our relationships and cause us to gain even more ground in life. Allowing them to defeat us will harm our relationships and cause us to lose ground and, for a time, may destroy our happiness.

When problems surface, sometimes they come so fast there is no time to collect the facts or write anything down. You have to analyze the situation speedily, formulate the best plan of action possible and begin to attack with all you've got. However, if time allows, Take a deep breath, thank God for trusting you with the problem and begin to gather your wits about you. Don't be melodramatic. Remain calm and collect as much information as you can. In times like this, you need to stop and write down all the facts and circumstances you know of surrounding the situation. Things become much clearer when you write them down on paper. Next, start writing down the assets you have at your disposal and every option available to respond to the situation. Then be sure to take the time to seek wise counsel. Solomon said, "Plans are established by counsel; by wise counsel wage war." (Proverbs 20:18) And, went on to say, "In a multitude of counsel there is safety." (Proverbs 24:6) Realize that we have nothing to lose by seeking counsel. You already, obviously, know what you know about the situation and have your own life expe-riences to draw from. Why not ask for advice from a well-respected veteran who has been battle-tested in the area of conflict you happen to be facing? An unbiased counselor is under no pressure and isn't emotionally involved so he can possibly see your options a little clearer. They will usually come up with options and angles you never thought of.

Solomon gives us a hint about the purpose of these unforeseen and unavoidable problems that come our way saying, "The refining pot is for silver and the furnace for gold, but the Lord tests the hearts." (Proverbs 17:3) Ore containing silver must be refined by the heat of a furnace to remove all the impurities and make it both useful and more valuable. "There are only two fires in the crucible of life," according to Dr. Doyle, "those that consume and those that purify." So we have a choice about these attacks, we can either let them consume us or we can let them purify us. Purification will remove the rough, unproductive attitudes and dispositions in our lives and will actually produce a blessing from these problems in due time. Some problems come to reveal and refine our character. Exceptional character traits often emerge but they cannot be produced by any other means. None of us like the heat but we can endure it better if we decide to be patient, let God have His way and continually look for the blessings while in the crucible.to see what He has in store for us. We can't do without problems in life. If we could, we would also fail to receive the benefits they bring us. Sometimes there are reasons for these problems that we will never know or understand while on this planet. We simply have to rest, knowing that our life, our breath and all our ways are in God's hands (Daniel 5:23) and that He knows very well what He is doing. He loves us. He alone knows best and has a better plan for our lives than anything we could ever think of for ourselves.. For this reason and many others, it is always best to pray about every situation and ask God for wisdom. On my knees, I have been given answers to problems that I would never have found any other way.

Once you have studied the problem, sought counsel and asked for wisdom, you must decide on the best time to respond. Then do it fearlessly with great resolve knowing that God "causeth us always to triumph in Christ." (II Corinthians 2:14 KJV) and that "The battle is the Lord's" (I Samuel 17:47) "In all these things we are more than conquerors through Him who loved us" (Romans 8:37) and the victory is ours.

What it means to have the character trait of being **ABLE TO OVERCOME ADVERSITY:**

- Having the mindset to see adversity as a blessing
- Not being discouraged or deterred by calamity
- Able to keep a victorious attitude in the face of overwhelming odds
- Not letting temporary affliction and reversals affect our outcomes in life

AGREEABLE IN NATURE-   Study start date: _____ Finish date: _____

Some people have the uncanny ability to put the wrong construction on everything. They doubt every-body's motives, are unhappy with where they are in the world and think everyone is against them. Some can even make the word *caustic* a thing of beauty. To them, happiness in life is quibbling, quar-reling, criticizing and cajoling. I think these fractious people really don't like themselves and that is part of the reason they are so argumentative. They already know that after you talk with them for a minute and get to know them like they know themselves, you won't like them either, so what's the use? They just rail on.

These are the people we all have been warned about who are walking the earth with the proverbial chip on their shoulder. Just being around them is like lying down in a pile of thorns, thistles, prickly pears and poison ivy. I don't care if you can take a running jump at a thorn tree and climb it backwards—and never get stuck. That was until you meet one of these people. You are going to get stuck just being in the vicinity. They are like a time bomb about to explode. Being around disagreeable people requires keeping your distance and treading softly, as if you were walking on egg shells. They must have forgotten that it will probably be the same people they so painfully perturb today that they will need cooperation from tomorrow, the next day and down the road for the rest of their lives.

If you have ever had to work with this kind of person, you found that their starting point in just about any discussion is being against everything. Nothing suits them nor do they like new ideas—unless, of course, they are their own. Why not rather work on being agreeable in nature. Look for the good points in another person's suggestions. Try to find common ground and work from that platform to resolve any differences. Always meet new initiatives with a positive point of view, always believing that you can overcome them. Agreement is the place of power in life. Truly working at being open, easily approach-able and helpful to others is what makes friendships work, groups function and life a blessing. One day, you will be glad you did.

All relationships begin with a first meeting and no one gets a second chance at making a good first impression. So, start out in a friendly way. Remember, the admonition, "A man who has friends must himself be friendly." (Proverbs 18:24) Making it our practice to smile when we meet people is also a good habit to start. If we look like we have been sucking persimmons all our lives, no one is going to want to be around us. How powerful is a smile? Just a smile can bring happiness to anybody—even to those who don't happen to like you. It is the universal code language for saying, I like you, myself, my job, where we are geographically and life itself. In addition a smile says I expect a positive outcome to this meeting, the situation we find ourselves in and our relationship. It also helps being pre-disposed to making life-long friendships with everyone we meet. Having this goal means we will always be ready to make investments in the lives of others in many ways, including being respectful, adding value to their lives and being patient with them. When meeting people we need to realize that both of us are human beings, with similar needs and aspirations, occupying the same planet, so finding something to agree about shouldn't be all that difficult. We should always be looking for common ground with other people. It should also be standard procedure before entering into a difficult meeting or confrontation to humbly ask God for wisdom.

In summary, we need to do our best to keep a mind-set of being flexible, negotiable and agreeable, not demanding that everything be done our way. Life is rarely ever perfect and neither are people, including us. So, we need to try to find something we genuinely like about the other person or group as well as something we can agree on. I believe a good goal is to endeavor to be like David, the shepherd of sheep who became Israel's greatest warrior, governor and king; a man who had a heart after God. When King Saul was looking for a musician to pull him out of depression, one of his servants who had met David said this to the king about him: "I have seen a son of Jesse, the Bethlehemite, a skillful musician, a valiant man, a man of war, prudent in speech (agreeable in nature), of a good presence and, behold, the Lord is with him." I Samuel 16:18

What it means to have the character trait of **BEING AGREEABLE IN NATURE:**

- Always starting out in a friendly way, being open, as if you might have missed something. (not being a know-it-all)
- Being respectful of everyone and be predisposed not to let another's rudeness or sharp words cause us to react negatively to them
- Realizing some people are truly a test and we are all going to meet some of them in life.
- Being intent upon agreeing with our adversary quickly if at all possible.
- Even if we don't agree with their overall position, look for at least one or two good points. Gladly tell them you agree with those points in their argument. It shows sincerity.
- Admitting it quickly when we find that we are wrong
- Not arguing about the unimportant, trivial points of life. We should pick our battles.
- Never interfering with another person's ways of being happy as long as it doesn't concern the work at hand. (If they like hot sauce on their ice cream, don't get in the way of that.)
- Looking for something to compliment the other person about and doing it sincerely. Everybody does something well and can do something better than we can.
- Considering everyone we meet to be a little bit better than ourselves. Everyone has gifts and talents given to them by God. Who can say their gifts are more important in the grand scheme of things than those of others?
- Letting people know you are always open to debate a subject calmly and respectfully but you refuse to argue
- Showing respect for the other person's right to have a point of view even if you don't agree with it. Realizing everyone in America has a right to believe anything they want—even if it is wrong.
- Letting the other person do most of the talking
- Trying our best to see things from the other person's point of view realizing that God uses conflict to bring people together
- Trying to put ourselves in the other person's shoes in our own mind even if it is for just a few minutes
- Always humbly asking God for wisdom before entering into a difficult confrontation
- Removing the harsh words and antagonistic attitudes that may exist in our own personality

ALERTNESS—   **Study start date:** _____ **Finish date:** _____

So many today live in a haze, a mist, a fog or a cloud, not realizing they are constantly vulnerable to being attacked. Certainly our enemy is on the prowl. He is crouched even at the door when we go out today (Genesis 4:7) and we are the target.

In addition to the eminent danger we face, things in life are made to give the appearance of permanence. However, quite the contrary, everything on this planet, except for the church, is in a state of flux. Change may come swiftly or it may come gradually but it is always part of the process in life. Companies, governments, political parties and families are rising and falling. It is said, "Whoever is first today, tomorrow shall be last." There will always be new inventions, new systems, new economic difficulties, new trends, new megatrends, new formulas and younger and faster guns coming up that will change the entire landscape in various fields of endeavor. Proverbs 27:24 tells us, "… riches are not forever, nor does a crown endure to all generations." We have only two choices. Be alert to change so you can respond to it in a timely manner, letting it work for the good of all or be crushed asunder by it like an on-coming steam roller.

Failing to be alert and careful about our environment and the systems around us, will allow the enemy easy access to steal our health, wealth, time and the opportunities of life. He can accomplish this by accidents, oversights, carelessness, by stealth or by the outright, open onslaught of a surprise attack. Having been a front line infantry commander in Vietnam, I have had to learn a bit about the importance of living ever at the ready, alert at all times. In war, there is no quarter. We will get no free pass from the enemy. Ignorance of the craftiness of our enemies pays its own ugly wages. Instead, we need to be like "the men of Issacar who were men who had understanding of the times to know what Israel ought to do." (I Chronicles 12:32) They were always awake and ever at the ready, watching for the signs, indicators and even the smallest movement or change. Once they recognized them, they also knew what courage and wisdom would have them do, either momentarily, or in the proper season.

The environment, the times, the economy and the enemy are constantly endangering man's existence on this planet. It has been that way from the beginning. Knowing this, we must be constantly alert, cognizant of the possibility of trouble when working with tools, implements, trees, large rocks, machinery, people who are in training, large animals, etc. Over the years, I have known several people who were killed while working on tree removal crews. They were crushed when a tree, cut by someone else nearby, landed on them completely unaware. Others I have known disabled the guards on their circular saws to gain a little speed, only to find themselves disabled, losing a few of their own, irreplaceable digits. I have, personally, entered a pastures on some ranchland and thought myself to be the only living creature there. However, I soon realized that I was mistaken about that and was soon being charged by an enormous, angry, hot-breathing bull, frothing at the mouth. Just the sight of that huge mass of well-horned and hoofed beef with two well-focused eyes coming my way at an extremely high rate of speed would have been enough to scare John Wayne, himself. Those hoofs were pounding the ground so hard it seemed to make the whole earth shudder. That experience frightened me enough as a young teenager to run like a streak of light and leap that barbed wire fence faster than I ever thought possible. Those oncoming horns were motivation enough for me.

Some things in life may sound a bit too trivial to worry about such as scraps of wood or other materials lying on the ground where men are working or pieces of wood lying around with the nails still in them. We have all seen these things on jobs before but you never know who might catch a bee sting on the ear and start out running without the first thought of looking at what might be in their path. Inadvertently, in their haste they might step on a rusty nail in a board that had been lying there. They probably won't get lock-jaw today but they will likely have to take a whole series of painful, expensive shots to prevent it. Proverbs 4:26 admonishes us to, "Make level paths for your feet and take only ways that are firm." This tells us that the minds God gave us, although excellent in many ways, are not capable of concentrating on the craftsmanship required by the job at hand and remembering the location of all the refuse scattered about on the ground. It is just not worth it for someone to step on something, stumble and sprain or break an ankle. We need to be alert, as leaders, to take every precaution to protect ourselves and our fellow workers. It is part of the job of a leader to ensure that those on their team perceive the inherent dangers, make preparations and wear the proper gear.

Operating heavy equipment such as front-end loaders, back hoes, motor graders and, of course, airplanes successfully over a period of time, requires vigilance, not only to carefully clear the standard check list before operating them but to also look for other signs of wear, tear and impending danger. We also need to take the proper precautions. A good friend of mine who is a general contractor, bought a large front-end loader several years ago that did not come with a protective cage or super-structure above the driver's seat. Being good friends, I had the freedom to demand that he not to even think about using that dozer, not even for a second, without buying a safety cage for it. Amazingly, he took that advice and the very first time he used it on a job, a huge tree limb fell right on top of the cab where he was sitting. According to his own words, that safety cage saved his life. That safety equipment paid for itself the first day in spades.

Another area in which we should be alert is to see trouble coming in the economy. There are economic services that give us indicators and graphs as to how the economy is performing. One can know what is about to happen from these indicators but it won't come to us by accident. It is our responsibility to sign up for these services and be alert to watch these reports in a timely fashion.

A great lesson in being alert was taught us about two thousand five hundred years ago by a Hebrew named Mordecai who happened to be living in Babylonian captivity at the time. When his brother and his brother's wife died, he accepted their young daughter, Esther, as his own and began to raise her from a very young age. As she began to mature, it became quite evident that she was going to be a very beautiful woman. Later on, King Xerxes divorced his wife, the queen, for insubordination and a kingdom-wide search was made for a successor. Many young women were selected to vie for his approval but only one would, ultimately be selected. In God's plan and unbeknownst to Xerxes, Esther, a Jewess, was the one chosen. Upon completion of the selection process she was moved immediately into the palace and Mordecai lost all contact with her. This, of course, was long before there were any of the efficient means of communications we are familiar with today. Being alert to the dangers of living as an alien in a foreign land, Mordecai had to find a way to check on her wellbeing and, of course, any

Haman walking out of the city gate in front of Mordecai

possible impending danger to his people. This led him to sit daily at the gate of the king's palace to hear the latest scuttlebutt coming out of the king's palace that was being noised abroad by his servants, cooks and guards. Sharing the king's secrets gave his attendants a certain sense of importance with all the peasants at the gate. While sitting there one day, Haman, the king's number two in command, walked by and

Mordecai, who of course being a Jew, refused according to the law of God to bow down to him as all the others did. It so infuriated Haman that he built a gallows seventy feet high on which to hang him. Later on he expanded his murderous plan to include all the Jews there in captivity.

However, waiting there at the gate daily and listening intently, Mordecai discovered, on one occasion, an assassination conspiracy about to be carried out against the king by two of his guards. He immediately reported it to Esther who advised the king so that the matter was quickly investigated and confirmed. Those men were quickly executed.

Later on, again while being alert, sitting at the gate, Mordecai discovered the pernicious, murderous plan hatched by Haman. This time, the assignation target was not the king but rather the entire population of Jews by Haman, himself. Again, Mordecai reported the insidious plan to Esther who was then able, although risking her very life, to make a wise appeal to the king and save her people. Esther's valiant appeal saved the life of her adopted father, Mordecai, and the lives of the whole nation of Jews in captivity there at the time. Had Mordecai not been alert, the story could possibly have ended very differently. As providence would have it, however, Haman, himself, was hung from the same gallows he had built for the hanging of Mordecai—seventy-five feet high.

What it means to have the character trait of **ALERTNESS:**

- Being aware of impending danger.
- Watchfulness for emergency situations (like trees falling on houses, brakes going out, etc.)
- Careful, cautious and circumspect
- Arranging to find consistent indicators that allow you to anticipate what the economy is doing
- A quickness to perceive a change in one's environment becoming dangerous
- Being ever vigilant, knowing the enemy always comes at a time when you least expect and your guard is likely to be down
- Realizing some things in life are more dangerous than they appear (examples–motorcycles, three wheelers, transporting mattresses in a pickup truck, etc.)
- Being ready to act quickly when trouble comes
- Quick to see both danger and opportunity

ALL-THE-WAY ATTITUDE, AN—   Study start date: _____ Finish date: _____

Life is not a single leap or a hundred yard dash but a marathon. It's a long-distance race, a test of endurance. To reach the goal we need an "all-the-way and then some" mentality. It seems like just about everything on the blue marble is harder and takes longer than we think. Few, indeed, are they who will do what it takes to succeed because they don't have just that—an all-the-way attitude. Sooner or later the world system grinds them down into powder and, thus, all their efforts come to a screeching halt. In a final act of desperation, they peter out and throw in the proverbial towel. They fold up their tent and go home because having this kind of a mind-set is contrary to human nature. All of us are wired prior to birth to seek instant gratification. We want all we can get and we want it the easiest way possible. Quite naturally, we want to take the path of least resistance and make the least effort possible to get by. This is simply human nature.

In yesterday's Atlanta Journal/Constitution (6/21/16) the front page news was an article by the head of the Georgia Highway Patrol instructor, a twenty year veteran of the force. He mentioned that twenty years when he went through the Academy nearly everyone who signed up made the course and became a State Trooper. Interestingly, last year, they had 2,700 young men and women start the course and only thirty made it. He said most of them just quit. What a change in attitudes in just twenty short years.

When I was a lieutenant in the 82nd Airborne Division, tradition had it that every time we met another soldier on the street or in garrison, we would salute those who out-ranked us and say with a loud voice, like we meant it, "All the way, Sir!" Why? Because we were in the business of fighting wars and war is a difficult but critically important endeavor. As a nation, we have faced many a competent foe. They have all been well trained and equipped—and none of them have ever given up easily. Their own lives, that of their families and friends and all they own and ever hope for is in the balance and as always, to the victor go the spoils. War is a life and death struggle and you can know of a certainty that the enemy is going to fight you tooth and nail to the very bitter or blessed end. Because of this, we must be willing to go harder, stronger and longer than our enemies or we will not be victorious. Many times, as a nation, as an army and, individually, as a soldier, we have not had what we considered necessary to face the enemy but we had to go with what we had and win anyhow. Attitude, as in everything else, is in fact everything in war! No matter the difficulty at the moment, we must acquire the mindset that we are going to go over the mountain, around the mountain or, if need be, we will dig our way through the mountain to accomplish our mission. We must overcome it and get past it—regardless! As young soldiers, repeating the phrase, "All the way, Sir!" time and time again, caused a can-do, all the way attitude to become engrained in our hearts and minds.to the point we thought nothing could stop us. It's a mindset. It's the kind of commitment with which you attack every task, assignment or mission that is given to you—every day for the rest of your life. In addition, what makes one valuable in the military and in civilian life as well is a person's ability to get the job done. In the military it is referred to as being mission oriented. The mindset that the mission is all that is important and that it must be accomplished—regardless of the cost. Other units in your area of operations may be relying on you to accomplish your mission in order to be in a position to accomplish theirs. Lives, many of them at times, may be in the balance. They are relying on you to get your job done. They don't want to hear a bunch of good excuses why you couldn't. They didn't give you the task for you to come back with a whole litany of excuses. The military is looking for a man who could get the job done every time and has no need of excuses.

Consider this for just a moment. Say you are an employer and have ten people working for you who are assigned various task from time-to-time. Nine continually report back with a well-documented list of reasons why they couldn't get the job done and why it was impossible in the first place. However one of them, no matter what you ask this person to do, he always gets the job done—no complaints and no excuses. Who is going to be your "go-to man?" Who is going to get the next promotion? Who is going to be put in charge of the department?

In the civilian world several things can get in the way of "getting the job done." Just one small item is the cost. Civilians are in business to make a profit, so if the cost of the project gets in the way of the profit incentive, the job comes, very quickly, to a halt. In the military, on the other hand, cost is not a factor because lives, winning the war and the nation's survival are at stake. Civilians are also moved off of certain goals, from time-to-time, because of political correctness and fear of public censure. In the military and the church, doing what is right is imperative, regardless.

Another deterrent to accomplishing the mission, is the time constraint. Few people ever even think of working past five o'clock, late into the night or coming in on a Saturday to get the task completed. The reason for this, of course, is their pay stops at five o'clock. However, remember this, those times you must work late seemingly without pay, will be rewarded greatly not in "over time" but over time. Forget yourself. Go all the way. Get the job done. Pull out all the stops. Go for it and get it done! One day you will be glad you did.

Yet another major impairment to having an all-the-way attitude oftentimes is fatigue. Just the distance of the race, the long hours, the heat, the constant press of the enemy and the discouragement of the world system, definitely wear on a person. Most people can lead just fine when they are well-fed, have plenty of energy and enough sleep. That is exactly why the Army Ranger School puts candidates through a couple months of enormous stress, starvation, sleep deprivation and pain to determine if they can stay focused on the men and their mission instead of caving in to the demands of personal survival. There is a very good reason for this. They want to find a person's pain threshold because in a real war, being surrounded by the enemy or in some other way cut off from your supply lines is a very real possibility. They may have to face the stress of horrendous heat, battles that last several days and nights (without sleep) or have to face the disturbing reality of running out of food and ammunition. Will you then tell your men its time to surrender or keep on fighting with knives and hand grenades? How will you react? My company in Vietnam went without food for three days and almost ran out of ammunition. Having no food was easier to deal with than the prospect of no ammo. What was worse, every time the Division sent a helicopter out to us for re-supply, the Viet Cong either shot it up or shot it out of the sky. They couldn't land so I asked them to put everything we needed in used 155 mm artillery canisters, fly over us fast, just above tree-top level, and drop it out on top of us. Thank God they did.

On military posts they have what are called Red Flag Days. This occurs every time the temperature and humidity both rise to a certain level. At that point a red flag goes up the flag pole and all training, work details and movement on the post stops, except for Ranger School. They continue on simply because there is no such thing as a Red Flag Day in war. The Army needs to know who can survive this and other things. One particular Red Flag Day while in Ranger School at Fort Benning, Georgia, we had to march from the Ranger Barracks to Victory Pond where our actual training would be conducted that day. It was so hot I could feel my brains cooking like scrambled eggs. One of the men in my platoon actually died from a heat stroke. Just another day of training. What one might have to endure in a real war might easily be that bad or worse. A friend I met years later told me the heat, stress, starvation and sleep depravation was so bad when he went through Ranger School that he actually prayed that God would send a snake to bite him so he could get out of there "honorably." Honorably meant having a good reason to leave without quitting. Well, God did answer his prayer but said, "No." Because of that, my friend pressed on, endured it all, graduated and went on to have a stellar military career.

Another hindrance to having this all-the-way attitude is either being unwilling or not knowing how to apply one's self to a task. You see, a person's life is described by Paul in the Bible as a race and he said in any kind of a race, everybody runs but only one gets the crown. He said if you are going to run, then run in such a manner that you win. Don't just be an also-ran. Those who desire to win realize that they need to train themselves to be temperate and disciplined in every area of their lives so they can endure the hardship and pain of a long race. He said it is a mistake to run with uncertainty, without a deep commitment to the prospect of winning or to fight as someone just beating the air; going through the motions. He concludes his discourse by saying, "I discipline my body and bring it into subjection, lest, when I have preached to others, I myself should become disqualified." (I Corinthians 9:27) On another occasion, speaking of our attitude toward our work, Paul said, "Whatever you do, do it heartily, as unto the Lord and not unto men. (Colossians 3:23) Realize it is the Lord God you are really working for even though you may answer to a mere man in this life. Realize you are really working for the King. Knowing this, everyone should strive for the highest possible standards, bringing every bit of creativity and persistence possible into the effort, to achieve extraordinary results.

Just as important, for any kind of human achievement in the race of life, we must learn to give it all we've got. Whatever you do, Paul is saying, do it with all your might and determination! This may sound a bit harsh, strident and grueling to make a habit of working in this manner every day on everything you touch. However, amazingly, in it you will find a great release. Extra strength comes and a much greater sense of satisfaction as well when we become an all-outer. Nobody wants or needs a half-way Jose.' They want someone who can get the job done and All-outer's are a rare find.

Although the mind of man may have a conscious aversion to working with all our might, when the work is done, we see the results and feel the satisfaction in our hearts, we realize, once again, that this is the only way to live and work. The easiest way and the only way to do anything in the long run, is with excellence and all our might. When coupled with integrity and diligence, this all-the-way attitude could possibly make you the most valuable person in your company. Remember, the measure of a man is truly how much others rely on you. Although we should work to be indispensable, nobody and I mean nobody ever really is—but its OK to try.

What it means to have the character trait of **AN ALL-THE-WAY ATTITUDE:**

- A completion, never-give-up, get-the-job done mind-set
- A conquering attitude
- An ever-victorious state of mind
- Expecting to go all the way in life—regardless of the obstacles
- Surmounting difficulties, setbacks, betrayals and enduring the waits and postponements life has for us along the way
- Determining that neither mountains, valleys nor the size or ferocity of the enemy will ever stop us

APPRECIATION — Study start date: _____ Finish date: _____

Sometimes, in a busy, helter-skelter world, we forget to show our appreciation for those around us by failing to praise them for a job well done. It is far easier to be critical but we can do better. We can be more thankful. It makes life so much better to honestly voice our appreciation by complimenting others for their work. Besides, we know that praise can really build up the other person and mean more to them than money. A great human need is respect in the form of appreciation. Without controversy, people respond better to appreciation than anything! Remember, people don't have to be on our team. Ours is not the only company, ministry or business in the world. So, we should be loath to find fault and quick to lavish sincere praise on those around us. Praising even the smallest improvement is always the right thing to do. Everybody wants to be appreciated and, believe it or not, everybody is always doing their best. Even a guy, passed out in cardboard condominium in a back downtown alleyway is doing his best. If he could think of a better way to be happy in life, he would be doing it. But in this particular case, we don't need to show them a whole lot of encouragement. We need to show them love, respect as a person and a better way.

Appreciation is simply giving thanks for the investments and contributions of others to our company, ministry, team or us individually. Solomon, the wisest person in the world, said, "A word fitly spoken is like apples of gold in settings of silver." (Proverbs 25:11) Learning how to show our appreciation to others in creative ways is something we all need to work on. Here are but a few:

- Thanks for the consistent effort
- You get an A+, go to the head of the class
- Your sales for the month were outstanding
- You really get the job done
- Your efforts really made a difference
- You make our company's vision come alive
- You are so thoughtful. Thanks.
- I'd like to clone you
- Thanks for sticking with it and making it happen while the rest of us were out
- Your perseverance is admirable
- You are killing our customers with kindness. Thanks.
- Your attitude always lifts our whole team
- I'm really proud you are on our team
- You're a champ
- You really go all the way and I appreciate it
- That was really a great effort
- You made your team members look good
- I have a lot of confidence in you
- It is a blessing to have you on our team
- Your efforts inspire our whole team
- Our customers have told me they appreciate your efforts to go far beyond what is required
- That was quite an accomplishment

We also need to be appreciative of God. None of us deserved to be born into the world and have the opportunities of life. As I write this, a dear lady in our church just had a premature baby by caesarean section that had to be put on a respirator immediately. The child had many problems and died just one day and one hour later. His only experience in life was pain. Most of us have all of our limbs, digits and faculties about us. All of this is the gift of God. None of us deserve today and none of us are promised tomorrow. Many of us have been through war. Some were wounded and some were not. Just getting through it alive is a great blessing.

One of my good friends was a Captain in 25ᵗʰ Infantry Division while serving in Vietnam. He was hit by a RPG (rocket propelled grenade) one day that instantly blew off both legs and an arm. His intestines were all over the place and it wasn't a very pretty sight. Because body bags were in short supply in those days, they scraped up what they could of his remains and wrapped it all in a rain poncho until he arrived by Medevac helicopter at the field hospital. Once at the hospital, his remains were finally placed in a body bag. A few hours later, a doctor was walking by and something told him to unzip this particular body bag and take the pulse of the corpse. This was not something he had ever done before. Amazingly, he found a pulse and ordered his attendants to put my friend on the operating table immediately. That began about fifteen hours of back-to-back operations just to get him stabilized. Later, he was shipped out to the Atlanta VA Hospital's Center for Multiple Amputees where he spent another twenty-two months undergoing another thirty-three surgeries. He has been in a wheel chair ever since but is still very thankful for his life being spared. Bet you never met anyone who" appreciated" the fact that he took a direct hit from an RPG. Today he is still thanking God for the direct hit of that RPG because that hot metal sliced through him like a hot knife in butter. Had he been hit in like manner with the shrapnel from an artillery round, he would most likely have died. The fire from that RPG explosion cauterized his wounds, stopped most of the bleeding and actually kept him alive. He still had some serious blood loss but, obviously, not enough to kill him. Thank God.

He never uses his situation for any kind of an excuse and has led an extremely productive life. He has been able to run businesses as well as be the District Director for the Veterans' Administration in Atlanta for many years. With his service time, eighteen years as District Director of the Georgia Department of Veteran Services, he had over forty seven years of service to our country when he retired. His name is Tommy Clack. His marriage produced two handsome kids, a son who became an Eagle Scout and an Army Ranger himself and a beautiful daughter who has brought him grandchildren as well.

Tommy has always been a hustler. At the age of eight he was working as a stocker in a supermarket and by the time he was twelve he was operating his own lawn service with nine employees. He will tell you, "Life is no accident. It is a daily choice and a daily gift." He will also tell you "Freedom isn't free." Be sure you appreciate it.

In 1973, Tommy and I had just recently returned from the Army and Vietnam. He happened to be the leader of the De Kalb County Jaycees when that was the premier young men's organization in our area. I was the president of the Rockdale County Jaycees in the same district. In those days the scope and portfolio of projects in Jaycee chapters made being a Jaycee president almost a fulltime job. I don't know what his chapter was involved in but ours was running a county-wide Empty Stocking Fund Drive, a Junk Car Roundup as well as writing a junk car ordinance and having it codified. We were encouraging the County to establish a Small Claims Court and to enlarge the one-man Commission to a three-man commission system of government, to name just a few. All of which actually happened. In addition, there was competition between the chapters on a multitude of other areas. At the end of the year one chapter in every district was always selected for the Best chapter award. I want you to know that Tommy's chapter, under his leadership, beat us soundly. Way to go Tommy!

He is truly a great leader and having just recently attended his retirement party, I can tell you there are several hundred other people whose lives he has touched who also happened to be there and who agree with me, Yes, he retired. Well, no, never. He is now the full-time CEO and Chairman of the Board for the Walk of Heroes Veterans Memorial in Rockdale County, Georgia. He is working hard to build it to its potential—a multi-million dollar project that can have a lasting effect on future generations. Tommy is outstanding and I appreciate him for being my faithful friend these many years.

What it means to have the character trait of **APPRECIATION:**

- Having heart-felt gratitude and praise for the work of others
- A favorable estimation of things done for us as gifts or in response to duty
- Responding appropriately for the help and investments of others in our lives
- Expressions of admiration and appreciation
- Communicating with others to say "well done"

ATTENTION TO DETAIL —   **Study start date: _____ Finish date: _____**

Life is simply a series of tasks completed. Sometimes we work for others and sometimes for ourselves but always for God. The secret to life is loyalty and the secret to loyalty is to always be working as unto the Lord. If we try to do our work well enough to present to God, be it our duty in friendship, marriage or as an employee, we need not worry about it being acceptable to men or women we report to here on earth. It will all be well. The sum total of all these tasks is what one's life will amount to. Of course we may start out a task just thinking in generalities and focus primarily on just getting the work done. Few indeed realize at the outset, the importance of getting everything done exactly right. We usually have to fail pretty dramatically once or twice before we see the importance of attention to detail.

I still remember a day in high school when a teacher explained the importance of writing legibly. He told of a great train wreck that occurred because someone scribbled a number down causing it to be misread by someone else. This same attention to detail is critically important in the military so the coordinates for a bombing run or an artillery strike hit the intended target, the enemy, and not the friendlies, non-combatants or a hospital. Even with all the modern technology and sophisticated weaponry on today's battlefield, we still persist in having more people killed and wounded by accident than we do on purpose. Certainly, a great deal of this is caused by human error and a lack of attention to detail. Every day mistakes are made in manufacturing, mistakes in sales because of simple, small mistakes or a number scribbled down that was misinterpreted.

A 1999 article from the National Academy of Science stated that medical mistakes, i.e., "medical malpractice," actually cause about 98,000 deaths every year. But that is just the tip of the iceberg. An even bigger problem is that a huge number of mistakes causing death or serious injury are covered up by the doctors and not even reported—for fear of law suits and other repercussions. Consider the seriousness of this problem. The study showed that more people die from medical mistakes each year than from auto accidents (about 43,450), breast cancer (42,300) or AIDS (16,500). The study further sited that "Doctor's notoriously poor handwriting too often leaves pharmacists squinting at paper prescriptions. Did the doctor order 10 milligrams or 10 micrograms? Does the prescription call for the hormone replacement Premarin or the antibiotic Primaxin?"[5] There are thousands of examples every year of doctors amputating the wrong leg, hand or finger. All these errors, omissions, mistakes and negligence is the sad state of affairs in one of the most highly trained, highly trusted and highly paid industries in our society. This fact is quite stunning when you consider that our medical system is dedicated first and foremost to "do no harm."

Another study done by a group of Harvard University researchers found that "four of every 100 patients in American hospitals are harmed while under care—most often because their medication or surgery is botched." This was the finding of a study of over 30,000 patients and their records in New York hospitals. Furthermore, it found that "14 percent of those who are harmed while receiving care die as a result of negligence or medical errors."[6] Amazingly, doctors are considered to be exceptional if they can be right with a patient's prognosis just 60 percent of the time. But, the medical profession is not alone in all this.

Just imagine how many mistakes could be corrected immediately in life if we would write more legibly and just stop for a few seconds to double check our work? Our CPA showed me how to double check entries in our computer system and just that created an amazing new world! It only takes a minute or two, but avoids the hours needed to rectify the damage done by undiscovered, incorrect, inadvertent erroneous entries.

Allow me to illustrate. A good friend of mine had won a contract to build a truck terminal in Jacksonville, Florida and asked another real estate broker friend of ours to go along with him for the ride since he was about to close on the real estate part of the transaction. Several of us were pilots and in years past from time-to-time would fly to various states to look at new development and building concepts. Anyhow, my friends left the airport near my house at about 4:00 A.M. and the pilot was kind enough to provide a sack of sausage-biscuits and coffee for breakfast. Before takeoff he completed his pre-flight check list in the dark, cranked the engine, received approval for taxiing instructions and a take-off from the tower. Once on the appointed runway, he shoved the throttle to the dashboard and they were airborne in a matter of seconds. Almost as soon as they had left the airport, they noticed the dense fog condition on the ground that the weather report had cited would be the case most of the way to Florida. However, they were flying well above it. About the time they had finished their biscuits, they turned on the cabin lights to stow-away the paper trash and the pilot noticed immediately that the windshield was covered with oil. Quickly glancing at the instrument panel, he saw the oil pressure gauge was going down rapidly. Knowing he couldn't make it much further and certainly couldn't land in the dense fog, he quickly turned the aircraft around, heading back to their original airport. However, the oil pressure continued to drop and the engine soon locked up. The pilot then set his flaps for the slowest descent possible and they prayed for God's help. I mean they really prayed. Soon, they were into the fog and visibility was zero. "At that moment," my friend said, "the Lord became the pilot and he became the copilot."

Soon, they hit the tops of some tall Georgia pines and both wings were ripped off, one right after the other. Then they hit another pine head-on and somehow it broke their speed and gently lowered them down to the ground like a hydraulic lift. (They found out later that the tree had a beetle knot in it that caused it to break just right for them.) When the plane hit the ground, it did so at a bit of an angle so they both were able to quickly exit the co-pilot's door in case the plane caught fire. Once they were out of danger, they sat on a dead tree trunk looking at the plane with their minds swirling, trying to contemplate the total disaster they had just somehow escaped. Amazingly, they discovered that both of them were just fine except for a very small cut one had on his hand. When they got their wits about them, they walked to a nearby farm house where they reported the accident and called for help to get home. The Federal Aviation Administration sent out inspectors right away to determine the cause of the accident. When they opened the engine cowling, they found the oil dip stick laying on top of the engine and not in the block where it was supposed to be. Every time the engine's pistons fired, the engine shot a little oil out of the top of the dip-stick shaft. During the pre-flight check, the pilot wasn't too concerned about checking the engine too closely because he knew that the airport mechanic had done the 1,000 hour engine overhaul the day before they took off. My friend had forgotten to take his flashlight that morning and skipped the engine compartment part of his pre-flight check because it was absolutely too dark. This caused him not to notice the missing dip-stick. The FAA inspectors determined that the cause of the accident was operator error which was, of course, a lack of attention to detail. God had mercy on my good friends that day.

We all have made mistakes in life though, haven't we? These two men are excellent and very faithful both in business and in the church. I told them they only survived because they were in covenant with God. My friend did such a good job piloting that plane through those pines and landing it perfectly on the ground, I asked him if he'd do it again just to see if he could do it as well the second time. Laughing, he declined any further demonstrations. Thank God for his mercy on my two friends and on me over a lifetime.

The Bible says, "He who is faithful in that which is least (the small things) is faithful also in much." (Luke 16:10) He can be given more. This is the law of God which He has written in nature and in our hearts. This law is great and is in operation every minute of every hour of every day. This is what it says: "For everyone who has (cherishes and counts what he has worthy of respect, proper care and maintenance), more will be given, and he will have abundance, but from him who does not have, even what he has will be taken away." (Matthew 25:29) In other words, he that is faithful in small matters will develop the gifts and talents to be competent to handle the much larger matters in life and business. That same person will obtain favor and will be given greater and greater concerns to manage as time progresses. By the same token, he who can't handle small things or thinks the small matters are too trivial to be concerned with, will never get past the small issues in life. He may even have the small things he despises taken away as well until he learns that every little thing does counts.

A true story is told about young Noel Borja of Malaybalay, Bukidnon, who would surely have been the youngest multimillionaire in the Philippines. As sole heir, young Noel had thirty days by statute to simply stand before the executor of his grandfather's estate so that he might account for himself (being alive) and receive the $116 million which had been left to him. However, unfortunately the executor's letter never made it to him because it was deposited in the dead-mail drop of the Bureau of Post until the deadline passed. Noel never appeared. How could this happen? He had recently decided to move from one boarding house to another while he was staying in Manila and didn't bother to leave his forwarding address. His failure to attend to the small detail of leaving his forwarding address, according to law, left him completely void of a basis for appeal. It may have only been a small task, a routine procedure, but it would have automatically forwarded his mail. It meant only filling out a short form but, none-the-less, it was not done. That fateful day Noel actually lost a whole lot more than the $116 million because of his failure to show a little attention to detail. He lost a much-improved standard of living, a myriad of new opportunities that would have presented themselves, vast opportunities to give, helping those in need, and an opportunity to be faithful on a large scale and multiply his new-found fortune phenomenally but, alas, the Scriptures are true.[7] He wasn't qualified to receive this great blessing because he, alone, disqualified himself.

Small things rule. I remember reading this insightful little statement somewhere years ago: in college. "For the loss of a nail, a horse's shoe was lost. For the loss of a shoe a horse was lost. For the loss of the horse a rider was lost. For the loss of the rider the commander was lost. For the loss of the commander the battle was lost. For the loss of the battle the war was lost and the nation fell- and all for the loss of a nail." author unknown

Our greatest hope in life should be to do all things, including the smallest things, with excellence so that, hopefully one day God Almighty might look down and catch us in the act.

What it means to have the character trait of **ATTENTION TO DETAIL:**

- Being alert to the fine points of life, personal relations and business matters.
- Realizing that it is all the small points being done well that make a great work or a large task one completed with excellence.
- Counting all facets of an operation, job or detail, even the small ones, as most important, significant and worthy of one's best efforts, art and concentration.
- Listening carefully to the instructions of our superior and writing them down so that we don't do what we think we heard but what we did hear.
- Getting our instructions right.

- Making a proper distinction to ensure the details required by our instructions, orders or commands are completed with zeal, excellence and perfection.
- Remembering that the sum total of all the small and large points of a project make the completed task either a work of art or a disaster.
- Realizing there are no "small things" in life. Everything is hugely important.
- A job well done well must be right from the bottom up.

ATTENTITIVENESS — (SEE ALERTNESS, ATTENTION TO DETAIL & THOUGHTFULNESS)

ATTITUDE, A POSITIVE—   Study start date: _____   Finish date: _____

There is so much negativity in the world, it is increasingly difficult to find people with a positive attitude. On any given day a person can be hit with the news that the house needs a new roof, they broke a tooth, the stock market fell 250 points and the thirteenth national, governmental scandal has been uncovered in two months. The national debt just reached eighteen trillion dollars, the President decided to cut our military by two-thirds and destroy half of our swiftly diminishing pile of nuclear weapons. The bank account is overdrawn by several thousand dollars and the dog got hit by a car. This is not something new. There has been trouble in this world since Adam ate the forbidden fruit in the garden. Job had a few troubles of his own.

He was minding his own business one day when a messenger came to his door with some bad news. First of all, he said the oxen were plowing the fields while the donkeys were feeding in the vicinity; all was peaceful and well. Then the Sabeans attacked and took them all away, killing every servants but this one last messenger who came to make the report. While the messenger was finishing his statement, another came right behind him saying fire had fallen from heaven and burned up all his sheep as well as all his servants watching them except for the one who came to give him this information. As he finished talking, another servant came and told Job the Chaldeans had just raided his camels and after killing all his servants but one, took the whole herd with them. Finally, while his words were still on his lips, yet another servant came and said that all Job's sons and daughters were banqueting at his eldest son's house when a whirlwind collapsed the building killed everyone except this lone servant who came to report what had happened. This is what you call trouble. He lost all his children, his business and his net worth went to zero in two minutes but it didn't end there. (Job 1:13–19) If this wasn't test enough, next the Lord allowed satan to attack his health. Soon he had the most painful boils imaginable from the top of his head to the souls of his feet. Then, to beat all, his wife and his friends came against him.

Today politicians are spending our nation into oblivion. While we are sitting on the largest oil reserves in the world here in America and the tree huggers won't let us drill like we should. They would much rather for us send our billions across the pond and buy our oil from the Arabs so they can buy bombs and send them back our way. Our economy is in the tank and industries capable of making actual products are almost non-existent in America today due to NAFTA.. On and on it goes, ad infinitum. But the point is, this is the only life any of us will ever have, the only economy we can really operate in and now is our time under the sun— no other. Always remember, there are busi-

nesses that make money in down markets and businesses that do well in up markets. Truly, God is the best businessman. In reality, the pendulum always swings in politics and the tax and spenders are on their way out. The longer it takes for us and start using our oil reserves, the more they will be worth and the more the Arab's supply will be depleted. Our reserves are so large that they will someday be our customers.

Clearly, in this world, there always has been and always will be trouble and it can come in some rather large doses at times. That is why attitude is everything. Attitude is altitude and attitude will either make or break us. Life will become whatever we think about. Everyone faces their problems with a certain, fixed mind-set. Some people are pessimists and others are optimists. If you think you can make it, you will; think you can't and you most assuredly won't. Remember, with God, our side always wins. Trouble never comes to stay—it comes to pass. With God and virtually nothing but a positive attitude, the world is your plum.

All of us face problems: this world, satan, our minds, the flesh and man's fallen nature, just to mention a few. Everything is automatically negative by nature. Every plant that sprouts its first root and sends up its first green sprig is born to die, as is every animal that takes its first breath. Everything is subject to age, decay, obsolescence and misuse by man—but there is hope.

All this tells us how critically important it is that we renew our minds with a powerful stimulus if there is ever going to be anything positive happen in the area of our thinking. Our minds can and must be renewed daily to work positively and productively. Thankfully, the most powerful success book of all time has already been given to us—the Bible. Every success book, in fact, that was ever worth reading was inspired by or derived in large part from this Book. The Bible is so powerful that it makes incredible promises to those who read it, follow its counsel and simply believe. It even tells us that no man can take the ground under our feet, no one can stand before us and that God will be with us if we will do this one, simple thing: meditate on the Bible day and night. Three times He commanded us to "be strong and of good courage" and said we could "prosper wherever (we) go" if we would meditate this book and not let the words of its contents depart from our mouth. If we would do this, we would have every reason to have a positive attitude because we would also have the Lord Our God with us wherever we go. Joshua 1:5–9 paraphrased

In addition to a positive attitude, this same Book fills our hearts with great expectation. It tells us "Whatever you ask for in prayer (your heart's desire)" you are to "believe that you have (already–past tense) **received** it and it shall be yours!" (Mark 11:24) The key word here is, "received." Oh, you will actually take physical possession of this thing you prayed for later but we are told here that the secret is to take mental and spiritual possession of it now. Act as if you have received it, rejoice and thank God for His goodness. This is an attitude of expectancy and it is required for our faith to operate and bring the things to us we are needing, desiring and asking God for. The physical manifestation will surely come. Scientists tell us that meditating on this Book affects the endorphins in the brain in such a way that we learn to accept and believe all God's promises, giving us success in life by having a positive attitude and hope that springs eternal. We face each new day with great expectation in the power of God. We know that even the bad things that come our way (and none of us are exempt from trouble) God can turn them around to "work together for good (for) those who love (Him and) who are called according to His purpose." (Romans 8:28) This just means that every dark cloud that encroaches on our path will have a silver lining! Besides the joy of being positive and someone people want to be around, this is the only way to live. Think about it. Not including suicides, people who are negative and depressed have about twice the death rate in every age category as people who are positive and happy. Also, positive people actually recover from surgeries and illnesses much quicker than depressed, negative people.

There is hope for everyone. Philosophers, for centuries, have agreed that people become what they think about. William James said that the greatest realization of his time was that "man can change his attitude by changing what he thinks about." Whatever you think, good or bad, is what you become. Two thousand years ago the Bible declared just this when the wisest man in the world said, "As a man thinks in his heart, so is he." (Proverbs 23:7) Paul, the apostle, warned us not to be deceived about this powerful principle. It is a promise from God and we know of a certainty that He will not be mocked about it by any man. He said, "Do not be deceived, God is not mocked, for whatever a man sows that will he also reap. For he who sows to his flesh will of the flesh reap corruption, but he who sows to the Spirit will of the Spirit reap everlasting life." (Galatians 6:7, 8) We are commanded to "Keep (our) heart (mind and attitude) with all diligence, for out of it are the issues of life." (Proverbs 4:23) The Master also said, "A good man out of the good treasure of his heart brings forth good things, and an evil man out of the evil treasure brings forth evil things." Matthew 12:35

You see the brain that was given to us at birth is actually a computer with two parts. One part, the conscious mind, takes in data like the weather, light, speed limits on the road, and instructions from our boss, etc. The other part, the subconscious mind, weighs, analyzes and makes decisions as to what to do with this information. Everyone's subconscious mind, regardless of where we might find ourselves in the world, has been pre-programmed by some system of belief or unbelief. Whatever you program it with, it will put out. If we program our minds with positive promises, thoughts of success and positive principles of living and working, we will make wise decisions. If we program it with pornography, violence, demented sitcoms on television, we can only hope to have a life of corruption to follow. Used correctly, we can program the computer of our mind to propel us toward positive results and predetermined, God-given goals.

For all this to work, we must be very careful what we think about because the second part of the brain is equally important: learning to be both careful and skilled with the words we speak. Thankfully, the words we speak will come forth as a result of the things we think about—the attitudes, thought patterns and values we consider important about life from the material we read and the things (videos, magazines, movies and television programs) we look at. Do you have problems in your life? We all do—every day! Now this is what the Master says to do about it. "For assuredly, I say to you, whoever says (speaks) to this mountain (your problems in life), 'Be thou removed and be cast into the sea,' and does not doubt in his heart, but believes that those things he says will be done, he will have whatever he says. Therefore, I say to you, whatever things you ask when you pray, believe that you receive them, and you will have them." (Mark 11:23, 24) He also said on another occasion, "By your words you will be justified, and by your words you will be condemned." (Matthew 12:37) What you speak about a problem, situation or circumstance in your life, will frame, form and finalize the ultimate outcome. Your words, not someone else's. Yours, are just that powerful. The Bible says, "Death and life are in the power of the tongue ..." But, thank God it doesn't stop there. It goes on to say, "and those who love it (understand this and let it work for them every day) will eat its fruit." (Proverbs 18:21) The positive words you speak go out of your mouth into the ethers and God's green earth affecting everything and everybody who hears it. Those words also go right back into your ears and down into the innermost being of your own spirit-man to encourage you and increase your faith. Words were what God used to create the universe and words are what He gave us to frame our worlds as well.

A positive attitude even works in the area of how we view others. Regardless of what we see in them, we can know that our attitudes have changed—and they will see this in us. God hasn't quit working on us so we can still expect the best and look for the best in the way of change in others. As long as we are still breathing, He is not finished with us nor is he finished with them. We were put here to be a positive influence on society and the whole world. We need to be salt and light.

Besides, if we expect it and start looking for it, something really good could happen to you today. God might give you an idea for a witty invention or tell you where to start digging for uranium. Today might be the day you get the idea to start a new company to meet a terrific need the world may have been waiting for. Remember, most ideas that solve huge problems are very simple.

What we are talking about here is the innate ability to take an optimistic approach to situations in life, even after hearing the negative reports, facts and having the worst environmental conditions. These things might well have defeated the ten other people who came down the road ahead of you but it won't defeat you. The world might have meant what it did to you for evil but our God will turn it around for your good. Having a positive attitude is knowing that the worst things that happen to you in life will always turn out to be the very best in the end. Every one of these problems have cleverly planted by God down within them the seeds of a much greater good! Our old flesh just doesn't get along that well with a life of total prosperity. When there are no trials, we don't need our faith. However, let there be a little trouble. Let there be some reversals, heart ache or the loss of a job or a loved one, and we get on our knees in half a second. We quickly go back to reviewing all the promises of God and start holding on to the horns of the altar.

The happiest people on earth are those who daily renew their minds by the Word of God. These people not only walk in love but live each day in victory and great expectation.

What it means to have the character trait of **A POSITIVE ATTITUDE:**

- A mind full of things that are affirmative
- Having a positive view of negative things
- Having great expectation
- Stimulating
- Always choosing to walk on the sunny side of the street
- Always seeing our cup half full and filling up quickly instead of half empty
- Marked by acceptance, affirmation and approval
- Always looking for the good
- Seeing opportunity in everything
- Knowing and believing that "with God, all things are possible." Matthew 19:26

UDACITY —   **Study start date:** _____ **Finish date:** _____

It's a fact. One certainly won't get very far in life without a little audacity. Now we are not talking here about the audacity of arrogance, rebellion or blatantly challenging authority but rather the audacity to venture out and accomplish new things.

The reason most people never accomplish anything much in life is simply because of the fear of failure and criticism. Some mistakenly think "If I never do anything, I will never have to worry about failing or being criticized." Wrong. That person is a failure already for not even trying. Besides, you don't have to fail at something to be criticized. You are going to be criticized in this life no matter what you do. If you try something and it works, you will be criticized because someone is jealous or thinks you should have done it differently. So then, if you don't attempt anything in life, you will very deservedly be criticized for that as well. The world is going to tell you to conform, be reasonable. Henry Ford warned us years ago that "A reasonable man will never accomplish anything great."

Right after getting out of the Army I worked in the building industry for a company that sold prefabricated homes. I was selling them to builders and my company told me how many they could deliver each month. The only problem was, the company couldn't get them built. Another company, then, hired me to be their sales manager and promised they could get them built if I could just sell them. However, part of their package was designing their entire line of houses. I had to make or supervise the making of every plan and blue print and I had only been in the home building industry just over a year. When I sat down to draw the first one, with my #2 pencil, T-square and little plastic triangle in my hand, I remember thinking to myself, "I'm not an architect." My next thought was "I am not a structural engineer and hey, I'm not even an engineer." (My college degree was to prepare someone to be a plant manager.) My next thought was, "I'm going to do it anyway. I'm going to give it my best shot." Houses back then were just a bunch of boxes stuck together, just four walls, a roof and a floor—no pizzazz. I had some creative ideas about building them with vaulted ceilings, exposed beams, clear-story windows, sunken great rooms and huge fieldstone fireplaces with large cedar beam mantles. I incorporated my ideas into those plans and guess what? We sold a lot of houses! What is more—miracle of miracles—neither the roofs nor the foundations ever crumbled on a single one of them. Praise the Lord! If I had listened to all the "Can'ts" that came into my head that day, I would have failed that test in my life! But I remembered something I read in college: "Fortune is a woman and therefore friendly only to those youths who with audacity command her." author unknown

On another occasion, when God and I built the Shepherd's House as a Transition and discipleship center for men coming out of prison and we did it debt free, never borrowing a penny. Right away, no less than five men came up to me over a period of time and were angry because I had built it. They said. "God told (them) to build it." I wondered then why they didn't? We could well use fifty more of them even today. While we built it, they stood off in the shadows, watched me struggle digging the footings, laying the blocks, framing the walls and floors, etc., and they never lifted even a little finger to help. They never drove one nail, threw one trial of sheetrock mud at a wall or donated a dime—and here they were mad at me. This didn't bothered me. Here we were getting lots of men saved a year with and only with God's help. Personally, I couldn't save a fly on my own. Many of these same guys I was preaching to for years in prison were getting out and really needed someone to be there for them on what was surely the happiest and hardest day of their lives. The day they were turned out on the streets from prison with no job, no friends, no money, no food, no telephone number and no place to go. Praise God we were there for them with the Shepherd's House.

The Shepherd's House

When people found out I was going to build the house (a $400,000 complex of two buildings) they asked if I had any money and I said, "No." Did I have any building materials and I said, "No." Did I have any help and I said, "No." Did I have a plan and I said, "No." They were stunned at my response. I just said, "God told me to do it and He will get it done." And, He did. He sent some faithful men to help and though it took a while, thank God I'm patient, we got it done. I certainly have no regrets. There is no telling how many men were helped in the house the Lord provided. Now we are finishing the second Shepherd's House which is much larger about 12 miles from the first one. What a joy it is. What did it take? In a word I suppose, audacity. Not the audacity of arrogance but an audacity of faith, hope,obedience and determination.

Charles A. Lindberg wanted to know, "What kind of man would live where there is no daring? I don't believe in taking foolish chances but nothing can be accomplished without taking any chances at all." What kind of person would ever want to be an Army Ranger and live a life of danger? Or join the 82nd Airborne Division knowing your mission may be to parachute out of a plane in the dark of night and take over a country as they did in Panama and Granada? Or on almost a daily basis in Vietnam, to get up and combat assault directly into the full physical strength and fire power of the enemy? I believe life following God is meant to be exciting.

What it means to have the character trait of **AUDACITY:**

- Having the boldness to stretch out beyond our experience, education, talents and comfort zone to accomplish what is needed or to meet a challenge presented to you in life
- The absence of timidity and fear
- The grace to charge your enemies and your fears
- Intrepidly courageous
- To be adventurous
- Daring
- To attack the enemy and your fears with reckless abandon
- To be marked by creativity and originality
- To willingly to take little and endeavor to make much
- To have the ability to set aside normal individual, cultural or historical restraints
- To have the courage to think outside the box
- To realize that we "can do all things through Christ who strengthen(s us)." Philippians 4:13

UTHENTICIY —   **Study start date:** _____   **Finish date:** _____

So many people today are like chameleons: they change colors based on whatever environment they might find themselves. They are one person today and another tomorrow. One on Sunday at church and another on Monday out in the work-a-day world; one person with the conservatives and another with the liberals. They become whatever person they need to be in hopes of having their approval. The problem, of course is, we can't please everybody in this life.

Others, unknowingly, go through life motivated by money, seeking financial gain first and foremost. Because of this, they stand for nothing so they fall for just about anything. We know money is deceitful (Mark 4:19) It is a mistake to seek riches because we always become like the thing we seek and think about most. Therefore, we would do well to seek the Lord and his righteousness. Matthew 6:33 tells us to "Seek first the kingdom of God and his righteousness and all these things will be added." What things? All the things the Gentiles seek—everything we might need in this natural, physical world. These things are given to us as a reward and are not to be sought as our objective. Riches have no eternal value and will not help us in the day of God's wrath. Aside from causing hypocrisy, another great danger with riches is the likelihood of our trusting in them. (Proverbs 22:4) We already have dominion, nothing to fear and access to all good things but from a completely different avenue the world knows nothing of. In Psalm 8:6 David said God made "(us) to have dominion over the works of (His) hands, (and) has put all things under (our) feet." And, the author of Proverbs 22:4 also promised us that "The reward of humility and the fear of the Lord are riches, honor and (the abundant) life." So riches, honor and life are God's rewards for those who choose to humble themselves and fear Him. If we will seek Him and love Him with all our heart, soul, mind and strength, everything we need will be provided, in due time.

Truth is we are all being conformed to something, either the world or Christ. Paul exhorted us "not (to) be conformed to this world, but be transformed by the renewing of your mind, that you may prove what is the good and acceptable and perfect will of God." (Romans 12:2) We simply need to seek the Lord and be like Him, as well as live and move and have our being in Him. He is who we are and we have our identity in Him. This is done very naturally every day as we meditate the Word day and night. (Joshua 1:8) We all may fall short from time-to-time but we are always getting better and there is no better, more effective way to success and no one better to be like. He never changes and we shouldn't either.

Here is what it means to have the character trait of **AUTHENTICITY**:

- One true to himself enough to be able to live life as an open book
- Someone who is trustworthy because they are what they say they are and will do what they say they will do.
- The real thing
- Not having a hidden agenda
- Conforming not to one's environment but to fact
- Not willing to bend or bow
- Genuine
- One not willing to change for even a million dollars
- Needing no veil over our face
- Living by the truth

- Being comfortable in one's own skin
- True to character to the deepest essence and to the nth degree
- Able to prove authenticity
- Fidelity to fact
- Peace with one's self enough to be who you are
- No adulteration, admixture or counterfeiting
- Not facetious
- Not putting on airs or giving a false impression
- Able to withstand scrutiny, inspection, questioning and the test of time
- Careful not to give a wrong impression
- Not a hypocrite

AVAILABILITY—   **Study start date:** _____ **Finish date:** _____

Having worked construction most of my summers growing up; as a mechanic, rebuilding an old Jaguar given to me by a friend in college, as well as working as a welder and machinist on several occasions during that same time, I have become, as you might imagine, a tool person. I love tools. Though expensive, I love them because of what they can do in terms of improved efficiency and capability. Tools will always pay you back in life and are, therefore, worth far more than they cost. There are also some tasks that absolutely cannot be performed without the right tool.

Generally speaking, there are many different tools on the craftsman's bench but not all have the same value or serviceability to their owner. Sadly some tools are for all practical purposes useless and unavailable for use, even though they are present on the bench, because they are either bent, broken or awaiting repair. Hopefully, upon being fixed, they will be useful again someday. But, today, the day you need them, they are virtually worthless, out of commission. Some are too rusty, bent and hard to work with. Still others are not a proper fit; too small for the big jobs or too large for the small jobs. Some, however, are expensive power tools, always kept by their owner in a special place because they can really be relied upon to get the job done effectively and efficiently. They are the owner's favorites. Some of these power tools are fairly universal in their application and quite able to speed the desired result. Still other tools are just plain missing when needed and can't be found. They are just unavailable and for that reason alone—are worthless.

People are much like tools. Some say they are tools the Lord can use—but, are they ready and available when needed? Others are so ticky, temperamental, high maintenance and difficult to work with, they have to be sidelined because they are just not worth the time and trouble to get them moving or properly directed. Others complain about jobs being either too big or too small for them. (Don't even think about asking them to carry out the garbage.) Other jobs require too much preparation, education, experience or technical skill and because of this, they would not be able to perform these tasks. What a happy day it is to find a worker who is flexible and trained well enough to be available for use in just about any capacity. Some even have a degree of humility, integrity, insight, prudence and understanding. One who is a tool the Lord can use. Some are filled with the supernatural power of the Holy Spirit. They never complain about the difficulties, the danger or the pay and are ready to get the job done come what may. These qualities actually make them extremely valuable.

Upon graduating from college, I remember one of my last unofficial acts before leaving Texas A&M University was to go to the hardware store and buy an electric drill. There are few poorer that a poor boy going through a state college at the end of the semester. College guys are for the most part poor but they are especially poor at the end of the last semester in college All their saving accounts for school have run dry. And, being a poor boy anyway, I can still remember how much it pained me to put up the substantial sum required to buy that drill. It was a lot of money to me but I knew it was worth it and have never, ever regretted it over the years. It was so expensive that I have always kept it in a safe place and have taken especially good care of it. The speed at which it operates and the power it has to penetrate thick metal is what made it well worth the investment. It has always been kept easily accessible because of its importance in construction or maintenance work. Through the years it has paid for itself many times over. Because of so much use, the bearings are beginning to grind a bit but, out of respect for its efficiency and the help it has been to me over the years, it still commands a prominent position of honor on my work bench. This is true even now after I have a better, more powerful, cordless drill. Yet, as I said, it still commands respect, gratitude and a place of honor on that bench. It has always been not only available but ready to provide a power solution to problem after problem. More than anything, it has always been available just when I needed it.

The world is always looking for capable people who are available in time of need. In any employment situation, it is a good idea to let the employer know that you are willing to work late if necessary or come in on Saturdays to solve problems or meet an important specific need for the company. If it is truly in your heart, you should tell them that as long as you are working for the company you are going to treat it as if it were your own and that you are willing to do whatever it takes to make it the most successful and profitable company in your market area. Employers aren't mind readers and unless you tell them, they won't know you are available and willing to go the extra mile for their business. This kind of loyalty and availability will mean more to them than someone's intellect, strength or beauty. Most of us may be woefully lacking in the latter but we can all be strong in loyalty and availability.

God, too, is looking for soldiers to send into important battles from time-to-time. He said, "The harvest is plentiful but the workers few." (Matthew 9:37) In this regard, one day years ago, Isaiah saw a vision of the Lord sitting on His throne with several seraphim hovering about saying, "Holy, holy, holy is the Lord of hosts; the whole earth is full of His glory!" The praise was so loud and powerful that the door posts of the temple shook and the room was filled with smoke. Momentarily, one of the angels flew over to Isaiah and touched his lips with a hot coal taken with tongs from God's altar. Upon touching him, he said his sins had been taken away so he was prepared and ready for the Master's work. Then he heard the Lord inquire, "Whom shall I send and who will go for Us?" Isaiah then made the proper response, "Here am I! Send me." (Isaiah 6:8) He was available.

Another time, Nehemiah heard from several people returning from Jerusalem how the walls were broken down and the gates were burned with fire. Heartbroken for his homeland, he prayed and asked the king to allow him to go back to Jerusalem so he could rebuild it. God and the king answered his prayer because Nehemiah was available and, though inexperienced, he was well up to the task. God always takes the willing and makes them able.

King David, hearing and seeing the giant Goliath railing at the armies of the living God, asked how long this had been going on and why no one had volunteered to kill him. After all, who could stand before God and his mighty men? Finally, he said "Is there not a cause in Israel?" What he was saying was, shouldn't there be something in Israel worth fighting for? Here was an uncircumcised heathen railing against God and His armies. Then he made himself available for the job and because he had prepared himself for the day of battle, he quickly and quietly eliminated Israel's foe. David had prepared himself by spending time with the Lord out in the desert tending his sheep. Unbeknownst to him at the time, he was also preparing himself by fighting the bear and the lion to protect his little flock. He was then ready, able, available and unafraid when God needed a man to fight the Philistine giant. Being faithful to protect a few sheep qualified him to shepherd a much larger flock later: the nation Israel.

There always have been and always will be difficult and sometimes dangerous jobs needing someone equipped, ready and available for the Master's use. Some, however, are equipped and ready but worldly entanglements greatly hinder their availability. When the world finds out that you can lead, manage and organize a bit, you have to be careful that frivolous activities with virtually no eternal value don't creep in and monopolize your time. They will have you so busy with fruitless activities in your community that you won't be able to answer the call from God when it comes. The good in life can oftentimes be the enemy of the best. Keeping one's self clear of these things puts you in the position of being available when God calls.

On various occasions, while in real estate here in Atlanta, I was offered positions like the presidency of the commercial real estate council, a seat on the County Planning Board, vice chair of the Georgia

Board of Realtors which nearly always led to the chairmanship the next year, etc. All of these positions were important, prestigious and could have been an opportunity to do considerable good but they were also secular and time consuming. Every one of them would have helped me in business but they all had one thing in common: little to no eternal value. Though humbled to even be asked, I had no peace from God to accept them. However, because my time was not consumed with all these worldly affairs, I was free later to accept God's call to serve as an elder in my Church, District Coordinator for One Nation Under God, President of the Full Gospel Businessmen's Fellowship, Director of Citizens for Protecting Our Children and others. By God's grace I was able to accept because the good had not gotten in the way of the best.

Secular pursuits are certainly not all bad. For it is usually in them that we start our apprenticeship in various fields and are able to hone our skills for the Lord's work. General Douglas McArthur said, "On the field of friendly strife are sown the seeds that on other days, on other fields win victory in battle." Elisha was plowing with twelve yoke of oxen when Elijah threw his mantle on him and called him into the ministry.

What it means to have the character trait of **AVAILABILITY**:

- Being present, accounted for and ready for immediate deployment or use
- Accessible
- Willing, trained, prepared and qualified to perform tasks
- Willing to assume additional responsibilities
- Ready, charged, activated and poised for use
- Ever sharpening one's axe to be ready when the Master calls
- Serving and available to one's own family first, then available for others
- Not being distracted or entangled by frivolous activities
- As a soldier, not entangled in civilian affairs
- Rejecting greed, ambition and notoriety that take us away from where God has placed us.
- Being ever in prayer for God to call

BATTLE, LOVING THE   Study start date: _____ Finish date: _____

We never go looking for trouble on this planet but it certainly has no problem finding us. Furthermore, the Master said, "In the world you will have tribulation." But, I'm so glad He didn't stop there. He went on to say, "… but be of good cheer. I have overcome the world." (John 16:33) "For whatever is born of God overcomes the world. And this is the victory that has overcome the world—our faith." (I John 5:40) Because "God … always causes us to triumph in Christ" (II Corinthians 2:14) we should never be afraid of a battle. They are for winning—not losing. In fact, we are promised that "A thousand will fall at your side and ten thousand at your right hand; but it shall not come near you." (Psalm 91:7) Truth is, the enemy is against you and God's purposes so if we are not being attacked, we must not be much of a threat.

If we don't learn to love the battle, life is probably going to be a miserable experience. The enemy will demoralize, discourage and defeat us at every hand. Life is full of battles small and large every day. Think about it though. Without a battle we can never have a victory and we must have a victory to vanquish the enemy, take in new territory and gather their spoil. Wars will be fought forever and although we don't instigate them, we must not grow weary of them. We must continue to fight the battles the Holy Spirit directs us to with all our might along with God's cunning and skill every day. Just as "the Spirit drove (Jesus) into the wilderness" to do battle with satan, He will likewise lead you, if you are willing, trained and prepared, into the battles of life you are to fight. (Mark 1:12) "Those who (make a diligent effort to) know their God" the Bible promises will "… be strong and carry out great exploits. (Daniel 11:32) Thankfully, "We don't war according to the flesh. For the weapons of our warfare are not carnal, but mighty through God for the pulling down of strongholds and the casting down arguments and every high thing that exalts itself against the knowledge of God …" II Corinthians 10:3-5

Life for believers has always meant a whole host of battles to fight. Life has always been a struggle and always will be. Why? Because the prince of the power of the air is loose in the earth and is always about doing what he knows best: "steal, kill and destroy" (John 10:10) as well as energize those he has taken captive to do the same. It is the devil's job to start the battles. It is our job to finish them. So, first of all, when faced with a battle, we should thank God for trusting us with the problem, ask Him for wisdom and then jump in and fight with God's help and the resources He sends. Then wait. Look to see what God is doing in the battle. He wants it to be a blessing in the end. See what He is saying and look for His redemption.

Before David was king of Israel, he was the shepherd of a small flock of sheep that he lived with in the wilderness. But, even there, he had to fight a lion and a bear to protect them. On another occasion his father sent him to take some cheese to the captains of Israel's armies to encourage them. They were engaged in a war with the Philistines at the time. While climbing the mountain where the Israelites were encamped, he heard this giant of a man from the enemy's side, in full battle array, railing against the armies of the living God. The Bible says Saul and all his soldiers were sorely afraid of this giant. David, on the contrary, couldn't believe their fearfulness and asked how long this had been going on. Someone said forty days. One of his older brothers overheard him asking about this reproach and tried to belittle him, accusing him of being insolent. He also did his best to send him back to take care of his "few sheep." But David asked the right question of all those standing by that day. He opined, "Is there not a cause?" What he meant was, is there not a cause in Israel worth risking your life for? We can't have an uncircumcised Philistine railing against the armies of the living God.

Immediately what David said was reported to King Saul who sent for him. Once there, Saul tried to discourage him like all the rest saying, "You are not able to go against this Philistine to fight against him; for you are a youth and he a man of war from his youth." (I Samuel 17:33) David replied that he had been keeping his father's sheep and when a lion or bear took one of his sheep he went after the animal and struck it all by himself, retrieving the lamb from its mouth. When it arose against him, he caught it by its beard and killed it. He said, "Your servant has killed both lion and bear; and this uncircumcised Philistine will

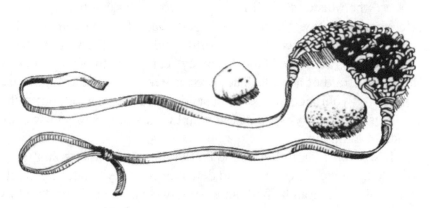

be like one of them, seeing he has defied the armies of the living God. The Lord will deliver me from the hand of this Philistine." (v, 36,37) So Saul told him to go after him and prayed the Lord would be with him. He even offered David his armor but he turned it down.

So David met the giant on the field of battle and instead of standing still or running from him, he ran to him. He took one of the stones out of his bag and hurled it right at his head. His slingshot sent that stone flying so fast that it sunk in his forehead, right between the eyes and killed him instantly. Just to assure all those standing by that he definitely had the victory over this Philistine, he took the giant's sword and cut off his head. When the Philistines saw their champion decapitated by a teenager, they fled in fear. The armies of Israel arose and went on the attack, shouting and decimating their enemies and plundering their tents.

Until the Lord returns there will always be conflicts, trouble, disagreements and wars. The wicked will try to take over the world but He made righteous men to ruse up and prevail against them. He made special provision for us to be victorious in the battles of life when we willingly demonstrate our trust in Him. We should rejoice when a battle comes our way because it is an opportunity for us to glorify Him for His faithfulness and receive a major blessing. There is also a rush of adrenalin to equip us with supernatural energy and strength during these trials. Battles are just serious opportunities.

What it means to have the character trait of **LOVING THE BATTLE:**

- Knowing that God created you to be a warrior and to overcome in the battles of life.
- Looking past the danger to the certain victory that awaits.
- Being thankful for each battle that comes our way and for God trusting us to win it.
- Though we do not seek conflict, we are promised it is coming to us on a reoccurring basis so we need to be thankful for the winning strategies of wisdom and God's love that have been given to us.
- Loving the battle for the opportunities it affords us to bring glory to the Name and increase God's borders upon the earth.
- Being thankful that God has given us superior offensive and defensive weapons as well as everything we need for victory, life and godliness. II Peter 1:3
- It is not becoming weary of the battles in life because we know God has always caused us to triumph in Christ Jesus. II Corinthians 2:14

EARING –   Study start date: _____ Finish date: _____

Many times in life, believe it or not, appearance is everything. Why? Because what people perceive is reality to them—at least for the moment. Appearance is also quite important in making first impressions because we never get a second chance to make a good first impression.

Any discussion about bearing would certainly include one's stature and making a habit of standing erect. Bearing is simply the appearance or manner in which a person carries or presents themselves especially while standing. So many people think they are standing erect when in actually they are not. The law of gravity is quietly and gently but powerfully and constantly working on each of us every day, causing us to stoop our shoulders, drop our head down and lean forward like an ape. If we let this go too long without attention, we will probably start dragging our knuckles on the floor as well. Standing erect is not always the easiest thing to do. Man's natural inclination is to slouch. If you have ever been on a drill team in the military, you already know that standing erect and keeping your head up is something one might think they are doing well until someone else observes and critiques you. We are not to stand erect to look proud but to look like God intended, walking erect, in all humility. Man is the crown jewel of His creation.

Some even in the military, sad to say, have the uncanny ability to put on a uniform and look exactly like a duffle bag. Others can easily don a uniform and look sharp as a tack because they have a sense of accuracy and perfection about them. One of the sharpest soldiers I ever knew was Sergeant Cockerel, a Tack Sergeant, in Ranger School back in 1968. Our entire class had just returned to Ft. Benning, Georgia from Eglin A.F.B. in Florida where we completed the Swamp Warfare Phase of Ranger Training and actually had our graduation. We were all so happy to have graduated and were breathing a huge sigh of relief after enduring one of the hardest tests of our lives. We were there just to turn in equipment and be processing out of the Ranger Camp. By this time, most of us had let a lot of things slide, thinking we had finally really made it. Milling around in the company street, we were waiting to march someplace that day. Then Sgt. Cockerel appeared on the scene out of nowhere with his starched fatigues. They always seemed to have creases like razor blades even after double-timing with us Ranger Candidates five miles in the hot sun. He always stood ram-rod straight, had his hair cut close on his head under a perfectly cocked black, Ranger beret. He had a big, really long cigar in his mouth and I promise you it always seemed to be perfectly at "Attention." He was tall, strong and the picture of military despotism (in the sense of a ruler with unlimited power). In those days, we thought Ranger Tacks had infinite wisdom and had almost as much power and authority as the Maker of the universe. There we stood in that dusty, gravel street, a happy but motley band of duffle bags. In addition, I might add, Sgt. Cockerel had a voice like thunder to match his persona.

Standing there in all his glory, feet apart with his hands on his hips and leaning into us he barked loud enough to shake the barracks, the ground and the eye teeth right out of your head. I can still remember it as if it was yesterday. He thundered, "Fall in formation! Roll those sleeves down and blouse those boots! Put out those cigarettes! Stand at attention! From the looks of you guys, they must hand those Ranger Tabs out to the cock roaches down in Florida!" Wow. He really rained on our parade. Although he might have been having a little fun with us, what he was mad about was our complete loss of military bearing. What he was really saying was—if you are going to be a leader and since truly, "Rangers lead the way," you need to look like it all the time. Nobody is going to follow a dizzy, dispirited band of dummies who look like they just fell off a turnip truck.

While out in the civilian world, an unusual thing happened to me in this vein. I had taken someone to a place of business and was just standing inside against the wall waiting patiently while most of the people were seated in the same waiting area. As was the case many times, I had on some old brown cowboy boots, wheat jeans, a western belt (but no big buckle) and a green golf shirt. Pretty modest attire for sure. I was just standing there thinking about absolutely nothing other than trying to be patient, when a little boy got up out of his chair and walked over right in front of me. He looked straight up at me with those big blue eyes and said in all seriousness, "Sir.... are you a U.S. Marshall?" I had to laugh and say, "No, indeed, son but thanks for the compliment." The only reason I mention this is that I believe the occurrence had a little to do with clothes and probably a whole lot more to do with posture.

Another field of endeavor where they certainly make a point of posture and appearance, and rightfully so, is the court system. Lawyers are required by statute to wear a suit and tie and lady lawyers must also dress appropriately, with what is called "proper decorum." How would we feel meeting our attorney in the court room, who you are paying big dollars by the hour to represent you before a stern old judge in a black robe behind the big wooden desk and there he is slouched over in a Hawaiian shirt, Bermuda shorts and flip-flops. It just wouldn't work.

Proper bearing also has to do with one's attitude. As leaders, we need to be happy but there is little place for being jovial and joking around. We should make an effort to smile at the people we meet and talk to each day, until that naturally becomes part of our personality. Failure to do this one, simple thing, could actually cost you two-thirds of your influence with people and will likely prohibit you from making friendships. People aren't generally attracted to unfriendly, sad, angry looking folk. They do have other choices in friends you know.

Whatever position one may hold or aspire to in life, requires you look the part. This includes proper hygiene, dressing with moderation commensurate with one's position and showing some attention to detail in the way we dress. Even in the civilian world, those who take the time and care to keep their shoes shined gain a lot of respect—on account of just that alone.

In summary, I'm not suggesting that we put on airs, certainly not. But, it is wise to invest a little time in learning how to tie a Windsor knot, keep the hair above the ears, and the back of your neck shaved. Remember, other people have to look at us all day long. We should make our appearance as neat and pleasing as possible so looking at us doesn't cause them any more pain than is absolutely necessary

What it means to have the character trait of **BEARING:**

- Comporting one's self with dignity
- Demeanor
- Decorum
- Standing erect
- Being noble in one's dealings, dress and disposition
- A proper attitude commensurate with one's position, situation and environment
- The overall manner in which one bears their office in life

EAUTY, A SENSE OF   Study start date: _____ Finish date: _____

Many go through life with little or no appreciation of beauty. Some can't appreciate the beauty and elegance of a golden palomino quarter horse racing across a green pasture, alternately kicking up his rear hoofs with a lot of dust and dirt, throwing his head straight up in the air and snorting—all this, as his white mane and tail swirl in the bright sun light. Some could see the Mona Lisa and think it no more than a few smudges of oil paint on an old canvas. Perfection and beauty never bothers them in the least.

When I first entered the real estate and building business, the president of our company was a man by the name of Jack Anderson. He had been an officer and a pilot in the Air Force prior to earning his law degree and entering the real estate business. At that time he was developing five large subdivisions, owned a huge builders' supply, a cabinet shop, a prefab house plant, a mortgage company, a real estate company and employed five field erection crews that were framing houses all the time. He was a great man and definitely had an eye for beauty. Though never ostentatious, it was readily apparent in his offices, the way he dressed, his cars, his airplane and the buildings he constructed. Jack was certainly dedicated to delivering quality but he always went well beyond that. One time he told me, "When you build something (any kind of a building), always spend five percent extra to put a little scrambled eggs on the front of it." What he meant was to go the extra mile and trim it out with some beautifully laid stone work, some well appointed mill work or some brass and glass to set it off. This extra touch would separate you from the rest of the field of builders who were simply putting pitifully plain pavilions up for sale. He said, "What you spend on this will always pay you back." You see, anyone can put a bunch of boards, bricks and mortar together to build a house but only those who can build beauty will stay in the business. Whatever you put your hand to should not only be neat but should also show, within reason, a sense of beauty.

My lovely wife, Donna, and I have lived in the house we now occupy for about thirty-three years. She first visited my house while we were dating. Much later she told me she couldn't believe it. She said "it looked like a machine shop." I had built a shelf system in the living room out of stained 2x4's and 1x12's. The stereo equipment on it was nice but looked a bit stark. There were no flowers or greenery in the yard other than a few shrubs and some grass. We live on some acreage but I had only mowed the grass about twenty feet out around the house. I must admit, the wooden shelf system was history soon after we got married. Quite often we receive compliments on the on the landscaping. My wife planted every flower, bush and nearly every shrub we have and it looks great. God knows to send us what we need—the perfect helpmeet with a sense of beauty.

Whatever we do, we should be trying our best to not only complete the work well but also to create a little beauty while we are at it. We shouldn't be doing things half way, We are to do everything we touch with all our might, "heartily as to the Lord and not to men." (Colossians 3:23) Even though we may turn our work in to a man here on earth, we need to do it like we would have done it for God, Himself. If you do it well enough to present to Him, human beings will be well pleased I assure you. We all need to develop our appreciation of beauty.

What it means to have the character trait of **A SENSE OF BEAUTY**:

- The orchestration of various parts in any medium that brings about pleasure to the mind, senses and spirit

- The ability to perceive those things that come together, the sum of which, forms perfection, symmetry, accuracy and beauty
- The ability to both appreciate and create beauty as distinguished from the debased, mediocre and profane
- The ability to put things together in one's chosen field such as art, building, music, management, etc. so that the quiet beauty of it is always present and clearly manifest to all

EING A ONE-WOMAN MAN—   Study start date: _____ Finish date: _____

One of the greatest enemies in life for a man or woman is the insidious, deadly temptation of marital infidelity. Due to the vicissitudes of life, the grass can easily, many times look greener on the other side of the fence. We wonder why this is so but upon closer inspection, we see the deception. When viewing the grass over the fence in the distance, one sees all the high grass on a horizontal plane between you and that other, distant location. However, when you get over there and look straight down at the same piece of ground, you see there are brown spots, voids, rocks, cracks and vacant spots all over the place. On the side view we see the tops of the few high patches of green grass sticking up.

Men, and it is men I am addressing here today, as this differs quite a bit for women. I also realize there is nothing a man can do about a wife walking off, leaving him, committing adultery or marrying another man. What we are talking about here is a man's *intention and commitment* to being a one woman man. If your wife cancelled herself out, go on or even if you failed, if you believe it is God's will for you to re-marry, do it with the *intention* in your heart to be, indeed, a one-woman man.

Men need to realize that they can easily be deceived by the enemy. Men are programmed to be attracted to the opposite sex so we need to be very careful as we trod our earthly path. It is fraught with danger. The enemy can send you a "Delilah" if you haven't purposed to protect yourself, don't know how to protect yourself or don't think you need to protect yourself. Falling into this trap can destroy your marriage, your career, your family and your life. No one thinks it will ever happen to them, however, statistics reveal that divorce is happening in fifty percent of marriages today. That includes both Christian and non-Christian couples. We also have documented evidence that it happened to President Dwight Eisenhower, President John F. Kennedy, President Bill Clinton and Sen. John McCain. More recently, Senator John Edwards, Governor Mark Sanford, Governor Elliott Spitzer and the list goes on ad infinitum.

Men, you must protect yourselves from the very real possibility of becoming involved in unfaithfulness and destroying your life and all you have worked for. A divorce can, and sometime does, ruin a person's life. Marriage is a mystery. Your partner becomes your other half spiritually and physically. I have known men who have committed suicide as a result of it. Just because you have been successful remaining faithful to your marriage vows, the temptations are not over. If you are breathing, you can still be deceived. The worst thing anyone can do is believe that you can't be tempted and that you can't fall. Just because you don't think you are interested in an affair doesn't mean that you aren't still on the enemy's radar as a viable candidate.

Mark Sanford, Governor of South Carolina, said in a TV interview recently, "It all started out so innocently," sending emails to this lady friend. Then the phone calls and notes started. Then they started discussing things and sharing personal problems, etc. That is just how this thing goes. Then lunch probably. Then… . Well we don't need go there. You got the picture. Here is this highly successful man being interviewed on national TV, the governor of a state with four teenage boys and a beautiful wife still fell for this trap. When asked by the commentator "What happened?" He replied, " I shouldn't have but I fell in love." He just let it happen. It cost him his marriage, will affect his relationship with his sons for the rest of his life, it cost him financially, it cost him his position as Governor and his political career Now he is wondering what he is going to do with the rest of his broken life. It has been about two years since all this surfaced but the trail of tears and heart aches has only just begun. He is left with shame that will never be wiped away.

Was his wife not a beautiful woman? Yes, she was and still is. She was far more than that. She had given him the best years of her life, four sons and had personally managed every one of his successful political campaigns. He simply allowed the devil deceive him by believing the same old lie: "The grass is greener on the other side of the fence."

You see it is all about ladders. Ladders, you say? What have ladders got to do with this stuff? Let me explain. Whenever we make a decision to buy a product or service, we usually do it by shopping around, using our prior experience, getting counsel from a trusted friend, etc. In the process we end up selecting someone on the top rung of the ladder in every field you can name. Where? In our minds. In our minds this person is our top choice. When it comes to a mechanic we know in our mind who we feel is the best in our area and that is who we use. When it comes to buying an automobile, we think we know which car is best for us. When it comes to selling property, we know someone who we think can do it better than anyone else in our community and that is exactly who we will call to represent us when we enter that market. You have someone on the top rung of the ladder of your mind in every field right now. When you decide to marry, you are supposed to have already checked out the prospects, narrowed the field, courted for a while, prayed about it, sought wise counsel and should have decided you can no longer live without this person. In other words, she climbed to the top rung of your ladder in competition with all the women in the world. You were then willing to make the decision to forsake all others and make a covenant with God to be devoted to her for better or for worse, until death do you part. She earned that place on the top rung of the ladder in your mind. Now you need to guard that place she has on that ladder. Don't ever let someone come along and take that wife's place away on *your* ladder. Guard it with your life! Only you can protect her place and only you can let some other woman that you *think* might be better take that place. If you allow this to happen, it will cost you far, far more than you will be willing to pay. You aren't just in covenant with your wife. You are in covenant with God, her family, your family, your children, your friends, her friends and the whole community you live in. Stay with it. You will be glad you did. Your decisions, either way, will affect many future generations.

There are some things in life that are so deadly, destructive, devastating and deplorable that you can't even come close to knowing their ferocity without experience them yourself. You need to do everything you possibly can to ensure that a marital failure never happens to you. Everybody loses in these situations. I experienced a divorce when my former wife left me first mentally and then geographically for another man who had tons of money. We were both real estate brokers and went out on appointments with people of both sexes all the time. We never fought and I just didn't think infidelity could ever happen to us because I was not unfaithful to my wife. Yes, I was faithful to my marriage vows over those nine years True, I wanted to be faithful and was committed to being faithful but was only faithful by the grace of God. Being a real estate broker, there were many temptations and many attacks but, I was able by His grace, to turn them all down. I always felt that my marriage covenant was truly a covenant with God. The enemy will always be trying to tempt you. He wants to get you in the right frame of mind. By that I mean to somehow get you to feeling sorry for yourself, make you angry with your mate and get you carrying resentment in your heart and plant resentment in your heart. He will also entice you to fall out of love and take her for granted. When we marry, it has to be forever and we must guard against letting ourselves fall out of love. We must guard our wife's place on the ladder of our mind. Don't let your wife's place on that ladder go to a woman who would entice you to break your marriage covenant and cheat on your wife. Be assured, if this woman will cheat with you to break up your marriage, she will probably cheat on you later as well. This is a pattern and has happened in nearly every case I know of. The danger of all this is so prevalent that one of the express purposes of the entire book of Proverbs being written was to deliver men from the insidious, immoral woman. Proverbs 2:16

Men, you may not be able to guard what your wife allows to get in her mind but you can certainly protect your own. If you ever catch yourself having thoughts about another woman, know that you don't have to continue in those thoughts. Continuing to muse on those thought will simply destroy you and your marriage. The wonderful thing about the way God made our brains is that we can only think about one thing at a time. If the enemy has sent you a wrong thought, call it what it is: a wrong thought, hate it and start thinking on something good immediately. Philippians 4:8 tells us what to think on if we want to live the abundant life: "Whatever things are true, whatever things are noble, whatever things are just, whatever things are pure, whatever things are lovely, whatever things are of good report, if there be any virtue and if there is anything praiseworthy—meditate (think) on these things," You and you alone decide what you will think about. Be aware that thoughts breed emotions and emotions breed actions and actions repeated for twenty-one days breed habits and habits soon become our character which then becomes our personality. Nobody ever fell in love with a woman that they didn't think about.

There are a number of things you can do to preclude falling into the enemy's trap. This doesn't have to happen to you. There are some precautions you can and should take I will recommend shortly. Friend, I take all of them. Just because I have made it this far without a personal moral failure in this area doesn't mean it could never happen. I haven't crossed over the finish line and into Heaven's gates yet. Now the adversary certainly meant having my mate fall into this horrible quagmire for evil but God meant it for good. Proverbs 12:4 tells it truly, "An excellent wife is the crown of her husband, but she who causes shame is like rottenness to his bones." Getting rid of an unfaithful wife is like getting rid of cancer in your bones.

Although it certainly didn't feel like a blessing at the time, my situation, with God's help, has actually turned out to be one of the best things that has ever happened to me. Because of all the turmoil and difficulties I experienced, I lost nearly everything I had worked for the first thirty-two years of my life. However, the main thing I gained was a personal relationship with Jesus Christ. I also learned that I was totally ignorant about what to look for in in a wife. That was my fault and I accept it. In some areas of life we are like the Germans. They say, "We grow too soon old and too late schmart." I sought advice from my Pastor, my father and studied the Word of God to find out what the Lord's will was for me in a wife and came up with twelve criteria. When I finished the list and looked it over, I said, "I don't deserve anyone that good." God's gifts to us are always far better than we deserve. I knew that finding a wife who met all twelve would have to be a miracle. I knew I didn't deserve anyone that good but I said, "It's God's will and I won't settle for anything less." I lived through a long dry spell after that commitment. No one came close to my blue print. Then, after five years, God sent me His best; one who met all twelve of His requirements. We have been married for thirty-one years now and it has been like heaven on earth. I soon found out she was as beautiful on the inside as she was on the outside. God blessed me far above what I deserve. It truly was a miracle.

After we married I found a math major to tell me the chance probability of finding a woman who met all twelve of those criteria in a city of two and a half million where we lived at the time. He calculated that it was one millionth, of a trillionth of one possibility in two and a half million. In other words, it didn't exist. However, whatever God's Word says He will perform. He is faithful.

A number of years ago, Bill Gothard was doing a seminar on why so many pastors and businessmen fell into this heinous trap of marital unfaithfulness. I am so indebted to him for all the wisdom he has given to me in so many areas over a lifetime. Here are a number of things you can do to avoid being deceived in this critical area and I gladly share them from memory along with some of my own. (Of course these are for married men)

- Never be familiar with a woman other than your wife
- Never share problems, jokes, etc. with a woman other than your wife
- Never rely on another woman for emotional support—call a man for prayer
- Do not call any woman on a regular basis other than your wife

- Never have lunch alone with a woman other than your wife
- Make a covenant with your eyes not to look lustfully upon a woman (Job 31:1) This includes magazines, videos, TV programs, etc.
- Never hire a Miss America for your secretary
- Never have another woman with you alone in your car
- Be especially careful when you are out of town and alone
- Once you are married, destroy every picture of every woman you have previously dated
- Guard your thought life. Do not think about any other women.
- Never counsel a woman in your office without another woman (preferably your wife) or a man present
- Once you are married and an old girlfriend calls you just to chat (right?), tell her very kindly that you are married now and it would be best for her not to ever call back.
- Remember there are a number of things only your wife can do for you and no other woman can. Keep it that way.

Another thing Bill Gothard shared was how fires get started. All fires require five components to get going: geography (a place to make the fire), combustible material, oxygen, time and something to ignite it. If you remove any one of these elements, it is impossible to start a fire. The same is true in a relationship with the opposite sex. If you make the effort and take the precautions to guard your life and guard your wife's place on the marital ladder in your mind, you can't have a moral, marital failure. We will never hear you say on TV something as foolish as "I knew I shouldn't have but I just fell in love." We all know how this happens now and it doesn't need to with us.

Never forget that a marriage requires commitment, hard work and as the man, a willingness to meet your wife not 50/50 but to give your mate 150. Someone said, "A man's love to a man's life is a thing apart, 'tis a woman's whole existence." Interpretation men: You are your wife's world. It means that you are going to have to makes some investments in her life. You must nurture her, protect her and cherish her as the love of your life. Unless she is double-working by having an outside job, all she has is you, the family and your home. You have all that plus your career and ministry. Marriage really can be like heaven on earth and I would say that you owe it to yourself and her to make it that way.

What it means to have the character trait of **BEING A ONE-WOMAN MAN:**

- Being faithful to one's marriage vows
- Purposing to stay in love with your wife
- Honoring your wife and showing appreciation for everything she does
- Preferring your wife and putting her desires and needs before your own
- Protecting your wife from dangers she may not even be aware of as the weaker vessel
- Making a covenant with your eyes and mind not to look or think lustfully upon another woman

BENEVOLENCE —   **Study start date: _____ Finish date: _____**

Sadly, in today's world, so many people have yet to find the joy and blessing giving brings. Most try their best to keep all they can and can all they get, not knowing that this will never work. They don't realize that God has written His law of blessing and reciprocity in all of nature. It is written not only in the trees, the dirt and the ethers but in the hearts of men as well. The basic principle of the law of physics is for every action there is an equal and opposite reaction. This is not only true in physics, it is true in a multiplied form in finances and human relations as well. We are also commanded to do unto others as we would have them do unto us. The spirit of benevolence manifests itself when we find ourselves willing to help others in their time of hardship with no expectation of repayment. Of course, the Lord will repay us in many ways.

There are only so many times as we trod the road of life that God will place someone in our path who is in great need. We must then decide how we will respond. We can chose to be like the priest and the Levite who saw a beaten, dying man in the ditch and just walked on by as if they had seen nothing. Or we can chose the part of the good Samaritan who went to him with compassion, met him on his own level there in the ditch and used his personal resources to deliver him. He was the true friend and neighbor. He was also the only one who experienced the joy of delivering someone who otherwise would certainly have died. The poor man had been left there exposed to the elements, half dead and naked. Besides, who knows? With the changing vicissitudes of life, it just might be us in that ditch needing help next time. You know, robbers don't have respect for anyone. They don't discriminate unless, of course, you don't have anything worth stealing.

Take note, stingy people never truly succeed in life. The wisest man in the world said, "He who loves silver (money) will not be satisfied with silver; nor he who loves abundance, with increase. This also is vanity." (Ecclesiastes 5:10) Money will never make a person happy. If a person's heart is set upon it, no matter how much he gets, it won't be enough. That's God's promise. Some people love money so much they can squeeze a nickel until the buffalo sheds a tear. They are locked up tight in the prison of selfishness and self-serving and what a horrible prison it is. The Bible admonishes us in Galatians 6:7: "Do not be deceived, God is not mocked for whatever a man sows, that he will also reap." This is such a rock-solid truth, that it is the only law in the Bible that God challenges the whole world to mock Him about it. It is inviolable. Consider that He created and owns the heavens, the earth and everything in it. It is all His alone, to do with as He pleases. He set up His own laws to operate it and they are truly, as I mentioned, inviolate. It is a fact, whatever a man sows in life, s.s., what he gives to others at work, at home and outside to others, from it he will surely reap, in due time. Paul clarified it a bit more when he told the Corinthians, "He who sows (or gives) sparingly will also reap sparingly and he who sows bountifully will also reap bountifully." (II Corinthians 6:6) Then he continued saying this one thing, giving, will actually cause God "to make all grace abound toward you, that you (will) always (have) all sufficiency in all things (and) may have an abundance for every good work." (vs.9:8) This is not just a law of nature, it is God's law of sowing and reaping. I have found it to be one of the most powerful laws I have ever encountered in my time on the earth. Why be here, take up space, eat the groceries and breathe the air and not be blessed while you are here—so you can be a blessing to your family and others?

One of our chief purposes in life is planting seeds and it is not the easiest thing you ever tried to do. For one reason, it is contrary to the self-centered, fallen nature of man. If we have physical seeds, be they seeds, things or money, we can certainly see them, count them and hold them in our hands. They are real and undisputedly ours but if we hold on to them for very long, there is a great likelihood that we will begin trusting in them, and looking to them to meet our needs rather than looking to God. Giving them to someone else, requires us to totally give up ownership. At that point, we have seemingly, physically, lost them for good. A farmer can't be digging up the seeds he's planted a week later. Those seeds have already germinated and completely changed character. We must also realize that the seeds we plant are far more valuable and powerful helping others or building God's Kingdom. This, no doubt, takes faith. But, when we start giving, several things actually begin to happen. God binds the devourer, we come out from under the curse and the windows of Heaven are opened wide. Those seeds we have sown He also multiplies back to us thirty, sixty or a hundredfold. He's just looking for faithful stewards who are willing to give to others so He can multiply it back to them and they can live to give again in the future, even more abundantly. When we give to those in need, we know that this is actually a loan to the Lord and He will repay. (Proverbs 19:17) Be always looking for good, fruitful ground to sow in. Don't wait to be asked. Let the Holy Spirit guide your giving.

Years ago I was out in the country fasting and praying for a few days at a friend's vacant lake house. I noticed a picture on the wall of a cold, winter, wilderness scene of a small snowy field surrounded by a forest. The field was covered with a hard layer of icy white snow but in the foreground was about a six inch, green tulip plant that had burst through that crust of ice and snow with the most beautiful purple bloom on top. All by itself, it spoke of the enormous power of the laws of nature. A seed is one of the most powerful things in the world. It will break up rocks, concrete and ice to come forth in its time. The caption under the picture was just as powerful. It said, "Judge the day, not by the harvest, but on the seeds you planted." Anonymous. It certainly stuck with me. You see, the harvest is the harvest. It is a blessing but it is over with taking it in. It has no more power to increase or multiply at that point in time. The part of that harvest we chose to make our seeds and sow, now they are really powerful. Nothing can stop them—neither time, nor space, nor wrong motives on the part of the recipients, they are full of the life force, zoy of God! Those seeds are going to sprout and produce with all certainty in time. It is the seeds we plant today that will multiply tomorrow. The ability and willingness to plant seeds in life is a great leveler. Some may have more strength, intellect or beauty but those things, although well and good, may help in a small way for a while but will never really produce in the end like giving. God rewards planters. It takes faith to give up those perfectly good seeds and plant them. In the Deep South, before the Civil War, Plantation owners were called "planters." Why not owners or harvesters one might ask? Because the most important part of the whole operation was planting. You had to know how to plant, the right seeds, at the right time, in the right ground and in abundance to reap a huge harvest. Planting is everything in farming as well as life.

The Lord has allowed me to be a test pilot for Him, in the area of giving. I have seen it work. Just an empty vessel sure enough but I am a witness. Having nothing to begin with other that a monthly pay check from various jobs, God has helped me in so many ways. He has allowed me to be an officer in the military, to found and own Creative Realty, Inc., Creative Builders, Inc., Creative Plan Service and Creative Publishing Company. He has also allowed me to found, and for Him to be a steward of, Creative Ministries, Inc., Manna Ministries, Bibles for Prisoners, Cars For Christ, The Shepherd's House, The Shepherd's Stores, Manna Ministries (Food for the poor), Seed for the Sower (Bibles for prisoners) and Greater Grace Church among other things. None of these organizations were inherited or passed down. I started all my businesses and ministries with virtually little to nothing but faith in God. He taught me the principles of being faithful in the small things, being faithful to others, having a servant's heart and giving. The success afforded in His providence was all Him and so very little of me. I am not that smart and nowhere near that capable. However, if you do things God's way, you can expect that He will soon come and run you down with blessings in His hands.

God loves everyone, including you. He wants to bless you more than you can imagine. He will do it for you just as He has done it for me and billions of others. It simply amounts to applying the principles laid down by the Master thousands of years ago which are still available today. Believe it or not, success is dependent more upon benevolence than anything else. Being a giver and having the joy of being a blessing to others in life is God's will for all of us. It builds our hope, faith to make it through the hard times and gives us great expectation for the future. Everything we will ever receive in this life will be by faith. When a giver, one in covenant with God pays, God answers his prayers. What a way to live! Christ came to give like no one ever before or since. He came to give us all things, not the least of which is a better way to live.

What it means to have the character trait of **BENEVOLENCE**:

- Having a heart inclined to do good and give to others
- Generosity with our time, talent and treasure
- A life of intentional acts of kindness

BOLDNESS —   Study start date: _____ Finish date: _____

At times, we will all be faced with enormous problems of one kind or another. Since retreat is not an option, we must, at those times, find a bold plan to overcome them. This is where the Timid Tommy's are left by the wayside and bold hearts rise up. Few are they who will even raise their heads when faced with impossible tasks, few resources and overwhelming odds. This is a time to pray and seek God's counsel and counter the enemy with a bold, creative plan. Basil Kinn once said, "Be bold and mighty forces will come to your aid." Boldness is not so much confidence in one's self but a belief that our cause is just, that God is in control and an assurance that we can do all things through Christ.

From time to time the enemy will come in like a tidal wave but this isn't something that has never happened before. It happens occasionally in everyone's life. But, Isaiah promised us, "When the enemy comes in like a flood, the Spirit of the Lord will lift up a standard against him" (Isaiah 59:19) That standard might be the Redeemer Himself, a friend or He may even use you, specifically. If we are on the side of truth, we can know that the devil is always our enemy and he never take a day off. What then, are we to do if we find ourselves in deep trouble? The first thing is to submit ourselves to God. The apostle James said, "draw near to God and He will draw near to you." (James 4:8) At that point, we must "Resist the devil and" we are promised, "he will flee… ." (James 4:7) He is a defeated foe. The Captain of our faith, Jesus Christ, defeated him on the cross and took the keys of death, hell and the grave from him too. Ask God for wisdom and, with His help, devise a plan. Be resourceful. Be bold, for the Lord your God is with you.

A prime example of the importance of making a bold plan occurred at a time just after David became king. Israel had come together at Hebron and there David was anointed king by the elders of all the tribes according to the Word of the Lord by Samuel, the prophet. The next step in building the nation was to take the Promised Land from their enemies. So his first priority was to take Jerusalem which happened to be securely in the hands of the Jebusites. It was so heavily fortified in fact, when David and his army arrived there, his scouts sent him word that the city was impregnable. It was so secure that the Jebusites boldly stated, "You shall not come in here …" (II Samuel 5:6) Their fortifications were so strong, they went on to say, if it was only defended by "the blind and the lame (they) will repel you." Not to be deterred, David devised a bold plan to circumvent their bulwarks. He figured one brave soul could swim under the walls through the water shaft feeding the city after dark, make his way to the gate, take out the guards and open the gate for his troops to enter unexpectedly. He just needed the one brave soul. Several times in life, people around you will be looking for a man to throw at a difficult task—so get ready now. Remember, when opportunity knocks, the time has already passed to get ready. This was such a critical mission, David let the people know that whoever would go through the water shaft and defeat the Jebusites, would become chief or captain of his entire army.

Joab was the intrepid warrior who climbed down in that water shaft, not knowing if there would be a long distances in it with no clearance for him to catch his breath. He didn't know if there were not some kind of iron bars or obstructions on the other end that would preclude his exit once inside of the city. He didn't know if the force of the water in that shaft would pin him to those iron bars causing him to find his own watery grave there. Neither did he know how heavily the entrance of that shaft on the inside of the city would be guarded nor how difficult it would be to take out the guards at the entrance gate. He didn't know if he would have the advantage of surprise when everyone knew a hostile foreign army threatening just outside. Something else he didn't know was how difficult it might be for one man to get the gate unlocked, being aware that it had to have been built battering-ram capable and having doors large enough to serve that whole side of the city. Nevertheless, Joab took the challenge. He swam through the water shaft, quietly killed the guards at the exit and opened the gate to David's awaiting army. His gallant action gave David's army the element of surprise and they easily took the city. Joab, as promised, became the Captain of the Host (commanding general) and had a long and distinguished career as David's commander. Just as all his other military leaders, he was chosen on the basis of just two things: his gallantry and loyalty to the king. David quickly established his kingdom in Jerusalem, the capitol city, and built his house there. He called it the City of David. If not a bold warrior himself, David, could never have devised such an audacious, risky plan to take the city by stealth. He was the greatest fighting soldier-King Israel ever had because the Lord God of hosts was with him. II Samuel 5:10

Whatever your personal fears might be, attack them. If the horse threw you, get back on immediately and go at it again. If you suffered a defeat in some other way, pray about it. Get wisdom from God, go back to the battle and fight on again. Your side wins in the end. Charge the enemy and they will scatter before your eyes. Remember, a poor army led by a bold leader can always defeat a strong army led by a weak one. The spirit of the leader is highly contagious. A weak leader will rarely attack so a decisive commander almost always gets to pick the time and location of the battle. By doing so he gains the best fields of fire (weapons fire), the dominate terrain and, last but not least of course, the element of surprise. Bold commanders spend precious resources on reconnaissance because, everything being equal, victory will always go to the commander with the best and latest information about their enemy. Weak leaders are more interested in running and hiding than planning attacks. Be bold. Never be afraid to take one big leap if that is what seems to be required because it is simply not possible to cross a large divide with two or three small steps. When the time comes for war and mortal combat, those who have experienced it know the adrenalin rush that comes as God's gift at those times and are able to better focus their consciousness, strength and intensity. It is then time to execute a bold attack against the enemy's stronghold without quarter, from one flank and then the next with all the firepower you can muster, until even hell's gates be broken to the ground. But first, as I mentioned, most importantly take time to pray, asking God for wisdom to make a bold plan.

What it means to have the character trait of **BOLDNESS:**

- Fearlessness in the face of hardship, difficult assignments and the enemy
- Intrepid
- A daring spirit
- Unafraid to take an audacious stand or approach
- Adventurous
- Conspicuously confident in the face of the enemy or trouble

AN-DO ATTITUDE, A—   Study start date: _____ Finish date: _____

As a leader, it is interesting to see how people react to new opportunities or, as it is interpreted by so many today, additional work. Most are stuck in the place of "I'm treading as fast as I can with just one nostril barely above water and one more ounce of work or anything else will, without a doubt, take me under." When asked to do something, they have learned to paint their faces with an incredulous look. Actually, new initiatives in any organization almost always begin with someone on the existing staff taking the lead. Opportunity in life always comes cleverly disguised as hard work, no pay, great risks and more responsibility. But opportunity usually only knocks once — so be ready. Besides, the leadership has already decided that this new initiative is critically necessary for the company's advancement; maybe even, survival. If you have been asked to take the lead, turning them down at this time is tantamount to deserting your leader in the face of the enemy. However, if we have decided that we are working for the Lord, the boss we are really serving is God. It is always much easier to say "Yes" to Him.

How then should we view added responsibilities in the work environment? First, realize that it is a great honor just to be asked to do anything new. Leadership has obviously already made the decision that you are the right person and are best equipped to handle the assignment, whatever it is. That's certainly a plus. They have seen something in you that leads them to believe that you can take on this task, solve the problems that will surely arise, gain the willing cooperation of your coworkers and bring the initiative to a successful conclusion. If we buck, claiming over-load, they are not likely to come to us with the next project and we will certainly cease to be the go-to man on staff. If they give you more responsibility, you can soon ask for additional personnel if it is justified. Another reason most people won't take a new project is the fear of criticism that will surely come from starting something new. Others are so afraid of failure they are permanently frozen in a do-nothing, take-no-chances mode. Perish the thought of being criticized—after all. Well, if that's your choice, enjoy the solitude of life at the bottom of the pile because nothing changes in life until someone is willing to step up to the plate and take a swing at whatever is coming next. Yes, someone has to accept the challenge and go with it. Someone has to rock the boat and challenge the status quo. You just simply can't make any progress in life, living in the past. Someone has always been, has to be and always will be the point of the spear leading the company into the future. This is what makes life is exciting!

Then again, so many people live such defeated lives that they no longer believe we can even get there from here. Those caught in this trap can think of a million reasons in a nanosecond why the project won't work and why we shouldn't even try. There is not one creative bone in their entire body. They haven't caught the fever of loving a new challenge, taking a chance, starting something new and different or finding a better way of doing something—just for the best interest of the company. Yes, there will be problems, there will be obstacles and there will be mistakes but, for a fact, if we come to a mountain today, we can defeat it in any number of ways. With a can-do attitude, we can go over it, around it or, bless God, if need be, we can tunnel through it. Mountains, come on because we've got something for you!

Be assured, our government doesn't spend millions of dollars training fighter pilots to fly planes that cost the taxpayers $190 million a copy, who are afraid to confront the enemy in fear losing the next dog fight. Our country doesn't drain the U.S. Treasury training Army Rangers who don't think they can accomplish the next assigned mission impossible. They are always looking for the man who thinks he can. Very often, that is the man who has his faith in God. David said, "By You I can run through a troop; and by God I can leap over a wall." (II Samuel 22:30) Paul was such a man, He established all the early churches in Europe with virtually no outside financial support. It was Paul who said, "I can do all things through Christ who strengthens me." (Philippians 4:13) He knew of a certainty that his "God shall supply all (his) need by His riches in glory by Christ Jesus." (v.4:19) His faith in God with its accompanying can-do attitude caused him to pen this statement of testimony for our benefit: "thanks be to God who always leads us in triumph in Christ ..." II Corinthians 2:14

Although we are not here to prove anything, God has placed us her to accomplish our purpose. We are here to do our job and it is in new opportunities and challenges that our ability is actually made apparent. New opportunities will define you. They will, in fact, reveal your creativity, vision, leadership, loyalty, strength and faithfulness. Leadership and all the Monday-morning quarterbacks in the grand stands will be watching you like a hawk because the new venture is a chance for the company to either succeed or fail and they have placed it all in your hands. Go with God's speed, wisdom and might.

Those in authority everywhere are always looking for a leader with a can-do attitude. They are looking for a man they don't have to beg and cajole to stand up to a task. Someone that always says, "Yes Sir, we can get this done. I will make it happen." Now, having accepted the job, it your responsibility to build the team and make the necessary adjustments. If you don't have enough man-power, go out and marshal a larger army. If you don't have enough equipment or provisions, you can always submit a request or go out and midnight requisition. They are looking for a leader who is not afraid to try new things or make a few mistakes. We all make mistakes. None of us are going to get it right every time but we can make corrections and use our mistakes to improve. Management is looking for a leader who can find consensus, build enthusiasm, find all the best-practices, innovate and create to a plan and come up with a stellar performance by the entire team. They are not looking for someone who will soon come back with a litany of all the best excuses why the job couldn't be done. They are looking for a man who has no need of excuses. They are looking for a man with a track record of success. They are looking for someone who can get the job done, with God's help, regardless. Leaders in every organization, every day of the year are looking for a Can-do Calvin, not a No-way Nate.

Remember this, those in authority know that there is only so much any one person can get done in a day. If they ask you to do more than is humanly possible, it's not a problem. They already know you are extremely efficient; so they will soon get around to allocating the resources you need to get the job done with excellence. So, attack. Pounce like a panther on the opportunities and duties that come your way in life. Receive them, every one, as assignments directly from God. Hustle like a wildcat. Say, "Yes. We can do it. ." If you keep it up, you will soon be the type of person who can say, "Don't ask me to do it unless you want to get the job done."

What it means to have the character trait of **A CAN-DO ATTITUDE:**

- A positive mind-set that says, "Yes, we can."
- Belief that God would not have laid this task at our feet unless He already equipped us.
- The mind-set of being more than a conqueror.
- Being positive about changes and new tasks
- One unafraid of failure, knowing that God, he can turn anything into a victory.

APABLE, BEING —   **Study start date:** _____ **Finish date:** _____

I t is easy to forget that all ability is simply and completely a gift from God. Those of us who can drive a car have been doing it for so long, we think nothing of it. Unless we are very careful, it is easy to think surely, everyone on earth can do this. Not so. Some don't have the motor skills or the vision required. Others don't have anyone to assist them with a car to learn or to apply for license testing. Still others don't have a satisfactory record of obedience to the law to qualify for a license. We need to thank God every day that we can drive. Aside from the fact that we all are born with some natural ability, we should make a concerted effort to become more capable in more and more areas of life. It is also well to remember that as soon as one rises to a level that they become incompetent in a particular field, their promotability comes to a screeching halt.

As a kid growing up in a technical society, my dad just happened to work in one of the most technical jobs around. He was a pilot in the Strategic Air Command. As you might imagine, the Air Force had to be on the leading edge of technology just to stay ahead of the U.S.S.R. As a teenager, he told me something I have never forgotten: He said, "Everything you learn you will use again in life." It may not seem like something you will ever need to use again but you will. In addition, abilities are cumulative. Learning one thing actually helps you learn something else down the dusty road of life. Increasing capabilities also produces self-confidence.

Here's just one example. During my last year in college, my degree in Industrial Technology required that I take an industrial safety course. Thinking I was soon going to be an Army Ranger, I was sure I would never, ever use that information again. What an exercise in futility this seemed to be. However, I gave my dad credit for being right on the basis of this being an exception to the rule. The rule was still valid but this was just an exception. Well, I took the course and did fairly well as did most everyone else and promptly forgot about the whole matter. Not a year later, after finishing several of the Army's schools, I was assigned to the 82nd Airborne Division at Ft. Bragg, NC. After I had a few days to organize my platoon, the company commander called me into his office to give me an assignment. Since the previous Brigade had been deployed to Vietnam en mass and we were a brand new unit, he said, "Lieutenant Menzies, I want you to write a Standard Operation/Procedure Manual (SOP) for safety for an airborne rifle company." My first thought was, my dad was right again. He was always right, matter of fact. Since I had taken the safety course and had kept the book, I was able to write a pretty good little manual. My company commander liked it so well, he even mentioned it in my efficiency report. Years later, when I was pastoring a large church and ministry, our staff started having too many accidents. I was able to write another Safety SOP and you would never guess—the accidents virtually stopped all because our people became safety conscious. That safety course was a great assist to me in life and was something I really thought was a waste of time. I was wrong.

To say life is a learning process is probably the understatement of the year. Learning is a life work—or should be. When we stop learning, we are dead. The more we learn, the more we are capable of learning and the more we see we have need of learning. In addition, society becomes more complicated every day. In the early 1900's it was a world of horses and mules, buggies and wagons. They had horse and mule drawn threshing machines. Before the turn of the 19th Century they were using steam tractors and by about 1906 gasoline engines had become part of the local landscape. My dad learned to fly in a biplane and later transitioned into four engine-bombers, air refuelers and jets. Today, we can barely keep up with computers, cell phones and the information technology revolution. It is all moving at light speed.

Learning how to build and drive a go-cart as a teenager, certainly made it easier for me to learn how to drive a car. Knowing how to drive a car helps immensely to master driving a semi–truck. I remember as a kid on a construction job on an Air Force Base up in Canada one summer, the superintendent needed somebody who could drive a semi-tractor/trailer rig. Nobody could. I volunteered for the job and remember climbing up the steps into that huge cab. It was huge. (I think I said that.) Just getting in the cab seemed like climbing a small mountain. The transmission had about fifteen gears and a high and low range. Somehow I got it going without dropping the transmission but you can know it was one more learning experience. That trailer looked like it stuck out behind the tractor for a city block. Pulling it seemed like driving a house down the road. All that helped me later to learn how to operate a back-hoe and front-end loader on a pipe line job in Texas. That thing had more levers than anything I had ever seen in my life and there was nobody to show me what the first one did. It was all trial and error—heavy on the error part.

Never be afraid of making mistakes. Everybody does. I tell all my employees everywhere I have worked, "If I don't ever catch you making any mistakes, I'm going to fire you, because if you never make any mistakes, you aren't doing anything." However, learning and mastering that back-hoe, what a contraption, later helped me have the confidence to learn how to fly an airplane. Wherever you are and whatever team you are on in life, situations will always arise that no one on the team knows how to handle or has any experience with. Always be willing to take the plunge when they ask for a volunteer. Being capable starts with being willing to stretch, to leave your comfort zone and be willing to make a few mistakes. It is an opportunity to learn and advance. Try it. Remember, 'Cain't never could do anything.' Give it all you've got. Give it Hell. Whatever it is will have to yield soon enough. No matter what you are learning, people always give you time to become proficient before they start judging your efficiency. Besides, you get a lot of points in life just for the boldness of stepping up to the plate.

For a person to really succeed in life today, they must love to learn. They must use the things they have already learned in other areas and apply them to help learn new things, grasp new concepts and new ways of doing things in other areas. Why? Because our world is constantly changing with ever-increasing speed. And, the world is forever looking for people who are capable of handling this changing environment and keeping their company ahead of things. Some people excel in learning concepts from books, conjugating verbs and can even, possibly explain the theory of relativity but they can't drive a nail. They can speak French and German but can't lead a crew of men to dig footings, laying block or frame a house. Today a leader needs to have a wide range of experience and abilities to function as the manager of just about any large concern. A general in the military or industry must have a general grasp of a whole lot of fields. Large operations today have a multiplicity of departments: finance, operations, vehicles, airplanes, taxation, maintenance, etc. To manage all of these successfully in a competitive marketplace, one must be experienced and knowledgeable in as many fields as possible. Unless a person becomes a dedicated learner, this just won't happen. That means we must not only be willing to learn but delight in learning to make ourselves more valuable to God and our fellow man.

Some, on the other hand, refuse to learn. Often the reason for this is a fear of failure. They worry that they might not be able to pick up something new, they don't want to leave their comfort zone or they fear taking on new responsibilities might open them up to failing in the new endeavor. Never, never, never be afraid to fail. Failing is actually really hard to do, nigh unto impossible, because whatever you try, even if you don't do so well at it the first time, you were still stepping out toward your goal in life. No matter what happens, you are better equipped to take another run at it, find a better approach and will likely succeed in the end. The only way we can be sure to fail is to refuses to even try.

To be promotable in today's society, one must demonstrate the ability to take risks and deal with people, technology and equipment as well as the laws of the land. The world, other than possibly the arena of scientists and researchers, is not looking for specialists but generalists. They are looking for people who can handle a generality of thorny issues, equipment and difficult people. You must also be able to handle trouble. Now I don't mean to give the impression that every day on a job is packed full of problems but they sure come around often enough. The person on the team who is capable, has demonstrated the ability to master new tasks, can easily get along with their teammates to build consensus and can consistently get their work done with excellence, will soon rise to the top. He will be the one the company leaders go to when they need a difficult task completed and, in due time, will soon be the leader.

In reality, we are all more capable than we think. .The apostle Paul said, "(We) can do all things through Christ who strengthens (us)." (Philippians 4:13) How many things? All things.

What it means to have the character trait of **BEING CAPABLE:**

- Able
- Having the various attributes physically, mentally and morally which are required to perform tasks
- Having the general capacity to learn quickly, become skilled and be efficient
- Able to apply previously learned information, concepts and skills to new areas of endeavor
- Able over time to master a multiplicity of tasks, skills and disciplines

AREFUL IN FRIENDSHIP—   Study start date: _____ Finish date: _____

Certainly a great danger that few young people recognize as they are growing up is the danger of wrong friendships and associations. Wrong friendships have an unbelievable, unseen power of contagion as well as the ability to entangle one as an accomplice in another person's criminal activity simply by being in proximity. The Bible says associating with a fool in their folly or even being in the vicinity is as dangerous as meeting a she bear robbed of her cubs. (Proverbs 17:12) A female bear can weigh from 200 to 1,400 pounds and, with her cubs, is even more aggressive than their male counterparts. They usually attack humans while standing and can be nine feet tall. More people are killed trying to run from them than the ones who stay and fight. People who have been bitten by a bear and were fortunate enough to actually live through it, say, understandably, it is something they will never forget. They say it felt like someone took a long two by four with a 30 penny nail driven through the end of it and then swung it as hard as they could and hit you in the head. Not a whole lot of fun but I said all that to say this. Wrong friendships, God said, are even more dangerous.

It is so easy for young people to miss the truth of all this. Paul said, "Do not be deceived; evil company corrupts good morals." (I Corinthians 15:33) The wisest man in the world, Solomon, said, "He who walks with the wise will be wise, but the companion of fools will be destroyed." (Proverbs 13:20) Fools are given to arguments, greed, cursing and debate. I was told never to argue with a fool because the bystanders may not be able to tell which one of us is the fool. Just being in the car or home of a person who uses drugs is extremely dangerous. If their home is raided or their car is stopped by the police and you are just present and it matters not that you aren't doing any drugs or that you aren't even aware that they are hidden somewhere inside, you too are guilty. You still get a felony, high fines and hard time in the clink.

Because of just one, young Hebrew girl choosing wrong friendships, a terrible incident occurred in Israel's history. Scripture commands that the Jews marry not only inside their nation but they are also restricted to wed only within their own tribe. This law maintained a pure blood line, the practice of the one true religion, and the inheritance of family lands. It also kept the nation from being polluted by the pagan practices of the heathen nations around them. However, on this tragic occasion, not being careful in friendship, Jacob and Leah's daughter, Dinah, "went out to see the daughters of the land." (Genesis 34:1) While in town, visiting with the other teenage girls, she was seen by Shechem, a Hivite prince. He took Dinah, raped her and tried to keep her for his wife. A Hebrew daughter being defiled in this manner, was a great offence to the Israelites as well as the worst thing that could happen to a young girl. Such an offense was an affront to the young girl, the family, the nation, their religion and their God. Had this been tolerated, the nation of Israel would have been absorbed into oblivion by the surrounding heathen nations.

As a consequence of one teenage girl not seeing the hidden dangers of wrong friendships, the whole nation, Israel, in its embryonic state, was placed in total jeopardy. Immediately after this happened, the young prince asked his father to get permission from the Israelites to keep Dinah for his wife. This heathen prince violating their sister was more than her brothers could stand. So, the sons of Jacob craftily devised a treacherous plan to defeat the Hivites saying that for the marriage to take place, all Hivites had to be circumcised. To obtain the approval of the townspeople, Hamor, the boy's father, and Shechem went to the gate of their city and spoke with the men saying: "These men are at peace with us. Therefore let them dwell in the land and trade in it. For indeed the land is large enough for them. Let us take their daughters to us as wives and let us give them our daughters. Only on this condition will the men consent to dwell with us, to be one people; if every male among us is circumcised as they are circumcised. Will not their livestock, their property and every animal of theirs be ours? Only let us consent to them and they will dwell with us." Genesis 34:21–23

So all the men of the city were circumcised and on the third day, when their pain was the worst, Dinah's two brothers, taking their swords, boldly entered the city and avenged their sister by killing every male in the town. They retrieved their sister, Dinah, and took all the townspeople had as plunder. They did this because they could not let their sister be treated like a harlot or for the nation to be polluted by foreign marriages. However, their actions also put the fledgling nation in danger of retaliation by all the Caananites and Perizzites of the land. Perceiving the danger, God spoke to Jacob and told him to take the Hebrew children to Bethel, to make an altar and dwell there. Scripture states that God had to divinely place a terror in all the cities round about them so that they did not pursue or retaliate against them. All this happened as the result of one young girl not being careful in friendship.

What was the result of this one bad decision? A teenage girl was raped and kidnapped. A family and nation were shamed. Israel felt they had to kill every man in a whole city in retaliation. The whole nation, Israel, was placed in jeopardy and came very near being absorbed into oblivion by another country. In the end, God had to divinely intervene to keep them from being attacked and physically annihilated by other nations.

Over time, I have seen so many fine young men and women who fell into the trap of wrong friendships with other young people who drank to excess, used drugs, used fowl language and engaged in illicit sex. Soon enough they were not only defending these practices but were involved in much of this themselves. The friends we choose have power. Proverbs 22:24 says, "Make no friendship with an angry man and with a furious man do not go, lest you learn their ways and set a snare for your soul." A person who has learned to get their way in life by railing, screaming and throwing fits has a spirit of rage in their soul. The only way you can deal with their rage is by fighting fire with fire. The problem is this spirit is communicable and you will be taken by it.

Another very important point about friendships is that loyalty is more important in life than anything else. The question is, are you going to be loyal to God or to yourself and the devil? The greatest gift you have to give is your loyalty to Him. Without that, nothing else counts and nothing else will work. Be loyal to God and your family first. God's enemies must become your enemies and His friends must be yours as well. Your fathers' friends should be your friends and his enemies need to also be yours. I'm not saying that you are to carry generational grudges but I am saying not to befriend your father's enemies as that can and most certainly will cause divided loyalties and will be misunderstood. By the same token, if you work for a company, your boss' friends should, likewise, be your friends and his enemies, the people you know have cheated, mistreated or spoken evil against him, are to be avoided for all the same reasons. The same is true in personal friendships. You can't play both sides of the street—and you shouldn't want to! Be a true friend. Let their friends be yours and leave their enemies to themselves. In the same vein, if you work for a company or an individual, stand behind them. Certainly no company and no man is going to be perfect. If you want to look for a chink in your leader's armor, you will surely find one. Do yourself a favor and try your best to see all the good in them you possibly can. Concentrate on that and always speak well of your superiors and your organization. Let them know you are loyal to them—come what may. There are some situations that are so corrupt, however, this impossible. So, if you can't be loyal, be gone.

Outside of the blessing of a Godly mate, close friendships can be one of the most precious gifts a person can ever have on earth. Sadly, some people go through life and never have one true friend. It is amazing how no one, I mean no one, would expect to get heat from their fireplace without putting wood in it and setting it afire. But in the area of friendships, they are not willing to make any investments whatsoever. Proverbs 18:24 tells us, "A man who has friends must himself be friendly ..." The King James Version says, "he must show himself friendly." which means making the investments of time, assistance, resources and loyalty that may be required from time-to-time.

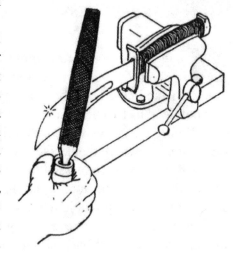

Friends should be selected and not haphazardly accepted because of convenience, proximity, the result of best affections or kindness to everyone. A friend should be chosen and accepted on the basis of esteem for their character and lifestyle. Close friends should be growing Christians. If your friend says he or she is a Christian yet is not interested in attending church, Bible study and living in a godly manner, they are not growing. They are dead. Find new friends. Know that "as iron sharpens iron,; so a man sharpens the countenance of his friend." (Proverbs 27:17) Copper, wood, plastic, lead and crystal don't sharpen iron. Only iron sharpens iron. You will soon be known by the friends you choose. Run with dogs and you will get fleas. Run with the wise and you will be wise.

What it means to have the character trait of **CAREFUL IN FRIENDSHIP:**

- Selecting friends wisely
- Having the wisdom to make close associations with people of character
- Well aware of the possibility of grave consequences brought on by wrong associations
- Choosing growing Christians for friends

C AREFULNESS —   **Study start date: _____ Finish date: _____**

Many go through life leaping before they look, making careless decisions based on emotions, without taking the time to consider all the relevant facts. We need to remember that every decision we make in life is really choosing among one or more options. The path we take will ultimately, like it or not, lead us to a destination. Some paths might also have ambushes set against us along the way as well. Before we go, we must carefully survey all the options and consequences and we better be certain we want to go where the decision will take us.

As humans we are blessed to have decisions to make in life. For this reason, we will, one day, be at a place that is the sum-total of all the decisions we have made. Decisions, as we know, can have consequences as well as possible rewards. Decision making is both an art and a process.

Since nobody knows everything and we all have a lot to learn about any subject you might name, we should never feel bad asking counsel from experts in their field. Someone said, "Ignorance is a consequence of being human. Not knowing it is even more atrocious." So true. The writer of Proverbs warned that, "Without counsel plans go awry but in the multitude of counselors they are established." (Proverbs 15:22) All the problems and trials of life are like small wars we each must wage. The writer says, "For by wise counsel you will wage your own war and in a multitude of counselors there is safety." (Proverbs 24:6) Their counsel will add to what you already know about the subject and give you several other viewpoints as well. Their wisdom will either deter or encourage you, giving you greater conviction about your plan. You have nothing to lose other than the small amount of time it takes to seek advice. But, know this, whatever you decide, you alone will own and either pay for a bad decision or reap the benefits of a good one.

Any discussion of carefulness in decision-making would require a word about what is known as the Ben Franklin close. This is a very simple method of reviewing all the pertinent facts about a decision, an opportunity in business or even deciding on a battle plan. You simply take a sheet of paper for each possible course of action and state that option on the top of each page. Under the stated option, you make two columns and put ADVANTAGES at the top of one column and DISADVANTAGES on the top of the other. Then start brain storming, writing down as many of each as you can. This exercise forces you to consider all the facts bearing on the decision. A prudent man, we know, gets all the facts before making a decision. Be sure to consider the long term consequences. Try to uncover all the unintended consequences of each option. Just the size of the columns of the facts will usually tell you quite a bit about what to do. You might also want to "star" some to give greater weight to the points that are crucial

Most importantly, pray and ask God for wisdom. James 1:5 says, "If any (man) lacks wisdom, let him ask of God, who gives to all liberally and without reproach and it will be given to him." We all lack wisdom and we all need to continually ask God for this great gift. Then, when you think you really have the answer, ask yourself if it is truly wisdom from God? Because "the wisdom that is from above is first pure, peace loving, considerate, submissive, full of mercy and good fruits, impartial and sincere." (James 3:17) Then pray over it for several days if the situation doesn't require immediate action. Major decisions should be prayed over for thirty days. Then, when you have peace and make your decision, go and boldly execute your plan.

Some things in life need special care and consideration. One such is children. They require careful supervision to avoid problems, accidents, loss and all kinds of danger in a world full of trouble. Even Jesus's parents, lost him for three days at the age of twelve. They had unknowingly left town without him and had to return to find Him. Happily, they found him listening intently to the wisdom of the priests in the temple.(Luke 2:42–46) Some people can be overly careful about natural or worldly things as was Martha and miss the more important spiritual part. (Luke10:41, 42) Other things that require special care are our mates (I Corinthians 7:32–34), our spiritual duties (Philippians 2:20) and shepherding the flock of God. John 10:11 and I Corinthians 12:25

Another area deserving special care, without a doubt, is machinery. Vehicles, airplanes and equipment require a special degree of attention and carefulness due to their size, speed and power. One summer during college I was working as a front-end loader and backhoe operator for a pipeline construction company in Dripping Springs, Texas. On this fateful day, I happened to be going from one site digging ditches to another a block away. Thinking it would only take a few minutes to get relocated, in interest of time, I decided not to put the lock pin in the backhoe arm base, attached to the rear of my tractor. That pin kept the arm from making any lateral movement. Then while heading down the road to the next location, I noticed the superintendent's truck parked on the side of the road and his arm out of the window signaling for me to meet and talk. I pulled my rig along-side, parallel with his truck, with mine on the pavement, I killed the engine, put the parking brake on, jumped down to receive instructions about the next phase of work. Thinking all was well, I jumped back on the tractor, cranked the engine, released the brake and let out the clutch in first gear to head down the road. Well, I didn't get but a few feet before I heard a loud crashing sound and felt that huge piece of equipment come to an abrupt stop. The problem was that all paved roads have a bit of a crown to them to assist water run-off and that meant the hydraulic pressure in the boom of my back hoe was slowly leaking down inside the system and the boom had, unbeknownst to me, crept over behind my boss's truck during our conversation. Upon exiting the tractor, I surveyed the damage on the back end of my boss's truck, expecting the worst. Amazingly, since the boom and bucket had mostly hit his bumper, the damage wasn't as bad as the sound indicated. Even more amazingly, I got out of that one with only an admonition to be more careful in the future and, thankfully, no pink slip. It certainly didn't do much for my feelings though. After that incident, I felt like I was about an inch tall. After all, this was the boss' truck I clobbered. In any event, I gained a new determination to be more careful and circumspect in the future. .

What it means to have the character trait of **CAREFULNESS:**

- Marked by caution and circumspection
- Taking the time to inspect and complete safety checks
- Unwilling to make careless moves or estimates
- Taking in consideration all the relevant facts and future consequences
- Cautious to double check to avoid errors and omissions
- Showing attention to detail
- Having prudence

AUTIOUSNESS —   Study start date: _____   Finish date: _____

It takes a while for young people to realize that they are living in a wicked world that is growing all the more wicked daily. This does not mean that there are not a whole lot of good people around. However, everybody who says well just may not be well. We need to get in the habit when making big decisions, of checking things out. Do your due diligence. Ask for references and vet them.

For example, in the financial world, it takes most people a lifetime to build an estate but it takes only a minute to turn all your hard-earned money over to a, so-called investment banker, the likes of a Bernie Madoff and lose it. Remember, it wasn't long ago (2008) that he was convicted for, not stealing millions or even hundreds of millions from his investors. He stole nearly 65 billion and is known for operating the largest Ponzi scheme in history of the world! He stole from thousands from sophisticated investors. As a matter of fact, he didn't care who he stole from or how many retirees, non-profits, charities, schools or retirement funds lost their money. What can we learn from this? As best you can, try to manage your own finances and investments. Check things out carefully before buying. If a deal sounds too good to be true, the rule is, it probably is. "The simple believes every word (people tell them) but the prudent considers well his steps." Proverbs 14:15

For most people, a lifetime of hard work, frugality and planning are necessary to amass an estate. Therefore, it is essential to, likewise, spend the time to do the research just as carefully to do the business of investing. As much as possible, try to find investments like rental homes, owning a coin laundry, buying and selling small pieces of land, etc. Your return on investment will be significantly better than the stock market or mutual funds and most importantly, you will always own them and they will likely not be going anywhere in the dark of night.

An interesting example of cautiousness can be found in the book of Judges. In Gideon's day, God was about to defeat the Midianite army but there was a problem. Giedon's army, of all things, was too large. It really wasn't all that large but large enough for the people to believe that they had fought for and won the victory themselves. God was about to give the Midianites into their hands and the true victor, of course, was God. To alleviate the problem, God told Gideon to send everyone home who was fearful and afraid. That day twenty-two thousand went home and only ten thousand remained. There were still far too many so God told Gideon to take his army down to the bank of a river to test them. The ones who got down on their knees, (who stopped being cautions even for a moment) and lapped up the water like a dog were to be send home. The ones who scooped up the water in one hand and drank it while continuing to be watchful about things around them, Gideon kept. Then there was only three hundred men in his army but it was this kind of men, the careful, cautious and circumspect that God would use to defeat the entire Midianite army. (Judges 7:1–23) It is important to note that Gideon's army was not chosen on the basis of who was the swiftest, the strongest or the smartest but for being cautious and circumspect. Caution does not deter one in the least from being fearless. It does, however, keep one from making foolish mistakes or falling for traps and ambushes In a real war, anyone who is not cautious will likely not be around very long.

Sometimes just building a wall, can quickly become extremely dangerous. During Nehemiah's time, just rebuilding the wall around Jerusalem enraged the enemies of Israel and caused them to do everything in their power to stop the work. His enemies tried mocking Nehemiah and his men, conspiracy, false accusations of tyranny, letters to the governors, threats, and they even planned armed attacks. These tasks will require great caution as well. Nehemiah's enemies threatened them ten times that it didn't matter what they did, saying, "From whatever place you turn, (we) will be upon (you)." (Nehemiah 4:12) Because of this Nehemiah positioned men with spears, bows and swords at the various openings of the wall while it was under construction. He cautioned the nobles, the leaders and all the people, "Do not be afraid of them. Remember the Lord, great and awesome and fight for your sons, your daughters, your wives and your houses." (v.14) So it was, when the enemy heard that they knew of their plan to attack and that God had brought it all to nothing, the people returned to their work on the wall but, with caution. From that time on, half of the people worked on the construction while the other half provided security wearing armor, carrying shields, bows, swords and spears. Even those working and carrying materials, situated themselves so that they could work with one hand and carry a weapon with the other. They were wisely cautious about the enemy's tactics but were confident that God was with them.

What it means to have the character trait of **CAUTIOUSNESS:**

- Being discreet and careful to check things out
- Not accepting information given at face value without verification
- Marked by caution and circumspection
- Being prepared and alert to the attacks of the enemy

HANGE, THE ABILITY TO EMBRACE— Study start date: _____ Finish date: _____

We all have a deep longing in our souls for everything in our environments to stay the same. We human being don't like change. However, God just keeps on moving the furniture around in our lives and in the whole world as well without asking permission. We've all heard it said, there are only two things for certain: death and taxes. Well, there are, regrettably, others and one of them is change. Every day there are new inventions. Growing up, I remember looking down the hall in my great grand-dad's house and seeing the wooden telephone box about two feet tall, sticking out six inches from the wall. About midway up on this contraption there was a black mouthpiece, a ringer crank on the side, along with a long chord and earpiece situated in a metal yoke receiver on one side. And, everyone had a party line. What a contrast to the cell phones of today with all the apps, flash lights, maps, directional finders, ask google, texting, email, weather, tweets and twitters, video and still cameras, just to name a few! What an improvement. Happily most change is for the better. We also see constant changes in the weather, earthquakes, warfare, a torrent of changing government regulations, medical advancements and, you name it. Change is coming. Seemingly every day our routine is decimated and we have to deal with a revolution in our plans. Today change is rarely a smooth continuum but more like a cataclysmic eruption.

Henry Ford built the Model T and then the Model A. He brought mechanized transportation to the middle class, to the majority of Americans. People bought them like hot cakes but about that time, the American public decided they wanted more style, color options, chrome and comfort. He told them, "You don't want to do this because it is really going to cost you." To which they replied, "Oh, yes we do. We'll pay it." The public got what they wanted and they really did have to pay for it too. Now the styles of automobiles have to change every model year.

Since change is coming, we may as well find a way to have it work for us, instead of against us. Because all markets are anticipatory, the analysts are constantly uncovering new facts and adjusting supply and prices. Obviously, if there is either an increase of oil coming on the market or a decrease in demand because of the economy, the price is going to plummet. Real estate and job markets as well as the price of shrimp in the seafood department of your local grocery operate the same way. For all this to work for us, and it is working one way or another all the time, we must find out about these changes before the masses. Then, we too can anticipate it.

In the days of the Medes and Persians, before they had court houses on the square, people conducted most of their business at the city gate. This was where proclamations were read, where real estate owner-ship was transferred by passing a shoe to the buyer in the presence of the city elders and men sat around to spit and whittle, tell jokes and hear the latest scuttlebutt about what was happening in the king's court. A Jew named Mordecai sat at the gate daily after his beautiful younger cousin, Esther, was selected to be the queen. He had raised her from childhood after her parents' death and was very concerned about her for good reason. They were both Jews living in a land of heathens and her nationality had not yet been disclosed to the king. Daily Mordecai sat dutifully at the gate with his ear to the ground, so to speak, to find out how she was faring in the king's court. It was there he discovered that two disgruntled guards had devised a plan to assassinate the king. He quickly got word to Esther who (giving Mordecai all the credit) in turn, told the king and saved his life. News concerning the business of the city and entire nation including all the edicts of the king, all privileged information, was revealed on a daily basis by the guards and others members of the king's court. They were just too willing to share all they heard from the king as well as his officers, attendants and magistrates. Certainly we don't need to sit at the gates of the city today but we should read the newspaper and trade journals. When we know change is on the way and it will, in fact, most certainly dramatically affect us all, we need to take the appropriate action to get ahead of it. We want to be sure we can not only be compliant but also, when possible, benefit from it. Failing to do so almost always results in loss, stiff penalties and sometimes other harsh, catastrophic realities.

Next, we need to make a quality decision right here and now to purpose, to be flexible. Face it, nobody comes normally and naturally fitted in this life to be flexible. We all want to cling to the past, what's familiar, what we like and the status quo. However, we soon learn that anyone who tries to stand still or become entrenched in the past will soon be run over by the steam roller of progress and be left behind in the dust of time. Instead, we should look for the good in the proposed changes as well as the opportunities that may abound because of it. We all need to practice being open to new ideas, new concepts and new ways of doing things. We should imitate the palm tree which is capable of bending in the high winds of hurricanes and not the brittle pine that snaps in the same gales. Be creative. Like they say, "Find a need and fill it." Then you can sell your new concept, inventions, books and gadgets to others who will definitely have need of them. We need to let the changing vicissitudes of life work for us.

In the 1970's Alvin Toffler wrote a book called *Future Shock* which predicted that change would increase dramatically in the last days, especially with the advent of the computer. Future shock is the resistance we feel when confronted with a new change, having to learn how to operate a new gadget or incorporate a new system in our daily routine. There are trends, we know, and, then again, as Toffler described, there are megatrends. These are major shifts that take years to complete. One such he mentioned was the loss of our industrial might in the northeastern states due to the increasingly high cost of heating fuel, union wages, benefits, pensions, and so on. Manufacturing plants are shutting down and they are padlocking the doors. Families that lived there for generations are leaving the "rust belt" in droves and moving to the "sun belt." This has been going on for years and will, very likely, continue for years to come. It accelerated significantly in the last decade because of the signing of NAFTA (North American Fair Trade Agreement). Most of America's manufacturing and engineering jobs left the country like a swift gust of wind for countries paying lower wages like Mexico, South Korea, China and Taiwan. One must be aware of these mega-shifts because they are going to dramatically affect jobs, housing, tax structures and just about everything else. Because of this evacuation, en masse, whole neighborhoods have been bulldozed in cities like Detroit. However, quite the contrary, the influx of people in the south has, as expected, driven up housing and land prices.

Some change, however, needs to be resisted. We know that evil is ever increasing in the earth, accompanied by new laws to promote and protect it. Who would have imagined, fifty years ago, that the Supreme Court would invent a dark, deep shadow of death in the Constitution, called the right to privacy, which, amazingly, allows women to kill their own progeny? Or that our government would legalize homosexual unions and give it the blessing of civil government? Knowing, all the while, that God hasn't changed His mind about it and never will. To Him and His followers, these are still abomination. We, as God's children, must stand against these things and let our voices be heard regardless of the consequences we might face someday. Psalm 94:16

Such an ungodly edict came in the life of Daniel one day. Though of royal birth as an Israelite, he found himself an obscure slave enduring the harsh realities of captivity in Babylon. As providence would have it, he and some of his gifted Hebrew brethren were summoned to serve in the palace of the king. The prerequisites for this appointment were that the young men had to be handsome, gifted in the knowledge of the day and quick to learn. It was there they were taught the language, literature and customs of the Chaldeans. Furthermore, the king appointed that they were to eat his delicacies and drink his wine for three years. However, Daniel determined in his heart not to defile himself with the king's food or drinking his wine. He made, rather, a wise and godly appeal to the eunuch who had been put in charge of them. He proposed, instead, that he and his brethren eat only vegetables and drink water for ten days. The eunuch was then to judge their appearance in comparison to the other youths who ate the king's table. At the end of those days, they were to be brought before the king and interviewed personally. He found them not only wiser than their contemporaries who ate the king's delicacies but also, ten times wiser than all the magistrates and astrologers who served in his court. So there, in the king's court, Daniel was not only allowed to stay but continued to demonstrate godly wisdom as well as the ability to understand visions and dreams. (Daniel 1:17) In all this, Daniel kept a clear conscience, staying faithful to his God..

Upon taking over the kingdom, Darius appointed 120 princes to bear rule who were accountable to three administrators, one of which was Daniel. Since he had a right spirit and because of his exceptional abilities, he so distinguished himself among the other administrators and princes that the king planned to give him charge of the whole kingdom. However, this aroused such jealousy among the other administrators and princes that they tried to find some fault in his handling of government affairs but, of course, could not. They found him faithful, trustworthy, incorruptible and never negligent. It was obvious that they would never find a basis to bring a charge against Daniel in the line of duty so they had to find something to cause him to be in conflict with the laws of his God. Thus they devised a plan they knew would eliminate him and presented it to the king saying, "O King Darius, issue the decree … The royal administrators, perfects, satraps, advisers and governors have all agreed that the king should issue an edict and enforce the decree that anyone who prays to any god or man during the next thirty days, except to you, O king, shall be thrown into the lion's den. Now, O king, issue the decree and put it in writing so that it cannot be altered—in accordance with the laws of the Medes and Persians, which cannot be annulled." (Daniel 6:7–9) The king liked the plan because it appealed to his pride and had it proclaimed throughout the land.

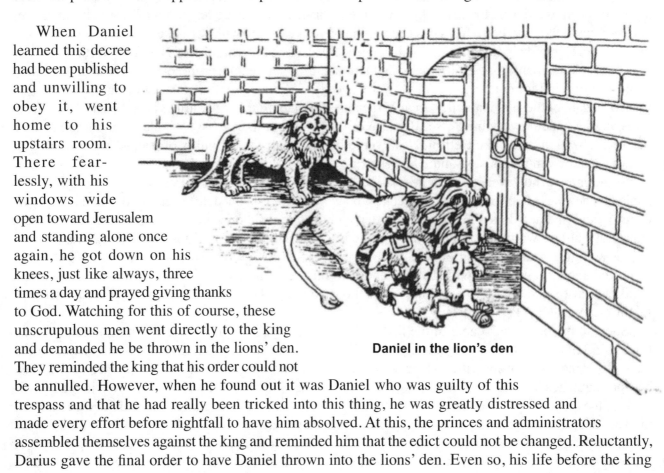

When Daniel learned this decree had been published and unwilling to obey it, went home to his upstairs room. There fearlessly, with his windows wide open toward Jerusalem and standing alone once again, he got down on his knees, just like always, three times a day and prayed giving thanks to God. Watching for this of course, these unscrupulous men went directly to the king and demanded he be thrown in the lions' den. They reminded the king that his order could not

Daniel in the lion's den

be annulled. However, when he found out it was Daniel who was guilty of this trespass and that he had really been tricked into this thing, he was greatly distressed and made every effort before nightfall to have him absolved. At this, the princes and administrators assembled themselves against the king and reminded him that the edict could not be changed. Reluctantly, Darius gave the final order to have Daniel thrown into the lions' den. Even so, his life before the king had obviously already served to increase the king's faith in God because he said, "May your God, whom you serve continually rescue you!" (Daniel 6:16) At that, a stone was placed over the entrance of the lion's den and it was sealed by the signet ring of the king and his nobles so that no one should remove it. Because of his steadfastness and righteousness, Daniel was afforded yet another opportunity to stand alone, this time in the lions' den.

Scripture states that the king fasted until morning—six to eight hours at the most. Though he tried to sleep but couldn't. At day break, he hurried to the lions' den and cried to Daniel in a voice broken with distress, "Daniel, servant of the living God, has your God, whom you serve continually, been able to rescue you from the lions?" Daniel answered, "O king, live forever! My God sent his angel, and he shut the mouths of the lions. They have not hurt me, because I was found innocent in His sight. Nor have I ever done any wrong before you, O King." (Daniel 6:20–22) The king was elated and gave the order to have him lifted from the den. No wound was found on him because he trusted in the Lord, his God. At this point, the law of retribution came quickly to bear as the king commanded that Daniel's accusers be thrown into the same den along with their wives and children. A testimony of Daniel's deliverance was the fact that the same lions crushed all the bones in their bodies before they even reached the floor of the den.

King Darius was so moved by this miracle that he wrote this decree to all peoples, nations and men throughout his kingdom: "May you prosper greatly! I issue a decree that in every part of my kingdom; people must fear and reverence the God of Daniel. For He is the living God. And he endures forever; His kingdom will not be destroyed, His dominion will never end. He rescues and saves; He performs signs and wonders in the heavens and on earth. He has rescued Daniel from the power of the lions." (Daniel 6:25–28) Subsequently, Daniel was promoted to ruler over the entire providence of Babylon and placed in charge of all its wise men. Furthermore, he continued to flourish as prime minister under the succession of at least four different heathen kings in his lifetime. Daniel 1:1, 5:1, 6:1 & 6:23

What it means to have the character trait of **THE ABILITY TO EMBRACE CHANGE:**

- Realizing that all humans have an inborn resistance to change that must be overcome.
- Being flexible in situations where change is possible
- Having the ability to change or modify one's life, business practices and procedures
- Flowing with the changes, mutations, permutations, phases, shifts and transitions of life
- Being cooperative and understanding
- Having a forward thinking mind set

CHARISMA—   **Study start date:** _____ **Finish date:** _____

Precious little is ever accomplished in life without enthusiasm and some degree of charisma on the part of the leader. There are all manner of things people can lay their lives down in the pursuit of but most choose something they see others are excited about. A person who is enthusiastic, who has also taken the time and expended the effort to be qualified in their field of endeavor, who knows what they want in life is simply the kind of person people are drawn to. In the military it is called being technically and tactically proficient or knowing your stuff. It is a fact that people who are fearless, confident and excited about their life automatically draw people to them. This phenomenon only occurs when people are happy and excited about life and what they are doing. Charisma does not happen without a positive attitude. Sad, disgruntled people are a drain on society. Their negative outlook and broken spirit is more than anybody can bear. Solomon said, "The spirit of a man (a positive attitude and the resulting faith) will sustain (a person) in sickness, but who can bear a broken spirit?" (Proverbs 18:14) Besides, people don't attach themselves to anything without getting emotionally involved with it and that takes excitement. A leader will never accomplish much in life without integrity and the ability to gain the explicit trust of others. For this ever to happen, they must have impeccable character and the ability to naturally convey enthusiasm to their associates.

You may have noticed that the leaders people follow smile confidently just about all the time. Why is this? Because they are happy. They are happy to be doing what they are doing. They have accepted themselves the way God made them and are comfortable living in their own skin. When engaged in conversation with people they smile because they are happy to be talking with them, they have a very positive expectation about the outcome of the project they are working with them on and their relationship with them in general. Leaders who have enthusiasm, accomplish and salesmen who have enthusiasm, sell. Their enthusiasm is a charismatic gift in itself. Paul told us in I Corinthians 1: 26 that God nearly always uses ordinary people. Then He makes the ordinary, extraordinary by filling them with the supernatural power of the Holy Spirit.

We see in the Apostle Peter a perfect example of the dramatic effect the power of the baptism of the Holy Spirit can make in a person's life. Before, there was no doubt, Peter knew the Lord because he had been with Him for the duration of His ministry on earth. He certainly had a revelation of the Kingdom but it was the baptism of the Holy Spirit that changed and equipped him for ministry. Acts 1:8 is a promise to all who will receive it. Here the Apostle Paul tells us, "… You shall receive power when the Holy Spirit has come upon you; and you shall be witnesses …" It certainly happened for Peter. His entire personality was transformed.

Before he was impetuous, after receiving the power of the Holy Spirit, he was meek.

Before he was unlearned, then he was enlightened.

Before he was fearful, then he was fearless.

Before he was haughty, then he was humble.

Before he was boastful, then he boasted about Christ.

Before he was a fumbling failure, then he came to know success.

Before he had a problem with foot-in-mouth disease, then he preached and had three thousand converts in a single meeting.

Before he represented himself, then he was able to give his life and all the glory to Christ.

After the gift of salvation, the greatest promise in the Bible is that of the Baptism in the Holy Spirit. Nothing else equals it.

Imagine being filled with the mighty Holy Spirit of God; being filled with the dunamus (dynamite) power of God. With the baptism, God gives us the power to witness and do the works of God. Being filled with the power gives us the ability to take self off the throne of our hearts and serve Jesus rightfully as Lord of all. This supernatural power fills us with the love of God which is His very essence. To receive this great gift, there are only four requirements. You must:

1. Be saved and believe on Jesus as your Savior.
2. Believe in the baptism and accept that it is for today (all God's gifts are received by faith).
3. Desire it with no deceit in your heart for personal gain. Acts 8:18–23
4. Ask for it. Luke 11:13

It is very important that we understand the importance of this last requirement, that of asking. It is not only printed in the Bible but it is in red letters because they are the words of Jesus. It is how all of life is to be lived. Jesus said, "… I say to you, ask, and it will be given to you; seek and you will find; knock, and it will be opened to you. For everyone who asks receives, and he who seeks finds, and to him who knocks it will be opened." Note the surety of this promise: "If a son asks for bread from any father among you, will he give him a stone? Of if he asks for a fish, will he give him a serpent instead of a fish? Or if he asks for an egg, will he offer him a scorpion? If you then, being evil, know how to give good gifts to your children, how much more will your heavenly Father give the Holy Spirit to those who ask Him?" (Luke 11:9–13) Of all the things a person could ask for, a job, a raise, a spouse, a healing, etc., Jesus singles out the absolute certainty of His promise to give the baptism of Holy Spirit to those who ask.

The baptism in the Holy Spirit also frees us to flow in our functional gift (I Corinthians 12) and really lets the Lord live His life in us as He wills—which is true freedom. The baptism is for everyone who wants to serve the Lord with power. Jesus even told all his hand-picked disciples to wait in Jerusalem until they had received it saying, "Behold, I send the Promise of My Father upon you; but tarry in the city of Jerusalem until you are endued with power from on high." (Luke 24:49) Even his hand-picked apostles were not to begin their ministries until they had received God's power. The Holy Spirit will:

- Teach you the things of God. I Corinthians 2:10–13
- Give you boldness. Acts 4:31
- Guide you. John 16:13
- Tell you of things to come. John 16:13
- Convict you of sin. John 16:8
- Comfort you. Acts 9:31, John 14:16–26 KJV
- Sanctify you. Romans 15:16 (Set you apart to serve God)
- Give you power. Acts 1:8
- The gifts of the Holy Spirit are real and worth far more than silver and gold. Seek, ask and receive them today.

What it means to have the character trait of **CHARISMA:**

- A confident, competent and enthusiastic, natural leadership style that engenders special loyalty and enthusiasm among followers
- That personal, magnetic type of charm or appeal of a leader's character
- Smiling when you talk
- An extraordinary gift given to Christians by the Holy Spirit

HARITY (Love) —   **Study start date: _____ Finish date: _____**

It's a fact. Few go very far in life, at least a life that is meaningful and enjoyable, without charity. Even if they do reach a few high points in politics or the world system, their end is usually corrupt, abrupt and horrifying. Life that is truly life, the real life God has planned for us, is mainly about giving and those who try to make it about getting are generally the losers. Most who gain their fortunes quickly as sports stars or those who win the lottery (so called) are ill prepared to cope with all the temptations and stresses caused by having a huge bounty foisted suddenly upon them. Greed is also a great curse. Trying to spend all one's fortune on themselves will ultimately choke a person to death. Truth is, if we will just think for a moment, a person can physically only sleep in one bed, in one house, on any given night. You can only eat three meals a day or you will blow up like a bull frog and get the gout. You can't drive but one car at a time. Having a fleet of fifty personal vehicles will soon become a nightmare of dead batteries, flat tires, huge insurance bills, problems with vandals, etc. Surely, rust, the moth, fire and thieves do come in to remind us that we are still here on planet earth. These same self-indulgent people should experience the joy of giving an $800 car purchased at an auto auction to the mother with four young children whose husband left her for someone else. That joy of giving a simple little car to someone in dire need, they would find, is greater than buying a brand new Rolls Royce when they have five or ten cars already.

Life should be a love affair and, yes, we should love life. The Apostle Peter told us very how to do it: "He that would love life and see good days, let him refrain his tongue from evil and his lips from speaking deceit. Let him turn away from evil and do good …" (I Peter 3:10, 11) Loving other people is also a large part of it.. He went on to say, " … have compassion for one another, love as brothers, be tenderhearted, be courteous, not returning evil for evil or reviling for reviling but on the contrary blessing, knowing that you were called to this, that you may inherit a blessing." (v.9) If we find a brother tempted or "overtaken in a trespass," Paul said, "you who are spiritual (should) restore such a one in a spirit of gentleness, considering yourselves lest you also be tempted." (Galatians 6:1) Paul encourages us to "look out not only for his own interests but also for the interests of others." (Philippians 2:4) and to "bear one another's burdens and so fulfill the law of Christ." Galatians 6:2

Life is about loving God, loving others, loving our work and living a life of giving. But it all begins with loving God. Without that, nothing else works. And how are we to do that? There is only one way for this to happen. We must ask Crist to come into our hearts, to forgive us of all our sins and save us. Then and only then will it be possible to do what the Bible commands, "'you shall love the Lord your God with all your heart, with all your soul, with all your mind and with all your strength.' This is the first commandment. And the second, like it, is this: 'You shall love your neighbor as yourself.'" (Mark 12:30, 31) When we love God with all our heart, keeping Him first in our lives, He lets us love other things with the same mighty flow. Then we can truly love our mate, our neighbor, our work and so on. Everyone wants to be loved and, no question, it is a powerful force. The wisest man in the world once said, "love is as strong as death … unyielding as the grave. It burns like a blazing fire, like a mighty flame. Many waters cannot quench (it), rivers cannot wash it away." Song of Solomon 8:6, 7 NIV

Love is all about giving and greed is all about getting. Giving God our tithes and offerings and then giving to those around us as we can, feel led and grow in this is what makes one happy. Oscar Hammerstein penned these words: "A bell is not a bell until you ring it, a song is not a song until you sing it. Love in your heart is not put there to stay. For love is not love until you give it away." We all possess not only some material things, even if it is only a few pennies but every one of us have also been given gifts and talents. Learning how to give at least some of those away is a great start in finding fulfillment in a purpose-driven life. This is so important Paul told the Corinthians to "Let love be your highest goal (in life)." I Corinthians 14:1 NLT

Loving our work and working as unto the Lord is also a part of charity as well as a great secret of success. The reason is simple and has to do with motivation. People who work for success, the love of money, notoriety, promotion or the boss' approval are actually setting themselves up for a many disappointments. The economy can crash and make financial success next to impossible. The boss can betray the hardworking man by hiring and promoting his nephew in his place. Those who are motivated solely by money need to know that it, alone, will never make you happy. Solomon, left those who love money and accumulating wealth with this promise: "He who loves silver (money) will not be satisfied with silver; nor he who loves abundance with increase. This also is vanity." (Ecclesiastes 5:10) They that love money will never get enough to satisfy them so they are doomed to a life of greed and discontent. Besides, money has a bad habit of making itself "wings (and) flying away like an eagle toward heaven." Proverbs 23:5

The solution to all this is to love God supremely and ask Him to give us a servant's heart. In this way we enjoy serving others and helping our superiors, co-workers and company. Love will drive people longer, harder and farther in their work than any other motivation. When we learn to serve others and work at our jobs as unto the Lord, we can never really be cheated or defeated. If the company goes out of business or our supervisor deals with us unfairly, it doesn't really matter. We still have the Lord above watching over us as well as His Word to perform His will in our lives. It is the Lord who we are working for who is faithful and true. He will use every occasion to show His mighty power and bless us anyway. For "we know that all things work together for good to those who love God, to those who are the called according to His purpose." (Romans 8:28) God will soon be fulfilling His purpose in another way and will ultimately use it all, to be a blessing to us. We don't need to hoard money or set our hearts on it because we know "Godliness with contentment (instead) is great gain." (I Timothy 6:6) Whatever we need, it will be there. Our "God will supply all your need according to the riches of His glory by Christ Jesus." Philippians 4:19

It would be virtually impossible to walk in love on this planet without loving our work because a third of our waking hours are spent doing just that. Loving our work is a great blessing. As a young lieutenant in the U.S. Army, there will probably never be anyone as formidable in our memory as our first company commander. My first commander in the 82nd Airborne Division was certainly no less and was, in fact, one of the greatest soldiers I ever had the privilege of working for. His name was Captain Alex Hottell (pronounced: Hot- tell) and he loved the Army. He was tenth in his class at West Point, a Rhodes Scholar, a German Jumpmaster, an Airborne Ranger and he drove a solid black, 1932 Rolls Royce. Besides all that, he was quite a likeable fellow and we all, officers and enlisted men alike, loved him.

As a side note, our unit was "C" or Charlie Company 1st of the 5th and somehow we became known as "Cobra Company." So I drew an icon for the company of a cobra coiled up with its mouth wide open and its' fangs out, of course. Since the 82nd was Airborne, I attached a couple of wings to the back of it and a streak of lightning coming out of its mouth. We ordered sweatshirts with this logo on them and, if I must say, it did look pretty neat. After a while the men got around to calling the CO (commanding officer) admiringly of course, Captain Cobra, We all had the greatest respect for him, his love for the Army and the work we were doing there. One week-end I had my platoon cut his nickname and the company's emblem out of plywood, paint it and affix it to his office door. He was quite surprised when he came in the following morning and inquired, of course, as to who was responsible for it but no one would confess—although I think he had his suspicions.

In addition to loving the Army, Captain Hottell was also a literary genius. He could write like no one I ever knew and had formulated an idea (which he never had time to implement) of how to win the war in Vietnam agriculturally. He was so efficient, he even wrote his own obituary before going to Vietnam—just in case. Amazingly, you will experience and get to know this great man quite well just by reading his obituary. He loved life, he loved the Army, he loved his work, he loved the mission and he loved his job. Tragically, he was killed in a helicopter crash in Vietnam. His extraordinary obituary appeared in the *Assembly,* West Point's alumni quarterly and follows here:

"I am writing my own obituary for several reasons and I hope none of them are too trite. First, I would like to spare my friends, who may happen to read this the usual clichés about being a good soldier. They were all kind enough to me and I not enough to them. Second, I would not want to be a party to a perpetuation of an image that is harmful and inaccurate: 'Glory' is the most meaningless of concepts (when men seek after it but God's glory is real- added by this writer) and I feel that in some cases it is doubly damaging. And, thirdly, I am quite simply the last authority on my own death. I loved the Army. It reared me, it nurtured me and it gave me the most satisfying years of my life. Thanks to it, I have lived an entire life time in 26 years. It is only fitting that I should die in its service.

We all have but one death to spend and insofar as it can have any meaning it finds it in the service of comrades in arms. And yet, I deny that I died FOR anything—not my country, not my army, not my fellow man, none of these things. I LIVED for these things, and the manner in which I chose to do it involved the very real chance that I would die in the execution of my duties. I knew this and accepted it, but my love for West Point and the Army was great enough—and the promise that I would someday be able to serve all the ideals that meant anything to me through it was great enough—for me to accept this possibility as a part of a price which must be paid for all things of great value. If there is nothing worth dying for—in this sense—there is nothing worth living for.

The Army let me live in Japan, Germany and England with experiences in all of these places that others only dream about. I have skied in the Alps, killed a scorpion in my tent camping in Turkey, climbed Mount Fuji, visited the ruins of Athens, Ephesus and Rome, seen the town of Gordium where another Alexander challenged his destiny, gone to the opera in Munich, plays in the west End of London, seen the Oxford-Cambridge rugby match, gone for pub crawls through the Cotswolds, seen the night-life in Hamburg, danced to the Rolling Stones, and earned a master's degree in a foreign university.

I have known what it is like to be married to a fine and wonderful woman and to love her beyond bearing with the sure knowledge that she loves me; I have command- ed a company and been a father, priest, income-tax adviser, confessor and judge for 200 men at one time; I have played college football and rugby, won the British National Diving championship two years in a row, boxed for Oxford against Cambridge only to be knocked out in the first round and played handball to distraction—and all of these sports I loved, I learned at West Point. They gave me hours of intense happiness.

I have been an exchange student at the German military academy, and gone to the German jumpmaster school. I have made 30 parachute jumps from everything from a balloon in England to a jet at Fort Bragg. I have written an article that was published in *Army Magazine* and I have studied philosophy.

I have experienced all these things because I was in the Army and because I was an Army brat. The Army is my life, it is such a part of what I was that what happened is the logical outcome of the life I loved.

I never knew what it is to fail. I never knew what it is to be too old or too tired to do anything. I lived a full life in the Army and it has extracted the price. It is only just."

After serving as a company commander in the First Calvary Division, Captain Hottel was pulled up to Division staff to write the history of the First Cavalry Division in Vietnam. He would rather have been out in the field doing the fighting with the men. Concurrently, it happened that my Ranger Buddy, Lieutenant Steve Grub, who was Aide to the Deputy Commanding General (CG) at the time. One day when he and the General were out in the helicopter overseeing the troops, they began taking anti-aircraft fire and Lieutenant Grubb's foot took a hit and almost destroying it. He then had to immediately return to the United States to convalesce. On Steve's recommendation and Captain Hottell's extraordinary record, he was selected to take his place as aide to General George Casey, who was also scheduled for promoted to Commanding General of the Division. However, one fateful day several months later, the General happened to be piloting the helicopter. He, Alex and other members of his staff were on their way to visit some wounded soldiers in a hospital and were traveling in terribly foggy weather. For reasons unknown to this day, their aircraft hit the side of a mountain, instantly killing everyone aboard—a huge loss for everyone, including the Army and our country. We all felt like both General Casey and Captain Hottell had the gifting, motivation and ability to have been Chief Of Staff of the Army one day. These men also loved their work.

It is important in life for all of us to learn to love your work for many reasons. To begin with, if you love your work, it will tell you its secrets. For some reason, loving work has never been a problem for me. I loved pulling weeds in a gladiola farm; loved being a bus boy, dishwasher, fry cook and, later, cashier and dining room manager in the Officers' Club on an Air Force base. I even liked digging ditches on a water pipe line in the dead of summer in Dripping Springs, Texas. I loved being a welder, machinist and gopher in the Cyclotron Institute while a student at Texas A&M University. I even loved flying planes and jumping out of them. I loved being a platoon leader, aide to a General and being a company commander in Vietnam. It always amazed me. I wondered why everyone didn't want to run a rifle company in battle. What a challenge—facing off with the enemies of our country in mortal combat. Later on I loved the real estate business and I loved the building business but there is nothing quite like being an evangelist and seeing God's resurrection power change men's hearts forever!

We all must toil at something so why not learn to enjoy it. Bill Gothard once said, "Find a job you love so much that you would do it for free and you will never have to work again." Great advice! When our work becomes a joy, we are then willing to invest deeply in education and training to prepare us to do it well. We will also be willing to go to work early and stay late and give it 110% effort and dedication. These kinds of investments in our career unquestionably produce great results and, amazingly, we also have the blessing of great enjoyment along with it. About this subject, E.W. Kenyon penned this insightful statement: "The measure of your love is how valuable you are to society." Work done well is always in demand no matter where you go. I don't know who said it but here is one final thought we should never forget: "To all who love, love is all the world." author unknown

What it means to have the character trait of **CHARITY:**

- To have love in your heart for God, life, your work and others
- Benevolence
- Loving life
- Walking in love
- Loving serving others
- Having a giving heart
- Doing intentional acts of kindness
- Goodwill and love toward all humanity
- Liberality toward the suffering and needy
- Having love in your voice (coming from the heart)

OMMIT, THE ABILITY TO—   **Study start date:** _____ **Finish date:** _____

Everybody wants to be happy in life. In fact, believe it or not, everybody is already doing their best to be just that. Even the drunk passed out in the ditch is trying his best to be happy. If het knew of a better avenue to happiness, he would be taking it. Until then, a bottle of Four Roses or T-Bird is going to have to do it. The super-rich buy rides on space ships to find a little happiness. Ted Turner bought up all the desert land he could out in the southwest. Why? To be happy—so he could say he owns more land than anyone else in the United States. Maybe all the mesquite trees, cactus, rocks, dirt, gila monsters, rattle snakes, jack rabbits, armadillos, tarantellas and scorpions will make him happy. Then again, maybe not. Especially when he gets his tax bills every year. Raw land is a vociferous, cash-eating alligator. Others collect hundreds of cars. But, cars won't make you happy either. We all need at least one but most of them depreciate like a falling rock, get banged up in accidents and rust out very quickly. Some seek worldly acclaim. But, worldly honor and acclaim won't make you happy either. People are fickle. They will run you for president today and tomorrow they want to tar and feather you and run you out of town on a rail. Still others seek wealth. Only problem is money won't make you happy. Here again, everybody needs some but if you love it, the Bible promises you one thing: you will never get enough. Steaks won't make you happy. You will get tired of them too after so many. Ice cream, likewise, is great but the law of diminishing returns starts to kick in after the thirteenth bowl full. The point is that people have searched far and wide and go to all kinds of extremes to find happiness within themselves. Sorry, living for "self" will never make one happy.

The good news is that the same God who made the universe, made the world along with you and me and all that is in it. He was also smart enough to make us fit in His universe perfectly—like a hand in a glove. We were made not only fit, but when following his plan for our lives, to also have meaningful lives full of success, security, purpose and happiness. Strangely, contrary to human nature, to find this kind of life we must learn to commit to things and people *outside* of ourselves. No man who has tried to live for self has ever found true, enduring happiness and tranquility. The ability to commit to others and this in harmony with one's convictions is, amazingly, what makes people happy. That is why the Master said it is "Better to give than to receive." Not just things like money and food but also your life. People who focus on themselves are usually the most miserable people in the world. After a short while they start thinking the whole world revolves around them.

Actually, the ability to commit comes from whoever it is you set your hope in. If you are the captain of your own ship and the master of your own fate, then you have only one choice, You will worship, serve and trust in yourself. If God is the head of your life and the director of all that pertains to you, then you will commit yourself to Him and His Kingdom and set your hope in Him. He is, after all, "a rewarder of the diligent seeker." (Hebrews 11:6) The writer of Proverbs said to "Commit your works to the Lord and your thoughts (plans and dreams) will be established." (v. 16:3) God will do it for you. The Psalmist said, "Trust in the Lord and do good." (v.3:3) "Commit your way to the Lord, trust also in Him and He will bring it to pass." (v. 3:5) You might as well commit to Him because your life, your breath and all your ways are in His hands anyway. Daniel 5:23 b

Once you have accepted Him as Lord and set your hope in Him, the secret to success and joy in life is one's ability to make commitments to God, things, people and entities outside of self. In the early 80's I took a trip to Israel with our church which was led by our Pastor, Paul L. Walker. Paul, by the way was a general for God and is still one of His generals today. At the time I was attending there, he actually pastored and preached at two large churches in the metro Atlanta area. He later became overseer of the world-wide Church of God and I never heard a better pulpiteer.) It was about his twentieth trip to Israel so we also had an excellent Israeli tour guide. Once while we were at Caesarea and broke as we often did for a time of prayer and introspection, I went down to the shore of the Mediterranean Sea and sat for a while on the beautiful sandy beach. It was a time in my life that I was at the point of seeking a deeper walk with Christ. Sitting there, with my hands in the sand, observing that beautiful blue sea, I felt something like barbed wire. Sure enough, upon closer inspection I had came across a rusted piece of barbed wire about four inches long. I picked it up and committed at that time to become, as Paul, a prisoner of the Lord. (Ephesians 4:11) As we know, Luke 14:33 says, "Whosoever he is among you that forsaketh not all he hath cannot be my disciple." At that point I thought I had committed everything: my life, my company, my home, family and finances to Him and surely there was nothing left. However, He said, "There is one thing you haven't yet given me." I was at a total loss as to what that might be. I asked, "What is it, Lord?" He said, plain and simple, "Your death." I stuttered for a moment in my mind and finally said, "I'll have to think about that for a bit." I was actually expecting to live to a ripe old age like most of my ancestors so I prayed about it for three days. Then I said, "OK, Lord, I give you my death. You give me the grace and I'll die for you and the Kingdom." You would think that a decision like that would be total bondage but not so. It was actually total freedom. I never worry now about dying of a disease, a bullet wound, or anything. I will be here until the Lord takes me. You see, there are some places and battles that God would take us to that we can't go if we are afraid of dying. Without a commitment unto death, we really can't follow Him fully.

Those who have been in the military seem to have an easier time with making commitments than most. They have already been trained to be mission oriented. They have been taught to commit to the mission they have been assigned because the mission (to take a hill, knock out a machinegun nest or take a city) is more important than anything, including human life. They have been told that they are to continue to fight and struggle even when they run out of ammunition. They are then to go at the enemy with their hand grenades, knife, bayonet and fists. They are instructed to go at the enemy even if all their men are wiped out. You are to go after them even if you get captured. We are to continue to resist and continue to mount the resistance in prison by trying to escape. The only time you are authorized to give up on the mission is when you, yourself, are dead. Someone might say, "That's kind of a cavalier attitude about the lives and welfare of the troops isn't it?" No. Not really. Yes, every soldier's life is important and I would fight to the death to save the life of every one of my men but, you see it is not the troops that are important in this case. The priority in war is the other troops around us and the people back home we are protecting. They are the most important people to be considered. It is these people we are there for. Failing to accomplish our mission and gaining our assigned objective may endanger a whole lot of other companies or divisions behind us and around us. The lives of far more people will likely be lost if we don't accomplish our mission. More importantly, the reason we went to battle in the first place was not for our own good or for the benefit of the Army but for the good of the country. This takes commitment.

Someone, somewhere must be willing to hazard and even sacrifice their own life to save the American people, our way of life, freedoms, all our women, children and the older people who have gone to war before us, who are still living. Some laid their own lives on the line to protect us when we were very small. What makes a person valuable in the Army is not their education, physical prowess or intellect so much as their ability. Their value is found in their ability to accomplish the mission regardless of the difficulty, casualties, size of the opposition, risks or loss of life. Being mission oriented is having the ability to commit to getting the job done, no matter what. No excuses. There is nothing to worry about, the battle is the Lord's and He always gives us the victory. I Corinthians 15:57

It is a wonderful, freeing thing to learn to commit in life. I mean to commit with reckless abandon. Second only to our commitment to God is a man's commitment to his wife. Men, we need to be a one woman man. Put her happiness before your own and commit to be faithful until death. Next commit to your employer to be loyal to the company. Tell him or her you are committed to it as long as you are there just as if you owned it. You are going to do whatever it takes to make it the most successful and profitable company in your market area. You are willing to stay late or come in on Saturday without pay. If they need you to do anything at all, the answer is "Yes" in advance. If you ever feel led to make this little speech, you better be sure you are willing to man up to it because the boss is going to watch you like a hawk to see if you are talk or walk. If your employer finds you are truly committed as a way of life and not as a way to promotion, you will undoubtedly be given greater and greater responsibilities. When the company has a difficult problem, they will come to you to tackle it because you know how to commit and they know you will get the job done. Make it your goal in life ***never*** to be asked to get anything done that you don't get done. Let getting the job done become your trademark. Be the one who can always be relied upon. You will be glad you did.

When you make a friend, commit in your heart to be the best friend they ever had for life. Do everything you promise them. Purpose to be a rainy day friend, not a sunshine friend. Look forward to the day when they might call you for help. Then again, you don't know, someday it might be you needing the help. A long-time friend of mine told me years ago that his best friend had let him down so bad that he prayed to God to send him another one. He says he met me the next day and I was the one God sent. We have been good friends for a long time now. After knowing him for twelve years he came to me one day with an astounding realization. He said, "Everything you ever told me you would do I could take it to the bank. You have never told me you would do anything that you didn't do." To God be the glory. That is commitment and all by the grace of God.

Along the same lines, the thing that is most important to me on the efficiency report written by my battalion commanders while serving under them as a company commander

Author serving as a company commander in Vietnam

in Vietnam was this simple statement: "He accomplished every mission I assigned him." One of them didn't know it but I specifically remember thinking toward the end of my tour there that he was trying me. He would ask us, as a company, to do incredible, next to impossible things. I thought he was doing it just to see if he could come up with something we wouldn't or couldn't do. One day he sent me a grid coordinate to get to by a certain time that was about five kilometers away. That was impossible. There was no way you could bust brush in the jungle to get there and he knew it. I didn't know then and don't know now what that was about or why that was so important but we did it. Had to walk down a river most of the way to do it but we got there. Everybody had leaches all over them but that was beside the point. This lesson has been so valuable to me. Because of what I learned in the military, this has been extremely helpful in the civilian world as well. I might have gotten out of the U.S. Army but I am still in the Army of the Lord. My bosses have all been free, of course, to make their requests but I won't say "yes" unless I have thought it through, counted the cost and prayed about it because I fully intend to keep my word. No excuse. Now know this. If you are still making excuses, you haven't learned how to commit. Once you commit, that's it. We need to be like the prophet Samuel. The Bible says, "The Lord was with him and let none of his words fall to the ground." (I Samuel 3:17) I only mention it to challenge you to become more valuable to God and your generation. It is only by God's grace this ever could have happened in my life. Without praying for God to help me as a young man of many, many broken promises, I would never have learned how to commit.

Commit to your church, your family and your community to make them better. Contribute your best work and your best ideas. Commit to spend time with your family. Not just quality time but quantity as well. Say what you mean and mean what you say. Follow through with what you say. What you will find is a life of service but along with it you will find success, fulfillment and true happiness. All this will happen because you are committed to people and things outside of yourself.

What it means to have the character trait of **THE ABILITY TO COMMIT:**

- The ability to accept a charge or mission and pledge to accomplish it without fail
- The ability to make covenant (with God and others)
- Being decisive, not equivocal
- The ability to give someone a straight answer.
- Letting your "yes" be truly "yes" and your "no" simply mean "no."
- The ability to make a promise and deliver decisive, deliberate, conclusive and targeted action.
- The ability to make a promise or to pledge one's self to a particular course, project, battle, mission or war and get the job done without fail—no excuses
- A refusal to give up after obligating one's self even if the slog is long and hard
- The ability to commit so one can be entrusted with a mission, personnel, resources and/or weapons
- Being mission oriented
- Remembering that winners commit and do not quit

OMPASSION—   **Study start date:** _____ **Finish date:** _____

The unregenerate man is self-interested by nature, caring only about himself. A person can certainly live that way and many do but it makes for a most unfulfilling, lonely life. On the contrary, the Master laid out a much better way. He came to bring us life that is truly life. Those in covenant with Him can be so blessed in this life that they will have sufficient to help all those God has placed in their path needing help while they are on this planet. Everyone, in the course of time, will be confronted with people in the throes of pain, poverty, trials and trouble. Although a good deal of their trouble will probably have been brought on by their own actions or inactions, we are to look past these things and see the need. These should be seen as opportunities to be a blessing as the Spirit leads. Each occasions is really a divine appointment. The Lord, Himself, admonished us to "Execute true justice, show mercy and compassion everyone to his brother." (Zechariah 7:9) For Him to give us such a direct command, it must be possible but we must also be willing to take up the challenge. Jesus said, "Those who are well have no need of a physician but those who are sick. Go and learn what this means; 'I desire mercy and not sacrifice.' For I did not come to call the righteous but sinners, to repentance." (Matthew 9:12, 13)

We, as God's children, are to be like Him. But remember, as worthless as all of us were, it was only, "Through the Lord's mercies we (were) not consumed, because His compassions fail not. They are new every morning." (Lamentations 3:22, 23) God, "being full of compassion forgave (our) iniquity." (Psalm 78:38) Jesus knows how we have been tempted. He, Himself, was tempted with everything the devil had in his black bag of tricks. In fact, if the devil didn't use it on Him while He was here, he can't use it on us. The writer of Hebrews said, "For in that He Himself has suffered, being tempted, He is able to aid those who are tempted." (Hebrews 2:18) He is able to have compassion on those of us who come short.

The prodigal son is one we need to watch. He was blessed to have a father full of compassion. Though he was rebellious and arrogant, his father honored his demand to take his part of the inheritance early and run. The prodigal ran and ran until, ultimately, he found himself at the bottom of a pig sty eating the pods the swine had rejected. If you have ever slopped pigs, you will know the good was all gone from them. But, amazingly, it was there in the mud, filth and stench of that pig sty, that he received the greatest blessing of his life, something he least expected: wisdom, a divine revelation. It finally occurred to him that he had totally destroyed his life all by himself. Weighing his options there, starving and knee deep in mud and pig dung, he determined that he would be far better off, even though he didn't deserve to be a son any longer, to return to his father's house and be a servant. Right there, he made the decision to return to his father's house, admit that he had sinned against Heaven and him and apply, hopefully, for servant hood.

Based on his son's actions and attitude prior to his departure, the father knew he would soon find his life on the rocks and would, no doubt, be returning. He was actually watching and waiting for him. Not to critique his every wrong but to welcome him home. When he saw him coming in the distance, the father had compassion on him and ran out to meet him. He hugged and kissed him. His son immediately confessed that he had been foolish, had sinned against him and Heaven, and no longer deserved to even be his son. His father wouldn't hear it. He told the servants to put the best robe on him, put a ring on his finger and sandals on his feet. He also ordered them to kill the fatted calf so they might all feast and be merry saying, "my son was dead and is alive again; he was lost and is found." (Luke 15:24) Though he had wasted all his inheritance on sinful living, his father looked past it. He was just thankful that he had returned home with a right mind. The son realized that the full wages for the lifestyle he led was death, which he had just narrowly averted. He came to his senses, returned home with a humble heart, a positive attitude and a grateful spirit and so received compassion from his father.

Doubtless, the highest calling of man on earth is to have compassion on his neighbors, knowing well that we "… all have sinned and (have fallen) short of the glory of God." (Romans 5:23) We often find ourselves in desperate need of mercy and compassion. As you know, there have always been the caught and the un-caught. Many of us have done enough prior to salvation, if convicted for all our wayward ways, but for the mercy and compassion of God, would never have seen the outside of a prison in this life.

Compassion was what the priest and the Levite needed when they saw the man who had been robbed, lying half dead in the ditch—yet they walked by. Compassion is what the Good Samaritan had for this poor man when he put all of his own plans on hold, going directly to him at the bottom of the ditch. He met the dying man on his own level. Furthermore, his compassion motivated him to save the man's life, take him to an inn and give the manager enough money to take care of him until he returned. Luke 10:30

Compassion is what Jesus showed when he went about the countryside and villages "preaching the gospel of the kingdom and healing every sickness and every disease among the people." (Matthew 9:35) Ever wonder why He healed every sickness and every disease the people had? He simply saw their need, was filled with compassion and blessed every one of them.

We see yet another example of this in Jesus' response to Peter's inquiry about how many times he had to forgive his brother. Peter offered up what he thought was a very generous "seven times," thinking this was the number of completion and certainly more than a gracious plenty. Besides, when someone struck one on the cheek, all you had to do was offer them the other and the scripture didn't venture anything past that so you are on your own to decide what you want to do next. But, Jesus said, "Until 70 times 7." Or, pretty much, as many times as they need to be forgiven. Then He shared a parable about a slave who was called before his king for nonpayment of a multi-million dollar debt. The king justly commanded by the laws of their day, that he and his family be sold to pay this debt. However, the man fell to the ground, begging for mercy in the form of a little time and promised to pay every penny. The king, moved with compassion, released the slave and, incredibly, forgave the entire debt. However the slave immediately went out and found a debtor who owed a very small amount, a penny-ante debt, grabbed him and began choking him for all he was worth. The other slave promised to pay back all as well—requesting a little patience. But, his creditor wouldn't hear of it and had him thrown in prison until he paid all he owed. When his friends heard of all this, they reported it to the king. He immediately called in the slave whom he had totally forgiven and shown so much mercy. Upon his arrival, the king asked him why he hadn't shown his fellow slave the same mercy he had received. At that point, the king was so furious that he had him delivered to the jailers to be tormented until he repaid all that was owed. The Lord's final statement was telling. "So My heavenly Father also will do to you, if each of you, from his heart, does not forgive his brother his trespasses." Matthew 18:35

What it means to have the character trait of **COMPASSION:**

- Heart-felt sympathy for another's distress, accompanied by the desire to alleviate or heal it
- Having mercy and sympathy for the weak and downtrodden
- The grace to look past a person's shortcomings, not forgetting our own, and help them anyway
- Having mercy for those in prison as if we were right there in the cell beside them
- Mercy for the widow and the orphan to alleviate their suffering

OMPETENCE —   **Study start date:** _____ **Finish date:** _____

Performing sub-par is something we have all found ourselves in the midst of doing at some point in life. Failing to be ready which would include not having the proper skill or understanding about a job usually ends in correction at best, failure or even dismissal at the worst. We have all failed at something. No one comes out of the starting blocks in life knowing enough to be ready to compete in a world that is all about the survival of the fittest. Succeeding in this life takes planning and preparation. Failure, however, is a great teacher, in and of itself, and is usually sufficiently painful that we don't want to experience it ever again. However, the proper preparation, training, study and mentorship in a desired field can usually bring forth not only competence but possibly even excellence at some point. They say if you will read a book a week about your chosen field of endeavor, after ten years you will have read over 500 books. At that point you will not have only become competent but could possibly be one of the most knowledgeable people in your field. So the question is not do you have the talent but this: are you willing to pay the price?

There is, however, one other book we really need to read if we want to succeed and win in the race of life. Without this one Book, we might gain knowledge but will likely become educated beyond our intellect in the process and fall victim to pride or some other terrible shortcoming. We were actually commanded to "study to show (ourselves) approved unto God as a workman that needeth not to be ashamed, rightly dividing (this Book which is) the word of truth." (II Timothy 2:15) This Book presents us with the most fantastic promise ever seen anywhere from anyone, any place, anytime on this planet. It says if anyone wants to be "strong and very courageous ..." and we all need to be, and if we want to "prosper wherever (we go)" (Joshua 1:7) all we need to do is this one thing. What is it? " ... Meditate (on this Book) day and night, ... observe to do according to all that is written therein; (and) then (we) shall make (our) way prosperous, and then (we) shall have good success." (Joshua 1:8) And, the most amazing thing—it is true.

What it means to have the character trait of **COMPETENCE:**

- A sufficiency of skills, knowledge and business acumen to succeed
- The mastery of and ability to perform in a certain field of endeavor
- Legally adequate or qualified to fill an office in government, position in business or take the witness stand in a court of law
- Having sufficient intellect, physical ability and knowledge of the properties of the work in a given field to function in a certain capacity relative to it
- Able to carry out orders, policy and procedure
- Having enough requisite ability to attain a certain state of readiness
- Being ready to compete
- Knowing your stuff
- In the military it is being technically and tactically proficient
- In sales, competence is the reason people buy from a salesman, even more than the quality of their product

ONFIDENCE—   Study start date: _____ Finish date: _____

onfidence in the flesh or one's own natural ability, resourcefulness, skill and strength is a very deceptive and dangerous thing. To some people their many abilities may seem to assure them of success and this certainly might work from time-to-time. However, sooner or later it will fail them on a grand scale. We are admonished in the Bible to trust not in princes (people), chariots, our sword or our own strength. (Psalm 20:7) Though it is both admirable and helpful to have natural ability, education and to constantly endeavor to improve our skills and increase our strength, still our trust must reside only in the Lord. In the battles we will all soon face, we must be ready to attack and defeat kings (or other enemies) coming at us with an army of 20,000 having only half that with us. (Luke 14:31) In the battles we face in life as Christians, we will almost always be outnumbered so our confidence must be in the Lord.

A good example of properly placed confidence is found in the story about King Saul's son, Jonathan, and his armor bearer during the time of his father's war with the Philistines. Jonathan had totally vanquished a garrison of Philistines the week before but apparently was still itching, even with all that action, for more. Without his father's knowledge, he asked his armor bearer to accompany him in a two-man attack on another enemy garrison. From their position at the bottom of a deep ravine, the two of them spotted the enemy high up on a rocky crag. At that point they were greatly outnumbered and the enemy held the valuable, military high ground. Jonathan told his comrade, 'Let's attack these uncircumcised (Philistines), perhaps the Lord will work for us, for there is no restraint to the Lord to save by many or by few.' (I Samuel 14:6) His armor bearer opined, 'Do all that is in your heart, I am with you, do whatever is in your heart.' (Interpretation: I am with you and will fight to the victory or unto death.) Then Jonathan devised a battle plan where the enemy couldn't possibly escape. He said, "When we show our position, if they say, 'Wait right where you are, we are coming after you,' we will hold our ground. But, if they say, 'Come up to us,' then we will attack. This will be a sign to us that the Lord has given them into our hands."

At that point they revealed themselves to the Philistine garrison and the enemy said, "Behold, the Hebrews come forth out of their holes where they had hidden themselves." Then they taunted them saying, "Come up to us, and we will show you something." So Jonathan and his armor bearer climbed the rocky crag on the attack. Together they fought the enemy back-to-back and there fell that day twenty of the enemy in the space of about half an acre and that was just in their first attack—so they made at least one more attack afterwards. Upon learning about this bold attack by these two intrepid Hebrews, the hearts of the Philistines melted in the cities, their soldiers trembled in the field and the earth quaked. I Samuel 14:1–15

This kind of confidence can only be obtained from one source. David said, "In God, whose Word I praise—in God I trust and am not afraid. What can flesh (mere men) do to me?" (Psalm 56:4) We are commanded in Joshua 1:7 and 8 to " … be thou strong and very courageous, that thou mayest observe to do according to all the law, which Moses, my servant, commanded thee; turn not from it to the right hand or to the left, that thou mayest prosper wherever thou goest. This book of the law shall not depart out of thy mouth, but thou shalt meditate therein day and night, that thou mayest observe to do according to all that is written therein; for then (and you might say only then) thou shalt make thy way prosperous, and then thou shalt have good success."

What it means to have the character trait of **CONFIDENCE:**

- Energized by a conscious reliance upon strengths and assets at one's disposal that have been tried and proven
- A state of certainty
- What enables mere men to confront and defeat giants
- A conscience assurance of one's ability to succeed in any situation
- Absolute trust properly placed in God
- A high state of friendship where one can be trusted to hold critical, valuable, highly sensitive and even secret or privileged information
- Faith and hope
- The knowledge that "One can (chase) a thousand and two can put ten thousand to flight." Deuteronomy 32:30
- The assurance that "A thousand will fall at your side and ten thousand at your right hand but it shall not come nigh you." Psalm 91:7
- Freedom from fear, failure or embarrassment

ONGENIALITY—   **Study start date:** _____ **Finish date:** _____

Too often in a fast-paced, me-first world, we meet people who seem to be about as friendly as a starving rattlesnake. They don't smile when they meet you and immediately, by their disposition, facial expressions, body language and negative attitude, they give you the impression that they haven't the least interested in you, your mutual interests or whether or not you might live or die in the next five minutes. They even make the word grump a thing of beauty. These people are self-interested and short-sighted as they move about the earth, content to live in their own little bubble seeking self-gratification. They think the whole universe revolves around them as its central focus and don't really care who knows it. Only problem is, somehow we all have to live on this planet and get along with the other occupants. Our future and our success on this big blue marble is, as a matter of fact, in the hands of other people. The way God set this up is the same people we meet today, we will probably run into tomorrow or the next day as well. So, we shouldn't mess in our own mess kit by being arrogant, inconsiderate, selfish beasts. Many people have and have lived to regret it very soon.

It has been said that we never gets a second chance to make a good first impression. So true. Upon meeting someone, it is just human nature for us to have our antennas up, to be sensitive to the needs, attitudes and disposition of the person we are meeting. This has been going on for so long, we don't even have to think about it. It is all happening in our subconscious minds. Within the first twenty seconds, we are going to form an opinion about this person and the other person, likewise, will have formed an opinion about us. This is just one reason why we usually ask (at least we should), how they are doing. Who knows? They might have the flu, the bubonic plague, their mother might have just passed away or they might have an appointment set up with their dentist for a root canal in the next thirty minutes. This kind of information is important—so we will know how to proceed, showing consideration to the other person's needs and situation. It is also just kind to ask. We should be quick to ask them about their life, their family, what they do for a living, where they live, etc. This shows we have a sincere interest in them as a person and helps us find common ground, interests, experiences, habits and tastes so we can make a connection.

It is so simple, even natural for human beings to revert to our base, fallen nature and look only after our own interests and, other than that, giving our best efforts to find fault with those around us. Some people are constantly changing their friends, mates and jobs but never, of course, think about changing themselves. Finding fault in others is so much easier. There is plenty of fault lying around out there. The only problem is, a good bit of it is usually our own so it is good to make a point of being agreeable, our very nature. Without vacating our own identity and belief system, this just amounts to making a conscious effort to be agreeable instead of contrary with people. All the while we should be praying for the wisdom to find common ground with others as well as to have a calm, happy, welcoming disposition. We need to naturally project to others that we are open to new ideas and new ways of doing things in order for them to even begin to have a willingness to share their hearts and ideas with us. We also need to let them know that we don't know everything and are teachable, open and negotiable on most subjects. We are the only ones who can let them know that we actually like hearing their ideas and looking at new concepts.

When meeting people, it is very important to look them directly in the eyes, grasp their hand securely and give them a firm hand shake. (Not too hard of course—but firm.) No lame, limp wrist, dead-fish hand-shakes please. A weak handshake and a far-away look gives the other person the idea that you have no confidence and no constitution. Also make it a point to initiate conversation by talking about something positive. Don't lead out with a complaint about a car wreck you just had or your uncle getting the hunna-huna disease. When meeting people, we also need to be careful not to appear to be stiffly formal or rigid. Don't be a perfectionist either. If we are expecting perfection in everyone we meet, we are going to be sorely disappointed. Instead, make an effort to be an old shoe type of person who is easily entreated and easily approachable. Wear a smile on your face and keep one in your heart. A smile simply let's others know, that you like yourself, expect a positive, happy outcome to the subject of your meeting and relationship. Everybody knows that you can't have a positive outlook on life and people in general unless you wear a smile on your face. A genuine smile is universal code language that tells people you naturally like yourself, your job and have a concern for other people. It will cause others generally, all things considered, to like you as well. And how much does it cost? Nothing.

Another important concept in the area of human relations is to remember that we have all been wrong from time-to-time and misspoke in times past, so it is best, unless we are in a court of law or something, not to try to do the "gottcha" deal. An old Chinese sage said to "Always allow the other person to save face." They will probably discover their error soon enough and you get no points in human relations for being the one who found them out and nailed them to the wall. It is best for us not to show irritation or aggravation when confronted with the wrong statements, actions or attitudes of others. Do not let their generally bad behavior affect your good behavior, nor allow it to drag you down to their low level. Better to live a more positive, pleasant, happy life. Make a friend and live a life of peace, love and joy. To do this, we will need to do our best to be considerate of others, as well as their wants and desires in life.

Some people, however, are just argumentative by nature; they love controversy. On the contrary, we need to enter a conversation, staff meeting or chance meeting on the street pre-disposed with the objective of being agreeable. This needs to be part of our very nature. Be flexible and a bit negotiable. We don't actually even need to get it our way every time. Be considerate of another's likes, preferences and allegiances. Their favorite brand of ice cream might just be all right too. Try it once. You might like it and make a friend along the way.

Having the proper attitude and being agreeable in nature, is far more important than what a person knows, were they were born or what kind of credentials they might or might not have. Facts, formulas, pride and prefixes to one's name build walls between people. A positive attitude and a humble, agreeable nature effectively tear down walls, fostering life-long friendships instead. Possessions, power and prestige quickly pass away but those who have a lot of friends are the richest people on earth.

Recently, my wife and I had dinner with Chuck McCrary and his lovely wife, Nola. I first met him when I got out of the Army and moved to Atlanta 42 years ago. We enjoyed a great dinner at our favorite restaurant and wonderful fellowship as always. What a blessing this man has been. At the time we met, he was a well-established builder and I was a nail driver in a pre-fab house plant. Not long after that, I moved into marketing and he was kind enough to teach me some of the finer points of salesmanship. I knew absolutely nothing about it. When I advanced to real estate sales, he and his wife bought the first five building lots I listed and later purchased the first large tract of land I ever sold. A few years later we became general partners on a land syndication and have always been the best of friends. When I branched out into the building business, he taught me invaluable lessons about how to buy materials inexpensively, how to build houses efficiently and effectively and how to avoid many of the sticky wickets in the business. We have never had a cross word—ever. When I was called into the ministry and started Creative Ministries in 1983, he agreed to serve as a director and advisor on the board. Even today, he is a great prayer warrior who can be called when I really need God's help. He knows how to believe and agree according to Matthew 18:19 and never lets go. I am so glad he was easy to get along with one sunny day in Georgia, 42 years ago. His wife died about twenty years ago and she, too, was a blessing. Then he married Nola and she is just like Chuck, a very congenial, kind and giving person. Chuck's congenial nature drew me to him years ago and we still share a unique, terrific, ageless, close friendship to this day.

What it means to have the character trait of **CONGENIALITY**:

- Having an agreeable, pleasant disposition
- Having an agreeable nature, always looking for similar tastes, likes and dislikes of those we meet
- Knowing how to co-exist with others harmoniously and pleasantly as far as it is possible within you
- Being genuinely friendly; interested in other people
- Generally sociable
- Possessing an attitude generally inclined to get along with others, showing love and genuine concern

ONSCIENTIOUS—   Study start date: _____ Finish date: _____

Human beings happen to be the only "animals" born equipped with a conscience. All others are ruled by the law of the jungle: kill or be killed. Other than humans, all of life on this planet is governed either by our place in the food chain or the law of the dominant (survival of the fittest). From early caveman, even humans were ruled by whoever could wield the biggest club. However, what the Creator intended was that people would walk in love and be ruled by absolute truth, what is right and their own conscience.

A man's conscience is his inner judge on moral issues. It is the intuitive sense that guides a person to choose between right and wrong according to some moral code of justice. Sorry, no excuse here. God, has written his laws on men's hearts and in nature so that we have no excuse before Him. (Romans 2:13-15) The conscience also operates as a person's gauge for being thorough in his duty as well as bringing forth excellence when completing tasks. The intuitive capacity of conscience guides a person to discern in much the same way as our eyes see and our ears hear. One's conscience is worth more than all the gold, silver and acclaim of all the men in the world and it must be followed and protected at all cost. The continued, knowing violation of one's conscience can cause it to be permanently seared.as with a hot iron. I Timothy 4:2

The Apostle Paul's practice of living in good conscience before God is something he claimed all those who knew him, in fact, witnessed. (Acts 23:1) He also told of the importance of holding "the mystery of the faith with a pure conscience" in I Timothy 3:9, going on there to say, "which some having rejected concerning the faith have suffered shipwreck." (I Timothy 1:19) We know that every human being came into this natural world in the same unredeemed state. We were "brought forth in iniquity, and in sin (our) mother(s) conceived (us)." (Psalm 51:5) We were born with sin in our members and because of this, we have all done some pretty despicable things. Therefore, our conscience must be cleansed and there is but one way to do it. "Through the eternal Spirit (Jesus) offered Himself without spot to God, (cleansing our) conscience(s) from dead works to serve the living God". (Hebrews 9:14) And, it is only with a clear conscience that we can have faith and draw near to God. (Hebrews 10:22) Through it we also receive answers to our prayers. Then we receive the incredibly, great privilege of the believer which is "Whatever we ask we receive from Him, because we keep His commandments and do those things that are pleasing in His sight." 1 John 3:22

Having a clear conscience has to do with more than even God. Once cleansed by the shed blood of Christ, it cannot be maintained without being obedient to civil government and obeying the ordinances of man. Paul told the Romans that it was very important for "every soul be subject to the governing authorities. For there is no authority except from God, and the authorities that exist are appointed by God. Therefore, whoever resists the authority resists the ordinance of God, and those who resist will bring judgment on themselves. For rulers are not a terror to good works, but to evil." Then he asks the question: "Do you want to be unafraid of the authority? Do what is good, and you will have praise from the same. For he is God's minister to you for good. But if you do evil, be afraid: for he does not bear the sword in vain; for he is God's minister, an avenger to execute wrath on him who practices evil. Therefore you must be subject not only because of wrath but also for conscience' sake." (Romans 13:1-3) This is true even to the point of paying taxes. Paul said, "Because of this (the need of a clear conscience) you also pay taxes, for they (these public servants) are God's ministers attending continually to this very thing."

Therefore, "Render ...to all their due: taxes to whom taxes are due, customs to whom customs, fear to whom fear, honor to whom honor." Romans 13:4-7

Maintaining a clear conscience is so important that we are told there will be no proper conduct in human relations without it. David's last words, given to guide his family to successfully govern the nation were these: "He who rules over men must be just, ruling in the fear of God." (II Samuel 23:3) Those words were actually given to him by the Lord. A leader who abdicates the moral high ground of truth and justice will, very likely, soon lose the authority to lead. We must all be answerable to the moral compass God placed in our hearts as well as being ever mindful that we must ultimately give an account to Him one day soon for our every thought, motive and action.

More importantly, however, neither will there be any true faith without it. Paul declared, "To the pure all things are pure, but to those who are defiled and unbelieving nothing is pure; but even their mind and conscience are defiled." (Titus 1:15) Without it there would be no avenue open to free and prosper us. The anonymous writer of Proverbs 28:13 stated emphatically, "He who covers (hides) his sins shall not prosper but whoever confesses and forsakes them will" on the contrary, "(find) mercy." Years ago, when I got saved, I knew I was certainly about as rank of a sinner as you might find. Though the Apostle Paul was chief of sinners, I could not have been far behind. My dad even said, "If you don't change your ways son, you will never see sixteen." Well, I'm sorry to say all my foolishness didn't stop with that admonition as a kid. It took the work of Jesus on the cross of Calvary.

I am certainly not proud of it but one sin I got away with for a while was cheating on some tests in college. Living in the Corps dorms, each outfit had a company clerk. He was responsible for keeping highly organized file cabinets full of tests that had been given by the various professors. We considered it sport to go out at night on recon, dumpster diving. For what? Our objective was to find the original mimeograph sheets the Profs used to make their tests. Sometimes, in retrospect, I wonder how much better I would have done in college if I had devoted as much time and energy studying instead. We had someone in the dumpster with flash lights looking through the trash. Someone else was in the bushes with a walkie-talkie keeping watch to alert those in the dumpster should the campus cops happen by so they could douse the lights. Sometimes, our plan worked marvelously. We had the entire test the night before. Actually, to our shame, we thought we were pretty clever. We thought we had outsmarted the professors.

It worked for a season and never came to mind for years and years —not even once until—until I gave my life to Christ in 1977. It was then I heard about Proverbs 28:13 and found my self convicted by the Holy Spirit and in possession of a college degree that I didn't earn entirely honestly. I prayed about it and, though living in a distant state, decided to mail my degree back to the President of my college, Texas A&M University, along with a letter confessing what I had done. This meant that I had to take off my college ring and remove being a college graduate from my resume. It was clear to me that I needed God's approval more than man's approval or a college degree. A whole lot of years and a whole lot of work had been done to get that degree and now–for seemingly nothing. This was a big decision for me at the time. I had great uncles, uncles, my father, my brother and numerous cousins who graduated from this school as well. There was also a great deal of shame in my heart.

About six months later, however, I received a package and a letter in the mail from the Vice President of Texas A&M stating that he had received my letter and degree and had reviewed my confession. He said he believed that now I was the type of person that they would be proud to have as a graduate of the University and asked if I would please receive my degree back with their blessing? How faithful is our God? He said if we would confess our sins we'd find mercy and I certainly received mercy and rejoiced in God's forgiveness. You see, I might have been able to get past man, my Profs and the school but I couldn't hide from God. He caught me red handed when the time was right.

What it means to have the character trait of being **CONSCIENTIOUS**:

- Being governed by the dictates of one's conscience (our inner-governor of right and wrong)
- Having scruples
- Moral turpitude
- A person's inner feelings that oblige them to do what is right
- Those inner feelings that enjoin us to do good deeds and dictate right actions

CONSIDERATE, BEING —   Study start date: _____ Finish date: _____

Rarely is anything significant on this planet ever accomplished in a vacuum. Even investors and inventors are usually assisted by others with their research. As life and tasks become increasingly more complex due to advancing technology, the more history, precedence and people must be taken into consideration to find the most workable and successful solutions to our problems. Life is basically a series of problems to solve and no matter how good you get at solving them, they will never stop coming at us. If there were no problems in life, we could just put all our families, businesses and churches on autopilot and wouldn't need leaders anymore. Due to the ever-increasing complexity of our culture, we are constantly, in fact, encountering more and greater problems in life. Failure to consider other people involved and to accommodate critical aspects of the solution before a final decision is reached may cause us to not only miss the mark but possibly have a total failure.

Being considerate of others is simply recognizing the importance of everyone in life's equation. People are important. Everybody must be considered if one wants to ever achieve any kind of success in life. Laws and regulations are important, capacities of the various pieces of equipment, natural resources being used, people and computers, for example, must be analyzed and care must be taken not to exceed their limits or failure will likely result. Furthermore, being considerate where people are concerned will certainly not only help on the project at hand but will also build a stronger relationship between you and your associates, fosters a sense of understanding, cooperation, respect and possibly a deep and lasting friendship. This kind of favor can and will be carried forward between the parties to future endeavors. We must consider what effect our actions and the changes we want to make will have on others in our company, being careful, as far as possible, not to cast others in a bad light.

It is said there are two things for certain in life: "Death and taxes." However, I would add a third: "Change." Everything in this life is in a state of flux even if it doesn't look like it. An effective leader must be able to make changes and do it with the willing cooperation, blessing and assistance of all those involved. However, many times in life, we will have ideas to innovate when, in fact, we are not the appointed leader. In either case, to implement change with a particular group of people, the players involved must, for the most part, feel like we (the agent of change) personally care about them, respect them and have already shown that we have their best interest at heart. We will need to consider the known goals of others around us and show them, if possible, how our idea fulfills their objectives. Being considerate is knowing that we must get others excited about our idea and that will be possible only if we have been excited about them and loyal to them in the past. You see, I firmly believe in upward and downward loyalty. It is a two-way street. Employees must be loyal to the leader and the company but the leader must also be loyal to the other workers there as well. This is critical because it is impossible to be an effective leader without having the resident ability to affect change smoothly, willingly and, as often as possible, gladly.

Wherever it is we find ourselves at this moment in life is the result of all the decisions we have made thus far. The most efficient way to make the best decisions is to consider all the points and forces that will come to bear on the various possible courses of action. Then we won't experience unintended consequences, abject failures or create intolerable situations for ourselves and others. An excellent way to consider all the forces that will come to bear and find quality answers to complex problems is what is called the Ben Franklin close mentioned earlier. All one need do is get out a pen and several pieces of paper. Write down each possible solution to the problem at the top of each page. Then make two columns on each page below the possible solutions and mark them "Advantages" and "Disadvantages." Now you can start brain storming. Write down every advantage and disadvantage to each prospective solution. Get help from other people and, hopefully, some with experience with the problem, if time allows. When you have written them all down, set it aside, let it go and sleep on it overnight. This will let your subconscious work on it and bring you even more ideas and clarity. Don't forget to list not only present consequences but the inherent risks and future consequences as well. In time you will gain conviction about exactly what course of action you should take.

One day a reporter was interviewing a highly successful industrial tycoon trying to find the key to his phenomenal business success. He asked, "How did you build such a large conglomerate that actually dominates the market?" He replied, "Good decisions." "How did you get to where you are today?" The businessman said, "Good decisions." Then he said, "Well then how did you learn to make good decisions?" He replied, "Bad decisions."

It is true, that we learn a great deal from our mistakes and we have all certainly made them. However, learning from mistakes is a very expensive teacher in terms of lost time, resources and pain. We definitely should learn from our own mistakes so we don't repeat them but it is much cheaper and easier to learn from the knowledge, experiences and mistakes of others. To find this information all that is necessary is to ask for the advice and opinions of those who are knowledgeable about the issue at hand, have had experience with it or who are currently involved in it with us. Always make a special effort to consult your key leaders in advance. Some people don't want to ask the opinions of others for fear that others will think they don't have all the answers. That can be solved very quickly, just tell them you don't have all the answers right off the bat. In fact, they will surely think less of you if you don't seek wise counsel or consider the opinions of those around you. When you ask another person's opinion, you are honoring them by showing that you value their ideas, experience and knowledge. Realize you still have all the wisdom you began with plus you will now have all the wisdom you learned from each of the other people you inquire of. "Iron sharpens iron." (Proverbs 27:17) Their ideas will test your tentative solution and help guide you forward. Now you are gaining wisdom. Asking their opinion is showing consideration to their status in the situation, appreciating their sage advice, and giving honor to them as a person. The Bible even says, "Without counsel, plans go awry, but in the multitude of counselors they are established." (Proverbs 10:22) It also says, it is only "by wise counsel you will wage ... war and in a multitude of counselors there is safety." Proverbs 24:6

Another way people have failed in the area of consideration is by thinking everyone else should be just like them and find their happiness the same, identical way they do. In other words, just think how boring this old world would be if everyone was just like us. How vanilla?

Yet another area of consideration that probably needs a lot of work in a society full of pride is how we actually think of others. Paul says in Philippians 2:3 to "esteem (or consider) others better than yourselves." The point being that everyone on the planet is important. Everyone has gifts and talents, all of which are needed in the master plan. Who are we and what makes us think our particular talents are more important than our neighbor's? In a word: pride. Think just a minute. Everybody we meet in life knows something we don't know. They have been places we haven't been. They have experienced things we have never experienced and can do something much better than we can. Why then should we expect others to be like us? We can learn from everyone and should consider them a little better than ourselves. This attitude of honestly esteeming others better than ourselves builds cooperation, friendship and mutual respect.

What it means to have the character trait of **BEING CONSIDERATE:**

- Being thoughtful of and taking into account the desires, knowledge, rights, opinions and preferences of others
- Considering the feelings of others and how things you may be doing or are considering doing will affect them and their interests
- Realizing that none of us live in a vacuum and in order to successfully navigate through life, we must be aware of, considerate and accommodative of those we interact with
- Being circumspect, careful and cautions in our approach to things—especially when affecting change
- Knowing you have little to gain and much to lose by interfering with another person's means of finding happiness.
- Discerning other peoples' pet peeves and avoiding them

ONSISTENT —   **Study start date: _____ Finish date: _____**

O ne quality rarely exercised in the world today is consistency. For example, a local business I frequent offers free coffee to their customers. However, in the space of a couple months I observed that twice the coffee was made but the burner was left off. Three times there were no cups. On three other occasions there was no cream. Twice there was no coffee made at all. A small thing you might say when it was free in the first place but it is the small things in business that make all the difference. Big problems are usually just an accumulation of a lot of small things gone awry. It is really better to be average consistently than to be excellent one day and poor the next. Far better, however, to be consistently excellent all the time.

I noticed a beautiful example of consistency during the last George W. Bush Administration when it was learned that our wounded veterans returning home from Iraq and Afghanistan were not receiving proper medical treatment and follow up. Who did the President put in charge of finding and implementing the fix? A medical doctor? The president of General Motors? No, an infantry soldier. He put the Vice Chief of Staff of the Army in charge to remedy this shameful medical non-delivery problem. He chose a man who had, over about a thirty year period of time, demonstrated a high level of excellence in every job he had ever been assigned. Here this general is, who you might think would have been a duck out of water, trying to regulate and improve the efficiency of a huge team of medical professionals scattered all across the United States. Remember, this man was trained to combat assault directly in the face of the full physical strength and fire power of the enemy on a daily basis. What did he know about the finer points of medical treatment and efficiency? In the same way he fought in a battle, he jumped right into the middle of this problem. He started listening to the soldiers who had problems as well as listening to the medical practitioners who had both problems and ideas. He made an extensive survey of the best practices that were successful at all the hospitals across the country and, most importantly, gained the cooperation and trust of all those in charge of the situation. Once the fix was ordered, he implemented and tested the system he designed. He then held a news conference. Present were some of the medical doctors along with all the chief non-commissioned officers and generals in the medical branch. That he had gained the full confidence, respect and cooperation of all these players was readily apparent. This general knew people, how to get along with them and how to consistently get the job done. When the news conference was over, there was no doubt that our soldiers, sailors and airmen were going to receive consistent medical treatment and follow through they needed from then on. No one was going to fall through the cracks in the future. That short, ten minute news conference let everyone know that the job was completed and completed with excellence as well. One could not possibly think that the President had chosen anyone but the right man for the job — an Army Ranger. This was a man, trained in hand-to-hand combat, demolitions, munitions, leading men, battle strategy and tactics who could consistently be relied upon to fix anything and accomplish the mission. What consistency. Amazing!

What it means to have the character trait of **BEING CONSISTENT:**

- Able to be relied upon without fear of failure or even the possibility of a poor performance
- Able to accomplish missions repeatedly and without fail — no matter what — with a high degree of excellence
- Having established an unfailing manner of performance

- Marked by a steady expression of not only professionalism but an example of character, belief, orders kept and customs met (performance that exceeds profession or expectation)
- Marked by steady conformity and harmony of operation
- An ability to keep continuity
- Free from failure, contradiction or variation
- Compatible with like kind or sample
- Always meeting or exceeding the mark or parameters of another's expectation be they senior, subordinate or peer
- "Jesus Christ, the same yesterday, today and forever." Hebrews 13:8

ONTENTMENT— **Study start date:** _____ **Finish date:** _____

Madison Avenue's main focus, although they will never tell you this, is to build discontentment in the hearts of people through its various advertising media. Truth is, people who are content with what they have don't buy and most of the products being promoted by advertisers are not essential to survival. Thus arises the economic or marketing necessity of engendering dissatisfaction with one's current state through advertising. If you already have a car, you probably don't need a motor scooter. But the ad crafters will show you a guy riding a motor scooter with a beautiful girl riding on the back. You get the inference I'm sure. A new scooter will help your social life. If you have a sufficient home paid for and the children have already left the nest, do you really need a bigger, fancier house? And on it goes— enticing you all through the lust of the flesh, the lust of the eyes and the pride of life. Henry Ford warned us years ago, we would be sorry if we let Madison Avenue get hold of the automobile and turn it into an object of fashion, style and pride. He said the price of cars would surely sky-rocket but the American people said, "No. We want style, dazzling colors, chrome and all the bells and whistles." But will the fancier, more stylish, more expensive cars get you there any faster? These advertising campaigns are unrelenting and so insidious that you don't even know when they have come upon you and gripped you in their tentacles. Everyone has been taken in by these schemes at one point in time or another. Having more extravagance simply means directing more of our resources to the less productive, less profitable and less important areas of our lives.

Paul, the Apostle, told us in I Timothy 6:6 what freedom and true gain was all about when he said, "Now godliness with contentment is great gain. For we brought nothing into this world, and it is certain we can carry nothing out. And having food and clothing with these we shall be content." Knowing God, pleasing Him and walking in the blessings of the Kingdom, are sufficient rewards for anyone. The temptations and lures of the world are a snare and cause people to be led astray into many hurtful lusts that often end, the Bible says, in destruction. The answer to this is so very simple that Paul told the Corinthians he was greatly concerned that their "minds (might) be corrupted from the simplicity that is in Christ" (II Corinthians 11:3) The plan we are given to find happiness, peace and fulfillment in life is fundamentally just this: "Seek first the kingdom of God and His righteousness, and all these things shall be added to you" (Matthew 6:33) In other words, we need not worry about how we are going to succeed in the world or how we are going to find food or clothing or a spouse. Rather we should focus on knowing, loving and understanding God and making Him our first priority in life. As we learn of Him and come to know His ways and will, we will begin to incorporate those things in our lifestyle and habits. We become a doer of the Word and not a hearer only. Then, in due time, He will add whatever He knows we really need. If we will just seek Him and his Kingdom, He promises, "all these things shall be added to you." What things? All the things that the Gentiles seek after, if we will but learn contentment and patience while seeking and putting Him first.

This is a lesson we must all learn otherwise we will be constantly led about by the spirit of the world instead of the Spirit of the Lord. Paul, himself, said, "I have learned in whatever state I am, to be content: I know how to be abased, and I know how to abound. Everywhere and in all things I have learned both to be full and to be hungry, both to abound and to suffer need." Why? Because he knew his source was not money, nor his current assets, nor a partnership with men or the government in power at the moment, but Christ. He simply said instead, "I can do all things through Christ who strengthens me." (Philippians 4:11–13) We are, at any moment in time where God has specifically brought us or permitted us to be. Our deliverance and our future is in His hands. If our ways are pleasing to Him, He is free to use His unlimited power to move us as He wills. For this to be so, our goal must be as Paul's: To know Christ and to "press toward the goal for the prize of the upward call of God in Christ Jesus." (Philippians 3:14) We do well to consistently remind ourselves to be content with the things we have. As we go through life, we certainly need to have an eye for quality but we also need the wisdom to avoid extravagance. We should be buying for utility rather than prestige value. Many times, the same product can be had, provide the same function at a much lower cost, leaving you far more capital to spend for other important items or investments in the future.

Long ago, John the Baptist was asked by his converts, while he was preparing the way for the coming of Christ, "What shall we do … ?" (Luke 3:10) In other words, how then should we live? One of the things he commanded them was to "be content with your wages." (v.14) He preached about this and many other things becoming known as a "voice crying out in the wilderness." Contentment must have a beginning point—a day you must drive your stakes down and say, "This day is square one for me. I will be content with food, raiment and my wages."

Face it, no one believes they are being paid what they are worth. This is just the way humans are built but we can overcome it. A person cannot possibly be content with food and raiment if their mind is constantly in a state of mental consternation over getting more pay. Contentment with all three of these must work together in unison. Give your pay to God. Let Him be the owner of all you have: money, possessions and talents. Then you can become a steward. Determine to work as unto the Lord and give your pay status to Him as well. According to Daniel 5:23, your life, your breath and all of your ways are in His hands anyway. He is the One who really controls everything but there is such a blessing in truly learning to be content. Otherwise you will live in this horrible mental state, suffering under the notion of being cheated which leads to a constant state of resentment, anger and pride. Contentment, on the contrary, leads to gratefulness, peace and joy. Sadly, you can never give an ungrateful person a pay raise

He was "the voice crying out in the wilderness."

and make him happy. No matter how much you pay him, he will always be ungrateful, wanting more. Contentment is found in hoping for God's best but enjoying and being thankful for what you have. The destruction of people, marriages, companies and civilizations past teaches us the grave lessons of greed and ingratitude.

Finally, contentment actually puts one in the position of being promoted and rewarded by his superiors. A wise man once said, "Beware of covetousness, for one's life does not consist in the abundance of the things he possesses." (Luke 12:15) Work as if there is no tomorrow. Give everyone 110% wherever you happen to be. Come in early to work and stay late. Give. Give. Give and the law of reciprocity will pay its wonderful dividends sooner or later. Those around you who haven't learned this law are going to constantly be tripped up, hindered and side-lined by the same resentment over the pay issue that you have already overcome. What many people don't know is that " … promotion comes neither from the east, nor from the west nor from the south. But God is the Judge: He puts down one and exalts another." (Psalm 75:6) Contentment and trust in God frees you up to be thankful for each and every opportunity to serve and every time we serve. Every time we serve the Lord, He will take care of our pay. Even when you donate your time, you will, one day be repaid. Helping others is its own blessing and brings tremendous joy to the heart. Even so, God will be a debtor to no man. He repays to all abundantly.

He has promised food and raiment. You know you will always have that but, more importantly, He said, "I will never leave you nor forsake you." Hebrews 11:5

What it means to have the character trait of **CONTENTMENT**:

- Having learned to be more than satisfied with the honor of knowing God, even if you have only food and clothing
- Realizing and having peace with the fact that regardless that there will always be people who have something better than we do. We need to learn to accept it.
- Having an eye for quality but the wisdom to avoid extravagance
- Being satisfied in your present state regardless of whether you are abased or abounding
- Feeling adequately supplied and satisfied with God's provision, knowing that in His divine providence, He probably has even greater blessings planned for you.
- Being satisfied with one's own possessions, not desiring our neighbor's
- Being satisfied and appreciative of one's wages at any point in time in our life
- Having supernatural control to contain one's appetites and desires
- Having found significance in something other than physical, transient things
- Freedom from greed, disappointment, discomfort and the worldly desire for "more and bigger."
- Having lost the desire to keep up with one's neighbor with respect to property, promotions, possessions, popularity and pecuniary rewards.
- Knowing that "Godliness with contentment is great gain." I Timothy 6:6

CONVICTIONS—   Study start date: _____ Finish date: _____

Most people, as they pass through life seem so very unhappy and usually don't know why. The reason in most cases is simply because they are constantly trying to be and do what everyone else wants them to be and do. Like the chameleon, they struggle to change colors depending on present company and contort to conform, based on whatever way the wind is blowing. Their problem is that they don't have any God-given convictions and without these, they will never truly have character. Why? Because character is the sum of the ethical, moral and mental traits that define each of us as a person. It is really the core, essential nature and system of beliefs that make us who we are. Having convictions and being true to those convictions deep within is what makes us genuinely happy.

There is an interesting parable in the Bible about ten virgins waiting for the arrival of the groom and the wedding party. What is often overlooked in this parable is that all ten were distinguished. Just about everyone remembers that five were wise and five were foolish but not that all were distinguished. You see, all ten had exhibited character traits that individualized and distinguished them as a person. Five were diligent to prepare, secure reserves of oil and trim their lamps; living always at the ready and waiting patiently. These were distinguished as wise and were ultimately blessed to go in with the bridegroom to the wedding but then the door was immediately shut. The other five distinguished themselves as foolish because they didn't bother to pay the price to prepare. They didn't understand the necessity or the urgency of it. They were not willing to deny themselves other pleasures in order to have oil in their lamps in anticipation of the groom's unannounced but expected soon return. There are many like them out in the world today who prefer rather to "run on empty," like the farmer who eats all of his seed and then, in a few months, finds himself having nothing with which to plant for next year's crop. While these five virgins were out frantically trying to buy oil at the last minute, the door to the wedding feast was closed and they could not enter in. (Matthew 25:1–13) They had no conviction in their hearts about the importance of maintaining reserves or being ready at all times—whatever the cost.

Besides having no convictions, another problem people have in this area is the difficulty, even impossibility, of having courage without godly, Bible-based convictions. Having such convictions is essential to effective personhood. We all have need of a guiding light as our moral compass. For this, one must first have a system of core beliefs, knowing exactly what they truly believe is important in life before they can stand and defend them. Like they say, "If you don't stand for something, you will fall for anything." Nothing in life makes a person happier or more fulfilled than knowing who they are and what they believe—standing to the death for their convictions. God-given convictions form character and character is the power to make right decisions in difficult circumstances, especially when no one is watching. To have integrity, one must first be true to himself. A coward, you see, dies a thousand times but those who have convictions only die once.

An essential exercise for everyone, I believe, is to sit down at some point and write out the ten most important convictions in life. Then make a list of the things you want your life to accomplish or count for and those things, beliefs or principles you really think are important. Take some time to do it now. Then set it aside and revisit your list again in about a week. If you still think you have the right ones, great! If you think of some better, more important, convictions, write them down. Finally, when you are satisfied with your core beliefs, then purpose to stand for those convictions regardless of what it may cost you. Keep your list in a safe place so you can review it from time to time.

Imagine what life would be like in the United States if everyone made a commitment to just one thing: the truth. To seek the truth, know the truth, practice the truth, tell the truth and defend the truth as a moral conviction. Just this one conviction would turn this whole country completely around. Besides, the truth is the only thing that will set you free, bless you and protect you as long as you live.

Sadly, America's deplorable condition today is the direct consequence of a lack of moral character among our people. The reason we have no moral character as a people is because we have no God-centered convictions and this will likely be the undoing of the nation. Thomas Jefferson said, "God who gave us life, gave us liberty. Can the liberties of a nation be secure when we have removed a conviction that these liberties are the gift of God? Indeed I tremble for my country when I reflect that God is just and that his justice cannot sleep forever."

What it means to have the character trait of having **CONVICTIONS:**

- An extremely strong, deeply held persuasion
- Total allegiance to a set of principles of right and wrong
- Holding to certain core beliefs in one's conscience
- Being fully convinced about something, so much so that you would die for these things
- Being fully persuaded to the point of personal identity with the concept or prospect

OOPERATION— 　　　　　　**Study start date:** _____ **Finish date:** _____

In a world of self-centered people, a cooperative spirit is hard to find—but so very valuable when you do. Having a team of individuals pulling in different directions all at one time is about the most inefficient organization one could ever design. There is actually a word for this creature: mayhem, a state of total havoc, confusion and disorder. This is not a very happy place for anyone to be, even temporarily and, certainly it is no place to live, work or be for any extended period of time.

On the contrary, cooperation is a beautiful thing. It is the ability to act in concert with others. It is to be teachable, approachable and agreeable in nature. It is the spirit of helping and good will. One of the greatest obstacles to people ever becoming cooperative, is their refusal to realize that the world does not revolve around them. Actually we must live together, work together and get along for anything productive to ever to happen. It is only to the unity of the Spirit, cooperation and agreement that God has "commanded the blessing." (Psalm 133:3) He never poured out His blessing on the unruly, uncooperative or the rebellious. He commanded His blessing to unity and cooperation.

Through unity strength

There was a time in history when everyone on earth shared the same language. Scripture records that a large number of them began to build in the land of Shinar. It wasn't long before they decided to build a tower into the heavens for the purpose of making a name for themselves. (Genesis 11:4) There certainly wasn't anything else up there in the sky they could harvest. The name of the tower and city was called Babel. The Lord observed what the people were doing and concluded that there was nothing they planned to accomplish, when working in cooperation with each other, even with a wrong motive, that could be stopped. The power of unity and cooperation was so great, God had no choice but to confuse their language, immediately causing them to scatter over the earth. On the other hand, people cooperating with honorable goals and motives, enjoy God's supernatural blessing.

Some have yet to learn that associating and working together cooperatively is where most of our mutual benefits as humans are derived. In God's hierarchal system of government here on earth, someone is always in authority and the rest are there to assist and learn. Most of us, even just starting out, think we know the best way to do most things. However, after working a while for other leaders, we soon find that most of them accomplish what needs to be done quite well using their own plans. It is also well to remember, that most of the time, the leader has more experience and time in the organization than anyone else on the team and they probably didn't get their position by accident. It is incumbent on us to show deference, such that whoever is leading the team can lead it their way. We should do our best to help make their plans succeed and be quick to give everyone else the credit. This is being a good team player. If we will just help everyone on the team and forget about ourselves, in due time we will be rewarded.

Wisdom, when first employed with a company, even if we think we might know a better way, is to hold our peace and defer to the leader's solution instead of trying to tell him how to run his railroad. It is not going to work well to always be telling people how they did it when you were up in New Jersey. In the military they had a name for the people who always knew how to do things better than the leader: a sharpshooter. Never ran into one myself but always heard they were around. No matter what the leader did or how he wanted to do it, they could always do it better, knew a better way and were quick to tell them so. Rather than being a rigid, do-it-my–way type who always knows best, it is good to be an agreeable sort. Someone who is easy to be around, easy to work with, teachable and flexible enough to go along with the leader's plan as long as the solution is not illegal, immoral or unscriptural.

Remember, we all started this life being very selfish and thinking our way was always best. It takes time to learn to be cooperative. To become truly effective at it, however, requires a servant's heart. It calls for one to realize that being a servant is actually a highly desirable office. A true servant's heart delights in promoting others and helping them succeed at their endeavors. You see, once we have proven our loyalty and willingness to cooperate over a period of time, the leader will, very likely, soon find a freedom to ask our advice and may turn whole projects or even the entire business over to us. When they hand us a project and we ask, "How would you like this project done?" If we have earned their trust and shown some effectiveness, they are likely to say, "Do it however you want." Sooner or later, perfect obedience and cooperation will win you perfect freedom.

What it means to have the character trait of **COOPERATION:**

- The ability to act in concert with others
- The opposite of having an independent spirit or being selfish or stubborn or being a glory seeker
- Delighting in helping those around you not only complete their work but also helping to make them look good in the process
- It is having a servant's heart and attitude
- The grace to hold your peace and let the leader lead the way
- Not demanding your own way
- To associate and work with others for the mutual benefits derived
- Not competing with the leader but choosing instead to assist, add your agreement and be a blessing to the overall scheme of things
- It is making the leader's decisions your decisions and trying to make them work out successfully
- Being a good team player
- It is delighting in making your associate, coworker or leader look good and making their solutions work out
- It is always giving the group and others the credit when things work out well

ORRECTION, THE ABILITY TO RECEIVE— Study start date: ____ Finish date:____

One of the hardest things for human beings to receive is correction. We all want to think we are doing just fine and have it all together. We all have to live with our inner self which is usually laboring under several misconceptions about us at the same time. The first misconception we believe about ourselves is that we always know what is best. The second is that we can do any job about as good as anybody else. The third is that everybody should like the job we did because we did our best. Fourth, we believe that everyone should like us because we are who we are. God made us and loves us. Finally, we don't know what we don't know so we don't see where we have any room for improvement anyway.

Most who grow up in a home with a loving mother and father, unknowingly suffer under the illusion that everybody in the world is going to love them just like their parents did. Oh what a rude awakening it is for those who leave home for the first time, join the military and step off the bus in the face of their kind-hearted and loving drill sergeant! (I'm being facetious of course) Here's this mountain of a guy with a huge chest and a small waist but with a voice loud enough to cause an earthquake any moment and he doesn't like you at all. I mean he really doesn't like you. Not the way you part your hair or anything. He doesn't even like it that you have hair and all-of-a-sudden you find out for the first time now that you have a tendency to slouch, your shoulders cave forward and you naturally droop your head like a buzzard. You thought you were pretty cool and now nothing, I mean nothing you do is right and he's got names for you that you never heard of. Some of these names you wouldn't hang on a mangy, old, flee-bitten dog. Now, for the first time, you feel like you might be something a little lower than a pile of whale dung on the lowest part of the ocean.

It was no better for those whose parents drop them off on the sidewalk at a military college with a few suit cases and a hand-me-down fan. This was right after the melting of the ice age and before air conditioning in the dormitories. Whoa! When those upperclassmen got hold of me, I thought I just ran into a tire shredder on steroids. They didn't like me or anything about me and it didn't look like that was ever going to change—at least any time during that century. Truth is there was a reason for their apparent dislike of this new, miserable piece of humanity the military was going to have to invest hundreds of thousands of dollars in to straighten out. Whether or not this was even possible was still in question at the time. Although they would rarely come right out and say it, there was at least a couple reasons for all of this. First they wanted us to improve and God knows we all had plenty of room for that. And, just as important, another equally good reason was they wanted to see if we had the inner constitution to even be able to take correction. Could we handle somebody getting into our stuff—and I don't mean your foot locker or your duffle bag. I mean getting under your skin and down into where you live. Would we shrivel up like a violet or could we stand tall, take it. Would we flinch at the first strong rebuke, fold up our tent and go home to mamma or would we take the chastisement to heart, fix what we could as quickly as possible and keep our mouth shut in the process. Like they said, "You gotta' be able to take it before you can dish it out" and they never quoted scripture, we know, most importantly, "Humility comes before honor." (Proverbs 15:33) Though it certainly isn't easy for anyone to endure this process, I really believe America would be a better place if all our young men had to do two years in the military just like they do in Israel. It is good for a person to learn that everybody in life is not going to love you or think like you.

Some correction is just going to come our way in life and much of it will not be delivered in the gentlest fashion. Not only that but this is the real world and the devil and some of his folk are still around who continue to do a lot of terrible stuff. Many of the people we meet out in the world don't like anybody very much; not even themselves. We had better become accustomed to running into them on a fairly regular basis. Wherever we work it might just be "the boss's way or the highway" and he may not even care to hear about how they did it back in Maryland. If one doesn't grow some thick skin in a mighty big hurry so they can take some correction, this new career of theirs is likely to come to an abrupt end.

Correction must come because we live in a complicated, highly technical world operated almost totally by convention, i.e., the standard practices of society or a particular industry's way of doing things. Convention allows us to work together successfully as a society. Things like putting the return address in the top left hand corner of an envelope, the forwarding address in the middle with a zip code and the stamp on the top right corner is all convention. Do it any other way and your mail will likely be held up, thrown out or, at best, returned to you in a few weeks.

The problem is, just starting out, many young people have no idea of what the world expects. We are a blank sheet of paper and need someone to teach us. Some things are hard to learn and even while we are learning, we will probably stand in need of some correction in the process. What we need to come to realize is that correction is good and we can't live without it. We all need correction to perfect our technique, attitude and understanding. A wise man will listen intently to instruction; no matter who offers the correction. If it is our friends or co-workers, we need to realize they are actually taking a big risk sharing their true feelings about our shortcomings in the first place. They could be risking their friendship with us just to share critically important, helpful information with us. Correction is a bit painful for all of us but we are compelled to receive it and make the necessary adjustments if we ever expect to progress.

Realize we are all humans with feelings but to get ahead and improve in life, we have to get past our feelings. Our minds naturally wants to reject the notion that we could be wrong or need improvement. That's just the fallen human nature we were all born with. I personally believe it is a good idea to write down the advice people give us, even if it doesn't seem spot on at the time. Take it home and put it in a file. Every so often open the file and review your critiques. Let the Holy Spirit speak to your spirit and then try wholeheartedly to receive it in a meaningful way. There are probably some good suggestions there you could improve on. It was likely meant for your good and should be given the utmost consideration.

Correction is so vitally important. A ship once set to sail from London to New York. Even before the captain gave the order to weigh anchor and shove off, he first set the azimuth on his ship's compass to plot their course at sea. When they left the harbor, he made their first correction, based on his maps and the stars, and set a new azimuth. They followed that course for several hours and, once again, he made another correction, setting a new course. Time and again, the captain would make corrections until one day, they arrived safely at New York harbor. Obviously none of his azimuths were correct. Their course, effected by the weather, winds and ocean currents as well as the condition, number and trim of their sails, required constant correction to make it to port. Actually, the captain never had the perfect azimuth but the sum total of all those corrections caused the successful result of reaching New York harbor safely for all aboard. Corrections were indispensable. It is the same for us as we trod life's pathway.

All of us have fallen short in life and have found ourselves in need of correction from time to time. We all want happiness in this life and Job told us where it could be found saying, "Behold, happy is the man whom God corrects; therefore do not despise the chastening of the Almighty. For He bruises, but He binds up; He wounds, but His hands make whole." Being made whole is what we, flawed, broken individuals really need.

The entire book of Proverbs was written to give young people wisdom, which is the ability to live life skillfully and avoid the pitfalls along the way. Incidentally, the youth department of a large church posted a sign that said, "Now is a good time to go out and make your million while you are still smarter than your parents." It is truly amazing that the older kids get, the smarter their parents become. In chapter three of Proverbs, the writer, Solomon, said, "My son, do not despise the chastening of the Lord, nor detest His correction; for whom the Lord loves, He corrects, just as a father the son in whom he delights." (v.3:11, 12) So correction may be painful for a little while but life would, certainly, be far more painful without it. The Master is saying, "listen." In chapter one, verse 23 of Proverbs the writer says, "Turn at my reproof; surely I will pour out my spirit on you; I will make my words known to you." If we would but stop, be open and listen, God would reveal His Word to us.

The majority, however, will not. Solomon said only "A fool despises his father's instruction but he who receives correction is prudent." (v.15:5) Most children have a problem with all this because, "Foolishness is bound up in the heart of a child; (but) the rod of correction will drive it far from him." (Proverbs 22:15) Yet some continue to stubbornly turn away. It is to those the Lord says, "They would have none of (My) counsel and despised My every rebuke. Therefore they shall eat the fruit of their own way, and be filled to the full with their own fancies. For the turning away of the simple will slay them, and the complacency of fools will destroy them; but whoever listens to Me will dwell safely, and will be secure, without fear of evil." (Proverbs 1:30–33) We are also given the promise that "He who keeps instruction is in the way of life, but he who refuses correction goes astray." (v.10:12) God's Word is clear, "He who hates correction is stupid" (v.12:1), will come to "poverty and shame." (Proverbs 13:18) If that is not enough, here is the end of the story: "He who hates correction will die." (v.15:10) On the contrary, "He who heeds rebuke gets understanding"(15:32), is prudent (v.15:5) and shall be honored. (v. 13:18) So correction or "Reproofs of instruction are the way of life ..." (Proverbs 6:23) As long as we occupy an earthly body, we are going to stand in need of correction. How we take correction will cause it either help or hurt us. If we really want to live life to the full, until it overflows, we must be teachable, quick to listen to correction from those around us and willingly take it to heart.

What it means to have the character trait of **THE ABILITY TO TAKE CORRECTION:**

- The act of listening, receiving and harkening to guidance, correction or critique
- Rectification
- Rebuke to bring one into conformity with a set standard or level of competency
- Responding appropriately to reproofs of instruction
- Having the humility necessary to take advice, correction and reproof
- To be freed from error

OURAGE —   **Study start date:** _____ **Finish date:** _____

As young people growing up, we find many awe inspiring, intimidating things cast round about us. In a highly technological, highly industrialized society, there are many institutions and career fields that look to be more than we can, at that early age, ever see ourselves being able to master. Not many of us are overburdened with tons of talent, Herculean strength, the speed of Mercury or a genius I.Q. like Einstein. We all, if we will be honest, start out life with doubts, feelings of inadequacy, wonderment and many questions. With about a fifty percent graduation rate today, young people wonder if they will even graduate from high school? We have all known people who didn't. Many wonder if they will graduate from college but for some of us, the question might rather have been, could we even get into one? Then, if we actually attended and by divine intervention we were able to graduate, the question became, would we be able cut the mustard when we go out on our first job? Could we get a pilot's license or "wash out" of the course? So many career fields are totally intimidating. To face the future in today's world, we need a whole lot of courage.

Most kids grow up consciously or subconsciously wanting to be like their dads. I remember as a teenager, observing my dad and wondering how in the world I could ever live up to the mark he set. As a squadron commander in the Air Force, he was in charge of two or three dozen Boeing KC-97 Air Refueling Stratotakers. There happened to be a special day one time, when they allowed us kids to tour one of planes. It stood five stories high and when you walked next to it on the tarmac, it seemed like a small city with wings and had four engines bigger than a Volkswagen Bug. Amazingly, it carried 9,000 gallons of aviation fuel in addition to its own fuel and still flew at four hundred miles per hour to refuel the Strategic Air Command bombers. This refueling had to be done while the bombers were in route to their targets anywhere around the world. Sitting in the pilot's seat, I was totally awe-struck. You have never seen so many gauges, dials, knobs, levers, screens, throttles, buzzers, lights and all kinds of avionics. Dad had some twenty or thirty of these planes along with a pilot, co-pilot, navigator and crew chief for each. As commander, he was also responsible for the huge maintenance staff it took to service, repair and maintain those birds in a total state of readiness. From time to time he would take his squadron or a large portion of them and fly to far-flung places around the world. Truly amazing. How could anyone manage a venture of this size and complexity? As a scrawny little teenager, hardly able to stay out of the principal's office and scared to death to talk in front of a group of people, I often wondered where I could get the courage to even try to follow in his footsteps?

Likewise, as kids, we wonder, if we could ever learn to drive a semi, a front-end loader, a back-hoe or whatever a particular job may require? Would we ever have the courage to start our own company, if we did we wonder if it would succeed or, to our shame, quickly disintegrate into a pile of ashes? Then, God forbid, if we ever had to go to war, how would we react to mortal combat? As young people growing up there are and will be many questions in our minds and huge mountains ahead for us to climb. Questions and wonderment about these things are both normal and necessary. Uncertainty about the difficulties that lie ahead encourages us to get prepared and do our best each step along the way in this ever-unfolding process of life. Actually, we find, successfully completing each step builds our confidence and gives us courage to face the future and all of its new challenges. This, combined with learning from our mistakes when failing occasionally, getting up and dusting ourselves off, and going at it again and again until we get it, also builds confidence. Learning how, in this way, to turn our failures into stepping stones instead of stumbling blocks is valuable information. I have never met anyone who hadn't failed at something before being successful. In fact Solomon said, "a righteous man falls seven times and rises again." (Proverbs 24:16) Success breeds success and so does overcoming failure so, as young people, we need to stack up as many successes as we can right from the beginning.

There are some troubles in life's seemingly never ending stream of obstacles that are, well, overwhelming, next to impossible situations for anyone. We will all face them. It may be health challenges, financial reversals, marital betrayal and many other things. Self-confidence is great and a necessary trait everyone must have, at least to some degree, but it just won't get the job done in some of life's situations. For these we will need super-natural courage.

An example of one of these seemingly impossible situations occurred in the life of David during a time when Israel was at war with the Philistines. At this point in the nation's history, both of their armies had gathered together at Sokoh, which was part of the inheritance of the tribe of Judah. The enemy is forever trying to camp out on the inheritance of God's people and this time was no exception. The Philistines were encamped adjacent to the armies of the living God on separate mountains with the valley of Elah between. Both were waiting for a sign from their god to attack. On this particular day, a giant, towering over nine feet tall, named Goliath, came out before the Israelites in full battle array. He struck an awesome figure, having a bronze javelin beam strapped to his back and a shiny bronze helmet that glistened in the sun. His spear was the size of a weaver's beam and just the metal point weighed more than 15 pounds. His coat of mail weighed over 190 pounds and had huge brass plates of shin-armor on his legs as well as a huge target, a piece of body armor made of brass on his chest, between his shoulders. His shield, so large it could cover nearly his entire body, requiring him to have a shield bearer to go before him and strapped to his side was also an enormous sword.

As he came out, he began to shout, defying the armies of the Living God and threw down a challenge. He said instead of both armies clashing, let each side chose one among for them as a representative. He, himself, would fight for the Philistines and the Isrealites could pick their warrior. The winner of this contest would determine the prevailing side. The losing side, of course, would become the servants of the victors. Then the Philistine said, "I defy the armies of Israel this day; give me a man, that we may fight together." I Samuel 17:10

When Saul and his army heard this, they were greatly distressed; stricken with fear. No one would take up the challenge. This occurred again and again for forty days. This heathen giant came out and challenged Israel but no one was willing to fight. The situation was so intimidating and terrifying, the whole army was paralyzed. No one, not even King Saul would step forward to save the nation.

About this time, David, who was one of the eight sons of Jesse. He had three older brothers whom his father had already sent to follow Saul in the war against the Philistines. David happened to be the youngest of Jesse's sons. His job at this time in life was to tend some of his father's sheep but on this particular day his father had sent him on an errand. He was to take some cheese, ten loaves of bread and some grain to the captains of their thousands (we would probably call these generals today) as a blessing and he was also to check on his three brothers, bringing news back to his father about them.

When David arrived, the armies were arrayed against each other on adjacent mountains and had already started railing and shouting at each other but the battle was not yet joined. Upon arriving at the camp of the Israelites, David left his gifts with the supply keeper and went to see his brothers. While little David was visiting them, Goliath came out once again and began his rant, defying Israel with the very same words as before but this time, David heard him. The giant was, no doubt, terribly intimidating because of his size, so at his words, the armies of Israel fled. The Israeli soldiers told David about the reward on Goliath's head. They asked, "Have you seen this man who has come up? Surely he has come up to defy Israel; and it shall be that the man who kills him the king will enrich with great riches, will give him his daughter and give his father's house exemption from taxes in Israel." (I Samuel 17:25) At this,

David sounded a little too interested in the proposition and his eldest brother overheard it. Embarrassed, he began to belittle him, inquiring as to why he was even there and with whom he had left the few sheep he was in charge of out in the wilderness. Then he accused David of having pride in his heart and rebuked him for insolence as a teenager for even coming down to the battle. David opined, "What have I done now? Is there not a cause?" He turned to others about him and inquired again, "Is there not a cause?" What he meant was could there not be a cause in Israel worth risking one's life to save it? Was not the cause of saving Israel and the Armies of the Living God from the defamation of this uncircumcised Philistine worth whatever risks it took? But those present turned and gave him the same answer. Then someone immediately reported the incident to Saul who called for David to come see him.

Upon his arrival, David said to the King, "Let no man's heart fail because of (Goliath); your servant will go and fight with this Philistine." Saul replied that he couldn't possibly do this, being just a teenager and here this giant was, a man of war from his youth. Discouragement had now come from the enemy, his brothers and, now, the King. David replied, "Your servant used to keep his father's sheep and when a lion or a bear came and took a lamb out of the flock, I went out after it and struck it and delivered the lamb from its mouth and when it arose against me, I caught it by its beard and struck and killed it. Your servant has killed both the lion and bear; and this uncircumcised Philistine will be like one of them, seeing he has defied the armies of the living God." Continuing on he said, "The Lord, who delivered me from the paw of the lion and from the paw of the bear, He will deliver me from the hand of this Philistine." Saul replied, "Go and the Lord be with you!" I Samuel 17:37

At this point, Saul tried to strap his over-sized armor, bronze helmet and coat of mail on him. David even attempted to hook Saul's sword to his side and tried his best to walk but the outfit was entirely too big. He then told Saul he hadn't tested it and took it all off. Picking up his staff, he headed out to the battlefield.

Once there, David chose five smooth stones from the brook in the valley of Elah and put them in his shepherd's bag. Keeping his sling in his hand, David drew near to Goliath in the valley. When the giant saw little David, he began to belittle him saying, "Am I a dog that you come to me with sticks?" And he began to curse David to his gods and saying, "Come to me and I will give your flesh to the birds of the air and the beasts of the field!" I Samuel 17:44

David replied, "You come to me with a sword, with a spear, and with a javelin. But I come to you in the name of the Lord of hosts, the God of the armies of Israel, whom you have defied. This day the Lord will deliver you into my hand, and I will strike you and take your head from you. And this day I will give the carcasses of the camp of the Philistines to the birds of the air and the wild beasts of the earth, that all the earth may know that there is a God in Israel. Then all this assembly shall know that the Lord does not save with sword and spear; for the battle is the Lord's, and He will give you into our hands." I Samuel 17:46, 47

Then the giant arose and came toward David who, at that moment, ran in his direction to meet him. Then David reached into his bag and pulled out a stone and placed it in his sling shot, hurled it at the giant and hit him squarely in the forehead. The stone was thrown with such force that it sunk deep into his forehead and, immediately, Goliath fell on his face to the ground. Having no sword, David quickly ran to the giant, pulled his and cut off his head. When the Philistines saw this, they fled as their champion was dead and had been defeated by a teenager with a sling shot. Emboldened by David's display of courage and triumph, the armies of Israel and Judah arose shouting and fighting, pursuing the Philistines all the way to the gates of Ekron. The rout of the Philistines that day was very great and all because the courage of a small boy who put his trust in God. Because of his courage on the battlefield that day, his life was never the same in Israel. This was the first of many battles that would cause him to become the greatest warrior in the nation's history.

The situation has changed very little today. The world is still desperately searching for men of faith and courage. One of the main reasons there is such a dearth of these men today is that most people go through life feeling woefully inadequate, fearful and afraid to fail. Why? They are looking to themselves for strength and trusting in man and his various contrivances for help instead of God. David said it would be this way when he penned these words: "Some trust in chariots, and some in horses; but we will remember (trust in) the Name of the Lord our God." (Psalm 20:7) The prophet Jeremiah also laid this problem out very clearly when he said, "Cursed is the man who trusts in man and makes the flesh (men, armies, weapons and the world system) his strength, whose heart departs from the Lord. For he shall be like a shrub in the desert and shall not see when good comes, but shall inhabit the parched places in the wilderness, in a salt land which is not inhabited." (Jeremiah 17:5–6) Their whole life is dying, falling apart and drying up like a sun-scorched weed in the desert. Every time they trust

more in man, their heart departs a little more from the Lord. But, on the other hand he goes on to say, "Blessed is the man who trusts in the Lord and whose hope is in the Lord. For he shall be like a tree planted by the waters, which spreads out its roots by the river and will not fear when heat (or a battle) comes; but its leaf will be green, and will not be anxious in the year of drought, nor will cease from yielding fruit." Jeremiah 17:7–8

There is only one place for any man to get this kind of courage. We find it in the first chapter of Joshua, where the Lord gave this command three times: "be strong and of good courage." But how can we do it? He goes on to tell us: "Only be strong and very courageous that you may observe to do according to all the law which Moses my servant commanded you; do not turn from it to the right hand or the left, that you may prosper wherever you go. This Book of the Law (the Bible) shall not depart from your mouth, but you shall meditate in it day and night, that you may observe to do according to all that is written in it. For then you will make your way prosperous and then you will have good success. Be strong and of good courage; do not be afraid, nor be dismayed, for the Lord your God is with you wherever you go." Joshua 1:6–9

In this chapter God made believers several incredible promises. You won't find a book anywhere else in all the world that will make you promises like these: First, every place the sole of their foot might tread, He would give it to them. (v.3) No man could stand before them all the days of their life. (v.5) They would prosper wherever they went. (v.7) He would make their way prosperous and give them good success. (v.8) And, finally, the best one: the Lord their God would be with them wherever they went. (v.9) I think everyone would agree that these are powerful promises and they are from the God of the Universe. They are for you and me as believers and they are for today.

There is, however, one stipulation. There is one thing we must do. The only place we can obtain this kind of wisdom, power and courage is from reading the Bible and meditating on it day and night. Of course no man could devote every waking moment to reading God's Word but we can read and study it daily. We can, however, fall in love with the greatest Book that has ever been written. We can memorize portions of it that pertain to our daily walk and then think about these passages while we work and travel about. We can keep them on the frontlets of our minds and refuse to let anything but the words of this Book come out of our mouths.

Some might say this is just a bunch of words from some dusty, two thousand year old book. Well, I can tell you from the experiences of a lifetime, that there will be many times we will have need of courage, not the least of which is in war. And having been in a war, I can tell you that this will not only work, it is the only thing that will work.

Our family has had a long succession of soldiers, sailors and airmen. A great grandfather, two great uncles, several uncles, my dad and my older brother all preceded me in the military beginning with the Civil War. My viewpoint in the Vietnam War was not from the rear echelons counting and issuing sox but on the front lines, leading rifle companies. Losing one American soldier in a war is way too many but by comparison, we have now lost over two thousand in Afghanistan but we had 58,000 killed in Vietnam. So it was a war. I also had the privilege of being assigned to the First Air Cavalry Division, which was the only airmobile unit in Vietnam. We were simply the only division equipped with sufficient air assets to move our units strategically by helicopter. Every time Division Intelligence would locate the enemy, they would pick up usually a company of men and insert us by helicopters into an open field right in the vicinity of the enemy. Other infantry units would travel toward the objectives assigned to them, breaking brush and whacking through wait-a-minute vines with their machete's in the jungle, at best, at about one mile per hour. By the time they got there, unless it was a supply base, the bad guys were usually gone. We moved toward our targets on helicopters immediately, at about ninety miles per hour, and there was usually somebody waiting when we got there. Only problem was, we couldn't get them to leave a light on for us.

Our sole mission on the front lines then and forever in the Infantry, was to close with and destroy the enemy. That interpreted means we were to daily find, engage and combat assault directly into the face of the enemy's full physical strength and fire power—and that without even a flak jacket. Although Kevlar was invented in the mid-sixties, they had not adapted for its current body armor use until the late 1970's. Because we were in contact with the enemy so much more than any of the other divisions in Vietnam, it comes as no surprise that we had the most enemy KIA's (killed in action). However, the increased enemy contact meant that we, as a division, also had the most friendly KIA'a as well. Thank God my companies had very few friendly KIA's but we had some. All we had for weapons most of the time was our small arms (M-16's), a few machine guns, hand grenades, some M-79 grenade launchers, a few LAW's (a light anti-tank weapons similar to a bazooka) and a mortar. Of course we could call in artillery and aerial fire support (cobra gunships and jets) but it was, oftentimes, a little late getting there in a jungle warfare situation. Now I'm not complaining. I volunteered for the Infantry, Vietnam, the First Cavalry Division and to be a company commander twice. I have absolutely no regrets and only gratitude for the opportunity to serve my country, help protect my neighbors, our allies, freedoms and way of life.

In combat situations, where both sides are equipped with automatic weapons, all kinds of high-explosives and trained for warfare, when they meet on the battle field, there will, as you might imagine, be some friction. The exhilaration of mortal combat gives you an adrenaline rush like nothing else, every time. There just happens to be several types of fear all men experience in life and a couple of them are actually positive. One is the fear of impending danger because, without it, we would not respond correctly to life-threatening situations. Everyone gets a bit scared in these situations and I was certainly no different. Some can manage that fear and some can't. What gave me strength during this time was something

I didn't expect. It was the scriptures I had to memorize when I was a kid in Presbyterian Church School for a number of years when we lived in Savannah, Georgia. But, don't think my parents sent me there to prepare for the ministry. That wasn't it at all. They sent me there because I had already gotten into so much trouble in kindergarten and the first grade that they didn't think I would ever make it in public school. I just barely made it in that Christian school.

Another source of courage was our family motto handed down from our ancestors in Scotland which says in old English: "Vil God I Zal." I believed in it so much that I had it engraved on the Randall fighting knife I bought and took with me into every battle. In today's vernacular the phrase means, If it is God's will, I will. Whatever He leads you to do, regardless of what type of trial or conflict it might be, if it is His will for you to prevail, you will. We know, "The battle is the Lord's." (I Samuel 17:47) and, "thanks be to God who always leads us (to) triumph in Christ …" (II Corinthians 2:14) Although I did believe in God back then, I was about as crude as any soldier but because I believed, He granted me mercy and was still my strength. I knew I would only make it through each battle by His will and grace. Though men died and were wounded all around me from time-to-time, I never got a scratch. This was absolutely no credit to me and any skill or ability that I might have had at the time but all to Him. Praise Him! He, alone, gave me the courage to do some of the things, I knew my men didn't want to do. There are some things a leader must do so that the men will know that you would never ask them to do anything you wouldn't do yourself. That's just how it works out in the real world.

Menzies Clan Seal

I wish I could tell you that I always knew what to do in every battle but I didn't. My men always thought I did but that wasn't always the case. The fog of war is such that you, as the commander, rarely ever know exactly what you are up against—especially in jungle warfare where you can't see more than ten to, at best, thirty feet in front of you. I just had to formulate the best plan I could with the limited information available and act on it. You couldn't just let your men sit there and get pounded by the enemy. They felt much better doing something constructive, executing a plan of attack they hoped would work and amazingly, it always did. Good thing God helped us. I truly believe that no leader has ever won a battle that God didn't allow him to. We men do what we can and might even give it hell but it all still rests in His able hands.

This world is in terrible shape today and has always been a mess. People out there are forever looking for a man to lead them. Thomas Jefferson told it truly when he said, "One man with courage is a majority." The world is looking for someone who is not afraid of anything. Someone who can face death, tragedy, betrayal, financial reversal, hardship and overwhelming odds and charge directly in the middle of it with humility and great trust in God. Meditating the Word will actually make you start feeling like David who said, "… by You (Lord) I can run through a troop (and) by my God I can leap over a wall." (Psalm 18:29) Now a troop is a number of soldiers, at least sixty to a hundred or more. David was, indeed, fearless; the reason being, God had made him some promises (you and me as well) and he knew that the enemy couldn't kill him before those promises were fulfilled. He also knew, that they couldn't take him out until they killed God first because the Lord was his protection. There is no way they could kill Him. Our God will protect us against great foes (Judges 7:7–23), great odds (I Samuel 17:32,50), when threatened (Daniel 3:16–18), in every moral crisis (Nehemiah 13:1–31, when facing death (Judges 16:28), before kings and presidents (Esther 4:8), in youth (I Samuel 14:6–45), in old age (Joshua 14:10–12) and certainly among our enemies. Ezra 5:11

Meditating on the Bible will, among other things, cause you to know God and understand His ways. Not only will you know the Word but you will know God too. In addition, we are assured that "People who know their God shall be strong and do exploits." (Daniel 11:32) They will be fearless and God, Himself, will call on them to go on important and sometimes dangerous assignments.

In life there will always be huge problems, conflicts and wars. Education, training, goal setting and the like are all great but never enough. One must have the courage to act. It is only by action that goals, plans, beliefs and desires can be turned into victory and accomplishment. It always takes courage to act because there is danger at every hand and critics galore just waiting to Monday morning quarterback your every decision. Let them. All the problems of life become much smaller if you don't try to dodge them but, instead, hit them head-on. They tend to crumble before your very eyes. The best defense has always been a good offense. Failure to act has never won a battle, has its own grave consequences and is truly just cowardice in the face of the enemy. Faith, on the other hand, is not just believing something in spite of the evidence. It is having the courage to act regardless of the consequences, throwing fear to the wind; knowing that God will surely give you the victory.

What it means to have the character trait of **COURAGE:**

- The moral and mental capacity to venture out into danger, difficulty, unfamiliar situations or mammoth projects
- The ability to persevere while under siege
- Fearlessness in the face of death, danger or difficulty
- The ability to overcome fear in the face of danger
- The intestinal fortitude to venture out into the unknown
- Brave
- Resolute
- Tenacious
- Able to withstand the continued mental and physical stress, constant unrelenting attacks and possibly even a lack of adequate resources outside of one's self, to meet the opposition
- The mettle ingrained in a person giving them the ability to get up and keep going when knocked down
- Total trust in God

OURTESY —   **Study start date:** _____ **Finish date:** _____

We, human beings, will never stop being just that, as long as we continue to take up space, breath in the oxygen and consume groceries here. We all have feelings and emotions, though subdued at times, which are still there and the little things people do or fail to do affect us. It will always be in order to be courteous to our fellow humans. Noble men treat all men well—especially the weak, handicapped and those under their authority. In the harsh world of business, politics, war and family relations we see today, courtesy, appropriately and sincerely given, is always appreciated and it never goes unnoticed. One can never get too rich, powerful or important to outgrow using words like "please" and "thank you." Courtesy and kindness are kissin' cousins. The lower a person's station may presently be in life, the more they notice the kindness and courtesy you willingly and sincerely extend to them. Sooner or later, a person will actually not only be known but also be remembered by how they treat those around them.

The Apostle Paul gave some sage advice to the Romans,. He said to "Be of the same mind toward one another." (Romans !2:!6) Treat all people alike. Don't pander to the powerful. Be courteous to everyone. In other words don't be haughty or arrogant. "Do not set your mind on high things …" Don't be the vainglorious type seeking high positions, the spotlight or the preeminent seat. All tasks in society are important. If you don't think the garbage collectors are important, let them go on strike for a few weeks and see how essential they are. Do your work with excellence all the while gaining knowledge and improving your character. Forget yourself and the future will take care of itself. Make sure there is no position too lowly. Practice this by doing menial tasks like carrying out your own trash at the office and that of the family at home. Work alongside your employees. Fill a few sandbags every now and then if that is what the troops are doing. Drive some nails and frame a few walls if you have a construction project going. Paul instructed us to " … Condescend to men of low estate." Associate with the humble people of society. Let there never be anyone who is not good enough to be your friend, considering others better than yourself. Regardless of their temporary position in life, their function is just as important as anyone else in the grand scheme of things. In the church, for example, every member is part of the Body of Christ. The foot is no more important than the eye or the elbow. We need to visit those in prison as well as the widow and the orphan. Finally, Paul said, "Do not be wise in your own opinion." There is too much to learn and we can learn something from everyone. Everyone and I mean everyone, knows something we don't know. Everyone has been some place we haven't been and everyone can do something better than we can. Someone said that "Ignorance is a consequence of being human but not knowing it is even more atrocious." We are all ignorant when it comes to the whole body of information there in the world today and can learn so much if we have a mind to. Common courtesy is always humble, polite and sincere. Acting as if we know more than anyone else is arrogant, prideful and conceited, the antithesis of true courtesy.

Ways to show courtesy are innumerable and most don't take much time. Things like remembering a friends birthdays by sending a card or giving them a phone call on their special day. Yours would possibly be one of only a very few cards or phone calls most people get. Take the time and make the effort to remember other peoples' names and use their name when talking to them. Make eye contact when speaking and, if possible, stop what you are doing and give them your undivided attention. Show them by your actions and attentiveness that you count them as a person of worth. Occasionally you might want to thank them for sharing their friendship with you and for meaning so much to you over the years. Perhaps you could buy them a really special gift. They will never forget it and will appreciate it for the rest of their lives.

In order to display courtesy, it is important to always smile when you meet people or greet them for the first time each day. If you don't smile, you will lose easily 90% of your influence with that person immediately. Not smiling will seriously damage your relationship. Aside from that, the offended party will usually make a mental note of the offense and could make a small-scale inquisition about why you are so unhappy in the future. They might be thinking, "What in the world is bothering this person who still hasn't learned how critically important it is to smile?"

When I think of smiling, my mind always goes to a business owner I know who was a little league coach for one of my sons. He naturally smiles all the time, which makes him a very pleasant person to be around. He certainly gets all my business in his chosen field, I also have a freedom to recommend him to my friends. I'm confident that using his services will be a pleasant experience for them. It is always a good idea to smile and act as if you are on top of the world even if you're not.

Truly, the people around us are the most important people in the world. People are more important than policy, products, plans, programs or promotions. Without the people in our lives, we really are nothing and have nothing. We are indebted to everyone we deal with every day. The people around us, our peers and those under our authority have tremendous influence on what we are able to accomplish and how far we go in life. Unsolicited letters of recommendation from peers and followers in business and in the military are one of the most powerful contributors to one's success.

Most good hotels even have courtier departments set up solely to treat their customers with courtesy, as nobility. They give them access to important information about the locale, tickets to plays, ball games, etc. not generally available to the public. All as a courtesy. All to show their customers how really special they are and how much they mean to the business they are trying to operate.

Be courteous. It is one of the really special joys of life you possess and that only you can give.

What it means to have the character trait of **COURTESY:**

- Polite, sincere, honoring behavior
- Considerations given those in high office
- Expressions of gentle, kind and noble communication
- Being considerate of others and appreciative of their assistance in both the smallest and largest things
- Giving consideration and appreciation of others in spite, sometimes, of the facts
- Overlooking the obvious shortcomings or failings of others from time-to-time and being kind anyway

REATIVITY—   **Study start date: _____ Finish date: _____**

S ince most of us didn't graduate from the school of trust funds, nor were handed everything as a member of the privileged class in life, learning the art of how to take little and make something, being creative, is very important. No question about it, my favorite movie over the years yet remains *Cool Hand Luke* and, the best scene in it was the infamous poker game. Paul Newman ("Luke" in the movie) slowly kept increasing his bets, tricking the other players to go a little more and a little bit more until he had them nearly betting the whole ranch. One-by-one the others folded thinking Newman really had something. The pressure was just too great for the last one as well and, finally, he folded. Then George Kennedy ("Dragline" in the movie) who was coaching the other players trying to beat Newman cried, clamored, cajoled, caviled and complained incessantly, trying to get him to show his hand. So, finally he laid his cards face-down, nonchalantly on the table and raked in the pot. Kennedy couldn't get to his cards quickly enough to turn them over only to find that he had—absolutely nothing! Not Jack! I mean nothing! Kennedy got so melodramatic in all his complaints, that Newman reluctantly explained his concept of winning saying, "Sometimes nothing can be a real cool hand."

That, now, is exactly the hand most of us drew with our first breath in this world. No genius, no rich parents and no special talent. My teachers could tell after the first, second and the third grade that I wasn't going to make Einstein mover over even an inch. And, if that wasn't problem enough, I was constantly in all kinds of trouble. My dad said, "Son, if you don't change your ways, they're going to put you so far back in prison, they'll have to air mail your lunch to you!" But, you know what? We aren't getting another hand in life. We're going to have to learn to deal with the one we've got. What was Cool Hand Luke's problem? Was it that he didn't have enough talent? No, he could speak, sing, fight and cut off the heads of parking meters real well. Was it that his mother didn't love him? No. She loved him so much over her lifetime, she felt sad when she had to give the home place to his brother, John, just before she died. Was it that he didn't have enough personality? No, everybody loved him—all the inmates, even the Captain (who was the warden) and all the guards. Was it that he didn't have enough determination? No, neither the enemy in war nor Drag-line in a prison fight could beat the determination out of him. The Captain, making him dig pits in the yard and days on end in "the box" couldn't break him. Neither the prison's barbed wire nor their chains could hold him. So what was it? Well, I believe the Captain had it right. What he had there was "a failure to communicate." Luke had the talent, the determination, the personality and the skills, he just didn't know how to communicate it to the world. Something all of us have had a problem with from time-to-time. So the real question for all of is, what can we do with the hand we were dealt in life to make it a winner for us, God and society in general? How can we find and communicate our little bit of talent in a meaningful way to the world?

Creativity might just be the answer. This is simply the ability to take nothing or very little and make something. It is a wonderful trait to develop and can be exercised in just about any field: the building business, the service industry, inventing, the military, politics and virtually anything you want to name. Many things in nature and society are replicated a billion times. Life is often so routine and mundane. So, it is a pleasant surprise when something new and creative comes along. Let's look at a few industries and areas where I have seen creativity work. .

In the building business you can take old houses that the owners consider obsolete, get their permission to tear them down (saving them the cost of demolition, transportation and dump fees, they will give them to you) and save the materials to build a house of your own. All you will have in all the material is some sweat, labor and some of your free time. Young people have a whole lot more free time than they have money for some reason. You can also go to the manufacturers of building materials and ask to buy their "seconds." This would be the products that came off the assembly line that weren't exactly perfect. They may be dented or scratched or otherwise not quite up to specs but plenty good for your home and can be purchased for pennies on the dollar. With a little discipline, a savings program, a plan, some knowhow and a vision, a person can build their own home—very inexpensively. My book and CD series, *How to Build a Debt-free Home* explains in detail how to accomplish this. What a blessing it is to help people avoid the curse of crushing life-time financial debt and bondage by enabling them to own their own home debt-free. What do you need? Very little. Just the ability to learn, some spare time and the willingness to sweat for few years along with some determination. But, what an accomplishment! To own your own home one day—debt free!

With so many inventions and systems already in use by society, few today have the boldness or courage to even consider trying to make a better mouse trap. Most men choose to dutifully get in the vanilla line for fear of being criticized by others for trying something new. Many others are so afraid to fail, they won't try anything new or creative. They just can't stand criticism and shutter for fear of being called a failure for trying. I tell my employees, "If you never make any mistakes, I'm going to fire you." In my mind, if they aren't ever making any mistakes, they are not doing much because everybody that's a "doer" is certain to make mistakes occasionally. When Thomas Edison tried 6,000 times to make a light bulb that didn't seem to work, he, too, was criticized by someone for his many failures. His response: "No, I succeeded in finding 6,000 ways not to make a light bulb before I found the right one."

In the area of real estate sales, one must decide early-on who they are going to represent. Are they going to work for themselves and burn both ends of the candle to get their brokerage fee or are they truly going to represent the seller, their employer, and do what is best for him? If you serve people, have a servant's heart and truly do your best by them, you don't have to worry, in this wicked world—they will notice. The moniker I put on our cards at my company, Creative Realty, Inc., was this: "Creativity in real estate stems from a sincere interest in solving the client's problem or filling his need. It manifests itself in service when attitude is coupled with experience, education and enthusiasm." What a joy to apply all your experience, knowledge and expertise to a client's real estate to make it worth more so you can get them the highest possible price in the market. Starting out with nothing, not knowing the players or having any product, sincerity in service resulted in virtual market dominance and a staff of eight brokers working in the commercial real estate business in about seven years. Thanks be to God! I would still be working in commercial real estate today if the Lord hadn't called me into the ministry.

In the residential real estate business, the problem I found was that people were building boxes that had little or no pizzazz. Builders were afraid to be imaginative or creative—just building the same old unexciting house over and over. My company, Creative Plan Service, designed and sold plans that had vaulted ceilings, rustic fireplaces, exposed cedar beam ceilings, clear story windows, sky lights, sunken great rooms and bonus rooms. We also had some killer energy packages that added very little to the cost of the home but paid serious dividends to the home owner in lower operational costs year after year.

The Bible illustrates the importance of creativity very well in the Parable of the Talents. In it, when the Master planned to leave the country for a time, he called ten of this servants in and gave each one of them ten minas (each was equivalent to only about twenty dollars). Then he told them to "Do business until I come." (Luke 19:13) This had to mean trading because when he returned he wanted to know "how much every man had gained by trading." (v.15) You see God made the universe, the world and everything it and then he told us the best business to be in on this planet is (drum roll here): trading. Profits are far better than hourly wages. It is so easy to get in the car business buying used cars at the auto auction barn (that sells to the public—some only sell to dealers). Oh, it takes a while to get used to the auctioneer's chatter but it is a huge opportunity to take a little and make much. We have had a ministry called Cars For Christ ® for years and I have written a book full of tips called *How to Buy a Used Car*. Most people don't realize it but they will buy, on the average, twelve cars in their life time. Say they marry and have two kids. That is forty-eight cars they will be buying in a life time. But, most people have several cars, a pickup, a boat and a project car. So becoming skilled at buying used cars (we aren't even going to talk about the insanity of buying a new one) is something we all need to learn for a whole host of reasons. Anyone who expects to buy 48 cars in a lifetime needs to be good at it.

How well does it work to be creative in life? As I was writing this, I took a walk into the living room to pet my dog, Ranger, and see my lovely wife. She just happened to be watching Home Shopping Network (HSN) on TV. Wolfgang Puck, a great chef, had recently invented a small, two pot pie cooker that makes a couple pot pies from either fruits, meat or left overs in six minutes. No, I wasn't really interested but my wife said "They sold completely out of the pressure cooker I bought yesterday and I'm sure glad I got mine when I did (just yesterday)." Hey, she was glad this guy sold her a pressure cooker she didn't have to worry about blowing up like a bomb and I am always happy when she makes us some really good food with it. You see, we like inventors and marketers. They make our lives better. We like the capitalistic system of free enterprise. Now, back to the two pot pie cooker, the lady then went on to say, "We have already sold 156,000 of these today." Just a creative idea. Nothing much new about a pot pie but Wolfgang Puck figured out how to make two small ones—fast—out of leftovers

Find something people need that will help them make their daily lives easier. You too can make a new widget, gadget or gizmo and sell it. You will be mightily blessed, hopefully, so you can be a blessing for God and a lost and dying world. Do an infomercial on TV and you will sell a gazillion of them. I heard an interview recently with the guy who started the infomercial industry the other day and you might be interested to know he has only made a little over

Front cover of our house plan catalog

four billion dollars—just making short commercials on TV and selling other peoples' creative ideas. Not bad for a guy who started out a po boy.

Creativity is all around us if we will just open our eyes. It just so happened that I was over to see a friend, Clarence Hall, today about something. He was actually the one who recruited me to join the Jaycees forty years ago and we have been fast friends ever since. Although he is a builder, the visit was not about him building anything for me. He has, to his credit, however, built over seven hundred homes and the last twenty years it has been all commercial, industrial and apartment construction work. Since we have been friends so long and mind you I never even brought up the subject of creativity or inventions during the conversation, but just as I was leaving, he said "Let me show you one of my little projects. I want see what you think about it." He had made and patented a small device to go on the end of an electrician's fish tape so they could run wires through conduit and turn corners without getting the tape stuck along the way. It was amazingly simple, inexpensive and quite ingenious. No doubt, if you are an electrician, you will soon be buying one. This man has been faithful to the Lord in many ways and I believe the Lord gave him this creative idea to bless him so he can bless others.

In the military, every war is different. The enemy, their tactics and weapons are different. The terrain and the foliage is different. The mission, likewise, is politically driven and it, too, is always different. In Vietnam, we were fighting an insurgency that moved, fought and transported their resupplies mostly at night. Since we had air superiority, they had to move under cover of both darkness and triple-canopy foliage. Our soldiers moved in the day-time and needed their sleep to be at peak performance the next day so we couldn't have them awake all night on ambushes along the Viet Cong's trails. Besides, our G.I's, in those days, liked to smoke, use mosquito repellant and shoot the bull. None of that is permissible on an ambush because, you guessed it, these things give away your location and will, in fact, compromise your ambush. Having studied a little about electronics and circuitry in college and having had a little experience dynamiting rock to put in a water line for a city in west Texas during the summer while in college, I designed what we called an automatic ambush. We did it with some commo wire, det cord, a spring, bailing wire, a few blasting caps, some claymore mines and a common, PRC-10 radio battery. We strung a spring-loaded wire across the path the enemy was likely to travel at night and rigged it to ground out the electrical circuit if the enemy either walked through the wire (increased the tension on it) or if they actually discovered the wire and cut it with a pair of pliers (thus decreasing the tension on it). If tampered with in any way, the circuit was completed and that would detonate the blasting caps in all the claymore mines. These above-ground mines were hidden in the bushes and when detonated would spray the path in both direction with thousands of ball bearings. It worked like a champ. My guys were able to stay in the relative safety of the NDP (Night Defensive Position) all night and get plenty of rest while they listened for these claymores blowing up in the night. The next morning we'd go out and police up the enemy bodies, weapons and ammo. We never had one of our soldiers wounded or killed with these devices. Now the enemy, well, there were literally hundreds we gave the opportunity to die for their country. It was either them or us and I was there to see to it our side and our country won. Thank God for a little creative idea. As leaders, we need to think and come up with ideas that will improve the lives of our people.

French President Charles De Gaulle was such a man. He fought as an Infantry officer in World War I until he was finally wounded and taken prisoner for the rest of the war. Released after the armistice, he rejoined his regiment. Later he was summoned to a staff job and then served in the army occupying the Rhineland. He was then reassigned to Lebanon and finally returned to Paris in 1931. During this time he wrote several books like *Edge of the Sword, Army of the Future* and *France and Her Army*. These writings revealed his intellectual and literary capabilities but actually got him crossed up with the staid, orthodox, military opinions of the army's leadership of the day. His strategy promoted the use of fast moving tanks and aircraft instead of the immobility of fixed fortifications like the berms, steel and concrete barriers and bunkers of the Maginot Line. This antiquated system of warfare later failed miserably at the feet of the German Blitzkrieg which meant "lightning warfare." Their strategy consisted of tanks and planes with the capability of speed, surprise and tremendous firepower.

In World War II, De Gaulle was promoted to Colonel and commanded a tank brigade. Soon he was made a brigadier general, commanding the only partially-formed 4th Armored Division. Later he was appointed to his first political position as undersecretary of state for war. In that capacity he conferred twice about strategy with Winston Churchill in London. However, when the then-current French leadership pressed for an armistice with Hitler, De Gaulle immediately departed to London and on June 18, 1940 made his famous radio appeal for the French continue their fight, putting himself at the head of the new Free French movement. Shortly thereafter, on July 7, 1940, a French court-martial tried him in abstention and sentenced him to death. When World II began, he remained the symbol of the French resistance to German occupation and an unflinching ally of the Western and Allied powers. Although his political career had many ups and downs, De Gaulle became President of France and then retired only to be elected President again later because he was, seemingly, the only political figure capable of inspiring the confidence of the people. At one point, he gave young leaders some sage advice with these words: "The leader must show that he has vision (creative ideas), act on a grand scale and thereby establish his authority over the generality of men who splash about in shallow waters." Coincidentally, today's Atlanta Journal-Constitution, August 18, 2013, has a headline for an article about an issue currently facing our city. It was a quote by Atlanta Mayor Kasim Reed saying, "We need a creative solution" for the new Atlanta Falcon football stadium. What do we need as a city? A creative solution. Politics is always in need of creative solutions—always has—and always will.

However, I believe, far and away, the best job in the world is to be a fisher of men. Jesus said, "Come, follow Me and I will make you a fishers of men." (Mark 4:19) You don't have to worry about it. You don't have to wrestle with it. Just believe, follow Him, seek Him, learn of Him because it is then something He will make you automatically. You will be his workmanship. You will, in fact, become a soul winner. It is not so much something you will do, although you will do it, it is something you will be. Know this, there is no greater joy in all of life than that of being a fisher and builder of men.

God will supply the creativity just as he has for our ministry. The Spirit has led us to take the gospel to those who are hungry and hurting in the prisons, jails and Youth Detention Centers. We have taken a platform trailer to downtown Atlanta and used free clothes, bags of potato chips, our gospel music band and open-air preaching to win many of those who are homeless and destitute to Christ. That coupled with one-on-one evangelism, handing out New Testaments and giving sandwiches to the homeless and the Lord's help usually provided salvation for anywhere from twenty to two hundred souls on a Saturday each month. The one prison meeting the Lord gave us grew at His hand into 125 each month at one point. He also added a good band of excellent preachers who help us preach these services across north Georgia. The Lord has led us to build the Shepherd's House to house and disciple troubled youth and young men, two Shepherd's Stores (thrift stores), Manna Ministries (a food for the poor ministry), a free Job bank, Cars For Christ ® a car donation ministry and a church—all from virtually nothing. We have benefited from the Lord's wisdom, power, creativity and favor. The battle has been His over these past twenty-five years but the victory has been ours (His gift). We can take no credit because it was really all God's work and it all started with virtually nothing but His calling. What does it prove? Just that God will supply fresh ideas, new concepts and creative wisdom to those willing to be available for His use.

What it means to have the character trait of **CREATIVITY**:

- Distinguished by the ability to create
- The ability to take very little or what others consider refuse and make something
- Being productive in virtually any environment or set of circumstances
- Guided by intuition, inspiration and fearless experimentation
- Able to create something that is new rather than simply imitate
- The ability to birth something into being or cause it to exist
- The ability to produce with one's imagination and skill
- Being bold enough to be imaginative and inventive
- One who moves in the future by inventing new concepts, approaches, systems, services and products
- The ability to think outside the box

- The ability to observe what others have seen for years and see something completely new and different
- The audacity to challenge the status quo in any field, service, product or system by making new things
- The ability to put several ideas together to make a distinctively new concept, product or approach
- The ability to take things made especially for one use and tailor or adapt them to fill a current need you may have in a totally different application
- Motivated by a sincere desire to serve others and to be a wise manager of God's resources
- The ability to make things and situations work in life that wouldn't ordinarily by using unique combination of things and systems
- The ability to see things from a new perspective

ECISIVENESS—   **Study start date:** _____ **Finish date:** _____

In the fast moving world we live in, being slow, timid and indecisive will ruin a leader. If you stand still in either the thoroughfares of the physical world or those of the business world, you will be run over by a truck, car, a new concept or a new regime. In such a fast moving world, few things are harder to live with than an indecisive, hesitant, fearful, slow-to-act leader. Though most things out in the world give the appearance of being etched in stone, *everything* is really in a constant state of flux. Nothing stays the same. Politically, the pendulum is always swinging from one extreme to another. New products are always making the old standbys obsolete. The old guard is going out and the new regime is coming in to take their place.

Certainly, the prudent man takes the time, if he has that luxury, to gather the facts and seek wise counsel. Once he has the latest and best available information, he can then make a timely, hopefully, wise decision. Decisiveness comes from the conviction that one has already sought counsel, researched the subject and has written down all the advantages and disadvantages of each possible course of action. It makes it so much easier as a leader to make decisions when he know that he gets paid, not to know everything or be right every time, but to make wise, calculated, informed and timely decisions. In life decisions cannot be avoided and neither can a few mistakes. Remember, a great medical doctor is only right about sixty percent of the time. Fear of making the wrong decision is what makes people indecisive. Don't worry. You will occasionally make mistakes but when you have done your homework, they will be rare indeed.

Oftentimes we find ourselves in situations, whether in business or in a battle, that are quite nebulas and difficult to discern. Because of the fog of war, one never really knows all the facts about the enemy or their plans but, when attacked, you, as leader, must quickly develop a plan and execute. Battles, for the most part, are never elegant things of beauty. They are, for the most part, just managed chaos; so any plan is better than no plan. The troops feel better occupying their minds, working in unison doing something that they hope will work. The alternative is just having them sit there getting pounded by the enemy's firepower. Who knows? What you decided with all your education and experience just might work! Especially with God's help.

Years ago, Australian philosopher Basil Kinn said, "Be bold and great forces will come to your aid." Only a steadily increasing diet of trouble comes to the hesitating leader. Decisions, made quickly but judiciously we find, transform into energy like knowledge turns into power. Indecision is anathema to just about everything, especially the victory. A rhyme I heard years ago about the fretful and fearful, was a dialogue between a couple of our fine feathered friends: "Said the Robin to the Sparrow, 'I think that I should like to know, why these anxious human beings rush around and worry so?' Said the Sparrow to the Robin, "I think that it must be that they have no Heavenly Father such as cares for you and me." Author unknown

In life we should never be afraid to take a bold leap if the situation seems to warrant it. You can't, after all, get across a wide chasm with two or three leaps when one is all you get. Be bold. Take the leap. Having goals, a good plan, and an understanding of the situation and our enemy are all important but never enough. One must have the courage to act. There are always risks with every decision. It is only by action that our goals, beliefs, passions, plans and dreams translate into success. Admiral William F. Halsey's personal motto was a quotation from Nelson: "'No Captain can do very wrong if he places his ship alongside that of an enemy... . The best defense is a strong offense, is a military principle,' said

Halsey, 'but its application is wider than war. All problems, personal, national, or combat, become smaller if you don't dodge them, but rather confront them. Touch a thistle timidly, and it pricks you; grasp it boldly and its spines crumble.'" [8] Someone once said that "Faith is not believing something in spite of the evidence. It is the courage to do something regardless of the consequences."

When Jesus found the money changers and those who sold oxen, sheep and doves for sacrifices inside the temple, he didn't call a committee, make a survey of public opinion or make a request for them to stop this practice through numerous different channels and methods. He made a whip out of some cords, turned over all the moneychangers, tables and drove them out post haste. Then he told them to "Take these things away! Do not make my Father's House a house of merchandise." (John 2:16) He made a decision and rectified the situation immediately.

Some people are cosmically confused in the face of challenges and adversity. A leader who is always hesitant, dithering, always reviewing his options while the ship is under attack, is quickly despised by those around him. A leader, just can't be timid in the decision making department. No matter what you do, realize that you will always be criticized. Even if you make good, timely decisions and even if you make the right decisions, you will never escape criticism in this world. Just accept it. You cannot please everybody. If you are throwing corn out to the chickens with your left hand, someone will always be there to say you should be doing that with you right hand. Then again, if you are feeding them with your right hand, there will be those who will say, you should be doing that with your left. Don't worry about it, just make the best decisions you can. Your track record over time will speak for itself. Tell the detractors the dogs might be barking till the cows come in but the train is still leaving town on time. However, without a doubt, the wisest thing to do when we are confronted with a challenge is to forget all the post mortems and quickly thank God for trusting us to handle it. Then give the problem back to Him and get about gathering the facts and asking Him for wisdom. With His help, make a wise, prudent and timely decision. Life is good for those who are decisive.

What it means to have the character trait of **DECISIVENESS:**

- Marked by the courage to make decisions regardless of the consequences
- A willingness to make decisions that one hopes will turn out well but, if not, it is knowing that the decision was based on the best information, counsel and analysis possible. It was the best decision that could have been made at the time and there is nothing to be concerned, worried, fearful or regretful about – come what may.
- Being resolute
- Having the strength of one's convictions with no fear of being wrong. If we are going to make a lot of decisions, as leaders must, we are just going to get a few wrong. . Sometimes the world system does the wrong thing, causing even the right decision not to work out but it will still be pleasing to the Lord. So it is the freedom on the occasion of a reversal to be able to say to yourself, "It matters not—I did my best."
- Firmness and speed in making deliberate decisions

EFERENCE—   **Study start date: _____ Finish date: _____**

It is so easy for most of us and especially young people, to be so taken with our own desires, ideas and ways of doing things, that we think our way is undoubtedly best. This is because we are all human beings and, regardless of the situation or circumstance, we all have developed our own ideas and ways of handling things. However, ours just might, perish the thought, not be the best way ever discovered on earth. It is also well to remember that every plan, approach or idea, no matter how plausible, has both advantages and disadvantages.

Over the course of time, almost everyone has been so taken with their own ideas that they think they are the only ones who are right or that their idea is the closest to it. They want to do their job, for example, the way they see it and not the way the supervisor assigned it. This, as we know, can lead to many problems, not the least of which is the possibility of the immediate loss of employment. This is especially true for those who seem to abound in their own, exaggerated sense of self-worth, emanating from unfounded feelings of superiority. In actuality, they are probably just proud, puffed-up, inflexible, self-centered and stubborn. These are the ones who have the most difficult time obeying instructions. They are rarely willing to ask for advice, much less take it.

Keep in mind now that there may be several reasons for those over us requiring work to be done a certain way. We may not be privy to these reasons and they may not all make sense to us at the moment. For example:

- The one in authority may be requiring something be done in an unusual manner that the Board of Directors, his superiors, are requiring.
- The job assigned might have to dove-tail with a task someone else is doing.
- The job might have to meet certain specifications set by the engineering department, the government or the purchaser's contract with the company, any one of which may stipulate other than what seems to be expedient or even reasonable.
- It could also be that the supervisor wants it a certain way because he has thirty years of successful experience doing it his way and is confidence it will work.
- The supervisors' way may take advantage of existing machinery, software, equipment, or inexpensive supplies already in inventory.

Nevertheless, it really doesn't matter in an employment situation. The one in charge is the one in charge and has the right to expect things done the way he wants. He has more than likely paid the price in terms of time, hard work and obedience to attain the position and the owners or directors of the organization think he is best able to guide the company successfully. When we are put in charge, we can certainly do things our way if we like. Possibly the fastest way to attain this position is by being obedient to carry out our instructions effectively and efficiently with a good attitude. Hopefully, when we do actually become the one in authority, we will seek input and advice from those around us and will try to be a solution provider to everyone we can.

Our objective, as an employee, is to be loyal and the best follower possible. High maintenance employees are usually the first to go in an economic down-turn. We should not only defer to our employer on procedure but also on unimportant issues like carpet color, who gets what office, etc. Never go to war over trivial matters. A large part of loyalty in any position is the ability to follow the supervisor's lead.

It is well to remember, the only reason we have a job is because his superiors think he has too much to do and needs additional help. If that were not the case, we would very likely not even be in the equation. So we are to be just that, a help to our employer, not a hindrance. It should be our goal as an employee to learn how to be the best follower possible and to make our supervisor's job easier, as well as to make the company a success. When we advance these goals and forget self, we will see great rewards.

An example of the importance of all this occurred when I was in the commercial real estate business selling a lot of problem properties owned by a large bank in the Atlanta area. The vice president I worked with was fairly knowledgeable about real estate and had been with the bank in this particular capacity for a number of years. After we had been working together for a good while, he felt a freedom to share his heart about how things were going there at the bank. On one occasion, he was particularly upset saying, "My boss is trying to tell me how to do **my** job!" Right there, a red flag was raised in my mind and I thought to myself, this man has had a long and productive career here and, unless he has a change of thought patterns, he is about to see all that come to an abrupt halt. Sadly for him, it did. It was no time before he was gone. Why? Obviously, the boss had the right to run the business any way he liked. The supervisor not only had to answer for what this man did but for what all his employees did as well. If he has to answer for it, he should be entitled to do it (drum roll here) his way. It is so much easier for us as followers to simply defer to those in authority unless we see an overwhelming need to make a recommendation. Unless what is being required is illegal, immoral or unscriptural, we should defer to the leader and do the job their way to the best of our ability.

When we think we might possibly have a better idea we need to learn how to make a godly appeal in a pleasing, productive and un-offensive manner. The first thing to remember is timing. Be sure you have been on the job long enough to prove your loyalty to both your supervisor and the company. When they know you have their best interest and the good of the company at heart, they will more than likely be open to your suggestions. In most environments it is good to have ideas and to try to be helpful. Sharing ideas and having a desire to make improvements are actually proof, in themselves, of our loyalty and sincerity. When making a recommendation it is always best to present it in writing and to list all the advantages and disadvantages. Don't show only the advantages because you can be certain the disadvantages of any proposal will soon arise after a policy is instituted anyhow. You don't want your leader or the company to be blind-sided by a failed policy. Once you have covered all the possibilities, make your proposal and leave it with the leadership. Tell him the final decision, of course, is his and whatever he decides, you intend to support. This takes all the strife, struggle and contention out of the situation because once he makes a decision, it is his decision alone and the issue is history.

A scriptural example of this approach occurred during one of the captivities. Daniel and three of his Hebrew brethren were selected to possibly serve before the king. During the selection period, they were required to eat food from the king's table and drink the king's wine. Daniel chose rather to appeal to his supervisor to consider an alternative diet. Note, however, that Daniel had also taken the time and made the effort to first gain the favor and good will of the chief eunuch in charge. His suggestion was that he and his other Hebrew brothers be allowed to eat vegetables which were healthier and drink only water for ten days and then for him to test them. The test was to see if their features didn't appear better and fatter than their secular counterparts who had eaten the king's delicacies. Of course they passed the initial test and were no longer required to partake of the king's table. In addition to that, when they were finally interviewed by the king, there were found to be none like them in the land in all manner of wisdom and understanding. They were ten times better than all the magicians and astrologers who served in the king's realm.

Deference is commanded in scripture. Hebrews 13:17 records these words: "Obey those who rule over you and be submissive, for they watch out for your souls, as those who must give account. Let them do so with joy and not with grief, for that would be unprofitable to you." When we have proved our loyalty to the company and the leader, they will, in time, almost always be willing to grant us more flexibility in how we do things. (Be sure to give this period of proving plenty of time) But, of course, we never deviate from policy or instructions without prior permission.

What it means to have the character trait of **DEFERENCE:**

- Regard for and obedience to a superior's preferences
- Respect due our elders
- Esteem for those who are our superiors
- To submit to someone else's wishes for respect
- Doing things the way the leader wants it
- The wisdom to avoid our employer's pet peeves

DEPENDABILITY—   **Study start date:** _____ **Finish date:** _____

We live in a day when so few actually say what they mean or do what they say. These people cannot be depended upon. This was something that really bothered me when I first got out of the Army and re-entered civilian life. In the military a person's entire worth, name, reputation and promotability was based on their being dependable and accomplishing either what they were told to do or said they would do and I mean—without fail. It didn't matter if you had to go over the mountain, around the mountain or through the mountain. This is called being mission oriented and is simply one's personal commitment to accomplish the assigned mission and keep their word no matter the cost. Sadly, in the civilian world most people will do what they say as long as it remains profitable or to their advantage at the time. Let that change for one second and their promise goes out the window, post haste. However, since time in memorial there has always been and always will be a great demand for a dependable servant. Masters are forever looking for dependable, faithful servants. Think for a moment how many times people tell you they will do something and fail to do it. It is an everyday occurrence. About the prophet Samuel, we know that he "grew and the Lord was with him and let none of his words fall to the ground." (I Samuel 3:19) This is the way to live and be of great value to your leaders. They and the success of their enterprise requires dependable people. It is also the only way to live at peace with ourselves and have a clear conscience.

Being dependable over the long term, however, requires a servant's heart and that, in and of itself, requires an abundance of humility. Many are those today, who endeavor to perfect the office of servant These nobodies, known today as the "Go to men" today, are not only used by God but business owners are proud to have working for their companies as well How valuable in a wicked world is a man who not only keeps his word but can always be relied upon gets the job done? Here is a short story about one of these Nobodies which is quite revealing:

> "**Fred Somebody, Thomas Everybody, Pete Anybody** and **Joe Nobody** were neighbors, but they were not like you and me. They were odd people and the most difficult to understand. The way most of them lived was a shame.
>
> All four belonged to the same church, but you couldn't have enjoyed worshiping with them. **Everybody** went fishing on Sunday or stayed home to visit with friends. **Anybody** wanted to worship, but was afraid **Somebody** wouldn't speak to him. **Nobody** went to church.
>
> Really, **Nobody** was the only decent one of the four. **Nobody** did the visiting. **Nobody** worked on the Church building. Once they needed a Sunday School teacher. **Everybody** thought **Anybody** would do it, and **Somebody** thought **Everybody** should. Guess who finally did it? That's right.... **Nobody**.
>
> It happened that a fifth neighbor (an unbeliever) came to live among them. **Everybody** thought **Somebody** should try to win him; **Anybody** thought
>
> **Somebody** should try to win him; **Anybody** could have at least made an effort, but guess who finally won him to Christ. That's right ... **Nobody.**
>
> **Anonymous**

"Nobody" could be depended upon to do anything. Amazing how self-interest and self-importance always seems to get in the way of being dependable. Humility and a servant's heart make it happen.

What it means to have the character trait of **DEPENDABILITY:**

- Worthy of being relied upon
- Consistent
- Reliable
- Able to follow and carry out instructions explicitly
- Loyal
- Always able to get the job done—no matter what
- A faithful supporter or follower
- One who is able to keep their promises even when it costs them dearly
- The ability to accomplish a job or a given mission regardless of the cost

ETERMINATION —   **Study start date:** _____ **Finish date:** _____

So many in today's world, having many electronic, mechanical and computerized assists to make life easier, take hold of tasks in a half-hearted manner. They are willing only to tap a toe in the water to test the temperature but are rarely willing to take the plunge. There should be no task too great for God or His people. Some can certainly be difficult while others are, indeed, treacherous, they must still all be tackled sooner or later for the will and glory of God.

All seems to be well on this planet until we set a goal or make a commitment to do something. Then it seems like all the demons of Hell are loosed. Everything that can go wrong will and that in a hurry. In the market place there are unethical competitors, in the home unruly children and in a marriage sometimes unfaithful partners. We can have equipment break-downs, attacks and higher taxes levied by the I.R.S., more government red tape and regulations, etc. Life is a test of the will. Do we have the will to win or not? There are some things which are worse than defeat, just one of which is compromise. It, for one, always leads to defeat because you are defeated already when you compromise. . Without determination, one can only expect a steady diet of failures because defeat only comes to the man who accepts it. We need not accept it. The biblical admonition is "only believe." (Mark 5:36) Regardless of the obstacles, we know that we "can do all things through Christ who strengthens (us)." Philippians 4:13

We see the poison of compromise in the life of Saul who was anointed by the prophet Samuel to be king over all Israel. At that very time he was commanded by God to punish Amalek for ambushing Israel when they were unarmed, coming up out of Egypt. Samuel said, "Now go and attack Amalek and utterly destroy all they have, and do not spare them. But kill both man and woman, infant and nursing child, ox and sheep, camel and donkey." (I Samuel 15:3) So Saul gathered three hundred thousand men and led them to a city of Amalek where they laid in wait to attack in the valley. At the proper moment, Saul pressed the attack of the Amalekites all the way from Hivilah to Shur which is east of Egypt. Although he destroyed all the people with the edge of the sword, he took Agag, king of the Amalekites, alive as a war trophy. He also took the best of the sheep, the oxen and the sheep, being unwilling to destroy everything as he was told.

At this, the Word of the Lord came to Samuel saying that He greatly regretted appointing Saul as King because he had not performed his commandments. This grieved Samuel such that he cried out to the Lord about it all night. He arose early the next morning as the Lord told him to go Carmel where Saul had set up a monument to himself. (always a bad sign)

When Samuel arrived, Saul said he had performed all the commandment of the Lord. But, at this, Samuel said, "What then is this bleating of the sheep in my ears and the lowing of the oxen which I hear?" Saul passed it off as the people sparing the best of the animals for sacrifices to God but had utterly destroyed all the rest. He actually thought 99 and a half would do with God.

Then Samuel said, "Be quiet! And I will tell you what the Lord said to me last night." Saul said, "Speak on." So Samuel said, When you were little in your own eyes, were you not head of the tribes of Israel? And did not the Lord anoint you king over Israel? Now the Lord sent you on a mission, and said, 'Go and utterly destroy the sinners, the Amalekites, and fight against them until they are consumed.' Why then did you not obey the voice of the Lord? Why did you swoop down on the spoil, and do evil in the sight of the Lord?" But, again Saul said he had obeyed the voice of the Lord but had only brought back Agag, the king, and it was the people who took the plunder and the best things which should have been destroyed to sacrifice to the Lord in Gilgal.

Then Samuel opined, "Has the Lord as great delight in burnt offerings and sacrifices, as in obeying the voice of the Lord? Behold, to obey is better than sacrifice, and to heed than the fat of rams. For rebellion is as the sin of witchcraft and stubbornness is as iniquity and idolatry. Because you have rejected the word of the Lord, He also has rejected you from being king." Finally Saul admitted that he had sinned because he feared the people and obeyed them rather than God. He then asked for a pardon and for Samuel to go with him to worship the Lord. However, Samuel replied, "I will not return with you, for you have rejected the word of the Lord, and the Lord has rejected you from being king over Israel." As Samuel turned to walk away, Saul grabbed his robe and tore it. Then Samuel said, "The Lord has torn the kingdom of Israel from you today, and has given it to a neighbor of yours, who is better than you." Saul then begged him to return and worship the Lord with him before the elders of the people.

At this meeting Samuel said, "Bring Agag king of the Amalekites here to me. So Agag came very cautiously saying, "Surely the bitterness of death is past." But Samuel replied, "As your sword has made women childless, so shall your mother be childless among women." At that, Samuel finished the business that Saul had been commanded to do. Clear eyed and unsentimentally, he cut Agag to pieces with the edge of the sword in the presence of the king's court. (What a bloody, awesome scene of God's judgment this must have been in an otherwise pristine and majestic court.) Samuel had the determination that was lacking in Saul but would definitely be found in the heart of his successor, David.

Then Samuel departed for Ramah and Saul to his house in Gibeah. From that time on, Samuel never met with Saul until the day of his death. Notwithstanding, Samuel mourned for Saul and the Lord also regretted making Saul king of Israel. His problem? No determination to follow clearly defined instructions in life.

What it means to have the character trait of **DETERMINATION**:

- The resolve to finish, without fail and regardless of the danger, discouragement, time, effort or cost whatever one starts
- The commitment to accomplish an assigned mission regardless of the cost
- The grit to stick with a task, project or battle until you have the victory
- To decide something unequivocally and definitely, with conviction
- A decision to stay the course and not quit or compromise
- The understanding that nothing great is ever accomplished without it
- Having the determination to always finish a task such that it becomes our trademark

EVOTION—   **Study start date:** _____ **Finish date:** _____

Everyone in this world is devoted to something. Some are devoted to drugs, others to alcohol, some to racing cars, some to skin diving and others to a thousand different things. Most, however, are devoted to frivolous activities, spending a lifetime seeking self-gratification. People are trying their best to find happiness and many still believe it will be found within themselves. It won't happen. You cannot make yourself happy. It, you will find, is a grand waste of time and resources. Some things are pleasurable for the moment but they don't satisfy the longings of the human heart. So, what is a frivolous activity? It is something that, one or two seconds after death won't matter in the least and certainly won't have any eternal value. It accomplishes nothing really important and will have no lasting effect.

As I write this on a Sunday afternoon, not as work but a joy and pleasure; actually; it is my worship to God for His faithfulness. I confess that later on today I will be watching the Super Bowl. Can I even tell you who won last year? No. Is my heart set on it? No. At this late date have I decided who to pull for? Someone asked me that question yesterday. The answer was and still is, No because I don't have a horse in this race. Will I enjoy watching it? Most likely will. Now recreation is fine in its place and we all need a little R&R occasionally but it needs to be limited to a certain appropriate amount of time and a minimal or reasonable financial commitment. When considering the infusion of all the time, effort and money in any recreational activity, we need to ask the question, "Is another human being better off because of this investment?" Proper devotion is, however, a total commitment to that which is meant to last even after death.

This old world has a way of getting turned on its ear time and again, before you can turn around. We saw it happen in the days before World War II when Hitler came to power and started knocking off nations like flies and killing all the Jews. Anyone who spoke against the regime was put in prison and most were killed. One such was a preacher devoted to God named Detrick Bonhoeffer. Some of the Christians who were still outside prison came to visit him and asked what the message of the church needed to be for their day. Thinking, of course, it would be some very deep theological gem, they were all ears to be sure. To which he said, "You need to teach people how to live in the world." So sage, so simple, so sublime. Why were the Germans and many other people on the planet killing people, robbing, raping, maiming, gassing, burning and bombing people off the face of the earth? Because they missed it. They didn't know how to live and succeed in the world. Realizing now that everyone, and I mean everyone, is already doing their best. That's right. Even the drunk passed out in the gutter still clutching a bottle of "Four Roses" in his clinched fist. This is his way to happiness. If he could think of a better way to find happiness and peace of mind, he would be doing it. His way may be flawed but it is all he knows and he is working it for all it is worth. To him, "Four Roses" was the answer to drowning all his troubles and escaping from the hard, cruel realities of life. He is devoted to it. His problem was that he hadn't learned the secret to success and finding true happiness in the world. He didn't know how to really live in the world. Tragically, his pursuit will ultimately lead to certain death. Who, then, would have the right information in regard to what we need to be devoted to?

We are very fortunate because in Matthew 25:14 the Master came telling us truly how to succeed and find happiness in the world. If I might paraphrase, He told the story of a nobleman who was about to travel to a far country, who gave varying talents to his servants based on their several abilities, and then promised to return later to see what they had done for him in the business of trading. Even by the master's own words, we know He considered this amount of money to be a very small matter and He wanted to see what they, left to themselves, could do with it. To one, he gave five, another, two and to the last, he gave one. The first went to work immediately and was able to double his by the time the master returned. To him the master said, "Well done, good and faithful servant; you were faithful over a few things, I will make you ruler over many things. Enter into the joy (or happiness) of your lord." To the one who had been given two, he commended in exactly the same way because he had doubled his as well. He started out with less, but still got his master the same return. Today we call it ROI (return on investment). Both of the servants who flourished never forgot who they worked for and whose talent it was. They delighted in being faithfully and fruitfully devoted to the master and had great joy increasing his kingdom. They were both devoted to the mission that was given them.

However, to the one who was given one—the picture changes dramatically. This servant hid the master's money in the ground. Upon the master's return, he gave it back to him and thought he had really done something—I guess because he didn't lose it or steal it. He told the master his reason for not doing any better was that he was afraid, thinking also that his master was an austere man who reaped where he hadn't sown and was the type who would gather where he had not scattered any seed. But the master, able to see into his heart, said, "You wicked and lazy servant, you knew that I reap where I have not sown, and gather where I have not scattered seed. So you ought to have deposited my money with the bankers and at my coming I would have received back my own with interest." Then he commanded that the talent be taken from him and given to the one who had ten. At that point, he pronounced the Law of the Kingdom in regard to success and happiness saying, "For to everyone who has (counts it valuable and worthy of one's best efforts), more will be given, and he will have abundance; but from him who does not have (what he has, he despises and considers insufficient of his best efforts) even what he has will be taken away." (v.29) Sorry, but it gets terribly worse. This man tried his best to lay all his sorry-ness off on the Master but God knows the heart. He told him exactly what the problem was. He was fearful, wicked and lazy. Then He commanded that this unprofitable servant be seized and cast into the outer darkness where there is "weeping and gnashing of teeth."

Note that success in this parable was determined not by the amount of grace each was given initially (grace being a number of talents in this case) but by what they were able to accomplish with the effort and devotion they put to it. Success in this life is all about production. The ones who succeeded were blessed with fruitfulness and were given much greater responsibility and something far greater in value that the world has overlooked for thousands of years. The profitable servants were allowed to enter into the master's happiness and those who practice this for a lifetime will be ushered one day into that same happiness for eternity! You see, what makes a human being happy is devotion to others and especially devotion to our Maker. Devotion to selfish goals and frivolous endeavors will not, for the most part, satisfy the longing of our souls.

Let's face it, we all start out in life so very selfish, looking out only for ourselves. In the crib we wanted our bottle, we wanted it right away and we tried to let everybody in the whole world know about it. The old "what's in it for me attitude" is still very prevalent in the world today. On the job, most people represent themselves and do just about as little as they can get by with to get to the next pay check. They need to realize that they were hired to represent the company and do what is best for it, represent not themselves but others. As we make others happy, the Law of Reciprocity demands that they will return our investments in their lives in a multiplied fashion and, amazingly, we will then find true happiness ourselves. People are working all kinds of systems to get ahead today. We just mentioned doing the least to get the most concept but there are many others. Working long and hard hours, gambling on the stock market or the lottery, partnerships, get-rich-quick-schemes, pyramids, chain letters. OPM (borrowing other people's money), PMA (having faith in faith instead of faith in God) and the list goes on and on.

However, what about exploring the concept of devotion? With this concept, we might consider working at a job, for a company or a boss as unto the Lord. Trying our best to be a blessing as a team player, always giving them 110%. Giving them our best ideas. Coming in early and working late when you feel like it. You would think that people would die of exhaustion and fall over dead if they stayed just a few minutes after five o'clock to finish a task. Some folk must be like Cinderella. They think they will turn into a pumpkin if they don't get out the door by the time the clock on the wall strikes five o'clock. What about being willing to come in on Saturday free and help with a construction project to facilitate a new line or help with the inventory. What about being loyal, obedient and devoted to management because in a Christian's life, management is actually the Lord? What about not saying but actually showing them that you are willing to go any distance, swim any sea, pay any price or climb any mountain to make their company, not you, the most successful and profitable company in your market area? What if you work to show God your faithfulness in the smallest things and an ability to get the job done, even the most difficult jobs, ask for nothing — not even any credit. What if your joy is really to see and join in the joy and happiness of your master? Will they not notice that something here is different? If you are always content with your wages, won't it be management's problem to lay awake at night concerned that the competition might try to hire you out from under them? Is the laborer not worth his wage? Will management not give you a promotion, raise your pay or put you in charge of a similar plant in another state? Do you, other than in difficult times, even need to ask for a raise? When our joy is not in being given ten cities to rule over but to see and enter into the master's happiness and give our thankfulness for any success we have seen to the Lord, we will be happy. Our future is assured. We might even be given ten cities to manage. Our confidence is in the fact that the Lord promised that working for Him and studying His Word would cause us "to prosper wherever you go." Joshua 1:7

First of all, before I even say this, know that I don't think anyone is indispensable. No one. However, with that being said, we all need to work to make ourselves just that, indispensable. Especially in bad economic times, we should try to find ways to make the company a profit as well as to find ways to become more efficient, streamline and thus save money. Look for new product lines to take on. Try to accomplish more and take on additional responsibilities to effect the same end and reduce the company's operating costs by being more efficient ourselves. Acquire new skills and certifications that will benefit the company. Don't be a glory hound. Refuse to accept honor from men and, certainly, do not be an apple polisher. Keep your integrity. Be quiet and wait for the Lord's promotion. It will come in due time. Our happiness will come from, as I said, being devoted to people and entities outside of ourselves.

Here are some ways we need to be devoted:

To God—First and foremost, to Him. He is really all there is. Husbands and wives will eventually die. Children will grow up, move out and build a life for themselves although we will get to enjoy, help and pray for them while we are here. Everything else you see is passing away quickly. When this short life is over, it is He whom we will serve forever. We are just here on earth temporarily for the purpose of finding Him, knowing Him, serving Him, learning to love Him, obey Him and then, one day to enjoy Him in Heaven for eternity.

To the Church—The fountain of life and all blessing. One might go it alone for a while and many are they who try it, but tidal waves are coming, earthquakes are about to erupt down the road. Huge problems you know not of are on the way and we won't be able to handle them apart from the Lord. We need to find our place in a church body and receive the joy of providing it our own, individual support. Why? "That we may grow up in all things into Him who is the head—Christ—from whom the whole body, joined and knit together by what every joint supplies, according to the effective working by which every part does its share, causes growth of the body for the edifying of itself in love." (Ephesians 4:15–16) It is in the church we learn the proper attitude of servanthood. It is in our devotion to a church where we hear and learn about faith because it comes by hearing. (Romans 10:17) It is faith we need to be saved, be creative, successful in the world, to please God and to live in proper relationship with our Savior.

To duty—To our office, job, industry, calling or ministry. If we are to make full proof of it to those we serve, we must execute our office with all our might, with all the skill, diligence and strength we can muster, pleading all the while for God's grace, assistance, wisdom and favor. We are never to fail by not doing for others what is expected of us.

To superiors—We are to honor them, cause them to prosper and make their plans succeed. We must try to be the best servant possible to them and be obedient to the rules of the company or ministry. We need to set our heart and mind to making their company the most successful and profitable company in our market area and treat it as if it were our own. Everybody is attacked at some time in life. True devotion is to be there for your leaders in their time of need.

To our spouse—Delight in them and really appreciate the gift from God they are. To be a one woman man or a one man woman. Place them above all others.

To family—Realize the blessing of family and invest time and energy in them. Honoring and respecting them, showing appreciation for the various members as well as in making your family the greatest experience it can be. Care for the needs of each one as far as is possible.

To friends—Love and serve your friends. Be available to them in good times and bad. Offer them sound, sincere, truthful advice. If we see them missing it in life, we must tell them the error of their way so they can get on to the come-back-trail. Share ideas with them that will cause them to prosper in their individual lives and business. Remember their special birthdays and let them know how much they mean to you.

To our country—To be loyal and willing to pay the price to keep it safe and make it better. Appeal to your elected officials to do and vote God's will, to support godly candidates, to stand up for righteousness and be heard in our community. Be willing to serve for the common good, looking for no credit at all.

What it means to have the character trait of **DEVOTION:**

- The act of being totally committed to things, people and entities outside of self
- Having an ardent, heart-felt love for others
- Freedom to work for others and cause them to flourish
- Fidelity
- Affection and loyalty to others and the various entities we associate with

ILIGENT SEEKER, A—   Study start date: _____ Finish date: _____

Everyone is seeking something in life; everybody wants something more than anything else. But, that person who is seeking the Lord more than anything is the one who is truly blessed. Those who seek worldly riches, honor and the approval of men are actually seeking their own reward. On the other hand, those who are seeking to know, honor and love God, will find that God, Himself, is, in due time, going to reward them. He also happens to be in a position to reward them with more than anyone else. After all, He owns the whole earth and the fullness thereof and can give it to whomsoever He pleases. Since He is the omnipotent Sovereign of the Universe, He can do whatever He pleases; whenever He pleases. Furthermore, He willingly and gladly has made his children promises and has never broken a single one of them. Here is just one: " … for he who comes to God must believe that He is …" That He exists and that He is alive today but even that is not enough. They must also "believe that He is a rewarder of those who diligently seek Him." (Hebrews 11:6) It is not enough to believe that God is real. Even the devil and his demons believe that. For all this to work, we must also believe that God has a reward for us that no man can give and no government can bestow. The life to come, in the presence of the Almighty will be unbelievable. It is not just anyone and everyone He intends to reward. He intends to reward the diligent seeker; the ones who seeks Him daily with all their heart by faith. Why? Because, the first part of the same verse tells us: ". . without faith it is impossible to please Him." Truth is, we know already, even in secular life, if a person really wants something, they will seek it daily and seek it diligently..

Even before I became a Christian, God had already been working on me by His grace. He allowed me to hear a message about Jacob wrestling with the angel of the Lord from the passage in Genesis 32:24. As the story goes, Jacob was left alone the night prior to meeting his elder brother to settle his accounts with him. Years before he had stolen his brother's blessing and swindled him out of his birthright. For this his brother had promised to kill him when their parents died. That night a man came and wrestled with him all night, even until daybreak. Jacob wrestled so hard, one version had it that he wrestled his hip out of joint. Another version says, Jacob wrestled so hard that the angel could not prevail against him and he finally touched his hip and put it out of joint. Then he told Jacob to let him go, because the dawn was breaking. But, Jacob refused saying he wouldn't let him go until he blessed him. At that, the angel asked his name and he, of course, answered, "Jacob." The angel opined, "Your name shall no longer be called Jacob, but Israel; for you have struggled with God and with men, and have prevailed." (v.28) Then Jacob wanted to know why he asked about his name but right there, the man blessed him.

It was because of this account about Jacob, that God began dealing with me about my own poor devotion to seeking Him. Up to that point in my life, I had sought to please the world far more than I had tried to seek the Lord and have His approval. It was at that moment that I purposed never to have to stand before Him someday in that condition. I knew I had expended a great amount of effort and had invested a considerable sum of money to pursue success in the world. I purposed in my heart to invest even more in God's kingdom. I would begin striving with all that was in me to seek Him and His Kingdom first. I decided to devote my diligence to seeking Him. Don't think I knew at the time that  Hebrews 11:6 was even in the Bible but diligence holds enormous power. It certainly levels the playing field of life and is a huge blessing for some of us who may not be as gifted as others. I always put a little star of David on the front covers of all my Bibles to remind me every time I saw it what I was about— being a diligent seeker. It also promises great benefits.

- **Diligence is required in seeking Him:** "Now devote your heart and soul to seeking the Lord your God." I Chronicles 22:19 NIV
- **Diligence is required in obeying Him:** "Ye shall diligently keep the commandments of the Lord your God." Deuteronomy 6:17 KJV
- **Diligence is required in keeping our own soul:** "Only take heed to thyself and keep thy soul diligently, lest thou forget the things which thine eyes have seen, and lest they depart from thy heart all the days of thy life." Deuteronomy 4:9 KJV
- **Diligence is required in keeping your own heart:** Keep thy heart with all diligence; for out of it are the issues of life.' Proverbs 4:23 KJV
- **Diligence is required in labors of love:** God is not unjust; he will not forget your work and the love you have shown him as you have helped his people and continue to help them. We want each of you to show this same diligence to the very end, in order to make your hope sure. We do not want you to become lazy but to imitate those who through faith and patience inherit what has been promised." Hebrews 6:10–12
- **Diligence is required in being found spotless:** "Wherefore, beloved, seeing that ye look for such things, be diligent that ye may be found of Him in peace, without spot, and blameless." II Peter 3:14 KJV
- **Diligence is required to bear rule:** "The hand of the diligent shall bear rule." Proverbs 12:24
- **Diligence is required for accumulating wealth:** "Lazy hands make a man poor but diligent hands bring wealth." Proverbs 10:4
- **Diligence is required for promotion:** "Seest thou a man diligent in his business? He shall stand before kings; he shall not stand before obscure men." Proverbs 22:29

The great promise of Matthew 6:33 is that we must seek "first the kingdom of God and His righteousness and (then) all these things will be added to you." What things are going to be added? All the things the Gentiles are seeking: houses, lands, husbands and wives, finances, children, etc. However, for all this to work, we must be diligent to keep our first priority just that—seeking God. Then we can face both the future and eternity with great expectation.

What it means to have the character trait of being a **DILIGENT SEEKER:**

- The grace to apply one's self to our first priority—seeking God—and keeping His kingdom first
- Having a heart after God
- Seeking to know Him and His ways
- Seeking to know and do His will
- Living a life to please Him
- Striving to be obedient to the Master's call and commands
- Striving to keep our heart pure and to be found spotless

DISCIPLINE —

Study start date: _____ **Finish date:** _____

A world where anything goes says, "Whatever feels good, do it." But with that mantra, how are we going to gain respect, build consensus or make any get anything meaningful accomplished? First of all, just anything won't do all the time and, for that matter, most of the time. Whatever feels good will lead us at light speed to problems, heartache, an early grave or a prison cell door slamming permanently right behind us. Clink! Truly, the flesh is weak and we have all tried taking the easy way out at one point in time or another. That is, until we found out that it wouldn't work and everything came crashing down around us like a truck load of rocks. Unfortunately, some people haven't realized this just yet.

In life, we must discipline ourselves to meet specific requirements, take care of needs and generally, get the job done. There are many thing our lives that must get done, a great number of them have to be done on a daily basis. Many are not the most fun or glamorous possibly but they might be the most needful at the time and the most beneficial in the long run. None of us will consistently do these things until we learn, usually through much pain and hardship, the benefits of the concepts of personal discipline and delayed gratification. Everyone would like to order some discipline "on line" but it can't be purchased pre-wrapped or in a bottle. It usually comes as a high price but that's good because what we have to pay the most for, we don't easily let go or forget.

The world has provided many instructors to teach us these concepts: parents, life experience, teachers, employers, nature itself and even our co-workers and friends. My dad was one of the best teachers. He had a belt that I was well acquainted with over time and learned far more from it than I had a mind to learn from it at the time. It was a very effective teacher of the hard to grasp notion that there is a price to pay for disobedience—and we probably aren't going to like it. Dad and I had a serious conversation just five minutes before he died. At the time of this, our last conversation, I had no prepared remarks and the thought of his old belt had never entered my mind. I told him that I loved him, that he was the best dad a kid could ever have and, for some strange reason at the time I said, "Dad, I deserved ever spanking I ever got and probably could have used a few more." That was because I needed so many whippings growing up, the thought just occurred to me that this could have been weighing heavily on his mind. I was, without controversy, the undisputed black sheep of the family. They say a boy is like a canoe. He behaves better when paddled from the rear. A good parent is a not just a provider but an adviser, a counselor and a disciplinarian when necessary. Five minutes after I had left the room, dad went on to his reward. I thank God for a father who refused to spare the rod. No telling where I would have wound up without him. He was an Air Force officer and a very disciplined one at that. I still keep the Bank savings deposit book which shows he deposited $200 a month for years and years to save for my brother's and my college educations. He never missed a single month—ever. Now that's discipline.

Discipline is something we all must learn. None of us were born with it but it is what makes for true sons so we best not forget it. Solomon recorded these insightful words: "My son, do not despise the chastening of the Lord, nor detest His correction; for whom the Lord loves, He corrects, just as a father the son in whom he delights." (Proverbs 3:11, 12) God is also our Father and Moses penned these words so we would, hopefully, learn to obey Him: "You should know in your heart that as a man chastens his son, so the Lord your God chastens you. Therefore you shall keep the commandments of the Lord your God to walk in His ways and to fear Him." (Deuteronomy 8:5) In the crooked, convoluted world we live in, harkening to God's chastening and instruction holds promise of a great blessing. In Psalm 94:12 and 13 we see, "Blessed is the man whom You instruct, O Lord, and teach out of Your law, that You may give him rest from the days of adversity, until the pit is dug for the wicked." We also know that "The complacency of fools will destroy them; but whoever listens to (Him) will dwell safely and will be secure without fear of evil." Proverbs 1:32b and 33

Another strange instrument of discipline God used in my life was the upperclassmen in the military college I attended. They might not have been the kindest and gentlest delivery system in the world but, they were effective. At the time I thought I was just trying to survive in an austere military environment. Without my even knowing it, they were teaching us things, valuable character qualities, like respect for authority, to reject self-pity no matter how bad things got, to be patience in adversity, the importance of being a team player, how to take correction and endure hard treatment, to be prepared, to do the hardest job first and to never ever give up—just to name a few. Amazingly, none of this had I intended to learn or probably even wanted to learn, nor did I know I was even learning it at the time but learn it I did if I wanted to survive. The upperclassmen said they were having us do all those push-ups, running us around the campus double-time in the middle of the night, etc., for our own good. Said they were trying to help us and teach us some things so we might even, believe it or not, grow up to be a man and be some semblance of a soldier someday. Well, they may have been helping us and later it truly did work out that way but it sure didn't feel very good at the time. We certainly didn't think all that was happening to us because the milk of human kindness was flowing through their veins. It looked and felt like anything but something that might have been good for us at the moment.

The author as a sophomore at Texas A&M

We find, however, that self-discipline is actually what causes us to succeed in everyday life, no matter where we may go or what we do. When consistently taught, discipline that is administered to another with his best interest at heart, will eventually cause that person to actually learn to discipline themselves. The flesh and the fallen mind we were born with always wants to take the easy way out. It just so happens that the best and the right way to do things is rarely if ever easy. The key to being a leader is learning to manage ourselves. It is discipline and determination, not desire, that will control one's destiny in life.

What it means to have the character trait of **DISCIPLINE:**

- The personal drive to do the hardest, dirtiest and least enjoyable job first
- The ability to focus one's attention and effort to do what is required or necessary as the priority of the moment
- The ability to deny the flesh and perfect one's moral character and mental faculties
- A system of rules that governs one's conduct
- Doing what you need to do before doing what you want to do
- Determining, like the farmer, not to eat all your seed so you will have some to plant for a crop next year. For non-farmers, this means opening a bank account and saving a percentage of what you earn.

- Training our mental faculties to do what is best, right and expedient
- The wisdom to look for the hard, more difficult paths in life.
- Positive, self-directed behavior patterns
- The ability to control one's appetites, passions and energies
- Mastery gained from the personal drive to enforce order and obedience.
- The trait that gives a person of value in any community, company, church or field.

DISPATCH—   **Study start date:** _____ **Finish date:** _____

The old saying, "Haste makes waste" is certainly true but there also needs to be a good balance between getting prepared and then executing a well thought out plan with expediency. Some people never can seem to come up with a sense of urgency in life about anything. They pretty well maintain a cavalier attitude about everything. They say they will get to it when they get ready to get to it and it will all get done some fine day if time permits. Their attitude is where the tree falls, there it will lie and never do today what you can put off until tomorrow— just some of the axioms they live by. No. We need to take dominion of our time and learn ways to maximize it to get the job done expeditiously and with excellence if at all possible. Time is one of the greatest blessings of life. None of us get very much of it even if we live to be a hundred and what little we do get, passes by "swifter than a weaver's shuttle." (Job 7:6) This being the case, we need to know how to use it efficiently. We need to learn how to guard against procrastination and wasting it. We also need to learn how to be creative in redeeming the time the world is so good at stealing through inefficiencies, unforeseen interruptions, broken appointments, etc. Wisdom is to start early and work a little extra every day. Never put off until tomorrow what we can get done right now. We need to execute with a swiftness as long as we have taken the time to prepare and check things out first. Our job is to think, pray, plan and work to build systems and get the proper equipment so our work can be done efficiently and effectively, as I said, with excellence. We need to see just how much work we can do in a day because the days are both evil and few but more importantly— because we work for the Master. We turn our work directly in to Him every day.

Dispatch is the ability to cut through the fluff, red tape, traditions of men and various hindrances so we can be efficient. As a leader it means having your equipment properly maintained at all times and organized to be available to the men when needed. It is training our team how to properly use their equipment as well as acquiring the latest technologies that work for them. However, for dispatch ever to become a reality one must first love their work. No one is going to become efficient at something they despise. On the contrary, when we love our work, it becomes a joy and, in time, will tell us its secrets.

What it means to have the character trait of **DISPATCH**:

- Executing orders from superiors with a sense of urgency, deftness and skill
- Executing (means to kill) details and duties one is given promptly and expeditiously
- Handling paperwork and mail only once if at all possible and putting the resulting paperwork where it goes immediately (into a good filing system).
- Never putting off until tomorrow what we can do today.
- Taking care of business immediately and efficiently
- To expedite—make the work flow quickly, with divine order. (Wasting no time.)
- Redeeming the time (Carry a book along to read for unexpected waiting periods or have an alternate project with you to work on)
- Making a daily list of duties and tasks, prioritizing them and executing them quickly so you can strike them from our list and get an immediate feeling of accomplishment.
- The ability to orchestrate systems, technology, techniques, equipment, personnel and scheduling to accomplish work speedily, accurately and efficiently.
- Pressing every minute to yield 60 seconds worth of blessing and fruit.

DOMINION—   **Study start date:** _____ **Finish date:** _____

When God created the heavens and the earth, He then created man in his own image and gave him special powers no other animal was to have. He gave commandment to Adam and all men after him saying, "Be fruitful and multiply; fill the earth and subdue it; have dominion over the fish of the sea, over the birds of the air, and over the cattle, over all the earth and over every creeping thing that creeps on the earth." (Genesis 1:28) Dominion over all creation was both man's commission and mandate from the beginning. Notice God's plan for man included a certain, specific sphere that he was to take dominion over: all the earth. The commandment to "subdue it" meant to conquer, wrestle into subjection if need be and bring it under control by the exertion of our will and strength. It was clearly God's plan that man be made in His own image to wield power. He was to rule and reign controlling all other created things. God so chose that His very own eternal purpose in the universe would be bound up with this creature He called man.

He also instituted a hierarchical system of government on the earth where man was in charge, under God's authority, of course. It is also important to note that He has neither changed His mind aboutit nor His design in creation until this very day. Later, at the fall, man rebelled against God and was burdened with several consequences which made his life here much more difficult. There are now thorns and thistles to deal with in the earth and the ground would no longer yield its fruit so readily. Only by the sweat of one's brow can we cause the earth to bring forth, bear fruit and make our living from it. This has still held true even after the industrial and computer revolutions. The world also the added difficulty of rebellion and its consequences built right into it. In addition to this, Man also has an adversary, satan, loosed against him in the earth as well. For all these reasons, therefore, for just about anything to go correctly on this planet, it requires a man to step up and take dominion. In order to make all the systems of the earth come to optimum productivity, bring God the greatest glory and mankind the greatest benefit, a person must truly be determined. Authority (dominion) was designed by God to be a good thing: to bless those who do well and to punish those who do evil. (Romans 13:3) However, all authority is from God and all those He places in authority are supposed to be ministers of good for Him. That means all judges, political office holders, policemen, corporate CEO's, middle management, moms and dads, etc., are under this same directive to take dominion over their spheres in harmony with His will and purpose.

We also have another burden to overcome. Since the fall, all men were shaped in iniquity and in sin our mothers conceived us. (Psalm 51:5) This means, of course, that we all have sin and rebellion working in our members. (Romans 7:5) This was certainly true of your humble correspondent growing up. We find this stubborn, rebellious spirit in most all animals of which horses and mules are a good example at birth. They all have to be broken. This thing is also found in the ground and the vegetation of the earth. Left to itself but given a reasonable amount of rainfall, most fields that aren't rocky will be totally taken over by wait-a-minute vines, thorns, thistles, weeds, shrubs and trees making it totally worthless for agricultural production. History has shown us that some men, in their lust for money, possessions and power will, without question, actually steal, kill and bear false witness to get what they want. For this reason, we must have those who bear the sword in society to maintain some semblance of law and order. The Apostle Paul went on in Romans 13:4 to say that those who bear the sword do not bear it in vain. This police power was placed here by God to be a mighty deterrent to those who think they can rebel against the ordinances of God and an ordered society.

Another very important place for man to take dominion is in their very own home. Joshua was certainly talking about dominion when he said, "As for me and my house, we will serve the Lord." (Joshua 24:15) It is up to the man of the house to bear rule. He is to drive his stakes down and bear rule in a kind, gentle and understanding way if possible. He is to make the decision to follow, serve and obey the Lord in all that transpires there.

The dominion mandate extends to every conceivable field of endeavor. A preacher once said, "If you have a thousand acres but only have forty in cultivation, don't tell anyone you have a thousand acres. Tell them you have forty." His point, of course, was that this is all you have taken dominion or control of, have producing or are managing optimally. Some other kingdom has the rest of it stolen, bound up in worthlessness and non-productivity.

Taking dominion is important in the military as well. A potentially catastrophic situation arose right after I took over my second company in Vietnam. Three days after assuming command, the battalion commander assigned my company to green line security duty on the brigade fire base in Quan Loi for a couple weeks. We considered this "cush duty" because it didn't require a whole lot of walking and busting brush on recon in the jungles every day. I assigned each platoon a certain equal number of bunkers to man and each of their soldiers had to post security so many hours every day. Their job was to watch the fields of fire in front of their bunkers to be sure sappers didn't crawl through the concertina wire, infiltrate our defenses and start blowing up our aircraft on the runway, ammunition dump, our fuel storage facilities or try to kill a lot of our people.

There was never even a suggestion from the base commander that I check my defenses in the middle of the night but it was my responsibility to be sure my men were "at the ready." The first night I got up at 2:00 AM and walked the green line. This was the dirt mound, covered with grass that connected all the bunkers and circled the entire fire base and landing strip. As the commander, I was responsible for everything the men did or failed to do so I wanted to be sure no one was asleep, making us easy prey for the enemy to come in and wreak havoc. The problem is that it is extremely dangerous to walk the green line in the dark. A soldier could actually have fallen asleep, be startled by the noise of you walking toward their bunker on the green line and spray you with their M-16 fire out of fear, drowsiness, reflex action or an abundance of caution. It was the old "shoot first and ask questions later rule" that no one was supposed to go by but some always did anyway. No matter the risk, in my heart, I knew I had to walk the line. The most amazing thing, as I made my check, I found five soldiers who weren't even asleep, they were A.W.O.L.! That's right, gone, gone, gone. I got their names from their respective platoon leaders and gave them all an Article !5, Summary Court Martial including a cash fine. In the case of serious violations like cowardice in the face of the enemy, leaving one's post as a sentinel such as this without being properly relieved, etc. there is a provision of the Uniform Code of Military Justice that allows commanders in the field to fine men on the spot, bust their rank if they think it's appropriate and put the verdict on their permanent record. No formal court has to convene, no board and no jury. Just the commander decides these things on the spot to keep the fighting effectiveness of the unit in tack. Failure to post your duty as a sentinel in the Army is a hugely grave offense because it leaves your fellow comrades in arms who are relying on you for security, completely vulnerable to the attacks of the enemy, I thought to myself, these Article 15's would surely do it and send a message to the other men that this would not be tolerated for one second. Well, the second night I hit the green line at 2:00 AM again and five different men were A.W.O.L. Frankly, I could not believe it. So I gave all them summary court martials as well, figuring that ten guys "Article Fifteened" as we called it, would immediately put an end to this. Incidentally, the whole time I commanded my first company I never experienced the first instance of anything like this. So the third night, I walked the green line at 2:00 AM again and, you guessed it, five different men were A.W.O.L. so I gave all them court martials too. About this time, I said to myself, "This is really crazy." I asked the first sergeant if he knew of anything going on and he said he thought it was a racial problem because all of those A.W.O.L. were black and in the last month or so something was written up in *The Stars and Stripes* news paper (The Army's newspaper for the Vietnam war theater) about racial problems over there. I knew that was not it but couldn't figure out what was going on. So, that morning I had the first sergeant call all the men in the company to my command post bunker. Never in my life have I ever been without some notion of what to say or do next. Can't say I have always been right but I have always had at least some idea of what to do next. I promise you, this time I didn't have a clue and not even a thought of what to do anywhere in my head. As I looked out the door of that bunker, I saw sixty or seventy of the meanest looking, battle hardened trigger-pullers in dirty, crumbled-up, jungle fatigues with automatic weapons, hand grenades and the most scratched up, dirty jungle boots you ever laid eyes on. Still, not having the slightest idea what to say or do, I just walked out there and hoped against hope for the best.

I started out by saying that having been with them for so short a time (only three days when this trouble started), they had not really had the opportunity to get to know me. Said I had been to every school the Army had and had already commanded another company in this very theater (war zone) and told them I knew how to run a rifle company (as opposed to a transportation company or a signal company). Said I had been told that we had a racial problem in Vietnam and in our company. For that to be the case in our company, I would have to tolerate it and I was not about to. The first day, before I had heard anything about all this, I had picked a black brother, "Booney" (was his nickname), to be my RTO (Radio/telephone operator) and that was the one person I would have to have been closest to every second of every day until I left. I also said that I was an Air Force brat and had grown up around blacks all my life—lived in base housing, went to the gym, the teen club, college, etc. with them ever since I was a kid. They were some of my best friends. I said no, we didn't have a racial problem at all. I told them we had a problem deciding who was going to run the company. If I was going to run it, and it was my job to keep every one of them alive, win our battles and send them home on the big iron bird (what we called those 707's), they were going to do what I said, when I said and exactly how I said. That was how it would be if I ran the company. Now, if they wanted to run the company, all they had to do was kill me!

That was the end of this kind of trouble. We never had another problem and everyone came together like JB Weld. We had terrific esprit de corps, very few casualties, won every battle and never called retreat. They knew I intended to take dominion of that company and nothing they tried would ever stop me. Fact is the men will do everything they can to keep you alive as the commander if they know you can lead them in battle.

It wasn't until a month or two later, that I found out what the problem actually was. Some of the Vietnamese women who were allowed to come on the fire base during the day to do the laundry, run the Post Exchange and give haircuts had failed to leave the base at night. The men who were A.W.O.L. were buying beer and shacking up with these women at night instead of doing their job, posting security for the fire base. Just as I expected, it wasn't a racial thing at all.

God gave us dominion over this planet from the beginning and, as I said, He hasn't changed His mind about it. Some seem to have lost the vision of how the stone cut without hands grew and "became a great mountain and filled the whole earth." (Daniel 2:35) So many today want to retreat in the face of all the "isms" (socialism, legalism, communism, Marxism, secular humanism, etc.). However, every time Israel considered retreat in the face of the enemy, they were rebuked by God for unbelief. You see, He put us here and gave us the victory! Remember the twelve man recon team that went in to spy out the Promised Land? Ten came back saying there were giants in the land and the Hebrew children were like grasshoppers in the enemy's sight. They basically said, they couldn't take the land and there was no sense in even trying. They were defeated before they even got started. Only two, Joshua and Caleb, gave a good report. They remembered that God had already promised to give it to them (Numbers 13:2) and said, "Let us go up at once, and possess it; for we are well able to overcome it." (v.30) The two who had the good report were allowed by God to go in and actually take the land of milk and honey. The rest were left to wander in the wilderness until they all died and their bones were bleached in the sun. They would never know the blessings of God or experience His plan for Israel.

What it means to have the character trait of **DOMINION**:

- Sovereignty
- The ability to subdue
- The authority, power and the faculties to rule
- Supreme power
- The ability to self-govern
- The ability to control, direct, limit and change
- Absolute ownership

REAMER, BEING A—

Study start date: _____ Finish date: _____

Unfortunately, many leaders live in the mundane, world of the possible, probable and practical. This happens, of course, for a variety of reasons, not all of which will we consider here but we will look into a few. To begin with, so many leaders are not excited about life and all the opportunities leadership affords because most just trying to get by. We should, rather, be on fire with the zeal of God, realizing every day is an opportunity to enlarge His borders on earth and do great damage to the enemy! This is our opportunity to start new ventures and build new things.

We are totally free in America to do just about anything we can imagine. We can build anything, grow anything, do anything and go anywhere we want.. There are no limitations and, besides, with God all things are possible. Let's turn that around a bit. Nothing is impossible with God. He owns everything and can give His resources to whomsoever He wishes. We know He owns the cattle on a thousand hills, the heavens and the heavens of the heavens are His, all the silver and gold is his and even all the pillars of the earth are His.

Other leaders happened into their positions by default, accident, inheritance, time in grade or, just simply, no one else really wanting the job at the time they were promoted. So many today don't really love their work and are doing their best to do just enough to get by. Loving your work has many benefits. If you love what you do, you will dream about it and it will tell you its secrets. You will have a burning desire to increase all your opportunities with the motive of helping your company, your leaders, your fellow employees, as well as the people and community your company or ministry serves as much as possible.

Still others would never, ever dare venture into the world of faith, dreams and the supernatural for fear of criticism or failure. Just think, if a project they started took a little longer than someone thought it should or something, God forbid. Someone might criticize them. Set your mind at ease. If you move with God, you are going to be criticized no matter what. That is just how it is. Even if your plans all work out right on time, pretty as a picture, which rarely is the case, you are still going to be criticized. If it goes badly or if it goes well, you are going to be criticized. Get used to it to the point that its like so much water falling off the proverbial duck's back. Succeeding at something will cause you to be criticized more than anything else. I have had several people tell me over time that the only way anyone could succeed in business was to cheat. How foolish is that. Cheating will get you put in jail. My God! Settle it for yourself, criticism just comes with leadership.

Other leaders want a job they feel like they, personally, can handle from one end to the other. Well, if your vision is something you can actually accomplish by yourself, you have the wrong vision. We need to keep on asking God for one so great that it would be impossible to complete without His help.

Being concerned about what people might think and say can really be a hindrance to a leader. May I share one of my own failings in this regard. Just prior to my senior year in high school I was contemplating running for an office in the student body. I actually wanted to run for president but thought: If I ran for that job and won and, I intended to win, I would have to do a lot of speaking, make a lot of decisions and would likely make a lot of mistakes. Some of you who know me today wouldn't believe it but back then I was terrified to get up and speak before a group of people. I would get so nervous sometimes that my mind would actually blank out and I would forget where I was in my talk. It was pitiful. My next thought was to run for vice president and then I probably wouldn't have to say anything or make any decisions and probably wouldn't make any mistakes or be criticized. So, foolishly, I chose the latter and won the office. The only problem was it turned out that I was exactly right in my prognosis. I didn't have to make any decisions, didn't have to do anything but show up at meetings, never had to say anything and I never got criticized. Holding that office for a year was a total waste of time other than it looked good on my resume for a few years. Later on, in college someone gave me the little statement that follows which has been attributed to several people, not the least of whom was President Theodore Roosevelt and it changed my life for good: I call it *The Man In The Arena*:

> "It is not the critic who counts, nor the man who points out how the strong man stumbled, or where the doer of deeds could have done them better. The credit belongs to the man who is actually in the arena; whose face is marred by dust and sweat and blood; who strives valiantly; who errs and comes short again and again; who knows the great enthusiasms, the great devotions, and spends himself in a worthy cause; who, at the best, knows in the end the triumph of high achievement; and who, at the worst, if he fails, at least fails while daring greatly, so that his place shall never be with those cold and timid souls who know neither victory nor defeat."

After reading that little statement about the excitement of really living life, I never wanted to be in the grand stands again. It was my desire to be that man in the arena, facing off with the other gladiators and the many lions out in the world. You see there will always be thousands of arm-chair-quarterbacks sitting in the comfort of the grandstands criticizing the man in the arena saying he should of zigged instead of zagged. He should of done this and not done that, on and on, ad infinitum. It is always easy, after the fact, to tell what someone should have done. Fact is, everyone makes mistakes. But mistakes aren't so bad. They cause us to grow in character, as well as gain valuable information while making them. I tell my employees all the time, if I every catch you not making any mistakes, I'm going to fire you. Why? Because the only people who don't make mistakes are the people who never do anything and that, friend, is the biggest mistake of all.

In his day, some said that Thomas Edison was called an inventor but really he was actually a dreamer. This visionary was accused of failing 6,000 times before finally succeeding at making his first incandescent light bulb. On the contrary, Edison said he succeeded 6,000 times finding ways that would not work before he found the way that did work so he could manufacture that little glass bulb that has been such a blessing to us and the whole world all our lives. I am sure he had the same trepidations, misgivings and fears applying for his first patent like everyone else who has ever tried it. He probably wondered where he would get the money up and who would ever listen to him without a high school or college diploma. Don't think he even finished grade school. Once he had the patent, he still wondered how he would ever talk an investment banker or an industrial tycoon into investing in his dream to manufacture of something to light houses and businesses that had never been tried before. Keep in mind now that there were virtually no electric generating plants or power lines to supply those dinky little bulbs at the time he invented them. But find help for manufacturing he did. Then he thought, "How will I ever market this fragile little glass bulb to a country full of people content with their coal oil lanterns and gas lights?" But he did. He put shoe leather to the pavement and beat a bunch of doors down. You see, it was his responsibility to put one foot out in front of the other every day by faith. It was his responsibility to think, dream and knock on doors until he knocked the right one. Funny thing, you always have to make your first invention and get it patented, manufactured and sold before you get your second. That is just how it works. The first one is always the hardest. God not only gave Edison the ability to invent and get patents, He also gave him the ability to manufacture as well as the ability to market those products successfully. A whole world has benefited greatly because of the persistence and perseverance of this one, great American dreamer.

On another occasion, Edison actually was burning the midnight oil (a candle in this case) trying to invent something completely different, when he messed up and accidentally knocked the candle over. This caused the molten wax to spill on some papers in the vicinity. Cleaning up the mess, he just kept on messing up and spilled some water on the paper. Then he noticed it beaded up and that the water would no longer soak into the paper. That, obviously, was how he discovered wax paper. Because of him the juice from the tomatoes on our turkey sandwiches never got mixed up in the chocolate cake our mom's put in our lunch sacks growing up. Go on Thomas, make some more mistakes will you please and bless the whole world with what you come up with. Don't worry, he did and has over a thousand patents to his credit in his one lifetime. That's not bad for a guy who dropped out of school in probably the third grade. I never was much in the math department but I think he has exactly a thousand more patents than I've got.

Another thing we don't want to overlook is that all of the opportunity in life is in the arena. There is virtually no opportunity in the grandstands unless, of course, you want to sell some programs about what the man in the arena is doing or get minimum wage selling some hot dogs and sodas. Most importantly, only the man in the arena will ever know in his heart what it really feels like to face the lion or that other gladiator with his life truly on the line. Only the man in the arena really feels the need to develop his skills and feels pressed to get stronger and better every day. No telling who or what he will have to face tomorrow. Only the man in the arena gets to feel that adrenalin rush, the exhilaration and only he will ever have the chance to be a winner. After reading that little statement about the man in the arena that I decided I would probably never get a railroad watch. God helping me, I would always be out trying new things, being creative, criticized and controversial. Hey, what a way to live! This is truly living.

Fear of failure is a huge deterrent to success in life but the fear of difficulty and the unknown are likewise, enormous obstacles confronting the mind and human spirit. Hope this may help. Someone said, years ago, when trying to decide what to do with one's time on earth, to ask this question. "What would you do in life if money and talent were not a factor?" Everybody worries so about not having enough money to do new things and very, very few have ever been burdened with a whole lot of talent. Certainly not me, I was the one, remember, who nearly failed the first, second and the third grade coming up. Gideon's life is a great lesson on facing huge obstacles. When the Angel of the Lord told Gideon to go out and vanquish the Midianites, he said, "My clan is the weakest in Manasseh (one of the smallest in all Israel) and I am the least in my father's house." (Meaning he was the runt of the litter.) (Judges 6:15) He was saying, basically, 'How am I going to do this?' The angel opined, "Go with the might you have." In other words, go with what you've got. You have God with

you. Don't despise the day of small things or small beginnings. (Zechariah 4:10) Besides, we have God with us and all his resources available by faith. Finally, of course, Gideon went with 300 and did what God said, totally vanquishing the enemy.

Finally, we need to realize that our goals in life should never be worldly, carnal, minuscule or mundane. We don't have to worrying about the small stuff. If we will but get our priorities in order and seek first the Kingdom, God has already promised to add everything we need. What do you mean everything? I mean everything the Gentiles seek. (Matthew 6:33) We are commanded in scripture to set our affections on the things above and let love be our high aim and goal in life. (I Corinthians 14:1) Everything we do is to be done to the praise of His glory. (Ephesians 1:12–14) We are to find our fulfillment in His Kingdom and pray that He might give us a project so big we couldn't possibly get accomplished without His help. (When you think about it, you couldn't get out of the bed in the morning without His help and every time your heart takes a beat, it has to go across God's desk and get permission.) But, that aside, we know that the Master said "the just shall live by faith" and that faith, not good works or being good, is the only way we can please Him. We are to be bold in the Lord and if we take time to know Him, fast and pray, He will call us out to do exploits. (Daniel 11:32) Just a few of God's dreamers were Abraham, Jacob, Joseph, Daniel, Peter and Paul. What a delightful crowd to get mixed up with!

Remember, when we stop dreaming, we stop the flow of the creative power of God in our lives and we are then for all practical Kingdom purposes … dead. So spend some time alone with God and be a dreamer. Ask Him to give you your dreams. As you continue to "Delight yourself in the Lord and He will give you the desires of your heart." Psalms 37:4

What it means to have the character trait of **BEING A DREAMER**:

- One who seeks God to know His will and prays for divine guidance in life.
- One who asks God continually, "What would You have me to do Lord?"
- One who envisions projects and sees new vistas
- A person who imagines great plans and future events
- One who deals in heavenly communications and visions
- One who imagines things most would consider improbable if not impossible
- A visionary

UTY —   **Study start date:** _____ **Finish date:** _____

Duty is a powerful thing. It can make a pauper a king while an absence turns a king into a pauper. In the military they say, "A man who serves his country well has no need of ancestry." Because David recognized his duty and was willing to risk his life to protect the few sheep he was shepherding, God saw in him the qualities that would someday make a king. Later, as a teenager, he saw it his duty to fight the Philistine giant Goliath to save the nation when no one else would. On the contrary, because King Saul failed to see his duty to be obedient to God, the kingdom was torn from him (I Samuel 15:28) and given to David.

Many are they who are capable of recognizing the duty of others and their own just quickly enough to dodge it. Such was Cassius Clay. He started training as a boxer at the age of 12 and beat Sonny Liston for the world heavyweight championship at 22. However, in 1975, shortly after this fight he converted to Sunni Islam. Shortly thereafter, he refused conscription into the U.S. Army on the basis of his religious beliefs and opposition to the Vietnam War. As a result, he was arrested and found guilty of draft evasion by a court of law. His title was stripped from him and he didn't fight again for several years. Because he refused to fight for our country, someone else had to fight in his place. Fifty-eight thousand men and women died for him to have the privilege of living in peace and enjoy his winnings. Many more than that were shot, had shrapnel wounds, were burned over much and some most of their bodies, lost limbs and many lost their minds (PTSD) serving in harm's way for Cassius. He later stepped into the ring two more times to take back the championship. Cassius could appreciate his desire to pummel another human being within half an inch of his life to regain his world championship and win the prize money. He could also see the need for heavily armed policemen to protect the ring during every fight and the door outside against unwelcome, non-paying intruders but he couldn't see the need beyond that for men and women in the military to protect our borders and airspace so he could have that fight and win those championship prizes. This will forever be to his great shame. It is true his appeal was fought by his attorneys all the way to the U.S. Supreme Court where it was overturned but the draft dodger title will never change. [9] You know, I know and he knows that no nation can survive without a military to protect it. They that bear the sword do not "bear it not in vain." They are actually "God's minister(s) … avenger(s) to execute wrath on him who practices evil." Romans 13:4

Many celebrities and pro athletes decided to do the honorable thing—serve their country in its time of need. Some are the likes of Humphrey Bogart who served in the Navy in World War I. Gene Hackman served in the Army in China. Ronald Reagan served in the Army in World War II. Johnny Carson was a sailor in World War II. Charlton Hesston was in the Army Air Corps in World War II. Mickey Rooney left in the middle of filming a movie to join the Army in World War II. Paul Newman served in the Navy in World War II. Johnny Cash served in the Army in the Korean War. Chuck Norris served in the Air Force in South Korea. Willie Nelson was a soldier in the Army in the Korean War. Clint Eastwood was also a soldier in the Army in the Korean War. Elvis Presley answered his draft notice and served honorably in the Army. Rapper and actor, "Ice-T" served in the Army as did "Mr. T." Kris Kristofferson completed Army Ranger training and served in Vietnam as a helicopter pilot. More recently, Montel Williams graduated from the U.S. Naval Academy and became a Marine Lieutenant. [10]

Pro Baseball star and the first to break the race barrier, Jackie Robinson, served in the Army quite honorably in World War II reaching the rank of lieutenant. Yankee catcher, Yogi Berra served in the Navy, participating in the D Day Invasion of France. Pitcher, Bob Feller, was the first professional athlete to enlist in the Navy in World War II. Heavy weight boxer Jack Dempsey served in the Coast Guard in World War II participating on board ship during the Okinawa invasion and attained the rank of captain. Heavy weight boxing champ, Joe Lewis, served in the army in World War II and was awarded the Legion of Merit for his service. Ace pitcher, Ted Williams, served as a Navy pilot in World War II and was later part of the air raid on Pyongyang, Vietnam. Heisman Trophy winner, Roger Stauback graduated from the Naval Academy and served as a naval officer in Vietnam. Bob Kalser, after being named Rookie of the Year, entered the Army and completed airborne training. He was later killed by enemy mortar fire in Vietnam. Pat Tillman left s promising football career with the Arizona Cardinals to enlist in the Army. He graduated from Ranger School and served in Afghanistan where he was killed during a terrorist attack. [11] Many other pro athletes served their country in its time of need with both honor and distinction.

However, when duty calls some people never seem to be home. We have a world full of people today who have strength sufficient to stand stalwartly demanding every right and government in the book but none to do their duty. Millions of young men in America father children and immediately abandon the mothers and the children as well as abdicating their God-given responsibility to protect, provide and train up mighty seed as the family head. We can know that neither happiness nor respect will ever come our way while our back is turned to our duty. On the other hand, duty empowers us to greatness. It equips us to do all things well because God never calls anyone to a mission, service or responsibility without giving them the grace sufficient to more than meet the task. Once we have fulfilled our duty, we will never look back with regret for having done our best, which is all He requires. Shirked, we will never forget having failed it.

Many desire position, power and recognition as did the disciples of old, arguing who was the greatest and went on striving to set at the right hand of God in Heaven. (Matthew 20:21–23) A couple of the disciples and their mother seemed to overlook the cup of suffering servitude in duty that these places of honor required or that the grace to endure this had to be given by God.

What is my duty you may wonder? Just by showing up on planet earth and accepting Christ, we are instantly called to many significant duties (just to name a few):

- To freely forgive all those who have wronged us
- To confess our faults
- To cast all our care upon the Lord
- To defend the helpless
- To run to the battle
- To meet the needs of our own household
- To be our neighbor's keeper
- To find our place and serve others in the Body of Christ
- To bear our cross daily
- To humble ourselves before the mighty hand of God

Sometimes our duty may be arduous, dangerous and costly but it is the only thing in life that will fulfill. We were all created to accomplish something important for the glory of God and rarely is it going to be done without a cost, care or inconvenience. Christ's duty was to be rejected, falsely accused, condemned, nailed to a cross and given the most ignominious death known to man on His errand of taking away all the sins of the world. He didn't shirk it but marched straight to it and that without a whimper. It was the will of God and it was His duty.

What it means to have the **CHARACTER TRAIT OF DUTY:**

- An obligatory task, service, conduct or function arising from one's position
- The responsibility of position
- A legal, religious or moral sense of obligation
- Something done as a part of one's job

ARLY, BEING—   **Study start date: _____ Finish date: _____**

Possibly one of the worst things a person can do to themselves, in the real world, is something seemingly as small as arriving late to work. When a person is late, the supervisor subconsciously places their name in a box in his mind marked "duds." Now duds are various types of ordinance (ammunition, hand grenades, etc.) that look like the real thing and are made almost exactly like the real thing but they have one problem. They won't go off. They won't detonate or perform as advertised. When you pull the trigger mechanism—absolutely nothing happens. That's why they are called duds. A person who gets to work late is automatically going to be a problem. The boss is going to be wondering if this is a one-time thing or if it is the beginning of a pattern that is going to keep on occurring over and over again? And if the leader can't count on someone to even get himself to work on time, how in the world can this person ever expect to be selected for leadership? He can't. If his tardiness is tolerated, it will become a contagion for the entire team. If he can't be trusted to take care of himself and his own business, why would the boss put him in charge of other people. So he can teach all his employees all the various reasons why nobody should be expected to get to work on time? Not happening!

In a book written about General Dwight Eisenhower called *Soldier of Democracy,* among many other things, his practice was shared about always being ten minutes early to every appointment in life. Having adopted this practice, I can tell you this has been extremely beneficial. First of all, the fact is, **if you are on time, you are late**. People have already started getting nervous about whether or not you are going to actually make it in on time. Every day you put them into the drama of wondering if last-minute-Charlie is going to sashay in the front door and bless the group with his presence before the clock strikes the bewitching hour or do we need to start looking for someone else to do his work? The only way you can be on time is to be early.

Another problem to consider if one still wants to make a practice of just being on time, is that our world is full of un-expected obstacles and hindrances. Sooner or later you are absolutely going to wind up being late. In due time, on the way to work you will have a flat tire or run into a train passing a railroad crossing. A million things can cause you to be late if you are always shooting for just being on time. Some other benefits of arriving early are having the opportunity to get your own work area, equipment and paperwork in order before the official time to start. Also, if you always plan to be there early, you are going to know what the details for the day are and you might even get to pick which one you want. You will also have the opportunity to help the leader—who always has more than he can do—get everything ready for the entire group. If something ever causes the leader to leave the premises at the last minute, guess who he will more than likely be put in charge? That's right, you—because you are the only one who knows what is going on. He can count on you because you are always there early. He doesn't even have to ask you to come in early and help get everything ready because you are already going to be there. You will also miss the absolute waste of time and frustration of sitting in the early morning, rush hour traffic.

Most people would never consider arriving at work early because they think they are not getting paid for the time. This is a clear sign that they are working for money instead of working as unto the Lord. A prudent man is admonished to look not after just his own things but also to look after the things of others. (Philippians 2:4) He is always willing, as a profitable servant, to do more than is expected or required. Five promotions, three bonuses and two pay raises down the road, you will be more than compensated for coming in early. And, all this when the only motive in your heart was to be a blessing, be cooperative, be ready and always do more than your share in the first place.

What it means to have the character trait of **BEING EARLY**:

- Getting there before the official start time or the beginning of a process
- Every crop has some low hanging fruit that is ready for the one to pick who arrives early
- Arriving before the competition
- Planning to arrive early at every appointment in life

EFFICIENT TIME MANAGER—   Study start date: _____ Finish date: _____

One thing we all get very little of is time. The Bible tells us our days are passing swiftly, quicker "than a weaver's shuttle" (Job 7:6) and that our whole life is no broader than the breadth of a man's hand. (Psalm 39:5) The Psalmist admonished us to, "Remember how short (our) time is; for what futility (God has) created all the children of men? What man can live and not see death? Can (a man) deliver his life from the power of the grave?" (Psalm 89:47, 48) Of course the answer to that question is a resounding "No." However, if we can learn to control our time, we can learn how to multiply it and take control of our entire life as well.

Be aware though because time is quite a deceptive medium. It makes the young think they somehow have an unlimited supply but it goes quickly and, like money, can be spent only once. We all have less time than we think. On many occasions we all have fallen prey the notion that there was not enough time to do a particular job right, but only later find that we had enough time somehow to do it over. Time and laziness tell us to put off as much as we can until tomorrow. When people get an inkling of how short life actually is, many times they complain about its brevity and yet they still act as if there is no end to it. We tell ourselves that we need to retire from our career early to be happy but the truth is, happiness actually comes from serving others. No sense quitting too soon because we have this promise from God: the righteous will "still bear fruit in old age; they shall be fresh and flourishing." Psalm 92:14

We think tough times will never end—but they do. You see, tough times won't last but over and over we find that tough folks will. Time also has a way of speaking to our bodies and telling us "slumber longer, sleep to the crack of noon. You deserve it and besides, you're not a morning person." And yes, time can and will lie to us in more ways than one. Solomon said, "Do not love sleep, lest you come to poverty; open your eyes and you will be satisfied with bread." (Proverbs 20:13) If we never learn the discipline of rising early, we will make precious little of our lives because the early morning is the most productive part of the day. The early morning hours are free from the traffic, buzz and hubbub of the outside world, where we can be alone to think our creative thoughts, study the Word, pray and receive guidance from God's Throne Room. This is why David asked God to "Teach us to number our days that we may gain a heart of wisdom." (Psalm 90:12) By numbering our remaining days, we all find that we have very few days of strength remaining. We hope for seventy years (three score and ten) of strength but even those are not promised to us. (Psalm 90:10) It is a good practice to carry a book with us or some alternative work in our briefcase in case of unforeseen interruptions and delays in our schedule. It is also good to multi-task. Keep a couple projects running simultaneously whenever possible.

In Luke chapter 12 we find the story about a rich man whose ground produced plentifully. However, this was a problem for him because he had so much stuff he didn't know what to do with it. His barns were overflowing but the thought never occurred to him to share some of his bounty with the less fortunate on the other side of town. He thought "within himself" and you might say—only about himself and decided to rectify the problem by tearing his barns down and build them much larger. Then he would "say to himself, 'soul you have many goods laid up for many years; take your ease; eat drink and be merry.'" Just as he finished his new construction project, thinking he had all things situated perfectly for himself, God intervened saying, "Thou fool, this night thy soul shall be required of thee; then whose shall those things be, which you have provided?" Then God said, "So is he who lays up treasure for himself and is not rich toward God." (Luke 12:19–21) We see here that the rich man made some wrong estimates. He overestimated the time he had remaining and wrongly thought it was all for him. He never asked God why he always gave him more than he needed and never thought to use his abundance to help those less fortunate. We can see clearly from this parable that our time here is most uncertain and totally, other than the present moment, out of our control.

Because of this, Paul said, "See then that you walk circumspectly, not as fools but as wise, redeeming the time, because the days are evil." (Ephesians 5:15) Time will get away from you in a second if you aren't careful so we need to make the most of every opportunity in life. As brief as it is, amazingly, with the wisdom of God there is actually time for everything of importance. Ecclesiastes 3:1–8

One of the secrets of time management is to grasp securely the present moment. Whittier said, "The Present, the Present is all thou hast for thy sure possessing; like the patriarch's angel hold it fast till it gives its blessing." Don't waste time on frivolous activities, things that yield no eternal gain. Certainly a little rest and relaxation is well. Everyone needs as a vacation now and then but time itself is short and not to be squandered. The Book of Proverbs remind us that sleeping one's life away is slothfulness and very dangerous because time is truly a gift from God. In Proverbs 19:15 we find these words recorded: "Laziness (slothfulness in the KJV) casts one into a deep sleep and an idle person will suffer hunger." This is a promise right from the throne room of God. One day the richest and wisest man who ever lived walked "by the field of the lazy man, and by the vineyard of the man devoid of understanding; and there it was, all overgrown with thorns; its surface was covered with nettles; its stone wall was broken down. When I saw it, I considered it well; I looked on it and received instruction: A little sleep, a little slumber, a little folding of the hands to sleep—so shall poverty come on you like a prowler and your need like an armed man." (Proverbs 24:30–34) Instead, if we will stay awake and get to work, we are promised abundance.

Decide now that you are going to hustle like a young wildcat in this life! And to pounce on your opportunities and duties of life, without any reservation, like a panther. You'll be glad you did one day. Try your best to make every second of every day pay and produce. Multi-task where possible. Realize that we will all give an account one day to the Master as to how we spent every second. Productivity is what this life is about.

Dr. Harold Walker made these important observations about time: "There are doctors who are committed to healing their patients, dedicated to the high ideals of their profession and lawyers who are committed to justice and to the worthy aims of their work. They are so motivated that they command the moments and the hours. They do not simply work to live; they live to work for the good of mankind. They find their joy in their toil and their satisfaction in work well done. Desire, dedication and discipline are the keys to your destiny. They are antidotes for the procrastinating spirit. By their power you will choose action and not inertia; doing, not waiting to do; and seizing the present, not letting it go by default."

In every company there are busybodies, joke tellers and sloths. When they come around to waste your time, just let them know you are working on something important and maybe you can have lunch sometime. Believe me, they will get the picture. We see these words recorded in Proverbs 14:23, "In all work there is profit. But mere talk leads only to poverty." In due time, the talkers and joke tellers will be getting more flexibility in their schedule, the opportunity to meet new people and the ability to see new places because they will be the honored recipients of pink slips.

Remember, God has no problem with time. His is a perpetual clock. "But beloved," Peter said, "do not forget this one thing, that with the Lord one day is as a thousand years and a thousand years as one day." It is men, this side of the veil, who are limited by time. He went on to say, "the Lord is not slack concerning His promise, as some count slackness but is longsuffering toward us, not willing that any should perish but that all should come to repentance." (II Peter 3:8, 9) The purpose of our time on this planet is to find God, accept Him, learn of Him and begin to enjoy, serve and share Him with others. Then, we will enjoy Him forever in eternity. True enough, a loving God set us all down here in a hostile, wicked, unforgiving world. He also set it up so that we would all have a need for food, clothing, shelter, transportation, security and many other essentials. In addition to all that, He made sure we would have to face impossible situations from time-to-time and find ourselves in desperate need of His help. All these things would cause us to look to Him because the only way we can overcome in this life is to become an efficient manager of time and obtain the great gift of the God kind of faith. Because, "Without (Him we) can do nothing" (John 15:5) but "with (Him) all things are possible." (Luke 10:27) Indeed, He can focus, direct and grant us favor as well as multiply our time in this one, short life.

What it means to have the character trait of being **AN EFFICIENT TIME MANAGER**:

- Refusing to waste a second of our life
- Paying the price to arise early each day and reap the benefits of working in the most productive time of the day.
- Redeeming the time
- Refusing to put off until tomorrow what we can accomplish today
- Multitasking
- Spending our time wisely so that we have a life well spent on projects that reap eternal rewards.
- Able to use time-saving efficiencies in life
- Knowing the appropriate time for a task so you are right on time

EFFICIENT, BEING —   Study start date: _____   Finish date: _____

There are only a certain, limited amount of resources that will come through anyone's hands in a life time. Some more than others of course but we all will only receive or manage a finite amount. There are also invisible forces, powerful laws of economics and supernatural laws of blessing that actually govern either the multiplication or diminution of the resources we receive.

One is the Law of Use which says: if you don't use something you will lose it, s.s.: use it or lose it. On this planet, everything rusts, breaks down, rots, catches fire, becomes obsolete or gets stolen in time if you don't use it. Another is the Law of Appreciation: that whatever we fail to value or appreciate will soon be gone because we see little worth in it so it will somehow be taken from us. Finally, there is the Law of Faithfulness. It says those who are faithful with small things will soon find themselves trusted with much larger things, entities and responsibilities.

One day I was walking through our living room while my wife was watching one of her chick flicks (where everybody falls in love and cries a lot) and noticed in this movie that a much older man was trying his best to help his grandson by telling him, I believe, how the cow ate the cabbage and where the bear eats the buckwheat. Then he made a statement that went right over the boys' head when he said, "Fortune is infatuated with the efficient." Well, he missed it completely but it didn't get past me. I said, "Now that is truth." It has been one of my favorite quotes ever since. Think about it. Fortune, God's providence, the breaks, blessings, call it what you will, always seem to come to those who are efficient managers of resources. Good things continue to happen to people who can take little and make much. People who are faithful in the smallest things even to watching their pennies seem to, in time, make those pennies add up to millions. It seems as if God's providence shines down upon them and they always receive the greatest blessings in life.

Greater responsibility can also be expected, day after day and year after year. God uses resources as His school house of faith. We must show ourselves faithful in the management of these mundane, worldly things before He will give us more of them. More importantly, we must be faithful in the worldly things before He will give us the far more valuable and powerful spiritual things. He also watches to see if we have learned to be faithful with that which is another man's before He gives us things of our own. Very, very few people are ever born with a straight flush for a hand. Most of us have to work our way up—which is a good thing. We get to see, first hand, that faithfulness and efficiency work wonders. We all need to have time to learn the importance of getting along with others in the workplace. The process also gives society time to file down some of our rough edges and correct a few of our character flaws before we get to the top. This is the reason why the Bible admonishes us, when selecting someone to put in authority, to make sure they are "not a novice, lest puffed up with pride he fall into the same condemnation as the devil." I Timothy 3:6

Remember, the Master was impressed far more with the widow's mite being donated than he was with all the money the rich were putting in the temple treasury. (Matthew 12:42) She gave her all and the others, though certainly important too in the scheme of things, gave out of their abundance. On another occasion, after He had fed the thousands with a few loaves and fishes, Jesus made a point of having his disciples go back and pick up all the fragments the people had left. Most importantly, in Matthew 25:14 Jesus gives us insight as to how we each will be judged for our time on this earth. It won't be on our grades in school, the size of our house or how many cars we have. In this passage, He told a parable of a land owner giving talents to several of his servants. To one he gave five, another he gave two and to the other, he gave one and then he went on a long journey. After some time he returned to see what each had gained by trading and to settle his accounts with them. To the ones who had received five talents and two, similarly, he said, "Well done thou good and faithful servant, you were faithful over a few things, I will make you ruler over many things, Enter into the joy of your Lord." (v.21) Their rewards were truly great!

But to the servant who had received just one talent and failed to invest it, use it or even put it with the bankers to gain a little interest, He said this after listening to his excuses. "You are a wicked and lazy servant, you knew that I reap where I have not sown, and gather where I have not scattered seed. So you ought to have deposited my money with the bankers, and at my coming I would have received back my own with interest. Therefore (he told his other servants nearby to) take the talent from him, and give it him who had ten talents." Then he pronounced the law of the Kingdom saying, "For to everyone who has, more will be given, and he will have abundance; but from him who does not have, even what he has will be taken away." But He didn't stop there. It got worse. He went on to say, "And cast the unprofitable servant into the outer darkness. There will be weeping and gnashing of teeth." This is what I call a life and death parable. The consequences of not applying the truths of this parable to our lives can be far reaching, a matter of life and death as well as eternal in scope.

Don't you love His words to those who were faithful over just a few things, "I will make you ruler over many things." Then the best part, good for all eternity: "Enter into the joy of your Lord." It is just simply the law of the Kingdom, the law He put in nature and the basic, bottom-line law of His universe. It is an iron-clad truth for everyone and it will never change. We are all just stewards over our little time, few talents and resources but regardless of what we have or don't have, never forget, "Among stewards it is required (not optional) that we be found faithful." I Corinthians 4:2

We need to be efficient not only with our resources and talents but also with our time. We should be careful it is not wasted or stolen by the inefficiencies of the world system but we should also try to use it skillfully, as well as multiply it where possible. We should always be trying to find ways to use the resources entrusted to us more productively. Keeping a book in your briefcase, for example, to read or balance your check book in case you get held up for an appointment so you can redeem that time. Make a quick "motion and time study" on any repetitive work you might be doing. Multi-task wherever possible. Assign someone to do the repetitive, time consuming but fairly easy tasks, the pick and shovel work, if possible, so you are free to do the creative, more productive work. Try to stay employed in fields that utilize your talents and spiritual gift so you are always "in your zone" as they say in athletics, as well as working in harmony with the way God made you on the inside. Your time will multiply when you are in your zone. Finally, work with a faith goal of being a hundred-fold believer. Try to multiply your resources and God's in this life as a hundred-fold believer for the benefit of the Kingdom. With His help, of course, all things are possible.

Being an efficient manager includes checking your equipment, animals, bank records, etc. to watch for any abnormalities. Do your due diligence on a daily basis, We are admonished to "Be diligent to know the (condition of our) flocks, and attend to our herds." (Proverbs 27:23) Today many of us have our horses under the hoods of our cars, Today, our electronic and motorized equipment such as chain saws, lawnmowers, well pumps, etc., need our constant attention and preventive maintenance.

Remember, "Fortune is infatuated with the efficient."

What it means to have the character trait of **BEING EFFICIENT**:

- Able to produce with little or no waste of time or resources
- Being the agent that produces an effect
- Being effective in relative terms considering, cost, energy, time, materials and money

- Able to take little and produce quantity, quality and the desired result
- Operating without producing any or very little waste or lost motion
- Having a dynamic system
- Having a good ratio of production to energy and resources expended
- Resourcefulness in reusing materials
- Being creative in taking something one already possesses, which was actually made for another use and rather than buying the right material or equipment, adapting or tailoring it to fit or answer the present need.
- Redeeming the time
- Wasting no time by doing alternative work when being detained by others
- Eliminating unimportant, frivolous activities in order to have more time and energy for the important, consequential, productive work
- Applying a time and motion study to your activities
- Multi-tasking effectively
- Able to see value in what others consider refuse
- Able to reuse partially used items (s.s.: taking condemned or obsolete buildings apart and reusing the materials, taking paper printed on one side, cutting it up and making note pads out of the remaining clean side)
- Able to take little and make much
- Daily checking your animals including all the horses under your hood.

EMPATHY —   Study start date: _____ Finish date: _____

We all receive unique, even strange assignments from time-to-time in life. Each one is a test and will either be a stepping stone or a stumbling block along our path to the future as leaders. A large part of turning these difficult assignments into a success is having empathy for those under our authority, as well as those above and around us who may or may not share our plight.

Nehemiah truly had empathy. While in captivity as a cupbearer to the King of Persian, he heard a report from some of his countrymen returning to Babylon from Jerusalem, his hometown. When he heard that all its walls were torn down and its gates burned to the ground, he just sat down and wept. But, he didn't stop there. He fasted and prayed for several days. Their hurts and failings became his. This was apparent as he stood in the gap for them in prayer confessing their faults to God as his own. He truly felt their plight and had great empathy for the city and his countrymen there. He was so moved by it all that, at the risk of his own life, he asked the King to allow him to return Jerusalem that he might rebuild it. Amazingly, the King granted his request.

Once back in Jerusalem, the compassion he had for those who were there and subject to his authority was patently obvious in everything he did. His heart was with the people as he worked right alongside them. Nehemiah even laid stones on the wall himself, with a sword in one hand and his masonry trial in the other. When his life was threatened on one occasion, as it was many times, the people wanted him to sleep in the temple at night for his own protection. He refused, telling them instead that the bugler would be with him and wherever the battle raged the hottest when they were attacked on the perimeter that was where they could find him. The bugler would signal their whereabouts.

When Nehemiah heard that the remaining Jews were put in bondage once again as a result of being charged usury by their own countrymen, he was outraged. He held a national, public meeting and demanded that these debts be forgiven. He reminded them that they had just come out of slavery to heathen nations and now, here they were putting their own brethren into bondage again. He made them record an oath before the priests, this debt forgiveness for the people as well as their lands and property. Then he shook out the creases of his robe and prayed that God would likewise shake out the house and possessions of every man who did not keep his promise.

He was so anointed for this work and such a gifted leader that the entire wall and all its gates were completed in just 52 days. Remember that he didn't even really have to get into all of this. Nehemiah had a cush job and was well protected as a cupbearer in the King's court far away from this kind of hard work, warfare and physical danger. However, he was willing to do this because he had a heart for his God and countrymen.

What it means to have the character trait of **EMPATHY:**

- Feeling what the other person feels
- The ability to use one's imagination to perceive another's state to the point that you become emotionally infused with their plight.
- That which causes one to be alert to the needs, feelings, fears and ideas of others
- The ability to love others right where they are
- Deeply caring for and being concerned about the plight and conditions of others
- The capacity to live outside of one's self, enabling one to live for others and become enthused about making their lives and your community better for your having been there.

ENCOURAGEMENT —   Study start date: _____ Finish date: _____

In my mind, the Apostle Paul was far and away the greatest of all the apostles. Because of the importance of his mission, he was heavily attacked by the enemy. It was given to him to not only know the will of God but to raise up all the Gentile churches, set the doctrine for all New Testament churches and write two-thirds of the books of the New Testament. He was so important to God's plan for man that Barnabus, one with the gift of encouragement (his name even meant Son of Encouragement), was chosen by divine guidance to go with him on his first missionary journey. (Acts 13:2) Barnabus was also a wealthy land owner who sold much of what he had and laid it at the apostles' feet. His name even meant Son of Encouragement.

Unfortunately, some people you encounter in life have the uncanny ability to point out your every fault. Along with this widely-held talent, they can also quickly catalogue in a matter of a few seconds every reason under the sun why you won't make it, can't possibly cut the mustard and shouldn't even begin to try. On the contrary, others, with the rare but wonderful gift of encouragement can catch you at your worst—down and about to take the ten count—and say just the right things to spur you on to victory. Those with the gift of encouragement and their innate hope and enthusiasm, have the ability to, time and again, help those around them snatch victory from the jaws of almost certain defeat. These are the kind of people you need down in the fox hole with you in a war. For this reason, we should be slow to find fault and abundantly gracious, even extravagant, in our praise of others. This is so important that the Master will judge us one day by the Master on our ability to encourage others. (Matthew 25:31–46) We are commanded in Scripture to visit widows and orphans, those in prison, the halt, hungry, thirsty and the poor.

Just about all of us can look back to our meager beginnings in life to a time when we truly wondered if we would ever be able to make it. Then, maybe, someone saw something good, however minute possibly, in us, and spoke a word of encouragement. Even against the constant flood of all the nay-sayers, that one bright little glimmer of hope found its mark in our hearts and gave us the courage to carry on. Because encouragement is so necessary and powerful in a dry, hopeless, forlorn world, we should be looking for all the good we can find in our neighbors and simultaneously be about the business of overlooking the bad as much as humanly possible. God has not appointed us to failure, defeat or wrath but to victory. And, He did it at the cost of bankrupting Heaven and the death of His own Son, to get it to us. (I Thessalonians 5:9) Paul said, "Therefore comfort each other and edify one another ..." (v. 11) Just one word of encouragement easily has the power to carry a battered and beleaguered soul over fully, forty miles of bad road. Use that power of encouragement given to you. Use it wisely and use it often. You might be the one to change a person's entire life and eternity.

We also need to learn how to encourage ourselves in the Lord daily, as David did. There are just too many bad hands dealt everyone in life not to have this ability. There are too many betrayals and too many disappointments. We can't count on someone always being there to encourage us. If we don't learn how to do this, the only other possibility is we will fall for the devil's secret most powerful weapon: self-pity. This is exactly what he entices people who are passed over for a promotion at work to get them to take the situation in their own hands and start stealing from the company. Self-pity is what he uses to entice wives who aren't shown enough attention to start cheating on their husbands, etc.

Certainly we have a large responsibility, as well as a great opportunity is that of encouraging our fellow man. But, far and away, the greatest encouragement any of us will ever get is from God and His Word. The writer of Hebrews tells us that His promises are unchangeable and that it is impossible for

Him to lie. For those who have taken refuge in Him, will "have (a) mighty indwelling strength and strong encouragement to grasp and hold fast the hope appointed for us and set before (us.)" in the Bible. (Hebrews 6:18 Amp Ver) There are two thousand promises in it and all of them without caveats as to age, education, ability, wealth or position in life. He says, "we have this (hope) as a sure and steadfast anchor of the soul—it cannot slip and it cannot break down under whoever steps out upon it—(a hope) that reaches farther and enters into (the very certainty of the Presence) within the veil, (Leviticus 16:2) Where Jesus has entered in for us (in advance), a forerunner having become a High Priest forever ..." (v.19) Our hope goes supernaturally through the veil from this life into Heaven and is anchored in Christ, the Rock of Ages, who cannot be moved and cannot fail. We can also read and meditate on the Word of God daily and when we do, we are promised supernaturally encouraged such that "No man can stand before us all the days of our life." (Joshua 1:5) We will "Be strong and of a good courage" (v.6, 7, 9), He "will make (our) way prosperous and ... (we will) have good success." (v.9) Furthermore, David said meditating on the Word, made him "wiser that (his) enemies,." (Psalm 119:97) gave him "more understanding that all (his) teachers" (v.99) and more understanding "than the ancients." (v.100) Since we know God is not a respecter of persons and the Word was sent to us as well, these promises hold true to encourage all of us today. Read the Word and be encouraged.

What it means to have the character trait of **ENCOURAGEMENT:**

- To inspire to achieve, advance and endure
- To give impetus for success and accomplishment
- Being loath to find fault but always looking for embers of hope in another's personality, gifts and talents
- To be able to see and amplify another's good points
- Having words in season, well-spoken
- Giving the downtrodden, disadvantaged and discouraged hope
- To inspire with added courage
- When others falter and begin to wane, it is the power to lift them up to not only finish the course but to go on to accomplishment
- Knowing that ultimately we will all be judged on our willingness to encourage widows and orphans, the thirsty, hungry and poor

ENDURANCE—   **Study start date:** _____ **Finish date:** _____

Many today are flagging, faltering, failing and falling to pieces in the battles of life. Apparently they didn't realize there were going to be so many crooks and crannies, trials and troubles, enemies and ambushes along this road called life. Truly, the only thing that passes quickly in this life is time—not troubles. The great news, however, is that we ultimately have the victory in all of them in Christ Jesus if we will but endure.

A good example of one ill prepared for the struggles of life is Esau. Although he was a skillful hunter and a man of the field, he couldn't withstand a few hunger pains and ultimately sold his birth right to his brother Jacob for a bowl of porridge. Hunger pangs can be hard to bear but they won't kill you unless, of course, you fail to find food for several weeks on end. As an able hunter and the man in charge of farming and growing the family's crops, Esau certainly had the necessary skill to find food fairly efficiently. He just simply couldn't stand to bear a little inconvenience, pain or hardship.

Endurance is the ability to withstand adversity; the ability to sustain a prolonged instances of suffering. It comes from the root word "endue" which means to infuse or to harden. Some define it as to don or to put on clothes, armor or weapons of war, whatever it is you don't have. It is the ability to sustain pain and suffering over an extended period of time. We all happen to be lacking in so many ways. No one "has it all" so it is the putting on of whatever character qualities we are lacking in certain situations in life so we will be able to endure the trial we are facing at the time. We may need to put on patience, forbearance, humility, wisdom, kindness or whatever is needed but we must always keep the victory in sight. Keeping the vision of Christ and His victory gives us the ability to keep on declaring victory in the face of virtually certain defeat. The enemy will tell us how weak we are and how the weapons of our warfare aren't bothering him. However, just remind him that it is in our weakness that the power of God is made strong!" (II Corinthians 12:9) We all need to tell ourselves "I'm going to make it" even when circumstances indicate differently. Make up your mind that you will never quit and that your trials won't break you; they will make you. Keep on speaking to that mountain of trouble in your life and keep on telling it to move and be cast into the sea. It will move if you don't faint and lose heart. It has to because God always causes us to triumph in Christ Jesus! II Corinthians 2:14

For this to happen, we have to get to the place in life where we love the battle. If you don't learn to love it, you are going to be real unhappy because everybody's life is full of battles, tests, trials and troubles and always will be. Besides, we can never have a victory without a battle. We can't take in any of the enemy's spoil or take control of his territory without a battle. It is only in a battle that we get that adrenalin rush and a victory. Remember, "From the time of John the Baptist until now, the kingdom of heaven has suffered violence and the violent take it by force." (Matthew 11:12) And, only "He whose work endures to the end shall receive a reward." Matthew 24:13

We find from the Word of God that endurance is a great blessing. It is not only commanded but it will also be rewarded. The gravel road we are to walk will certainly not be an easy one. Jesus said, "You will be hated by all for My Name's sake. But he who endures to the end will be saved." (Matthew 10:22) We have to be "be strong in the grace that is in Christ Jesus" (II Timothy 2:1) because we "must endure hardship as a good soldier of Jesus Christ." (v.3) All are dealt our share of trials and troubles and all are betrayed from time-to-time. However, in time, if we will keep the faith and let Him, God will cause it all to come together for good for us. Romans 8:28

Paul exemplified this saying, "I endure all things for the sake of the elect, that they also may obtain the salvation which is in Christ Jesus with eternal glory" (II Timothy 2:10) He also recalled "the former days in which, after (the Hebrews) were illuminated, (they) endured a great struggle with sufferings: partly while (they) were made a spectacle both by reproaches and tribulations, and partly while (they) became companions of those who were so treated " as well. Hebrews 10:32, 33

Paul's endurance was ultimately rewarded as ours will be. He reminded Timothy that he endured the "persecutions (and) afflictions which happened to (him) at Antioch, at Iconium (and) Lystra—what persecutions (he) endured. And out of them all the Lord delivered" him. (II Timothy 3:11) James, the Apostle, gives us great hope in this regard as well saying, "Blessed is the man who endures temptation; for when he has been approved, he will receive the crown of life which the Lord has promised to those who love Him." James 1:12

It is up to us what we will do with our lives. We can hide on the sidelines or in the shadows but we are the only ones who can make sure our life is about the real thing. Paul warned us not to "look at the things which are seen but at the things which are not seen. For the things which are seen are temporary, but the things which are not seen are eternal." (II Corinthians 4:18) Pray now to grow in the area of endurance so that God can later throw you into the battle where He might need you. Spend time now to know Him because those who know Him "will be strong, and carry out great exploits." Pray that God will call you out for an important mission. (Daniel 11:32b) Make the most of the present time because "We are receiving a kingdom which cannot be shaken, (therefore) let us serve God acceptably with reverence and godly fear." Hebrews 12:28

What it means to have the character trait of **ENDURANCE:**

- The grace to press on bearing with much suffering to the finish line
- The ability to withstand all manner of hardships and adversity
- The ability to reject the complaints and pains of our own body. It will tell you that you are too tired and are finished when you can still keep going. Listen to the strong man of your spirit.
- The ability to endure suffering without complaint. Learn to speak faith and victory to your life, body, enemies and battles.
- The ability to declare victory in the face of seeming defeat and all types of negative news and information

NERGY—   **Study start date:** _____ **Finish date:** _____

S ince the speed of the crew is always the speed of the leader, it is understandable that those in authority out in the world are forever looking for people who have a lot of energy. The leader's energy level is highly contagious by virtue of his position of authority.

A friend who was very successful in the retail business was very interested in the energy level of job applicants. He made a practice of watching job applicants as they exited their cars in the parking lot to come in for their interview. If they were reticent to make their exit from their car and didn't have a click in their step coming in the store like they had some energy, he would eliminate them from consideration immediately.

Leaders are always out in front. In fact the word *leader* means "first" or "out front." To stay there any length of time you must have the energy to go farther, faster and longer than the rest of the team. You have to come in earlier and stay later. You've got to be willing to pay a greater price than the rank and file. If you are looking for a job where you will have to do just your fair share of the work, leadership is not for you. The leader always has to do more than anyone else. He has to think, dream up, research and hammer out a plan, train the team, acquire all the tools and materials they need early each morning, supervise, encourage, counsel and work alongside them. Then at close of business, he will probably have to maintain the equipment, seeing that everything is put away and begin preparations for and buying the material needed for the next day.

Leaders need a ton of energy just to overcome all the negativity in the world on a daily basis. To be a person of action, you have the stamina to seize the moment and always get the job done—to persist without exception. To do this and more, you are going to need plenty of energy and endurance.

For all these reasons, leadership courses in the military emphasize physical training as well as endurance. The leader must be equipped to endure hardship because warfare over the centuries has taught us that our enemies are going to do their best not only to inflict pain, death and hardship but also to diminish or if possible cut off our resources and supply lines. They will try to do inflict physical and mental damage on us, as quickly as it is in their limited power to do so. This is accomplished by psychological warfare, destroying the enemy's production of materiel (military-industrial complex) and food sources. In a real war-time situation, as a soldier, you may have to do a fourteen mile march with a full back pack, weapons, a three day supply of ammunition, rations and water, along with all your basic equipment and weapons as well having to carry some things that belongs to other members of the unit. The mortar platoon and the machine gunners can never carry all the ammo they will need. In addition to that, the tactical situation may dictate that you have to go without food or water or both for several days. When the enemy continues to shoot your re-supply helicopters out of the air, at some point headquarters will stop sending them as they did from time-to-time in Vietnam. I didn't mind the occasional few days without food so much. It was nearly running out of ammunition that I didn't care for. One time it got so bad the choppers had to just fly over and kick out the ammo and water in 155 Howitzer canisters along with a few cases of C rations.

Those in leadership know that certain people who face physical exhaustion, sleep and food deprivation will come completely unglued. Due to their lack of energy and intestinal fortitude, they immediately forget to keep their mission and men first and soon cave in to the pain of starvation and lack, becoming totally engrossed with self-preservation.

Other than genes, there are, happily, many other things that contribute to a person's energy level. One of which is whether or not you are working in your functional gift (there are nine of them found in I Corinthians 12) because we need to be acting in harmony with the way God has made and motivated each of us. Another factor that contributes greatly to a person's energy level is whether or not they like their work and feel it is meaningful to them and to society. It is hard for someone to maintain a certain momentum doing something they dearly hate. However, we always seem to have the energy to do more of what you love and feel is meaningful to society and God. Actually, everyone's work is important.

I remember years ago the sanitation department of the city where we lived went on strike. The garbage didn't get picked up for two weeks and it kept stacking up, ever increasing in its ability to cast off an aroma. At the end of that episode no one had to tell people in the community that the sanitation workers were important. We got it. What I am talking about here though is that you, yourself and nobody else, must believe in your heart that what you are doing, your own work, is important.

Another reason for a lack of energy and a reason some people fall into a lethargic lifestyle is that there may be no requirement for physical activity in their particular field of endeavor. As time progresses, more and more people spend an ever-increasing amount of time every day tapping on computer key boards as well as being progressively more desk and office-bound, sedentary jobs. If so, a one hour exercise regimen three to five days a week should be considered. Go to any local gym and find a personal physical trainer to set you up with a one hour or so work-out program. Gym membership is incredibly inexpensive for all the benefits to your health. If that doesn't work for you, they will set you up on an exercise program you can do at home which can be done with or without equipment. You might also want to invest in some kind of cardiovascular exercise machine because you really need to take care of your heart! Studies have shown that people with a sedentary lifestyle have less heart mass, meaning that exercise and especially cardiovascular exercise is very important. Remember, there is a price to pay for not exercising properly. If you don't, your body has censors that tell the brain you are dying and they will start shutting down your various organs earlier than normal. Your body and your bones will ache, you won't have any energy and your mind will start collecting cobwebs. Soon you will feel decrepit, have an aversion to any kind of physical activity and start thinking you are old. Exercise keeps your weight down, moves life and cell building blood through your body, gives you a greater desire to eat less as well as keeps you toned and fit.

What good is it for you to prosper in life and be a leader if you don't have your health? You won't enjoy life. You might want to think about what kind of a physical body you would like to inhabit twenty years from now (should the Lord tarry)? Would it not be the one you currently occupy, hopefully, trim and fit? Therefore, we best take care of it. It is also no doubt a given that we have all had our excesses over time and from time-to-time failed to exercise properly but wouldn't right now be a great time to start being as good stewards of our health, the very best we can?

Yet another reason people have so little energy is an improper diet and not drinking enough water. To properly hydrate the body, you need to drink at least 32 ounces of water a day in addition to what you get through other liquid intake with coffee or tea. Water is necessary for the body to make the blood that carries energy and building materials to the various cells throughout the whole body.

Finally, eating too much or eating the wrong things certainly contribute to a low energy level as well. Not eating a proper breakfast is a significant cause of an energy deficiency. Breakfast is the foundation of your day's energy and good health. Going without breakfast is like failing to put any fuel in your body's gas tank and then going out to do a full day's work. We will also agree that some foods are better for us than others. Some actually have very real, metabolic, medicinal value and will not only help maintain your physical health but can also build it up over time. My lovely wife, Donna, has had me on what I call the "Breakfast for Warriors" for years. We are all warriors in this world for God or we should be. The other day I decided to look into what all is in this basic, quick bowl of cereal and the things it actually does for you. It will make you feel like you can whip your weight in wildcats. Here it is. Try it (the breakfast that is). I believe you will like it: Just in case you want to try it, I have printed it at the bottom of this article because I want you to enjoy life and live a long time.

What it means to have the character trait of **ENERGY:**

- Having plenty of "get up and go."
- The capacity to work, act, perform and keep right on with it all over an extended period and in the midst of great difficulties, facing immense obstacles
- The power to exert one's self vigorously over an extended period of time
- Having a capacity for work
- Stamina
- The basic inherent physical fuel, physical strength and mental resources to keep driving on when your body is telling you it is through

BREAKFAST FOR WARRIORS

By Winston & Donna Menzies

SOME KIND OF DRY ORGANIC CEREAL: (Non-sugar coated)
OATMEAL SQUARES (Quaker) or
FLAX PLUS (Nature's Path) Granola Cereal or
ALL BRAN (Kellog's) or
MULTIGRAIN SQUARES (Casdadian farm) or
ORGANIC SMART BRAN (Nature's Path) or
OPTIMUM (Organic- Nature's Path) or
Whatever non-sugar coated, organic kind you like

FRESH BLUEBERRIES—Good for the brain and the eyes, has vitamins and helps the circulatory system. Blueberries are FANTASTIC! They are the most powerful and potent fruit on the planet! The ten top health benefits from blueberries according to Women's Fitness web site are as follows:

(1.) It has the highest antioxidant capacity of all fresh fruit. It has lots of Vitamin C, B complex, Vitamin E, Vitamin A, copper (a very effective assist to the immune system and also highly anti-bacterial), selenium, zinc, iron (also promotes immunity in the blood), generally boosts the immune system and prevents infection.

(2.) It neutralizes free radicals known to cause disease and aging of the body. Blueberries are #1 in the world of antioxidants primarily due to its pigment, Anthocyanin.

(3.) Helps reduce belly fat, reduce factors for metabolic syndrome and cardiovascular disease.

(4.) Promotes urinary tract health. Blueberries have a compound of heavy molecules known to inhibit the growth of colonies of bacteria such as b-coli that try to build colonies on the lining walls of the urinary tract. They also have a few anti biotic properties that contribute to this effect as well.

(5.) It has been proven to preserve vision. They are high in anthocyanosides which have been found in studies to retard visual loss. Three or more servings a day helps with macular degeneration which is the primary cause of vision problems in older adults.

(6.) Good for brain health. The anthocyanin, vitamins A, B-complex, C and E, zinc, sodium, potassium, copper, phosphorus, magnesium, manganese and the selenium among other things can prevent as well as heal certain brain disorders. All these prevent the death of neurons (brain cells) and restores health to the central nervous system. They can even cure serious problems with Alzheimer's disease to a considerable extent.

(7.) Helps protect against heart disease. The high fiber content of blueberries, the brilliant antioxidants and the blueberry's ability to dissolve "bad cholesterol" make it the perfect dietary supplement to cure many heart diseases.

(8.) Cures constipation and helps with digestion. The roughage or fiber of blueberries assist in warding off constipation. The sodium, copper, vitamins, acids and fructose all help to improve digestion.

(9.) Helps cure cancer. Blueberries contain compounds like Pterostilbene (good remedy for liver and colon cancer) as well as Ellagic Acid which along with Anthocyanin and some other antioxidants such as copper and vitamin-C can actually do miracles to both prevent and cure cancer.

(10.) Other helpful factors. Blueberries also keep you active and alert as well as in a good mood as an effective antidepressant. You won't need to spend as much on medicines and blueberries produce no known negative side effects. [12]

CINNAMON POWDER—Half a tablespoon a day lowers blood sugar (especially type 2 diabetes) and cholesterol levels. It helps with safe weight loss. It gives natural menopause symptom relief for women. Cinnamon helps reduce the spread of leukemia and lymphoma cancer. It has an anti-clotting effect on the blood. Half a tablespoon of cinnamon powder used along with a tablespoon of honey every morning can give significant relief from arthritis pain. It also fights E. coli bacteria in unpasteurized juices. [13]

WHEAT GERM (2 tablespoons)—Has various healing effects due to its vitamin E and folic acid content. It helps with hormonal disturbances. Expectant and nursing mothers use wheat germ to prevent miscarriages and premature births. It helps with heart problems. Wheat germ's vitamin E content contributes greatly in the area of cell regulation as well as stopping blood clotting problems. Wheat germ helps with obesity. It does this by healing hormonal disturbances which, in turn, assist in curing weight problems caused by unsettling hormones. Helps heal an enlarged prostate because it has the ability to decrease inflammation with its essential fatty acids. [14]

HONEY (Raw & local)—about a tablespoon—It is good for its B vitamin and helps with allergies. In addition it is also a wonderful natural sweetener since the body does not have to break it down like sugar. It helps considerably to sooth a stubborn sore throat. It also gives a huge natural quick energy boost for work and athletic events. Honey is made up primarily of natural sugars (carbohydrates) and water along with enzymes, vitamins, minerals and amino acids. It also contains a number of phenolic acids and flavonoids that work like antioxidants going about in the body scavenging for and eliminating free radicals. [15]

SOME 2% MILK—It is a complete food for the young animals of each species including humans. It also adds calcium for strong bones in all ages. It gives us milk sugar or lactose which aids in the growth of the beneficial bacteria in the digestive tract. Milk also gives us riboflavin, protein, iron and vitamins A, B and D. [16]

According to gotmilk.com, a recent study by the American Psychiatric Foundation revealed that a lack of sleep was the most overlooked health problem in America. The resultant sleep deprivation damages our memory and our wellbeing through a lack of alertness. A protein found in milk can improve the quality of our sleep and improve our alertness the following day. People who are having problems sleeping should drink a glass of milk before going to bed at night. [17]

2 or 3 CUPS OF COFFEE—Coffee was recently found to cause the tips of our brain cells to stay alive and thus stave off Alzheimer's. Some recent studies have found that coffee (from the Journal of agricultural and food Chemistry) contains soluble fiber of a type that can actually lower cholesterol. It only contains one gram per cup which is small but counts each time you have a cup and adds to the already growing stack of positive coffee news. Harvard researchers just recently completed extensive research which found that regularly drinking coffee will significantly lower a person's chances of having type 2 diabetes. The more one drinks, the lower their risk becomes. Despite coffee's generally bad reputation for causing heart problems, recent epidemiologic studies have found no such connection. Some actually found coffee can be medically protective. The Journal of Clinical Nutrition stated that people over 65 who drink four or more cups of caffeinated beverages (mostly coffee) had a 53 percent lower risk of heart disease than non-coffee drinkers. It has also been linked with a reduce risk of gallstones, liver cancer, Parkinson's disease and cirrhosis. [18]

Eating an egg, a piece of toast and some grits occasionally is good too.

NTHUSIASM —   **Study start date:** _____ **Finish date:** _____

So many people fail to succeed in life because they never get excited about the potential a productive life can hold. Opportunity on this planet abounds for the enthusiast. It takes energy and enthusiasm to climb mountains and surmount obstacles. Lazy, disinterested people never get anything done in life because there is nothing they are really fired up about doing.

On the contrary, the whole world is a plumb, ripe for picking, to the enthusiast. Opportunity abounds. It truly does. All we need to do is what we have always been told, "Find a need and fill it." Norman Vincent Peale once said, "The whole world belongs to the enthusiast who can keep cool." It is important to have enthusiasm so deeply lodged in our heart that it becomes part of our personality. Once there, it never wanes and makes us who and what we are. Charles Swab, the great early American industrial tycoon penned these words: "A man can succeed at almost anything for which he has unlimited enthusiasm." If you stay motivated, it won't be long before the competition fades, the doors that been resisting you crack open and you find success like a finely wrapped package sitting on your doorstep. You just have to love whatever it is you are doing, get excited about the situation and stay at it. The great philosopher Emerson remarked, "As for me, I believe that enthusiasm is the spice of life... . . Nothing great is ever achieved without enthusiasm."

Arnold Toynbee said "Apathy can only be overcome by enthusiasm, and enthusiasm can only be aroused by two things: first, an ideal which takes the imagination by storm and, second, a definite intelligible plan for carrying that ideal into practice." Actually there is a third: a zeal and zest for life itself and the opportunity each day holds to create, build, invent, motivate and encourage others. There is so much in life to be excited about. Sure, there are temporary set-backs, hold-ups, disappointments and seemingly immovable obstacles but in time they can all be overcome. A quote from *The Catholic Layman* I found years ago stated that, "Every man is enthusiastic at times. One man has enthusiasm for thirty minutes—another has it for thirty days—but it is the man who has it for thirty years who makes a success in life."

No one wants to be around the eternal pessimist. People never have and never will like those who are always negative, who have nothing but criticism and condemnation for everything and everybody. No, the world always has its "Help Wanted" sign out for a man who is excited about lifer and is always ready to tackle a difficult problem or situation—just for the thrill of being a servant and the joy of turning things around for good. They are looking for someone who believe in people, who believe and still has hope no matter how many times he gets knocked down. The world is seeking a man who is always enthused about life who can always get the job done. Henry J. Kaiser, the great industrialist, said, "When a tough, challenging job is to be done, I look for a person who possesses an enthusiasm and optimism for life, who makes a zestful confident attack on his daily problems, one who shows courage and imagination, who pins down his buoyant spirit with careful planning and hard work, but says, 'This may be tough, but it can be licked.'"

It may sound strange but I have loved just about every job I have ever had. That includes my first job which was pulling weeds on a gladiola farm in Bellevue, Nebraska. I've lived in southern California, Arizona, Texas, Georgia and Florida as well as a number of other places and I tell you it seemed like it got hotter in Nebraska in the summer than anywhere. Everybody ought to weed gladiolas for a while. All day long we were on our knees in the hot sun crawling between the rows of those gladiolas pulling weeds. I was only ten and all the other boys were twelve or older but I loved it. Besides, I was just proud to have a real job and we were making big money, 75 cents an hour. Loving that job might have had something to do with my enthusiasm. Over time, I have hired out for a bus boy, waiter, dishwasher, fry cook, builder, cashier, ditch digger, soldier, back-hoe operator, jack-hammer operator, demolitions man (blasting rock), block mason, framer, machinist, welder, ranch hand, carpenter, sheetrock hanger, concrete finisher, building designer, commercial real estate broker and a preacher just to name a few. For some reason I liked every one of those jobs and thought they had great value to society. The only job I really disliked was KP duty in the Army. I would much prefer to be issued a rifle and a couple hand grenades and go to the front lines with the troops than be on mess hall duty. With the possible exception of KP, I have never had a day when I wasn't fired up and enthusiastic about going to work and doing a job. What a blessing to live like this.

At fifteen, our family lived on an Air Force Base on the northeast end of Canada and that is spelled "c o l d." Seemed like we had snow on the ground most of the time. The base was so far north that there were no roads to it. You could only get there by boat or airplane. It was a pretty big air base, kind of like a small city. It was my great fortune at the time to get a job in the Officers' Club as a bus boy on Saturday mornings. I was so proud of that job. Our uniform was black slacks and shoes, a white shirt, a white sort of captain's jacket and a black bow tie. I really loved that job and thought I was as important as the President of the United States to do that work. Besides, I was up to $1.25 an hour by that time and couldn't have been happier or more enthused. Before long, however, the clipper operator (the dish washer had a big conveyor operated steam cleaner) quit so I got his job and hired one of my buddies as the busboy. Not long after that the fry cook quit and I moved into his job, moved the bus boy up to clipper operator and hired another buddy to be the bus boy. Bob Hope came up and did a show from time-to-time and I even got to fix breakfast for Anita Bryant! Then a little later, the dining room manager and cashier quit so, you guessed it, I took that job, moved the clipper operator to fry cook, the bus boy to clipper operator and hired another little buddy to be the bus boy. I, for one, was too young to even get a driver's license but here we were running the entire Officers' Club on Saturday mornings. None of us knew what we were doing but we were eager to learn and were all thrilled to have a job. The force behind that whole thing, although we probably didn't know it at the time, was enthusiasm.

Wherever I go people ask, "How are you doing?" I always tell them "So good I can hardly stand it!" I say it so sincerely, enthusiastically and naturally and they are expecting a much less optimistic report in such a hopeless world, they usually respond, "Really?" To which I usually say, "Really! But it's getting better!" And, it truly is. A good many have actually said, "How can you be so happy?" or "I sure would like to have some of that." What an opening!!!

Count your blessings. Write them down. I really mean it. We are all so very blessed and life is full of opportunities for all of us. He made you for a special purpose. You have been given a genius to do something great for the world. Step out with excitement and get it done with enthusiasm. It doesn't even cost a thing to be enthusiastic and it may be one of the most valuable assets a human being can possess. Today is your day! Go for it!

What it means to have the character trait of **ENTHUSIASM**:

- Being fired up
- Being excited
- Being highly motivated
- Having an optimistic view of things
- Having a feeling of overwhelming optimism and excitement about something, your work or life in general
- The feeling that inspires and energizes one to passion, zeal and great fervor
- An attitude that inspires one to give themselves wholly, with reckless abandon, to whatever they are involved in

EXCELLENCE—   **Study start date: _____ Finish date: _____**

Excellence, doing things with a high standard and achieving beauty is what the world is in search of. The best of everything is always a winner. It is the mark to shoot for and will pay you well en every currency known to man.

On the other hand, poor performance is not something anyone knowingly shoots for but can occur very easily for a variety of reasons. Oftentimes, poor quality work is the result of having little talent for the job. However, more often it is the result of a lack of ambition, the lack of a high personal standard of performance or working for the wrong person.

Little talent—This is a problem most of us have at least to begin with. Certainly very few people are ever born overburdened with an abundance of talent. However, we can train, we can apprentice, we can be teachable, we can ask questions, we can read books and we can hone what little skill we do have. If talent was a pre-requisite in life, very few things would ever get done and even fewer would be done well. The world has always been looking for a man with 25 years' experience and a master's degree who is no more than twenty years old. To overcome this, the Bible says, "Whatever your hand finds to do, do it with (all) your might …" (Ecclesiastes 9:10) Do your best! Give it all you've got. Remember, no one ever felt good about doing a job half-way, just to get by and we never regret having done our best.

A lack of ambition- In Matthew 25:14 the Master laid out His plan for man on planet earth. He said we would all be judged, not on how many talents we had been given but how we had multiplied what talent we have. You know the story, how the Master was going to a far country and left varying talents with his workers. Two doubled theirs and one hid his in the ground. The two who doubled theirs were rewarded with much greater kingdoms to rule and the one who had only one, did nothing with his. He tried to blame his poor performance on the Master but, in reality, he was just lazy and full of fear. His bad attitude and lack of ambition resulted in the loss of his talent and finally resulted in being cast "into outer darkness where there is weeping and gnashing of teeth." Don't be afraid to set high goals for yourself. It costs nothing to shoot for the stars. .Once your goals are set, you just have to work toward them knowing the results will be rewarded in many ways. This is a motivating factor in life, in and of itself.

Working for the wrong person- Most people are working for money in life which means they are working for themselves and for what's in it for them. To them, life is all about what they can get and not about working for favor or serving or being a blessing to others. Paul told the Colossians3:23, "Whatever you do, do it heartily (with all your heart and might), as (unto) the Lord and not to men." Don't be a man pleaser and don't work for money. If you love money, the wisest and richest man who ever lived promised that you would never get enough. Turn your work in to God every day. If your work is done well enough to be turned into God, Himself, you won't have to worry about what your boss right here on earth might think about it. Pleasing God should be our standard of performance.

What it means to have the character trait of **EXCELLENCE**:

- Living and working at the highest efficiency and having a high standard
- Being above average or superb
- Meeting the mark of being the best of its kind
- Having no defects
- Striving toward the highest mark

- Being made valuable because of quality, performance or service
- Attaining to a higher standard of performance, expectation or beauty
- Being outstanding
- Delivering quality
- The highest standard of perfection
- Making your work conform to a quality suitable to hand in to God, Himself, who is actuality our real Boss.

AIR, BEING OR FAIRNESS— Study start date: _____ Finish date: _____

The world never has been fair and, for the most part, never will be. However, as a leader, being fair needs to be our hallmark. A lack of it, on the other hand, will cause us to lose the moral authority to lead. Having unjust scales, breaking our word and not fulfilling our promises destroy relationships.

It is a simple fact, almost every follower, subordinate and employee in the world, sooner or later will ask themselves these four question ns about their leaders:

1. Do they really care about me?
2. Will they treat me fairly?
3. Are they real, humble and approachable?
4. Do they have the ability, experience and knowledge to improve my life as well as my service to God and others?

Whether or not our leader is in politics, the military, business, the church or the home, like it or not, these questions are forever being asked by people and demand answers in the affirmative. For a person to perform well and do their best, an environment must be created where workers feel they will be treated fairly and have the opportunity to advance and thrive in their personhood. These questions actually have to do with their very survival.

One of God's greatest commands to leaders in answer to this basic human need is found in Micah 6:8. Here leaders are commanded to, "Do justly, love mercy and walk humbly with (our) God."

People simply must trust their leaders. For this to happen, the leader, first of all, must be just, as I said, in order to have the moral authority to lead. Subordinates must know that their leader will always be fair and equitable. No matter who or what is involved in any situation, they must know the leader will always be fair and will consistently be found on the side of "right." They must believe that even when the circumstances make it look like the leader may have done them wrong, before all the smoke clears, they have found them to have been fair for so long, they won't believe the bad report. They know there must be a reason things appear to be a certain way. However, they also know that, in time, there will be a vindicating circumstance that will show the right thing had been done or that the situation will be made right for them in the end.

Another large part of leaders being fair is for them to love mercy. Mercy is truly powerful force and always triumphs over judgment. (James 2:13) Yes, there is a time for judgment but we, as leaders, should always be looking for excuses to be merciful as long as possible.

Finally, humility must be a central component in a leader's personality and style as well. We can't expect someone to be humble with their fellow man or those under their charge if they are not first humble before God. A fair leader will not twist, color, distort or do torture to the facts in any situation for personal advantage or try to protect some particular person or group. A good leader will first gather all the facts about the situation, listen intently to both sides and then make a timely, fair decision.

What it means to have the character trait of **BEING FAIR**:

- Working, responding and conforming to established rules
- Staying within the proper bounds

- Being equitable
- Doing the right thing regardless of the cost
- Hating injustice and discrimination
- Allowing and facilitating the redress of grievances by subordinates
- Judging according to prescribed standards without deviation
- Doing those things that are right, sound and proper
- Endeavoring to make decisions that are incontestable
- Doing one's best to give equal, even-handed treatment to all involved
- Unbiased
- Being honest and impartial
- Free from prejudice
- Not inhibited by favoritism or self-interest

AITH— Study start date: _____ Finish date: _____

So many people actually think they can live this life and navigate its pathways without faith. They believe that raw strength, ability and intellect will suffice. If God really created the heavens and the earth (Genesis 1:1), could anyone really think that He would be so foolish as to let the wicked prosper in this world without Him more than the ones who live by faith? Not so. Sooner or later each person will encounter a mountain too high, a valley too wide, a task too great or a race too long and arduous for man's frail frame. Some might even be dealt an unseen swift and heavy blow of betrayal, divorce or an economic collapse that wipes out a business or a whole litany of other possibilities that have happened to people in life.

Faith is what makes sense of things that absolutely defy reason and make no sense whatsoever. Faith believes in a loving God who can turn the harshest mistreatment and our worst personal failure into our greatest success. It is called the transcendent glory of God. Faith simply believes that "all things, work together for good to those who love God, to those who are the called according to His purpose." (Romans 8:28) No matter how deep the problem, stop and thank Him for trusting you with it. Be patient and praise Him for the solution while serving Him without complaint. He will, in time, bless you unbelievably. No matter what you believe God can do, He will do far better. That's right, no matter what you are believing for, no matter how impossible it may be, "He is able to do exceeding abundantly above all that we ask or think, according to the power that works in us." (Ephesians 3:20) What power is that? God's power. God's resurrection power at work in us!

Few people have ever suffered more that Job. This man was upright, feared God and shunned evil. Though he was the greatest man in all the East, in a matter of minutes, raiders killed all his servants, took all his livestock and then, all his sons and daughters died in a tornado. That was not the end of his sorrows, however. He had painful sores come upon him from the top of his head to the tips of his toes until his body was covered with worms and scabs. His skin was broken and festered with infection and skin worms. When his friends saw him in this condition, they could hardly recognize him. All they could do was just throw dirt on their heads in unbelief, sit down and weep, saying nothing because they could see how greatly he was suffering. His wife even told him to curse God and die. He said if anguish and misery could

Job scraping skin worms

be weighed on scales, his would surely outweigh the sand on the seashores. He lamented, "God has made me a byword to everyone, a man in whose face people spit." He was totally misunderstood by his wife and closest friends. But, he had faith in the midst of it all saying, "Though God slay me, yet will I trust

Him. Though the skin worms consume my flesh, yet in my flesh I will see God and not another." (Job 19:25) He kept the faith, trusted God and feared Him in the worst of all circumstances and in the end God doubled all he had. Amazing.

We all have faith and we all start out with the same mustard seed size of faith. The question is not whether we have faith but how large we will allow ours to grow? Until it moves mountains? God never intended for us to trust in man and man's flawed and failed institutions and contrivances in life. He intended for us to build our lives by faith. In this regard, He said, "The just shall live by faith." (Habakkuk 2:4) The world cannot compare with what God can do with a man's life who is led, energized and motivated by faith.

What it means to have the character trait of **FAITH**:

- That which empowers the allegiance to fulfill our duty to a person, company or Sovereign.
- The belief, trust and loyalty to our God
- Acting on what you believe
- The rock-solid belief in something that cannot be seen or for which we find no physical proof
- That which brings heaven and earth together
- Absolute confidence in the promises of the Master
- Something truly believed
- Being fully persuaded
- Believing you have already received the thing you are believing for before you have it
- It is the title deed to things hoped for
- It "is the substance of things hoped for, the evidence of things not seen." Hebrews 11:1

FEARLESS, BEING—   Study start date: _____ Finish date: _____

There are only two types of people in the world: Those laboring under a spirit of fear and those living in the freedom of the Spirit of life in Christ Jesus. Faith in God is the only true defense against fear. Four hundred and fifty times the Bible tells us not to fear. The phrase, "Fear not" is God's most often repeated command. The reason is that fear is such a powerful debilitating force. It immobilizes a person, makes the blood vessels constrict and keeps one's adrenal glands pumping hormones into the blood stream. Fact is we human beings can only respond to situations we are confronted with in life either in faith or fear. There are no other options. In addition, fear and faith cannot co-exist. They are completely incompatible forces, concepts, mindsets, spirits, and motivations. When we are afraid, we need to say, "I know in whom I have believed and am persuaded that He is able to keep that which (I) have committed to Him until that Day (the Day of Recompense)." (II Timothy 1:12) Hopefully, we have already committed our life and everything we have got to God. We are wise to do so because for every fear there is a corresponding promise in God's Word to overcome it. If a person is fearful, it is because their heart is not yet in agreement with God's Word in a particular area. Fear activates the devil and energizes his kingdom much like faith moves God. Job said, "The thing I feared most is come upon me." (Job 3:25) Also, most of the energy expended on fear is lost because they say about 92% of the things people worry about never happen anyway. S.I. McMillian tells us there are fifty-one diseases directly related to fear and any or all of them can kill you. Fear also has torment. Most importantly, however, it robs people of the blessings, power, healings and promises of God.

We see how important it is for Christians not to be fearful in God's selection of the army Gidon raised to fight the Midianites and Amalekites. Gideon was camped at the well of Harod and was hopelessly outnumbered by the enemy which was encamped just north of them on the hill of Moreh. At the beginning of God's selection process, Gideon's army consisted of 32,000 men. Then God said, "The people who are with you are too many for Me to give the Midianites into their hands, lest Israel claim glory for itself against Me. Now therefore, proclaim in the hearing of the people, 'Whoever is fearful and afraid, let him turn and depart at once from Mount Gilead.'" Immediately twenty-two thousand men headed for their homes. Then God said they still had too many and had Gideon send them all down to the brook where he would test them for being battle capable. All those who stuck their faces in the water and lapped it up like a dog were

sent home. Those who drank it by the handfuls, being ever watchful, careful and cautious were allowed to stay. Thus, momentarily, he was down to only 300. Of course Then God gave them the battle plan of attacking the enemy at night with trumpets and torches inside of pitchers. They were to blow their trumpets, break their pitchers at the proper moment and charge down the hill attacking the enemy shouting, "The sword of the Lord and Gideon." (Judges 7:18) Of course the enemy would be immediately thrown into confusion and total victory would be the Lord's. However, this was such a bold, dangerous plan that God knew the fearful couldn't stick with it. They would likely have started murmuring and complaining if not going into total mutiny at the last minute thus foiling His plan and endangering the whole army. However, with the proper number of brave soldiers, the plan worked perfectly. The enemy fell into mass confusion and began fighting each other with their swords. Then, whatever remained of them fled?

As to fearlessness, King David was, without a doubt, the greatest warrior Israel ever had. The Bible tells us "Saul has slain his thousands and David his ten thousands." (I Samuel 18:7) It also says God "(trained) his hands for war and his fingers for battle." (Psalm 144:1) When challenged for forty days, it was David who volunteered to fight the Philistines' champion, Goliath, when no other soldier in all Israel would. In fact, when all the men in Israel's army saw him, they fled immediately in fear and anguish. However, when David saw him, he ran toward him and the entire Philistine army. He reached in his bag and pulled out a smooth stone and killed the giant with his slingshot. The stone hit Goliath squarely between the eyes and down he went like a sack of potatoes. David then took the giant's sword and cut his head off." (I Samuel 7:51) When the Philistine army saw their champion beheaded by what seemed to be a young lad, they fled in fear. This single act of bravery energized the entire Israeli army to attack and vanquish the enemy. The point the Bible is making here is that fearlessness is indispensable for all of us but especially among soldiers.

Fear is the enemy of faith and was first mentioned in the Bible just after the flood. (Genesis 9:2) In the world we have many real and imagined enemies. Since they usually hit us unexpectedly, they are quite capable of striking fear in the heart of men. There are actually many fears: 1) Fear of lack 2) Fear of death 3) Fear of failure 4) Fear of impending danger 5) Fear of disease 6) Fear of the people 7) Fear of falling and 6) the Fear of God. We should never forget that fear is the enemy of faith so let's see how they can be overcome.

Fear of lack. The Bible says, "There is no fear in love, but perfect love casts out fear, because fear involves torment. But we know he who fears is not made perfect in love." (I John 4:18) Perfect love knows that "all things work together for good to those who love God, to those who are the called according to His purpose." (Romans 8:28) Dr. Dyer said, "There are only two fires in the crucible of life: those that consume and those that purify." We decide which one of those fires all our troubles will be. They can burn us up and make us bitter or clean out the dross and make us better. Bitter or better, the choice is ours.

Fear of death. This is probably the greatest unknown for all mankind. The fear of death is great for those who have not entered into eternal life through Jesus Christ. The Bible says, "To live is Christ (to live for Christ, as His representative) and to die is gain." (Philippians 1:21) When Christians die, they will be with God in ecstasy for eternity. Concerning ourselves about death is certainly not productive because we have absolutely no control over it. The number of our days are held in the providence of God and we can be comforted to know He makes no mistakes.

Fear of failure. Many people are afraid to make a mistake, afraid to fail or afraid they will fall to temptation and are completely paralyzed by it. There is really no power over failure or temptation other than the personal discipline and grace given by the Holy Spirit. Jesus promised us this help saying, "If you love Me, keep my commandments. And I will pray the Father, and He will give you another Helper (the Holy Spirit) that He may abide with you forever. The Spirit of truth, whom the world cannot receive, because it neither sees Him nor knows Him; but you know Him, for He dwells with you and will be in you." John 14:15–17

Fear of impending danger. Self-preservation is the strongest emotion given to man and is actually a healthy response in the face of danger or threatening circumstances. About it, Isaiah reminded us of God's promise: "Fear not, for I am with you; be not dismayed, for I am your God. I will strengthen you. Yes, I will help you, I will uphold you with My righteous right hand." Isaiah 41:10

Having experienced war on a daily basis for an extended period of time in the Infantry, I can tell you that the fear of impending danger is real. Unlike other branches of the military which are, for the most part, ordinarily a distance from the enemy, our mission was to close with and destroy them. For us that was not something you could did from a distance. Battleships and fighter jets can but not soldiers. Sooner or later, every war has to be won by the foot. You have to control every square foot of the real estate and that means occupying it with boots on the ground. Closing with the enemy for us meant that we had to find them, focus our supporting weapons fire on them if we had the chance and then combat assault directly into the face of their full physical strength and fire power. Although I was close to death on many occasions and subject to not only a stray bullet, a well-directed one or flying pieces of shrapnel on almost a daily basis, somehow I never really thought I would die. I was afraid many times but there is a difference in that and being afraid you will actually die. Having had to memorize scripture in a Christian school at a young age, I found myself repeating the 23rd Psalm in my mind quite frequently. The Bible also gives us the promise that "A thousand may fall at your side and ten thousand at your right hand but it shall not come near you." (Psalm 91:7) Similarly, our Scottish family motto of old is "Vil God I Zal" which in today's vernacular means: Will God I Shall. I believed if it was God's will, that my company would overcome the enemy in every battle and thank God He made it happen did but if not … so be it. I just knew that my life was in His capable hands. It was totally out of my control. War, to me, was not about killing the enemy so much as it was about protecting my own men and our country. My ancestors fought for my generation in the Revolutionary War and both World Wars. My dad fought in World War II and the Korean War. They protected me in my youth and Vietnam was simply my turn to protect them in their old age, as well as defending all my neighbors, our freedoms, our land and our way of life. How others dealt with and lived with ever present danger, I don't know but having faith in God certainly worked for me.

Fear of disease: People who are afraid of disease or illness are known as: hypochondriacs. They are consumed by their fear of diseases they haven't even been infected with. For all of us, about diseases, God has given us these promises: "Unto you that fear my name, the son of Righteousness shall arise with healing in his wings." (Malachi 4:2) "It is the Lord who heals (us)." (Exodus 15:26) "He forgives all (our) sins and heals all (our) diseases." (Psalm 103:3) and "… by (His) stripes (we) were healed." (I Peter 2:24) If we were healed 2,000 years ago, we still are. It is so readily available for God's people Matthew 15:26 describes healing as "the children's bread." It is not something extra or miscellaneous but something so important and readily available that it is captioned as similar to our daily bread.

Fear of the people. Needing man's approval and being afraid of what people might think about us is a tremendous burden on people that must be dealt with to become successful in life. Proverbs 29:25 admonishes us that "The fear of man brings a snare" but it also gives us the remedy: "whoever trusts in the Lord shall be safe." We can also pray for a forehead like God gave Ezekiel, one "like an adamant stone, harder than flint." (Ezekiel 3:9) We can't serve God if we are bound up with care about what people might think or say about us because we can either please God or man but we can't please both.

Fear of falling. This is a fear we are all born with and it helps us to have the sense to avoid dangerously high places. It is actually a healthy fear but it can be overcome to a large degree. There are a number of training exercises the military conducts in the airborne, ranger and seal schools to enable men to navigate and traverse high places. This is done by making and using rope bridges, repelling off of cliffs and out of hovering aircraft as well as jumping out of airplanes with a parachutes. If it were not possible to overcome this, no one would ever jump out of an airplane even with a parachute.

Fear of God. Not all fear is bad. There is indeed a holy, reverential kind of fear, the fear of God. This Spirit empowers us to hate wickedness, sin and every evil way. Jesus warned us "... not (to) fear those who kill the body but cannot kill the soul. But rather we are to fear Him who is able to destroy both soul and body in hell." (Matthew 10:28) This very positive, reverential fear gives us the power to:

- Depart from evil. Proverbs 16:6
- Hate evil. Proverbs 8:13
- Prolongs our days. Proverbs 10:27
- Have strong confidence. Proverbs 14:26
- Provide us a place of refuge. Proverbs 14:26
- Makes itself a fountain of life for us. Proverbs 14:27
- Turn us away from the snares of death. Proverbs 14:27
- Free us from envy. Proverbs 23:17
- Lead us to life. Proverbs 19:23
- Cause us to be satisfied. Proverbs 19:23
- Cause us not to be visited by evil. Proverbs 19:23
- Have God's angels protect us. Psalms 34:7
- Have no want. Psalm 34:9
- Give us wisdom and knowledge. Isaiah 33:6
- Have stability for our times. Isaiah 33:6
- Have the strength of salvation. Isaiah 33:6

The wisest man in the world said, here is "the conclusion of the whole matter: Fear God, and keep His commandments; for this is the whole duty of man." (Ecclesiastes 12:13) Serve Him, live to please Him and commit all your works into his merciful, powerful, loving hands. This is the way to truly live.

Isaiah 43:1 goes on to give us three good reasons to never have to fear things in this world or what might happen to us in life. First, God said, I have redeemed you, and that for a purpose; second, I have called you by name and third, he said, "You are mine." God takes care of that which is His. Paul stated very clearly, "God hasn't given us the spirit of fear but of power, and of love and of a sound mind." II Timothy 1:7

In times of crisis, turbulence and adversity, leaders are called to the forefront. When a difficult, dangerous or controversial job comes along, a leader always answers the call and steps forward to tackle it. When others are paralyzed, they just step up and take the reins. Rather than asking others, they generally just do it. Leaders have learned over time to naturally do things that are uncomfortable and dangerous. Doing new things and launching out into unchartered waters is their forte. Leaders stand for what is right and go against the tide, willingly doing what is unpopular when necessary.

What it means to have the character trait of **BEING FEARLESS:**

- Being free from the torment of personal doom, disease, accidents or loss
- Freedom from fear
- Freedom from the dread of public opinion or the need for approval
- Confidence in the greater protecting power of God
- Confidence in one's ability with God's help to overcome our enemies and every adversity
- Confidence in the face of the enemy or a threat
- Not being startled or paralyzed by a foe
- An absence of dread

FINISHER, BEING A — Study start date: _____ Finish date: _____

I t is so easy to start something. Anybody can start a project. The hard part is finishing. Once you begin, many unforeseen problems and circumstances are sure to crop up. That is why the Bible counsels us to count the cost before we start to build a tower so you can be sure you will have enough to finish it. It also says, "The end of a thing is better than its beginning." (Ecclesiastes 7:8) And, before you go to war, first sit down and decide if you are "able with ten thousand to meet him that cometh against you with twenty thousand." (Luke 14:31) As Christians, we should never expect the odds to be in our favor. Life is rarely fair but our God is more than enough to help us overcome in any situation.

Having the courage to accept and start a task is important even commendable. Working at it diligently with all your might is important as well but more important than anything is finishing it. The trait that makes one valuable in this life is being a finisher. Someone who can be assigned a task and be relied upon to finish it without fail and with excellence is what makes one invaluable in the world today. We need to be so committed to finishing every task we start that it actually becomes our trademark in life. Leaders are always looking for people on their team they can hand projects and problems to and forget about them.

What it means to have the character trait of **BEING A FINISHER:**

- Determining to finish every race, contract, project, agreement or battle you start
- Realizing anyone can start something but the difficult part is finishing it
- Realizing that once you declare yourself to start something in this world, everything that can oppose and discourage is coming to hinder so be ready.
- Realizing that God always gives us an anointing of the Spirit equal to or greater than the task assigned.
- Being mission oriented: always accomplishing the mission no matter what it costs
- Crossing the finish line
- Bringing something to its final end
- Not accepting half way or even 99 and a half percent
- The final state of being completed
- Embracing the old adage that "Quitters never win and winners never quit"
- Realizing we always have the victory in Christ Jesus

FLEXIBILITY—   Study start date: _____ Finish date: _____

We all live in a world occupied by a whole lot of other people. Inasmuch as we would all like to have everything our way all the time, paradoxically, the more we try to have it so, the less likely it is this will ever to happen. For us to live here successfully, we are going to have to learn to be negotiable on some things. Just one of the other problems we were all born with is that all of us think we know how to do things the best way possible. Well, the fact is there is just about nothing that has ever been done that couldn't be improved upon. So for that reason alone, we should remain open to new ideas, new ways of doing things and stay teachable. No one has a corner on all the best ideas and if people know we are open, flexible and approachable, they will likely share their ideas with us. If not, forget it.

For example, if our boss wants something done a certain way and doesn't ask for input, we need to do it his way. Most bosses probably got there by doing things right more than just growing old and out-living their predecessor. For the most part, bosses don't like folk, especially up-starts and new-hires, trying to tell them how to run their railroad. If we will just show enough deference to do it the boss's way (as long as it is not illegal, immoral or unscriptural) for a period of time, wonder of wonders, he or she will no doubt start asking for our input or even let us do some things however we like. Our first test on any job is to show that we can be obedient and that will take some flexibility for all of us. Never forget this. The only reason we have a job is because our boss, as efficient as he may be, can't possibly get all of his work done that he is responsible for and his superior has authorized him our slot to help. Furthermore, we will probably never have a position that we can say: "This is my job." We all work for others. Even when we own the company, we have directors, stock holders, employees and the public to answer to. No one owns a job and no one is indispensable. Regardless of how good we are, we hold our job only temporarily. The reason I mention this is for us all to operate with a certain degree of alacrity, to continue to be flexible and please our superiors. We will be glad someday we did.

Sometimes the instructions for the job at hand may look silly and may not make a whole lot of sense. But who knows that the boss's superior hasn't called for it a certain way for a reason. It could be that it has to dove-tail with another project or product someone else is working on. It could be in the buyer's specifications that way so be flexible.

When working with others it is always wise to be an agreeable, informal, easily approachable type person. If everyone thinks they are going to run into a hornets' nest every time they approach your work-space, don't be surprised if your part of the world becomes a bit chilly and void of human traffic. We all need to be good listeners and easy to get along with. Being a stuffed shirt, stiffly formal Joe won't get you anywhere. Smiling and being interested in others, their pursuits, their ideas and showing a willing-ness to learn from them cause's relationships to flower. Show them you are flexible and will gladly try something someone else's way.

The boss also needs to know that you are going to be flexible enough to try to make his plans work out no matter what. Even if it doesn't work, he needs to know that you will always try your best to make it work if at all humanly possible. This is where flexibility morphs into loyalty and loyalty pays huge dividends in life. None of us have ever been right all the time so we need to leave our leader room to be wrong on occasion too – that is, just as long as it is not illegal, immoral or unscriptural.

Should you become the boss, your employees need to learn that you are flexible enough to consider their ideas and that you won't be offended by their knowledge, talent or experience. They will help you if you are open to new things and are willing to give credit where credit is due. If they do come up with a winner, let everyone know who was really responsible for the idea and how much you appreciate both them and it.

Besides all the other reasons to be flexible, we know the world around us is changing all the time. For this reason alone, we need to be ready to change what we are doing in a moment. If the market changes, we have got to change with it to remain viable. In our mission outreaches, we need to be flexible to change our plans, strategies and even places to minister. There are seasons in life, nature, work and ministry.

What it means to have the character trait of **FLEXIBILITY:**

- Being willing to yield to a proper influence, a better plan or the excellency of wisdom
- Being pliant
- Being able to conform to changing environments, situations, conditions, leadership styles and personalities of those around us
- Being able to bend in a storm like a palm tree, so you don't break like a pine tree but, at the same time, not compromise
- Having the necessary deference to do things the boss' way as long as it is not illegal, immoral or unscriptural
- Not being stuck in one's ways
- Not being formal
- Easily approached or entreated
- Being capable of learning new concepts
- Able to accept new ideas and new ways of doing thing
- Being agreeable in nature

OCUS, THE ABILITY TO —   Study start date: _____ Finish date: _____

As human beings, we are strange creatures. We all have a wide range of interests, desires and motivations. Just for example, we often try to be in several places at one time and try to do several different things at once. It has been said, "This one thing I do, let me do it well" and it'is certainly good advice. Therefore, the ability to focus is an extremely valuable human trait. No one I am aware of has ever succeeded in life without the ability to focus. This includes the ability for us to set boundaries for ourselves as well as the discipline to consistently swallow the most undesirable pills we have on our schedules first each day. Focus is the ability to set aside other thoughts, musings, incentives and enjoyments to do those things, though not be pleasurable momentarily, for the hope of possibly achieving a much greater long-term benefit.

Today's highly technological environment offers people a wide spectrum of choices, allurements and distractions to keep one from doing the next, most productive thing oiur lives might require. Since most required tasks are not pleasurable, focus, combined with grit and self-denial, is necessary to succeed in the world today. Once imagined, nothing great in a complex world will ever be created, patented, produced and marketed without a lot of long-term, disciplined focus. Neither will speeches, sermons or services be provided to anyone, rich or poor, without focus. Getting a formal education is not enough. Someone said and I believe it, "A formal education will make you a living but self-education will make you a fortune." To be a success in any field, one must be dedicated to it, dream about it, read books about it, be trained and educated in it at least to some extent. We must also love it and do it for others with a servant's heart but, most importantly, we must stay focused on it. Jumping from one career field to another every few months or years will never lead to success or serious accomplishment.

Of one thing I am confident, few people reading the things I write still believe in the big bang theory: that there was a big bang one day and something as intricate and complicated as a F-16 was created instantly with all its electronics, avionics, hydraulics and jet engines. Or a Rolex watch with all the fine works, wheels, springs and jewels it takes to operate. How ridiculous. Focus, remember, is the one and only reason the tortes beat out the hare in the great road race. Fine art, leading-edge computer programs, advanced weapons systems, challenging books, developing meaningful personal relationships and even having a good time on the ski slopes require focus. Like I said, it is critical to success but without it, you are likely to drive yourself crazy on the way to the poor house.

What it means to have the character trait of **THE ABILITY TO FOCUS:**

- Concentrating on one thing at a time
- Concentrating on one's chosen field
- The ability to limit our thoughts to the one central thing or task at hand.
- The ability to commit wholly to the current priority being emphasized and pursued.
- That ability to concentrate long enough to create convictions sufficient to make hard choices, stand for something against great opposition, build things that are consequential and, generally, have a life that makes a difference.
- The ability to give 100% of your concentration and effort to one thing at a time.
- The ability to get excited about the task at hand regardless of how little pleasure there may be in it by seeing clearly the overall end goal.

- Putting emphasis, thought, energy and action to the number one priority of the moment.
- Totally consistent persistence
- To adjust our spectrum of choices to the wisest, most critical or important need.
- To limit our attention by self-discipline

FOLLOW THROUGH—   Study start date: _____ Finish date: _____

Many are they who start projects with a bang, tons of gusto, a whole lot of flash, flitter and flying sparks but few are they who finish them. People's lives are full of fits and starts, joining's and commitments, goals and promises but few get any further than just past the starting line and the hollow pop of the starter's gun. They are all a flash in the pan with no guts or grit. No staying power or determination to get the job done. Many hindrances always seem to get in the way. Sometimes jobs are actually completed but even then we need to remember that no task is really finished until all the tools or equipment have been serviced and returned to their proper place. Nor is it completed until the reports have been filed. Fact is, follow through will either make or break you in life.

In the technical, industrialized society we live in few jobs can ever be accomplished without tools. We are all, homemakers included, having to deal with lots of tools. In today's world, everything needs to have its place and every place needs to have its thing—so we will be ready for the next task and can find what we need next in an efficient manner. We need to make up our minds to put everything back in its proper place immediately, while we have it in our hand, so we don't have to waste valuable mental time later studying the issue, re-prioritizing the time to do it and then making the same effort that was needed to get the job done in the first place. It's like the old proverb says, a stitch in time saves nine. Sure you can get by momentarily without sewing the garment immediately that has come loose or putting a new sole on those shoes but by not taking immediate action, the job is probably going to get much larger and you might even permanently weaken and damage the material, the equipment or the shoe to the point it becomes a total loss and has to be thrown away.

A lack of follow through in business today is a huge problem. There are only about three reasons people avoid following through on things and none of them are good. First, is time. They think there isn't sufficient time to do a job right the first time. But, for some strange reason they can always find the time to do it over. No. If there it time to do something, there is time to do it right even if you have to work late. Get it done, done right and behind you. Another, is laziness. Some people were born lazy, are easily fatigued and never seem to get rested. Remember, laziness is a powerful enemy. It, alone, can steal all the blessings God, Himself, has in store for you in this one short life. We need to learn to love our work, enjoy strenuous jobs, even getting dirty and sweating. All work is honorable and none of these things will kill you. It was Napoleon who gave us the insight that "Courage is not really as important in a great soldier as the ability to endure fatigue." And, the third reason is not having a goal of excellence. To anyone with the belief that anything will do, less is always best. Until you have a goal of working as unto the Lord and turning in excellent work to the Master, you will never have sufficient motivation to do things right and get the job done, regardless.

Follow through includes developing effective filing systems so you and your fellow workers can easily find things at a later date. It includes designing and building racking, stacking and storing systems and labeling things properly to begin with. Remember, just a little organization goes a long way. It pays dividends over and over again in the future. In many ways, neatness is its own reward and will also likely keep one from getting tripped up on all the clutter at a later date. No one, absolutely not one respects a nasty, sloppy leader who leaves trash and paraphernalia strewn out all over the work place. Follow through is thinking ahead when you turn a bulk mail mailing in to the Post Office and getting the plastic postal trays you will need for your next mailing while you are there instead of having to come back for them again later.

Follow through also includes cleaning up one's work area immediately after finishing a project. It is also doing things immediately, like turning in the required reports. Some people have the hardest time making reports when failure to make the proper, timely reports can get you fired. Most of the time, our superiors have to make their own reports from the data we supply them and not turning them in when needed, in a timely manner, can put us quickly behind the eight ball. Not making proper reports can cause your company or ministry to lose customers, privileges and opportunities for good. It doesn't need to be all that hard. All you have to do is get the forms. Put them in your briefcase or car and make up your mind to do the reports immediately and shoot them out by mail, email or fax. This puts the issue behind you immediately so you won't have to clutter up your mind worrying about reports that needed to be made and are already late. Never let anyone, your boss included, ever have a reason to call you for a report. Let follow through and making timely reports be one of your strong points.

Remember, the only thing in life more worthless than an idea on which no action has been taken is one that time and materials have already been invested in but was never quite completed.

Let follow through be your trademark.

What it means to have the character trait of **FOLLOW THROUGH:**

- Being a great turtle but a sorry rabbit
- Taking a motion, once started, without interruption, to the concluding point of the arc
- Finishing a task without fail, regardless of the hindrances, obstacles, enticements to quit or fatigue
- Learning never to take "No" for an answer when charged with a mission or beginning a t a s k of your own
- Realizing that most projects require more than one frontal attack so it is being ready to mount several flanking maneuvers, find a basic load of true grit and a ton of patience to go along with it to stay at it until you succeed.
- Staying with a project to the glorious, victorious end.
- Seeing to it that you keep your word and promises in all you do, no exceptions
- Continuing through all phases of a task regardless of what is required or what has to be sacrificed
- Personally checking to be sure things are accomplished by those under our authority
- Always getting the job done. Not half-baked but done with excellence!
- Seeing to it that all the smallest details of a job are done right
- Keeping a suspense file for matters that need to be completed at a later date or on a recurring basis
- Never, ever, failing to accomplish a mission given by a superior

FOLLOWERSHIP—   **Study start date:** _____ **Finish date:** _____

Some people believe they will establish themselves and receive promotions on the job by showing the supervisor that they have all the best ideas and can do everything better than anybody else. No. That will never work. When you first take a job, it is best to keep your ideas to yourself unless you are asked. Use what you know on your own work. Forget yourself and focus, whenever possible, on making your co-workers and your boss look good. Now having great ideas and doing things with excellence is definitely important but what will advance your career and cause you to be appreciated more than anything else is something little known or taught today: followership. This has to do with following and documenting instructions in writing so you not only accomplish a given task with excellence and expedience, but do it right, the way you were instructed. You may think you have a better way but first you need to build a bond with your leader. The one in authority needs to know that you will do as you are told without going into a dissertation on the subject and telling everyone how they did it where you came from. A huge part of succeeding as a follower is finding great joy in making others successful and helping to make their goals and dreams come true. Every supervisor has likes and dislikes and has developed a number of pet peeves over the years. These may be small or even large things they hold to be really important for their organization to function properly and succeed. Take note of these things and act accordingly. Be pliable, flexible, responsive, cooperative and observant.

A significant part of followership is having a goal of being the best follower possible and, as I mentioned, finding great joy in making others look good, be successful and helping make the goals and dreams of others come true. A dangerous place to be is to ever think of your work at a company as "My job." No one ever really owns a job. Besides, none of us are ever indispensable. Our job is just a small part of the boss' job. We are there to shoulder part of their workload, make their job easier and them, successful. Yes, we should work every day to become indispensable to our company and leaders, do the extras, add value wherever possible but we must always remember that we can all be replaced.

Followership is also building a track record of getting the work done every time, on time. This will make you a valuable asset to any organization and is another area where so many people seem to miss the mark. They find it easier to say, "We didn't have enough time, enough manpower, enough resources, etc." The person who has follow-through and is mission oriented will always find a way to get the job done. Well, almost.

Remember the example of Daniel. He was a captive servant in a foreign land which is, in and of itself, a huge political disadvantage. Notwithstanding, he was selected by the king to be above all the presidents and princes of the land. Why? Because "an excellent spirit was in him." (Daniel 6:3) Furthermore, the Bible records that he prospered as prime minister under at least four different kings. (Daniel 1:1,5:1,6:1, 6:28) He probably didn't like their pagan beliefs; their course, heathen ways; their arrogance or their religion but he was able to keep his head straight and, other than a trip to the lion's den, prospered in his job. He even overcame that trip to the lion's den quite handily with God's help. Do your own job well, of course, but help those around you succeed in their pursuits. Forget about yourself. In time, you will be rewarded.

Another important point is to always try your best, and this can be hard at times, to like your supervisor. As I mentioned, they are all humans too and, as such, have their failings, quirks and short-comings. If you want to find fault with your boss, you certainly can but you are a fool to do so. He's probably not going anywhere anytime soon so you better get along with him. Look, instead, for the good things about your leaders. Be thankful and center your thoughts on those things. Watch your heart. If you can't respect the person, respect their position. I'm sure Daniel didn't like what he saw in all the Babylonian kings he worked for but, he worked in a manner such that he found favor with them all. If you don't like your boss, he will know it with lightning speed. Things like body language, facial expressions, tone of voice, attitude, etc., will tell him. In addition, the wisest man in the world gave us some sage advice in this area long ago: "Do not curse the King (your boss in this case), even in your thought; do not curse the rich, even in your bedroom; for a bird of the air may carry your voice, and a bird in flight may tell the matter." (Ecclesiastes 10:20) Your boss probably wasn't born yesterday and might even have more experience toiling in the industry than you do. If your leaders know you don't like them, you have put yourself in dangerous territory and are likely to pick up a pink slip soon like the billions of others who have made this same, fatal mistake before you.

Realizing everyone already has a lot to do on any job, most employees get real down in the mouth and start feeling persecuted when they are asked to take on any additional work or responsibilities. No, this is the time to get excited. Remember, responsibility comes to those who seek it. Responsibility is the door to leadership. If you aren't into getting more responsibility (which can easily be interpreted more work), you are going to be stuck right where you are for a very long time. If you ever really do become overloaded, the powers that be will likely send you some assistants to help but never complain about being trusted with more and greater responsibilities. Accepting new tasks with a certain degree of alacrity is hugely important. Followership is realizing that we, as human beings, volunteers or employees, are simply tools in the hands of God and our leaders. They need to know we are ready to take on new things and go with them faithfully into the next battle with excitement, loyalty and enthusiasm. Those who have to be coaxed, prodded or pulled along, dragging their heels, kicking and screaming all the way, will likely be shuffled to the side quickly and let go at the first opportunity.

As an added plus, when you have demonstrated the ability to follow instructions joyfully, explicitly and without resistance, it won't be long before the leader will start asking for your advice and giving you jobs to supervise all by yourself. When you ask them "How do you want this done?" One day they will say, "Do it however you like."

What it means to have the character trait of **FOLLOWERSHIP:**

- Obedience
- Loyalty to the leader
- The desire and ability to make the leader's plans come to fruition and succeed
- Looking ahead and making the leader's job easier
- Being cooperative
- Being one easy to lead, a low maintenance follower
- Being excited about receiving new tasks and responsibilities
- Being willing to follow the leader
- Being grateful for the leader's positive points
- Being observant of the leader's likes and dislikes
- Having attention to detail and following instructions implicitly

FORBEARANCE—

Study start date: _____ **Finish date:** _____

Today's world is an angry place. Many who don't know the Lord see all that they have, all they have worked for and all they love on this earth being diminished, dismantled, decaying or destroyed. They are just plain angry right from the get in their day-to-day lives and this is inevitably, constantly spilling over into their personal relationships. If you don't do everything just like they like it and do it instantly, you are necessarily, automatically "the enemy" and are dead in the water. They immediately take your head off—if not physically, albeit verbally.

But it is well to remember, we all have sinned and fallen short. We, too, have changed our beliefs over time and today we may not even agree with ourselves—at least who we were a few years ago. We, too, have made mistakes even accidentally over the years. So we all need to be patient with others and more understanding when our neighbor fall short. We don't need to allow their little idiosyncrasies to cause us to react to them. The wisest man in the world said, "The discretion of a man makes him slow to anger, and his glory is to overlook a transgression." (Proverbs 19:11) So we would do well to cut people a little slack, endure a few provocations, and forbear a while to give them a chance to make some corrections. This, of course, doesn't mean that we have to compromise our beliefs but we certainly don't have to pursue all of our preferences and pet peeves with everyone around us either. God's grace may allow us to give people a little space to be themselves. After all, they are probably accepting us, warts and all too.

God's patience and slowness to anger, has been demonstrated over the eons with many people, tribes and nations. When the Hebrew children came out of Egypt, totally defenseless, they were attacked and ravaged unmercifully by the Amorites. However, because their iniquity was not complete, God's righteous anger waited three hundred years to repay them. (Genesis 15:16) King Saul was charged, during his reign, by God with the responsibility of rendering total recompense upon this people. .It was at this time that Saul "gathered an army and attacked the Amalekites, and delivered Israel from the hands of those who plundered them." (I Samuel 14:47) Vengeance is His and not ours.

During another time, we know Lott had lived for years among the people of Sodom

**Abraham observing the destruction of
Sodom and Gomorrah**

and Gomorrah, observing what they did daily to the point that it vexed, as you might imagine, his righteous soul. All the while, God withheld judgment. Then He had a conversation with Abraham in which it was made known to him that the outcry of the sins of these two cities was so great that He had just about come to the point of destroying them. Abraham then interceded for them, knowing his relatives, Lott and his family, lived there. He first prayed that God wouldn't destroy the towns if there were fifty righteous in it. God's reply was that He would spare it. Then Abraham continued to lower his figure in various increments, posing the same question until he got down to ten, at which point God still agreed to spare it. At that, however, both went their ways and the conversation was over. Shortly thereafter, God sent two angels to Sodom who were nearly attacked by the homosexuals of the city. It was then that the angels told Lot, to take his wife and two daughters and leave immediately or they would be overtaken by the evil of the city and be destroyed by God's impending judgment. They were given fair warning and told to leave immediately. They were not to even look back. Of course, as we know, Lot's wife didn't obey and upon looking back, was turned to salt while the others escaped.

Time and again, the Hebrew children rebelled against God, threw His law behind them, and killed His prophets who witnesses against them, so He "delivered them into the hand of their enemies, who oppressed them." (Nehemiah 9:27) However, in their agony, when they cried out for His help, He "heard from heaven; and according to (His) abundant mercies … gave them deliverers who saved them from the hand of their enemies." (Nehemiah 9:27) Yet, again and again, "for many years (He) had patience with them, and testified against them by (His) Spirit in (His) prophets, yet they would not listen; therefore (He) gave them into the hand of the peoples of the lands. Nevertheless in (His) great mercy (He) did not utterly consume them nor forsake them; for (our God) is gracious and merciful." Nehemiah 9:30

Even the people of Nineveh, who God, after having sent His prophet Jonah to prophesy their certain destruction, held his anger once again. When the king passed a decree and published it throughout the land to repent, fast and seek God, He relented. They went on a total fast, both men and their beasts. No one was allowed to eat or even drink water. The people covered themselves in sackcloth and cried out mightily to God, turning from their wicked ways. God saw all this and relented from sending the huge disaster He had promised upon them. (Jonah 3:5–10 summarized)

In the area of forbearance we need to be imitators of God, Himself, and His forbearance with the whole world, which is not to be despised. However, some still actually do despise His forbearance and longsuffering. Speaking about our God, who is infinitely wise and can make no mistake, Paul asks, "do you despise the riches of His goodness, forbearance and longsuffering, not knowing that the goodness of God leads you to repentance?" (Romans 2:.4) God sent forth Jesus Christ "as a propitiation by His blood, through faith, to demonstrate His righteousness, because in His forbearance God has passed over the sins that were previously committed, to demonstrate at the present time His righteousness, that He might be just and the justifier of the one who has faith in Jesus." Romans 3:25, 26

Not to be overlooked, God is, on the other hand, not slack with His promises. Peter remarked, "beloved, do not forget this one thing, that with the Lord one day is as a thousand years, and a thousand years as one day. The Lord (again) is not slack concerning His promise, as some count slackness, but is longsuffering toward us, not willing that any should perish but that all should come to repentance. But the day of the Lord will come as a thief in the night, in which the heavens will pass away with a great noise, and the elements will melt with fervent heat; both the earth and the works that are in it will be burned up." (II Peter 3:8–10) Since we know all these things are so and "all these things will be dissolved, what manner of person ought you to be in holy conduct and godliness … ?" v.11

How then should we live? By daily being patient with others in our midst. Having self-restraint, knowing we too have had and still do have our own shortcomings. We need to give our neighbors space and time even as God has given us time to improve and make amends. Dealing with others, we are to abide in His grace. We can with His love working through us, "bears all things, believes all things, hopes all things, (and) endures all things." (I Corinthians 13:7) Paul said, "I, therefore, (as a) prisoner of the Lord, beseech you to walk worthy of the calling with which you were called, with all lowliness and gentleness, with longsuffering, bearing with one another in love, endeavoring to keep the unity of the Spirit in the bond of peace." (Ephesians 4:2, 3) Remembering, we are not in this by ourselves. "There is one body and one Spirit, just as you were called in one hope of your calling; one Lord, one faith, one baptism; one God and Father of all, who is above all, and through all, and in you all." v.4–6

Malachi asked this penetrating question, "Who can endure the day of His coming? And who can stand when He appears?" (Malachi 3:2) How do we prepare for His soon coming? We should look for, greatly desire and hasten it. We also know only too well, that even our bodies have aches, pains, bruises and diseases from time-to-time and we all find ourselves in need of the Master's healing touch. So too, we should be ready and willing to be forbearing, gently minister healing faith as we have the grace to other parts of the Body of Christ. We must leave the deceitfulness and trickery of men and speak "the truth in love, (that we may) grow up in all things into Him who is the head—Christ—from whom the whole body, joined and knit together by what every joint supplies, according to the effective working by which every part does its share, causing growth of the body for the edifying of itself in love." v. 15, 16

If we look for faults in our co-workers and friends, we will surely find them. We can look for a chink in our boss's armor and we will, no doubt, find a few. Wisdom, I believe, however, is to be thankful for having as good a boss, environment and work-place as we do and work in it as a mission field. No matter where we go to find work on this planet, we will not likely find perfection. Probably people there will still be people and it won't quite be utopia just yet. Bloom where you are planted is the wise admonition. Make a difference where you are and remember, the reason diamonds shine so bright when set in mud or some other flawed medium is that the contrast is so great —especially under the light of the Sun. The darker and murkier one's surroundings, the brighter our light appears to shine. So, forebear with your neighbor in love and shine with the light of Christ, bringing glory to God!

What it means to have the character trait of **FORBERANCE**:

- To have patience with the shortcomings of others without being provoked
- To be pre-determined to endure with others
- Having self-restraint
- To be willing to overlook small offenses
- Delaying action
- Holding back
- To be patient with others while they are still in their learning curve
- Realizing that love covers a multitude of sins
- Having the ability to endure slights and omissions
- Having the ability to grant mercy on occasion

ORGIVENESS— **Study start date:** _____ **Finish date:** _____

or those of us who live in this world, we have a promise from the Master: "Offenses must come." We will have trials, troubles and tribulation. We will be offended and know very well what we would like to do about those who offend us. But, amazingly, He also said the best way to handle these fiery trials, succeed in life and cause the blessings of peace, favor and goodwill to come our way both now and for eternity is to forgive.

Many lives have been ruined and eternities lost because of a failure to obey this one command. Un-forgiveness is deadly. If we don't forgive one who has offended us, what we are doing spiritually is sitting as the judge and chaining that person up but that is not the worst part. Far, far worse is that you have also, possibly unbeknownst to you, imprisoned yourself as well. How? Because you have to hold the other end of the chain and will be carrying them with you in your heart of hearts wherever you go. You will be chained to them psychologically until you let go by forgiving them. You are permanently connected to them on their miserable level. The whole wretched incident is branded indelibly on your brain both consciously and subconsciously. Your mind is locked in the low-life dungeon of turmoil and hate with the tormentors. Even if you don't say a word to the offender, you will be submerged in a steady stream of mental strife, ugliness, hurt, self-pity and anger. James told us where this will take us. Where there is "strife there is confusion and every evil work." (James 3:16) Un-forgiveness has caused people to do some horrible things, even murder. We are not likely to accomplish much in life if we are bound up in strife, confusion and thinking about every evil work. The best approach for us, of course, is to forgive our enemies completely from the heart and truly ask God to bless them.

When faced with an offending brother one day, Peter came to Jesus and asked, "Lord, how often shall my brother sin against me, and I forgive him?" Thinking seven was the number of completion and certainly a gracious plenty, he said, "Up to seven times?" Jesus opined, "I do not say to you, up to seven times, but up to seventy times seven." (Matthew 18:21) In other words, un-forgiveness is so dangerous, insidious and deadly, divine counsel is to forgive almost unendingly. For this to really work, we should forgive those who offend us completely from the heart but don't stop there. Take the next step. Sincerely ask God to bless them. Like Joseph of old, we should "Bless and curse not." That first prayer to forgive them from a sincere heart is a powerful and effective one for sure. However, most of these heinous acts have been almost indelibly imprinted on our brains. The other person is truly forgiven but rarely can a total cleansing of the deep recesses of our consciences be accomplished with one fell swoop as qne quick prayer. We must keep praying for this person and blessing them every time they come to mind. Keep it up until you don't think about them or the situation anymore. When you sincerely pray for God to bless them, just a part of His blessing may be some correction in their life that will bring them to repentance. But that's God's business, not ours. Ours is to forgive and keep on forgiving until they don't come to mind anymore. Then you are free so God can forgive you. You see the only kind of forgiveness any of us will ever receive is the "even as" kind. Even as we forgive others, so will the Master forgive all of our trespasses. (Matthew 6:12, 14–15) It has been said that "Forgiveness is man's deepest need and highest achievement." Regardless of the hurt and damage someone has caused you, God is well able to repay you completely in another form or fashion. If you will just forgive them, one day you will be able to look back on the incident and say, "I thought that was the worst thing that ever happened to me but it turned out to truly be the best." God can turn it around for your good. Just think for a minute about all we have done wrong. Coming up, I was a rounder and I mean I was so bad most people thought there was not hope even in Heaven for me. Remember, "To err is human but to forgive is divine." Paul was the chiefest of sinners, because the Bible says he was, but I wasn't trailing too far behind. Not a problem. God has sufficient grace and mercy for all of us

There are three things men are absolutely incapable of doing in this short life: bearing burdens, serving two masters and retaliation. Every time I ride a horse and growing up in a family of ranchers and having horses over a lifetime, was quite often most of the time, I would always come to the same conclusion. This animal had to be especially made by God to both carry burdens and for a man to ride. They are the perfect height, temperament, construction, strength and can actually become a good friend to you just like many people have dogs and cats. But man is a horse of a different garage when it comes to bearing burdens. We don't do well at this at all.

Soldiers in Vietnam had the hardest time getting used to a 60 pound rucksack. The human skeleton and its support system just can't handle it. It wasn't meant to. Neither can we carry the even more burdensome worries and offenses of life. The Bible says we have a sure remedy for these things. We are to cast them all on the Lord and let Him carry them. (I Peter 5:6) Worry can and has caused many a man's early demise.

The third thing, which un-forgiveness brings is retaliation and men are simply incapable of seeking their own revenge. If we decide to become a self-appointed vigilante, we will screw it up every time. The Lord said, "Revenge is mine, I will repay." (Romans 12:19) If a person even tries to dig a pit or to roll a rock down on someone, our God is skilled, powerful and wise enough that He can cause the one who dug the pit to fall into it himself and the one who thought of rolling the rock to be the one actually hit by the exact, same rock. (Proverbs 26:27) What a mighty God we serve! You would think a person who is able enough to dig a pit would remember where he dug it and not fall into it himself. Rather, what we are commanded to do is forgive them immediately, forget the whole matter and, in so doing, make room for the Lord's vengeance. We do this by forgiving the person from the heart, blessing them and forgetting the entire offense. Vengeance becomes the Lord's business. He is well able to do what is best and will bless you mightily in the end. Remember, King Saul's hateful attempts trying to take David's life actually caused him to be elevated to the crown. Joseph's mistreatment by his brothers, Potiphar and his friends in prison caused him to be promoted to prime minister. Haman's plot to kill Esther, Mordecai and the whole Jewish nation, brought about his own swift demise and Mordecai's promotion to second in command under the king. Pilot and the chief priests may have crucified our Lord but they caused Him to be given a name that is named above every name that is named.

What it means to have the character trait of **FORGIVENESS**:

- To freely forgive the trespass of a neighbor, friend or enemy
- To forgive an offender, extinguish all feelings of resentment and forget the matter entirely
- To grant a full pardon and forgetting about it completely
- To free a debtor from any claim you might have against them
- To grant relief from a debt
- To remit a penalty
- To cancel a charge

FOUNDATION BUILDER, A —   **Study start date:** _____ **Finish date:** _____

Many people go through life wondering why others are succeeding all around them but they are not. Of course there are many reasons but one key reason is a failure to understand the importance of being a foundation builder. It could also be called: preparation. The wayfaring man on the street looks at those who are constantly driving by in automobiles and wonders why not me? Where is my car? Well, that person driving by has taken the time and paid the expense necessary to build some foundations. They are not running their life or their car on empty. What if the farmer ate or sold all his corn? There would be no seed for him to plant for the next year's crop. Obviously, you can't eat up all your seed in life and expect to succeed. Every one of those people driving by in a car either has a down payment made on it and their payments current so they are building equity. Or, it is paid for. They have obviously secured a driver's license, purchased a license plate, kept good tires on it, etc. They couldn't even have put it on the road without their insurance policy paid up to date. This, in and of itself, is a foundation. They probably have an apartment somewhere for which their rent is paid as well as having a security deposit on account with the landlord and the utility companies. If they have a home, it is either paid for or they, likewise, have made a down payment and their payments are current. All these things are part of their foundation as they travel through life, giving them stability, protection from the elements, pleasure, efficiency and peace of mind. They also very likely have a "rainy day" fund they are growing in the bank to help out in case of the unexpected expenses that might crop up. Foundations give one's life efficiency, stability and power to meet contingencies.

In every field of endeavor, I am sure you will agree if you have been out there any time at all, there is fierce competition. Competition is good. It forces us to improve our serve and delivers increasingly better products and services to the public at lower prices. The person or company offering the best product or service at the best price will soon prevail in the market place. Remember this, all business sooner or later goes to the strong hands. The race of life doesn't always go to the swiftest and the strongest, chance and providence certainly enters in occasionally but those who are the strongest in any field, you will find, have usually taken the time and paid the price to lay a proper foundation. That foundation could consist of a number of things like gaining a good education, for one. Cavett Roberts, the late-great leadership coach said, "School is never out for the pro." One's foundation also includes other important things like one getting the necessary training and experience in their particular discipline, being certain to be properly capitalized as a business before starting out and having a backlog of good will among our customer base. It also includes having a servant's heart, a good character training program for our staff, good research and development and a superior product, excellent advertising and a powerful sales staff, just to name a few. In the same way, those in the military who advance well, are the ones who have taken the time and paid the price to build a proper foundation. That would include getting a good education from a reputable institution, they must read a lot of biographies and books on warfare, attending every school the military has related to their field and taking the time to gain character. This puts them in the position of being able to bring more to the table than time in grade and an empty uniform, hat and brief case.

Most people, keep in mind, are only interested in spending what they have on their own personal pleasures. We are warned about a preoccupation with pleasure in Proverbs 21:17 saying, "He that loves pleasure will be a poor man; (and) he who loves wine and oil will not be rich." God never gives anyone an abundance to spend on themselves, only to be a blessing to others. There are really only two types of people you will find in the world: those who can spend money and those who can grow it. Give a hundred thousand dollars to two different people and one will have it spent in no time. The other will use just enough to get by and invest the rest. Come back in a year and one will be stone cold broke and the other will have a hundred twenty thousand or more and will still be growing it like Jack's bean stalk—right into the sky. Yes, everybody spends their money on something in life but before anyone will ever invest in building the various foundations necessary to succeed, they must first realize how critically important this is.

Money to invest in a foundation is hard to come by because there is always something else we could spend it on that would make us feel better and appeal to our senses in addition to the government's taxes attacking it incessantly. It takes discipline to deny one's self and save part of our seeds. I keep the old bank savings account register that my dad used while my brother and I were in elementary school, Junior High and High School. Every now and again I pull it out and marvel at it. For years and years he saved $200 every month to put us boys through college—and he never, ever missed a single month. Incredible! What discipline! That was back in the 1960's when $200 was a lot of money. Wisely, he also required us to get jobs after school when we could and during the summer so we could learn the dignity and blessing of work, new skills, help save for our educations and so we could pay for half of it ourselves. He's already gone on to his reward but if you are listening, I say, thanks again dad.

Surely no one would invest in anything unless they thought it would have any value to them. Some investments, such as reading career-related books to build one's foundation, may not pay off immediately but they certainly will over time. Another thing my dad did was to let us boys buy any book we wanted to read. Once we finished reading them, all we had to do was bring him the book and the sales ticket and tell him that we had finished reading it. He would pay us for the book and let us keep it for our own libraries. Way to go again dad! He also told us "Whatever you learned, you will use it again later in life." After many years now, I can tell you that was a true statement. The body of knowledge you gain can also be applied to every task, assignment or job you are given until you graduate from this life. Not everything in every task but, sooner or later, you will use it. There is an inscription at the U.S. Air Force Academy that says, "Man's flight through life is powered by knowledge." So true but knowledge comes neither cheap nor easily. One must be willing to pay the price.

In building construction the foundation always determines the size, use, life, longevity and height of the building. The foundation is actually the most important part. All kinds of steel pilings, re-bar and concrete must go underground for a building to reach very far toward the heavens. In fact, the foundation of a sky-scraper will go into the ground a good percentage of its overall height in order to withstand the wind shear of hurricanes and the tremors of earthquakes. This expense must be made but will likely never be seen or appreciated by the passers-by or the occasional visitors to the building. Most visitors just notice the marble floors and walls, the beautiful glass and brick exterior. However, when the next hurricane and hundred fifty mile an hour winds come by, they will all be glad the builder didn't cut any corners on the foundation. Hopefully, the building will stand.

The day I was writing this, I noticed an article in the Atlanta Journal-Constitution by staff writer, Chip Towers.[19] It was about Aaron Murray, the very successful, current, University of Georgia quarterback. His strength, speed, decision-making skill and arm is causing pause among many a NFL scouts. Lots of little kids are wearing the number 11 jersey, the coeds swoon when he walks by and even his teammates are impressed. However, they see him differently than you might imagine. One of his wide receivers and closest friends, Tavarres King, said, "He's a nerd. He's always studying, and he already knows so much. It's hard to even talk to him outside of football because it's always going to get back to football, whatever we're talking about." Another teammate, Michael Bennet said, "He's got some weird study habits when it comes to quarterback. He's in here (at the football complex) all the time. He spends a weird amount of hours in here. He's here five or six hours a day. It's all football with him." True, everyone will have to admit that he's a tall, strong, smart athlete with some guns for arms. Regardless, this is not what has made him the record-setting, Bulldog quarterback. It is his serious approach to preparing and building a foundation that has launched his meteoric rise. True, he might be a nerd but according to the article he might be "the coolest nerd on campus."

Georgia coach, Mark Richt said, "Aaron just prepares really like no one we've had." And, he's had some good ones like David Greene who left Georgia with the record for the most wins in NCAA history and then there is Matthew Stafford, a NFL #1 draft pick and many other greats. He continued, "We've had guys that work hard. All of our guys work hard at preparing, but Murray just takes it to another level in how he prepares for the game." He is also a great student. As a fourth-year junior, he already has an undergraduate degree in psychology. He is already into his graduate studies in his major of industrial-organizational psychology. This just happens to be a doctoral program where students can get a master's degree along with it. He has already found that his academic studies are paying dividends on the football field as well. He is writing a paper on the successful leadership qualities of other NFL quarterbacks. Aaron set a school record of 35 touchdown passes last year and this year, he is off to a terrific start having passed for 1,092 yards and is leading the SEC in points and total yards per game. This young man no doubt has talent but has multiplied that talent by taking the time and effort to build his foundation.

Success in anyone's life depends upon having three critical elements: having a true foundation; having a sufficient foundation and, finally, using the right building materials. The Master laid it out for us quite well when he warned us to be very careful how we build. Foundations are so important to Him that He built twelve under Heaven and every one out of precious jewels. He was talking here not only about constructing buildings but also how we are to build our very own lives, careers, businesses and families. Everybody will be building their lives with some kind of material and on some sort of foundation which is the philosophy or belief system we choose. Some will even try to build with no foundation at all thinking they will save the money and get by, not realizing that their work is soon going to be tested by the elements. Regardless, even attempting to build without a foundation is, in and of itself, actually a belief system or philosophy about life. We would probably have to call it the fool's building method. Amazingly it is the very one the majority of people out in the world have unknowingly adopted. However, it is definitely not recommended. Luke, the apostle, recorded the Master's teachings on the subject of foundations thusly: "Whoever comes to Me (seeking advice about their life and success) and hears My sayings and does them, (not being a hearer only but a doer), I will show you whom he is like; he is like a man building a house, who dug deep and laid the foundation on the rock. And when the flood arose, the streams beat vehemently against that house and could not shake it, for it was founded on the rock. But he who heard and did nothing (with the Master's advice) is like a man who built a house on the earth without a foundation, against which (trouble came) the stream beat vehemently; and immediately it fell. And the ruin of that house was great." Luke 6:47–49

By the grace (divine favor and revelation knowledge) God had given him, Paul was a wise master builder who laid the best and only true and lasting foundation there is: Jesus Christ. He said we who follow after Him must be very careful how we build on His foundation. "For no other foundation can anyone lay than that which is laid, which is Jesus Christ." Although some will try, he points this out: "Now if anyone builds on this foundation with gold, silver, precious stones, wood, hay or stubble, each one's work will become clear; for the Day will declare it, because it will be revealed by fire, and the fire will test each one's work, of what sort it is. If anyone's work which he has built on it endures, he will receive a reward. If anyone's work is burned, he will suffer loss; but he himself will be saved, yet so as through fire." (I Corinthians 3:11–15) There are several things worthy of note here. Every house (which is a life) will be tried by fire (the tests, trials, troubles, and tribulations of life). Don't miss that word "every." Nobody coming to this planet will escape the fires and trials of life. It will, in fact, reveal what kind of builder we all are, what we have been building with and the kind of foundation we have been building on. The all-important, final point is telling: did our work endure the test of time and fire so we were able to make it to the end? The true reward is at life's end and it is eternal!

What it means to have the character trait of being **A FOUNDATION BUILDER:**

- The subsystem or base relied upon for a building, business or life to be supported and advanced
- A base of support
- The underlying background of study, preparation, finances, friendships and developed skill required to found a business
- The concrete, steel and masonry substructure for an edifice
- The support upon which a business, building or a life both stands and is able to endure the tests of time

FRANKNESS—   **Study start date:** _____ **Finish date:** _____

We live in such a politically correct world, it is hard sometimes to find people who will tell you the truth or what they really believe about anything. They are so afraid they are going to offend someone or be ostracized they can't give you a straight answer. Their solution is to stutter, stammer, send up some smoke screens and beat around the bush. If they ever do give you an answer, it is about as worthless as a four-finger glove. What a breath of fresh air it is to find someone who is willing to call a spade a spade anymore.

I believe the main problem people have in this area is caused by a failure to sell out and fall in love with the truth. According to Paul, not receiving "the love of the truth" is probably the greatest failing of mankind not just for the present but for eternity as well. (II Thessalonians 2:10) Years earlier David said, "Buy the truth and sell it not." (Proverbs 23:23) It is worth more than all the gold on the planet.

What is wrong with just telling someone the truth? And, letting the chips fall where they will? Why not just lay it on the line. Hopefully, they will be a big boy and receive it. Don't sugar coat it, twist it, paint it a different shade of grey, bend it or do torture to it, just tell it like it is—being, of course, as gentle as you can in order to make your point. Being frank doesn't mean one must be so to the point of brutality. Tact certainly has its place but it never trumps the truth; especially "speaking the truth in love." (Ephesians 4:15) Besides, Proverbs 27:9 (NIV) tells us " . . the pleasantness (value) of one's friend springs from his earnest (sincere and frank) counsel."

What it means to have the character trait of **FRANKNESS:**

- Honesty of expression
- Having unmistakable clarity
- Succinct
- The courage, confidence and character to tell it like it is
- Not mincing words
- Sometimes not telling people what they want to hear but what they need to know
- Sincere, free, forthright counsel

RIENDLINESS —   **Study start date: _____ Finish date: _____**

Someone made the statement and it is true, "Anything you start out wrong, never turns out right." This is especially true in friendships. Why? Because we never get a second chance to make a good first impression with everyone we meet. If we approach a new acquaintance with a sour puss—like we've been sucking on persimmons all our life—what else could they possibly think? We are probably exactly what we are representing ourselves to be, a person who meets people and doesn't think enough of them or their friendship to even smile. A smile, by the way, is the universal sign language that says to people: I like you. I like myself. I like being here. I am confident about this meeting and believe something positive is going to come from it. Proverbs 18:24 tells us truly, that "A man who has friends must himself be friendly." Now I'm not trying to tell you how to live. You don't have to smile when you meet people and you don't have to eat or breathe either—but there will be consequences if you don't. If you don't smile, your demeanor will, in fact, be making this kind of a statement: I don't like you, I don't like myself. I am not happy being here. I am not confident about this meeting and I don't think anything positive is going to come from it.

In life, sure, there comes a time we must take a stand for who and what we are but, remember this,: he who treads softly and makes friends will go far. Like they say, an ounce of honey draws more flies than a gallon of gall. Although I am convinced that most of these grumpy goats can't see it, in their mind there is nothing whatsoever wrong with being more caustic than battery acid. They go all the way through life and, because of this attitude, never even have the first good friend. Philosophers out of antiquity past such as Aristotle, Cicero and Montaigne believed that friendship was truly the pre-eminent institution as humans go. They believed that friendship was indispensable to a person's life and that every friendship actually has positive societal, business and political effects. Incredibly, they also believed (although I am not recommending it) it is so crucial that a person could go through life without honor, justice or marriage but not friendship. Having friends and being a good friend, I believe, is what makes one truly rich in this short term lease each of us have on planet earth. Friendships are one of the greatest comforts of life and he who invests in his friends is wise.

One of my best friends for many years now and still a great friend today, told me long ago that we actually have an account with every person we meet in life and at any point in time we will either have money on account with them or be overdrawn. He cautioned that we should always leave a little money on the table. Never, never ever put yourself in the position of being overdrawn. What he was saying was to take people to lunch among other things. Show them some sincere interest and kindness. Don't worry about who paid the last time. It is always an honor to bless a friend. It should be our daily objective to encourage them, let them know we appreciate them and do our best to add value to their lives. We should be sincerely interested in them, their family and their pursuits. We should be predisposed, trying our best to help them accomplish their goals in life. We should look at every person we meet as one worthy of being not just a friend but a life-long friend and be willing to make the investments of the time and resources necessary to make that happen. We should make it a point to never be able to find a person who is not good enough to be our friend.

Here are ten ways to make friends:

1. Smile when you meet people or talk with them. Begin things in a friendly manner.

2. Remember the person's name. It is the most important word on earth to them and should be very important to you as well. Make the effort.
3. Discuss but refuse to argue about debatable issues.
4. Be a friendly, relaxed, comfortable person who is easy to be around. Don't lay down a lot of rules for others or be demanding about having things your way all the time. Be negotiable especially on small matters.
5. Practice being a good listener. Encourage other people to talk about themselves and their interests. Ask questions.
6. Don't be a know-it-all. Show people that you have a lot to learn and plan to always be learning in life until the day you die. Let them know that you can learn from everyone. Seek humility as a life goal.
7. Be an interesting, principal, exciting, stimulating person yourself so people will want to be around you.
8. Realize we all have rough edges in our personality and work to eliminate them. Take the criticisms of others to heart.
9. Genuinely make others feel important.
10. Never interfere (as far as this is possible) with another person's means of being happy.

Here's a poem about friendship that gives us all something to shoot at:

"I'd like to be the sort of friend
  That you have been to me;
  I'd like to be the help
  That you've been always glad to be;
  I'd like to mean as much to you
  Each minute of the day
  As you have meant, old friend of mine,
  To me along the way."

Guest

What it means to have the character trait of **FRIENDLINESS:**

- Showing kindness and good will
- Smiling (the indispensable, universal sign of friendliness)
- Showing a sincere interest in the pursuits, well-being and state of another's affairs
- Being cheerful and comforting to others
- Finding ways to help your friend's business, children and ministry succeed
- Doing all those things befitting a true friend
- Being there in our friend's time of need

RIEND, A RAINY-DAY—   Study start date: _____ Finish date: _____

W e know for a man to be truly rich in this life, he must first be rich toward God. (Luke 12:21) This notwithstanding, one of the greatest riches a person can have here on earth is our friends. True friends are certainly a delight, a great gift, a blessing and a comfort as we travel this cold, hard, sometimes difficult and perplexing path of life.

The bible picture of true friendship was that of David and Jonathan. Theirs was wonderful and it was experienced amid a time of the greatest turmoil, political intrigue and trepidation at the highest levels of government and unending wars. David and Jonathan were constantly fighting battles from within and without the kingdom. Their greatest problem was Jonathan's father's desire to kill David because he had been anointed king by the prophet Samuel. Through all of this, the depth of their friendship was such a blessing David said that Jonathan's love "was wonderful, exceeding that of the love of women." (II Samuel 1:26) Jonathan even withstood his father and called him out for trying to kill David without a cause. Although he relented temporarily, Saul soon continued his pursuit of David with 3,000 of his finest soldiers. Being divinely guided and protected by God, he narrowly escaped death time and again. However, when the news came to David that Jonathan, his brothers and his dad were killed in battle, he tore his clothes, wept and fasted until that evening. He knew his best friend in all the world was gone and there was nothing he could do.

Years later, after David had defeated the Philistines and established his kingdom, the thought occurred to him to see about honoring any possible remaining descendants of his good friend Jonathan. There was no law, tradition compelling his to do this. It was for no reason other than respect for Jonathan's devotion as his true friend. So David inquired of his staff, "Is there still anyone who is left of the house of Saul, that I may show him kindness for Jonathan's sake?" (II Samuel 9:1) They soon found a descendant of Saul by the name of Ziba. He came to the King and told of a long forgotten son of Jonathan named Mephibosheth who was lame in his feet and living in Lo Debar. This was a dry, barren place where there was no pasture. Life for this young man, as an invalid who obviously could not work\ and make living at a time when society was supported only by an agrarian economy, was pretty bleak. It might be well to note in our time of mechanized wheel chairs, that they didn't even have the non-motorized variety at this time in history. Invalids had to be carried about mostly on stretchers.

Mephibosheth's injury occurred when he was five years old. His nurse was gripped in fear and shock when she had gotten news that Jonathan and his father, Saul, had been killed by the Philistines. Since they were still under attack and in haste to flee, she grabbed the boy up and accidentally dropped him in such a manner that it made him lame for life in both of his feet.

Upon learning about him, David commanded that the young man be brought to his house immediately. Upon his arrival, he told him not to be afraid or have any misgivings (because of David and Saul's conflicts). He just wanted to show him kindness for his father Jonathan's sake. David immediately restored all the land of Saul, his grandfather (as a king, he had considerable holdings). He also invited Mephibosheth to eat at his table for the rest of his life. This was all so startling to the young man that he said, "What is your servant that you would look upon me any more than a dead dog?" At this, David commanded Ziba, Saul's servant, that he had just given to his master's grandson all that belonged to Saul and all his house, some of the choicest land in the country. Then he commanded him, his fifteen sons and his twenty servants, to work the land for him so he would always have food to eat. Further, he told Mephibosheth that he would eat at his table, not merely as a guest, but as one of his own sons. The life fortune of this disadvantaged young man changed in a moment because of one thing, the sincere devotion of his father's friend and that, long after his father had died. David proved to be not only a rainy-day friend but a friend in war and times of great trepidation. Yes, a friend who was yet a great friend even years after Johnathan's passing.

One thing we need to remember about being a rainy-day friend and helping others in time of need is that their need will never arise at a convenient time. We are all busy and have a barn full of projects ongoing as well as a whole lot of pressing things already scheduled for each day. But to be a rainy day friend, we must be predisposed to stop what we are doing, throw our schedules to the wind and go to our friend's aid. If we don't realize the call for help is probably going to interrupt our plans and be an inconvenience, we will never be able to respond as we should.

Nobody plans to be a sunshine friend but there is more to this than just desiring to be a friend to our neighbor when all is well and they want someone to go fishing, share some tickets to a ball game or go waterskiing. We should desire rather to be a rainy-day friend; one who wants to be there for our neighbor on their worst day—when the world has them pinned and is going for the ten count. When all hell has broken lose against them, all have forsook them and they are broke, betrayed, hired-out and renting. That's when worldly friends are so quick to disappear but it is truly the best time to show up as a friend. People rarely forget the help given them when they are down and out. Just being called upon and being able to deliver is its own reward.

What it means to have the character trait of **BEING A RAINY-DAY FRIEND:**

- Taking the mantle of a servant in difficult times and circumstances
- Gladly being there for our friends in their time of need
- Being predisposed and mentally ready to help others when it is not convenient
- Being willing to go the second and the third mile
- Having the goal of being the best friend our friends have ever had
- Realizing that it is a great honor to be called on by a friend to help
- Taking great delight in being a tool of deliverance in the hands of God

FRUGALITY —   **Study start date: _____ Finish date: _____**

America has been blessed for so long that many have actually become wasteful with our bounty. Before the current Great Recession, Americans stopped saving and were actually spending on the average 103% of what they made. Few think anything of leaving the lights on in multiple rooms in their house when they are only occupying one. In the course of a year, all those lights left on can come to a considerable sum. Over time, fortune always smiles on the efficient. Certainly faith and giving have a tremendous effect on a person's finances no doubt but so does frugality. "Waste not, want not …" as they say and we must also learn to "use it up, wear it out, make it do or (or sooner or later you will probably have to) do without."

Understand that everything we have, both small and great, has been entrusted to us, as a gift from God, Himself, and is to be managed carefully and efficiently. One day soon we will be called before Him to give account of our stewardship. Frugality, we know, is being faithful with our finances, using wisdom in the management of our material wealth. You see, finances is God's school house of faith. He trusts all of us with a certain amount to see how we will handle it. Will we spend all of it like a drunk sailor on liberty or will we respect it as a gift from God to give Him back His portion, conserve, invest and multiply the rest by managing it wisely? The Master is focused on frugality as a test of the hearts of men. We see these words recorded in Luke 16:10-12. "He who is faithful in what is least is faithful also in much; and he who is unjust in what is least is unjust also in much." God made the heart and he knows how to judge it. He then goes on to reveal how this is the key to His willingness to give us even greater riches ssying, "Therefore, if you have not been faithful in the unrighteous mammon, who will commit to your trust the true (spiritual) riches?"

The Bible also promises us that there are seasons in life and every season is not harvest season. We are also assured that there are storms on the way to try every man's house to see of what sort it is. God wants to know what it is made of as well as what it has been built upon. All this is to encourage us to be very careful how we build and sow for if we sow to the wind, Scripture tells us we will surely reap the whirlwind.

Without controversy, every human being will only, over a lifetime, receive a certain finite amount of money.—and no more. Some spend every dime and spend it fast, as soon as they get it. Others spend it faster than they get it by borrowing against the future. One of the failed philosophies of the world is that of trying to borrow your way to great riches. It doesn't work. Now if you are looking at someone who may appear to have done it, remember, if they are still alive, the complete story has not yet been told. Many calamities may yet be awaiting them. Besides building your estate on borrowed money always makes you the servant of the lender (some can be pretty ruthless) and it always keeps you in a very vulnerable, slippery place. Furthermore, it makes no provision for depressions, recessions, physical ailments, a temporary loss of work, etc. Interest on loans never takes a holiday. It must be paid on Saturday, Sunday, holidays as well as the times you are sick and can't work. You can't have a rainy day borrowing your way to a fortune and the Bible promises all of us that we will have our share of those dark days. How do I know? Well, primarily because I read this in the Word and it just so happens that I have a ton of real-life experience as well.

At one point in my younger years, I was about $300,000 in debt. We had a nice home that I had built and nice cars but I had no boat, airplane, motorcycle, mountain house, lake house or condo on the beach. All of my debt was in real estate investments. They were all working out fine at the time until something cataclysmic came out of nowhere which was totally outside of my control. It had nothing to do with anything I had done. Believe me. I was only smart enough to get into all that much trouble but not at all smart enough to get out. I turned to the Lord and promised Him if He would get me out I'd never do it again. At that point I took all I knew about business and threw it in the trash. I started doing everything He said do in the Bible. I spoke to that mountain of debt (Mark 11:23), worked my tail off, and believed God for His promise that I could "owe no man anything but to love him)." (Romans 13:8) Within a few years, He miraculously paid everything off and pulled me out of the fire like a red-hot branding iron.

God's system of blessing is for Him to find us faithful in the small things He has given into our charge. When He sees us faithful, He gives us more and more. In the Parable of the Minas, He said to the servant who had been faithful with a few minas, "Well done … because you were faithful in a very little, have authority over ten cities." (Luke 19:17) Remember now, that a mina was a very small amount of money. (Sixty minas made a talent.) God is so serious about this principle that He decided that a person who had demonstrated skill and self-discipline with about $20 could well manage ten cities at one time! Not only that but He also gave him the ten cities.

Frugality is learning to live on less than you make and always save a portion for the future. You will never have the resources to take advantage of the opportunities of life that will surely come your way if you don't learn to save. If you ever hope to start a business, you must know how to conserve resources. If you ever want to get a loan from a banker, he is going to be watching to see if you have learned to live on less than you make and save some of what you have made. Your savings account will give him the answer. Bankers don't want to loan someone money who hasn't shown they have the discipline to save and deny themselves. They just might flake out with the first sign of trouble or go to Hawaii on vacation with their money.

Another crucial aspect of frugality is seeing value in things that others consider refuse. Old houses, for example, can be torn down in one's spare time and the lumber, doors and windows saved for a future home or piece of rental property. Cars needing work can be picked up for a song at auction, fixed or painted in your free time and sold for a considerable profit. Learning how to do some construction is also a way to save and get ahead. For an example, anyone can learn how to roof a house either with the asphalt butt shingles or the new metal roof systems. Neither system is all that complicated. Volunteer to help a roofer for a day free and you can learn all you need to know about it.

Owning cars and houses are virtually necessities today and so important to every person and family, I have written a book on both subjects: *How to Build a Debt-Free Home* and *How to Buy a Used Car.*

Another important part of frugality is making a practice of buying with an eye toward utility value instead of prestige. Good, two or three year old cars are, as you know, much cheaper than the brand new ones just off the show-room floor and they still have most of the life left in them. Let someone else have all the prestige and take that high depreciation the first few years. You might be saving 30 to 40%. Some cars are known for their serviceability and utility and can be bought for a song in comparison to what one would have to pay for a Rolls Royce. You can buy a gold Rolex President watch today for $34,800 with 7% sales tax, you are out the door for a paltry $37,236. (This one doesn't have any diamonds.) About ten years ago, a fella I knew had a Rolex that wasn't keeping very good time so, of course, he took it to a jeweler to have it cleaned and adjusted. The bill was over $800. On the contrary, you can buy a good Timex for about $35. That's $37.00 with tax and it's on God's 60-cycle electricity so it never, ever needs to be adjusted. Besides it has a light on it, several stop watches, a lap timer, keeps your calendar, tells you the time around the world, has two alarms, tells you the day, month and year, etc. just to name a few of its functions. Quite a good investment as a time piece and if it ever stops working, just change the battery or toss it and get a new one.

Another area to consider is learning how to buy wholesale. This can be done by getting to know the wholesalers in your area, finding the wholesalers on line or buying direct from the factories in your area.

Of course another way of stretching one's finances is learning how to buy and operate the equipment to do the things needing to be done in your business and home rather than hiring everything out. Most tools and equipment can be purchased at a pawn shop for 30–40% of retail and are still about like new. If you get a bad unit, which can happen occasionally, they will just about always take it back—so no worries there. This enables you to do the job yourself, save the labor and overhead of the company likely to have been doing the work—and you still own the equipment so you can do it again and again in the future when a similar need arises.

Most importantly, being frugal allows God to bless us. Then we can use the finances He gives us to be a blessing to others. In addition we will have an inheritance to leave to our children's children. Malachi 3:10, Proverbs 13:22

What it means to have the character trait of **FRUGALITY:**

- Able to conserve resources
- Not wasteful
- Using economy when expending resources
- The ability to be content, curbing one's desire to always have more and bigger
- The ability to see value in things others throw away
- The creative ability to convert something made specifically for one use to meet another need
- Knowing a penny saved is worth far more than a penny earned
- Knowing that being faithful in the least things is the test God gave us to be granted stewardship over much greater things
- Knowing how to keep resources properly protected during storage for a later use
- Knowing that fortune always favors and smiles on the efficient

GENEROSITY—   Study start date: _____ Finish date: _____

Solomon, the wisest man in the world, made us aware of something very important he observed: He said, "It is good and fitting for one to eat and drink, and to enjoy the good of all his labor in which he toils under the sun all the days of his life which God gives him; for it is his heritage." Ecclesiastes 5:18) In other words, it is his portion and joy. "As for every man to whom God has given riches and wealth, and given him power to eat of it, to receive his heritage and rejoice in his labor—this is the gift of God. For he will not dwell unduly on the days of his life, because God keeps him busy with the joy of his heart." (5: 19) What a blessing to know the secret of life that is truly life. Being generous is one of the greatest blessings life has to offer.

Then he went on to point out, "There is (also) an evil which I have seen under the sun, and it is common among men: A man to whom God has given riches and wealth and honor, so that he lacks nothing for himself of all he desires; yet God does not give him power to eat of it, but a foreigner consumes it. This is vanity, and it is an evil affliction."(Ecclesiastes 6:1, 2) Their love of money becomes so great they can't bring themselves to spend any of it for fear of the loss of it from their estate. Not only will they not give a poor invalid a crumb off their table, they can hardly even spare a crumb for themselves most of the time when the only reason God gives an abundance to a person is for them to share with others.

A good friend of mine had an uncle who was a multi-millionaire. At one point he had over a thousand employees and over twenty accountants just to keep up with it all. He had service industry corporations, silver and gold mines as well as a number of apartment complexes which he bought and sold on a regular basis. Later in life he decided to sell the apartment project where he was living but retained in the contract a life estate in one of the apartment units. The agreement was that he had to live there continuously. If he ever moved out, his life estate ended. At this point in his life, he could have bought one of the finest homes in the world, but he could not part with that one, little apartment unit. It became something like a jail cell that he could never leave. Imprisoned by his own greed, he finally died between its four walls.

Today some of our politicians want the people in America to give more taxes to the government so they can give it to whomsoever they choose. That happens to be their own constituents and ever so generously. However, this is not what the Bible suggests. In the book of Acts, Ananias and Sapphira didn't get into trouble for not paying their taxes or for not giving enough to the Church. They got in trouble for lying to the Holy Spirit. They promised to give something to the Church that was theirs alone to give but kept back part of it for themselves. Prior to making this promise, they were under no compulsion to do or give anything. (Acts 5:1–11) There are many today who are selfish, stingy and much like the rich man who refused to give the beggar Lazarus even one crumb off of his table. (Luke 16:20–25) Giving is to come from the spontaneous kindness and compassion of one's heart, not the calculating, largess of a conniving politician seeking to build a voting bloc.

We have this promise from God. Take note: "The generous soul will be made rich, and he who waters will also be watered himself." (Proverbs 11:25) We were also told that he who "uses unjust effort (chicanery) to … (increase) his material possession(s) gathers it for him (to spend) who is kind and generous to the poor." (Proverbs 28:8 Amp Ver) Truly, "God loves a cheerful giver." (II Corinthians 9:7) In deed He does but you don't really get the full flavor of what He is saying here unless you read it in the Amplified Version: It says, "He takes pleasure in, prizes above other things, and is unwilling to abandon or do without a cheerful (joyous, prompt-to-do-it giver)—whose heart is in his giving." Life and all of nature are designed and empowered by God to reward the generous soul. Proverbs 22:9 tells us "He who has a generous eye will be blessed." Why? Because, "he gives his bread to the poor." He gives to people who cannot possibly repay him, expecting and requiring nothing in return. Then, God, Himself, will undertake to multiply it back to him.

What it means to have the character trait of **GENEROSITY**:

- Having a willingness to share
- Being free handed
- Someone who is cheerfully generous
- Being a conduit and not a reservoir (that stagnates)
- One who sows bountifully
- Benevolent
- A liberality of spirit to give to others expecting nothing in return
- Magnanimous
- Characterized by a spirit of giving. One truly generous is in covenant with God as a tither and giver. God gives them tremendous grace equipping them to be ever more able to give. II Corinthians 9:6–15
- Marked by an abundance of fruit as a result of past giving

ENTLENESS—   **Study start date:** _____ **Finish date:** _____

The world is in to winning by intimidation and taking what it wants by hook, crook or, if necessary, by force. Amazingly, in such a fierce, dog-eat-dog, get out of my way world that is all about getting what it wants at any cost, God has called us to gentleness.

We were admonished by Paul in I Timothy 3:6 not to give authority to a novice, the reasons for which are almost endless. First of all, the beginner doesn't understand the complexities of leadership and the interconnectedness of life and its problems. They certainly don't understand human nature and haven't had the time it takes to gain valuable experience in business, the ministry or human relations. They won't know the value of money or the importance of building consensus with their team. In addition, they likely haven't had time to work through many of the temptations of personal passion and are not only prone to fall prey to some of these temptations but most assuredly will. Most importantly, however, a novice, placed in a position of power, will become puffed up, inflated by their own ego, and generally lifted up with pride. It is so tempting to the novice to use their new-found power to solve every problem with an arbitrary, mighty fist. The Bible is replete with examples of princes who ascended to the throne at a very early age because of the untimely passing of their fathers and then we are told, time and again, of all the havoc this wreaked upon the nation because of their arrogant leadership style and foolish decisions. This is why banks, for example, are reticent to take on new builders. They aren't sure this new builder won't take the construction draws they give him to complete a home and use the money to go on a vacation to Florida instead of paying their bills on the house. Novices also tend to be a bit dictatorial, having a tendency to use the power of their newly gained authority to rule, as I said, rather than effecting change through wisdom, understanding, encouragement, consensus, cooperation and gentleness.

King David was, without a doubt, the greatest soldier and political leader Israel has ever had. His prowess in both of these areas was known far and wide. He was King of Israel all by himself (with God's help of course) with no congress or Supreme Court to answer to and never even had to face the voters in elections. He could do anything he wanted and could treat anyone just about however he wanted with few limitations. Even with all he had gone through as a shepherd of sheep defending his flocks out in the wilderness, fighting the bear and the lion, being chased by King Saul like a flea in the desert and all the battles he fought for his country, he still got tripped up with Bathsheba. Then he went on to fail so badly in his position of authority that he even had her husband killed. Just one problem. A bold prophet, Nathan by name, confronted him with a parable showing him his sin. Verbally, he painted David the picture of a rich man who had many flocks but was so greedy that he who took the one little ewe lamb, the personal pet of a very poor man, for his own use. This was not only the poor man's only lamb, it was also his only possession. He had bought it, fed it personally and grew up with it such that it was like a child to him. This rich man mercilessly took it and slaughtered it to furnish his feast for a traveling dinner guest. When Nathan asked David what should be done to one in his kingdom who had committed such a heartless act, he responded in anger. "As the Lord lives, the man who has done this shall surely die! And he shall restore fourfold for the lamb, because he did this thing and because he had no pity." (II Samuel 12:6) Nathan pointed his finger right at the King and opined, "Thou art the man!" Grave consequences came upon him because of his selfish sins, not the least of which was the sword not departing from his house until he died. Yet he remained a great king in Israel even with the rebellion and civil war his sins had caused his son, Absalom, to instigate.

All these experiences, however, led him to make an important statement: It wasn't his prowess in battle, his gift of leadership, his physical strength or agility, his wisdom or understanding that had catapulted him to national prominence. Amazingly, summing up the secret to all his success, he said, "Thy gentleness (God's) has made me great." (Psalm 18:35) The ability to have the position and almost total power over peoples' lives but the grace to set it all aside for a season when trying to bring correction or improvement in the lives of one's constituents. It is the maturity to try every other tool at one's disposal to bring correction and improvement in the lives of others gently rather than using the brute force of executive power. It is doing everything you can to avoid having to bring the hammer down. He knew, however, that in some of the most difficult cases, this might still have to be done but only as a last resort.

Paul, the most preeminent of all the apostles, came pleading with the Corinthians to make the corrections needed in their lives, not by his authority as an apostle, or as one who moved in the gifts or as the principal leader of the church. He made his plea "by the meekness and gentleness of Christ." II Corinthians 10:1

Certainly we have all benefited from the kindness of our benevolent benefactor, God, Himself. Because of this, He wants us to treat our neighbors with the same gentleness He has shown each of us. He is the standard. You see, He didn't deal with us by the strictness of the Law but granted us an imperfect righteousness. He actually gave real value to a righteousness that should have, according to the Law, been none whatsoever. He remembered our frailty and what we were made of and refused to levy what would have been heavy but fair penalties according to rhe Law. He gave us mercy with gentleness along with more and more chances, time and again.

In Matthew 18, Peter had just asked the Master how many times we were to forgive a brother who had offended us and suggested seven times thinking seven, being the number of completion would be a gracious plenty, especially in the area of being offended by someone. Being a man given to rage and capable of cutting off your head or your ear with his sword and really would rather settle things that way, the truth be known, was really stretching here to learn gentleness in the form of forgiveness. But, amazingly, Jesus said we needed to be willing to forgive our brother not seven times but "Until seventy times seven" or 490 times. Then, to help him see this and make his point, he told peter a parable about our responsibility in the sensitive, trying area of enduring offenses by our neighbor.

It seems, there was a certain king who settled accounts with his servants from time-to-time. On one particular occasion, a servant was brought before him by his exchequer who owed him ten thousand talents. We might, in today's dollars, just call this a multi-million dollar debt, a debt so great he could never ever really expect to repay. He owed so much that the king ordered the sale of all he had including his wife and children in order for the account to be paid, at least to some extent. At that point, the servant fell to his knees worshipped the king and begged for more time, promising to pay the entire amount. At this, the king was moved by compassion and, amazingly, actually was so gentle with him about the matter that he forgave him the entire amount. That servant walked out the door with his family and his freedom as a free man but also with a completely clean slate.

It wasn't long, however, before this same servant went out on the street and found a fellow servants who owed him a hundred pence — we could say a penny ante debt in today's terms. He immediately grabbed the man, began choking him half to death and demanded immediate payment of the entire indebtedness.

His servant, likewise, fell to his knees begging for patience and promised to pay every penny. However, he refused to give him a moment's time and had him cast into prison where he was to stay until the debt was paid full. This was both hypocritical and cruel. Hypocritical because he had just been forgiven a far greater indebtedness and cruel considering prisons back then were not at all like the ones we have today: florescent lights, central air, indoor plumbing and three hots and a cot. But in one respect, they were similar. They were about the worst place on the planet to think about raising serious money and paying off a lot of indebtedness.

One of their fellow servants who had seen all this transpire became very disturbed about it and went to his Lord and told him all that had gone on.

After hearing the man, the Lord called in the one to whom he had shown mercy and said, "You wicked servant, I forgave you all that debt because you begged me to. Shouldn't you have had mercy on your fellow servant as I had on you?" At this, his Lord was wroth and commanded that he be given over to the tormentors in the jail until he had paid all he owed him. Then the Master made His concluding statement: This is how my heavenly Father will treat every one of you unless you forgive every one of your brothers their trespasses.

Some people, as we have all experienced at one time or another, are like the proverbial bull in the china closet as they go through life. Being honest, we, too, have actually played this very part ourselves from time-to-time. Realizing this, when in leadership, we should always try using less power than we think is necessary to effect needed changes or improvements. If nothing or very little happens, we know that it can always be ratcheted up later if absolutely necessary Teddy Roosevelt said it was good to "Walk softly but carry a big stick." (The hope, of course, is that you won't have to use the stick.) Be gentle if you can. Benjamin Franklin, I believe said, "Always try to take hold of things by the smooth handle." That too, is some good advice.

What it means to have the character trait of **GENTLENESS:**

- Having the soft or gentle touch dealing with policy, human failings, our neighbors and the issues of life
- Not being of the baser human nature: cruel, mean, harsh or strident
- Being kind, understanding and amiable
- Moderation and temperance in judgment and relations with our neighbors, friends and employees
- A trait of the honorable and distinguished
- A demeanor suitable to people of a high social station in life
- Being free from strictness, sternness, harshness, cruelty or violence
- Using less power than you think is necessary, as long as possible, to get things done
- Remembering King David said, "Thy gentleness has made me great." Ps 18:35
- Having "the meekness and gentleness of Christ." II Corinthians 10:1

GOAL ORIENTED, BEING—   **Study start date: _____ finish date: _____**

I'm going to begin this with a startling statement: We are all humans. That's right. That was the earth shaking statement. Now I knew you were only too acutely aware of this but I have a reason for saying this. Remember, scientist say we are all just 75% water and the rest dirt. Certainly not a whole lot to be proud of so we can see it doesn't take a whole lot to get involved in this game we call life. I respect everyone and understand that we are all made in the image of God but, we are all still humans. Even men like George Washington, and Abraham Lincoln were just human beings. Albert Einstein, Ike Eisenhower and Alexander the Great were just—well, humans. Sure, they came, saw and conquered in their time but they all came from dust, lived a little while under the Sun, died and went back to dust. I don't say this in any way to be disrespectful. I have great respect for all these men but we are going somewhere with this.

Furthermore, we know, as human beings, God gave us all a mind. Brains are good but they sure are funny to look at when taken outside of our boney heads as scientists are want to do so often. Now I have said all that to say this. Without goals our minds soon turn to mush. Without goals in life, the press of the battle, reversals, betrayals, hard times and fatigue as well as the constant barrage of negative stimuli can cause us to quickly become despondent, depressed and discouraged. So many people play out their lives like the proverbial ricochet rabbit, bouncing off this bad news and that, blown here and there by every turn of events. Without goals, their destiny is decided by the series of inadvertent accidents and avalanches of trouble coming into their lives. The Bible tells us bluntly: "Without a vision (goals) the people perish." (Proverbs 29:18) Humans, simply cannot survive on this planet without goals. But, with goals burned by the Spirit deep within our hearts, our

Without a goal to reach for, men will perish

whole being is moved by an unseen, inner drive that propels us through the same difficulties, fatigue and betrayals to very efficiently bring our hopes and dreams to fruition. Our minds are incredible computers programmed to work constantly, 24/7/365, to bring us the things we desire—even while we sleep. Truth is, we all have to learn how to navigate purposefully through life. Just like you drive a car where you want to go with your mind and eyes, we must guide our lives with goals and the eyes of our faith.

All of us, as human, also possess something else that is extremely valuable, if we are still breathing, which is called a life and it will either be used or abused. It can be abused with drugs, alcohol, illicit sex and a thousand other things, not the least of which is a person not having clearly defined goals. Not having goals cause's people to get discouraged, wallow in self-pity and make horribly stupid decisions. Often I ask people I have never met what they think the devil's most powerful secret weapon is and they never get it. I mean never. The answer is self-pity. This insidious, invisible enemy of all mankind is highly ranked in the devil's bag of tricks because in using it, he makes us feel we have every right, when betrayed or done wrong, to feel sorry for ourselves and retaliate. People never even see it coming. And, how many people over time has he used it on to not only defeat but destroy? The answer is: likely every human being who has ever arrived on earth. We have all been taken by it as children and some still fall prey to it throughout their entire lives. Self-pity can cause someone to steal from their company (for being passed over for a promotion), cheat on their spouse (because he or she isn't giving them enough attention) and do a million other stupid things including commit suicide. It is a fact, the lives of people without goals will rarely ever amount to a hill of horse manure.

On the other hand, your life can be used constructively to build, accomplish, thrive and bless others. In fact, your life can be a blessing to a lot of people. God loves you. He has placed desires in your heart only you and He know about. He wants you to have them even more than you do. He hid them there, deep in your heart and you need to find them in order to find your life. As we know, everybody is different. What floats one person's boat won't help the next person flop their mop. So you need to find these desires and let God help you fulfill them. That is what life is really all about and what makes life truly life as God intended it.

I also believe that everyone was born with at least one talent given by God. We see this very effectively presented in the Parable of Talents. (Matthew 25:14 and following) Take careful note that this is also a life and death parable—having life and death consequences in the lives of people depending on what they do with their talent. Joni, for example, has no use of her hands but is able to make the most beautiful, incredible oil paintings by holding the paint brush in her teeth. George Washington Carver used his life to study the little peanut and found all kinds of great things in it that just keeps on blessing the whole world. Me, I'm just here to help you become great. I live to win souls and make others great in the eyes of the Lord. Hopefully, with God's help, we can all add a little value to people's lives and help them get where they want to go. The brains we were given will be used in everyone's life to either make us or break us.

Some people spend a whole lifetime on this planet and never learn how to use their brains! Others (and I'm one of them} spend their entire lifetime learning how to use their brains. And, the good news is you don't really need much of one. You just need one. Some people are actually too smart. They tend to rely too heavily on their brains and, as a result, aren't willing to give life the hard work and toil it requires. Like my dad told me frequently growing up, "Your brain was put there for more than a hat rack." I must have been in the hat rack mode most of the time as a kid. Our brains are there to be used with wisdom, prudence, knowledge and God's guidance to accomplish great things—primarily to help others. We are actually here to make the world a better place. There is something unique that you can give the world that no one else can.

Besides not using their brains, another reason people never get anywhere in life is just plain fear. Fear of failure is a powerful, debilitating force. All of us have been fearful at to some point in our lives. Don't worry about failure. We have all failed at something. But, remember, the transcendent glory of God is so powerful that it can actually cause the worst things that have ever happened to us turn out to be the best.

Another thing that commonly causes people never to do anything is a perceived lack of resources. They may think, "How can I do anything without a whole lot of money, equipment and personnel?" They forget that God owns everything and He can and will give it to whomsoever He pleases. Men want to borrow lots of money and do the "big box" thing, getting themselves hopelessly in debt. On the contrary, God wants to show us how important it is that we "despise not small beginnings." He wants to show us how to start things out very small, get them right from the bottom up and build a company in the strength and wisdom of God.

Yet another worry people are consumed with, causing them not to set meaningful goals is a perceived lack of talent. Matthew 25:15, the Parable of the Talents, speaks to this as well. From it we know everyone has at least one talent and that's all we need. So the question is, if money and talent didn't matter, what would you do with your life? Like a man said, "Everything you need is right under your nose and it is so obvious you can't see it." Make a plan and plan big. Set your goals high and go after them with God's help and all of your might.

How do we get started in all this? First, we need to invest some time in prayer and get God's goals for every area of our lives. At the end of this Character Trait you will find a set of short range goals (one year) and some long-range goals (five years) for your life. Now we have already said your life is important so take the time. You are worth the trouble. Make your list, write it down and pray over it. Get a blue-print for your life from the Bible and plan things like you want them to be. Check your progress and update them every year. Here are eight critically important things we need to do immediately to have a new beginning and God working with us:

1. **Be willing to call a spade a spade.** Truthfully identify the situations in life you are unhappy about and if you are satisfied with where you are, you're really in bad shape. God can't steer a parked car. So many people are parked at a place called Status Quo on Mulley Grub Alley, paralyzed, afraid to move. Get some goals, get in gear and get outta there.

2. **Clarify your own desires in life.** Write them down and pray over them. Spencer Johnson said, "A goal is a dream with a deadline." While you are getting your goals down, be sure to ask God for His goals for your life. Cut out all that stuff that won't matter a hundred years from now or one second after death. Recreation and vacations are fine in proper perspective. You need these but not a whole life full of them. Cut out the frivolous activities. Don't let the world pour you in its mold and use you up doing a whole pile of eternally-inconsequential things. To be a well-rounded person, you need goals in every area of life: Spiritual, personal, educational, financial, family, home, vocational (work), church, ministry and physical fitness.

3. **Honor the things you desire.** Dr. Noel Langdel once made this statement: "If you want something in life, all you have to do is honor it. Whatever you honor, you cultivate; you water prune and in the season thereof you produce the fruit."

4. **Know right off that your mind will try to betray you.** Your brain is going to tell you "Don't take a chance, it is far too dangerous, you have set your goals way too high, you could fail and make a fool of yourself." Laugh at fear and go right on! We all have to outwit our brains!!!

5. **Love the work, love the battle and love the fight.** It's worth it! Someone said, "Not the quarry, but the chase, not the trophy, but the race." Enjoy the fight because we win. The victory is ours in Christ Jesus. Enjoy doing quality work for others. Fall in love with adding value to other people's lives, encouraging them and helping them attain their goals – asking nothing.

6. **Once you have your goals in writing, dedicate them to God.** Release them to Him. Lay it all at God's feet. Put God on the spot to carry out His Word. Trust Him to bring it to pass.

7. **Speak to the mountain.** The problems you face with your goals is your mountain. Speak to your problems and goals and command them to be and do what you desire. It is not good enough to just have faith. You must have enough faith to speak to your mountain. Really, right out of your

mouth. Mark11:22 says, "Have faith in God. For assuredly, I say to you, whoever says (speaks) to this mountain, 'Be removed and be cast into the sea, and does not doubt in his heart, but believes that those things he says will be done, he will have whatever he says. Therefore I say to you, 'whatever things you ask when you pray believe that you receive them, and you will have them.'"

8. **Rejoice.** Get in touch with what it would be and feel like if you got it. Be thankful. Rejoice and be exceedingly glad!!! Even before it actually happens. Don't ask me why. Just do it. It works!

Faith, goals and serving God are a powerful combination. It is how God wants us to live and work with Him—using our minds, goals, hard work, faith, love and perseverance. Faith is the only way this will work. The writer of Hebrews said, "The just shall live by faith ..." and this is also the only thing that pleases God. (Hebrews 10:38) If it will work for me, it will work for anyone.

What is possible with faith? Anything. Absolutely anything. You can do anything with God's help—even the seemingly impossible. Now go at it. When you do, you will find life that is truly life. The real deal that God intended. Life will be exciting! God will even cause you "to ride upon the high places of the earth." (Isaiah 58:14) Praise Him!

What it means to have the character trait of **BEING GOAL ORIENTED:**

* Regularly making a written list of our faith goals in life
* Constantly seeing the finish line in the race of life
* Keeping the goal in mind and never letting it fade regardless of time, trouble or circumstances
* Using delays and reversals to make a concerted effort to double-down at critical moments to score points in the game
* The ability to count pain, distractions, difficulties, hardships, temporary losses, heat, cold, betrayal and injustice as nothing but temporary imposters in order to press on to the goal and your sure reward

SEE ONE & FIVE YEAR GOAL OUTLINES BELOW:

ONE YEAR GOALS
(Short Term Goals)

From: Date _____ to _____

Name: _____

I. SPIRITUAL:
    1. Time in Word daily: ___ min./day
    2. Prayer time ____ min./day
    3.
    4.
    5.

II. PERSONAL
    1. Developing my functional gift
       which is _____.
    2.
    3.
    4.
    5.

III. EDUCATIONAL
    1.
    2.
    3.
    4.
    5.

IV. FINANCIAL
    1.
    2.
    3.
    4.
    5.

V. FAMILY
    1.
    2.
    3.
    4.
    5.

VI. HOME
    1.
    2.
    3.
    4.
    5.

VII. VOCATIONAL (WORK)
    1.
    2.
    3.
    4.
    5.

VIII. CHURCH
    1.
    2.
    3.
    4.
    5.

IX. MINISTRY
    1.
    2.
    3.
    4.
    5.

X. PHYSICAL FITNESS
    1.
    2.
    3.
    4.
    5.

FIVE YEAR GOALS
(Long Range Goals)

From: Date _____ **to** _____
Name: _____

I. SPIRITUAL:
    1. Time in Word daily: ____ min./day
    2. Prayer time _____ min./day
    3.
    4.
    5.

VI. HOME
    1.
    2.
    3.
    4.
    5.

II. PERSONAL
    1. Developing my functional gift
      which is _____.
    2.
    3.
    4.
    5.

VII. VOCATIONAL (WORK)
    1.
    2.
    3.
    4.
    5.

III. EDUCATIONAL
    1.
    2.
    3.
    4.
    5.

VIII. CHURCH
    1.
    2.
    3.
    4.
    5.

IV. FINANCIAL
    1.
    2.
    3.
    4.
    5.

IX. MINISTRY
    1.
    2.
    3.
    4.
    5.

V. FAMILY
    1.
    2.
    3.
    4.
    5.

X. PHYSICAL FITNESS
    1.
    2.
    3.
    4.
    5.

GRACE—　　　　　　　　　　**Study start date: _____ Finish date: _____**

race has a several definitions but here we will consider only divine gifting, which are the gifts that can only come from God. There are actually quite a few things in life that one can only receive from Him: salvation, the Holy Spirit, the fruits of the Spirit, wisdom, godly character, a prudent wife, etc. Some things you can receive reading about them in a book, from an education in school, or buy in a store. However, the best things in life only come from God, Himself. These are the blessings conferred on people by our merciful, all-knowing, benevolent Heavenly Father.

His grace is sometimes called "unmerited favor" and that is so true because none of us deserve it. However, that in no way fully describes God's grace. True, no matter how good a person might be, how much good they might have done in this world for others or even if they have been willing to give their bodies to be burned for some noble cause, these piddly things, in the realm of divine justice, would never amount to a hill of horse feed. The price of the greatest grace gift, our salvation, was so high that God had to sacrifice His only begotten Son and bankrupt Heaven to get it to us. Honestly, I can write these words and say these things, knowing what it is that I am saying but have no idea of the immense cost to God and His Kingdom to bring us so great salvation. We, mere men, think in terms of dollars and cents, millions, billions and trillions, worlds and galaxies, and this wouldn't get us within tem million light years of the true cost. The cost was too high for us to comprehend. The fact yet remains that we were all born with a fallen nature and sin in our members. None of us, deserved to receive this amazing grace.

It was only by His mercy and divine providence that any of us have enjoyed so great salvation and every other gift of his grace subsequently. Paul told us it was "by grace (we) have been saved through faith and that not of (ourselves); it is the gift of God, not of works lest anyone should boast." (Ephesians 2:8) It is completely separate from His love and mercy as Paul also said. We were all dead in our trespasses and sins and all here means all. "But God, who is rich in mercy, because of His great love with which He loved us. Even when we were dead in trespasses, made us alive together with Christ (by grace you have been saved) and raised us up together, and made us sit together in heavenly places in Christ Jesus, that in the ages to come, He might show the exceeding riches of His grace in His kindness toward us in Christ Jesus." (Ephesians 2:4–7) Mercy was the compassion by which God was moved to provide us, the lost, a Savior. If mercy could have done it on its own, He would never have sacrificed His only begotten Son to accomplish this, the most difficult, costly and painful feat of all time.

More real, eternal and true, the gifts given by God's grace are to be distinguished from worldly gifts. James made this when he penned these words: "Every good and every perfect gift is from above, and comes down from the Father of lights, with whom there is no variation or shadow of turning." (James 1:17) What this means is that there are other prizes, seeming gifts and preferments that man can confer on another person. There are other things that we might think we have lucked upon on the path of life, others might have been given us and still others we might think we worked for and earned. Though pleasant for the moment, these pale by comparison because they are so temporary and fading. God's gifts are truly real, serve a divine purpose and they last for eternity. Some things we have here for the moment. They look like they are ours. We might even be able to have our name engraved on them or have the title for them in our name at the court house. But, we also know that these things are subject to the moth, rust, fire and the thief, functional obsolescence, depreciation, rot, wear and discentegration. God's gifts, again, are eternal, pleasant and beneficial beyond our finite minds to imaginations, calculate or understand.

We earthlings love human merit. We like to point to how well we did in school (some of us might have a hard time doing that one). We might like to point to how well we were prepared or how fit we were for a certain task or mission, God's grace excludes all human merit, requiring but one thing: faith in the Risen Savior. Any admixture of grace and human merit vitiates His

plan and power to convey salvation to the unworthy candidate. Even despite our imperfections after salvation, His grace continues to provide our safety and protection even in a world where satan is the prince of the power of the air. Once saved, we enter a sort of divine, protective cocoon of God's grace made necessary because of our ignorance, at that point, as babes in Christ, of both the weapons of our warfare and the tactics of the satanic kingdom laid out and focused on us. However, even at the moment of salvation, still having many flaws, grace makes the saved person perfect in God's sight because of our position in Christ. He is all our righteousness, by faith. Instantly, we receive Christ's merit and standing before God at Christ's expense. This is only fair in God's divine system of justice because Christ took all our sin on Him so that we could be washed thoroughly clean by His blood. What a glorious plan! What a glorious gift! (Romans 5:1, 8:1, Colossians 2:9, 10) Therefore, at the moment of salvation, believers are no longer "under (the) law but under grace." (Romans 6:14) We instantly become "dead indeed to sin but alive to God in Christ Jesus our Lord" (Romans 6:11) Realizing our standing and having faith in our position "in Christ" make grace a reality in the believer's daily walk and life. There will still be the possibility in one's life for rewards to be given at the hand of God for our faithfulness and holiness but this fact in no way changes the truth of God's infinite, instantaneous, unmerited and unforfeitable salvation.

Without a doubt, the one thing of the greatest value to us in this life is grace and our benevolent Creator has a certain amount allocated, in His providence, for each of us. The question remains, however, is how much of that grace will we be willing to receive? Some, tragically, will sin past their day of salvation and will completely miss out on grace because "Spirit shall not strive with man forever …" (Genesis 6:3) They are truly blessed who seek Him early and with all diligence (Hebrews 11:6) but those who have received grace need to use it beneficially. Paul admonished us, saying, "We then, as workers together with Him also plead with you not to receive the grace of God in vain" II Corinthians 6:1

God's delivery of grace happens to also rely heavily on our own, individual opinion of its value. In Matthew 13:12 we see these words recorded: "For whoever has (That is appreciates, cherishes, nurtures, uses and counts of great value something), to him more will be given, and he will have abundance; but whoever does not have, even what he has will be taken away from him." This is God's law of increase and it will never change as long as we are on this planet. Our God is a wiser manager of resources, gifts and talents and wants to place them in the hands of those who will be most faithful to not only use them but take care of them and see that they multiply.

Our faith and response to tribulation in life also has a direct bearing on the amount of grace we receive. Paul penned these words to the Romans: "Therefore, having been justified by faith, we have peace with God through our Lord Jesus Christ, through whom also we have access by faith into this grace in which we stand, and rejoice in hope of the glory of God. And not only that, but we also glory in tribulations, knowing that tribulation produces perseverance; and perseverance, character, and character, hope. Now hope does not disappoint because the love of God is shed abroad in our hearts by the Holy Spirit who was given to us." Romans 5:1–5

Another great promise in regard to receiving grace is found in I Peter 5:5 where Peter tells us clearly, "God resists the proud but gives grace to the humble." Not only the proud and arrogant are the subject of this passage but those who openly and notoriously continue in sin after they have been shown the light. They are those who are hearers only and are not doers of the Word. But, those who receive more grace, truly see their need of God and His provisions. They see themselves in desperate need, unable to do anything without His guidance and help. They receive more grace. And, then He openly declares, in the next sentence, His plan for those who see reality for what it is: all is God's and we are nothing and can do nothing without it. Peter says, "Therefore humble yourselves under the mighty hand of God, that He may exalt you in due time, casting all your cares upon Him for He cares for you." (I Peter 5:6–7) Don't worry about anything, God is in control and has never made a mistake. Life won't always be a bouquet of roses. Certainly, there will be many trials and persecutions but, in the end, it will be infinitely worth the trouble because Heaven will be our reward and there will be countless blessings of His added grace along the way.

What it means to have the character trait of **GRACE:**

- The state of sanctification granted by divine grace
- God's enabling power
- A sense of proper action, propriety or being right
- Every good gift that can only come from God
- The ability of one to be considerate and understanding of others

RATEFULNESS or GRATITUDE—   Study start date: _____   Finish date: _____

In a free economy, everyone (at least by design) has a job and is serving others in some fashion in order to earn a living. When the performance and kindness of members of our society exceeds our expectations, gratitude is born. The capitalist meritocracy we happen to live in, to some extent, over time, pays people what they earn or deserve. Over time it has created an elaborate reward system with pay raises, bonuses, promotions, corner offices, free vacations, etc. but what humans want and appreciate even more is just a little gratitude. When it is birthed in the human heart by the performance or acts of another person, and appreciation is actually extended to them, it means more to people than money. Gratitude is actually the invisible but powerful force that glues us together as a society. What could mean more than a letter of appreciation or a thank you note in the mail? Very little.

However, so many things are given out by our nanny state government that people have lost their sense of self-reliance and gratitude. Many today think the world owes them a living: free housing, food, fuel, medical care, education, telephones and so on. We are now seeing the generational theft of opportunity, freedom and upward mobility from a whole segments of our society. Many take the good fortune of having sound bodies and minds, friendships, jobs, living in a free country and all the opportunities of life here completely for granted. Remember, none of us did anything, rang any bells, jumped any hoops or met any qualifications whatsoever to merit being born into the world. Every one of us is here at the behest of God's mercy, grace and pleasure. So whatever any of us have has to be more than we deserve because we don't really deserve anything. All we have is purely gift from the Master. Truth is, we should be grateful to wake up each day, breathe the air and see the light of day.

An attitude of gratitude is so important because it allows God to bless and multiply whatever we have. Whatever, we are not grateful for, be it our job, spouse, dog, health or life, likewise gives the enemy the right to come in and do what he does best: steal, kill and destroy. Whatever we are not thankful for in life, we can very well kiss goodbye. That's just the law of gratitude. Love it; more is in store. Loathe it; you lose it.

It is also important to realize that none of us could have made it alone and that there is no such thing as the "self-made man." We all had parents, foster parents or guardians, a first grade teacher, friends who showed us how to ride a bike or a horse, tie our shoes, make a sling shot, do our two plus two's, etc. None of us have anything except what was given to us by God in His divine providence. All talent, skill, I.Q., healthy bodies, etc., came as a gift directly from Him. As the ready writer, inspired by the Holy Spirit, said, "Every good gift and every perfect gift is from above, and cometh down from the Father of Lights, with whom is no variableness, neither shadow of turning." (James 1:17) Gratefulness is remembering all this and showing it by first of all being thankful and, then using our blessings to bless the poor and finally, remembering, honoring and serving, those who have helped us along the way.

Ingratitude has long been a problem among us mortals in these Last Days and it wasn't any better when the Master walked the earth. He healed ten lepers who had the flesh rotting off of their faces, hands and all over their bodies. Certainly all were thrilled to be healed—but. only one of them, that's right, only one out of ten returned to give thanks. That's only ten percent and that number wasn't chosen by the Holy Spirit at random. It likely has a whole lot to do with the true situation as it relates to the hearts of men. God help us. And, the one who returned to give thanks was a Samaritan, not even a Jew. He had no part in the commonwealth of Israel or any right to receive healing mercies by the hands of their priests. He didn't deserve anything as a foreigner, and yet was grateful.

A good example of the proper attitude of gratefulness is found in the life of Jonathan and his people, Israel. At one point, the nation was in a horrific war with the Philistines and other than Saul and Jonathan, the Army had absolutely no weapons of war and not a single blacksmith in the land to make any. This required the whole Israelite Army to use farm implements: axes, sickles and the like which were, at best, poor, make-shift weapons and in short supply at that. Not only this but, just as importantly, they were always outnumbered by their enemies as well. In and through all of this, Jonathan had greatly distinguished himself as a warrior on many occasions. At this particular time, he and his armor bearer had just returned from attacking a Philistine garrison all by themselves and had killed twenty of them in the first attack and then went back after them again. (I Samuel 14:14) The Bible doesn't tell us how many they killed in the second attack but the rest of that Philistine garrison high tailed it and ran. That ought to tell us something. Then, under Saul's leadership and while Jonathan and his armor bearer were still out fighting the enemy, the Army went to battle against the Philistines at Gibeah. The Lord was with Israel that day and put the enemy into such great confusion that they began to attack each other with their own swords. The rout was so great, many Israelite soldiers came down from the mountains and the surrounding countryside to assist in this attack on the Philistines.

Then Saul made a rash and foolish oath that really angered the people. He said, "Cursed is the man who eats any food until evening, before I have taken vengeance on my enemies." (I Samuel 14:24) This meant that no one could eat their own food or take of any of the food they found with their slain enemies to refresh themselves during the few momentary breaks while in mortal combat, being in one battle right after another. This made no sense. What is worse, the curse was upon all Israel's soldiers, including those who didn't even know the oath had been made. Obviously, they didn't have typewriters, memos, radio communication or fax machines back then. With thousands of soldiers crawling all over the various mountains and valleys, only a few around the King's headquarters actually got the word. For Saul to hold those who hadn't even heard about the edict accountable to it was ludicrous.

Later that day the Army came to a forest where honey was dripping to the ground, probably falling from a bee hive in the trunk or limb of a tree. Jonathan had caught back up with the main element by this time and, for one, had certainly not heard of the King's foolish edict. Honey being quite a welcome sight to any soldier, he stretched out the staff that was in his hand and gathered some of the honey on the tip. Then he put it in his mouth and his countenance immediately showed his enjoyment. Astonished at all this, men in the vicinity told him of his father's edict. About this time the people were exhausted, famished, about to faint and in no condition to do battle. Totally frustrated, Jonathan told the men how foolish he thought his father's edict was and wondered how many more of the Philistines would likely have been killed if the people had been allowed to eat freely and regain strength. Though the rout had been great, it could have been much greater. They had already driven the enemy from Michmash to Aijalon, a considerable distance not just to be traversed on foot but they also had to do it in the heat of battle. The soldiers were so famished that they killed many of the enemy's livestock and ate them along with the blood.

When Saul had been told about the people falling on the prey and eating the blood with it, he said, "you have dealt treacherously; roll a large stone to me this day." Then he told the people to spread out among the troops and have everyone slaughter an ox or a sheep but not to sin against the Lord by eating the blood. So that night they had a great slaughter and Saul built his first altar to the Lord.

Then Saul wanted to make another attack on the Philistines but the priests persuaded him to inquire of God first. However, God didn't answer him that day. So he took this time to ask the chiefs of the people what the sin was all about that day saying, "As the Lord lives, who saves Israel, though it be in Jonathan my son, he shall surely die." But, no one would answer him. Then Saul began to cast lots between himself and the people and finally between himself and Jonathan was taken. Saul then told Jonathan to tell him what he had done. And how he had tasted a small amount of honey on the end of his staff and agreed that, according to his father's edict, he now must die. Saul then replied, "God do so and more also; for you shall surely die, Jonathan."

But, the people objected and out of gratefulness for all Jonathan had done, time and again as a mighty warrior of Israel, came to his defense saying, "Shall Jonathan die, who has accomplished this great deliverance in Israel? Certainly not! As the Lord lives, not one hair on his head shall fall to the ground, for he has worked with God this day." What the Philistines couldn't extract from Jonathan, the breath of life, on a thousand fields of battle, his father was willing to take on the whim of a foolish oath. So it was that the gratefulness of the people actually rescued Jonathan from certain death. His crime? Breaking the foolish, frivolous edict of his father, of which he was totally unaware.

What it means to have the character trait of **GRATEFULNESS:**

- Heartfelt appreciation for things received—even the small things
- Having a form of humility that expresses itself in gratitude
- Taking the time to personally thank those who have helped us
- Willingly making investments in the lives of others
- Realizing the world doesn't revolve around us and that we need to be thankful for every kindness
- Realizing that if any of us got what we deserved for one second, we'd all be in Hell and it hot
- Showing thankfulness by making the most of every opportunity in life
- Endeavoring to give back more to those who have helped and had mercy on us, especially remembering them in their time of need
- Being a faithful friend to those who have befriended us
- Remembering that the greatest blessing of friendship is not what our friends can do for us but what we can do for them.

HAPPINESS —   **Study start date:** _____ **Finish date:** _____

Some people truly go through life looking like somebody just shot their best friend, stole their car and ran over their dog. They don't seem the least bit capable of appreciating any of the blessings that have come their way. Their favorite past time is singing the "Somebody's Done Me Wrong" song by telling everyone all their sorrows. Being around these sad-faced misfits is usually a pain few can endure.

On the other hand, there are people who, regardless of the circumstances, manage to wear a continual smile from the inside out. These people have decided to be happy all the time regardless. Even when things go wrong, they keep on smiling because they know that sooner or later it is all going to turn around and work out for their good. (Romans 8:28) They have probably seen their fair share of trouble, betrayals and reversals in life but have learned to be thankful for the good times and they realize that, for most of us, the good far outweighs the bad. Probably they have also come to the conclusion that the world doesn't revolve around them and that they are never going to get everything their way in life anyway. That would be totally narcissistic; not even reasonable. They realize that nobody gets to eat all the candy and if they did, they would get very, very sick. They much prefer to walk on the sunny side of the street, appreciate their friends and the fact that God has been good to them. Far better than they deserve.

L. Richard Lesseor once opined that "Happiness is like a butterfly. The more you chase it, the more it will elude you. But if you turn your attention to other things, it comes and softly sits on your shoulder." Happiness is realizing that we probably don't have all the gifts and talents in the world and it is ok that we weren't born with a silver spoon in our mouth. This just means we will probably be blessed to have a little more humility and might be allowed to acquire a bit more character as we trod this earth because of it. It is also realizing, however, that each of us have some gifts and at least one talent. Yes, we have all made some mistakes but we also have our own personal DNA code, our own sweet blush of innocence and a genius to give this world something no one else can. We just need to find our gift, be thankful for what we do have and regardless of the current state of the world around us, get started using it to serve others and bless our current generation. Truth is, we are all going to be about as happy as we have a mind to be. That's where it starts. Next, we need to count your blessings and name them one by one, as the old song goes. When you believe you are happy, speak it out loud. Nothing will work unless you SPEAK IT!!! What you say will go out into the eithers, back in your ears and down in your heart. It is a process that needs to take place daily for "Out of the abundance of the heart the mouth speaks." (Luke 6:45) So the place to start after taking dominion of our mind is speaking cordially to everyone you meet. They always ask you "How are you doing?" I just tell people the truth: "So good I can hardly stand it!!!" They usually say, "Really?!" like they can't believe anyone could be living on this planet and be that happy. I tell it so strong and truly that, yes, they believe me but they are really digging for the how part. Of course I say, "Really! But it's getting better!" Sometimes, they say, "I sure would like to have some of that!" That opens the door to a conversation. I might even tell them "If you'd been where I've been, done what I've done, been forgiven of all I have been forgiven of, know who I know and were going where I'm going, you'd be that happy too!" Just think, I commanded two front-line rifle companies in Vietnam. So many of my friends in Ranger School were either shot or killed in that war and I never even got a scratch! I could go on but won't.

A word to the wise, if you are going to be a leader, you need to realize as soon as possible that people don't want to be around folk who aren't happy. They certainly don't want to work for them and get a steady daily diet of their sorrow, scorn and sadness. Choosing to be happy is the only way to really, truly live. It will probably even make you live longer. Being happy and excited about life is a winsome attitude and God lets us decide just about how happy we are going to be. Here are some ideas that will contribute to your happiness:

- Knowing God and taking Him with you wherever you go
- Focusing on the good instead of the bad everyday
- Making life-long friends and being thankful for them
- Having the pleasure of being a true friend, especially in their time of need
- Being grateful
- Gaining character so you can feel good about who you are
- Having stood for something noble in life
- Having accomplished something meaningful in life
- Having someone to love
- Knowing that 95% of the things we might worry about will never happen and that it is a sin to worry anyhow
- Having the courage to admit our mistakes and say, "I'm sorry"
- Having the ability to consider every person you meet as little better than yourself
- Having the freedom to give everything you touch 110% of your effort, devotion and creativity
- Knowing that you can't ever meet anyone who is not good enough to be your friend
- Realizing that who you are has nothing to do with your greatest accomplishment or your greatest failure in life Both are imposters.
- Realizing that if God is on your side it doesn't matter who is against you. You already have an unfair advantage and the victory!
- Being thankful that you are alive
- Even if you have ruined your whole life, you can still get up, dust yourself off and start over. You have the author's prerogative of re-writing the second edition.
- That in an ordered society there will be rules wherever you go and a one-time decision to obey them all will cause you to have more favor, peace, blessing and, ultimately, liberty than the alternative: rebellion;
- Realizing that money, in and of itself, has never made anyone happy and that the wisest man in the world, Solomon, made those who chose to chase and love it a promise: they will never get enough.
- Knowing that whatever you say or do will be an example to someone, somewhere, someday.
- Living every day as if it is your last, because it very well may be. And, if, in fact it was, it is realizing that in this one life you have been well overpaid.

What it means to have the character trait of **HAPPINESS**:

- The emotional state triggered by continual feelings of well-being, good fortune, an ordered life, self-acceptance and success
- Serving God with reckless abandon
- Contented living
- Having the prospect of ultimately possessing the desires of one's heart
- Contented enjoyment of life and one's lot in it
- Being enthusiastically optimistic and settled in life
- Being good natured, positive and friendly
- Being hopelessly optimistic

HARD-WORKING—   **Study start date: _____ Finish date: _____**

In this life we all will soon be known by our work or the lack there of. You can't avoid it because this just naturally happens a part of the process of everyday life. Those working around us quickly observe and form an opinion about our work ethic. It is really not something people think about so much as it is something that just happens sub-consciously. When the going gets tough some faint, others quit and still others get fired but some use it for an opportunity to go to the next level in the company. As the old adage goes: When the going gets tough, the tough get going and the tough get tougher. Our attitude toward work affects multiple aspects of our lives. It says a lot about our character and also happens to be the very thing God and the world will use to judge and reward us. Nobody has ever gotten an award for sleeping consistently to the crack of noon or for taking the most exotic vacations. No. We reward people for their work.

In the Army we used to have some guys, from time-to-time, who were so lazy they couldn't carry their own shadow. They didn't want to dig their fox holes in the NDP (Night Defensive Position), didn't want anything to do with filling sand bags and wouldn't even clean and oil their own rifles every day in a monsoon climate where it rained torrents twice a day. That is pretty amazing when you consider that the weapon they were so reticent to clean, the fox holes they only half dug and the sand bags they weren't willing to fill were the very things they expected to save their lives in the next fire fight. There have always been and always will be those who are lazy, who always find themselves too light for heavy work and too heavy for light work.

Work is not a new thing. The whole concept of "work" was levied upon the human race at the Fall in the Garden of Eden. God cursed the ground and told Adam that from then on, he would eat his bread only by the sweat of his brow. Compared to the ease they enjoyed prior to the fall, I am certain it appeared to them to be a huge curse. However, that is all behind us now. In reality, work is actually a blessing today if we will it be. The secret to work is not to avoid it but to make it every bit of the blessing it can be. It is how each of us paint or write our life's story on the canvas of the world. This is so important the Apostle Paul told the Thessalonians they needed to learn to work with their own hands. (I Thessalonians 4:11) All work is honorable. Furthermore, it is so important in an ordered society, he went on to say, if anyone refused to work, they should not be allowed to eat. (II Thess. 3:10) Sounds a little stern but work is how we earn our rite of passage here, how we obtain the blessings of life, increase in abundance, help our neighbors and prosper in the earth. We are admonished by the writer of Proverbs that in all work there is profit. (Proverbs 14:23) We also have a promise that the person who develops skill and diligence in their work will be so abundantly blessed in this life that they can also be a blessing to others. This is so much the case, that the writer said, "See a man diligent and skilled in his work? He shall stand before kings, he shall not stand before obscure men." (Proverbs 22:29) These are the kind of people kings seek out to oversee their own business interests as well as the kind of people they want to honor and set up as example of those who bless to the commonwealth. There is also another thing kings kind of like about them. They also happen to be the ones capable of, well, paying taxes.

Regardless of the job, everyone where you work has a reputation and is known by their work ethic. They are either known for being a slacker, one that does only what they are required to do when others are watching, or known as one of those who work hard. These are the ones who will do their part, your part and anyone else's part and will stay at the task no matter how difficult until they get the job done. It is important to have a reputation for being a hard worker. These people are both highly respected in life and are also in short supply. Doing a hard day's work has many benefits. It is fulfilling, produces a good pay check, promotions, good health and, among other things, causes a person's sleep to be sweet as well.

Since my father was in the Air Force, our family lived everywhere and once even in Canada for a couple years while I was in high school. The particular air base we lived on happened to be so far north, it was accessible only by boat or airplane. That's right, there were no roads to that place. Not even a pig trail! That meant all the really heavy equipment and building materials had to be shipped in by boat. During the summers, my older brother, Steve, and I got jobs working construction. One time we worked down in the hold of a huge ocean-going freighter that was full of 99 pound bags of cement. (They quit making them that heavy a long time ago.) The ship's crane would lower an empty pallet down in the hold and it was our job to load it up in two shakes with all the bags of cement we could. I was only 15 or 16 back then and my little scrawny frame, soaking wet, wasn't even 160 pounds. Every time you would set one of those bags on the pallet, it would let out a little "poof "of cement dust into the air.

After a while it became really cloudy down there with all that wonderful cement dust in the atmosphere. It also got hot during the middle of the summers and especially hot down in the belly of that ship. Soon the shirts came off and our bodies were covered from the top of our heads to the bottoms of our boots with a slippery, slimy skim of gray cement dust—hair on our heads and all. Perry's (our dad) two little tow-head boys soon became gray headed. Fact is if those Portland cement hair-do's we got down in the hold of that ship had ever dried out and hardened, we might have had to wear them for the several months. Those bags of cement nearly wore my little rear end out but I certainly didn't let anybody know it. I was trying my best to keep up with the big guys! They used to say in the south, "If you can't keep up with the big dogs you need to stay up on the porch." I didn't want anything to do with staying on the porch, sittin' in a chair, being quiet or being without a summer job was no place to be.

Once we got the ship unloaded, we thought things were about to get a whole lot better. Nope. Not so. They put us to batching (mixing) concrete and no, they didn't have any big batching plants like we have in the U.S. They just had a large antique mixing contraption with a big bucket that dropped down to be filled up regularly with cement, sand and gravel. That thing never did seem to get full. It was just one big hungry monster all the time. Being the youngest, my job most of the time was to shovel the gravel into that hopper of that beast—all day long. Did I say that it got hot up there in the summers? Try shoveling #57 gravel all day in the hot sun. Metal shovels don't like going through gravel. They pitch a fit. It was a fight but a good one. Taught me for the first time what an honor it was to have calluses on my hands. By the end of that first summer I was also so skinny I looked like I traded legs with a Kildee and the Kildee got my hind quarters.

Later during college, Steve and I both worked on a pipe line in Dripping Springs, Texas a little town west of Austin, digging ditches. I don't think there were over twenty buildings in the whole town counting the residential homes back then. It was just a wide spot in the road its only claim to fame in those days was that Willie Nelson did open air gigs in a huge cow pasture pretty regular. The one thing that little town could do real well was get hot. It was hotter there during the summer than a $2 pistol in downtown Dallas. And, I don't think it ever rained but maybe one time that whole summer and I promise you I never saw Dripping Springs drip one drop. No, not even one. But, thank God for those experiences and thank God for a good job to help pay for my education. We were into making the big bucks too—I think $1.75 an hour. You know it's good for us to learn what hard work looks like and to feel the sense of satisfaction and accomplishment it brings.

We did have a little excitement once. They gave us a huge air compressor, along with a pneumatic jack hammer and drill to bust up the rock. What they didn't have around there in water they made up in lots of rock. We would break up what we could with the jack hammer and then drill holes in the rock, pack it full of dynamite and then lay cyclone fencing over the top of the whole area so the rocks didn't fly so far when we shot it. We liked to see just how much dynamite we could pack into those holes. One time we packed it real heavy, set the blasting cap, hooked up the wires and trailed them back to the pump-handle dynamo box (like they had in the old western movies) that sent the electric charge to the blasting cap. That time we went a little overboard with the dynamite because it blew that entire cyclone fence apparatus way up in the air and got it tangled up in the telephone pole wires way up above it. We saw a bunch of sparks fly, some wires broke and it all, along with some of the phone lines, finally fell to the ground. We didn't think much of it but about 15 minutes later helicopters, state police and federal agent cars, what seemed like ever cop in five counties, were swarming around us like a bunch of bees after honey. Seems those telephone poles were carrying top security lines that went out to LBJ's ranch right down the road and in those days he was the Pres. They wanted to know what happened. Of course we told them we must have just got a little too much dynamite in that charge. They said, "Ok but be more careful next time." Whew—that was a close one. We'd never been that close to being in so much trouble before so we went back to work. Dad told us boys time and again that there was some trouble you could get into that they'd put us so far back in prison that they'd have to air mail our lunch to us. I wasn't real sure about it at the time, but after seeing all those cops, patrol cars and helicopters, I thought that this was one of those things that was getting us a little too close to all that "air mailing your lunch" business.

You know some jobs are so bad, that there is actually something good about them After you have done a few of them for a while, all other jobs look a whole lot easier. Hard it was but in all honesty, I loved it. Through these jobs I had early in life, I learned that hard work was not a bad thing but was actually a joy to me. Although I thought there probably must be something wrong with me because I've loved every job I ever had. Well, except KP in the Army. Only had KP twice and someone else can have that job. I'm just not cut out for kitchen work. I'd rather you'd give me an M-16, a couple hand grenades, some ammunition and send me out with the troops. However, each job was an opportunity to improve myself, learn new disciplines and how to operate different equipment and well as to contribute and bless others and I knew one thing for sure: I had a lot to learn.

What it means to have the character trait of **HARD WORKING:**

- Volunteering to take the heavy end of a load needing to be carried
- Willingness to arrive at the job early and stay late to get it done
- Not being afraid of any kind of work
- Being pre-disposed to giving every job we are assigned 110% effort
- The ability to go at your work with all your heart
- One who is willing to work long and hard and maybe even get dirty along with it
- Willingness to do whatever it takes to beat the task instead of letting the task beatyou

HEART— **Study start date:**_____ **Finish date:** _____

Many go through life afraid of their mother-in-law, their shadow, the devil, the dark and the deep blue sea. Fear of failure and criticism also loom heavily upon their minds. They can't go hard, they can't go fast and they can't go long because they have a heart problem. Mostly, they just can't go because they are wearied constantly in their minds. After all, what if they tried something and failed? What would people say and wouldn't they make a fool of themselves? No. Actually, not. Who cares what people say? There are going to be some who will criticize you either way. It doesn't matter if you succeed or fail, win or lose. You can count on that. Get used to it. I, for one, don't believe you can ever fail when you honestly try, giving it your best effort. You always learn a bunch from a failure and are far better prepared to take a run at it again from a better angle, the next time. You just have to love the battle, love the race, love the fight and thank God for every opportunity to step up to the plate and take a swing at the ball. We'll have to agree, we are not going to accomplish much in life, sitting on our blessed assurance in the dugout.

What a person becomes in life depends to a large extent on whether or not they have heart. Not the circulatory organ that pushes blood through our veins, arteries and capillaries but the hidden place where a man's courage, audacity and grit resides. The place the fortitude comes from with which we faces all the battles, prospects, opportunities, and tests of life. Some take a look at life with all its difficulties, discouragements and sometimes undeserved attacks and recoil into a cocoon of self-protectionism, never to venture out in life again. They rarely try anything or make suggestions in life as to how things can be improved for fear of criticism. They have an even greater fear of making a mistake or putting themselves in the position of, God forbid, being wrong. Life doesn't excite them. They figure, what's the use? To them, life is a drag, thinking it is probably going to rain on the hay crop before harvest tomorrow, the mare is likely going to miscarry and prices at the market will probably be down by the time they get their produce there. They really don't think you can even get there from here without falling in a pot hole or blowing a tire on the trailer.

On the contrary, one with heart loves life, people and all the opportunities living on this planet affords. They believe that whoever has something to do today and is thrilled about it, will be given more to do tomorrow. They love to play the game, take reasonable risks and help others even when there is seemingly nothing in it for them. They are always willing to take a run at something they have never tried. This attitude is always a winner because they find out that they will either like the new thing better than what they had or they will have even greater conviction to stay with the old. Either way, the new-found knowledge is a gain. They are always fired up and motivated. Not only are they always game for new things. They are willing to play the game even in the rain, freezing cold or the red-hot sun and go at it again and again until they win. They are the optimists who rarely make excuses because they always do their best and see their mistakes as opportunities to learn and improve. They give everyone and everything 110% and believe that everything is going to turn out for the best in the end.

Heart, in the spiritual sense, is the innermost core of a person's being. It is where we find the reservoir of the very life-power that strengthens the whole man. It is where we gladly and willingly purpose to do certain things or, just as importantly sometimes, resolve not to do them. The heart is the center of our thoughts, understanding, estimates and deliberations. It is, according to the Word of God, the seat of a person's love (I Timothy 1:5) and hatred. (Leviticus 19:17) In it we also find the seat of the conscience, the place where natural laws are written, as well as being our personal repository of divine grace. We find in it the center of all moral life and our moral condition for everything from the love of God to self-destructive, debilitating pride. It is both the laboratory and factory for the issue of all good and evil, be it thoughts, motives, words or deeds, as well as the place where all of man's good and evil treasures are kept. It is, most importantly, the dwelling place of Christ (Ephesians 3:17) for those who have received Him. Keep in mind too that "out of the heart proceeds evil thoughts, murder (and) adulteries." (Matthew 15:19) Until He reigns supreme as Lord of lords and King of kings in our hearts, we will never see the peace, production or the unlimited potential He has for us. Our heart is the very thing we are commanded to keep "with all diligence" because "out of it spring the issues of life." (Proverbs 4:23) The prophet Ezekiel gave us this promise from God more than two thousand years ago: "A new heart I will give you and a new spirit I will put within you; and I will take the stony heart out of your flesh and I will give you a heart of flesh, (Ezekiel 36:26) And, it's not a mysterious, hard or far away thing either. "It is not in heaven, that you should say 'Who will ascend into heaven for us and bring it to us, that we may hear it and do it?' But the word is very near you, in your mouth and in your heart that you may do it. See, I (the Lord) have set before you today life and good, death and evil. In that I command you today to love the Lord your God, to walk in His ways, and to keep His commandments, His statutes, and His judgments, that you may live and multiply; and the Lord your God will bless you …" "But if your heart turns away so that you do not hear, and are drawn away, and worship other gods and serve them, I announce to you today that you shall surely perish; you shall not prolong your days … I call heaven and earth as witnesses today against you, that I have set before you life and death, blessing and cursing; therefore choose life, that both you and your descendants may live; that you may love the Lord your God, that you may obey His voice, and that you may cling to Him for He is your life and the length of your days …" (Deuteronomy 30:12-20)

What He just said was that our life does not, as we might think, consist of things that we can see. Life that is truly life, real life overflows from our invisible relationship with Christ when we enter into it by accepting Him as our Savior. All we have to do is stop and say, Lord I repent of my sins, I realize you died for me on the cross and paid the full price for all those sins and they are surely many. I ask you to come into my heart right now, to save me and be the Lord of my life. Then just thank Him for being your Savior. Now that you have experienced the new birth, set your priority to seek "first the kingdom of God and His righteousness, and all … things shall be added to you." Matthew 6:33

What it means to have the character trait of **HEART**:

- The entirety of one's personality which includes drive, devotion, intellect, character, motions and resolve
- The essence and centrality of one's being
- One's willingness to strike out at venture on something new
- Being fearless, audacious and resilient
- The ability to accept certain risks in life
- Curiosity and excitement about new things and the opportunities of life
- The willingness to take a chance
- Having a heart like God

EART AFTER GOD, A— Study start date: _____ Finish date: _____

Every person on earth is seeking something in particular out of life more than anything else. Actually, whatever someone really desires or wants, we will, in fact, be found in their heart. Most live for comfort, security, physical pleasure, greatness, the approval of men or the love of money. In short, they live for themselves. Others in the United States today are drunk with democracy and actually worship it. Certainly I like it better than communism, a monarchy or a dictatorship but democracy is just another flawed and fallen system of government. I would much prefer a theocracy—the kind God intended for us to live under—where He actually led the nation by directing the prophets. Most people today live by the polls. They want to be in the "main stream" so they can have the approval of men. Regardless of what they call it, ultimately, if we live for ourselves, our life won't amount to much for God. On the contrary, Peter, a man who had a heart after God, rejoiced that he was counted worthy to suffer for the Name.

As a very young man, I seemed to get into trouble all the time. I didn't go to jail but, no doubt, should have. As I have taken time to reflect on those younger years, I now know why. I didn't know who I was, I didn't know where I was going or why I was here. Unknowingly, I thought that success in life was having a good time and the more I tried to have a good time the more trouble it seemed like I found myself embroiled in. Fundamentally, I lacked a proper goal in my heart. From Scripture we know that the heart is the innermost reservoir, seat and center of a man's natural being. It is where we hide God's law and His righteousness. (Psalm 40:8, 10) It is the seat of all love (I Timothy 1:5) and hatred. (Leviticus 19:17) The heart is the center of all thought, contemplation and deliberation. (Nehemiah 5:7) It is where we begin to understand, gain and store all wisdom and prudence. (Proverbs 8:5) It is where all estimates (Proverbs 16:9), feelings of affection and plans (Proverbs 16:9) are made and kept. It is also the center of our moral life from our greatest affection and love for God (Psalm 73:26) to the rancid, soul-destroying pride that can also lurk there (Ezekiel 28:2) if we aren't careful. As such, it is the place where we determine value, place affections, begin to treasure things and set goals in life.

For human beings, goals are tremendously important. Apart from divine inspiration, we must realize that we are going to encounter and accept many false objectives and deceptive goals in life. Once accepted, they cumber men about and take them swiftly, albeit usually unknowingly, down the wrong path to disillusionment, dissatisfaction and destruction. We don't have to go far to find them either. They are in our minds. Scripture states that "There is a way that seems right to a man (in his own mind) but its end is the way of death." (Proverbs 14:12) Some think illicit sex, for one, will satisfy but it won't. In fact, it always ends in death: unwanted pregnancies that either ends in infanticide or huge child support payments, broken homes, the contraction of diseases like syphilis, gonorrhea, AIDS, etc. but ultimately in death. God's way leads to life and it to the abundant full, life that is truly life. Fulfilling, productive, peaceful, contented, secure and honorable life. For this reason, we are admonished in the Bible to be very careful what we set our affections on. Not on things of this world because they are so transient and temporary, passing away quickly. Most are either consumed or worn out with the using but, we know from Scripture that they will not satisfy. It is so important to make the right choices, Jesus said, "For where your treasure is, there your heart will be also." (Matthew 6:21) Our hearts were made by God to operate like computers working constantly, seeking and searching, even while we sleep to bring to us the things we treasure and desire most. Setting our hearts—is one of the most important things we will ever do on this planet.

From the lives of Saul and David we can gain considerable insight about the importance of setting the heart. First Samuel 10:26 tells us how Samuel anointed Saul to be king of Israel. Scripture records that he went home to Gibeah and "A band of valiant men" …" whose hearts God had touched" went with him. That is exactly what is needed today: a band of valiant men whose hearts God has touched! You see, a man who has truly been touched by the Master, will have a heart after God. A few years later, however, it also says that when the Spirit of the Lord had departed from Saul he became very depressed. On the advice of his staff, he began looking for a skillful player of the harp to sooth his nerves. Concurrently, we know that David, a simple shepherd of sheep and only a teenager at the time, had already gained a reputation for being a musician and a psalmist. As soon as Saul's notice was published abroad, one of his servants made this report to him: "Behold, I have seen a son of Jesse, the Bethlehemite, a skillful musician, a mighty valiant man, a man of war, prudent in matters, agreeable in nature and behold, the Lord is with him." (I Samuel 16:18) This passage gives us great insight into what it takes to have a heart after God.

First, we must be true sons. We must be born again and have a new heart filled with God's love. God doesn't have any grandchildren, only true son's and daughters. We can't depend on our father or mother's relationship with God, however strong it may be, we must have our own.

We need to be a man or woman of praise. David loved to praise the Lord. He worshipped Him with the harp and the lyre while he was out with his sheep and wrote nearly all of the Psalms. He danced in the streets in jubilation with most of his clothes off for the arc of the covenant having been returned to its proper place, Jerusalem. Even if we can't all be musicians, we can certainly delight in making a joyful noise, singing praises from our heart to God! Our heart-felt praises are beautiful to Him even if we do miss a few notes here and there.

We must be strong. David was a "mighty, valiant man." To be strong, we must spend a great deal of time with the Lord—in His Word, in prayer and praise. When we know what we have in God, we will be fearless just as David was. We will be skilled with God's spiritual weapons and will not need or want Saul's pile of military scrap iron because "the weapons of our warfare are not carnal" or worldly. (II Corinthians 10:4) They are mighty through God.

We must be warriors, people dedicated to a cause. When no one would fight Goliath, David asked this heart-penetrating question of his countrymen, "Is there not a cause in Israel?" What he was saying was, 'Is there not something going on here worth dying for?' 'Isn't anyone willing to risk their life for our country, God's will, and His honor and glory in the earth?' A man with a true cause is committed to the will of God even unto death. When we personally accept responsibility for the success of

King David dancing in the streets of Jerusalem

God's kingdom, God automatically gives us the mantle of authority. An old Chinese sage is reported to have said, "The wisdom of this age is to find out what God is doing (in our time) and throw yourself into it bodily." That means without reservation, measurement or care—with reckless abandon. Too many supposed men of God today never join in the battle. Why? Because they are too afraid of what it will do to their reputation and their bottom line. The newspaper might call them a liar or a buffoon, say they are "misrepresenting things" and say that everything they are saying is "false." They might even cartoon them and, another problem, like some preachers have told me there's the problem that, "Their parishoners just might not understand." Get real. It's the devil and the world's job to discredit and persecute us. Forget about it! Count it all joy! This stuff comes with the territory. Our reputation is in God's hands. (Daniel 5:23) Let's get with the battle. Matthew 28:19 tells us explicitly what God wants done in our time. Jesus said, Go into all the world teaching and preaching the truth, commanding people to observe and obey it, making disciples of all men. That is what He was doing 2,000 years ago and that is what He is doing today. And, we to continue doing this in a wicked world " ... even to the end of the age." (v.20)

A man after God's own heart is also "prudent in matters." He is cautious, circumspect and wise. As a young man, I promise you, I was not cautious—nowhere even near it. I drove everything I had so fast I flipped it in no time. One Christmas my parents gave me the most beautiful English racer bicycle you ever saw. It seemed like it had 25 gears and was all black and crome. The sun never set on it before I flipped it. When I was ten, I saved my money from a summer job pulling weeds on a gladiola farm in Bellevue, Nebraska and built my first go-kart. It consisted of a used washing-machine engine, a bicycle sprocket, some bike chain, four *Radio-Flyer* wagon wheel and some 2x4's. It would really go! But it wasn't long before I drove it so fast I turned it over. One time, just for the thrill I jumped off a tower next to the Guadalupe River in New Braunfels, Texas right into the river only to break a toe, flew planes and jumped out of them every chance I got—40 times in a year. I volunteered twice to command rifle companies in Vietnam. Not a very cautious person, to say the least. However, once I was saved, God began to deal with me. Although I am still willing to take risks, it is only at God's command. Furthermore, a prudent man discerns the spirits and looks into the heart of things. Such a man is also skillful in the handling of resources and is not wasteful or extravagant.

A man after God's own heart is "agreeable in nature." That is, as long as we are agreeing with God's Word, he is easily approachable. He is meek and humble, open to new ideas and new ways of doing things.

A man after God's heart is a giver. David had a heart to build a temple for God but was denied that privilege because he had blood on his hands. He did, however, allow him to provide all the building materials. All the gold, silver, bronze, wood, stone and even the real estate, David donated. Even though he was not allowed to build it, God gave him credit for it by faith because he had the desire in his heart to do it. God is a giver and to be like Him, we must love to give not only the tithe, but offerings as well. (II Corinthians 9:6–8) This is when life really gets interesting.

A man after God's heart bears fruit. This is so important that John 15:1 tells us you can't even prove to be a disciple unless you bear much fruit. Our whole life should speak of fruit—fruit everywhere for God! Fruit that will remain.

Finally, one thing we know for sure about the man of God, is that "the Lord is with him." King David was "wrapped up in the bundle of life with the Lord (his) God." (I Samuel 25:29) He always "saw the Lord ever before Him, even at his right hand." Because of this, he was able to say, "I shall never be shaken. I shall never be moved." After all, God said, He "will never leave (us) nor forsake (us)." He didn't say we wouldn't have to go through the fire—just that He would be with us and lead us through it to victory.

What then should be our response? Just this. Here am I Lord, send me. I'm not the greatest and I don't even have anything much to offer. Surely others could do things better but I'm available and I believe You can do anything you want through me. D.L. Moody once said, "Give me ten men committed to the will of God and I will turn the world upside down." I believe this is not only possible today but that it is also the will of God.

From David's life we see the importance of serving God with a whole heart. Many times the Bible says David was "a man after God's own heart." Upon selecting him from among his brothers to be king, the Lord told Samuel the prophet, "Look not on his countenance or on the height of his stature because I have refused (Saul)' for the Lord seeth not as a man seeth; for man looketh on the outward appearance but the Lord looketh upon the heart." (I Samuel 16:17) It is true, most people "glory in appearance and not in heart." (II Corinthians 5:12) But, Peter told us, "let (it) not be the outward adorning of braiding the hair, and of wearing gold, or of putting on apparel but let it be the hidden man of the heart in that which is not corruptible, even the ornament of a meek and quiet spirit, which is in the sight of God great of great price." I Peter 3:3,4

Jesus spoke to this saying, "Thou shalt love the Lord, thy God with all thy heart and with all thy soul and with all thy mind. This is the first and great commandment." (Matthew 22:37, 38) The simple fact is that throughout time, "men have done evil because they prepared not (their) heart to seek the Lord." (II Chronicles 31:21) The Bible further states in Job 9:4 that "God is wise in heart and mighty in strength. Who has hardened (his heart) against Him and hath prospered?" No one. What does it mean to have a heart after God? Simply stated, it is to have a heart that is broken to its own way of doing things. It is having a heart that is contrite, grieving and penitent for one's own sin. It is having a heart that has found wisdom in seeking God's perfect will and delighting in it as the answer to every problem in life. It is having a born-again heart that gladly inquires of the Lord for His leading before doing things. This attitude of the heart will lead all those who possess it to live a life pleasing to Him. Ultimately, it will usher them into the presence of God to live in ecstasy for eternity.

It all starts, of course, with getting rid of our stony hearts and gaining a heart of flesh that can love and know Christ as our Savior. It is as simple as praying this prayer with all your heart: God please forgive me for my sins. I believe that Jesus died on the cross for my sins, God raised Him from the dead and He is now seated at the Father's right hand in heaven. Jesus, please come into my heart right now, save my soul and be the Lord of my life. Thank you Jesus for saving my soul. It is that simple and now we need to take the next step and ask, by faith, for a heart after God.

What it means to have the character trait of **A HEART AFTER GOD:**

- Totally devoted and dedicated to God
- Sold out to God's will
- One who lives for God's approval alone
- Always ready, on call, to carry out exploits for Him

HEART TO BE A BUILDER, A—   **Study start date:** _____ **Finish date:** _____

In life there are only two kinds of people: builders and wreckers. These are also sometimes referred to as givers and takers. Like a raging fire that always wants more, takers can never seem to get enough which is just happens to be the nature of that particular beast. They are always eager to get but never even a thought or any willingness to give in return. They are so consumed with self-interest and so busy taking that most places they have been for any period of time begins to look like a hoard of locust has just recently passed through. Remember, if we are not blessing others and a part of the solution, we are most certainly part of the problem. Quite the contrary, givers are always wanting to give. They want to build things, improve places and build other people up. They want to make everything they touch better for their having been there. The best part of all this is that we get to choose which type of person we want to be!

We all have a short lease on this planet and it truly will be over for us here sooner than we think. Then, when all is said and done in life and we stop at the end of the trail to look back, what will we have to show for all our effort? Have we left a barren waste-land of scorched earth in our wake? Have we consumed a lot of groceries and banged up a bunch of rusted out cars? Or do we see buildings completed that are still standing; organizations we started, increased and strengthened still performing; systems and procedures improved wherever we have toiled, lives changed, mended and built up? Are the towns we lived in a little better because we were there to help?

Even as a little kid in kindergarten, I remember taking a hammer, some nails and few pieces of 2 X 4's and building a battle ship on the sidewalk in front of our house. It had gun turrets and cannons sticking out everywhere (made out of nails). If you saw it, you certainly would not have been impressed but it was as big as my imagination and so real to me. I have always been taken by building. Early in elementary school days, I was building treehouses and forts out in the woods. Several opportunities opened up during the summers of high school and college to work construction. I have always been interested in building things but a little poem I heard about the time I was a lieutenant in the Army changed my life forever. Building would no longer be limited to sticks, bricks, concrete, steel and rebar.

"I saw them tearing a building down,
a gang of men in our busy town.
With a 'Yo heave ho' and a lusty yell,
They swung a beam and a whole wall fell.
And I said to the foreman, 'Are these men skilled,
As the men you'd hire if you were to build?'
And he laughed and said, 'Oh, No indeed,
The commonest labor is all I need;
For I can easily wreck in a day or two
What builders have taken years to do.'
And I thought to myself as I went my way,
Which of these roles have I tried to play?
Am I the wrecker who walks my town,
Content with the labor of tearing down,
Or am I the builder who works with care
That my town may be better, because I've been there?"

                        Anonymous

What it means to have the character trait of **A HEART TO BE A BUILDER:**

- A heart to design and build better buildings, systems, procedures, laws, teaching methods, books, etc.
- To own the thrill of organizing and ordering construction
- To join materials according to a systematic plan to create beauty and efficiency
- Being the cause force for construction
- Seeing life as an opportunity to improve everything around us
- To increase, improve, enlarge, strengthen and beautify
- To initiate, orchestrate and harmonize activity
- To contribute to the general increase and improvement of things where we are
- Finding great enjoyment and satisfaction in building facilities to house and help others

EART TO HAVE INFLUENCE—   Study start date: _____   Finish date: _____

When properly exerted, leadership should result simply, naturally and effectively in influence. In a word, leadership is influence. Without a doubt, the greatest thing we leave to others when we are gone is the influence we have had in their lives. Certainly one of the greatest opportunities God has given us as we trod this blue marble to influence others by the power of example. Very little will probably ever be accomplished in this regard until we develop a servant's heart along with a burning desire to make others great, especially in the eyes of the Lord. We must stand for the truth and help others stand to do the same. Hopefully, with God's help, we will have a part in influencing future generations to stand for the way of truth as well.

It is so easy in a natural, physical world of pressing demands and crushing physical needs, with rising prices, frequent shortages and corruption all about, for us to lose perspective of what is important. We as mere men know nothing about what is important unless we have guidance from the Lord. Since He created the heavens and the earth and set us here for His purpose, it might be wise to take note of what He said in this regard. What follows here is one of the most important statements given to man: "Ye (you and me) are the salt of the earth; but if the salt have lost his savor, wherewith shall it be salted? It is henceforth good for nothing, but to be cast out and to be trodden under foot of men." We are not only salt but we are something else as well: "Ye are the light of the world. A city that is set on a hill cannot be hid. Neither do men light a candle and put it under a bushel but on a candlestick; and it giveth light unto all that are in the house." Then he gives us our life purpose and a command: "Let your light so shine before men, that they may see your good works and glorify your Father which is in heaven." (Matthew 5:13–16 KJV) Truly, we are here to make a difference and to have influence. Salt gives meat flavor and preserves. Without the salt and light we provide in this world, two things would happen. First, this world would corrupt with lightning speed and contagion would set in for a quick decay of whatever is left. For our lives to count, we must take the blessing of our having influence seriously and develop that God-given capacity.

We all, before salvation, had a sphere of influence and after being saved, still do. The question is: What are we going to do with this great gift from God? Will we expand it to bless as many as possible with the light or hide it under a bushel? You see the world works pretty-much on the mushroom principle: Keep everyone in the dark and feed them full of mush. Don't ever let them know what you know or they will take your position. But that is not the way God's Kingdom works. In the Kingdom of God, we take the light we have and give it generously to others letting God place them in the Body as He wills. We are here to bless, share, give, encourage and equip as we take our stand in a wicked and dying world. All of us will be judged one day on how well we have carried out our commission to be salt and light.

Many who have come before us have had great influence. By faith Abraham became the father of many nations. During his lifetime, William Wilberforce defeated slavery in England. Henry Ford changed the American mode of transportation. John Wesley set a high mark as an evangelist, winning thousands to the Lord and significantly changed the way we worship God in song. The Wright Brothers ushered in the whole era of flight. Thomas Edison gave us over a thousand patented inventions, most importantly, the light bulb to brighten our way. Thanks Tom. Compare that for a brief moment with my patents: zero. All of these had a purpose in life and fulfilled it. You too, have a unique purpose and in the total overall scheme of things, your life is just as important as any other.

Improperly used, our lives can have a corrupting, negative effect on people with positions of authority through the power of black mail or a bribe. One can also have their nature and abilities negatively affected by being under the influence of alcohol or drugs. Even worse, would be to use the gifts and talents God has given us to enter into a life of illicit activities which are now increasingly accepted practice in America. In this last election cycle alone, three states voted to let people grow and sell marijuana and three voted to forbid any future laws outlawing sodomite marriages. End Time prophecy is being fulfilled.

However, to have any lasting impact, one must be committed to live a life of influence. Berthold once made this startling statement: "Talent is cheap; dedication is costly." A work must be deep ever to go wide and a work void of excellence is simply a work void of sacrifice. There is always a correlation between the cost paid and the impact made. The sacrifice of a lot of time, study, prayer, hard work and service goes into making a lasting contribution to society. And, probably little will ever happen in our lives in this regard until we find a purpose powerful enough that motivates us not only to sacrifice but also be willing to die for it.

Twenty-eight years ago I answered the call to the ministry. At the time God had already been gracious enough to give me a very successful commercial real estate company. He also allowed me to attend just about every real estate school in the country and even became a certified commercial investment member (CCIM) of the National Board of Realtors. My desire was to learn all I could about it so I could use it to help my clients in every transaction I was involved in. We had eight brokers working for the company at one point, were debt free and all my brokers and agents were believers. It was a blessing to have a business that was built on the Rock. Our weekly sales meetings always started with a Bible study. (Today, nearly all of my agents and brokers are in the ministry in one way or the other. I am grateful for God's work in their lives.) I truly loved the real estate business because it allowed me to make like-long friends and make a bold stand for God while serving the real estate needs of others. Amazingly, twelve years into all that investment of time, treasure, effort and learning, the Lord called me into the ministry. Immediately, as a man under authority, I sought the blessing of my earthly father and pastors on this new calling. My pastor agreed immediately but it took a couple years for my earthly father, who I honor, to give me his. Seems, his step-father was also an itinerate preacher and they didn't do very well financially. He saw that the Lord had already given me a very good business and with the opportunity to preach in the jails and prisons. A calling to help people in and out of prison and jail without a penny to their names, didn't look very promising when I had a family to provide for. I didn't know how the Lord would provide, I just knew if He called me to it, He would provide whatever I needed. When he finally gave his approval, I gave up all my business interests and started living by faith.

Everyone exchanges their life for something. At the age of forty-four, I decided to follow God's calling and exchange mine for a life of influence. The first year, was pretty rough but, we never missed a meal unintentionally. However, the commitments to Christ were plentiful. We saw over 500 come to the Lord. The second year it went up to 1,150 and just kept climbing every year. Praise Him! The financial blessing finally started coming but our ministry has never been about money. At the time of this writing, we are seeing the Lord build our eighth building for the ministry debt free. We have trusted Him for the knowledge of how to be wise managers of resources to build physical properties as well as wisdom to build an effective teaching and preaching ministry. It has been all of Him and none of me. Nothing much though is ever accomplished in God's Kingdom without sacrifice. Over the years I got to see the inside of a jail as an occupant and not a preacher twice because of standing against infanticide in America and I have never regretted it for a minute. God always adds the grace to make it a light burden to carry. Even the jail time, probation and fines for standing against infanticide were nothing compared to the blessing of doing God's will. Think about it. If no one considers the killing of our own pre-born babies as what it truly is, murder, nothing will change. When we started coming against it the majority of Americans were pro-death. Now that has turned around completely: the majority is far more pro-life. At the time, we started this years ago, I determined to pray and come against the Ponce de Leon Abortion Mill here in Atlanta and purposed never to quit until they were closed. Well, a few years after I made that commitment, the State of Georgia closed their doors. Upon inspecting their facility one time the State found that it was so filthy they could never trust such a sorry bunch to clean it up and keep it that way. So the State closed them down (by the hand of God) and that for good.

Right after answering the call to the ministry, one of my real estate broker friends called and said, "I heard you gave up your business and went into the ministry. Tell me it ain't so." I said, "It is definitely so." Bless his heart, he might have thought I was half crazy but now had reason, possibly, to be sure of it. Here I was leaving a viable and successful, professional business to go preaching in the prisons and jails. Another time, about seven years after going into the ministry I was in the building inspection dept. of the city getting another building permit. I was wearing my blue jeans and muddy boots at the time. Another broker friend and competitor from days gone by, dressed in his business suit, was there in the office and saw me. A few minutes later he came over and asked, "Winston, have you ever missed the real estate business?" I replied honestly, "Never for one second." There is just nothing greater than winning souls and building the Kingdom for God. Why He chose me I will never know—until I get to Heaven. God had to do some serious scraping the bottom of the barrel to come up with me and could, obviously, have done so much better picking a whole lot of others. But I am, in deed, grateful for His trust, help and grace. The Lord has truly been gracious to allow me to serve in a lot of industries: construction, the military, real estate and, now, the ministry. I have loved every job I have ever had but none as much as the ministry. It seems to require everything I have ever learned and that all accounts for about half a percent of what I need each day. The other ninety-nine and a half comes from God's grace—or I would never make it a minute. Our hope is that some day I may have had some influence in the lives of people before God calls me home.

What it means to have the character trait of **A HEART TO HAVE INFLUENCE:**

- To use the flow of spiritual, intellectual and moral forces one is gifted with to extend light and salt to others.
- To possess the moral and spiritual authority to educate, encourage and equip others to become greater for their own benefit and that of their generation.
- To have the ability to change people and society without the use of coercion, physical exertion or the power of command.
- Realizing the only thing we can leave behind is the influence we have had on others.

EART TO HONOR, A —   **Study start date: _____ Finish date: _____**

Today some people wouldn't give an ant any credit if he ate a bale of hay. How can people be this way, you ask? They don't respect themselves and through the eyes of their, depraved hearts, cannot possibly respect or honor anyone else. They think everybody else is just like them; seeing no good in anyone. In times past, some have actually shared with me the belief that the only way businessmen can get ahead or make a profit is cheat. What a sad perception but this kind of thinking has been going on for a long time. Remember, the unprofitable servant in the parable of the Talents said of God, Himself, that He was "a hard man" when God is love. He went on to say He "reaped where he hadn't sown and gathered where He hadn't scattered seed." (Mt 25:24) This is impossible. God created the Universe and all that therein is. Everything that exists is a seed He has sown. This servant judged God out of his own heart to be just like him. He already admitted being fearful but God, who knows our hearts, said his problem was that he was wicked and lazy.

As we go through life, we should look, instead, for the good in others and we should start with our own parents. Sure, no one is perfect and we have been right there in the house to see some of their flaws the whole time we were growing up. However, just as we would like to be forgiven for all our mistakes and have them forgotten, we should stop and count all the ways our parents have been a blessing to us. We should count all the ways they have done well in life themselves and give them credit for in our own minds first. Then thank them and give them honor at every opportunity.

As promised, we all have had our own trials and troubles. Job was no different except that his trials were so great that the rest of us will likely not ever have any room to complain. He was blameless, upright and the greatest man of all the men in the East and yet the Lord granted satan the right to test him. In a matter of minutes he lost a thousand oxen, fourteen thousand sheep, six thousand camels, a thousand donkeys and, last but not least, seven sons and three daughters. His went in minutes from being the wealthiest man in the East to a net worth of zero. This not sufficing the devil's thirst for troubles, he was later granted permission to touch his body with painful sores from the top of his head to the soles of his feet. His entire body was clothed with worms and scabs. All his "friends" quickly blamed him for all these troubles. This notwithstanding, his wife even said, Why don't you "curse God and die?" In all this Job did finally complain a little but he never stopped trusting and honoring God. Unable to understand the reasons for all this adversity, he said, "Though He slay me, yet will I trust him …" (Job 13:15) "And as for me, I know my Redeemer lives, and at the last He will take His stand on the earth. Even after my skin is destroyed, yet from my flesh I shall see God; whom I myself shall see and not another." (Job 19:25–27) In and through it all, he honored God with his faith. In the end, however, we know "the Lord made him prosperous again and gave him twice as much as he had before." (Job 42:10) His relatives and friends finally came to him with their consolations and gave him gifts. He fathered seven sons and three daughters once again and the daughters were the most beautiful in all the land. He lived to see his grandchildren unto the fourth generation, living another 140 years and died a truly blessed man.

We can know that whatever and whoever you honor in this life will one day honor you. It is simply the law of reciprocity God has placed it here in all the earth.

Good things rarely happen by accident. Someone has to be the procuring cause. Some people, I realize, have had horrible bosses and pastors. If you are where you can't honor your leader, leave. Go where you can so you can grow and be blessed. Never forget, as I said, whatever and whoever you honor will, in fact, honor you in time. I am thankful that I can honestly say, all my bosses (and they are many) have been great and my pastors have been princes. Respecting and honoring them has been a joy and something that just came naturally.

Today is the day to honor others around us. Don't put it off. Give them their roses now instead of when they are six feet under.

What it means to have the character trait of **A HEART TO HONOR:**

- Honoring your father and mother is the first commandment with a promise. God thought this was important enough to not only make it a commandment but then to also give us a promise for our obedience: our days would be long upon the earth.
- Highly esteeming those around you; especially your parents, employer and the leaders God has placed in your life
- The ability to consider all others better than yourself because humility demands it and, secondly, because their gifts and talents are just as important to the accomplishment of God's mission and purpose on earth as ours.
- Realizing there can be no honor without forgiveness because none of us are perfect. We all make mistakes. To have a heart to honor you must first have a heart ready to forgive.
- Realizing all life on this planet is about relationship and there can be no relationship without honor
- Realizing that all men have clay feet, it is the ability to look past the small human defects and see the greater good
- The ability not to be looking for a chink in your leader's armor because if you are looking, you will surely find it
- Having enough good in you to see the good in others.
- Concentrating on and being moved by the greater good in a person's life rather than fixing on a small defect.
- It is giving honor to whom honor is deserved
- Honor can be deserved for excellent character, purity, sacrifice, awards on the field of battle or sports, education, a good work ethic, achievement, holding high office, superior performance, making quality products, being a parent, being a friend, being an acquaintance, etc.
- Heart-felt thanks that comes from realizing what good leaders we have been blessed with knowing you could, except for the grace of God, have been serving under Hitler, Stalin or Hugo Chavez.

HEART TO KEEP RANK, A—   **Study start date:** _____ **Finish date:** _____

So many people today and especially younger folk, are offended by those in authority over them in the home, society, school and their place of work. Beware because, what starts out as resentment can often turn into anger, then jealousy and will usually in the end, turn into rebellion. It has caused some to rebel and even attempt to usurp the leader's position of authority. Obviously, there will always be people in the world with more authority than we have at any particular point in time. If we first despise their position and then begin looking for a chink in their armor, we will surely find one simply because all men have clay feet. However, I, personally, have been blessed by God's providence to serve under some great leaders—truly generals for God in the military, in business and the church. For this privilege, I will be forever grateful.

My first company commander in the Army was Captain Alex Hottell, a man among men. An Airborne Ranger, tenth in his class at West Point, a Rhodes Scholar, a German Jumpmaster and British national diving champion two years in a row. When I knew him back in 1969, he drove a solid black, 1932 Rolls Royce. Our Company was C Company (Cobra Company) 1st of the 508th Battalion in the 82nd Airborne Division. We were a newly formed company since the previous Brigade had deployed to Vietnam. It fell to me to design our company insignia as a coiled up cobra with wings (we were an airborne unit) with a streak of lightning coming out of its mouth. It was entirely our idea to call our commander Captain Cobra. We all loved him and were so honored for him to be our leader. He died in a helicopter crash defending our country in Vietnam. I still miss him even to this day.

Next I was aide and business manager for Major General John R. "Uncle Jack" Deane, Commanding General of the 82nd Airborne Division. He was a graduate of the U. S. Military Academy, a great leader who not only commanded our nation's 16,000 man, first response, airborne task force but also led the only airborne, tactical jump fighting our enemy in Vietnam as Commander of the 173rd Airborne Brigade. He entered the Army as a buck private and retired a four star general.

The Broker I first worked for in civilian life was Jack Anderson, President of Allied Properties. He had a BS degree and a law degree. He was a captain and a pilot in the Air Force before going into business. When I worked for him, he was developing five huge subdivisions, two mobile home parks, had five framing crews stick building houses, a prefab home manufacturing plant, a huge building supply store, a mortgage company and a real estate company. Jack was known for building quality homes and taking care of business.

I was also honored to serve as an elder under Dr. Paul Walker, Pastor of Mt. Paran Church of God in Atlanta, Georgia. He grew the congregation from a few hundred people to a membership of 2,500 and was one of the most effective pulpiteers I have ever heard. He was a great leader and later became overseer of the entire, world-wide Church of God.

I also served as an elder at Victory Tabernacle where Pastor Franklin Walden grew that church from a tent meeting to a congregation of about 500 while also serving at the same time as an evangelist all over the United States and Canada. He was a man God worked through to perform many miracles. With God's help, he healing the sick and even raised one from the dead. He won thousands and thousands to Christ in his life time. Though he never had more than a seventh grade education, he still became a builder before going into the ministry, a legendary pastor and wrote and published over thirty books.

Now I said all that to say as great as these men were, if I had had a mind to, I probably could have found a fault or two in each of them but I just wasn't looking for any. I was honored to serve under them.

If we are going to live on this blue marble and prosper, we have to understand authority. We need to know that God put it here for our good. He put a hierarchal system of leadership here so we could live in harmony, be taught and flourish as well as to learn how to work for our leaders as unto the Lord. Authority was divinely established to guide and successfully manage people and resources. Those in authority are also here to commend those who do well and punish those who do wrong. If one can understand this concept, they will soon find that those in authority would like to bless, prosper and grant them incredible favor.

What it means to have the character trait of **A HEART TO KEEP RANK:**

- Not resentful of those who bear rule over you
- Having a desire to honor one's superiors.
- Having the wisdom to look for and be thankful for all the good in our leaders and a refusing to look for and find faults
- Gladly being in willing submission
- Serving contentedly with excellence in the post you are given knowing that in due time, you will be rewarded
- Not allowing the favor or familiarity your leader grants you to cause you to fall into the slightest degree of contempt
- Serving not for promotion or a pay-raise but to honor those who are our authorities
- Knowing how to honor one's superiors with integrity and a grateful heart. No apple polishing
- Working with the motive of making our leaders look good
- Respecting the position even if you have problems respecting the person
- Being like the men of "Zebulon … who went out to battle, expert in war with all weapons of war, stouthearted men who could keep ranks (with an undivided heart)." I Chronicles 12:33

HEART TO KNOW GOD, A —   **Study start date:** _____ **Finish date:** _____

Our loving Heavenly Father has given His children the ability to learn and know many things. Of course, some things are important and some are not. Truly, the most important thing to know while on this planet is, actually, not a thing but a person: God, Himself. The truth is, He has revealed Himself to us and has given us the ability to know Him personally, Actually, we were all put here to find Him, know Him, serve Him and enjoy Him both now and for eternity. Unquestionably, a person who knows and understands God has acquired the most important knowledge obtainable. In this natural world, finding and knowing God is not simple because, in His infinite wisdom, He made Himself invisible. This alone causes many to say "There is no God," "God is dead" and "There are many gods." It also allows them to believe that they can get along in this life without Him. Actually, we all start out on our own, alienated from God but at some point He grants us the grace to call out to Him. At some point we must ask forgiveness for our sins and for His Son to come into our hearts and be the Lord of our lives. Although critically important, this is just the first step of our lifelong pursuit of knowing Him but it is certainly the beginning of a wonderful, personal relationship with the Creator of the Universe.

Another obstacle in the way of finding Him is the simple fact that although He is a person, He is not like man at all. God is all powerful, all knowing, ever present, inscrutable, eternal, unchanging, unequaled, incomparable, all-wise and love itself personified. He is capable, competent and creative beyond description. His powers are so immense that He can breathe stars into existence and sling them into their proper orbits in His Universe in a moment. Scripture tells us, "By the word of the Lord the heavens were made, and all the hosts of them by the breath of His mouth." (Psalm 33:6) What a God we serve!

Yet, at the same time, man is just a vapor. We are less than nothing but God is so humble David asked the question: "Lord, what is man, that You take knowledge of him? Or the son of man, that You are mindful of him? Man is like a breath; his days are like a passing shadow." (Psalm 144:3, 4) " … O Lord … You are very great: You are clothed with honor and majesty Who cover Yourself with light as with a garment, Who stretch out the heavens like a curtain. He lays the beams of His upper chambers in the waters, Who makes the clouds His chariot, Who walks on the wings of the wind …" (Psalm 104:1–3) Our stark insignificance by comparison, is what provoked Job to say, "What is man, that You should exalt him, that You should set Your heart on him, that You should visit him every morning and test him every moment?" (Job 7:17) God is capable of hearing and answering the prayers of all His creation, managing the entire universe, sending rain in its proper season, as well as rendering justice and vengeance on every human being. He can do all this and much more at the same time and none of it is the least burden to Him. In his perfection, He is incredible, beyond our ability to even imagine.

In some ways God is similar to man but in most He is radically different. His thoughts and ways are totally different from man's. He said, "' … My thoughts are not your thoughts, nor are your ways My ways, … For as the heavens are higher than the earth, so are My ways higher than your ways, and My thoughts than your thoughts." (Isaiah 55:8, 9) Although this is true, He still graciously allows us to know many of His ways. He sends us His Word and reveals His will to us in nature and many other ways, if we will seek Him. This is so important because even in Moses' time, the people knew God's acts but only Moses knew His ways. The people saw God demonstrate His power to Pharaoh and even to part the Red Sea. They knew the "what" but not the "why." Only Moses knew God's ways. Thankfully, they are not past finding out. The Lord, Himself, said, "Stand in the ways (at the crossroads of life) and see (look, open your eyes and be observant), and ask for the old paths (the ancient ways), where is the good way, and walk in it and you shall find rest for your souls." (Jeremiah 6:16) We human beings oftentimes find ourselves at a crossroad in life and don't know which way to go. He said stop and look. Seek the Lord for His guidance and He will show us His way. And, His way is the ancient way. Not a new way, a new wave or a new trendy solution. His way is the way everlasting and it never changes. It was right in the beginning and it is still right today. Man's way is forever changing but not God's. As we practice this process of finding God's ways, we become more and more knowledgeable about it. And, hopefully, more and more capable of knowing His will, practicing it and succeeding in life. Instead of having disaster after every start and a life full of controversy and lack, He promises we will "find rest." He said "rest for (our) souls."

God definitely wants us to know Him. In fact, His Word says "He is a rewarder of those who diligently seek Him." (Hebrews 11:6) This is important because, knowing this, we really only have two choices. We can either go through this life trying to bless ourselves and make it on our own or we can let Him lead and guide us to the green pastures and still waters. If we chose ourselves as boss, we are immediately at the mercy of a crooked, perverse world and have only the few fleeting things we can acquire with which to bless ourselves. On the other hand, if we chose the Lord, He is seated far above us. He owns the earth and the fullness thereof, all the gold and silver, the cattle on a thousand hills and everything else. Even promotion we find "comes neither from the east nor from the west nor from the south. But God is the Judge: He puts down one, and exalts another." (Psalm 75:6) If we will set ourselves to gain a servant's heart and to be content having just food and clothing (I Timothy 6:8), we will place ourselves in position for God to use us as He wills and receive His blessings. We also know that " . . the eyes of the Lord run to and fro throughout the whole earth, to show Himself strong on behalf of those whose heart is perfect toward Him." (II Chronicles 16:9) We can either try to be strong enough to defend, serve and reward ourselves or we can seek God, forget about ourselves, serve others and let Him send us His blessings, favor, strength and protection.

There is no place more important to know God than on the field of mortal combat. I don't believe there is anyone who was in combat with their enemies more than David. After all he had seen, he wrote these words, "A thousand may fall at your side, and ten thousand at your right hand; but it shall not come near you (the believer). Only with your eyes shall you look and see the reward of the wicked. Because you have made the Lord (your) refuge, even the Most High, your dwelling place, no evil shall befall you, nor shall any plague come near your dwelling; for He shall give His angels charge over you, to keep you in all your ways. In their hands they shall bear you up, lest you dash your foot against a stone. You shall tread upon the lion and the cobra, the young lion and the serpent you shall trample underfoot. Because you (have chosen to know Him and have " set (your) love upon Me, therefore I will deliver him; I will set him on high because he has known My name. He shall call upon Me, and I will answer him; I will be with him in trouble; I will deliver him and honor him. With long life I will satisfy him, and show him My salvation." (Psalm 91:7–16) What promises we have from the Maker of the Universe.

The Apostle Paul gave up everything for one goal: to know God. Everything he thought was gain, he counted as loss to know Him. His one ambition and goal in life was to "know Him and the power of His resurrection, and the fellowship of His sufferings, being conformed to His death, if, by any means, (he could) attain to the resurrection from the dead." Philippians 3:10,11

Our God is so gracious that He set each of us here on the Earth with the task of searching Him out. Although we can have a knowledge of God, we certainly can never know Him completely. Scripture declares that He is so vast in His nature that He is, to a large degree, incomprehensible. (Job 11:7, 36:26; Romans 11:23) However, Scripture also states that God is constantly revealing Himself to men and has put this knowledge in His Word, in nature and within the grasp of all human beings willing to make the effort to seek Him. The best we can obtain is a partial knowledge but this will not be a deterrent to the diligent seeker.

Significantly, a part of knowing and experiencing God is sensing His presence with us. King David practiced God's presence seeing the Lord ever before him, even at his right hand and because of that he said he would never be shaken. Nothing the enemy brought against him would move him. (Acts 2:25) When we have the Lord with us, nothing will move us either. On another occasion David said, "He alone is my rock and my salvation, my fortress; I shall never be shaken." (Psalm 62:2) A personal knowledge of and a personal relationship with God is the best experience man can ever have on this planet. It will totally change a person's nature and give him incomparable strength. He desires fellowship with men and we at any time we like can "enter His gates with thanksgiving and into His courts with praise." (Psalm 100:4) We can also take our petitions directly to Him in prayer.

Some, in God's providence, have been granted more favorable attributes and earthly possessions in this life than others. However, great wisdom, riches and strength can oftentimes be a hindrance as well. These things have been known to blind men on earth, distract them from the true source of unlimited power, hindering their knowledge of Him. The Lord actually warned us about this saying, "Let not the wise man glory in his wisdom, let not the mighty man glory in his might, nor let the rich man glory in his riches; but let him who glories glory in this, that he understands and knows Me, that I am the Lord, exercising loving kindness, judgment and righteousness in the earth. For in these I delight." (Jeremiah 9:23) We are admonished here to have such a close relationship with the Lord that it becomes the very thing we boast about. It is OK to have wisdom. It is fine to have strength. It is well to have great riches but knowing Him causes all things to pale and become inconsequential in the light of our knowledge of Him. All these things will pass away with time and certainly with end of our time on this little planet but our knowledge of God will be with us throughout eternity. It is our only sure possession.

What it means to have the character trait of **A HEART TO KNOW GOD:**

- Knowing Him Jeremiah 9:24
- Knowing His Son John 14:6
- Knowing His grace Ephesians 2:8
- Knowing His Word Psalm 1:1–3
- Knowing His will Romans 12:2
- Knowing His ways Hebrews 3:10
- Knowing His leading Isaiah 48:17b
- Knowing His mercy II Corinthians 2:1–4
- Knowing His love Ephesians 3:17–19
- Knowing His peace Philippians 4:7
- Knowing His rewards Hebrews 11:6
- Knowing that He exercises loving kindness, justice and righteousness in the earth. Jer. 9:24
- Having His presence with us Acts 2:25

EART TO LISTEN, A —   **Study start date:** _____   **Finish date:** _____

Listening is a critically important skill that needs to be perfected by all of us in life. The Germans had some idea about life and I believe they had it right: "We grow too soon old and too late schmart." We all have a lot to learn and I mean all. In order to continue learning in life, we must realize how desperate our need to learn really is and a large part of learning is becoming a really good listener. This is increasingly difficult in today's world. It is becoming far more technical and complicated, requiring us to know a great deal more each day just to function normally. At the same time, every day there is also a corresponding increase in the many distractions and demands competing for our attention. We are constantly in an environment of TV's and radios blaring, text messages, emails and phone calls coming in, tweets and twitters, bells, buzzers, whistles and beepers going off. It is not only courteous to be a good listener but it is also smart for us to stop what we are doing and listen when someone is speaking to us. It's a fact, you can't talk and listen at the same time. That is just the way God made our brains. It is also important not to crowd the other person in the conversation. Give them time to finish because they are going to be watching to see if you are going to extend them this very basic courtesy or start walking on their conversation. Make up your mind that you are going to go overboard to hear the other person's points of view. We also need to realize that they are only going to be giving us the tip of the iceberg about whatever it is they are sharing with us. They don't want to give you any more than you are willing to take so sometimes you will need to draw out their innermost feelings with questions. Know that their deepest feelings and fears are barricaded up in their heart of hearts and closely guarded. Therefore, you will need to be gentle and sincerely interested in them as a person for those to ever be shared with you.

Listening to others may well include body language, eye contact, tone of voice, attitude, facial expressions, pauses, voice inflections and emphasis. A good listener knows that we, as humans, communicate with more than just our voice. They also make a point of listening for something equally important, what people don't say as well.

An important area we need to improve on in the area of listening skills is hearing criticism. Truly, one of the most valuable things we will ever have the opportunity to receive in life is constructive criticism. Those who are kind enough to give it to us may not sound very kind to us at the time because correction is never a pleasant thing. The other person, unless they are in authority over us, could be risking their friendship to give us, what they believe, is helpful information to make us a better person or more successful in life. Take it to heart. But, remember, we are human just like everyone else. We really don't want to hear it and have all, over time, lulled ourselves into thinking we are doing just fine. Realize now that everybody, just out of self-preservation, has a natural inclination to resist correction and criticism. Believe it or not, none of us have it all right. So, we need to count the criticism of others extremely valuable and write it down so we can't brush it off. This will require us to face it and, hopefully, start trying to look into the matter and correct the problem.

Wives are great for giving us correction and that's why they are oftentimes called "heavenly sandpaper." It has also been said that every woman has 25,000 words she needs to get out every day and if she doesn't, she is going to be very unhappy. So, you men would be wise to become really good listeners. Plan to spend quality time listening to your wives every day. There is nothing they love more than sharing a cup of coffee and for their man to be listening to them. Wives really do know a lot and are constantly finding new, really helpful things going on in the world to share. When they are talking and the TV is on, when you can, turn the volume off and be attentive to her for a minute.

One final thought speaking of listening. I picked up the paper this morning and noticed where the cops had just busted a couple guys for possession of $1.4 million worth of cocaine in the Home Depot parking lot just a few miles from my house. The reason they got caught was because of the listening skills of the officer who happened to pull them over. Seems a Spanish guy and his sidekick were driving a semi-truck with a car carrier on the back of it (as a decoy) to make a drug drop here and the tractor had a secret compartment in the ceiling of the sleeping loft. They were stopped because of something as small as a burned-out tail light but they got caught because of something even smaller. Upon talking with them, the officer said one of them told him they were planning to buy some cars from Peach State Auto Auction in Loganville and sell them in Mexico. The way the officer knew something was up was that the one doing the talking "would not make eye contact with (him)" during the conversation. His voice didn't have a convincing tone, he kept looking away and his hands started trembling nervously. The deputy called out the K-9 unit and the rest, of course, is history. Good thing this cop knew how to listen.

What it means to have the character trait of **A HEART TO LISTEN:**

- To maintain eye contact and truly hear
- To hear others thoroughly with undistracted, careful attention
- To be alert to body language of the other party and their tone and voice inflections
- To give a willing ear to hear with undivided attention
- The act and art of listening
- To hear not only what people say but what they don't say is also very important
- To pay attention to sounds as well as meaning
- To pay heed to the words, attitude and facial expressions

HEART TO PREPARE FOR BATTLE, A — Study start date: _____ Finish date: _____

In America we have been basking in freedom for so long, the majority of our citizens think it's free. Most people think it is always going to be sunshine, lollipops and roses forever. Remember it was complacency, a lack of morality and an entitlement mentality that rotted the foundation of the Roman Empire. It was one of the greatest empires the world had ever seen and this caused its total destruction. Despite appearances, freedom isn't free and we are all probably going to see more trouble before we leave this planet. In fact, we are promised trouble in this short life. We are not just talking about national military conflicts but we are promised trouble in our own personal lives and businesses as well. It is not at all a matter of if but when it comes and how much. Truly, no one can succeed in life, a family or business unless they can handle trouble. We are promised that every house (and a house is a life) is going to be tried by fire and as painful as these fires may be, they also happen to be extremely beneficial. Just as silver and gold are perfected by fire for the removal of all the dross and impurities, the human spirit is purified by the trials of life. We all have defects and various hidden faults some of which we may know about and some of which may not have been revealed to us yet.

Now though every day may not packed with trouble and because we are alert to the fact that new and bigger battles are on the way, we should always be preparing to be a better soldier tomorrow than we are today. Even civilians should be soldiers of the Lord, preparing to fight, as Paul did, the beast at Ephesus. Some will pay the price to train and will be ever learning and preparing and some will not. My dad told me while I was growing up, "Whatever you learn in life you will always use again someday." Time has proved him right.

Though, admittedly, I didn't progress very far in the Boy Scouts due to frequent family moves in the Air Force and other interests, I did take their motto, "Be Prepared" to heart. I quickly found that failing to be prepared on a camping trip, for example, wouldn't cost anyone else probably but it would cost me if I forgot to take various critical items along. Not preparing can be extremely costly, not just on a camping trip but in every area of life. I thought I understood this, but evidently not too well as I would soon see after high school.

At that time I wanted to attend Texas A& M University and be in the Corps of Cadets. All my family graduated from A&M but since I didn't apply myself in high school I was not accepted to attend. Actually had to attend a smaller college in Texas for a year in hopes of obtaining a high enough grade point average to get into A&M. This was my first experience with a big failure in life and I took it to heart and tried my best to right my ship. I hit the books, got on the drill team at Tarleton State College and studied military science. When they had the particular try-out for the Drill team I attended and three of us actually made the cut. They said we were all marginal and were going to need a lot of work. I think this is what they told everyone so they would be properly motivated. However, in my case, I believe it was true. Actually made pretty good grades and, unexpectedly that year, set my heart on something as crazy as becoming an Army Ranger and "living a life of danger." I gave it my best and was somehow selected Best Drilled Freshman in the Corps that year. Texas A&M also accepted me to attend my sophomore year and I thought all was well but it was just the quiet before the storm.

At the beginning of the next school year I was assigned to a unit in the Corps and that was when the stuff really hit the fan. Having had a lot of friends all my life, I found myself a one-man-island for the next three years. No matter how hard I tried, the Corps culture would not accept me because I had not been a freshman there and that was that. It didn't matter how much I suffered and how much we were hazed on the drill team at another college. That was it—end of story. There I was, paying another huge price for not doing my best and not being prepared in high school. It was really something. I was an outcast in a military cast system. Though it was tough, quitting was not an option with me so I stuck it out and learned far, far more from the experience than I ever expected. God knows how to prepare the perfect scenarios to correct our character defects. Years later looking back, it was one of the best things that has ever happened to me. It has been said that "In every adversity is planted the seed of equal or greater good." During that time, I studied my regular courses and especially military science and kept on sharpening my ax, as they say. I began reading lots of books about the military, the art of war and successful military officers. I prayed for God to give me just one opportunity to compete on a level playing field someday.

After two years all my Corps classmates from A&M and I were sent to ROTC Summer Camp at Ft. Sill, Oklahoma along with 2,000 other college seniors. Now honestly, I never thought I was the strongest, swiftest or smartest, far from it. Really. I did, however, have faith though and believed in prayer. Knowing we would be assigned a number at the end of that camp based on marksmanship, physical endurance tests, peer ratings, military science and tactics tests, leadership, etc., I asked God to help me be number one. Really, I promise, I didn't think I was the best but I just kept the faith. Ok, so I didn't come out #1, I was # 2 but was still first among all those in my class at A&M. Because of the standings at camp, the Commandant promoted me to a staff position above nearly all of my peers. I made up my mind to continue preparing for the future. The Army even helped me with free flight school which enabled me get my pilot's license. I was getting ready for the next battles of life. Dr. Doyle once said, "There are only two fires in the crucible of life, those that consume and those that purify." We can either let our problems make us bitter or better and the choice is ours. I decided to forgive everyone, let it all go and opt for the latter.

While attending A&M, the war in Vietnam was raging hotter and hotter. All of us in the Corps knew that in a few short years we would graduate, be commissioned, get a little training from the U.S. Army and be air-dropped on a battlefield somewhere in Vietnam. Knowing this should have given all of us an intrinsic desire to learn all we could about our trade. No question about it, very soon I would be involved in my own shoot-out at OK Corral. Only difference was, Wyatt Earp's gun-fight lasted a matter of minutes and mine, I figured, would carry on, off and on, for about a year. Once we were in contact with the enemy every day for 51 days in a row. No shower and no change of clothes either. You see, the Infantry is charged with the job of closing with and destroying the enemy. What this means is that we have to find them and since they are likely not going to come to us, we must combat assault directly in to the face of the full physical strength and fire power of the enemy—sometimes on a daily basis. Of course we have our own weapons and fire support as well but this is a very direct form of combat. Unlike sitting in the cockpit of a fighter jet, sitting in an armored tank or firing artillery rounds from inside a fire base's secure perimeter, the Infantry's battles are up front and personal. There was no question that I would soon be facing off against the best lieutenants the North Vietnamese Army and Viet Cong could field. For that reason, I thought it best to attend every school the Army had: Airborne, Ranger, Jumpmaster and Pathfinder School I also made a special effort to go to the firing range. I continued practicing until I fired expert with just about every weapon in the Army's arsenal except the .45. Caliber pistol. Couldn't seem to get that one to do all I wanted. Why do all this work and study? I was truly headed for what you might call ultimate warfare—a battle unto death. For this new venture as a young man on the military path of life, I fully intended to be prepared.

I didn't know it at the time but there have long been others who prepared and trained for battle as well. The Bible talks about "Seven hundred select men (among the Benjamites) who were left handed; every one could sling a stone at a hair's breadth and not miss." (Judges 20:16) There were also those who volunteered for David's army at the most dangerous time: while he was yet a fugitive from Saul. Three thousand of King Saul's finest soldiers were chasing David like a flea in the desert. However, David's new volunteers "were armed with bows, and could use both the right hand and the left in hurling stones and shooting arrows …" I Chronicles 12:2

Sure enough, upon graduation from college, some training at the Jumpmaster, Airborne and Ranger schools and a stint of garrison duty with the 82nd Airborne Division at Ft. Bragg, NC, I was given orders for Vietnam. About that time I requested entry and was accepted into the Pathfinder School at Ft. Benning en route. That school taught some pretty important military concepts and I wanted to learn all I could.

One day during a short break in the training, we happened to have a helicopter hovering above us to demonstrate something they were teaching us at the time. On my own, I quietly picked up the radio handset and asked the pilot if he could teach me how to call in aerial rocket artillery—as if he was a cobra gunship in close support of a rifle company. Directing a cobra gunship was really not a company commander's job but that of the Artillery Forward Observer, a lieutenant assigned to him. Even so, I wanted to understand the concept since it was very likely something that would be going on in the middle of my battlefield. Since the pilot had just returned from Vietnam, of course he was glad to be of assistance. He instructed me to always bring the gunship in parallel to the front area of the battle line to make his gun runs and to have him break away toward the enemy side when peeling off the target. The reason for this was that when exiting the target area, the cobra was right over the enemy and in the most vulnerable position of his run on the target. The underbelly of his aircraft was, at that point, completely exposed to enemy fire and he would also be at the closest range to the enemy as well. He advised me that the pilot would not take his finger off the trigger shooting rockets as he peeled off in hopes of keeping the enemy's heads down until he could fairly well make his exit and clear the target area. He knew as soon as he stopped firing his rockets, the enemy was going to pop up and engage his aircraft with all they had in hopes of shooting him out of the sky. We practiced a couple runs and I thanked him for his trouble and willingness to train me but I never thought I would really have to use that information.

Then, a few weeks later I was on what we called "the big iron bird," a large personnel aircraft (probably a 707 or 747), taking a huge load of us young soldiers to Vietnam. As providence would have it, I took my assigned seat next to a lieutenant Smith (different name), who I had, of course, never met before in my life. It was a fairly long flight across the Pacific Ocean and we both knew we were about to face our first baptism by fire. Although we didn't bring up the subject, neither one of us knew how we would respond and were, understandably, wondering within ourselves how we would react to a real, live enemy with real, live ammunition. Fact is, no one knows. This was, however, going to be the real deal—sure enough. He asked me what I expected to be doing in the 'Nam and my reply was that I was hoping to command a line company in the First Cavalry Division. ." He said basically, "Are you crazy? You can get killed doing that. Besides you have to be a Captain." (I was a lieutenant.) I said that I had volunteered to go into the Infantry Branch of the Army and had been preparing (seemingly) all my life for this, being a military brat and having gone to a military college. I told him I had been recommended for it and had asked for the job besides. Then I asked him what he was hoping to do. He said he had a "rear job" all lined up. That meant a rear echelon, cush, support job probably driving a desk at some fairly safe, rear brigade or division fire base. I wished him well and he, likewise. Upon arrival in Vietnam, he went his way for equipping and indoctrination as an artillery officer and I went a different route as an infantry officer. We didn't expect to see each other ever again on this planet. The U.S. Army was huge back then. It had more troops than at any time except WWII, more boats than the Navy and more airplanes than the Air Force.

When I went through the 1st Cavalry Division Firebase and was blessed to spend a short while with my old Ranger Buddy, Lieutenant Steve Grubb who, after having been a platoon leader there in the 1st Cav. was selected to be aide to the Commanding General (CG). He and my first company commander in the 82nd Airborne Division, CPT Alex Hottell, preceded me to Vietnam by about eight months since I stayed and served six months as aide to the CG there and then went on to Pathfinder School as I mentioned. It was really a blessing to see Steve again. I also spent a few hours with CPT Hottell who after commanding a company in the 1st Cav., had been promoted to Division Historian. A Rhodes Scholar, Hottell could write like no one I had ever seen before. We had become fast friends and he gave me a NVA lieutenant's pistol belt his company had captured as a gift that day (which I still have and cherish). I didn't know it then but that would be the last time I would ever see him. A few months later, Steve was riding around in the helicopter with the CG and got shot in the foot with a 51 caliber, anti-aircraft machinegun round. His foot was so messed up he had to go back to the world we called it (the U.S.A.) and CPT Hottell was selected to be his replacement in the aide's job. Tragically, just a few months later, Hottell and the CG were going to visit some wounded soldiers at a hospital by helicopter when they got into some fog and accidentally slammed their chopper into the side of a mountain. Everyone on board was killed instantly. What a loss! We all thought the world of CPT Hottell and General Casey. They were both terrific officers with unlimited potential. Both of them were outstanding, extremely competent, could do anything and were also very likeable men.

After our short visit, I was quickly assigned to a battalion and flown to the fire base. I was there no time at all before the Battalion Commander had a helicopter take me out to assume command of a rifle company. Strangely, my unit had no Artillery Forward Observer when I arrived. However, three days later a logistics helicopter landed to bring in our re-supply and, in the process, I noticed a young lieutenant exit the aircraft. He quickly headed toward my command group. The closer he got, the more I thought this guy looked a whole lot like the lieutenant I sat next to on the airplane. As he got closer I knew it was, indeed, him. He saluted and said, "LT Smith reporting for duty, Sir." (The Lord has, Himself, cleaned up my language since then) I said, "What the Hell are you doing out here? I thought you were going to get a 'rear job." He replied, "No Sir, it didn't work out and I am assigned as your Artillery F.O. (Forward Observer)." Of course I welcomed him to the unit and tried to accommodate him but knew right from our previous conversation that he really didn't want to be out front and probably had not trained or prepared himself very well.

The very next day, while on a ground reconnaissance mission, we spotted a platoon of North Vietnamese soldiers with two .51 caliber machine guns. Since we saw them first, I had Lt. Smith engaged them with artillery and I ordered up a cobra gunship to give us close aerial fire support. I had the lead platoon combat assault until they made solid contact. Then I had them begin to lay down a base of fire and had the second platoon advance alongside them until they were receiving too much fire as well. Once in close proximity to the enemy in battle it was standard procedure for the company commander to have his Artillery Forward Observer right next to him so they could coordinate. It was his the FO's job to bring in (fire) the artillery from the battalion fire base as well as to direct the cobra gunship (aerial rocket artillery) in on the target. Since the enemy was to our north, the flight pattern he gave the pilot was to make his run echo, whiskey and break Sierra. This was language using the Army's phonetic alphabet (so the enemy couldn't understand what we were saying very well) meaning the pilot was to come in on the target and make his runs from east to west and break south. Only problem was that he had the cobra's gunship breaking out in the wrong direction because the enemy troops were north of our position. I said him "Negative. Have him break November (north)." He said, "No, I've got it right." So I told him again and he still wouldn't change it. Since time was extremely short at that moment, I grabbed the phone set out of his hand and quickly told the pilot, "This is Bright Knight 6 (the call sign the Battalion commander had given me.) come in echo whiskey and break November, break November. Do you Roger, November?" He said, "Roger, November." If I hadn't done that in what was the very first fire fight for both LT Smith and me, I probably wouldn't be writing this story today. Our company truly routed the enemy that day. We gave fourteen of them the opportunity to die for their country, captured their two 51 cal. machine guns, a bunch of other AK-47's and B-40 rocket launchers along with a quite a few SKS rifles. Not a single one of my men even got a scratch. I was so thankful that I began to prepare, a few years earlier by learning to fly a plane in college and getting "checked out" on how to bring in aerial rocket artillery in Pathfinder School. Had I not, I assure you that I wouldn't have had the confidence to over-rule my FO's instructions to the cobra pilot or taken charge of the pilot's aircraft and his gun run as well. Not only that, but my whole company of sixty or so men would probably have been wiped out for the most part that day from the gunship's rockets. Only God knows but I probably wouldn't have made it through my first battle. For me that day, there was not work-ups, no OJT, no time to watch someone else do it first, I had to get it right the first time—in my first battle.

Yes, as you might imagine, Lieutenant Smith and I had a little talk. After that. I told him from then on, he would do exactly what I told him, and that immediately, or I would give him a summary court martial on the spot. That was not going to happen again. He knew very well why. The reason for this was, as the commander, I happened to be the one responsible for everything both he and the whole company did or failed to do. I told him if I was going to be wrong, I would be wrong in the future for my own mistakes and not his. He got it and we never had another problem after that. He actually did a pretty good job as my FO after that first fiasco.

Am I thankful for being prepared? Yes, I am thankful today and was back then too. However, make no mistake about it; our victory that day came from the Lord. Scripture states, "The horse is prepared for the day of battle, but deliverance and victory is of the Lord." Proverbs 31:21 AMP VER

Why might all this be important? I can say with assurance that every discipline or field of endeavor in the military and civilian life requires training and preparation to be proficient, competitive and successful. If you are going to be a plumber, pilot, preacher, builder, lawyer or engineer, you must prepare. Learn all you can about your chosen field. Go to every school your industry offers. Read a book a month about it. In ten years you will have read 120 books related to your specialty. In time you will likely know more about it than just about anyone else in the field. You will need all the tools and knowledge you can get because business is itself a form of competitive warfare. One day you will need everything you ever learned not only survive but to make a difference. Your competitors are going to do everything they can not to just take a deal or two away from you but to obtain an advantage in the market place and put you out of business. Don't let them. In the computer age, you are going to be competing against millions of people and businesses around the globe, most of whom you will never even see. Be prepared. Besides, whatever you learn, you can apply to every task or problem that comes your way for the rest of your life! But the most important book to read is the Bible. Joshua 1:8 gives us an incredible promise. If we will meditate on the Bible "day and night (and) observe to do according to all that is written in it. Then (we) will make (our) way prosperous and then we will have good success." (Joshua 1:8) You will also have "the Lord your God with you wherever you go." (v.9) Furthermore, you will "be strong and of a good courage "(v.6) and "no man shall be able to stand before you all the days of your life" v.5

Of one thing I am certain. God expects all of us to do our dead level best with whatever we've been given. He won't tolerate anything less. I have had to learn this the hard way and hope that others can learn from my mistakes in the area of preparedness. So in life, as the Army slogan said, "Be all you can be." You will never regret learning all you can or doing your best at a job. It pays incredible dividends both now and in eternity.

What it means to have the character trait of **A HEART TO PREPARE FOR BATTLE:**

- To prepare by study, discipline, instruction, research and drill to accomplish various tasks
- To prepare one's self in life by pruning, chastisement, schooling, experience and personal reading
- Having an intrinsic desire or inner motivation to improve and learn as well as gain special tools to overcome and be victorious in the battles of life
- To make one's self proficient, fit and qualified for a task, position or career
- To be equipped for warfare

HEART TO STAND ALONE, A —   Study start date: _____ Finish date: _____

Many times in life, things on this planet have had the ability to go south so quickly and badly it is totally astounding. Even more amazingly, on those occasions, you will find that most of the time no one around you is willing to take a stand for the truth. Much of the reason for this is the way we were all made. We humans, being gregarious, have a tremendous need for acceptance by the group. It is an incredibly powerful motivating force. One of the hardest things for us to do is to elect, for the sake of truth or what is right, to stand against the group or against the entire world if need be, for that matter. Surely, part of the reason is that a decision to stand also means you will likely face ridicule, rejection, repudiation, persecution and will probably be ostracized from the group.

Standing alone against all of society takes great courage. That kind of courage usually comes primarily from two things: strength of conviction (grace) and a decision to stand in life for what is right no matter the cost. Though not evidenced much today, it is vitally important. It is said, "If you don't stand for something, you will probably fall for anything." Besides, how we live is how we die and how we die is how we live. We also know cowards die a thousand deaths but the brave only once.

Years ago a friend handed me a copy of an article torn out of a magazine called *The Teaching Home*.[8] It was about a young scribe named Athanasius who lived long ago. This little article has had a most profound effect on my life. This young scribe had no credentials, no position, no external traits that made him noteworthy and certainly had not been to seminary He, seemingly, had nothing that would distinguish him as someone important. He was just a scribe—one who, day after day, was trusted only with copying text, word for word. It was not given to him to decide doctrine, judge, teach or preach—just copy text. I think I have read this little article a thousand times and it has worked an incredible work in my heart over the years. I am certainly no Athanasius but I sure want to be.

DAD *Contra Mundum*

"A long time ago there was a pernicious fellow named Arius who troubled the church. He taught that our Lord Jesus Christ was not the eternal God, the Second Person of the Trinity, but rather was a created being, not the same essence with the father. Needless to say, this foul heresy, if accepted by the church, would have destroyed Christianity, if that were possible.

The Council of Nicea met in 325 A.D. to resolve the challenges put forth by Arius. More than 300 leaders of the church gathered. Some were followers of theheretic Arius; others held to the orthodox doctrine. Arius and his disciples were eloquent in their defense of their blasphemies—so eloquent that some of those who believed the orthodox doctrine were intimidated into silence. Who would defend the deity of Christ?

A relatively young man, small of stature but great in faith and intellect, was in attendance—Athanasius by name. Technically, he attended as a scribe, not as a leader of the church. When others were silent, Athanasius arose and delivered a powerful, irrefutable defense of the orthodox doctrine. This great champion of the faith won the day, and the Nicene Creed proclaimed, 'We believe in one God, the Father Almighty, Maker of all things visible and in- visible. And in one Lord Jesus Christ, the Son of God, the only begotten of the Father, that is, of the essence of the Father, God of God, Light of Light, very God of very God, begotten, not made, being of one substance with the Father.'

During this tremendous challenge to the faith, Athanasius virtually stood alone. Other believers believed as he did, but none fought as he fought. At one point a friend said to him, "Athanasius, the world is against you.' This warrior replied, 'So be it. Then Athanasius is against the world!' Athanasius *contra mumdum*–Athaniasus against the world.'

Well, that's all fine and dandy, we fathers say. The guy lived 1650 years ago, and confrontation was expected then, but we have progressed to the point where we look upon that sort of thing as being a bit uncivilized. We fathers don't want to have a reputation for being contentious. 'tis best, we fathers believe, to roll with the punches and try to get along. We fathers no longer have the strength of our convictions because we no longer have convictions. Athanasius seems strange to us today because he believed something to the point of personal inconvenience. He almost single-handedly defended the orthodox doctrine at Nicea. He boldly challenged the ambivalent Emperor Constantine who wanted Arius readmitted to the church. Athanasius was falsely accused of sabotage, witchcraft, graft and murder, he was attacked in his church several times and was banished from the realm on at least five separate occasions. Athanasius, no doubt, could have lived a quiet, peaceful, comfortable life except for one little problem—he believed something! Athanasius believed something and was willing to defend that which he believed. He gave no thought to his own personal comfort when the object of his belief was attacked. What Athanasius believed was the truth of God; thus he received grace to stand against the world in defense of God's truth. The twentieth century, no less than the fourth, has heresies which would supplant the truth of God, idols which would receive the worship which is due to God alone, pagan philosophies which would deform and destroy the people of God. In the fourth century, *one man* prepared himself to stand for God, and the purity of the church's doctrine was preserved.

Today, there are innumerable abominations which would seek to capture the minds of God's people. And who will arise to defend God's truth? Perhaps we will not have our names written in the history books as did Athanasius, but every father can stand before his family as God's representative and proclaim and defend God's truth.

Perhaps our efforts will not influence the entire church as did Athanasius's, But they can bless and prosper our family. Perhaps we will not turn back the forces of darkness from every corner of the world, but we can say, 'In this my house, God's truth will be established, honored, and praised. The blasphemies of the world will not breech the sanctity of this place. When the pagan philos- ophies of our age seek to capture my family, I will stand against them and, by the grace of God, defeat them and destroy them.'

Athanasius went to the council of Nicea as a scribe and a helper. He left as the champion of God's truth. He was prepared and his preparation was re- warded. Every father has a little flock to guard and nurture and cherish. Dad must be prepared, must study God's truth, because the enemy will seek to snatch the lambs from the little flock. Little lambs can't fight this fight; they need a shepherd, a guardian, a champion, a warrior to protect them. They need someone to stand, if need be, against the world. Dad *contra mundum*— Dad against the World!"[21]

By Dr. W. David Gamble

(Reprinted by permission from American Reformation Movement, 7341 Clairemont Mesa Blvd., San Diego, CA 82111)

What it means to have the character trait of **A HEART TO STAND ALONE:**

- A heart that has counted the cost and is prepared to stand alone for truth and what is right
- The ability to forsake the approval of all men for the approval of one man, our Lord and Savior, Jesus Christ
- The ability to go it alone in life even if no one joins you
- The grace to forsake all for what is right

HEART WILLING TO SUFFER, A — **Study start date:** _____ **Finish date:** _____

As a believer, we will all be called on to suffer persecution for the Name to some degree. Persecution has simply been described as God's income tax. It is indeed a great honor to be counted worthy to suffer to any degree for that Name. James said we should "count it all joy when (we) fall into various trials" for the testing of our faith. (James 1:2) Jesus told us there will come a day when they will actually deliver us up to councils and we will be brought before governors and kings for His Name's sake. He went on to say we "will be hated by all for (His) name's sake. But He who endures to the end will be saved." (Matthew 10:22) God promised us grace for these things if we have the right heart, when they come to us.

In today's technical world, there will also be little to no success in the workplace without suffering in both preparation and service. Everybody wants to win the race, get the prize and have the million dollar business but precious few are willing to pay the price. The price, simply stated, in every field of endeavor is preparation and suffering–and that doesn't come cheap. If there is no pain, there will likely be no progress. In a world full of couch potatoes, those willing to prepare for battle, practice for tournaments, suffer for a cause or their religion or lay a foundation for a career, are few and far between. Suffering may not be one of the most glamorous of concepts out in the world today but it may be one of the most important obtaining success. You see, successful people are the ones who are willing to do the things unsuccessful people refuse to do. Success in business or any field of endeavor, comes from preparation, faithfulness, hard work, long hours and years of obtaining and improving one's character. All of these things will come only one way and can be summed up in one word: suffering. No body, for example, wants to remain faithful when they feel like they have been slighted. Well, there is a character trait that will solve that problem in an instant: forbearance. No matter where you might work, things are never going to go exactly your way all the time and your boss is never going to see everything just like you do. In these times, let it roll off your back like so much water down the drain, double down, remain faithful and go back to work. Know that the boss will probably find the truth about it all later and get it corrected in the future but keep your head down and keep driving on. You'll be glad you did.

Obtaining success in life is no secret. There are principles of success out there that work over and over for anyone who is willing to work them. You can pick them up from supervisors, co-workers, books, magazines, newspaper articles and especially the Bible. In fact, most success books are just reiterations of principles author has taken from the Bible

Sometimes on the job a person might be confronted with a boss or two they don't respect, care for or even like. Most will not be willing to serve them as unto the Lord and wait for God's promotion process to kick in so they just quit. They immediately lose all that seed time and planting they have done there. I call suffering in this way eating dirt. I knew a fella in the real estate business that moved his license from one company to another every six months. He always had a problem about this or that and didn't get it his was so he got up and left. It happened over and over. To get anywhere in this crazy world, one must be humble and willing to eat a little dirt occasionally. You aren't going to always have it just like you want it everywhere you go in life. In addition, you have to pay your dues in most career fields. If you can't respect your boss, at least realize all authority on the planet comes from God and respect their office. Forget who they are and what they are and turn your work into them as unto the Lord. (Colossians 3:23) It sure makes working for them a whole lot easier. God will take care of them in His time, don't worry. The leader will likely make some discrepencies up to you in time.

A case in point is a good friend of mine, we'll call him Dave, who went to work for a major corporation the day he graduated from college in an entry-level sales slot. Being a people person and one of the most efficient and capable people I have met, he always exceeded the sales quotas given him and naturally made life-long friends both inside and outside the company. He never worked anywhere else all of his adult life. There were, however, many problems there and he faced a number of personal challenges from both those around and above him. He certainly earned it but they paid him well and during this time he accepted Christ. Otherwise, he might not have had the grace to stay with it. The man who had taken over as President of the company had several well educated sons just a little younger than Dave working there as well. Problems kept cropping up. Nepotism crept in even more. Then one of the territory managers got involved in an illicit relationship with another staff member. One of the leaders of the company told Dave, "If it is not hurting the company financially, you need to just forget about it." To this Dave replied, "If we have to have that conversation, we don't need to have that conversation. If you allow that kind of stuff to go on, a whole lot of worse things are going to start happening." Instead of reacting to these people and because he had no direct control or influence over them, he just personally refused to compromise and started praying for them. His prayer was for God to arrest them, come into their lives and deliver them.

Another time, one of the owner's sons started tapping Dave's phone line and listening to his conversations as well as those with other officers of the company. When the equipment was found, verified by other leaders of the company and all of this was reported to the president. He then confronted his son, who promptly denied it. The president of the company got back with Dave and said, "He told me he didn't do it and I have to believe him." Dave left all this with the Lord and persevered, continuing to do an excellent job. A few years later when the president retired, because of Dave's production, perseverance, organizational ability and character, incredibly, he made Dave president and CEO of the company. He worked for that company for over forty years, starting out, as I said as a salesman and ended up CEO and the largest stock holder in the company. God certainly rewarded his tenacity and willingness to suffer wrongs.

What it means to have the character trait of **A HEART WILLING TO SUFFER**:

- The ability to postpone gratification and endure hardships to obtain a future goal
- The ability to take criticism, punishment, death, pain or take a loss in order to stay consistent with one's character and beliefs
- The ability to labor long, hard and even under duress in order to obtain
- The ability to pay a price for success, excellence or to win a contest
- The willingness to pay the price to incorporate success principles and character in one's life

HEART TO TAKE A STAND, A —   Study start date: _____ Finish date: _____

In a society like ours here in America, many things are decided by the ballot box, so many, in fact, that most people are scared to death to take a stand against the majority for anything. Sadly, being politically correct is the order of the day for most. How tormenting it must be to be bound by the shackles of public opinion. True freedom is to live in pursuit of the truth, dedicated, unflinchingly, to its advancement, whatever the price.

Just think, the majority has almost never been right. Ten of the twelve spies who went in to search out the land of Canaan were wrong. They said "We are not able to go up against the people (of the land) because they are too strong for us." (Numbers 13:31) Only two, Joshua and Caleb, got it right. Caleb's report to Moses was, "We should by all means go up and take possession of it, for surely we shall overcome it." Only Noah and his family had it right when it was time to build a boat. Other than his little family of eight, the whole world was wrong at that moment and paid the ultimate price for being wrong. Jesus told all His followers, "Stay in Jerusalem and wait until I send you power." There were thousands of Christians by that time but only the minority, 120, waited in the upper room for the fulfillment of the promise, the Day of Pentecost. When Jesus went to the cross, all His disciples had it wrong, forsook him and departed.

Back in my early twenties I read a book my Niccolo Machiavelli called *The Prince* and *The Discourses* which happened to be required reading at West Point back then. It is actually two books in one, written years ago by an advisor to a prince for the purpose of giving him insight on how to be a great king. Among many other things, he said it is far better in life for a prince to be decisive and choose a side. Human nature is to vacillate and defer for fear of making a mistake or making those on one side of the issue or the other unhappy. He opined that in most situations, all things being equal, you have a 50/50 chance of being on the winning side, whatever you decide. If the side you chose wins, to the victor goes the spoils. If you fail to take a side, you can never win. Even if the side you chose should lose, and you retain your head, you are still at least respected greatly by both sides as being a man of conviction.

Don't know why it is but it seems like everyone I had a fight with in school growing up, when it was all over and the smoke cleared, we ended up respecting each other all the more afterwards. And besides, like they have always said, "A coward dies a thousand times but the brave only die once." If you refuse to take a stand, you won't be respected by either side. Cowards and fence straddling milquetoasts are despised universally.

There is no freedom like the freedom of being true to God and yourself. You won't even like yourself if you don't stand for something. Being a true friend is the stuff life-long-friendships are made of. Equity and truth make it our duty to be a true enemy of those not on the side of right. Being on the side of right is the part we are all to play in advancing society to its rightful place. It is so fulfilling when you stand with others in their plight on the side of truth and see it all the way to victory. God is asking the same question of men today: "Who will rise up for me against the evil doers? Who will stand up for me against the workers of iniquity?" Psalm 94:16

What it means to have the character trait of **A HEART TO TAKE A STAND:**

* Willingness to stand when others retreated to the shadows
* A willingness to stand no matter what the cost

- Having a forehead like flint
- Realizing the majority has just about never been right
- Willing to risk one's reputation for the side of truth and right
- Being sold out to God unto death

HEART TO WORK FOR FAVOR, A — Study start date: _____ Finish date: _____

Unfortunately, most people in the world work just to complete a task. Many just work for "eye service" and do only what they must to get by. A few work do their work with excellence, motivated strictly by the money and the hope of a promotion so they can make more money. It's all about what's in it for them. Equally sad is the fact that people who work for money are not aware that they will never be happy simply because nobody ever thinks they are paid what they deserve. This is a never-ending search for something that is just not out there. They will never get paid enough and will never find the Land of Pay Utopia. Working for money binds and imprisons one in the chains of self-centeredness and making daily decisions through the myopic lens of "What's in it for me?" Although there is certainly some satisfaction for everyone in a job well done, it pales in comparison to the opportunity of working in this world for favor.

People who work for money are trying to please flesh and blood person, namely their boss. Working for men is, in and of itself, quite difficult because all men are imperfect at best. They have their own problems and are usually hard to please. Incidentally, men, as we know, will also let you down but… . God won't.

There is, however, a plausible alternative: working as unto the Lord. Those who work for the Lord work to please Him. They work for His favor and are able to work in love. They not only want to do a job well but, along with it and more importantly and in addition, want to please the leader God has placed over them at a particular time in life. Since they work for the Lord, every leader is in the place of God in their hearts and minds. Now think just a minute, if God was really their boss, how hard would they work for Him? Would they get to work early, stay late, be willing to endure difficult circumstances, dangerous duty and toil at small tasks without recognition? Yes, I expect they would.

Walking in divine favor

Certainly everyone needs money but money won't make you happy and will quickly evade your grasp. "When you set your eyes upon it, it is gone." It has the built in capacity to "make itself wings, like the eagle that flies away toward heaven." (Proverbs 23:5) When you work for money, all you will ever receive is that small amount of money, a few atta-boys and maybe an occasional pay raise.

If, on the other hand, you work for favor, there is no end to what may come your way. Nehemiah worked as a slave for a heathen king. When he needed to return to his hometown to rebuild the walls, the king not only let him go, gave him all the timber for building the gates, letters to the governors along the way to give him favor and ultimately setting him over the entire task. Mainly the king wanted to know how soon he could come back because he liked having him around. Before asking the king for all the materials and permission to go, he prefaced it all by these revealing words: "If I your servant has found favor in thy sight …" (Nehemiah 2:5) Nehemiah had made himself liked, trusted and almost indispensable. Note, he didn't ask, "If I have done a good job." No, no, no. He asked, "… if I your servant has found favor in thy sight."

Daniel also wise enough to find favor working under six heathen kings as well as the chief of the eunuchs. He was promoted, in the end, to supreme president over all the presidents of the land. Joseph found favor as a slave under Potiphar such that everything in his realm became his responsibility. The only thing Potiphar thought about is what he might want to eat next. When thrown in prison, falsely accused by Potiphar's wife, Joseph soon found favor in the eyes of the head jailer and was placed in charge of everything in the prison. His friends might have forgotten him but God didn't He subsequently became prime minister, second only to pharaoh. After the death of her husband, Ruth found favor in the sight of Boaz because her reputation for being a loyal and faithful servant to her mother-in-law. More importantly, as Boaz was about to bless Ruth personally, we see where he said her reward was really coming from. He stated, "The Lord repay your work, and a full reward be given you by the Lord God of Israel, under whose wings you have come to trust." Ruth 2:10–12

If we will learn to work for favor and to honor our leaders as we would God, Himself, He promises to "bless (us and) … with favor (He) will surround (us) as with a shield." Psalm 5:12

Working for favor results in:

- Heart felt appreciation shown a subordinate by his leaders
- Tokens of love, appreciation, partiality and kindness usually shown openly and conspicuously by a superior to a follower
- Unbelievable advantages, preferences, care shown to and promotions given to a loyal and devoted servant
- Being placed in positions of high trust and responsibility far beyond what might be commensurate to one's skill, age and experience

What it means to have the character trait of **A HEART TO WORK FOR FAVOR:**

- Making it our goal to learn to be the best follower or servant possible
- Making it our goal to be a profitable servant (one who always does more than is expected or required)
- Always working with the motive of making those around us great in the eyes of the Lord.
- Always helping others around you finish their tasks well and giving them all the credit
- Always thinking of things you would like to see in an employee and doing them yourself
- Always thinking ahead to what the leader and your group needs next and making it easier for others
- Being a permanent volunteer. Tell your leader if he ever needs anyone to volunteer to do anything, especially difficult tasks and things no one else wants to do, you are volunteering.
- Purpose to be so efficient and effective that you become your leader's "go-to man"; the one he always thinks of for the "mission impossible"
- Although you never mention it, letting the fact that you always get the job done be your trademark in life

- Knowing that there is only one time we can be a blessing to our leader and bring honor to his company, business or ministry and it is right now
- It is having the goal of making your company the most profitable and successful in your market or area (even if you make it happen and don't get an extra dime). Do it in love. Do it because you and God can. Do it to be a blessing and be thankful for the opportunities you have been afforded. Life is not all about the money. Forget about self—"God is a rewarder of the diligent seeker." Hebrews 11:6
- It is important to look for the good in your leader. Nobody is perfect. Be thankful for the good you see in him and show him respect. Overlook his flaws and maybe God will overlook some of yours.
- Some followers are high maintenance: stubborn, selfish, uncommitted, cavalier, contemptuous, argumentative, and indifferent They can't follow instructions, always know a better way, sloppy, etc. Make a list of what you don't want to be like.
- Be an easy-to- lead follower who is responsive to help in times of trouble and loyal in times of testing and adversity.
- Give everybody 110% all the time on everything
- Refuse to forsake "mercy and truth . .(in fact) bind them around your neck, write them on the tablet of your heart … (then you) will find favor and high esteem in the sight of God and man." Proverbs 3:3,4
- Remember, he who earnestly seeks good for those above, around and under him, will find favor. Proverbs 11:27
- Gladly give credit to all those around and under you for their contributions. "Bless and curse not" as Joseph did.
- Serve with excellence to honor and bless but do not be an apple polisher. Keep your integrity.

When time passes and you have moved on to other tasks in life, you will always be able to look back and it won't be on all the awards, promotions and bonuses you received from a job well done that come to mind. What will make you shed a little tear of joy for your service is the tremendous bond of mutual trust, respect and admiration you shared with your leader and the difficulty of the tasks that were placed in your hands. You will remember how much joy you brought to your leader and how thankful he was to have you on his team in the battle. Those things are permanently etched in the heart and are never lost by the sands of time. Why is all this so? Because a loyal and faithful servant is truly rewarded in all ways, not the least of which is the heart.

For fear that some will miss the reality and power of God's favor, please allow me to give Him the credit for a few of the things He has done in my life. I have never been the smartest, strongest or swiftest at anything. It is all God's favor.

- At Tarleton State Univ. God favored me to be a member of the drill team and was later designated Best Drilled Freshman in the Corps
- While at Texas A&M He enabled me to start the Society of American Military Engineers. It grew to over 200 members in two years and accomplished quite a bit. Our club was presented the Distinguished Student Post Award.
- The summer before my senior year at A&M, I attended R.O.T.C. Training Camp at Ft. Sill, Oklahoma with a group of other college seniors. God allowed me to be rated number two out of 2,000 and first of my classmates at Texas A&M.

- Was nominated by my Brigade Commander to compete against the best platoon leaders of the other two brigades to be aide to the Commanding General. Well, God let me get the job and later the General gave me an Army Commendation Medal.
- God gave me a company command in Vietnam as a lieutenant (a Captain's job) and another they promoted me to Captain.
- In the field there in Vietnam, it seemed like we were in contact with the enemy all the time. On one occasion we were in a battle of some sort for 51 days in a row—without a change of clothes or a shower. My command group was always right in the middle of the two platoons spread out on the front edge of the battle line. My mortar platoon was to our rear and the enemy knew the commander was right in the middle with three radio men with whip antennas sticking up in the air next to him. I was holding the phone sets directing the battle all the time. Most of the enemy's fire went to the middle and toward the mortars going off. That was where I was. No telling how many thousands of times I have been shot at. People were getting shot and killed right next to me but, thank God for His amazing favor, I never got a scratch.

I believe that God pre-ordained a plan for my life and work if only we will accept it.. Only by His grace I have experienced favor far more than I deserve which has enabled me to work on accomplishing that plan. I could go on and on about His favor in business and the ministry. What a way to live! If He could do all this for me, think what he would do for you?

ELPFULNESS — **Study start date:** _____ **Finish date:** _____

Have you ever worked with a group of people to accomplish a task and felt like you were right in the middle of a den of rattle snakes? Some of those team members might even have been so brazen as to let you know that they were only there to do their specific job description and were not about to help anyone else on the team. They were doing their task and that was it. This is not helpfulness and these are not the vibes we want to be sending out.

On the other hand, we would do well to be telegraphing a spirit of meekness, sincerity, cooperation and congeniality. Other folks not only give that impression but show by our actions and attitude. Still others are glad to be there for us and are happy to help anytime we might have a need. Not only that but when the job is finished, they are happy to give others all the credit.

Our coworkers should feel that we are always ready to go the extra mile to help them. For this to be a reality, we need to maintain a deep desire to help and make others look good as well as to make their job easier over the long term. To do this in a wicked world, we must have the heart of a servant. Helpfulness is an attitude as well as a state of mind. It is not waiting to be asked for help but is always looking for every opportunity to be of service to someone.

A servant's heart is the key but a true servant's heart can only be received as a gift from God and, therefore, like everything else in God's Kingdom, one must ask for it and receive it by faith. We are all born selfish by nature so this attitude can't just be "put on." It shouldn't be this way but, amazingly, even the best service we give others, many times in life, will not be appreciated. For various selfish reasons: jealousy, competition, biases, etc., some will fail to respond as they should to the help we have freely given them. Regardless, a servant's heart is a winsome attitude everywhere and all the time. Ultimately, it will be rewarded—even if not in this life. Go ahead; do the work and forget about yourself. Helping others and the satisfaction it brings is its own reward even if there were no other immediate or long-term benefits. "Finding a need and filling it" is exactly what a servant's heart has made a habit of. Don't be surprised if this attitude causes you to stumble, unexpectedly upon many great ways to serve. Opportunity has always been cleverly disguised as hard work, no pay, no recognition and a lot of responsibility. Rather, it is always a joy to even attempt to be a blessing to others.

None of us are here on this earth very long. Our time is shorter than any of us think and it is up before we know it. However, when looking back, the times we cherish most are the times of serving and really helping others without anyone else knowing it.

What it means to have the character trait of **HELPFULNESS:**

- Endeavoring to be of assistance to those around us
- Thinking about how we can help our coworkers and doing it cheerfully and covertly
- Taking on the office of a servant to others, desiring no recognition
- To further and advance someone else's cause
- To give relief
- Volunteering to take a turn when we don't even have the requirement
- Privately taking great joy in making others look good and succeed
- Making one's self useful
- Looking for opportunities to assist
- Going beyond what is expected or required to do

HONESTY— **Study start date:** _____ **Finish date:** _____

I t seems today, that honesty has all but completely disappeared in America— from the outhouse to the White House. A person who will tell you the truth, no matter what, is a rare find in the world today. However, the very survival of our entire society and governmental system is based solely on trust between its citizens. The basic ability to rely on the truthfulness of the words, statements, reports and promises of others and to work according to outlined procedures and functions with others. Without honesty no society can exist. There can be no community without mutual reliance among its contributing members. For this reason, a truly honest person is highly valued in society today.

There has to come a day in the life of every human being when they stop the merry-go-round in life and make the decision to drive their stakes down and start telling the truth. This is the birth place of honesty—where they decide that they will no longer bend the truth, color it, shade it grey, twist it, tell half of it or otherwise do it torture but be straight up honest at all times.

Theirs then becomes a life that God can bless.

- What it means to have the character trait of **HONESTY**:
- Being truthful
- Having integrity
- Veracity
- Having scruples
- Being reputable
- Moral rectitude
- No admixture
- Being frank and sincere
- Being free from fraud and deception
- Being candid, upright and innocent
- Straightforwardness
- Not bending, coloring, shading, twisting or otherwise doing torture to the truth
- Character that is upright in planning, communication, record keeping and actions
- Telling the truth even when feeling inadequate
- Making a report accurately even when confronted with the very real possibility of being found out for having done something foolish, shameful, wrong or embarrassing
- Not cheating on tests
- The wisdom to make yourself accountable for things that belong to others by keeping receipts for everything that costs more than 10 cents
- Not taking what does not belong to you
- Giving others the credit they deserve and not taking it for yourself
- Unwilling to cheat no matter how high the stakes or bribe

OPE—   **Study start date: _____ Finish date: _____**

Ever wonder why so many people seem to fail in life? Why, when placed in a difficult or trying situation, they suddenly "snap" and do the wrong thing. The main causes for failure is people lose hope for a very specific but little known reason. God has designed life so that we will all be tested and sooner or later and our situation will, in fact, look hopeless. It is going to look like we are up against a wall and there is no way out. The other problem is that most people have their hope in this present world. Actually, you see, everyone has hope. The problem lies with what they have placed their hope in. To get ahead, most trust in education, skill, a well-paying job, banks, the government, contrivances like partnerships, doing a good job, etc. They are trying to find these elusive things called success, security and happiness. Actually, there is certainly nothing wrong with gaining an education or doing a good job, for example, but our hope must be in the Lord and not this present world. Why? Because this world and its systems are failing, falling apart and dying all around us. Ostensibly it tries to give every assurance that we can trust in it but the world and its systems can never be relied upon. We will lose hope quickly if we trust in it. Hopelessness sets in and soon becomes despair and then moves one quickly to self-pity. Self-pity, though not a permanent state, happens to be the devil's most powerful secret weapon. In a world that is rarely fair, injustices can quickly motivate people to become self-appointed vigilantes. They want to rectify the situation, feeling like they have been wronged and have every right to in their own mind, and take justice in their own hands. Soon they begin engaging some of the most despicable acts known to man. This is the same motivation behind people deciding to steal from their companies, hire hit men to kill their mate or business partner and many other terrible acts not worthy of mention.

Those with their eyes on the world system can't help but lose heart because all its systems are based on three things: fear, death and selfishness. Everything in the world is dying. Every blade of grass that springs up out of the ground is born to die, as is every living thing. Plants start dying the moment the seed germinated in the ground. When the cells of a man and woman unite in the womb for the first time, the newly created being starts the dying process as well. Every child born of a woman is dying. Nations are dying, having a life expectancy for the most part of less than two hundred years. Businesses are dying because of any number of forces impacting them. Their products are becoming obsolete, they may experience the problem of an internal moral failure or increased competition, just to name a few. Because of selfishness, no one is satisfied and neither can they be apart from living for God. The stock market wants more profit. The banks want more interest. The drug addict wants more and more powerful drugs. The greedy want more money and the list goes on. Everything is dying, nothing satisfies, nothing lasts and nothing is sufficient. Why? Because the world just will not satisfy.

But, praise God, there is hope! In Romans 15:13 we find these words recorded: "Now may the God of hope fill you with all joy and peace in believing, that you may abound in hope by the power of the Holy Spirit." Paul starts out by saying, "Now." Aren't you glad our God is not a god of tomorrow or next year but the God of Now and wants us to have hope and have a faith that makes things happen right now. (Hebrews 11:1) Then we find that our God is also quite an authority on the subject of hope. He doesn't just know somewhat about it, He isn't just an expert on the subject of hope, He is "The God of hope" who is able to fill us with all joy and peace in believing. Enough hope that we may abound in it. Keep in mind now that to fill means full that means something is so full it can't receive any more. But, this passage goes on to say that we can also "abound in hope." To abound means to have a rich, abundant supply or to overflow with something but this, for anyone, only comes about through God, by the power of the Holy Spirit. We are talking about a power so great it is no less than God Himself being involved as well as the resurrection power of the Holy Spirit. Hope is one of the most powerful forces known to man and all believers actually possess it to some degree. What we are talking about is the contented and joyful expectation when one's faith has attached itself to God's will and for it to come to pass regardless of the situation. . Hope defies reason, common sense, time, physical limitations, the laws of nature, circumstances and all odds. Hope is the size of the sail on a person's ship of faith and it is able to drive them through life and over life's obstacles..

In regard to hope, man has only two choices and we find them listed in Jeremiah 17:5. We can either be cursed or be blessed. Because, "Cursed is the man that trusteth in man, and maketh flesh His arm, and whose heart departeth from the Lord." The man who sets his hope in the world, trusting in men, man's systems, machines, contrivances, weapons and institutions is already cursed by God, Himself. "He shall be like a shrub in the desert, and shall not see when good cometh, but shall inhabit the parched places in the wilderness, in a salt land and not inhabited."

The other choice is, of course, to be blessed. Jeremiah 17:7 says "Blessed is the man who trusteth in the Lord, and whose hope the Lord is. For he shall be like a tree planted by the waters and that spreadeth out her roots by the river, and shall not see when heat cometh, but her leaf shall be green; and shall not be anxious in the year of drought, neither shall cease from yielding fruit." Now a tree planted by the river is alive, growing and secure. In the year of drought it doesn't even need rain but continues to bear fruit because its roots go down and tap into the invisible water table below ground by the stream. The world system has no provision for drought, war, disease, divorce, etc. There is no relief for disasters like tornados, fire or deceit which is out of control in the world today but God's system does. He says that those who build upon the Rock in their personal, business, family and financial life will never cease to bear fruit. This tree will be alive, will stand for something and will not be moved. Psalm 46:4 goes on to say, "There is a river, the streams whereof shall make glad the city of God." When trials, trouble, deceit and discouragement come against us, as surely they will, we have a river to drink from that will forever make us glad, so glad that we will never, ever lose hope. The important thing, as mentioned, is where our hope is placed.

Psalm 78 admonishes us to listen intently to the words of God and the importance of every father teaching their children to teach their children the most important lesson of their life. What is it? To "set their hope in God and not forget the works of God." (Psalm 78:7) We are to teach them about all His marvelous acts and His mighty deliverances of old. Then he warns us of what will happen to those who fail in this regard. He says, there will always be some who do "not set their heart aright, and whose spirit (is) not steadfast with (Him)." (v.8) They will be like the children of Ephraim (a tribe of the Hebrew children) who "though being armed and carrying bows, turned back in the day of battle." (v.9) Why were they found to be cowards? Verse 22 tells us: "Because they did not believe in God and did not trust in His salvation (which includes deliverance)." Not having set one's hope in God, anyone would be terrified in the face of mortal combat. Like the Ephriamites, as this Psalm says, they will run like cowards. Just everyday life on the planet today can get pretty testy and can, at times, be totally overwhelming for those who haven't set their hope in the Master.

What does it mean to set one's hope in God? It is simply to love Him with all your heart, mind and soul and to put Him and his Kingdom first. It is to realize that your life, your breath and all your ways are in His hands anyway. (Daniel 5:23) For that reason alone, we have nothing to fear. It is to know that all we have or ever will have both now and eternally will come from Him. He alone is the rewarder of the diligent seeker. (Hebrews 11:6) It is for us to humble ourselves under His mighty hand and know that we are here just to please Him. Then, when all our ways please Him, we will live our life to the full, until it overflows. He becomes our God, our master, provider, protector and deliverer. With our hope in God, He is all we will ever need.

It is important to note that God always uses the most impossible situations to prove His point. In this regard, Abraham was chosen as our example. Abraham, was not just a faith man, he was the father of faith and the friend of God. This is important because we know the just must live by faith and that faith is the only way we can please Him. However, faith can't operate alone. It needs the help of a couple other agents. One is love because Galatians 5:6 tells us "Faith worketh (operates) by love." This means we need to first start using our faith, not for ourselves, but to believe for the needs of others.

Another indispensable ingredient needed to operate our faith, of course, is hope. In this regard, "Faith is the substance of things hoped for and the evidence of things not seen." (Hebrews 11:1) Faith is not the substance and evidence of just anything and everything but only those things hoped for. Hope is the invisible image of what faith will bring into fruition. Hope is a contented and joyful expectation! Romans 4:18 says, Abraham "hoped against hope" That is he hoped without any basis according to human understanding but "Against hope" he "believed in hope." He hoped against hope (because all the facts said, "No.") He still believed God and "became the father of many nations, according to that which was spoken …" The facts of his circumstance were crying out in hope against the hope that was in him. His wife's womb was dead and he was about a hundred years old himself but, praise God, he wouldn't consider his own body. He only considered the Word of God that was spoken over him and he knew God was not only able but would definitely somehow make His promise good. Later, we know, he

Abraham about to sacrifice his son, Isaac

was tested to see if he would be willing to sacrifice his only son, the son of promise, for God.

Ever wondered why there is usually a lapse of time, a void, an expanse or a waiting period between the giving of the promise and the performance of most important things we are believing for in life? Well, there are now and always have been many unbelievers who want things to happen too. Not being rooted and grounded in faith, serving the Lord for love's sake. They have not died to self and are not willing to endure hardship or persecution for the Word's sake. Their hope quickly fades, shrivels up and is blown away by the wind in times of testing. These are the times when all the natural indicators point to hopelessness and death as they most often do in trials of faith. They quickly give up and go back to trusting in the world system. This is why the Word says it is only through faith and patience that we inherit the promises. (Hebrews 6:12) God is not a rewarder of everyone, just the diligent seeker who has patience. (Hebrews 11:6), These are the ones with true grit who will serve Him even if it appears they are about to be burned up in the firey furnace, devoured by lions or have to live in caves and wear sheepskins for clothes. Their hope in God is not diminished. Hebrews 11:1 tells us that faith is both "substance" and "evidence" but not of just anything. "Faith is the substance of things hoped for and the evidence of things not seen" but hoped for anyway. Having hope is crucial in the area of faith because without hope our faith is hopeless.

Every one of us, if we are still alive, is now fully embarked upon our own voyage of faith in life. We are all riding in our very own ship of faith and most of us have set our compasses and sails for the Harbor of Heaven as our destination. The size of our sail is the exact size of the hope in God we have in our hearts. Since the sail is always what our faith gets behind to move us along in the spirit really, the bigger it is, the faster and more surely we go. We will all, sooner or later, find ourselves out on the raging sea with huge waves of depression, discouragement and despair pounding against us. These aren't just little slaps at the sides of the ship, they can become tidal waves capable of capsizing our ship so we must have an anchor and the one we need is described in Hebrews 6:19. The "hope we have as an anchor of (our) soul, both sure and steadfast, and which enters the Presence behind the veil." This is a hope that is out of this world. It leaves this universe and goes off into eternity, into Heaven and anchors itself under the Rock of Ages, under nothing less than the Throne of Jesus Christ in Heaven!!! There is no failure or dying in Heaven and certainly not under the throne of Christ. His rule is without beginning or end and His promises are from everlasting to everlasting. When we are anchored in Him, our ship will never capsize. All our hope is in Him alone! I Peter 1:3 says it this way: "Blessed be the God and Father of our Lord Jesus Christ, who according to His abundant mercy has begotten us again to a living hope through the resurrection of Jesus Christ from the dead." Yes, the fountainhead of the hope we have is anchored in nothing less than the death, burial and resurrection of Jesus Christ. Nothing in the universe could be more real, more powerful or more sure than our hope when it is in Him. Where is this hope? The only place it will work and that is Christ in you. "Christ in you the hope of glory." Colossians 1:2

What it means to have the character trait of **HOPE**:

- Great expectation
- The power of man's soul to endure
- Confidence in something happening when there is no assurance or visible possibility of it
- Longing for something with the assurance of obtainment
- To expect against all odds, with great desire for good things to happen
- Trust in God's promises that they will surely come to pass
- Reliance upon the unseen forces of the Almighty
- Being anchored in Christ!

OSPITALITY—   **Study start date:** _____ **Finish date:** _____

In days long ago, before civilization and population centers began to build inns, it was considered one's duty to accept, lodge, feed and even protect a traveler who might have happened by and stopped at one's door. When treated as a guest of the family, the stranger often developed a bond of friendship that lasted, in many cases, from generation to generation. The Law of Moses commanded this of the Hebrew children: "The stranger who dwells among you shall be to you as one born among you, and you shall love him as yourself; for you were strangers in the land of Egypt: I am the Lord your God." Absent this kind of admonition, because of man's fallen, fearful and selfish nature, foreigners who happened among them would likely have been rejected or discriminated against in many ways. Job, one of the most blessed men of his day, received God's favor for a number of reasons, not the least of which was his compassion for the poor, the down trodden and the wayfaring man. The Bible records that, "… no sojourner had to lodge in the street" because Job "opened (his) doors to the traveler." Job 31:32

The importance of this duty under the law was carried into the New Testament under the law of love. Paul, while outlining some of the more important duties of Christians in Hebrews 13:1, penned these words: "Let brotherly love continue. Do not forget to entertain strangers, for by so doing some have unwittingly entertained angels." Foreigners who cross our path in life may be put there as a test of the faith, love and hospitality we have in our heart. From this we see they could actually be angels.

The consequence of neglecting the law of hospitality is shown in the story of David's confrontation with Nabal and Abigail in a time of war. David and his men were continually risking their very lives to protect the Israelites and supplies for his men were scarce. Nabal, on the contrary, was living in Carmel in total prosperity. Although corrupt and crafty in his business practices, He had great possessions, not the least of which were his three thousand sheep and a thousand goats. David and his men were in the wilderness and very hungry about this time so he dispatched ten of men to seek some assistance from Nabal who was shearing the sheep at the time. Nabal was also mightily blessed with a beautiful wife, Abigail, who also had the grace of good understanding. The men were told how to go to Nabal in David's name and make a gentle appeal for help in whatever form he might be hospitable enough to provide them. When they arrived and spoke gently according to David's request, Nabal replied as if he didn't know who David was and further inquired as to why he should take the meat, bread and water he had for his shearers and give it to strangers? Upon hearing this from his returning servants, David commanded four hundred of his men to put on their swords and accompany him while the other two hundred were to stay with their baggage.

Incidentally, one of David's men told Abigail what her husband had done and his total disregard for all David's kindness and protection. He also said David's army was marching against Nabal and his house because he was such a son of Belial. She immediately had five sheep dressed and gathered two hundred loaves of bread, five measures of parched corn, two hundred cakes of figs, a hundred clusters of raisins and two bottles of wine and had her servants take them to David on donkeys. Abigail instructed her servants to go out to David before her and mentioned that she would be along right behind them. When she came down over a hill, David and his men met her and recounted his disdain for Nabal's horrible treatment of his men and disregard for his protection. Seeing his fury, she jumped off her ass and fell face down at David's feet. She admitted that her husband had acted very badly but that she had not been present and had not seen these young men. Then she mentioned the blessing she had just sent to David and his men and asked for him to forgive the trespass of her husband and recounted all the good she knew David had done in his life. She prayed that all David's house would be secure and his enemies would be as a rock slung out of his slingshot. She said it was her desire that this occasion not be an offense to him, that he would not shed this blood without a cause and that he would soon be ruler over all Israel. She concluded by asking David to remember her when the Lord had dealt well with him in the future.

At this, David blessed the God of Israel for sending her that day. He also blessed her personally and for her advice turning him from avenging himself against her husband with his own hands. Had she not come, her husband and all his house would surely have been dead by morning. David then said, she should go in peace to her house because he accepted what she had brought, had harkened to her request and had accepted her person as well as her petition. .

However, when Abigail returned, she found her husband was banqueting like a king. She wisely waited until the next morning when Nabal had awaken from his drunken stupor to tell him of the great peril they faced and what she had done to avert it. It was then that his heart failed him and became like a stone. About ten days later, the Lord struck Nabal and he died.

When David heard the news, he blessed the Lord for avenging Nabal's contempt and for keeping him from returning his wickedness on his own head. He also sent word by his men to Abigail asking her to be his wife. She, very humbly, returned with the men on her ass with the five maids who attended her. This woman's hospitality saved the lives of all who were in her house, caused the Lord to avenge her husband's contempt and elevated her to be a queen in Israel.(I Samuel 25:4–38(Hospitality is a powerful thing.

In Titus 1:8, hospitability is listed as one of the qualifications for elders. It is also cited in I Peter 4:9 as one of the ways we are to show fervent love for others in that, specifically, we should be "hospitable to one another" and do it "without grumbling." God has given all of us the gift of grace in many different ways so that each of us can minister to those in need and bring glory to the Name. Again, when describing to the Romans how Christians are to walk in love, Paul said we need to be ready to distribute "to the needs of the saints (and be) given to hospitality." (Romans 12:13) This command was also given in the book of Hebrews, admonishing us not to "forget to entertain strangers, for by so doing some have unwittingly entertained angels." (Hebrews 13:2) The writer also commands us to remember the prisoners but not just remember them, we are to remember them as if we are chained right there in the prison with them. And, to remember "those who are mistreated" as well because "you yourselves are in the body also." We are all connected in the body of Christ.

Although hospitality may be a great command, it is also a great joy to extend. None of us go this way but once. Any good we can do for others needs to be done now because these opportunities are momentary and will likely not come again. We must do whatever good we can now, while the power to help and bless is still in our hand. Through the gift of hospitality, God allows us to be His hands extended to a lost and dying world.

What it means to have the character trait of **HOSPITALITY**:

- Greeting people in an accepting, positive, kind way
- Being happy to meet the physical needs of strangers on a short-term basis
- Being willing to help with food and raiment
- Being respectful, affable and courteous
- Giving guests a warm, cordial and generous reception
- Offering guests comfortable accommodations
- Making others comfortable in our environment
- Not overstaying one's welcome
- Leaving meaningful gifts of love and honor

HUMILITY —

Study start date: _____ **Finish date:** _____

The environment and earth suit we humans were reared in beckons us to seek the praise of men, money and the power to rule over others as our source of security. Yet these things, in and of themselves, are temporary, fleeting and totally incapable of satisfying the human soul. The world says, "Trample others if need be so you can take what they have or rise up and rule over them." It is easy to see where we have come in society today just by reading II Timothy 3:4–5. We can "know this, that in the last days perilous times will come. For men will be lovers of themselves, lovers of money, boasters, proud, blasphemers, disobedient to parents, unthankful, unholy, unloving, unforgiving, slanderers, without self-control, brutal, despisers of good, traitors, headstrong, haughty, lovers of pleasure rather than lovers of God, having a form of godliness but denying its power. And from such" we are commanded to "turn away!" There is no better description of the cancer of pride in the hearts of men. What is worse is that it won't end well. We know that "God (Himself) resists the proud but gives grace to the humble." I Peter 5:5

With pride having the power to make God our adversary, we can only pray that He would help us find the perfect antidote, humility. As such, it is the most desirable commodity in the universe, the absolute highest of the spiritual virtues and the hardest to lay hold of. Every act of love first requires a certain degree of humility, to give it life. We must first cease thinking about ourselves in order to take our time and resources and give them, out of charity, to someone else. The greatest act of humility of all time was Jesus giving up from his throne in Glory and humbling Himself, coming down to earth and walking toward his cross for thirty-three years. "He humbled

"I then, your Lord and Master, have washed your feet; you also ought to wash one another's feet."
John 13:14

Himself and became obedient to the point of death, even the death of the cross." (Philippians 2:8) What we are talking about here is the love of God being poured out on the world and everything. Paul is saying in this passage is really about humility. Love motivated it but humility was its essence. He said, "Let this mind be in you which was also in Christ Jesus." (v.5) What mind is that? Lowliness of mind—humility.

Though made equal with God, He centered instead on "(making) Himself of no reputation (humility), taking the form of a bond-servant (humility) and coming in the likeness of men. (He left His throne and glorified body in Heaven) "And being found in appearance as a man, He humbled Himself and became obedient (humility) to the point of death, even the death of the cross. (no greater humiliation on earth) (v.6–8) But it didn't stop there, His humility caused something to happen that had never occurred before in the universe. It goes on to say, "Therefore, God also has highly exalted Him and given Him the name which is above every name, that at the name of Jesus every knee should bow, of those in heaven and of those on earth, and of those under the earth, and that every tongue should confess that Jesus Christ is Lord to the glory of God the Father." (Philippians 2:9, 10) He humbled himself more than anyone else in all of history and God did what He promised He would do when he sees humility, He highly exalted Him.

If you could take love, put it in a pot and boil it for a while, effervescing whatever comes off, the residue you would be left with at the bottom of that pot is humility. It is the essence of love. Love is also giving. Giving is humility because it is dying to the power of the gift you have in your hand with which you might bless yourself and planting it, instead, in the life or ministry of another. Humility is also the ability to admire the good in others and actually see them as better than ourselves.

This flesh, which is what we call our earth tent (along with the mind) says, "rise up, climb up, be the greatest if you want to succeed in this world." Quite the contrary, the Spirit says, "You must decrease in order to increase." Truly, the way up is, in fact, down and down is the way up. We must first humble ourselves to a time of testing, education, discipline and training to qualify for leadership. To make progress in this world one must quite often take a step backwards in order to make two forward. And we will rise no higher in life than we are willing to humble ourselves. Authentic leadership is only advanced servant hood. We must, as I alluded, desire to decrease for God to increase in our life and ministry. We also know that it is the meek (humble) who will inherit the earth. (Matthew 5:5) Our motivation to lead should be driven by a desire to serve others and help them succeed. In time, this desire to decrease and take on the office of a servant may cause something else to happen in the Spirit realm. Jesus said, "Whosoever would be greatest among you, shall be your servant." Matthew 23:11

Of all the character traits, humility is the most difficult to truly grasp because it is so contrary to human nature. If you think you ever have it, you have probably lost it already. For example, humility is nothing like orderliness which can be attained by lining our shoes up in the closet or our pens and pencils in the desk drawer. Humility is much higher, more honorable and infinitely more valuable but far, far more difficult to obtain. It is the grace that opens the door for all others to be added. The reason for this is that it gives us the heart attitude of brokenness, receptivity and the hunger to improve, as well as the correct attitude of total dependence upon God. Humility is also the ability to die to self—and our old flesh is not willing to die but so much at any one point in time. We have to seek humility like a drowning man swimming to the surface is wishing only for his next gasp of air. If you will do this, I promise that it will bless your life in more ways than you can imagine. To receive it, we must be delivered from the curse of pride since it the source of all sin, sickness, selfishness and shortcomings. To find humility we must ask God to reveal every vestige of pride, self-reliance and the desire for the approval of men. It we, for just a moment, could be granted the power to see in the spirit realm exactly what pride is doing to each of us, we would plead to God with all that is in us. We would be willing to pay any price, go any distance, for this poisonous snake to be torn from its deadly hold on us. Pride is captivity and death whereas humility is freedom and life.

When I finish this little string of words I am so feebly putting together, I shall take my own advice and, once again, pray for God's help to grow in humility so He can add the grace.

What it means to have the character trait of **HUMILITY:**

- The grace to willingly and gladly decrease so God can increase in our life.
- To have a broken and contrite spirit
- To glory in weakness knowing that it causes the power of God to be made strong
- The end of evil, deception and sin
- The one condition that causes grace to be added to our lives
- To be and to do nothing of ourselves
- What causes the Spirit of glory and of God to rest upon us
- The willingness and ability to be an empty vessel in which God can show forth His glory
- The ability to consent to be nothing
- Knows humility's chief lesson: "Learn of me for I am meek and lowly in heart."
- Knows "In the mouth of a fool is a rod of pride but the lips of the wise will preserve them." Pv 14:3
- To totally cast away self and let God be our all in all
- Makes the word "servant" become a glory and an honor
- Desires to add value to the lives of others
- The discipline, grace and desire to serve and bless even those who try to vex and despitefully use us
- The one condition for fellowship with the Lamb of God, Jesus Christ
- To be willing to pay the price as the member of a group to keep the unity of the Spirit in the bond of peace
- When offended, as Joseph, it is to bless and curse not
- The ability to follow a superior's orders even when you think you have a better way, unless the orders are immoral, illegal or unscriptural
- To know that we will never have more grace or faith than we have humility
- The essence and basic building material of love
- The place where we realize that we will be absolutely nothing apart from Him.
- The ability to esteem others better than our self
- The ability to say, "I am nothing"
- The ability to gladly receive correction
- The ability to return soft words when faced with anger and wrath
- The ability to hold our peace when being corrected and not answering back
- Knowing that the way down is actually the fastest and only sure way up
- Is the power to denying self
- The power to make others great in the eyes of the Lord
- Total dependence upon God in every area of our life
- Taking pleasure in all trials, distresses, corrections, weaknesses and wrongs
- To know "the humble also increase their joy in the Lord." Isa 29:19
- The mark of a gentle, kind and lowly spirit
- The beauty of holiness
- The ability to hate pride, arrogance, the haughty look and every evil way
- Knowing that those things that are highly esteemed among men are an abomination to the Lord
- Childlike—the one condition for living and abiding in the Kingdom of God

INDUSTRY —   **Study start date:** _____ **Finish date:** _____

One thing is certain, none of us have much time on this planet and even the time we do have passes by with lightning speed. That is why we are admonished by the apostle Paul to "(redeem) the time (because) the days are evil." (Ephesians 5:16) Hel was saying we should take the greatest advantage of our time because it is not only working against us, on our short excursion here, but life is also full of many unforeseen difficulties and time-wasting distractions. There is a lot of "hurry up and wait" and a never-ending series of offers to engage in frivolous activities that are fantastic opportunities to waste this valuable asset that we all have too little of.

Industry means to engage in activities that are productive and consequential. Benjamin Franklin, one of the most inventive and industrious men of colonial American, said for us to, "Lose no time, be always employed in something useful, (and to) cut off all unnecessary actions." I had a roommate one time who loved to watch cartoons on TV. He was a full grown man, keep in mind, and I really couldn't figure it out. It was only much later that I finally understood this for what it really was. He had a lots of business and personal problems and watching those cartoons, if you can believe it, was his escape. It allowed him get his mind off of reality. Only problem, it was a waste of time and totally unproductive. There are a lot of entertaining, engaging, unproductive activities in life that the flesh (fallen nature) loves to enjoy. If we didn't have to eat, the very motivation the Bible says causes people to go to work, we would all be lazy. I mean fulltime couch potatoes, just laying around and hollering for someone to fetch us some ice tea, popcorn, a steak or some ice cream and all this at regular intervals.and posthaste.

A major contributor to industry in anyone's life is finding work that you truly like, believe in and actually enjoy. If you love your work, it can becomes a work of art on the canvas of your life. We all want to make it as beautiful and meaningful as we possibly can—given our limited time, talent and resources. I have never had any overabundance of talent. However, I have been blessed to love just about every job I ever had and have always said, if you love your work, it will tell you its secrets. So, you can believe that my only talent is probably diligence in the form of industry. Anything you work at steadily and faithfully will, in due time, begin to take shape and start working for you. If you love your work it won't be hard for you because it will be a joy. Production, building and creating will become a passion in your life.

Solomon, the wisest man in the world said, "He becometh poor that worketh with a slack hand but the hand of the diligent maketh rich." (Proverbs 10:4) Now slack doesn't mean lazy. That is another whole category of people who are discussed in another place. He is talking about the one who actually shows up for work nine to five instead of five to nine. This is about the person who works with a limp wrist and a slack hand. This person might call himself working but he is really just marking time and doing, half-heartedly, as little as he can to get by. What we need to do is set our hearts to give 110% to every job that comes our way. Consider every job as an opportunity to learn and improve your service. Make each one a stepping stone to excel to the next level instead of a stumbling block to fail. Go in early and stay late even when the time is off the clock. Know this. It is impossible to give and not receive in due time. It is the law of reciprocity—and it is set on autopilot in nature like the law of gravity. If you don't get some speed on you and become industrious, your place will always be at the rear of the pack. People in management all know the speed of the leader is the speed of the crew. Not everyone in every generation is going to understand this. That is why we are warned that "riches are not forever, nor does a crown (or an inheritance) endure to all generations." (Proverbs 27:24) After the fall in the Garden, God told Adam, that life from now on wasn't going to be so easy from that point on and only by the sweat of our brow, would we eat our bread.

Another reason industry produces wealth is called the compound effect. This is so powerful, some have called it the eighth wonder of the world. It works like this: whatever you produce in life starts to give a return such as interest on money in the bank or residual income on investment property, etc. As you reinvest your profits in other ventures, pretty soon, you are getting a return on the return of your return of your return's return. Obviously, over time this can have quite a powerful multiplying effect. Solomon also said, "He who tills his land will be satisfied with bread, but he who follows frivolity (partying, playing computer games and just hanging out) is devoid of understanding." (Proverbs 12:11) Then he made both groups of people a promise: " … the lazy man will be put to forced labor (either on a chain gang or, at best, working for minimum wage)" but "the hand of the diligent will bear rule." Proverbs 12:24

Now there is nothing wrong with a vacation every now and then or hobbies enjoyed in moderation. Just don't become a professional vacationer or hobby-horser. You will burn up all your seeds and the time we would otherwise have for sowing. We must imitate the ant who needs no supervisor. He goes out diligently collecting in summer—even when it's hot. Those little guys just keep right on going. And, you know I've never seen a picket line in front of an ant hill or one of those little fellas out front with a sign that says ostensibly, "Hungry, will work for food." Truth is they already know you don't have any work for them. They just want a hand out. Ants, however, know how to find work and they always have plenty of food.

What it means to have the character trait of **INDUSTRY:**

- The ability to work steadily, redeeming the time.
- Diligence combined with skill in one's employment, objectives or in the pursuit of a task
- Systematic, consistent, orchestrated labor that produces value
- A mindset that refuses to waste time
- The antithesis of slothfulness

NITIATIVE, TAKING THE—   Study start date: _____ Finish date: _____

Many people go through life seeking to do just what is required in their job and no more. They want a job description and if anything falls outside the boundary, it will not even be considered. This is such a terribly myopic view of our responsibility in life. Yes, we can do the bare minimum and most do just that, but they will also miss out on all the excitement and blessings in taking the initiative in life. There are all kinds of opportunities out there still today. They are, however, usually very cleverly disguised as additional hard work and responsibility accompanied by little or no pay.

There is so much needing to be done out in the world today. When the Apostle Paul had to depart from Crete on another missionary journey, he left Titus there to "set in order the things which were lacking and to appoint elders in every city." (Titus 1:5) Paul needed these men to finish the work he had started. Wherever you go on this blue marble there are tons of things that are lacking. There are so many things right where you work needing improvment. They are just sitting there waiting for someone with a little initiative to come along and tackle them. To do that, however, someone cannot be afraid of work or the criticism that accompanies making changes for the better. You just can't own the character trait of initiative without being criticized. When you start moving the furniture around in a company or a community somebody is not going to like it. Criticism just comes packaged, part and parcel, right along with it. No matter what you do in life you will be criticized. Fact is, you don't even have to do anything. If you just sit on your thumbs through life you will be criticized. However, you can really expect to catch it if you ever haul off and do something as radical as to have the audacity to take the initiative. The reason is that you will always be rocking the boat; threatening the status quo. You will indeed become a controversial person. Not to worry, Jesus, Peter and Paul as well as all the disciples were controversial people. They ushered in a changes in religion that caused controversy everywhere they went. The question is simply whose approval is it that we seek? God's or men? The motive behind everything we do in life should be to simply bring glory to the Name. (I Peter 4:11) If you, in fact, do that, you are going to bring on the heat so you had best be ready. Question. When you leave your company, will it be better because of you having been there? When you leave you community, will it be better because you have been there? Will they miss you? When you leave this planet, will it be better because you were there? Or did you just suck up the oxygen, eat the groceries and take up some space geographically while you were there?

Some years ago, I was president of the Jaycee chapter in our town. Our hope was to make our community better than we found it. That year our chapter started a movement to shed our county of the single-commissioner form of government. We wanted a three-man commission model so there would be less chance for corruption. It was not well received by some at first but we got it passed and that is exactly the form of government we have today. We also set up a committee to work on forming a small claims court to have some smaller matters come before a magistrate judge so small subcontractors who had done work for a builder, business or homeowner could get paid. Up to that time, they had to hire a lawyer to have their case presented before a judge. Going to court usually cost them more than their contract were worth, thus forcing them to accept whatever crumbs they could get. We took the small claims court concept to our county legislative delegation. They liked it, wrote the legislation to enact it and it was done. We still have a Magistrate Court in our county today. We had many other initiatives too numerous to name.

About this same time I had just started out in the real estate business selling houses in a new subdivision our company had developed. The man who bought the house at the entrance had a daughter who had gotten into a head-on collision and totaled her car. He parked it on the grass in his front yard.

Nothing I said or did would convinced him to move it. No one wants to live next door to a junk yard so the whole subdivision was up in arms about it. So I did a little research and drafted a junk car ordinance modeled after some I had found across the country. I went to our single-man commissioner and laid out my case for a junk car ordinance for our county and he said, "Sounds like a good thing, Winston, but I just don't want to do it." At that, we bade each other good day and parted company. After laying a little groundwork, about a week later I called him and asked if I could reserve the conference room next to his office for a Thursday afternoon at one o'clock on a certain day about a week later. He called out to his secretary to check the date, told her to make a note of it on their calendar and said, "Yes." Then I asked him if he would be kind enough to be there as well and he agreed.

The day of the meeting arrived and the commissioner entered the room at the appointed time and sat down at the head of the conference table. At that point I introduced him to the presidents of just about every civic club in the county and most of the presidents of the major home owners' associations. I simply said, "Bobby, you are probably wondering why I have asked you to this meeting today." He nodded. "I said, we'd like to have a junk car ordinance in this county." He said, "OK, Winston, take it to the county attorney. Have him look it over and when he is happy with it, I'll sign it." I thanked him and the meeting was over in less than five minutes. Our chapter also sponsored a voluntary Junk Car Roundup and had a lot of fun with it. In about a two week period, we retrieved about two hundred cars that had littered our community for years.

That same year, I was serving as a director on the regular Chamber of Commerce and was appointed to a three-man committee to look into whether or not the Chamber should back the building of a county hospital. It was quite a controversial issue at the time. The other two men on the committee were so afraid of what people would think if this, that or the other thing happened. After more than ample time for research and discussion I said, "Look. All I know is it is at least a 45 minute drive from the county line to the nearest hospital and we are forever going to have kids like me falling out of trees and breaking their arms. We are going to have young mothers needing a hospital nearby to have their babies. I am for building one here and I am always going to be for building one here. We can run a hospital in our county as well as anybody in the next county. You all can decide whatever you like but I have made up my mind." That got them off of dead center and we finally voted unanimously as a committee to recommend building the hospital here. Subsequently, the entire Chamber also voted for its approval. Next, the county had a referendum on it and, again, voted for approval as well. It was built here and has been a blessing for years.

Looking for opportunity in life? Looking for a new business venture? They say (and it's true) the best way to start a new business is to find a need, something no one is doing, and fill it. It takes initiative to look outside of our comfort zone and outside of our sphere of responsibilities since we all probably already have a full plate anyway. It takes initiative to start doing something that is not expected or required, something that needs to be done but nobody is doing or wants to do. In addition to all that, it takes boldness to work past the fear of failure because there are risks involved in every venture and an avalanche of criticism that is sure to come as well. But that is what makes life interesting. Besides, if you can ever obtain the grace sufficient to take the initiative in life, the whole world will be your plumb.

What it means to have the character trait of having **INITIATIVE:**

- Taking the initial step in commencement of work or a large project
- The thought and willingness that initiates action, meets a need or solves a problem

- The fearlessness to start new things, be creative or do things differently than has ever been done before, regardless of the resistance and heat that will surely come from the defenders of the status quo
- The ability to see a need and fill it without constant supervision or prodding
- Being innovative
- Having the desire to make lasting, unique contributions wherever you may work or live
- The sincerity and innate drive to improve things around oneself even when, seemingly, no reward will come to you
- The ability to "bloom where you are planted" without coaxing and prodding

INNOVATIVE, BEING—   Study start date: _____   Finish date: _____

It has always been said, "There are two things for certain in life, death and taxes." But, there are really three: death, taxes and change. Nothing stays the same. Everything in this world is in a state of flux. The pendulum is constantly swinging in politics, first one direction and then the other.

Throughout society, there are constant changes, movements and trends and, according to Alvin Toffler, in his book, *Future Shock,* there are also "megatrends." Megatrends are huge movements going on in a country, economy, market or demographics that, once begun, take years to complete. Just one mentioned in his book was the shift of America's population from the Rust Belt in the north to the Sun Belt in the south. We all need to be aware of these megatrends so we can prepare ourselves and respond favorably to their impact. Every one of them will have far reaching effects. Either we will anticipate them and benefit from these changes or we will be rolled over by them like an on-coming steam roller.

Some people are reticent to change anything around them. They are so terrified of criticism and the possibility of a little temporary failure that they freeze up completely. These folks would rather live in the cold, dark but comfortable closet of the status quo and antiquity. There, they will never feel the stinging arrows of criticism that are sure to come for daring to improve something or stand up for what is better or right. They can stand still in the sunshine of time and refuse to be an innovator for a moment but, they will soon be crushed by the fast-moving locomotive of change.

Thomas Edison was given a gift by God to make over a thousand, incredible, patented inventions. Not only was Edison a gifted inventor, but he also had the talent to manufacture his inventions as well. Then again, no matter how valuable all this ability to invent and manufacture was, it would all have been absolutely worthless had he not also had the talent to market those products to the world. Thomas Edison was a master of innovation. Every time you take a sandwich out of the wax paper that kept it clean and crisp and the mayonnaise from getting mixed up with the chocolate cake in your lunch bag, thank Thomas. The next time you are groping around in the dark trying to find something in your closet and turn on the light switch to facilitate your search, send up a little prayer of thanks for the innovative heart of Thomas Edison. He has made life a lot easier for all of us and certainly lived a great life during his time on earth.

The innovator, by definition, must be a different breed. He sees himself as forever the stealth R&D (research and development) point man, refusing to fall for the conventional thinking on anything. He questions the validity of every product, process, procedure and philosophy, always thinking outside the box. He is constantly seeking input from those in other fields of endeavor whose minds haven't been trained and corralled by the disciplines of his own industry. He is consistently questioning everyone: customers, users, employees and even people on the street. He is constantly substituting other things, pieces to the puzzle, materials (new alloys, plastics, polymers, etc.) always trying to go the old way one better. He does motion and time studies, tries to combine two good ideas, breaks the routine on purpose and gladly tries new ways of doing things. Innovators are willing to take chances and even fail on occasion because they know that this is the only pathway to success. Criticism doesn't bother them in the least but they do tend to get rid of the nay-Sayers they find around them very quickly. They are also alert, keeping a pad of paper with them everywhere they go so they can write those ideas down immediately (before they forget them). Earl Nightingale said, "Ideas are like babies. Nobody gets very many so you better take good care of every one you get." Remember, one good idea can be worth a million dollars and possibly change the whole world for the better.

In the area of products research and technology, someone is always going to be building a better mouse trap. Everything from cars and computers to buildings and toothbrushes are constantly being improved. The old is forever being "one bettered" and replaced by the latest and greatest widget, gadget or duma flitch. In the fast-moving, industrial and computer age we live in, time is of the essence and cost saving is king. If your new product, system or method can do one of these two things, you are going to be in like Flint. That is, if you can do one thing more: innovate.

One of the main problems encountered by the inventive mind is stubbornness and a general resistance on the part of the public to accept this whole process of change. Toffler called this phenomenon "future shock." This is what all of us in the older generation felt pounding on our brains when we had to learn to operate our first computer. We knew we had to do it and we knew we could do it but we certainly didn't want to do it. The buying public may see the new product or idea but they are naturally more familiar with, invested in and comfortable with the old. Things in their lives, were going along just fine thanks and they don't really want anyone rocking the boat. So the innovator must be adept at building critical mass in the mind of the target constituency so that this new product is worth the cost, the re-training of personnel and time it takes to switch to the new. This can be done very well and fairly easily, by using what is called the Ben Franklin close. You simply take out a sheet of paper and make two columns. At the top of one column, you write "Advantages" and on the other, of course, "Disadvantages." Then you start listing every pro and con that comes to mind. Remember to always be faithful to list every disadvantage you can think of as well. The public and the market are going to find all the flaws in the course of time anyway so honesty is, as always, the best policy. Besides, those listening to your proposal or even reading it, will even be more convinced to accept the advantages you have given if they know you are sincerely and honestly showing them the down-side as well. People just don't want to go through the pain and price of change unless someone, the innovator, can show them it is well worth their time and effort. They must be convinced this "new thing" will make them a winner. In the free market system we live in, we must always get the willing cooperation of all who are involved or invested in the new idea, product or system.

To stay competitive in this fast moving world, one must become proficient at innovation or we can fully expect to be left behind and that, in short order. Therefore, it is critically important that we learn how to sell these new ideas, products and concepts to our coworkers and leaders. Some of us may be reluctance to think of ourselves as salesmen and may never have wanted to be a salesman but a salesman we all must be in this life. As you know, nothing happens until a sale is made here in the U.S. In reality, we all have to sell ourselves to get a job, sell our company's products or services, sell our boss on the job we just finished, etc. Guys, if you every want to get Susie to say "Yes" to that age old question about marriage, it might be an idea to shine up those salesman shoes in the closet and work on improving your presentation.

I remember one summer in college I was recruited to sell encyclopedias, door-to-door, in San Antonio, Texas. I went from one community to the next every day knocking on doors, getting the brush-off and being chased by dogs. I was so good at this, my first selling venture, that I never sold the first set. No. Not one. Nada. Didn't figure I was cut out to be a salesman at all. However, when I went into the civilian world years ago after leaving the Army, I had to go into sales once again—reluctantly of course, as you might imagine. With that back-log of experience as a salesman, can we say lack-luster performance selling (or not selling) encyclopedias, my mind was really wondering if being a salesman was ever going to be a possibility for me. However, I still enjoyed eating at that time and needed to provide a few vittles and a roof over my family as well, so I studied the concepts of selling. There was no lack of good books on the subject and, believe it or not, I was actually able to start selling, saw myself helping people selling and started having fun doing it.

Again, while on the subject of encyclopedias and change, it was announced just this week that *The Encyclopedia Britannica* was going out of business. Wikipedia, the "Great Wicki," now free on the internet, has just pushed that fine publication over into the scrap heap of obsolescence. The founders of this truly fine encyclopedia were probably some of my ancestors across the pond in Scotland. I also happen to have a set in my library and it is an incredibly excellent publication. Tons of hours and millions of dollars have gone into making it what it is but, sorry guys, change is upon us once again.

Remember, we are all just human beings and, as I said, reluctant to change. I'm certainly no different. I have, no doubt, made the mistake of not being open to change as much, if not more than most. Years ago I had a commercial real estate company and a copier salesman came calling on me to, of course, sell us a better copier. Unbeknownst to him, he had at least three obstacles to hurdle: first, we already had a perfectly good copier that was paid for. Secondly, the new one he was selling was very expensive and thirdly, I was happy with our old one. Initially, my thought was to follow my first impulse and say, "Thanks but no thanks" but I have forever burned in my conscience the picture of a cartoon about a certain salesman I saw years ago. In it, the salesman was approaching a king outside of a small tent he had erected to house his new invention and keep it shrouded temporarily. He was trying to interest the king and create a new market for his newly invented weapon but didn't want anyone looking at it until the proper moment. All the knights, knaves and everyone standing around were, of course, decked out in their medieval body armor with lances, shields and swords in hand. The king, when asked if he would be interested in this new invention and unable to see inside the tent from his vantage point in the cartoon, said, "Not interested!" However, the flap was turned back on the front of the tent so that you and I, the readers, could see that the weapon inside he wanted to sell was actually a Gatling gun. (one of the first machine guns) The weapon the king refused to even consider was such a giant leap in military technology that it could have saved many of his subjects' lives, won many a battle a whole lot quicker and cheaper in terms of everything from men, materiel, money and time. Wars, you know, have always been expensive propositions to prosecute. So with the king's error in mind, I told the salesman in my office, "Go ahead and let's see what your copier will do." His little pride and joy, was one of the first with a series of automatic collator bins to separate and sort the various copies of multi-page documents. Our contracts in commercial real estate were always many pages to cover all the contingencies, special stipulations, laws, building codes and regulations, inspection periods, engineering tests, financing, title work, etc. and there had to be a bunch of copies to sign and leave while negotiating back and forth between buyers and sellers. You always had to leave a signed copy with the prospective purchaser before presenting that offer to the seller. If the seller made even one small change, it had to be initialed by the buyer. Then the contract had to be signed and a copy left with him. The rest of the copies had to be carried back to the purchaser for his approval. This scenario could easily play out many times before there was actually a complete "meeting of the minds" and what is commonly referred to as an agreement or a deal. When I saw the time my staff would save not having to collate copies anymore, this young salesman immediately got some ink out of my pen on the bottom line of his sales order. Thanks to that salesman, we moved into the future and all lived happily and more efficiently ever after in the Land of Oz.

Today, corporate presidents say being innovative (a form of being creative with the power to take action) is the most important character trait of a successful executive.

What it means to have the character trait of **BEING INNOVATIVE:**

- The ability to affect change
- To introduce something new and different
- To substitute a new device, system, idea, concept, method, product, tools or piece of equipment,

- To be known and characterized by the ability to find and implement new things
- Always being curious about things, ideas and processes.
- Always open to new ideas, new concepts and new ways of doing things
- The ability to see even greater potential in people, products, systems and techniques.
- Not the desire for change just for change's sake but seeking change to benefit your company and society in general
- The burning desire to affect a change and improve something
- The force that creates progress
- The desire to leave society and life better than you found it by your own small contributions, inventions and improvements
- The force that moves creativity and progress forward
- To introduce new, creative things
- Is never being satisfied with the status quo
- To realize there will always be a better mouse trap
- To realize it is the leader's job to get his people ready for change because it is inevitable
- To realize nothing is ever going to improve unless there is a change
- To realize change in life is inevitable
- To realizing creativity and innovation create all change
- The ability to implement and convince others to assist in the implementation of new products and ideas.
- The ability to withstand the torrent of criticism that will surely come when any new product, service or idea is introduced regardless of whether they are good or bad
- The power to risk rejection and failure to pave the way for the introduction of new things.
- Creativity in developing and introducing new concepts, products, systems and techniques.
- It is the ability, confidence, finesse and social skill necessary to successfully implement changes and ideas on a daily basis
- Creativity is the ability to develop new ideas but these are worthless unless one is able to innovate those ideas in real life and market situations
- An absolute necessity in order to remain competitive and to survive in our fast-moving world today.

NSPIRING —

Study start date: _____ **Finish date:** _____

In a world full of trials, toil, turmoil and trouble, leaders are needed who can inspire people. This is true in every family, company, a church, military unit or political subdivision. Actually, we are all going to have dark days when it seems like everything is turning to mush. Things sometimes have a way of getting so down, dirty and out of control that most people give up and lose all hope. This is exactly where our nation was at the end of the Carter administration in the early '80's. Long lines at the gas pumps, nothing much was selling all across the country and the economy was in the pit. That's when we needed a leader to rise up, cut through the fluff and spark the imaginations of our people with his enthusiasm, faith and clear cut, achievable goals. That's when Ronald Reagan came galloping up on the American landscape to run for the Presidency against the peanut farmer from Plains. I remember the time well. The economy was a train wreck at election time. All the way up to election night the pollsters and pundits said Carter was well out ahead and had won the race. Even the night of the election they still had him winning handily. The next morning, however, the nation awoke to headlines saying that it was the movie star, the governor from California who had won and won strong. Ronald Reagan took over in a big way. What Carter couldn't do in all his years in office, free the Iran hostages, Reagan did his first day. Later he told Gorbachev to "Tear down that wall" dividing Germany—and he did. Having lived through all that I, for one, was thankful for an inspiring leader who gave this country hope. And, yes, he really did change things for the better—right away! He rode up on his white horse and put the whole country on the come-back-trail In no time the economy began to take leaps and bounds. He was so inspiring that they began to call him The Great Communicator.

As I said, life is not always going to be easy. We will always need leaders to take us through the tough times who demonstrate confidence in their actions. Remember, in your own personal life, every time you solve a difficult problem or win a battle, it just makes you that much more confident when you step up to face the next challenge. After a while, winning gets to be a habit and it helps immensely to start dealing with things with a track record of past successes.

This is exactly what David, as a young man, did when facing the giant, Goliath. He volunteered to fight the giant to remove the disgrace this heathen had put the Armies of the Living God. All the Israelites (including King Saul) refused to meet him on the battlefield. When told by Saul that he couldn't do this thing as a mere lad, David started pulling a few things out of his bag of past successes. He said, "Your servant used to keep his father's sheep, and when a lion or a bear came and took a lamb out of the flock. I went out after it and struck it and delivered the lamb from its mouth; and when it arose against me, I caught it by its beard, and struck and killed it. Your servant has killed both lion and bear; and this uncircumcised Philistine will be like one of them, seeing he has defied the armies of the living God." Saul was inspired. He could only reply, "Go, and the Lord be with you!" (I Samuel 17:33–37) David was one who always led by example on the battlefield. He proved to be the greatest fighting warrior in Israel for all time.

When you show endurance, fearlessness and a track record of creativity overcoming obstacles, people will soon come to believe that victory is still achievable themselves; regardless of how bad the situation may be. Having spiritual, mental and physical stamina naturally inspires those who follow you to believe that they too can reach new heights. Someone who is willing to tackle impossible situations when necessary, just plain inspires confidence. No question about it, intolerable situations are going to continue to crop up in everyone's lives. The thing about them, as they say, is sooner or later they all have to be tolerated. Someone has to rise up and sort them out. Faith knows that there is nothing impossible with God. No matter what He calls you to do, you cannot fail.

A leader must have the ability to quickly analyze the situation and formulate an achievable plan, even when few think there is even a remote possibility of winning. Then he must have the confidence to communicate that plan in such a manner to build consensus in the organization and make it happen. Then the leader must continue to lead, being willing to do a large part of the dirty work, in addition to demonstrating courage in the face of the enemy. In war-time battle, when men on the front lines are given the command to combat assault into the face of the full physical strength and firepower of the enemy, in each man's mind, it always boils down to this: Do I believe my leader can take us to victory in this?

In the companies I commanded in Vietnam, an unusual thing, that you would never expect, happened every time we made contact with the enemy. Now I would have thought that the eyes of every soldier would have been fixed on the enemy firing at them. Their full concentration, it seemed, would have been on watching their movements or trying in all that dense foliage to see them because they were the ones shooting live bullets at them. I was never told this in all my military training, but when contact is made with the enemy, most of the men will be looking at their commander, It never ceased to amaze me. Other than for each, individual's belief and trust in God, Himself, their hope rests in you as their leader. You hold their lives in your hands.so their confidence is in you! If they make it through this battle, you are the one they are looking at to take them there. It is also a fact that on any given day, the best soldiers led by a poor general can easily be beaten by average soldiers led by a great general. I also believe most great generals are made and not born. Neither servants nor soldiers have ever been and never will be greater than their master.

What it means to have the character trait of being **INSPIRING:**

- The ability to encourage, impel and motivate those we lead
- Executing our plans and orders fearlessly with the most ardent zeal inspires those around us
- To move or challenge a person's inner being to accomplishment beyond what one originally believed might be possible
- To engage the intellect and emotions of those who follow us to achieve higher goals
- To infuse with supernatural or divine power to spur people on
- To affect another in a positive way
- To bring out the best in another person or group

INSULT, THE ABILITY TO OVERLOOK AN— Study start date: _____ Finish date: _____

This trait is so very important because of the hostile world we live in today. The Bible describes our position as Christians living here "as sheep among wolves." We are sheep among wolves, plural, and wolves on the attack are always fierce, extremely wily and as deadly as they can be. They have long, sharp fangs while sheep have none. Wolves are fast movers while sheep are slow and have absolutely no defensive capabilities. So we, according to this similitude, have to be wise in order to live, survive and thrive in this environment. King David said, God will "prepare a table before me in the presence of my enemies." (Psalm 23:5) So we shouldn't fear our enemies, just know how to deal with them. He also said he prepared himself for this by meditating the Word day and night, and it made him wiser than (his) enemies." (Psalm 119:98) Why? Because in this life, we are always going to have enemies. If you name the Name of Christ, for that reason alone, you will automatically have enemies. So be it. In a lost and dying world, it is only reasonable to expect that we are going to have an insult hurled at us on occasion so we must learn how to navigate in a world gone crazy. It is a hostile environment especially if you are on the front lines of the Army of the Lord. God is not preparing us for R&R. He is preparing us for battle. You will be cartooned, called a liar on the front page of the paper, labeled a radical, etc. when all you are doing is living the normal Christian life—being salt and light. If we can't handle these insults, we just might allow the enemy to escalate the incident to the point of an altercation or worse. God wants us to be ready for this. Proverbs 24:10 gives us this warning: "If you falter in times of trouble, your strength is weak."

We know a hot temper comes part and parcel with the flesh. We all have to deal with this problem. Proverbs 14:17 reminds us that "A quick-tempered man acts foolishly" and will likely make a fool of himself over the smallest provocation. We need to be careful not to let others make us angry. Solomon said, in Ecclesiastes 7:9, "Do not hasten in your spirit to be angry, for anger rests in the bosom of fools." We have all been provoked to anger many times in life but we need to watch these times very carefully. We can be enticed into words and actions that can ruin our whole life and testimony. We have to learn to be angry but sin not. (Psalm 4:5) And, Proverbs 19:19 NIV warns, "A hot tempered man must pay the penalty." So many lives have been destroyed by allowing hot words with some fractious, peevish, truculent person to escalate into blows, law suits or even death. Whole lives and careers are often ruined by a few hasty words, not properly handled.

Patience is the goal in life. James 3:8 says, the tongue no man can tame, "It is an unruly evil, full of deadly poison." It sounds like it is impossible but we find this admonition in James 1:26: "If anyone among you thinks he is religious, and does not bridle his tongue but deceives his own heart, this one's religion is useless." So we must learn to take dominion of it. It may be a small member but, left to itself, it can set on fire a world of iniquity. It can be done because Colossians 1:9 says we can "be filled with the knowledge of (God's) will in all wisdom and spiritual understanding; that (we) may walk worthy of the Lord, fully pleasing Him, being fruitful in every good work and increasing in the knowledge of God; strengthened with all might, according to His glorious power for all patience and longsuffering with joy." When we have reached full maturity in the faith we will know it, not by the size of our house or bank accounts but when we have "patience and longsuffering with joy." That's the proof. Paul and Silas were singing praises to God in the Philippian jail and thanking Him for counting them worthy of being persecuted for the Name. Proverbs 19:11 tells us "The discretion of a man makes him slow to anger, and his glory is to overlook an insult." And, "He who is slow to wrath has great understanding, but he who is impulsive exalts folly." Proverbs 14:29

Let's consider the power and danger of reckless words. One of the greatest lies ever told is the childhood rant that goes, "Sticks and stones will break my bones but names will never hurt me." Wrong. Wrong. Wrong. Reckless, hateful words have destroyed friendships, business relationships, marriages and churches. Proverbs 12:18 says, "There is one who speaks like the piercings of a sword, but the tongue of the wise promotes health (brings healing)." We have all said things we wished we hadn't. It is all the more evident when the words we spoke were repeated back to us. The reason for this response was because hearing those words repeated, they didn't sound good at all. But, by then, it was too late. We can't retrieve those words because the damage was already done. We all need to learn to stop and think before we speak. Proverbs 15:28 says, "The heart of the righteous studies how to answer, but the mouth of the wicked pours forth evil." James, the Apostle, said, "Be swift to hear and slow to speak ..." (1:19) If we are reticent to speak, we will have more time to cool down and study our answers. God, in his infinite wisdom, gave us two ears but only one tongue. A good plan to follow any time you are not sure what to reply or find yourself a bit angry, is count to ten (to yourself).

Another helpful practice in all of life and especially helpful in the area of confrontations is to always smile. This will help us several ways. First of all, smiling automatically conveys to the others involved that you are a friendly person. That's important. It also helps them to know that you are confident in yourself, you aren't at all worried about the confrontation, and it also gives them the notion that you still believe a positive resolution to the encounter can be found. Besides, you might as well look like a winner and winners smile. It always confuses the devil when we are happy. Why shouldn't we be happy? Our side always wins. "Whatever is born of God overcomes the world. And this is the victory that has overcome the world—our faith." (I John 5:4) Everything is coming together for our good. "A cheerful look brings joy to the heart, and good news brings health to the bones." Proverbs 15:13 NIV

In times of provocation it is so very important to return a soft answer. It overwhelms our enemies. Proverbs 15:1 tells us, "A gentle answer turns away wrath but harsh words stir up

anger." It is so powerful that Solomon said, "a gentle tongue breaks a bone." (Proverbs 25:15) When you have been provoked and people expect you to come back like a scorching whirlwind or a streak of lightning but you instead have a gentle response, it is totally disarming. God knew it and wrote it in the Book. Proverbs 15:21 says, "The wise in heart will be called prudent and the sweetness of the lips increases knowledge" (Proverbs 16:21) Furthermore, "A wholesome tongue is a tree of life, but perverseness in it breaks the spirit." (Proverbs 15:4) We know "A man finds joy in giving an apt reply—and how good is a timely word!" (Proverbs 15:24 NIV) An apt response in a heated exchange is a thing of beauty. Proverbs 25:11 says, "A word fitly spoken is like apples of gold in settings of silver."

We see a few illustrations of this in everyday life. There was a young lady who said to John Wesley, "I think I know what my talent is." And, he said, "Tell me." She said, "To speak my mind." He opined, "I think the Lord would be pleased if you would bury that talent."

On a windswept hill of the English countryside, there was a church yard with a drab, gray, slate tomb stone that had this faint etching written on it: "Beneath this stone, a lump of clay, lies Arabella Young, whom on the 24th day of May (in some certain year) began to hold her peace." (She died) And it goes on to say, "If your lips you would keep from slips, five things observe with care: To whom you speak, of whom you speak, and how and when and where." We need to be careful what we say and how we respond to an insult.

What it means to have the character trait of having **THE ABILITY TO OVERLOOK AN INSULT.**

- Knowing that not handling insults correctly can cause the loss of jobs, friendships and can possibly in death.

- Being ready for insults and false accusations in life is wise because they will surely come.
- Realizing we live in a world full of lost, angry people who are led about by the prince of this world.
- Remembering our goal is to be patient in our trials and troubles.
- Remembering the tongue needs to be our main focus in a provocation.
- Always counting to ten to yourself in a provocation to allow time to consider well your answer.
- Always smiling in the face of adversity.
- Responding with a gentle tongue

NTEGRITY —   **Study start date:** _____ **Finish date:** _____

Of the billions of people who inhabit this planet, amazingly few possess true integrity. So many today can be bought and sold for a song. What is equally amazing is that there are many who would rather make $50 under the table than $100 straight up, on top. Why? I guess they just love darkness and deceit and feel more comfortable operating in that realm. This is to imagine knowing that corruption always has consequences built right into the act. Numbers 32:23 says, "Be sure your sin will find you out." A failure to have and demonstrate integrity in all of one's actions will actually remove from a person the moral authority to lead and might even cost them their job. Once a person's integrity has been compromised, it is hard, nigh even impossible, to ever get it back. Thank God, our God is the God of the second chance.

Everybody is trusting in something to get ahead in life. Some trust in skill, others in education, still others in deceit and so on. The best choice, without a doubt, is to trust in the Lord, follow His counsel and start doing what is right every time—all the time, especially when no one is looking. To truly succeed in life requires something most don't know about–the blessing of the Lord. No one can live well or long without it. Any other course in life is reckoned to be as likely to succeed as one building a house on sand. And, down the road of life there will be many unseen storms, tornados, hurricanes, financial and economic national tsunamis, business and possible marital betrayals, on and on ad infinitum. Whereas building one's house on the rock, which is really truth, love and integrity, will not only stand these and other horrendous tests in life but will also add the Lord's blessing. His power is so great that one small bit of favor from the Lord can wipe out years of poverty, sowing to the wind, and every other kind of foolishness. In addition to causing you to succeed in life, it will also cause others to respect you but, just as importantly, will cause you to respect yourself.

During the Clinton Presidency years, the deceit unearthed in the White House by his impeachment actually shook, to the core, the faith of many in our government, including our young college students studying journalism. About that time one of our greatest syndicated, journalists, Jack Anderson, was about to retire after a forty year career of covering our various Presidents. He had seen the best and the worst. Jack was being questioned by some aspiring college students on TV who asked him what could be missing in our society for this to even happen?. Then they asked what advice he would give them starting out in life to shield them from this kind of moral failure. He said the problem was basically the absence of a moral code of right and wrong. We all must adhere to a code for living. Then he gave them some simple but sage advice, the same he had always tried to live by: " If it is not true, don't say it; if it is not right, don't do it and if it is not yours, don't take it." I believe he had it right.

What it means to have the character trait of **INTEGRITY:**

- Being honest and true
- Doing what is right and telling the truth even when it is not comfortable, popular, profitable or convenient and may even be embarrassing
- Doing what is right when no one is watching
- Keeping your word
- Refusing as King David did to "set any wicked thing before your eyes" and to "hate sin, wickedness and every evil way."
- The condition of soundness

- Having no admixture or rottenness under the surface
- Strict adherence to God's moral code
- Telling complete truths and not half-truths when a half-truth would distort the facts
- A willingness to admit to and correct one's errors even when we find them after-the-fact and regardless of what it costs you.
- Incorruptibility
- The capacity to be unwavering on points of honesty and truth

INTREPID —   **Study start date:** _____ **Finish date:** _____

Interestingly, how King David chose his chiefs among the captains, which we would call generals today, was not by seniority, ancestry, political connections, education, brute strength or a strikingly handsome appearance. He chose them strictly on the basis of loyalty and demonstrated bravery and skill when greatly outnumbered in battle. This is so important, Churchill once said, "Without courage all other virtues lose their meaning." David's generals had to be intrepid. Of these great chiefs, David had three.

Chief of them all was Adino, the Eznite, who lifted up his spear in one day and killed eight hundred men. Having commanded an infantry company in Vietnam on two occasions, I can tell you that killing eight hundred men in the heat of the battle is no small task. The mission assigned to the infantry since time in memorial is to close with and destroy the enemy. Interpreted, that means to combat assault directly into the face of the enemy's full physical strength and fire power and that, in Vietnam when I was there, had to be done on almost a daily basis. At one point during the Cambodian invasion, we had contact with the enemy fifty-one days in a row without a shower or a change of clothes. I only mention that to tell you from my experience no one ever volunteers to be die in war and give up the thing most precious to them: their very existence. Men will fight to protect their life with all that is in them. In a fray where hand-to-hand, spear-to-spear or spear and club-to-sword combat takes place, there were doubtless others in the vicinity on the enemy's side, who were shooting at Adino with their bows, throwing spears and hurling stones with their sling shots. To take out eight hundred men in a single day would have been extremely exhausting physically and mentally. Keep in mind that rarely if ever during battle, is it a fair fight. You can be assured that the enemy soldiers didn't line up, single file, to take him on, one at a time. Oh no. He always remained one man with a spear but the enemy surely tried, on several occasions to gang up on him with three to five or more against one. He had to be extremely alert and agile to manage all those in the fight at hand as well as, being circumspect to watch for the other arrows, stones and spears coming his way from several other directions as weell. Some of those projectiles were coming at him at speeds of well over a hundred miles an hour. The constant adrenalin rush and tests of physical strength had to be horrendous and terribly exhausting. His accomplishment that day was, no doubt, impressive and for that reason he was made the chief of all David's captains. II Samuel 23:8

After Adino was Eleazar, the son of Dodai, the Ahohite. He was one of the three who were with David that fateful day they defied the Philistine army which had set themselves against them for battle. This was at a time when all the armies of Israel had completely vacated the area. Only David and these three were left to face an army of hundreds or even more. The Bible records that Eleazar rose up and stood his ground, refusing to back down. He fought so hard against the Philistines that his hand clung to his sword. They continued to take the battle to the Philistines until "the Lord brought a great victory for them." As the armies of Israel returned that day it was only to strip the spoil from those who were slain. Eleazer was not only a mighty man, he was intrepid. II Samuel 23:9, 10

Then came Shammah the son of Agee, a Hararite. On this particular day, the Philistines gathered together in a troop or mounted cavalry unit comparable to a company of infantry soldiers today. Keep in mind, however, that although the bible is true as it is written, the definitions of some words change in their usage over the years and this is especially over the last two or three thousand years. Suffice it to say, it was a large number, fifty to a hundred men at the time and they were probably mounted on horses. Shammah took his stand in the middle of a field full of lintels or beans, after all the inhabitants of that area had fled in the face of the attacking Philistines, and defended it. He continued to rout the enemy until, again, we see these words recorded in the Bible, "the Lord brought about a great victory." Against unbelievable odds, he held his ground and defeated them all. II Samuel 23:11, 12

There were many others. Honored among them was Benaiah, the son of Jehoiada, the son of a valiant man from Kabzeel, who had done many mighty deeds. Once he killed the two sons of Ariel, the Moabite. He also went down in a pit on a snowy day and killed a lion, single handedly. In addition, on another day, he killed a very impressive Egyptian warrior.who had a spear. Benaiah, having only a club, so he snatched the spear from the Egyptian and killed him with it. II Samuel 23:20, 21

Without a doubt, our resident courage and skill will only take us so far in enormous battles like these. All of these battles would have been considered impossible but our God specializes in these kinds of things to show His power and faithfulness to men. These men had to have something more. To fight as they did and refuse to back down even when greatly outnumbered, they had to have a revelation of the promises God for battle in Joshua chapter one. Three times in Joshua chapter one, He told Joshua to "Be strong and of a good courage." Realize now that there will be times of trouble in all of our lives when we will be totally outnumbered and seemingly, by human standards, overwhelmed. We must be ready and this short passage tells us the one thing we must do for this to happen for us. We must meditate on His Word day and night. He went on to say He was giving the ground under his feet. He said, every place the soul of his foot might trod. (v.3) and that "No man (would) be able to stand before (him) all the days of (his) life." He also promised never to "leave (him) nor forsake (him)" (v.5) and that He would be with him "wherever (he would) go." (v.9) War is no walk through the park. People are constantly being killed and seriously wounded in this kind of close combat. It is a contest unto the death. These men, no doubt, also had revelation of God's promise in Psalm 91:7 where we find these words recorded: "A thousand may fall at your side, and ten thousand at your right hand; but it shall not come near you." They had to believe in God's miraculous keeping power and that His promises are the same yesterday, today and forever.

One other thought in all this that we need to remember is that just one of God's names is Adonai-Jehovah, which means:sovereign. There has never been a battle and never been a nation in all of history that God didn't give the victory to one side or the other. It means He has power and control over all our lives and battles. Their side or the other. As a case in point, it is recorded in II Kings 5:1 that there was a certain commander of the armies of Syria, a heathen country, whose name was Naaman. Although he and his nation served other gods, he, personally, was a great and honorable man who was always victorious in battle. The Bible goes on to tell us why, "because by him, the Lord had given victory to Syria." He seemingly had everything, in addition to being a "mighty man of valor." He was the highest ranking military officer in his country and he had the confidence of not only the king but all the people. He had victory in all his battles, honor and integrity, a wife and certainly sufficient finances, among other things, but he did have a problem. A big problem. His facial features, his ears, nose and lips were rotting off because he also had leprosy and no hope of a cure. That was until his wife told him of a prophet in the land of Israel who could surely heal him.

As it happened, a young servant girl who was attending his wife whom his armies had captured on a previous raid in Israel told him of a prophet named Elisha. For a man stinking, rotting and dying from leprosy, there could not have been much better news. With the king's blessing, he went to Israel and, though reluctantly, followed the prophet's directives and was totally healed. What is the point of all this? That our life, our breath and all of our ways, whether it be health and healing or life and death in battle, is in God's hands. (Daniel 5:23 paraphrased) He alone holds the victory in all things.

Though all the generals mentioned were brave, cunning, intrepid, strong and highly skilled in battle, all their victories still came from the Lord. You can attend the best military schools, acquire the best weapons and even prepare your "horse … for the day of battle but victory rests with the Lord." (Proverbs

21:31NIV) And, for all of us as well, all our victories will come from the Lord and "… nothing restrains (Him) from saving by many or by few." I Samuel 14:6

What it means to have the character trait of being **INTREPID**:

- Brave
- Audacious
- Fearlessly resolute
- Dauntless in the face of an overwhelming enemy force
- Having personal courage and intestinal fortitude
- The ability to endure and prevail in a great conflict

OY or JOYFULNESS—   **Study start date:** _____ **Finish date:** _____

How can we live in a world full of war, deceit, terrorist attacks, up and down economies, constant change and often disappointment? We definitely can but we will need real joy.

Happiness, of course, depends on a happening. That is, it can only be brought on by external, natural or worldly happenings or circumstances. Joy, on the other hand, is internal because it is energized from the inside out. Joy is the delight of mind caused by the confident, grateful and contented state of the believer. It is also internalized and energized by the Holy Spirit as just one of the manifestations of the Spirit's power and fruit. (Galatians 5:22) It is the result of fulfilling our purpose and helping others by using our God-given gifts to invest in their lives. In addition to all this, joy is brought on by knowing that our life, our breath and all our ways are securely in the Lord's hands. (Daniel 5:23) We know that everything that might happen to us will turn out, ultimately, for our good. (Romans 8:28) We believe this is so because "There is no fear in love (as) perfect love casts out fear …" (I John 4:18) When we know God loves us and our life is in His capable, unfailing hands, we have nothing to fear and fear has no place to attach itself. Thus, it is actually "the joy of the Lord (that) is (our) strength." Nehemiah 8:10

Joy is also an inner knowing that God is always watching over us and thinking about us. Psalm 139:17 and18 records this clear statement from God: "How amazing are your thoughts concerning me." The Psalmist David agreed that we can have hope in this life, saying, "… my heart is glad, and my glory rejoices; my flesh also will rest in hope. For You will not leave my soul in Sheol (hell), nor will You allow your Holy One (Jesus) to see corruption. You will show me the path of life; in Your presence is fullness of joy; at your right hand are pleasures forevermore." Psalm 16:9–11

Someone might ask, "Is walking in joy all that important? Is it ok for a Christian to be walking around with the mullie-grubbs or to have a chip on their shoulder? Well, God gave some tremendous promises to His children in Deuteronomy 28:1–14, called the Blessings of Obedience. These blessings are incredible! Then verse 16 and following catalogues all the curses of disobedience. They are just as horrible as His promises are magnificent, it there could ever be equality in opposites.. One of the reasons the disobedient didn't receive God's blessings was recorded in verse 47: "Because (they) did not serve the Lord (their) God with joy and gladness of heart …"

If there were no other promises, and the Bible is replete with them, just II Corinthians 2:14 would be enough to keep us joyful all the way through this life: Paul said, "Thanks be to God who always causes us to triumph in Christ and through us diffuses the fragrance of His knowledge in every place. For we are to God the fragrance of Christ among those who are being saved and among those who are perishing." We have so many reasons to be joyful. Though we, as believers, cannot "see Him, yet believing, (we) rejoice with joy unspeakable and full of glory, receiving the end of (our) faith—the salvation of (our) souls." (I Peter 1:8) It is also a confidence we have that "all the promises of God in Him are Yes, and in Him Amen, to the glory of God through us." (I Corinthians 1:20) We can build our lives on the unchanging, unfailing Rock of God's Word. Storms and trials will surely come in life, but those who build their lives on the Rock will endure and prevail in the end. In His final conversation with the disciples, Jesus, as you would imagine, chose his words carefully.

He could have dealt with a thousand other things at that moment but instead He spoke of joy saying, "As the Father has loved me, I also have loved you: abide in My love. If you keep my commandments, you will abide in My love, just as I have kept My Father's commandments and abide in His love. These things I have spoken to you, that My joy may remain in you and that your joy may be full." (John 15:9–11)

Therefore, we can conclude that true joy is found in loving God and keeping His commandments as well as living and moving and having our being in Him. He also made them a great promise: "… you now have sorrow; but I will see you again and your heart will rejoice and your joy no one will take from you. And in that day you will ask Me nothing. Most assuredly, I say to you, whatever you ask the Father in My name He will give you. Until now you have asked nothing (by faith) in My name. Ask and you will receive, that your joy may be full." (John 16:22–24) This is the believer's privilege. What a promise! Believers can ask whatever it is that they need for the kingdom work and He will grant it. When we help God advance His kingdom, He will provide whatever we need. There is a joy of the spirit (Acts 15:3) given us when souls are saved and baptized and churches are established. Furthermore, we know that in the fullness of time, all "the kingdoms of this world (will) become the kingdoms of our Lord and of His Christ, and He shall reign forever and ever!" (Revelation 11:15) Even so come quickly Lord Jesus!

What it means to have the character trait of **JOY:**

- Delight
- Bliss
- Imperturbable gladness
- Experiencing great internal pleasure
- Internal felicity brought on by fulfilling our purpose in life
- The emotional state brought on by feelings of success, well being, strength and the prospect of good fortune
- The assurance of possessing something long desired

UST, JUSTICE OR BEING JUST— Study start date: _____ Finish date: _____

Few things bother people more than an unjust, hypocritical leader who shows partiality to various individuals or groups. The late Lieutenant Colonel David Hackworth, one of the greatest and most highly decorated commanders in Vietnam told us truly, saying, "Justice is the hallmark of a successful leader and injustice, the companion of the mediocre." This is so important, someone that said, "We should wrong no one by doing injuries or omitting the benefits that are our duty." Justice and its brother, truth, are the foundation of society. Without them, relationships between people cannot exist. Something is truly just only if it adheres to the principles of faith but it must still be administered with compassion. Justice without compassion is cruelty and compassion without justice is no justice at all.

In respect to justice, we are to be like God. Of Him Moses said, "He is the Rock, His work is perfect; for all His ways are justice. A God of truth and without injustice; righteous and upright is He." (Deuteronomy 32:4) Justice is also part of divine wisdom for "By (it) kings reign and rulers decree justice. By (it) princes rule, and nobles, all the judges of the earth." (Proverbs 8:15, 16) By it thrones and systems of government are established as well as maintained.

I am sure we will all agree that any man about to die would certainly choose his last words carefully. These were King David's and they were actually inspired by the Spirit of the Lord through him saying, "He who rules over men must be just, ruling in the fear of God." (II Samuel 23:3) It might be a short sentence but it is full of meaning and insight. This is some of the best advice any leader could ever ask for. Justice is the hallmark of any leader. We don't have to wonder why Abraham was chosen to be the patriarch of God's people. We were told very explicitly in Genesis 18:19. He was chosen "in order that he may command his children and his household after him, that they keep the way of the Lord, to do righteousness and justice …" The desire to be just is such an integral part of Godly leadership and condition precedent to having faith that God, Himself, decided that "The just shall live by faith" (Hebrews 10:38) but that faith would be the only way for us to please Him. Hebrews 11:6

Some think life is complicated, and sometimes it may seem to be so in such technical world, but it's really not. It is not even about keeping the Ten Commandments or the other 2,000 laws of the Old Testament. Would anyone like to know what it takes to receive the Lord's blessing in life? What is required to have God's favor in this life? Micah 6:8 tells us very succinctly what is good and what the Lord requires: "… To do justice, and to love mercy, and to walk humbly with thy God …" That's it. It's not a whole lot of rules or difficult to understand formulas or philosophies. Just three things. These are not just three suggestions or three requirements but should be three overarching, burning passions in the heart of every leader. Three things that should really fire our furnace. Three things that not only fire your jets but cause the after-burner to kick in as well, so let's take them one-by-one.

First, to "Do justice" means that leaders must be about justice, equity and truth in all they do. Having a fair weight, honest scales and being truthful in all they get involved in. The world might try to convince us it is better to fudge a little or shade the truth somewhat but it isn't. It is always best to be just. This is what brings God's sure blessing in our lives. We also know for certain that our sin will surely find us out. (Deuteronomy 32:23) And, there is no end of blessings for being just, not the least of which is having a good reputation and a clear conscience.

Next, we must "Love mercy." We can't do justice without mercy because it is such an integral part of it. If we love mercy, we will be looking for every reason available to be merciful. Mercy is showing compassion to an offender, someone in distress or someone who is subject to our power. Mercy in God's

Kingdom is so powerful it always triumphs over judgment. Just look at God's plan of redemption. We deserved death but if we truly repent and cry out to Him, He lets the fact that His Son died for us cover our sins and imputes His Son's righteousness to us as well. We inherit Christ's blessing, His righteousness and His standing for eternity— and all at His expense!

Third and finally, we are to "Walk humbly with (our) God." This is to walk with God as our Father, realizing that the Father knows best. It is to believe that His plan for our life is not only the right plan but the only plan for our life that will work. It is a better plan than anything we could ever dream up on our own. It is to walk with Him with lowliness of mind, considering others better than our self. To willingly have our power, prominence and independence totally destroyed is true humility. It is to realize that God is smarter than we are and to always walk in the fear of the Lord. To be humble is the key to obedience and, ultimately, true freedom. We also know that "God resists the proud but gives grace (favor and every worldly and spiritual blessing) to the humble." (I Peter 5:5) It is the only way to live.

What it means to have the character trait of **BEING JUST:**

- Conforming to a standard of truth, equity and reason
- Conforming to what is morally good and upright
- Something that is lawful and legally correct
- Administering impartially and fairly according to existing rules, standards and laws

INDNESS—   **Study start date:** _____ **Finish date:** _____

nce, years ago, when I was ten, my parents took our family on a tour of New York City: Radio City Music Hall, Madison Avenue, the Empire State Building, etc. I admit, it was all quite spectacular. However, having lived in the South most of my life, I was used to people speaking and greeting one another as they passed by on the street. They always said, "Howdy" where I grew up in Texas, which was obviously short for "How do you do?" or "How are you doing?" It just meant that they were interested in you and how you were making it. Who knows, you could be sick or have a problem they could possibly help you with? It is really a public show of kindness and caring between human beings who in most cases didn't even know each other. I liked it back then and I still like it now. However, the stark difference of people not speaking on the streets of New York combined with their being curt in their conversation, made me not want to stay in the South. When you spoke to them, they would look at you like you were three bricks shy of a full load. This made me realize at an early age the enormous value of a little kindness. We all get caught up in the hustle-bustle, fast pace of today's electronic, computerized world and forget to show other people kindness and respect we should as fellow human beings

Proverbs 19:22 tells us, "What is desired in a man is kindness." Few things in life are sweeter than showing others a little kindness. It is good to also remember that those who are out sowing kindness will reap a perpetual crop of joy. Kindness always makes you feel good, no matter if you are on the giving or receiving end. It is the icon of a person's loving heart and its seeds planted today promise a brighter tomorrow. It is also the oil that takes much of the friction out of our lives. We should never worry about showing kindness too soon because we don't know when it will definitely be too late. We need always be kind. It costs so little and means so much.

What it means to have the character trait of **KINDNESS:**

- Having an empathetic nature
- Being affectionate
- Having and showing humility while genuinely caring
- Loving
- Solicitous
- Employing gentle words
- Telling people you care about and appreciate them
- Sending a card to recognize a happening in another's life
- Inclined to be very helpful, compassionate and considerate
- Having a forbearing and nurturing nature
- Desiring to meet another's need, give aid or relief
- A gentle nature

EADERSHIP—   **Study start date:** _____ **Finish date:** _____

Leadership is something there is, no doubt, a dearth of in today's society. It certainly should not be so because there are far more great leaders who are made rather than born. So there is hope for all. Few, indeed, are those who are born with all the outward accoutrements of strength, intellect, appearance and the ability to articulate their points of view. Even having all those in most cases there are two things most lack. First, the ability to organize, develop workable plans and have a winsome attitude. Secondly, and, most importantly, character. Many make advancements and are able to achieve recognition for their leadership for a season but sooner or later, they are tried by the fires of life. Once weighed in the balance, they are found wanting and fired. Leadership for most everyone who sincerely wants to be a good one, must be studied, learned and practiced in the heat of the battle on the playing fields and battle fields of life on a daily basis. Not many are willing to pay the price to not only learn leadership but to discipline themselves to incorporate each of its points into their personality. An even fewer percentage are there are who make it a life study to find these points of leadership and rejoice over them every one as having found a nugget of gold. Finally, those who are self-confident enough to stand up, make a decision, disseminate their plans, follow through, hold people accountable and then take the heat from the nay-Sayers and obstructionists, are extremely few in number. Most would

rather keep their heads down and wait for someone else to come along and take the lead so they can avoid the controversy, criticism and condemnation that comes along with doing what is right.

Remember this, you will never be happy in life until you become what God put you here to be. If God made you an eagle, don't expect to ever be happy bouncing around on the ground like a Bull frog, bumping your …well, posterior every time you take a leap. No, God didn't even make us an eagle, He made us the crown jewel of his creation. He made the universe and while He was at it. He made you in His image, just like you are, to fit into it like a hand in a glove. If you are a man, He created you to be the leader so become the best one you possibly can. If you are working out in the world, apprenticeship is a valid season of life but God made you to be the head and not the tail. (Deuteronomy 28:13) If you are in the church, he made the man to be the leader, teacher, preacher and the elder. (I Timothy 2:12) If you are in the home, He established you as the head of that family. I Corinthians 11:3, Psalm 78:1-11

There are really only two kinds of leaders: first, those who desire to lead for the sake of the power, prestige and personal gain. These are the "rulers of the Gentiles" who love to, like the Master said, lord their power over people they control. (Matthew 10:28) The other kind is, of course, the servant-leader, the ones who lead in love, to serve and bless. They don't see themselves in leadership over but in service under their constituents as well as the leaders they report to and the Lord, Himself.

We see the latter in the Roman centurion who asked Jesus to heal a paralyzed servant who was residing in his home. Although this centurion was a well-paid, powerful Roman captain, he was concerned enough about one of his servants that he afforded him all the comforts of his home. He also took time out of his busy schedule to become his advocate with the Great Physician. Jesus was so moved by the centurion's appeal that He immediately agreed to come to his house and heal him but, amazingly, the centurion objected. With uncommon humility he replied, "Lord, I am not worthy that you should come under my roof. But only speak a word and my servant will be healed. For I also am a man under authority, having soldiers under me. And I say to this one, 'Go.' and he goes, and to another, 'Come." and he comes; and to my servant, 'Do this' and he does it." (Notice the most significant thing he saw about his authority: he didn't see himself as a man "in authority" but a man "under authority.") The centurion saw himself serving and never forgot for a moment the leaders who were in authority above him and his position as one to serve not only them, but those under him. He had total faith in the system of servant leadership that is the hieratical system that God had placed here on earth. He was so confident it would work, he told Jesus to just speak the Word. His was a mantle, not of iron-fisted rule but that of humility and servant leadership. Jesus stood amazed and said, 'Assuredly, I say to you, I have not found such great faith; not even in Israel.' 'Go your way; and as you have believed, so let it be done for you.' And his servant was healed that same hour." Matthew 8:5–13 (condensed)

This kind of servant leadership was written about some twenty-five centuries ago by the Chinese sage, Lao-Tse. He told us, "The reason why rivers and seas receive the homage of a hundred mountain streams is that they keep down below them. Then they are able to reign over all the mountain streams. So the sage, wishing to be above men putteth himself below them. Wishing to be before them (hopefully—for the purpose of serving) putteth himself behind them. Thus, though his place be above men, they do not feel his weight, though his place be before them, they do not count it an injury."

When confronted by injustice in his generation, a true leader, will rise up and lead the charge against it. He must also be a visionary, willing to make large and sometimes bold plans. According to former army general and president of France, Charles De Gaulle, the leader must not be afraid to act even, when necessary, on a large scale—wide open to public scrutiny and criticism. He said, "the leader must aim high, show that he has vision, act on a grand scale, and so establish his authority over the generality of men who splash about in shallow waters."

Our generation, like all others, is looking for leaders to give clear answers to real problems. The Apostle Paul said, "We know that the whole creation groans and labors with birth pangs together until now." (Romans 8:22) "For the earnest expectation of the creation eagerly waits for the revealing of the sons of God." (Romans 8:19) They are groaning under the power of corruption, greed, futility, deceit, sickness and the law of sin and death crying out, in their subconscious for liberty and someone, a real leader, with real answers, to come and set them free. Colonel V. Doner put it this way: "It (the whole creation) is waiting for someone to point the way, from listlessness to purpose, from futility to hope, from despair to vision, from alienation to commitment, from fear and anxiety to strength and courage of great convictions." They are looking for someone to use their leadership to deliver them and influence them to go in the right direction.

A true leader has discipline and is willing to do the things failures refuse to do. He:

- Always carries the tools of a leader: pen and paper
- Arises early every day to spend time alone with the Lord, in the Word and prayer.
- Retires early at night so he lives in the most productive part of each day.
- Always plans to arrive ten minutes early for appointments.
- Looks ahead, prays ahead, plans ahead and stays ahead.
- Makes a prayerful, prioritized list of his daily duties and goals.
- Is alert, careful, cautious, and circumspect and is always prepared.
- Is teachable, ever determined to learn and able to be taught by everyone he meets.
- Never stops sharpening his axe.
- Seeks the Truth, knows the Truth, loves the Truth and lives by the Truth.
- Accepts responsibility for all his men do or fail to do.
- Sets the pace and shoulders more than his share of the load.
- Always does more than is expected or required.
- Defuses problems and remains calm, confident and undramatic in adversity.
- Is open, approachable, flexible and easily entreated.
- Is just, above board and honest in all his dealings because he fears the Lord God.
- Makes every second of each fleeing minute yield its blessing and lets not one get away.
- Is careful to make very few promises but keeps his word regardless of the cost.
- Is a true friend, a true father, a true husband and a true leader.
- As a man under authority, is totally loyal and obedient, discerning the will of his superiors.
- Thinks only on the good things and believes the best of everyone.
- Always works as a servant to make others great in the eyes of the Lord.
- Prefers others above himself.
- Has given his own problems to the Lord so he can concentrate on those of others.
- Has learned that there is no problem or task that patience, prayer, persistence and God will not solve.
- Never, ever quits until he GETS THE JOB DONE.
- Seeks not the world but sets his affections on wisdom, humility, faith, character, understanding and the glory of God.
- Has, in the long run, a calming, prospering effect on all he sets his hand to.
- Is always openly grateful for the assistance and contributions of others.
- Can be trusted implicitly with anything and will one day hear these words: "Enter into the joy of the Lord thou good and faithful servant."

Here is what it means to have the character trait of **LEADERSHIP:**

- Having influence
- Taking responsibility for the task and your group's success or failure
- Having the capacity and qualifications to lead and inspire
- Able to set the example
- Having the ability to build and train leaders under one's authority
- Being out front

LIVING IN THE MOST PRODUCTIVE PART OF THE DAY

Study start date: _____ Finish date: _____

Because we live in a free country, thank God, we are presented with many choices. We always have at least two choices wherever we turn. We can either chose to take the easy path which our flesh craves or the road less traveled, disciplining ourselves to do what it abhors. In most cases the road less traveled is far more productive. Just one choice we face every day of our lives is whether to sleep until the crack of noon or to get up early. Many will tell you that they are just not "morning people." No. That is not the problem. I don't think I have ever met a single person who was actually born with the desire to get up early when their flesh is still wanting to stay in the soft, warm bed. My body has never, ever wanted to get up early one day in my whole life. I just have to tell it what to do. This may all seem very insignificant but it is actually one of the most important decision of our lives. Given the fact that most people sleep about the same seven or eight hours a night, we are free to place them in our day wherever we like. The old adage: "Early to bed, and early to rise makes a man healthy, wealthy and wise" is much more than poetic folklore. It may well decide how much one gets accomplished in life. There is, *in fact,* a most productive and a least productive part of each day. Consider the two choices:

One person gets up at 7:30 AM, throws his clothes on and races to the office with the newspaper under his arm, gulping down a cup of coffee and a sweet roll, works his eight plus hours and gets home about six or six thirty. The kids want to play ball, the phone rings and the telemarketers want to sell him siding, insurance, and whatever else is under the sun. The wife wants to talk and if she doesn't get out her 25,000 words a day, she is going to be upset. He really wanted to watch the news but the neighbor calls, wanting him to help fix his cheap lawnmower, and on and on it goes, ad infinitum. There is no time to be alone with God and no time to read God's Word or pray. The kids go to sleep about eight or nine and he is dead tired, so he and his wife watch TV until the late show is over and go to bed at midnight. The whole day is a blur as he dashes like a lightning streak dealing with one societal demand or crisis after another. No time to prepare, pray, study, plan, organize, get ahead of the bill paying, write the relatives or prepare a Sunday school message.

On the other hand, another person arises early, about 4:30 AM or so and has time alone with God. He gives Him not only a tithe of his days' time but the first fruits of his time as well. He knows the Lord's pattern is that He has always desired, even requires, the first fruits and the first born of everything. This man has time to read the Word, pray, organize, study, write, pay bills and generally get ahead of the day. This is the reason the old proverb says 'the early bird gets the worms.' Thankfully, not many salesmen call at 5:00 AM, the kids don't want to play, mamma doesn't want to talk (she's still sleeping) and you have time to give God the best part of your day. About four or five days a week he can even hit the gym for an hour or so. He still gets to work early at about 7:00 or 7:30 AM to start working on the day's projects but he has already gotten some of his work organized at home. He works until 5 or 5:30 and goes home. Since he already gave God the first part of his day, he now has a perfect freedom and a clear conscience to play ball with the kids, spend time with his wife and tell her how blessed he was to find such a wonderful, beautiful lady to be his bride. He can hear about her problems and even take a few phone calls in time to sit down to supper with the family. He can listen without distraction to what is bothering the kids and even see the evening news. Then he can get to bed by 9:30, giving his body plenty of rest, and arise early the next day, ready and excited to meet with the Lord. Realize now that some folk must work at night but the concept of prioritizing our time holds regardless of the time of day we actually do these things.

Remember, there is a certain season a farmer can plant and, likewise, a season to reap. No wise farmer plants in the winter and reaps in the summer. Similarly, there is a time to rest and a time to plant in our own daily lives if we want to be as productive as absolutely possible. Every person has only so much time and the Bible tells us our days are few and speeding away like a rocket ship. Our energy, efforts, prayers and time are the only seeds we have with which to plant and we can plant them in any part of the twenty-four hour day we choose. If you, like the farmer, plant them in the least productive soil, you might get a crop but it will only be stunted and deformed, if you get a crop at all. On the other hand, if you plant your seeds in the most productive soil and in the proper season, you can expect a bumper crop. In addition, what you produce every day is added to what you produced the days and years before so you will start enjoying the compound effect. How powerful is this? It is said that the eighth wonder of the world is compound interest and it works with time just like it does with money. What if you got that kind of effect with your whole life?

Why is this so important? Because, as I mentioned, none of us gets much time on the blue marble. Moses showed us in Psalm 90:10: "The days of our lives are seventy years; and if by reason of strength they are eighty …" Then again, some get the eighty and more but he says later in this passage that those who get a few more years will have little to boast about because their days will be full of "labor and sorrow, for … soon (we are all) cut off and fly away." That is why Moses prayed at the end of his days in Psalm 90:12 (NIV) to "Teach us to number our days aright that we may gain a heart of wisdom." This is so we can see that the days we have in our years of strength are very few and we need to be good stewards of them. That is, we need to get the most out of each and every one of them and not let them slip away. Here is the exercise Moses recommended:

365 days per year
- 8 holidays per year
-104 weekend days
253 days per year

70 years of strength promised
-_____ your current age
_____ your years remaining
x 253 days per year
_____ Days of strength remaining

No matter how many days of strength you come up with, it won't seem like very many and you will certainly want each one of them to be productive.

What it means to have the character trait of **KNOWING TO LIVE IN THE MOST PRODUCTIVE PART OF THE DAY:**

- Knowing just as there are seasons to plant and seasons to reap, there are better times to plant our daily efforts in life
- The ability to discern the time we choose for our daily activities as good ground or bad
- Knowing that it pays in life to arrive early, be prepared and live at the ready
- Realizing which part of our is the most productive

OVE/ see CHARITY

LOYALTY—   Study start date: _____ Finish date: _____

We are told in the Scriptures, "Know this, that in the last days perilous times will come." And, how will we know we are there? It tells us explicitly. " … People will be lovers of themselves, lovers of money, boasters, proud, blasphemers, disobedient to parents, unthankful, unholy, unloving, unforgiving, slanderers, without self-control, brutal, despisers of good, traitors, headstrong, haughty, lovers of pleasure rather than lovers of God." (II Timothy3:1–4) We see all of these things today but probably worst are the traitors. Those who loudly profess their loyalty but their heart is far from you. This kind has been here since time in memorial. Those who say they will be with the unit, company, ministry, church, etc. until hell freezes over but they don't have the foggiest notion what that means and the least intention to follow through. When you boil it all down, loyalty is really the essence of life. It is what life is really all about. Are we going to be loyal to ourselves and the devil or loyal to God?

First, we need to dispel a terribly erroneous notion here. So many today want to be totally independent. Actually, no one ever really is. No one ever really works for himself. You might be the boss or you might own your own company but everyone works for and serves others in this life. Every company has customers to serve, employees and a staff to look out for and take care of, a board of directors to answer to, etc. Sooner or later, the depth of our loyalty will be plumbed by the trials, troubles, temptations, market pressures and military threats of life. These things will, in time, cause the hidden motives of every heart to be revealed. Those things men try their best to cover up and hide, the Bible promises will be shouted from the housetops. (Luke 12:2, 3) We will all be known, sooner or later, for who and what we really are.

Loyalty is an extremely rare commodity in the world today. It may be a trait rarely found but it is still indispensable in life. It is the ability to be steadfast in service, friendship and faithfulness to others. It can't be hidden because it is exposed by everything we do or say. It comes out in one's attitude, body English, eye movement and tone of voice. For anyone wanting to be a success in life, loyalty is crucial. It is the most precious gift you can give your leader and without it all else is worthless. Now I'm not calling for apple polishing or blowing smoke. Keep your integrity. But, think about it a minute. Let's make you the boss for a minute. You have ten people working for you and only one is loyal. Nine are just self-seeking opportunists. Which one would you promote? Which one would you want to keep in the hard times when you have to let nine of them go? Employers would far rather have one average employee working for them who is loyal to a fault than a hundred talented people who are really only looking out for themselves. Besides, knowing that your leaders can count on you, that they need, appreciate and trust you implicitly is one of the greatest rewards life has to offer. Truly, if we are going to work for someone, we would be wise to look for the good in them and speak well of them. No one is perfect. Now you have a choice. You can either focus on their few short comings or be thankful for all the good points resident in them. However, if you can't be loyal to someone, then do yourself and them a favor—be gone. I'll say it again, If you can't be loyal, be gone.

Years later, looking back, the thing that is real that I got from my service to my first company commander, as aide to the Commander of the 82nd Airborne Division and as the S-1 (Personnel Officer) for the Brigade Commander at Ft. Ord, was not the tremendous Officer Efficiency Reports (OER's) they gave me, the Army commendation medals they gave me, the promotions these things caused or the pay raises that came as a direct result. What is most precious to me was the loyalty and devotion I gave them and they returned to me in time. It was how much they trusted me when they weren't around and the enormous tasks they put in my hands; even the mutual love and respect we shared. Truth be known, it was probably only on account of loyalty that every good thing in the military happened to me in the first place. I certainly wasn't perfect. A whole lot of people were far more capable but loyalty was a free gift that only I could give them for my service at the time. I was also blessed with some good commanders in Vietnam. Although I rarely saw them, because we were always deployed in the jungles operating as a separate rifle company on search and destroy missions, I can tell you that loyalty even works long-distance. Amazingly, the one thing that means the most to me of all that was said by one of my commanders in my OER's was a solitary, little statement: "He accomplished every mission I assigned him." That was my intention from the first moment I took command of each company. No matter what it took. As a commander I was responsible for everything my men did or failed to do. Don't guess I need to say that in a war, that is sometimes, because of the enemy, not easy. They like living on this planet too but God gave the grace. True, I had some great platoon leaders, some awesome soldiers and some fantastic air support.

Certainly another huge assist was God. I truly knew that I would only make it if it was His pleasure—though undeserved in my case, as it might have been. Our family motto, as I have mentioned, is "Vil God I Zal" which means "Will God I shall" or "If it is God's will I will" do, accomplish or gain the victory in anything I might be pursuing at the time. Here is something you need to write down in your book. The victory in every battle that has ever been won on earth was given by the hand of God. He gave us every one. Proverbs 21:31

Not being a faithful friend, family member, employee or mate cannot be made up for by other deeds, enormous cash payments, boxes of candy, dozens of roses or a litany of other positive character traits. Loyalty is a duty. It is indispensable to building and maintaining relationships. It is what makes who we are either real, imagined or fraudulent. A man void of loyalty ceases to exist. Loyalty actually arouses one to true manhood, meaning and purpose in life. Only by a man's willingness to invest himself as well as his intellectual, physical and moral resources generously and unreservedly beyond his own narrow circle of self, is it possible for him to become valuable to others, emerge as a leader or make a significant contribution to society. Neither man nor community can exist without loyalty. Truly, no man can be rich unless he is first rich in friendship with God (Luke 12:21), which is our most important relationship. However, in earthly terms, a man is rich only if he is rich in friendships with others and there is no way to keep and maintain life-long friendships without it.. Indeed, very few in life are blessed by the Creator with great intellect, strength or beauty, but all these things are quickly overcome by loyalty. We can all choose to make that our most outstanding trait or not. It begins with a decision only you can make.

In life it is loyalty that causes you to be picked for important jobs and promoted in the work force more than anything else. Opportunists, gold diggers and traitors are a dime a dozen (or less) but a man loyal to a fault is truly a rare find. How often do we run across the one who makes his boss' friends his friends and his boss' enemies his own. We have been told and it's true that "People will say they will be with you through thick or thin but when it gets a little too thick, they start to thin out." Where the battles of life rage the hottest is precisely the point where our loyalty will be tested again and again. If it fails at that point, it never really existed in the first place. What we love the most and who we are faithful to will soon be manifest. Life is just set up that way. There are no secrets for long.

This one thing called loyalty is what makes service to others so sweet and satisfying in life. Whoever we work for on this planet, we should work for as unto the Lord and in the name of the Lord. (Colossians 3:17, 23) What a joy it is to acquire a servant's heart and lose one's self in service to others. It is such a blessing to be an extension of a leader's personality and make his wish our command. What freedom there is in losing one's self and deferring to the leader's instructions. It is the most precious and fragile thing and is to be preserved and defended at all cost in every human relationship. Therefore we should make a point of avoiding any action or speech that would cause our loyalty to ever be questioned. Loyalty only exists by the most fragile cord and can be destroyed, often irretrievably, in a moment.

Another important part of true loyalty is being there for our leader in his time of need. We always want everyone to be there when we are in need. Remember this, there are times in every leader's life when the enemy, the mutinous, the world system, the jealous and the false accusers will come against him. We should be watching for these times to support and defend him (as long as what he is accused of is not illegal, immoral or unscriptural). They say, "When the tide goes down, the rocks begin to show." When the going gets rough and the times get testy, the motives of men's hearts are going to be exposed. It is in those times that our faithfulness to our friends and our leaders is most important.

In the military the minimum requirement has always been loyalty to the group and obedience to the commander. However, for any organization, military or otherwise to be healthy, strong and vibrant, there must be both upward and downward loyalty. The subordinates must be loyal to the leader, and, in turn, the leader must be loyal to his subordinates.

What it means to have the character trait of **LOYALTY:**

- Faithfulness to the one to whom fidelity is obliged or expected
- Faithfulness to one's God, sovereign, belief system, cause, leader, lawful government, ideal, political party or custom
- An issue of the heart
- The unnatural ability to deny self and remain steadfastly loyal to entities and persons outside of one's own selfish interests.
- The ability to deny self and serve others when it is not easy, convenient or immediately beneficial
- The one trait that causes a person to gain and retain responsibility
- The trait that makes one valuable to God, society and its organizations
- The trait that causes one to be promoteable
- Unwavering allegiance
- Dedication to others and their interests
- Sincerity
- Being there for your friends and leaders in their time of need
- Fidelity of heart and trust
- Faithfulness to one to whom fidelity is obliged or expected

EEKNESS— **Study start date:** _____ **Finish date:** _____

Meekness is a preeminent grace of the soul, the character quality first and foremost exercised in *submission* to God. It is here that one accepts His dealings, teachings and commands gladly without resisting. It follows and has a very close connection with humility. Jesus said, "Take My yoke upon you and learn of Me, for I am meek and lowly in heart, and you will find rest for your souls." And, this is the way we will know we have found the right yoke: He says, "For My yoke is easy and My burden is light." (Matthew 11:29, 30) "Therefore," the Apostle James said, "lay aside all filthiness and overflow of wickedness, and receive with meekness the implanted Word, which is able to save your souls." (James 1:21) It will, indeed, take effect. "Who (some may ask) is wise and understanding among you? Let him show by good conduct that his works are done in the meekness of wisdom." (James 3:13) They will, "with all lowliness and gentleness, with longsuffering, (be) bearing with one another in love, endeavoring to keep the unity of the spirit in the bond of peace." Ephesians 4:3, 4

One excellent example of meekness is Moses, who the Bible says "… was very meek above all the men who were upon the face of the earth." (Numbers 12:3) Certainly, he was meek but he was not weak. Having been the son of Pharaoh's daughter, Moses was also extremely able and knowledgeable of all that was taught by the scholars of Egypt. However, when he was fully grown, he went to his own people who were slaves and, having compassion, began to look upon their burdens. In defense of his people, Moses killed an Egyptian and when the crime was exposed, he quickly fled to the land of Midian. His meekness allowed God to continue teaching him for the next forty years on the back side of the desert. Later he was used by God to lead the Israelites through various difficult and dangerous trials, journeying through the desert for another forty years.

Meekness is power and ability under God's harness and control. It teaches us that our Father knows best. Though first extended toward God, it manifests itself toward men as well. To both those in authority and even those in power who are evil—meekness is knowing that God is well able to chasten and purify His people.

It was this same spirit of meekness we saw in King David's life when he fled Jerusalem at his son Absalom's rebellion. David knew he could easily defeat his son but he left town at great cost to himself and his kingdom instead to keep from having to take his life. This decision caused him great loss of property and certainly resulted in many of his subjects thinking he left in defeat or in fear of Absalom's army. He gave God room to have His way with Absalom and his rebellion.

On another occasion, David allowed Shimei to curse him, throw stones at him and kick up a bunch of dust in his presence. Remember now, David was the greatest warrior in all of Israel's history and certainly needed no help to personally take Shimei's head off or put him in his place. However, in this situation David was flanked by his mighty men on both the right and left. One of his lieutenants said, "Why should this dead dog curse my lord the king? Please, let me go over and take off his head!" (II Samuel 16:9) David said, "… Let him alone, and let him curse, for so the Lord has ordered him. It may be that the Lord will look on my affliction, and the Lord will repay me with good for his cursing this day." v.10–12

Meekness is what caused Job to say, "Though He slay me, yet will I trust Him." (Job 13:5) "And though after my skin worms destroy this body, yet in my flesh shall I see God, whom I shall see for myself, and mine eyes shall behold and not another …" (v.19:26) No mortal man in recorded history has ever suffered more than Jo, yet he would still trusted God with not only his life but with his eternity as well.

Having had only two, what one might call "bad things" happen to me in life, I learned that what we mortals see as bad, God is always working it for good. In each case it seemed at first the worst things that had ever happened to me. Both, in time, however, turned out to be the very best. For this reason I have learned to thank God for two things in every adversity: First, I thank Him for the trial. And, Secondly, I thank Him for trusting me with it. This poem by Grant C. Tuller says it far better than I:

The Weaver

"My life is but a weaving, between my Lord and me,
I cannot choose the colors He worketh steadily.
Ofttimes He weaveth sorrow, and I in foolish pride
Forget He sees the upper and I, the under side.

Not till the loom is silent and the shuttles cease to fly,
Shall God unroll the canvas and explain the reason why.
The dark threads are as needful, in the weaver's skillful hand,
As the threads of gold and silver, in the pattern He has planned."

Meekness enables us to be taught and, most importantly, to remain teachable. It shows us how little we know and how much we need learn; so much more no matter where we are in life. It also lets us realize that there are some lessons that only God can teach us. Meekness, further, teaches us that nothing can happen to us in life without God's approval. For our heart to take even one more beat, the matter must first cross God's desk for approval. It also gives us assurance that whatever happens to us will come together for good in the end. (Romans 8:28)This thing is so powerful that the Orientals have said, "Meekness compels even God, Himself."

This great gift of meekness allows us to always see others as better than ourselves. Though we may possess a few gifts and talents (and we all do), it is the ability to see that other people have them too and not regard our own as any better than anyone else's. Besides, everyone's talents are needed in life as well as the Body of Christ. Further, it causes us to realize that everyone we meet can be our teacher. We realize that they probably have been some place we have never been. They may know something we don't know. They can do something better than we can, so why not learn from them?

What it means to have the character trait of **MEEKNESS**:

- Lowliness of mind and spirit
- It is to gladly realize that we have all made mistakes and have many shortcomings
- It is realizing that in our limited, flawed condition, whatever God's providence allows us to accomplish in life is all by His exceeding great mercy and grace
- It is to expect and require nothing
- It is to be at peace when everything around you is going wrong and no one understands you
- The ability to endure injury or insult patiently as well as not being resentful or retaliatory
- To be mild mannered
- Totally trusting of God's providence
- Not arrogant or haughty
- Submissive to authority
- The ability to gladly defer to those in authority
- Having a teachable spirit
- Being obedient
- Open to learning new ideas and new ways of doing things

MISSION ORIENTED, BEING —   **Study start date:** _____ **Finish date:** _____

A mission is defined as a goal, task or objective to be accomplished whether it be assigned by the military, a business, a church or a humanitarian group. It can be a single or a multifaceted task or a sequence of goals that need to be accomplished over a period of time. In the church it could the assignment of the task to build a mission housing a ministry in a foreign city or a mission in your home town called a home mission, with the ability to begin conducting outreaches, ministry or hold crusades. In business, it could be the assignment to go into a certain trade territory to sell a product with the goal of achieving a certain sales volume within a given period of time. In the military it can be the assignment of an enemy target to one aircraft on a given day or an objective assigned to a combat unit, be it a squad, platoon, company battalion, division or army to take out a specific objective, unit, petroleum or ammo dump, fort, city for example, on a certain day. Being mission oriented is to dedicate ourselves to an assigned mission. Specifically, it is the ability to remain totally committed to the goal assigned until it is accomplished, regardless of the cost, loss of life, the time required or how many obstacles are placed in our way.

In business, for example, missions or objectives are to be met in much the same way. Things like sales quotas, target dates for opening new plants or markets must also be met but with the precondition that the whole process happen in a timely manner and with safety for all being of primary importance. It is also understood that in business, where making a profit is the primary goal, the mission is to be continued only as long as the assignment remains profitable.

In the church, the mission is to be accomplished regardless of the cost. Lives are in the balance and the church's work extends out into eternity. A good example of the cost of missions work can be seen in the life of Jim Elliot. He and his team were committed to the evangelism of the Waodani Indians in Ecuador during the early 1950's. On January 4, 1956, upon flying their small plane in and setting up a base camp in the vicinity of the Indians village, they were visited by a group of Waodani warriors who killed Elliott and all four of his companions. These missionaries all lost their lives to the very ones they were trying to win to Christ. Long before Elliott died, he stated his belief in the importance of mission work saying, "He is no fool who gives up what he cannot keep to gain that which he cannot lose." After he died, his wife, Elizabeth, along with other missionaries (and on another occasion, the son of the missionary pilot, Nate Saint), returned and continued to work with the Indians. One of the natives who participated in the murders actually became an evangelist himself and helped lead most of the tribe to the salving knowledge of Jesus Christ. They accomplished the mission.

In the military, an assigned mission is to be accomplished without fail, regardless of the cost in material, finances or lives. Being mission oriented, is such that once a mission is assigned, it is one's responsibility to accomplish regardless, without excuse. Regardless of the opposition, one is to attack and keep on attacking even when out of ammunition, even when all one's men are dead and, yes, even if captured. A soldier must never give up. Even while in captivity he is to lead the resistance and try his best to mount an escape in order to attack the enemy again. Loss of life is not as important as the mission because your unit may be guarding, protecting or be expected to attack in unison with other sister units in an orchestrated invasion. Giving up your position may allow the larger, friendly unit you are part of to be flanked or even encircled. It may also allow the enemy to cut off your army's supply lines. In any of these cases it is easy to see that your small loss could preclude a much larger loss of life and maybe even the failure of the army's overall mission. In the military, usually a lot of other people are counting on you so failure is not an option. Not only are other units in the service counting on you but so are the people back home, the millions of women, men, children, babies and old folks who need and are counting on our protection. All life is important but better a few in the military to give their lives so the whole nation is not bombed or plundered by raiding bands of savage heathens, Marxists or communists. The only time a soldier is authorized to give up on his mission is when he is dead. I don't mean to be brutal here but war is hell. However, there are several things worse than war: losing, slavery, tyranny and torture are a few. This can't happen.

Being mission oriented is something taught as an absolute necessity of very early on in the military. Leaders are to carry out the orders of their superiors regardless of how long it takes, or whatever may be required. You are never to proffer excuses or say, "We didn't have enough time, men, material or ammunition." If you didn't have enough time, you should have started earlier or be willing to stay later. If you didn't have enough men, marshal some or deputize some. If you didn't have enough materiel, requisition more or go out and buy some yourself or "midnight requisition." Not enough ammunition? Requisition more or take if from the enemy and shoot it back at them in their own weapons. But, never, never come up with excuses. A good leader has no need of an excuse because he always accomplishes the mission. There is no excuse for not accomplishing the mission. Being able to accomplish the mission makes a leader valuable in the military and the civilian world as well.

Remember, in life authority and responsibility always goes to the strong hands. Some companies go out of business in various markets and all their business goes to the stronger, more able and capable companies that yet remain. When a problem surfaces in business, the leader always looks for someone who has always accomplished every task that has ever been assigned because they know one thing for sure: that person will always get the job done—regardless. This is a huge asset or mind-set people formerly in the military take into the civilian work-place. Having the ability hang with a task regardless of the circumstances and get things done makes a person extremely valuable to any organization.

Just yesterday I saw the owner of a security company speaking on TV who, in his prior employment, had been in the upper echelons of law enforcement in New York City. He was talking about hiring people for the company he started for the purpose of doing investigations. He said, "Send me every soldier coming out of the military you can. I'll take every one I can get. They already know to respect authority, get the job done and say 'Yes, Sir.' and 'No, Sir.' automatically to their customers and the public, etc." or words to that effect. He went on to say, "There are a whole lot of things they already know and don't have to be taught." Although he didn't use these words, one of the traits he alluded to was being mission oriented.

What it means to have the character trait of **BEING MISSION ORIENTED**:

- Being totally dedicated to completing an assigned task
- Focused and determined to complete the assigned goal regardless of the difficulties or costs encountered
- Moving on the assigned task and not being deterred by counter influences or obstacles

MOTIVATION —   **Study start date:** _____ **Finish date:** _____

Have you ever wondered why one person is so highly motivated they succeed in life at everything they touch while another person hasn't got enough get up and get a cup of coffee? We can look at two different people but all we see is the outside. They may appear to be similar in size, physical strength, education, etc. They could also score about the same on an I.Q. test, but are, in fact, very likely totally different when it comes to their ability to accomplish things in life. Physical, mental and educational attributes are not what makes the difference. We would need to go inside their hearts to know what kind of motivation they have. We can't tell from appearances which one has an excitement for life, a craving for a challenge or a drive to master difficult assignments and face off against the impossible. One person goes to work waiting for the five o'clock chime and the other goes there to learn new things, make changes for the better, to improve efficiency, open up new opportunities for the company, improve the company's competitive edge, take things to the next level and, generally, make a better mouse trap. One is bored to dickens with life and the whole miserable work-a-day-world scene and the other is thrilled at all the prospects. One will soon be getting a pink slip and the other will likely be promoted to either president of the company or the branch manager in a new market area.

The difference in a word: is simply, motivation. The one with the motivation could actually have far less talent and while the others has tremendous abilities. Motivation trumps ability every time. One just wants to get by—thinking they are doing the company a favor showing up at work on time, blessing them with their presence so he can have the opportunity to grumble about the low pay and poor prospects. The other is there to make a difference for everyone concerned. He is there to treat the company as if it were their own and make it the most successful and profitable company in their market area. He sees all obstacles as opportunities and thanks God for trusting them to solve them. Sure, he sees all the garbage and injustice out in the world but these things to him are miniscule compared to the vast array of glowing opportunities and challenges awaiting him. People with motivation love their work, they love people, they love their job, they try to love their boss and they love to try their best to make a difference. They are always looking for a better way to do things because they are working for God and working simply to be a blessing. They are always willing to do more than is expected or required, laying down 110% effort on everything they touch. Success, you see, doesn't depend on talent, as much as it does desire. How much do you want to succeed? If you have enough desire, you will work diligently at improving yourself and you will get what you need to succeed. You will read the books, take the courses, study all the areas of your interest and do your best to become an expert in the field you have chosen. You will give it all you've got every day and you will love your work. And, remember, when you love your work, your work will tell you its secrets.

Highly motivated people, you need to know however, are generally not well appreciated by many of their peers simply because their performance sets a higher standard for everyone. It may even shine a light on the others' miserable lack of motivation. An example of this was seen in the life of David. He was sent by his father to carry some supplies and food to his two elder brothers and some cheese to the commanders of the Israeli Army who were all at war with the Philistines. This would be somewhat like taking them a box of Snickers candy bars today—just a little refreshment and encouragement amid the austere life of soldiers at war. Then just a teenager, David climbed the mountain where the Israeli Army was camped and heard the giant, Goliath, the champion of the Philistines, railing at the armies of the Living God in the valley below. He dared someone to come down and fight him and no one would.

David asked how long this had been going on and they told him forty days. When little David volunteered to take him on, Eliab, his oldest brother began to ridicule him saying, "Why did you come down here? And with whom have you left those few sheep in the wilderness? I know your pride and the insolence of your heart, for you have come down to see the battle." (I Samuel 29:28) No. He had come down just to deliver a blessing to his brothers and the captains of the Army on his father's instructions but now, incredibly, he was about to be the only Israeli in the battle. David's response was, "What have I done now? Is there not a cause in Israel?" (I Samuel 17:29) Interpreted, this meant: Is there nothing sacred in our nation worth risking your life and dying for, our women and children, our neighbors, our sacred honor, the honor of God? Is there not a motivation here to fight? He was not happy that an uncircumcised Philistine was allowed to mock God, His nation, army and people. When David's words were reported to King Saul, he was immediately summoned to Saul's tent. Before Saul he said there would be no need for any man's heart failing them about this Philistine, he would fight him by himself—and did. He was the only one in the nation with the motivation sufficient to risk his life to deliver the country from this curse. Remember, the reward Saul had posted for anyone willing to do this was great riches, the hand of his beautiful daughter in marriage and his father's house exempted from taxation. David showed all the world that day that he had the motivation and the gear to take on any problem the nation had. He had the motivation long before he came to the job.

At the turn of the 20th century an interesting young cadet enrolled at Virginia Military Institute by the name of George C. Marshall. He was, in fact, highly motivated before he arrived there. He was so highly motivated that he was the only cadet in the school's history to graduate without receiving a single demerit. Early on, he set his standards high. As an Army officer, Marshal said "He was tough because he believed men wanted to belong to a highly disciplined, hardworking, business like organization they could be proud of and boast about. The stricter, the better within the prescribed hours." He advanced quickly through the ranks to become Chief of Operations of the 1st Army Corps, establishing himself as a dynamic leader and a terrific logistician. The very day Pearl Harbor was attacked, he, coincidentally, was installed as the Chief of Staff of the Army. During World War II he was promoted to General of the Army and was responsible for selecting most of the generals during this critical time when the ranks exploded. All his selections had to be ratified, of course, by the President. He was also responsible for the training of all our soldiers, seamen and airmen as well as the manufacture and delivery of all the supplies, arms, ships, tanks and airplanes to the Allied forces. This, certainly, was a mammoth task, in anyone's estimation. As a five star general he would tell the commanders about these tasks under him, "I'll be out to see you soon. If I find you doing something, I'll help you but if I find you doing nothing, only God will help you."

After the war, he became ambassador to China. Later he was appointed Secretary of State and Secretary of Defense where he formulated what later became known and enacted into law as the Marshal Plan. This was a herculean operation to rebuild all of war-torn Europe, supplied by air from the United States. For this and many other initiatives, he was awarded the Nobel peace prize.

Motivation, after salvation, may be the most important thing a person possesses. It is available to anyone, the whosoever wills that is, who are willing to do what it takes to get it. When Moses died, God told Joshua, Moses' aide, a young man at the time, that his day under the sun had come. He needed to rise to the occasion and become a great leader himself because they were about to go in and take the land from several heathen king. For this enormous task he would need to be strong, courageous and, you could certainly say, highly motivated and God then told him how to get it. He assured him that the plan He was about to give him would cause every place he set the sole of his foot would be his and that no man could stand against him all the days of his life. Furthermore, God promised not to leave him or forsake him and that whatever he did would succeed. He said, "Only be strong and very courageous, that you may observe to do according to all the law which Moses My servant commanded you; do not turn from it to the right hand or the left, that you may prosper wherever you go. This Book of the Law shall not depart from your mouth, but you shall meditate in it day and night, that you may observe to do according to all that is written in it. For then you will make your way prosperous and then you will have good success. Have I not commanded you? Be strong and of good courage, do not be afraid, nor be dismayed, for the Lord your God is with you wherever you go." Joshua 1:7–9

What it means to have the character trait of **MOTIVATION**:

- The inward drive that produces outward results
- The impulse to get out of bed early and conquer the world
- The thrill of changing things for the better in society
- The drive and confidence to initiate things that have never been done before
- The willingness to stand for the truth
- Drive
- Zeal
- Having high goals and expectations
- Enthusiasm and the intestinal fortitude to go all the way
- Incentivised by an internal drive

MOXIE —   **Study start date: _____ Finish date: _____**

In today's world knowledge is abounding such that many people are becoming educated far beyond their intellect. Few have any moxie—which is to know what to do with knowledge and how to make it work in practical life problems and situations.

An example of a complete lack of moxie today is our government's recent quest to require a license to do everything up to and almost including getting out of bed in the morning. Until a year or so ago in Georgia, a person didn't have to have a license to be a builder. Ostensibly, of course, the state said it was needed to protect the public from sorry builders. It might, indeed, provide some additional protection, albeit at an enormous expense but it happens to be in an area where it was not needed. The market weeds out bad builders immediately. First of all, even if the person hiring a builder is not wise enough to check his pedigree, these same people are probably going to get a bank loan in the process. If a builder doesn't deliver a good product or fails to stand behind his work—just one time, the bank will cut them off in a second. In addition to that, the disenchanted home owner can put a sign up in his yard, blast the builder on the internet or call a TV station for an interview in front of the property. No builder can stand that kind of report or reputation and will be out of business very quickly. In addition the county building inspection office requires a review of the plans and specifications. Even beyond that, they inspect every part of the construction while it is in progress to be sure things are done right. Think about it for a moment, since this law was enacted in Georgia a couple years ago very few new buildings have been built. That means just about every building in the state has been built by an unlicensed builder and there was rarely ever a problem with any of them.

So the state decided that a builder's reputation, experience, quality and customer service will no longer count and quality assurance will be better handled by someone's ability to take courses and pass a test. Of course the home buyer will also have to pay their pro rata share of the cost of the Builder's $500,000.00 liability insurance policy and the huge pre-paid workman's comp. policy, license fee, plus the cost of continuing education classes every year. This all might have worked in a time where builders did twenty to fifty houses a year and could amortize this added expense over this large number of houses. However, now that residential building has all but stopped in this state, few builders can afford the $10–14,000.00 up front cost required to take a small remodeling or an occasional house to build even on a pre-sale. We have lawyers with no business experience and no moxie making laws like this that detrimentally effect and shut down entire industries. Requiring a builder to have a license just creates another level of government bureaucracy, more red tape, more fees and more government employees for the public to pay. This simply causes buyers to pay more for their new home.

I won't even get started on Presidents Carter and Clinton along with Congress passing the Community Re-Investment Act that required banks to make loans to NINJA's. That's people who have no income, no credit, no job, no bank account or credit and then making them loans they do not qualify for or can in any way afford. This one foolish move, primarily caused our recent economic collapse, shutting down nearly the entire home building industry and immediately bankrupting the insurance companies that stood behind the loans.

Similarly, not long ago the state started requiring a license for septic tank operators. An engineer friend of mine decided to take the septic tank operator's test along with his dad who had been in the business for over forty years. His dad could walk out in someone's back yard, look at the soil, survey the situation and know instinctively, in a matter of minutes, how to correct the problem in the least intrusive and expensive as well as most effective way. The engineer's dad made a 70 on the test and he made a 100. What did all this testing prove? That the son was better at taking tests that the father—nothing more.

Growing up, my dad always told us boys to make good grades in school—which was only right— but I rarely did. However, he also told us that "Out in the world, for some people who were able to get a college education and make excellent grades, this still wouldn't make it all happen for them. Education is not enough". He said, "You've got to have moxie and some people have little to none of that."

During the Cambodian Invasion back in the Vietnam War days, my company, after some pretty fierce resistance, took over a major Viet Cong base camp. It was so large, we found out later, that the folk up at Division Headquarters dubbed it "The City." The NVA had tons and tons of rice, weapons, ammunition, communications equipment and other munitions and stores too numerous to name. We also captured fourteen duce and a half trucks (a huge truck with six wheels capable of carrying a two and a half ton pay load.) None of those trucks would run and my men found absolutely no keys or tools. I was busy seeing to it that all the rice, munitions and equipment were destroyed so we could get out of there before we started taking mortar fire again. While most of us were executing on that, a couple men asked to see what they could do with the trucks. I had absolutely nothing to do with it but in the space of about 45 minutes, those red blooded, young American soldiers of mine, with all the shade tree mechanics they learned in their back yards working on flat head Fords and Chevy V-8's, got all fourteen of them hot-wired and purring like a kitten walking on cotton. Now that's moxie. I called the Battalion Commander on the radio, requested a cobra gun-ship for close aerial fire support in case we ran into trouble and got permission to drive all of those trucks back to the Battalion fire base. We put a machine gun on top of the cab of each truck and had the best time making that run at pretty high speeds—for duce and a half's—back to the fire base. Those men were so excited, they were whooping and hollering, waving handkerchiefs tied to the flash-hiders on their rifles and hanging off the sides of those trucks as we drove into the entrance of the base camp. Oh happy day!!!

What it means to have the character trait of **MOXIE:**

- Intuitive know how
- The ability to navigate successfully through the sticky wickets of life
- Finesse
- The ability to make 2 plus 2 equal 4 out in the world—in real life
- The ability to look ahead and see future unintended consequences
- The ability to make decisions on your feet
- Having common sense—which is not at all common today
- Practical knowledge
- The ability to coordinate information, systems, resources, equipment, policies and human personalities along with your faith to get the job done efficiently and effectively.
- The ability to take virtually nothing and make something
- The wisdom to hear both sides of an issue before making decisions
- The wisdom to list all the options available to you in a certain situation and then catalogue all the advantages and disadvantages on paper for each
- When broadsided with a huge problem in life, it is the presence of mind never to feel sorry for yourself but to thank God for the problem and trusting you with solving it.
- When trouble comes, it is the ability to land on your feet like a cat every time.

EATNESS —   **Study start date: _____ Finish date: _____**

eatness starts, with one's personal appearance but it certainly doesn't end there. In life, every man, we know from Scripture, is building a house. We are all builders because one's family is referred to as a house in the Bible. For instance, it tells us of the house of David which was more than a residential structure. It also included his wives and children, his finances, his authority, governance, livestock, chariots and his work. We also know that no life or house can stand without a foundation or it will soon fall to pieces. An important part of building a foundation of all we do in life is neatness. Neatness and organization are integral parts of each another. Having a place for everything and everything having its place is very important.

Most people appreciate neatness whether they are neat or well organized themselves or not. It is both pleasing and gentle on the mind to see that all things are in order in someone's home or work area and not in need of cleaning, sorting or storing. A well-ordered environment is indicative of a well-ordered mind. Truly, if we can't order our environment or work area, how will we be able, as a leader, to organize the affairs, production and work areas of others? To qualify for leadership we must showing an affinity for neatness. Providing neatness and organization is the leader's responsibility. If we aren't providing that, what is it then that we have to offer? Oftentimes people will actually refuse to work for a leader who isn't organized. It drives them crazy to pick up, sort out, clean up and organize their leader's mess or look for his lost items.

Can other positive character traits make up for a lack of neatness a leader's life? According to a front page article in the September 2, 2013 issue of *The Atlanta Journal-Constitution* the head of a major department of the City of Atlanta government was fired recently for incompetence and sloppy business dealings. She was in charge of the critically important business of running elections and record keeping. The official investigating the situation and making the decision to fire her said he found her office staff "in disarray and lacking discipline." He also said he made the decision, among other reasons, because "The department looks unorganized and inefficient" and he was "unsure if much respect exist(ed) between the staff and management." This director's lack of organization and neatness made it impossible for her to be respected by either her staff or the public she served. In addition, the appropriate forms were not available at the polls and thousands of records were not being recorded properly. Luke, the apostle, gave us some valuable insight about human nature when he said, "He who is faithful in what is least (the small things) is faithful also in much; and he who is unjust in what is least is unjust also in much." Luke 16:10

Pig Pen is one of Charles Schultz's most interesting Peanuts characters—and so appropriately named as well. He just seems to have a spirit of filth and confusion swirling about him. Wherever he goes, he takes it with him. We can certainly all improve in this area but remember this. Just a little organization goes a long way. It will breathe life into your company, organization, family or ministry. It makes people feel good about your organization, you as the leader and themselves when things are neat and orderly. It makes them feel important, well considered and provided for even when provisions are scarce.

Early on and even while serving on a precision drill team, I must admit that my first experience with neatness and organization in a military college left me feeling their ideas about this were a bit over the top. They said everything in my foot locker, things like my toothbrush, t-shirts, sox, etc., all had to be in the same place just like everyone else's in the entire U.S. Army. Then, a few years later, in my first fire fight with a real enemy in Vietnam, the importance of all this came cascading down on me in my mind. My leaders were right again and I was wrong. You see, I didn't know that the enemy was probably going to blow up half my stuff right off the get. When I realized that I would probably only be dealing with half a deck or less, the importance of knowing where things were and how to get to them quickly became real clear to me.

What it means to have the character trait of **NEATNESS:**

- Having a well-groomed appearance
- Having a habit of cleanliness and orderliness
- Simplicity of design
- Trim and functional
- Realizing we never get a second chance to make a good first impression.
- Marked by good taste, moderation and simplicity
- Systematic
- Orderly storage of supplies, files and materials
- Realizing anybody can be a builder but only those who can make beauty and be neat will be able to stay in the business.
- A detest for filth, sloppiness and disorder
- Realizing that this quality and beauty are admirable
- Realizing everything must have its place and every place needs to have its thing
- Manifesting orderliness, cleanliness, care, preparation and attention to detail.
- Realizing neatness is a spirit and a habit
- Able to chose clothes that are appropriate, attractive and neat.
- Shows one has a sense of beauty

O, THE ABILITY TO SAY— **Study start date: _____ Finish date: _____**

In this anything goes permissive world we live in today, few people are willing to utter one of the smallest words in the dictionary: no. Though small, this little word can have more to do with one's success and freedom in life than many others. There is just something in all of us that wants to tell people, yes. It's human nature to want to make everyone happy and grant their wishes. For this reason, few people actually have the moral courage, when necessary, to utter this simple, little, two-letter word. If one never gains the fortitude to speak this little word, they will soon be swallowed up by corruption and compromise. They will also be hindered from doing what man was placed here to do in the first place: subdue the Earth and take dominion. Keep in mind that refusing to say "no" when we should means that we will automatically be saying "no" to a lot of other things (rules and regulations) and "yes" to a whole host of things that this decision will set in motion.

From the beginning, there have been rules given for us to live by. Wherever you go in life, there are boundaries—most of which are for our own good and protection. Lines on the side of highways are there to show us where the smooth pavement ends. Go past these, even accidentally, and we will likely either run off into a ditch or a guard rail on the side of the highway. They are there, obviously, to keep our vehicles from careening end-over-end down a steep embankment to an abrupt, possibly deadly stop.

In the Garden of Eden, Adam and Eve were allowed to do whatever they wanted—almost perfect freedom with only one prohibition: they were not to eat the tree of good and evil. Beguiled, Eve couldn't tell satan no, Adam couldn't tell Eve no and both got themselves kicked out of the garden paradise that they had taken so completely for granted. Life was too good on Easy Street. That was not, however, the worst of it. Many other penalties were also incurred: the ground would no longer yield its fruit so easily, there would be thorns and thistles to deal with, a woman's pain in childbirth would be increased and enmity was lodged between man and woman, human beings lost their innocence and instead of being clothed with light, had to start wearing fig leaves and animal skins. Life would not be a picnic in Paradise again on this planet for a long, long time.

You see, if, down the road of life, you come upon a fence that says "Bad dog." Remember that the sign was likely put there **for your benefit** as well as the owner's. Yes, you can still jump the fence if you are spry enough, dumb enough (and I certainly have been on occasion myself in other settings of course) and have a mind to. But, don't be surprised if a huge dog with a big mouth loaded with lots of long, sharp teeth takes a big chunk of meat out of your posterior. Oh, and this admonition doesn't have to do with only jumping fences, it applies to every rule given to us in life.

The Bible has provided many admonitions for our benefit so that we might obtain favor, victory, success and peace in this short life. Generally speaking, however, we are all still in position to break the rules every day, everywhere we go. True, we can break them—but only at our own great peril and detriment. Most people break rules for several reasons: because 1) the judgment and penalty phase for wrongs committed in life is oftentimes so long getting here, 2) so many are blinded by their sins to think they are going to get away with it, 3) we were all born with a sin nature, 4) no one likes someone telling us what to do—it is just human nature, and 5) finally, because all of us start out in life wanting man's approval instead of God's. Some good advice is to learn the rules wherever you go. If you work for a company, ministry or business, keep the rules and you will also find peace, prosperity and promotabiity along with the very beneficial habit you have gained by doing so, .

Walled cities in days of old were put there for two reasons: First, to keep their enemies out and, secondly, to keep the good people, their children and animals in and secure. These physical boundaries served a very useful purpose and actually worked fairly well until gun power, aircraft and atomic bombs were invented.

The need to be strong and very courageous is not something new on planet Earth. It has been a necessity for every leader, family head, business owner or spiritual leader since Adam was created in the Garden of Eden. It was also a need during the prophetic ministry of Ezekiel to whom it fell to prophesy to Judah during their seventy year exile in Babylonian captivity. God told him to open his mouth and eat the scroll He gave him which was the Word of God. Then He told him to go to the house of Israel and speak these words to them. God already knew that they wouldn't listen to Ezekiel, however, His grace compelled Him to send his prophets again and again. God gave him first a warning and secondly, a spiritual gift. The warning saying, " ... the house of Israel will not listen to you, because they will not listen to Me; for all the house of Israel are impudent and hard-hearted." (Ezekiel 3:7) This, however, would not diminish in the least his responsibility to deliver the message to them. Then God told Ezekiel, "Behold, I have made your face strong against their faces, and your forehead strong against their foreheads. Like (an) adamant stone, harder than flint, I have made your forehead; do not be afraid of them, nor be dismayed at their looks, though they are a rebellious house." (v. 8, 9) So, he continually went forth and spoke the words of prophecy to the people, whether they received it or liked it or obeyed it or not. It was the truth, it was for them and they needed to hear it. The responsibility for the outcome was on their heads at that point and not the prophet's.

As leaders in a difficult, dark day we are blessed to be here by God's divine providence. There is no doubt that the battle has heated up hotter than ever before—just before the Lord's return to take His people. It would be well for all of us to pray for God to, likewise, give us a forehead of flint so we could be delivered from the people. Fast and pray for it. Ask God for it. Then thank Him for it believing you have received it. Do this every day for a good while, thanking God that you have been delivered from the people. Get ready because there will be many times you will be called upon to take difficult stands for the truth. Many times you will be required to stand alone and say, "No." You will be required to stand for God in a not so far distant place—even your own home. That is why Joshua said, "As for me and my house, we will serve the Lord." (Joshua 24:15) It was not just some high sounding platitude he was speaking to be politically, religiously and socially correct as a Jew. He was stating his determination that day, to drive his stakes down, to follow God and His rules for his home. He had just announced to the people coming into the Promised Land that they needed to put away the foreign gods of Egypt and, likewise, decide for themselves that very day whom they would serve. It was there, at Shechem, that the people made a covenant to serve God. (v.25) He then took a large stone and set it under an oak tree by the sanctuary of the Lord as a memorial of the covenant they had made. It would be a witness of the covenant and of their disobedience if they ever refused to obey God. A forehead of flint they would need.

The most important person we need to learn to say no to in life is.... . ourselves.

What it means to have the character trait of **THE ABILITY TO SAY NO:**

- Having the intestinal fortitude to stand against the tidal wave of compromise and take a stand
- Having the character to stand by one's duty to preserve those things and rules under our charge
- Having the ability to say "No" when asked to do something wrong or go where you shouldn't go
- Having the determination to please God and not men
- Having the character to be able to stand alone in life

BEDIENCE—   **Study start date: _____ Finish date: _____**

Even as infants, we all start out in the world refusing to obey the rules and have a strong dislike for anyone telling us what to do. That simply comes with the fallen nature of man. In time we must learn that living together successfully with others in an ordered society requires rules for everyone. Hopefully they are well thought out, sensible rules formulated by people with knowledge, understanding and experience in the field. Of course we are not suggesting that anyone obey rules that are illegal, immoral or unscriptural but even when they are not considered the best rules in the world, they will still, most likely, contribute to some degree toward order and efficiency.

Consider this for just a moment. If there was no rule about what time kids had to meet the school bus each morning? The driver would be running his route all day wasting a whole lot of time and resources hoping to catch a few kids here and there. Furthermore, the teachers could not assemble their classes for instruction, would have to teach the same things over and over to the few, here and there as they dribble in. Teachers could never get a solid head-count in time for the cafeteria to prepare the lunches. On and on it goes—mass confusion. Rules are required and very helpful in society for many reasons.

We know the three pillars regarding authority are clearly stated in Scripture: all authority is instituted by God. Those who resist His ordinances bring judgment upon themselves and those in authority are here to do two things. They are to bring wrath to evil doers and, hopefully, on the alternative, blessings and promotion to those who submit and do well. Those who bear the sword, the police and those in the military, do not "bear the sword" (guns today) in vain. They are actually ministers of God for the good of society. (Romans 13:1–7) If there were no police or sheriff's deputies around, I promise you there are many who would overnight begin going from house-to-house raping, maiming, pillaging, killing and burning. If there was no military, other countries would invade us at will to make us their tribute paying minions. Their presence deters law-breaking.

Wherever we go, there will be those who are in authority and rules or guidelines already in effect. Every city, state, country, business and family must have rules. We can live in contempt of these policies if we like but only to our detriment. It is a wise practice, when coming into the employ of a company to find out what their rules are and immediately show respect for authority by following them. This takes us off of the path that leads to our own sure and swift demise and, instead, places us in a position to be commended and promoted by management. It is just that simple. We don't have to like all the rules, we just have to obey them. In time, our obedience will make us useful and we may soon be asked to carry out certain important and, sometimes, critical tasks. We will also gain the right to an audience with authority to quietly make a godly appeal with reasons as to how the poor rules could be improved or eliminate entirely. Of course, wisdom would be to always include the final stipulation by the one making the appeal that he would leave the final decision, whether or not to change the rule, solely the leader's prerogative.

Samson was a Nazirite, one set apart for the service of God as a judge and deliverer. Ostensibly, he was heir-apparent to the high office of national deliverer, having all the accoutrements as well. He was blessed of the Lord in many ways even to the point of his birth being announced by an angel. He was strong and he was handsome. For the task of delivering the Hebrew children from Philistine bondage, he was also given a terrific, super-natural anointing of the Spirit. Though he was courageous enough to take on thirty to a thousand men singlehandedly, he lacked one thing: obedience. This moral weakness manifested itself in many areas, not the least of which was making a god of beautiful women such that he constantly pursued and slept with harlots. Instead of accepting the high and noble calling of leading the nation Israel out of captivity, he wasted his time and strength on affairs with women in disobedience to the revealed will of God. Though he knew God's law and was advised not to by his parents, he still took a bride outside the nation Israel. He went on to touch the carcass of a dead lion which was also forbidden for Nazirites. He was not, as Nanazirite, to partake of wine or strong drinks, to eat any unclean thing or to let a razor cut his hair—all of which he did. For his disobedience as one to whom God had entrusted so much, there would be a great price to pay.

While he was sleeping with his head in the lap of Delilah, another one of his Philistine women, she surreptitiously had his locks shorn—taking him out of covenant with God and causing his supernatural strength to depart. The Philistines seized him, gouged his eyes out and bound him with shackles of bronze. In a moment, he lost his freedom, his eye sight and was made to grind grain, around and around, imprisoned like an ox in a threshing granary. However, his hair began to grow again. Then one day, as providence would have it, the lords of the Philistines assembled in their temple to offer a great sacrifice to their god, Dagon, supposedly thanking him for delivering Samson into their hands. When the spirits of the people were high, they called for Samson to enter-tain them. After they had summoned him from prison to perform so they could taunt him, they set him between the pillars of the temple. Samson then told the servant that held his hand to put him where he could feel the pillars supporting the temple so he could lean on them. The temple was packed that day with men and women as well as the officials of the Philistines for this gala affair. There were about three thousand people just on the roof who had been watching Samson perform. Then he called upon the Lord saying, "O Sovereign Lord, remember me. O God, please strengthen me just once more and let me with one blow get revenge on the Philistines for my two eyes." (Judges 16:28) Then he reached out and braced himself against the two center pillars upon which the temple rested, one with his right hand the other with his left, as he made his final request to die with the Philistines. When he shoved those pillars will all his might, the temple fell on the officials and all the people in it. Thus, he killed in his death more of Israel's enemies than he did in his whole life. .

The thought remains, what would Samson's life have been like had he been obedient to God's plan as the victorious commander of the army of God's Chosen People. What kind of blessing would the beautiful, faithful wife from among the Israelites, have been to him—who would have done him good all the days of his life? Only God knows but we can wonder. For a lack of obedience, Samson got the devil's worst instead of God's best. He also missed out on the blessing of being a great deliverer of God's people. To whom much is given, much is always required.

An extremely clear example of obedience was explained to us in the Army Ranger School years ago as a parallel to the breeding of a responsive, obedient strain of Arabian stallions. The trainers would teach the horses to obey the command to "halt" over and over. Then they would take water away from the herd being trained for a day or two and then release them in the desert nearby. A good distance away was a water trough and they would splash the water in the sight and hearing of these great horses. Of course the herd would immediately stampede toward the new found source of water. When they were within fifty yards of the trough, someone in the vicinity would give the command to halt! The horses that obeyed were harnessed, given water and allowed to continue breeding to produce an obedient blood line. The horses that failed to obey the command, were shot. Then the process was repeated again and again.

Obedience is essential in life. Who will we obey, God or ourselves and the devil?

Samson's revenge

What it means to have the character trait of **OBEDIENCE:**

- The act of carrying out orders and fulfilling the spirit of rules more than the letter.
- The realization that we will find rules wherever we go in life and understanding that obeying them contributes to the order and productivity of the group as well as placing us in line for promotion and blessings.
- The first requirement to be of value to any organization.
- In the military, the minimum requirement is obedience to the commander and loyalty to the group.
- Submissiveness to the desires, restraints and commands of one's authorities.
- Realizing that obedience is the quality of obedience makes one extremely valuable in the work place, military and Church.
- The trait that qualifies one for leadership.
- The necessity and wisdom of obeying instructions explicitly.
- Carefully taking notes when superiors are giving instructions and making requests. To realizes how important this is because our mind will forever want to do things "our way" and not the way we were instructed.
- The joy of pleasing superiors (David's men who risked all to fulfill his desire for a drink from Jacob's well).
- Refusing to deviate from orders

OBSERVANT —

Study start date: _____ Finish date: _____

Truly, some people go through life with their head in a cloud, a mist, a fog or a haze. They seem to be completely unaware of what is going on around them. They have no idea where the bear ate the buckwheat, how the cow ate the cabbage or who might be doing what to whom. In every large group of people there are always some incredibly unaware individuals. This was no less the case in the Corps of Cadets at Texas A&M University where they actually had a name for these kind of folks: "two per centers." There was always about two percent in the group who didn't know the uniform of the day, the drill, what day it was or the even the time of day. They might have looked like fairly intelligent human beings ostensibly but on the inside the lights, unfortunately, were out.

To succeed in life, one must be observant. We need to know the rules and regulations where we live and work and observe them in our everyday walk. Violating simple rules can cause one to be reprimanded, lose trust with co-workers and superiors as well as opening ourselves up to the likelihood of losing our job and a great opportunity in life. Every job, however small, should be looked upon as a great opportunity, a chance to learn new skills, improve our serve, better understand human nature as well as be a stepping stone to future opportunities instead of becoming a stumbling block.

We also need to learn the skill of making positive changes in an organization that will, as far as possible, not create enormous turmoil and animosity along with it. However, if the need for change is great or truth is attacked, we need wisdom to know when to be willing to fight for it to the death. Knowing the rules of the game is crucial in sports. Oftentimes games are won or lost on the turn of a single rule governing one play. You will find that knowing the rules is especially helpful when you get engaged in competition with someone who is bent on making the rules as they go. Be observant to learn the rules in whatever you are doing.

In just about every business, knowing what the weather will be doing for the next few days is very important. It will likely determine the kinds of work that will be most productive, decide scheduling, equipment requirements, what to wear and many other things. Being observant will do little good if we don't also know the importance of carrying a pen and pad so we can make notes of important points, prices, people, phone numbers, statistics, market fluctuations and wisdom sent our way by others. In an increasingly complex, technical society, our lives are constantly impacted by a steady stream of numbers that must be captured immediately, analyzed and acted upon to survive and, hopefully, thrive.

Though knowing and observing rules is important, we must be observant to know even more than that. If we aren't observant, we might find ourselves walking down the proverbial primrose path to a black eye. You might be observing the rules as a driver passing through an intersection, knowing that you might have the right of way but that doesn't mean you will be a winner. The other driver may not be thinking or able, for any number of reasons at the moment, to do what is right. They could be tuning their radio, texting or arguing with someone on their cell phone. You could have the right to go through that intersection but you could also be, as we know, dead right. Regardless of "rights," it is always best to be circumspect, cautious and careful. Look twice every time you cross an intersection.

This brings to mind a time when I was seven years old and had just been blessed with my first bike. Having also just learned how to mount it and get going by myself, I was riding down the street on cloud nine in our housing project on the Air Force Base in Tampa, Florida. Something totally caught my attention off to the right causing an abrupt change in my immediate plans. Not paying attention to what was ahead, I crashed into the back of a parked car. That car didn't move a sixteenth of an inch and there I was on my brand new bike crumpled up in a pile, all tangled up behind the back bumper of that car, flat on the pavement. I pulled myself together, got to my feet as quickly as I could and looked around to see if anyone saw my most recent stroke of genius. Thankfully, apparently not. My bike was alright but my pride, knees and legs had definitely taken a hit. How stupid not to be looking where I was going?! My shins, knees and elbows were done great damage and, at the time, I couldn't remember ever experiencing so much pain. At that point, I realized the importance of being more observant of objects in front of my bike and learned that I could not afford, ever, even for a moment, to let my concentration be side-tracked from the path ahead. Painful as it was, that little experience proved to be a great blessing throughout my life whether I was riding a horse, flying a plane, steering a boat or driving a car.

A year or so later my dad was taking the family on a Sunday drive. It was a beautiful, summer day in the south and my mom noticed a house off to the right with a yard full of beautiful red flowers. She quipped, "Honey, look at the beautiful gladiolas" and pointed in that direction. He glanced over and enjoyed the sight immensely—that is until our car crashed into the back of the vehicle in front of us. Quick as I am, in my young mind, I connected the dots between this experience and the one that I had had with my bike accident and realized, again, the importance of being observant, alert and undistracted while operating vehicles on the road.

Society tries so hard to give the impression of stability. They build marble office towers, form corporations and "firms" to give sense of credibility and longevity to businesses. However, regardless of appearances, the observant will notice that the world is changing rapidly around us all the time. Nothing stays the same. Corporations come and go. Everything but the Word of God is in a constant state of flux. Some are even trying to change it. Realize now too that not all change out in the world is bad. Some changes are certainly positive. Although there are dangers and problems incumbent with change sometimes, there can also be great opportunity. Markets and economies are changing constantly. An astute entrepreneur who is alert and observant can find opportunities in up as well as down economies and markets.

It has always been important in the business world to be informed but in today's highly technical society, everything is moving so fast that it is all the more crucial. We need to know what is going on but we also need a steady stream of new ideas and stimulation. Remember, markets and businesses are always anticipatory to coming changes as well as breaking news. We too should be observant and analyze what effect it will have on future events, various businesses, prices, politics and so on. Whatever you have to pay for news and information will certainly pay you back many times over in the days and years ahead. We need to stay ahead of the power curve instead of being beaten by it from behind.

Years ago a good friend of mine, the late Larry Burkett, founder of Christian Financial Concepts, had a creative way to gauge economic trends. He had a system of calling the various paper and plastic bag manufacturers and would graph their numbers. Since nothing happens, as they say, until a sale is made in America, following the retail end of our society made a whole lot of sense. Trends could be identified very rapidly. It is of the utmost importance to know what the economy is doing

A great source for looking behind the scenes to know what is really going on in the economy is a composite index called the PMI Report (Purchasing Managers Index Report). It is produced by my friend Dr. Don Sabbares, of Kennesaw State University, in Kennesaw, Georgia. His economic team collects data from all over the southeastern United States in six categories: new orders, production, employment, supply deliveries, finished inventory and commodity prices. Then they crunch the numbers together and come up with an index figure for Georgia and another for the Southeastern United States. Their monthly report is timed for release along with the Institute of Supply Management Report (ISM) out of Tempe, Arizona that covers the nation as a whole. With their figures you can readily see movements of the economy each month and can clearly and easily see the latest trends. He has also tracked businesses that had observed the trends and stayed ahead of them. His data proves that these companies have continued to be profitable while others went broke. You see, in business we need to be doing exactly the opposite of what the rest of the world is doing. If they are selling, we need to be buying and vice versa.

In the United States, we are extremely proud of our Constitution and rightfully so. Our founding fathers were incredibly wise to provide us such an enduring and beneficial document. To be a good governing document, however, it had to allow for measured change with many checks and balances. The founders also warned future generations that this type of government was not suitable for a corrupt, irreligious people. Congress, had made many changes to this document over the years as it should. However, we need to remember that the actual Constitution as amended, is now much different than the one written on parchment they handed to our nation over two hundred years ago. We, who believe in our country being one nation under God, need to be observant and ever vigilant to stop encroachments and other attempts to change our form of government and way of life. We need to be faithful to take a stand for freedom, self-reliance and individual responsibility—the principles that made our nation great. To do so, we must first be observant and then willing when we see the need arise to suffer, sacrifice, stand and even give our lives to protect the foundation of this great nation.

What it means to have the character trait of being **OBSERVANT:**

- Paying close attention to everyone and everything around us
- Keen observation of the inner workings of things and inter relationships of cause and effect
- Studying one's surroundings with keen interest
- Alert to change, trends and market movements
- Not living with your head in the sand
- Not hearing only the words people speak but being attentive to their voice inflections, appearance, facial expressions and body language.
- Having discernment
- Recognizing change and considering its ramifications, secondary effects and meanings

OPTIMISM—   **Study start date: _____ Finish date: _____**

Because we are living in the Last Days and television's advancements, there is a ton of negative information being shot around the world on the 24 hour news cycle. In addition there is the printed page
and news flashes on your cell phone that can just about drowns people in the quicksand of negativity and
hopelessness. We are, if we will listen to it, hit with one negative blast right after the other. Even so, we
need to be alert and informed so listen and read we must with moderation. What all this news is telling
us is, just as the Scriptures tell us, that all the foundations of the world are out of course and are now
cracking, crumbling and falling apart. The whole world is drowning in a sea of envy, debt, greed and
religious hatred. A whole lot of people don't even think there is any sense trying to do anything in such
a wicked world. Some young families are afraid to bring children into such an evil world.

Amazingly, the way to not only survive but thrive in this world is to be an eternal optimist. Sure, there
are problems in the world but we still have God and with Him all things are possible. As long as we are
still breathing, it doesn't matter how bad things might look at the moment. In Christian tennis, we are
on the winning side, the ball is always in our court, it is our serve and we don't ever have to quit until
we win. We must believe that there are opportunities in up markets and as well as down markets. When
you are surrounded by your enemies as General George Patton was once in Europe during World War II,
we can be as thankful as he was saying, "Now we've got them where they can't get away." The optimist
who believes in God knows "A thousand may fall at your side, and ten thousand at your right hand; but
it shall not come near you …" (Psalm 91:7) He realizes that every adversity can work for us just like a
small grain of sand in a mussel shell to produce a beautiful pearl in time. And, in the mind and heart of
the optimist, hope always springs eternal.

Life is such that there will be trials, temptations, and the winds of adversity blowing against us from
time-to-time. These winds come to sift everyone on earth to see what we have been building upon as well
as what we have been building with. Have we been building on sand with wood, hay and stubble or have
we been the wise master builder, erecting our fortress on the Rock with gold, silver and precious stones?
(I Corinthians 3:10) These winds blow to separate and sort all things in the lives of people just like winds
out in nature sort the wheat from the chaff. It has never been a case of if these winds will come, just
when. However, the good news is that just like the major league umpire in baseball calls every pitch as
it passes over the plate, we, too, make the calls in our own lives. It doesn't matter what the batter thinks
about a pitch or what the fans think, or what those watching on television think or even what the coaches
might think. It only matters what the umpire thinks and, friend, it is going to be whatever he calls it.
When something comes our way in life, we have the God-given right to call it whatever we will. Sure,
we are going to get some curve balls, wild pitches and even some bad balls from time-to-time. But, it is
still whatever **you call it**. Call it good in your life and it will be good. Call it bad and it will, likewise,
be just that, bad. Certainly it is only human nature not to like it when God starts moving the furniture
around in our lives. The best thing to do, however, when we have an enormous problem come our way is
to thank God for trusting us with it right away and then thank Him for giving you the wisdom to handle
it. Thanking God takes a lot of the pressure off the situation and off of you as well. Then you can start
looking for the solution and all the good that will come from it. The more you do this and the more you
see it work, the sooner you will master it. From my experience, the absolute worst things that have ever
happened to me have always turned out to be the best in the end. Trials have gifts for us in their hands

that we cannot afford to live without. We can't receive them, however, unless we are willing to accept the trial along with all its pain, work, struggle and acquiring the perseverance necessary to conquer it.

What it means to have the character trait of **OPTIMISM:**

- Trying to see some good in everyone and everything.
- Knowing that God can cause even our mistakes to work for our good if we are following Him in our calling and fulfilling our purpose (Romans 8:28)
- Always anticipating a positive result regardless of the circumstances
- Believing that problems are just situations God is trusting us with to help us grow, accomplish and reach a higher plane
- Knowing that no matter how difficult life may get, God will always make a way where there is no way
- Knowing that every adversity has planted in it the seeds of a greater good.
- Expecting the best out of everything and everyone
- Realizing that optimism is shown, heard and communicated in one's tone of voice

RDERLINESS: SEE NEATNESS & ORGANIZATION

RGANIZATION—   **Study start date:** _____ **Finish date:** _____

In order to succeed in life, we need to get the most done in the shortest amount of time. The reason for this, too, by the way, is that very few have been gifted with a whole lot of talent and none of us, even if we lived to be a hundred and twenty, have very much time. The best way to get a great deal accomplished then is organization. Without it, we would all be running around like a bunch of chickens with no plan and no direction. We would soon have too many eating and scratching and not enough covering up. Then, of course, everything starts to stink. Just a little organization, on the other hand, goes a long way. Focus increases, productivity increases, the morale of the troops increases, unity increases and the strength of the group seems to multiply. Suddenly anything becomes possible.

Being organized is actually not all that difficult. It only takes a few extra minutes initially to lay the necessary groundwork but these little things pay huge dividends over and over again in tie. Some things that help is to have a set time to do daily and monthly tasks. Organizing a filing system for paperwork is no more difficult than purchasing an inexpensive alphabetical divider system from an office supply store and a used filing cabinet from a thrift store. As far as tools and equipment are concerned, we need to let everything have its place and every place have its thing; then we will always know where to find what we need.

At times, while in the Corps of Cadets at Texas A&M University, I thought my superiors might had gone a little overboard with organization on occasion. For example, everything in our footlocker, had to be in just the right place: socks, toothbrush, underwear, everything. Later on, in my first battle in Vietnam, the importance of all of this came on me like a load of bricks. I then realized that the enemy was probably going to blow up half our equipment right away. Once you are dealing with only half a deck, you certainly want to be able to quickly find what you need out of what is left. The fog of war is real. Soldiers in combat, must be trained to be organized so they can find what they need in the middle of this kind of what is commonly called "managed chaos." Order and organization is a foundation, in and of itself. To the soldier, it is crucial. To the business manager in a highly competitive world, it is certainly no less important.

One of the most important jobs of a leader in any organization is to train up the next generation of leaders succeeding him. They need to know that one can only qualify for leadership by being efficient and able to organize the small things. Good organization always starts with the small things. The Master even said, "He that is faithful in that which is least is faithful also in much." (Luke 16:10) All this begs the question, how can a person who can't organize a small thing be counted on and trusted to organize a huge, complicated, inter-related, functioning entity? If a soldier can't organize his foot locker, how is he going to manage a 16,000 man airborne division with artillery, armored cavalry, signal corps and communications units with encrypted messaging, a parachute packing unit, tanks, aircraft, trucks, a computerized tactical operations centers and radar. Now add to all this the complete re-supply network and maintenance organization along with ability to feed this unit while on the move, under fire.

Organization is a beautiful thing. It gives you and everyone in your company a sense of strength, knowing that the organizational tools you and those with you took the time to provide will pay manifold dividends to all, time and again, now and in the future. Things like setting up a filing system; a blank paper, stationery and envelope store; office supply stores; a business form supply and so forth, are huge time-savers, everyone in your organization can benefit from.

One of the greatest and best organized leaders in Biblical history was Nehemiah. As far as his resume was concerned, he had no experience with organized management. He was not a five star general, a neurosurgeon, a world-class bronc rider, a pilot or a mountain climber. Nehemiah was just a cup bearer. It was his job to set the king's table and serve him wine, water and whatever else he desired. Just another Hebrew slave in Babylonian captivity, he was well down the road of life and had never built anything, not even a dog house. But, one day some men had just come from Israel and he inquired as to how things were back in Jerusalem. They said it was horrible. The walls were torn down completely and the gates were burned with fire. Everyone was discouraged, distressed and disheartened. So he immediately began to fast and pray about the situation and God laid it on his heart to return to Jerusalem, rebuild the wall and begin to restore their nation. Ridiculous. How was a slave with no money, no experience and completely unknown by the people in Jerusalem going to accomplish this? He immediately inquired of the king saying, "If it pleases the king, and if your servant has found favor in your sight, I ask that you send me to Judah, to the city of my fathers' tombs, that I may rebuild it." (Nehemiah 2:5)

Favor, not ability or track record, was his ticket to even be allowed to attempt such a difficult task. He certainly didn't work for money because, as a slave he didn't make any. He didn't work for glory. There was certainly none of that for someone in his position, just a cup bearer. However, he was likely very organized because kings didn't keep people around them who were not sharp and highly organized. The king's first concern was not the wall or the cost of building it. He wanted to know how soon Nehemiah could get it done and get back because he liked having him on his staff. Nehemiah asked, "If I have found favor in your sight." He had obviously learned to work for favor—to please his superiors and cause them to like, trust and depend on him. When he set a time, the king gave his approval, financial support and blessing.

Nehemiah quickly returned to Jerusalem but was wise enough not to reveal his purpose to anyone. He obtained either a mule or a horse and chose to ride the perimeter of the city at night. In so doing, he could make his notes and design the city's walls however he wanted without interference or being discovered. He laid out the gates by name and the general location for all the walls. He organized the construction by families and made each responsible for the rebuilding of the wall in front of their own homes. This gave each of them the most incentive to complete the work as soon as possible so they could benefit from the security the wall would provide. By placing the head of each family in charge, the wives, children and even the old people pitched in and helped out on some part of the construction from morning to night each day. Every family saw the families adjacent to them doing a great work and everyone was thrilled to have a part. Excitement about all the progress soared. This was all so much the case, that despite enormous opposition, scarcity of funds and materials, false accusations of treason about him to the governor and threats against his life, Nehemiah and his people rebuilt the wall around Jerusalem in only 52 days.

What it means to have the character trait of **ORGANIZATION**:

- The segregation and ordering of like items.
- To let everything have its place and every place have its thing.
- To put things back in their place immediately. (i.e.: put trash in the refuse receptacle immediately so your work area is always neat, clean and orderly.)
- To "make level paths for your feet"—keeping your work area free of clutter.
- To provide structure
- A system which coordinates the various parts to act in concert and function in unity
- A plan to carry out coordinated, synchronized, accurately timed activities
- Planning ahead, making a **written plan** and working your plan.

- Investing the time now to implement time-saving systems and concepts that will pay re-occurring dividends in the future.
- Practicing neatness and order.
- To label things, putting things in folders and filing them by topic.
- Cleanliness.
- Making a "To Do List" each day along with a list of materials and tools needed

PATIENCE —   **Study start date:** _____ **Finish date:** _____

We live in a fast-paced world today where people have been used to shake and bake chicken, instant grits, microwave meals and minute rice for far too long. There are instant credit checks and now just sign and drive car deals. People are pursuing the American dream and want everything it took their parents fifty years to achieve—right now. Patience is definitely not a quality we humans are born with. It is, in fact, a common tendency among humans to want everything not only now but yesterday. Some think that the whole world needs to stop and bring it all here right now because they showed up on the planet. The only problem is that the world doesn't revolve around us so we must learn to wait and do that waiting very patiently. We just as well get used to it now or we are going to have to learn this lesson over and over again, the hard way.

For us mere men, the race of life can sometimes be quite strange and complicated. There are many false objectives, detours and pot holes in what seems to be a very long road. There are also many deceptive influences arrayed against us, endeavoring to control our lives and entice us to leave the King's highway. The world system also requires a whole lot of training, certifications and credentials to make any progress at all. Because of all these things and more, the race of life seems long and arduous—unless, of course, your last name is Rockefeller, Hunt or Trump. But that's just what we in the proletariat think. But, don't be deceived, we need to remember, that those who inherit fortunes will have challenges and temptations far beyond what most of us will ever face in life. Inheriting a fortune almost instantly will most likely allow that person to escape the times of testing and apprenticeship we worker bees must endure. However, the life-lessons we learn in humble service to others will pay us far more in the area of patience and character for the near term and will very likely even bode well for us financially in the long term. The ones who generated those family fortunes not only had the skill sets, the grit and the character requisite to create them but they also had the discipline and business acumen to maintain and preserve them as well. While, on the other hand, those who have inherited fortunes, most likely do not. So you see, the School of Hard Knocks is a really good one and we should never be ashamed of the diploma we earned there although you may never be printed on a sheep skin. That diploma is usually etched in your heart.

For those just beginning the race of life, as I said, it can look quite confusing. There are times when we seem to be working hard and doing all things right but see little to no results. We seem to be treading water and making little to no progress. The natural tendency, mind you, is to give up and say, "What's the use?" And, throw in the proverbial towel. We have all been bombarded by those thoughts. Well, the whole world, for some reason, has it set up to make it look that way quite often. I think now, after some years, it is so that we might gain greater faith and skill. But, even though things seem to be taking forever, believe it or not, everything is still, most likely, working and still moving, albeit it invisibly, according to plan. We are winning even though it doesn't look like it. Every barometer and indicator may say we are losing—but, our side still wins in the end—if we will just stay the course and not give up.

One thing a person who has endured it can never forget is the trials of the Army's school for young boys called the Ranger School. Actually it was their training school for special ops and tactical units, and is conducted under the most adverse conditions imaginable for their soon-to-be combat leaders. It was, without a doubt, the hardest thing I have ever had to endure in my whole life—even real warfare with live bullets, B-40 rockets, bungee pits and bombs couldn't compare. They told us you had to be in the top levels of the Army in leadership to be accepted by the school and then you also had to volunteer. I found out much later that only 42% of any Ranger class ever graduates and many times far less. It is nine weeks of starvation, endurance, physical exhaustion, sleep deprivation, intense training and mental anguish. At the time we, at least I, didn't know why it was so hard but later I found out it was so that the Army could know who would stay mission oriented and continue to look out for their men instead of caving in to the demands of "self." You see just about anybody rested, well fed, full of stamina and happy, can lead on any given good day. Not so when things are hell-bent otherwise. On top of all that there are many studies, physical tests (called obstacle courses) and the rigors of patrols one must pass. No slack.

Just to give you the drift on this thing, there are Army regulations dealing with heat and humidity. When both of these indicators reach a certain level, a red flag is hoisted up the flag pole and it is then mandated that all work details and training on the installation cease immediately. Officers' Candidate School stops, Pathfinder School stops, Jumpmaster School stops, Airborne School must cease as well as every other outside work detail. On a red flag day everyone has to return to their barracks and stay there until conditions improve. Not so in Ranger School. Ranger training never stops. On one particular red flag day, we were double-timing on a forced-march from the Ranger Barracks to Victory Pond, several miles away. It was so hot my brains (what little I have) felt like they were frying—kind of like scrambled eggs. I had never experienced that feeling before even working construction in the hot summers of Texas and never again since. I happened to be the platoon leader that day. About half-way there, one of my men fell out and was lying beside the road. I motioned for the medic truck, which was always following us on forced-marches, to come up and they immediately checked him out. His face was purple and the medics took him on from there. Well, he died.

Most of the time in Ranger School is devoted to tactical exercises where small units are conducting simulated missions like ambushes, knocking out missile emplacements, destroying a base camp, etc. Each Ranger candidate gets the opportunity to lead such a patrol five times. You never know when you will be told to take over so you have to memorize the field order (battle plan for the patrol) and be ready to lead and accomplish the mission without even a moment's notice. In that capacity you have to show sufficient leadership in a changing, simulated, war-time environment to get a "pass" from the grading Tactical Officer. Among other things, it is critical that you pass at least three of those patrols.

Well, we were about two-thirds into the course and into the Swamp Phase down in Eglin A.F.B., Florida and I don't mean out behind the Officers' Club. We were deep in the swamps. That air base is actually a huge place in terms of square miles. I had already lost forty pounds—and I didn't have them to lose. I had pneumonia (hope this doesn't gross anyone out) but was coughing up blood and could hardly even see straight out of my sunken eye sockets. They sent me to the doc who said that was exactly what I had, pneumonia, and he was sending me to the hospital to convalesce. That meant I would have to—what we called—"Recycle" and that was not going to be an option for me. At that time, we had never heard of anyone who had to "Recycle" who ever made it. I just said, "Sir, there's no way I'm going to recycle unless it's in a pine box. Until then, I'm driving on." He just looked at me. Just out of the field I'm sure I looked like a rag-tag, crumpled up old duffel bag that had been stuck in a mud puddle and then half-baked out in the sun. No shower and no change of clothes for quite some time prior to this trip to see the doc. He, in his clean, shiny and neatly pressed doctors' outfit, stethoscope and all, looked at me like I had to be the biggest idiot in the Army if not the whole world and released me to go back to my unit. It didn't get any better either, slogging through those swamps and wait-a-minute vines, day and night. At that point, I had passed two patrols and failed two. My mind was about to explode wondering how I had screwed up two of them so bad that I failed. About then guys were failing their third patrols right and left and they were sending them, heart-broken, back to the base camp. I knew I had to pass the fifth and final patrol when it came up or else. I was sick as a dog and I'm sure I was a pretty site. I was wet as a freshly dunked rat from wading through those swamps, skinny as a bean pole and coughing up blood. I was exhausted, my feet looked like hamburger meat from being in wet boots and marching miles and miles into what seemed like eternity, was continually falling asleep and my mind was "warping" from a lack of food intake. You see when you don't get enough to eat, the blood system can't carry the requisite nourishment or energy from the stomach to the brain for it to function properly so you begin to hallucinate. This is when people start seeing visions of things like an oasis, a hamburger or any number of other things. Believe it or not, I started seeing banana splits. Don't know why. I probably never had more than one or two in my whole life up to that time. I liked butterscotch Sundays. But I was seeing banana splits. I told myself at the time, if I ever got out of there alive, I was going to eat some banana splits. (I have kept that promise too.) We were all starving so bad about that time that a football player from West Point started eating snails—raw snails. Starvation does strange things to people. He got so sick they sent him to the hospital and, of course, we never saw him again.

Just another of the many problems caused by starvation and physical exhaustion was hypothermia. At the time no one in my class died from it but, over time twenty-two men in the Swamp Phase did. The brass was stumped about it because the water wasn't quite cold enough to cause a person to expire. They finally sent a team of scientists and doctors down there to study the problem and found that a severe lack nourishment (which creates body heat among other things} actually causes hypothermia to occur at slightly higher temperatures. For that reason and because the Army was losing precious active duty time, they started allowing the Ranger candidates more food in the Swamp Phase. Those who actually graduated in our day were so depleted and beat up, they were not physically fit enough to report to their next duty stations.

We had patrols what seemed like virtually day and night. They said we were supposed to get two hours of sleep a night but can you really get any decent, deep sleep in the rain or in the bottom of a muddy fox hole—no blankets or pup tents allowed—thank you very much? I can still remember walking single-file in my patrol, with my eyes fixed on the two, small pieces of reflective tape on the back of the guy's patrol cap ahead of me—so I wouldn't get off the path and fall out. I was sound asleep with my eyes wide open and I was seeing a banana split ever so often. When we stopped or started maneuvering, I would awaken and start thinking. My mind said I wasn't going to make it. My body said I wasn't going to make it. My stomach said I wasn't going to make it. My record up to that point said I wasn't going to make it but I remembered a story (this really gets deep philosophically) when I was a termite about the little engine that could. I'm sure you've heard it. This little locomotive was going up this hill that was, of course, way too steep and it didn't look like there was any way to make it. But it kept on saying, "I think I can. I think I can. I think I can." So I started speaking to myself so nobody could hear me saying (even though I really didn't believe it), "I'm going to make it. I going to make it." (Don't ever tell anyone I did this now.) Bet I said it a million times and then my final patrol opportunity popped up. We thought those Tac (tactical) Officers were only about the sharpest people on the planet. Sure, they were tough but had to be really good to be selected for the Tac job. I guess maybe the heat was getting to him but I'm sure the milk of human kindness wasn't flowing through his vein that day because they were all tough as nails. Anyway he gave me a "pass." That was probably the happiest day of my life up to that time. Ranger School wasn't over then but that was crucial. After Ranger School, everything in life has seemed a whole lot easier. Like they say, "I wouldn't take anything for it but I would never go back and do it again." Patience under trial always pays off if you can just hang in there. I will never forget the small piece of advice a Ranger Tac gave our company in the very beginning. He said, "Close your mouth and your mind and keep your feet moving; you will be there on the day of graduation." Interpretation: There would be many days and times your body would say it is far, far past spent, your mind would have already left and your feet, a decimated, bloody mess, were shouting a refusal to take another step. Many days and times I said to myself, "Just don't even think about it." Some things are too dangerous to even think about. And, definitely don't make the fatal mistake of verbalizing your situation. Don't think, don't talk, just put all you've got in taking that next step forward. Don't stop. Patiently endure. Keep your feet moving! James said trials, temptations and tribulation, the testing of our faith builds something extremely valuable: patience. James 1:3

Patience is so important that Paul told the Galatians "not (to) grow weary while doing good …" (Galatians 6:9) Why are we being warned? Because we, as humans, have every tendency and likelihood in life to do just that—grow weary while doing well—and start feeling sorry for ourselves. Then Paul gives us a promise: " … in due season we shall reap if we do not lose heart." He did have to bring up that word "season." We earthlings want to plant and reap in the same season if not the same day. But the law of the harvest is that you can't reap in the same season in which you are planting. We must learn to be patient.

Matthew 7:7 gives us the secret to success in life. It is all about patience in asking, seeking and knocking. The Master gives us this promise: "Ask, and it will be given to you; seek, and you will find; knock, and it will be opened" to you. No caveats, no exceptions and no conditions—all promises. So we can see how iron-clad this is, He then gives us three completely ridiculous examples as fathers. He says, what father would give his son a stone if he asks for some bread, or a snake if he asks for an egg? Then he concludes by saying, "If you (men) then, being evil, know how to give good gifts to your children, how much more will your Father who is in heaven give good things to those who ask Him!" Evenw we mere men know how to give good gifts to our children and, as God's children, how much more can we expect our Heavenly Father to give good things to us? He will, but the secret is to ask Him and never stop asking, seeking and knocking. Don't ever give up. What He is saying is that once you really get patience, you will never lack for anything. How valuable is that?

One of the best examples of patience in the Bible is the life of Noah. God told him to build an ark and build he did. He "did everything just as God commanded him." (Genesis 6:22) He even stayed at it for a hundred years—just he and his family of eight. They gathered and sawed all the wood, they drilled holes, made pegs and pounded them. They dug up or bought the pitch and spread it between the beams for water sealant. They built like there was no tomorrow and, no doubt, drew the ire of the locals. He must have been quite prosperous because, in addition to providing for his family, he funded the whole project all by himself. Noah was also faithful to preach to the townspeople for that same length of time and never had a single convert. He didn't lose patience, however. The Master had spoken to him and he was going to complete the task he had been assigned. The town's people continually laughed him to scorn saying, "Hey Noah, that's a fine boat you are building but did you

The ark rests on dry land after 40 days

forget something? There is no water around here. Ha-ha- ha-ha ha!" Surely there were hot days and cold ones. There were trials, there were shortages of this and that from time-to-time and probably times even Noah thought a hundred years was a long time to stay at something, but God had spoken. When He speaks to you, you never forget it, so he carried on. Undoubtedly, he had discouraging moments and days. Noah kept right on building through all manner of hardship, public scorn and rejection. But, one day he finished it and knew the time had come to load up all the animals and his family. Amazingly, the Lord closed and sealed the door and then the rains came. They came and they kept on coming. The water began to rise until the townspeople came knocking on the side of the ark crying out to please let them in The water kept rising and their knocking more rapid and their cries grew louder and more desperate, pleading to let them in, but the Lord had closed the door. Then the knocking and the cries ceased as the ark rose in the waters. Thank God for the patience and obedience of Noah.

This same attitude of patience should also be practiced in our business and finances. We are to avoid all get-rich-quick schemes, one of which is the lottery. Our government knows just exactly how naive its subjects are so they devised the lottery. As I am writing this it was announced on TV that they were having the largest in history at about $650,000,000. People were lined up in the streets, wrapped around buildings, standing on the sidewalks everywhere across America where they sold these tickets. What they were not told was that the probability of getting the winning ticket was about the same as the chance of a person getting bitten by a polar bear and a Kodiak bear on the same day! There was also some research done on all the lottery "winners" to see what had happened in their various lives that they weren't told about either. It was one disaster after another. Most lost all their winnings within a relatively short period of time. All we need to do is keep on being faithful in the small things and the big things will take care of themselves. We need to receive the joy of being found faithful as unto the Lord on a daily basis with whatever has been given to us. Remember, "An inheritance (or windfall) gained hastily at the beginning, will not be blessed in the end." (Proverbs 20:21) "Wealth gained quickly will dwindle away, but the one who gathers it little by little will become rich." (Proverbs 13:11 NET) We also know, "A faithful man will abound with blessings, but he who hastens to be rich will not go unpunished." Proverbs 28:20

If we will just press on, with all patience and never give up, the Lord will send us help or give us supernatural endurance and wisdom about our situation. We will succeed. Plan to make patience your strong suit. The Master wants us to be like Him. "God is love" (1 John 4:8) and first of all "love is patient." I Corinthians 13:4

What it means to have the character trait of **PATIENCE:**

- Having the capacity or having developed the habit of being able to wait
- Having the ability to endure pain, trials and hardships without complaint
- Having the ability to hold on regardless of the provocation, difficulty, length of the trial or opposition experienced
- Not being impetuous
- Being able to wait until God gets ready to do something
- Faith under pressure
- Refusing to ever give up

ATRIOTIC—   **Study start date: _____ Finish date: _____**

In America we have been mightily blessed by God with a great and fruitful land. It has many natural resources, inland waterways, thousands of miles of sea coasts, rich farm and ranching lands, interstate expressways, borders that have been somewhat protected on the east and west by oceans and peace for many years with the nations to the north and south. We have a climate with seasons and, for the most part, with God's favor, we experience the blessing of good rain fall. These are just a few of the favors God has granted us. Americans should love this land. Not only is it great but we also have the added blessing of having economic freedom, including the right to own property. Property ownership is one of the secrets of our economic success and one of the primary concepts that has made our Country great.

We have the largest economy in the world; a large, highly skilled work force, numerous fine educational institutions as well as the finest and best equipped standing and reserve military forces in the world. In addition to all this, until recently our systems of business, government and religion were based totally on individual freedom. Our people are completely free to live wherever they want, work wherever they want, buy whatever they want, worship God however they want, vote for whatever governmental official we want and even serve in the military if we want. Individual freedom, self-reliance and responsibility, have been the hallmarks and the foundation of our success in America. Most importantly, we are a nation that was founded on the motto, "In God We Trust." From the time our founders began to draft our Constitution and Bill of Rights, we have believed in the importance of divine intervention among nations and the importance of God's blessing on our land. As to our Christian heritage, Virginia's Governor Patrick Henry said, "It cannot be emphasized too clearly and too often that this nation was founded, not by religionists, but by Christians; not on religion, but on the gospel of Jesus Christ." Many others knew this country was founded on Christianity as well. There are a great many profound statements by some of the signers of the Declaration of Independence. One of which, Charles Carroll said, "Without morals a republic cannot subsist any length of time; they therefore who are decrying the Christian religion … are undermining the solid foundation of morals, the best security for the duration of free governments." It is also important to note that on the first day of our nation's existence, our first president, George Washington, gave us a prophetic warning in his inaugural address saying, the "propitious smiles of Heaven can never be expected on a nation that disregards the eternal rules of order and right which Heaven itself ordains." The Supreme Court's recent approval of the wanton killing of preborn children and sodomite marriages has now placed our national security and the lives of those in our Armed Forces in serious jeopardy.

It is so very easy in a prosperous land like ours for the people to begin to take all their blessings for granted and forget who gave them to us. They may also think that they will be preserved indefinitely at no cost or sacrifice. This memory loss and ingratitude is not a new phenomenon. Just before Israel was about to go into the Promised Land God was freely giving them, Moses spoke this solemn warning: "So it shall be, when the Lord your God brings you into the land of which He swore to your fathers, to Abraham, Isaac and Jacob, to give you large and beautiful cities which you did not build, houses full of all good things which you did not fill, hewn-out wells which you did not dig, vineyards and olive trees which you did not plant—when you have eaten and are full—then beware, lest you forget the Lord who brought you out of the land of Egypt, from the house of bondage." Deuteronomy 6:10–12

God had just delivered Israel from four hundred and thirty years of slavery under the heavy hands and whips of Egyptian tyrants with them not having a single weapon known to man. He parted the Red Sea, gave them water from a rock in the middle of the desert, manna and quail from heaven, clothes and shoes that didn't wear out for forty years and led them continually with a cloud by day and a fire by night. Then He took them into the Promised Land by yet another miracle, that of parting the river Jordan, and gave them a miraculous victory over Jericho, the heavily fortified city of the Canaanites. They didn't have any weapons as I said, and no one had any military training or experience in warfare. They simply had to be faithful to stand on God's promises and obey His commands. Then He gave them this warning because there is something in the fallen nature of man that is inclined to forget where our blessings come from and who gave them to us. He said, 'Beware when you are full and your cattle are waxing sleek up to their bellies in green pastures, you have homes and vineyards, etc. Don't forget the One who brought you here.' Time and again, Israel did just that. They forgot the God who delivered them. As a result, they paid a great price, sometimes even to the point of losing their land, homes and freedom, being taken into captivity. Remember, all victory is from the Lord. This is just one more reason the Bible says, "Blessed is the nation whose God is the Lord." Psalm 33:12 NKJV

Likewise we in America, if we want to long succeed, need to remember to be thankful for all our blessings, to truly appreciate this great country and keep it ever present on our national conscience that these blessings and freedoms are not free. They will only be secured at the price of eternal vigilance by a grateful people, willing to pay the price and do whatever it takes to keep it that way. We must be willing to fight for freedom and let our voices be heard when tyranny begins to encroach. We need to vote and pray. We should be thankful for our Second Amendment right to bear arms. This past week the 9th U.S. Circuit Court of Appeals, the most liberal in the Country just ruled that the 2nd Amendment right to bear arms doesn't extend to carrying concealed handguns. This morning we got up to the news that 50 are dead and 50 more are wounded last night by a radical-Islamic terrorist in an Orlando, Florida bar. Wonder how many would have lived if just one person had a pistol and used it?

This, however, is not the biggest problem. Our government can be an even greater threat. A well-armed citizenry is a major contributor to deterring foreign attacks on our homeland as well as tyranny from our own government. We must never forget or fail to appreciate the investments and sacrifices of those who have gone before us to create and secure our form of government and the God who has given it to us and allowed us to live here. Recently I was asked to speak at the Walk of Hero's Veterans Memorial Park here in Conyers, Georgia. My task was to address the Gold Star Moms, the ones who had lost a son or a daughter in a war. Now stop for a second. What do you tell those Moms who lost so much, who hold their children so precious and dear? Of course, I told them that no one has paid a greater price for our freedom than they, other than their child whose very life was taken. I also told them that even though war is Hell, which it certainly is, there are a lot of things worse than war: terrorism (9/11), oppression, tyranny and slavery just to name a few. Freedom on this planet comes only at a very high price and they had certainly paid the highest price. Here is the cost just in lives in some of our major wars as part of the price our nation has had to be willing to pay for us to be here today[22]:

Revolutionary War	4,435
Texas War of Independence	704
Mexican War	13,283
Civil War	439,035
World War I	116,518
World War II	405,399
Korean War	54,246
Vietnam	90,220
Iraq	1,938
Afghanistan	1,474

Freedom is not cheap and it certainly isn't free, as some might think. Every one of those listed above were the son or daughter of some young mother who taught them their numbers, colors, shapes and how to tie their shoes. They were fathers, sons and daughters whom their dads worked, sometimes two and three jobs to provide a home, transportation, food, clothes and an education. They all had sisters and brothers, aunts, uncles and grandparents who thought the world of them and coveted great hopes and expectation for their futures. They were, however, for the most part, not able to realize their hopes and dreams because of the huge, final, unforgiving cost of war. Those who gave the ultimate sacrifice in warfare are to be honored. It is a price far too high all by itself but it doesn't stop there. Many others were wounded, some seriously to the losing of limbs or their eye sight. Others were burned over much of their bodies and still others wounded with trauma to the brain, etc. Today, due to improved medical care, the seriously wounded but living with major handicaps usually exceeds the number actually killed in war. The cost in terms of dollars can't compare but our financial costs are incredible as well. For us to be able to sit here in peace and read this, there must be sentinels all around the globe standing guard, some flying jets, others carefully watching radar screens in tactical operation centers, many standing guard and many on patrols or in fox holes. Still others are operating our spy networks behind the lines in other nations, thousands are aboard battle ships and so on. Let us always be thankful for our military and such a great nation to live in where we still enjoy more freedom than any other country on earth.

What it means to have the character trait of being **PATRIOTIC:**

- Having loyalty and love for one's country
- Having a love for the land, rivers, mountains, sea shores and people
- Love sufficient for one's country to be willing to serve and do our duty
- Having an appreciation for our rights to bear arms and of property ownership
- Honoring the sacrifices and contributions of our ancestors.
- Respecting and supporting the authority, aspirations, goals and interests of our nation
- Honoring and flying Old Glory
- Being devotion to one's country

EACE —   **Study start date:** _____ **Finish date:** _____

We live in a very chaotic world. There is stress, strife, corruption, rebellion and murder everywhere. Whole cities are going bankrupt and a number of states are teetering on the verge of it as well. Companies, families and nations are falling apart. Millions and billions held in trust by financial managers in the stock market are stolen from their clients. There is wickedness in public school systems, the General Services Administration, the Secret Service, the military, the U.S. Justice Department and even religious institutions. But, the Bible tells us all the foundations of the world, especially the ones men make, "are out of course," meaning they are out of level. (Psalm 82:5) Anything built out of level will, at some point in the construction process, fall over and come tumbling down, simply due to the law of gravity and the power of its own weight. But, in this same world each of us must learn how to build, function, navigate and get along. Thankfully, God has His own way of building that won't fail. He wants to show us how so we too so we can have "a strong city." (Isaiah 26:1) A righteous people which "keeps the truth may enter in" and He goes on to say, He "will keep him in perfect peace, whose mind is stayed on (Him.)" (v. 3) As we keep our focus on Him, learning of Him, loving Him and pleasing Him, we will have peace even in the midst of a storm. We will have peace in the midst of a battle. We will have peace even when we are falsely accused and betrayed.

Where can peace be found? First of all, peace is actually not a thing but a person, Jesus Christ. Isaiah said He would be called the "Prince of Peace." (Isaiah 9:6) Paul, in his day, told the Ephesians, "He, Himself, is our peace." (v. 2:14) Jesus said, "Peace I leave with you, my peace I give to you; not as the world gives do I give to you. Let not your heart be troubled, neither let it be afraid." (John 14:27) And we are told to let "the peace of God rule in your hearts and minds." Colossians 3:15

One of two things is, in fact, going to rule in everyone's heart and mind, either peace or fear. We are the only ones who can decide which it will be for us. We can choose to worry, however, it has been said that about 90% of all the things people worry about never happen. It has also been proven that worry is highly detrimental even to our physical health. On the other hand, we can let "the peace of God which transcends all understanding … guard (our) hearts and minds in Christ Jesus." (Philippians 4:7) This decision is not always easy with all the fiery darts the world is constantly hurling at us. However, since the battle is the Lord's we must constantly "(cast) all (our) cares on Him because He cares for (us)." (I Peter 5:7) Not half our cares, three quarters or even ninety-nine percent of our cares and worries but all of them. Every time they come back, cast them there again. Don't roll them over on Him but cast them like a rock or like a fisherman casting his line. Cast them! We can always have the assurance that whatever happens in any situation, our lives are still in God's hands. But for this to work, what comes next is so important.

We must be very careful what we choose to think about. The battles of life are won or lost between our ears—in the mind. One good thing about the way God made our minds is that we can only think about one thing at a time. So when a bad or negative thought occurs, immediately start thinking on something good and this will erase it. Whatever we think about all day long is what we will become and what Job feared most, he said came upon him. Paul told us what to center our thoughts on: "Whatsoever things are true, whatever things are noble, whatever things are just, whatever things are pure, whatever things are lovely, whatever things are of good report, if there be any virtue, if there be any praise, think on these things." (Philippians 4:8) Refuse to think on anything negative. We will soon find a life of quietness and peace. Where the Spirit of the Lord is there is peace.

We know we are all going to have trials and problems in life. However, we cannot find the answers to these problems which is truth, wisdom and understanding without having peace along with it. Peace is quite simply the result of doing the will of God and peace is one of God's greatest gifts. As believers, we can have peace "that passes all understanding." (Philippians 4:7) As leaders, the peace or the agitation, fear and uneasiness we harbor is highly contagious to those around us. Having a peaceful, friendly attitude makes a leader approachable and easy to follow.

In order to have peace in our relationships with others, we must first be dealing with everyone according to truth. Having truth, honesty, a fair measure and uprightness in all our dealings bring peace in and of themselves. Conveniently, using these, we never have to remember what we told someone or keep two sets of books. Next, we need to realize that life for everyone can be extremely difficult and hard to manage at times. It can only be mastered with wisdom and none of us ever seem to have too much. That is why Solomon said, "Wisdom is the principle thing, therefore get wisdom." (Proverbs 4:7) "All things you may desire cannot compare with her. Length of days is in her right hand, in her left hand are riches and honor. Her ways are ways of pleasantness and all her paths are peace." (v.3:15–17) When we find wisdom, we will also find, along with it, understanding. Yes, Solomon did say, "Wisdom is the principle thing" but he also said, "… in all your getting, get understanding." We need to find out not just what people are saying but how they really feel about things. A significant part of having understanding in all our relations with other people is for them to know that we have their best interest at heart and that we are going to treat them fairly. That kind of trust and a spirit of understanding will build unity. It is through unity we experience strength and peace in relationships.

What it means to have the character trait of being **PEACE:**

- Having the fruit of a clear conscience
- Having harmony, trust and fairness in personal relationships
- Being free from disquieting, oppressive and fearful thoughts and their accompanying emotions
- The absence of anarchy and rebellion
- The resulting state of harmony among people in a community as a result of good government, laws and customs
- Having restored relations, a pardon and harmony with God
- Having a state of quiet, mutual concord and tranquility existing between individuals, families, companies and nations

PEACEMAKER, THE HEART OF A— Study start date: _____ Finish date: _____

Isn't it amazing how some people can make trouble where there is none? This is where wars come from: greed, hate and animosity. Some are said to love arguing so much that "they will argue at the drop of a hat, hand you the hat and knock it right out of your hand." All this for just a chance to bicker. They love a controversy so much that they can take a small smoldering ember of agitation between two people and turn it into a raging forest fire of lost tempers. Still others have an uncanny ability to put the wrong construction on everything and, by their very nature, make everyone angry. Now trouble in this world is something we are all guaranteed. Since it is not a case of if, but when it is coming, knowing how to handle it and get the victory over it is a talent we all need to work on.

A peacemaker is one who is adept at de-escalating a controversy and defusing it as one would a ticking time bomb. Being able to do this in the midst of raging tempers, for the best interest of everyone involved, is a special gift. The first priority when two people or groups are at odds, is to stop the rhetoric for a moment, calm everyone down and encourage them to start listening to reason. Begin in a calm, humble and friendly way to find out what the bottom-line issues of the controversy are in the first place. Getting a handle on what exactly the problem is can be a large task, in and of itself, since the first casualty in any conflict is usually the truth. Often people have at least two reasons for the things they do: one that sounds good and the other is the real reason. You will also need to immediately let both sides know that you sincerely want to help them because a solution will help everyone. We know a prudent man gets the facts so he can de-confuse the problem. By using a pen and paper, jot down the issues at hand. Seek to have each side, as calmly as possible, describe their view of their points of disagreement without inter-ruption or debate from the other. It is important to practice being a good listener and not allow anyone to raise their voice in these discussions. They must know, hopefully, from past experience as well as your calm and sincere attitude, that they can trust you to help and be on the side of truth. They also need to know that you truly care about them both, personally, and as a group if that is what you are dealing with.

Once you have found the core issues and both sides have calmed down for the moment, try sincerely to remove the bones of contention. First correct any misunderstandings because these are usually the root of the problem. So many problems between people are fomented simply by misunderstandings and, over time you can be assured that we are all going to be misunderstood sooner or later. A fire will go out if you remove the logs that have fueled it in the first place. Then correct any obvious injustices if you have the power to do so or have them agree on a path to correct them very quickly. Next, try to find common ground because points of agreement will bind people and groups together quickly. Few people or groups in America who are close enough to each other to argue are without at least some similarities, as well as common needs and goals. You can also appeal to a higher motive such as the good of the company, their usefulness to the company, their testimony and their reputation in the community, etc. Appeal to honor. The writer of Proverbs penned these words, "It is honorable for a man to stop striving (arguing), since any fool can start a quarrel." If one or more of the parties to the disagreement happen to be leaders, it might be well to remind them that "Mercy and truth preserve the king (or leader) and by loving-kindness he upholds his throne." (20:28) We are also admonished to "do good, seek peace and pursue it" (Psalm 34:14b) Finally, to those who will do this, we have this promise: "Blessed are the peacemakers, for they shall be called sons of God." Matthew 5:9

What it means to have the character trait of having **THE HEART OF A PEACEMAKER:**

- Able to deescalate trouble and tension between warring factions
- Able to find the misunderstandings and the root of the problem so there can be reconciliation
- Able to gain the trust of warring parties to find a way to bring peace
- Able to find common ground
- Able to reconcile factions at variance
- Able to "take hold of things" Ben Franklin said, "by the smooth handle."

EOPLE PERSON, BEING A—   **Study start date:** _____ **Finish date:** _____

A man was asked by a friend how the Lord was treating him and he replied, "The Lord is treating me fine, it's just His people that I have a hard time with." Certainly we have all had our troubles with fellow occupants of this big blue marble. But, we all start out in life with a whole lot of rough edges. That's probably why God gives most of us wives which some have aptly described as much needed heavenly sandpaper. There are just some things each of us can do in life that will work extremely well at irritating the hound out of everyone around us. The sooner we learn what these are and eliminate them from our personalities, the better life will be for us because everywhere we go, people are the same. I've lived all over the United States and in many parts of the world. What I have found is if you like people, and you like where you are, for the most part, unless you are acting like a half-wit, they will like you. Now if you just basically don't like people and don't like where you are living, they will be only too quick to show you the door. I believe everyone should read Dale Carnegie's book, *How to Win Friends and Influence People,* and read it several times. Even though it was written in 1936, it is still really one of the greatest books ever written on the subject of human relations. Why does this book not ever get old? Well, because people are the same today as they were in 1936 and about the same as they were in 1592. You treat them right and they will love and help you. But, if you rub them wrong more than once, look out, that boomerang is probably going to hit you squarely in the back of the head my friend. Now as good and as great as this book is, it will not help if you just, basically, don't like people. The book is about the psychology of human nature but you can't put a band aid on cancer. You can't fake not liking yourself or other folk.

Almost everyone wants to succeed in life but few have ever learned the importance of really liking other people. Just think about a few of the things you will be needing during your stay here on the planet. You are going to need things like food, shelter, a job, a pay check, transportation, someone to love, a meaningful life, etc. Now unless you have found a hideout nobody knows about in the back of a national forest, you are probably going to need other people. There was a time when one of the scribes came to Jesus and asked, 'Which was the first or greatest commandment?' In other words, what is our basic and most important instruction while here on earth? He replied, "The first of all the commandments is … 'Love the Lord your God with all your heart, with all your soul, with all your mind and with all your strength.' This is the first commandment. And the second, like it, is this, 'Love your neighbor as yourself.' There is no other commandment greater than these." (Mark 12:29–31) In other words, learn to like yourself, because you can't like anyone else if you don't first like yourself. Now I didn't say to get stuck on yourself or to start thinking that you are the greatest gift to ever to come down the dusty road but to like and even as the Bible says, love yourself. All the while, most importantly, don't forget, we are still to consider others better than ourselves. Philippians 2:3

One thing that will help us learn the importance of being a people person is getting a firm hold of the fact that none of us knows very much, without help from other people. Absolutely not enough to survive and certainly not enough to thrive while here. Today knowledge doubles every twelve years so we have much to learn. However, no one learns very much by accident and certainly precious little if they aren't at all interested in learning. Therefore we must see clearly our need, how truly desperate we are to learn and how important it is to learn from others who are far wiser than we. It has been said that the greatest treasure overlooked in America is the untapped wisdom of grey-headed men and women. Society just seems to discard them, never asking them to share the treasure of their wisdom stored up from a life-time of experience, learning, hard knocks and study. We just run up on all the same old stumps day-after-day and year-after-year. Our generation thinks it's cool to act like we know everything. No. I believe it is like a wise man said, "Ignorance is a consequence of being human. Not knowing it is even more atrocious." I did so poorly in high school—partly because of not applying myself but mostly because I wasn't the sharpest knife in the drawer, when I heard that little quote about ignorance, it was no great leap for me to immediately declare my total ignorance. That was years ago and I have been learning like a wild man ever since. Have I arrived? No. And, yes, I have learned a few things but I still see myself like the beggar Lazarus at the rich man's table in Luke 16:20. I still need to ask God every day for a crumb of wisdom off His table just to make it. I still don't know my right hand from the left and certainly don't know how to get out of the rain without help from God and my friends. Thank God I see my great need to learn. I am truly bankrupt apart from Him and His wisdom. Most of my friends know that I stand ready to learn from them. Please help!

One of the first rules in relating to people or becoming a people person is to learn not to interfere with someone else's means of being happy. If they like eating worms and they have been doing it a long time, leave them alone. I'm certainly not saying you have to do it but if they haven't died from it yet, let them eat worms. Don't try to convert everyone to your way of doing things or your ways of finding happiness. Leave that alone. There is no percentage in it. None.

It is certainly important that we learn to enjoy interacting with other people. As I mentioned, liking people is not something you can fake. At some point, we must stop and acknowledge what a blessing it is to have friends and interact with other people. As you know, in prison, to punish those who get out of line, so much has already been taken from them, they don't have a whole lot of options here. The worst thing they can do to them short of taking their life of course, is to put them in solitary confinement. That removes them from the general population so they can no longer interact with the other prisoners, no more going to the mess hall, sharing jokes about the guards or going out on the yard, playing gin rummy, etc. For those of us who are free to have all the contact with others we'd like, it would be well to understand that a large part of our own, individual happiness comes from relating to others: seeing their smiling faces, asking how they are doing, etc. Remembering their birthdays and special times, being there for them in their time of need. There will never be enough of those times and they are so special.

One thing that causes some people trouble relating to others is not confronting their mutual problems head on. I often advise people to put the skunk on the table. Be tactful but never beat around the bush, acting like there isn't a problem when you know for sure there is one. If you leave the skunk under the table, he is definitely going to start stinking up the place—if nowhere other than in your own mind. Two people can never get along, walk together, enjoy fellowship or accomplish anything much unless they work out their individual differences, find understanding and come into agreement. Like they say, "Through unity strength." Believe me, it is worth the temporary trouble and inconvenience to address your problems.

Another hindrance to our fellowship and the enjoyment of our relationships with others is sometimes caused by people trying to be something or somebody they are not. Just be yourself. You are, in fact, the person God made you to be. Everybody else is taken so just be yourself. After he made you, he threw away the mold. Trying to be somebody else is just plain impossible. You can and should incorporate the winsome ways that contribute to good interrelations with other people and make these things an integral part of your own personality over time, but you can't imitate someone else. It is fine to be yourself and a whole lot easier. God made you and He loves you so go on ahead and like yourself. Then people can learn to like the real you. When they see you are confident being the real you, they will actually be drawn to you. Developing godly character will also cause others to value you as a person and a friend.

Yet another way to enjoy people is to look for and see the good in them. Everyone has at least one gift and some people even more than that. Compliment and honestly encourage them in their gift. Just today, my lovely wife, Donna, received a note that thanked her sincerely for her gift of encouragement. The words were heart felt and the card even had lots of little sparkly confetti inside that spilled out on the table when I watched her open it. That is the joy of people liking and enjoying people. So show sincere appreciation for another's accomplishments. Be glad for them. Clip that article about them out of the paper and send it to them with a note saying you are proud of them and honored to be their friend. Remember their birthdays. Compliment good work and try your best not to be critical. Unless it is obviously important, overlook small offenses and injustices. This is not a perfect world we live in. If you try to make it perfect, you have a big job ahead.

In the world, one thing we will all certainly encounter is difficult, hard to get along with people. If we are going to endure successfully all their provocations, we must see them as our ministry. Their attitude and objectionable personality is often a cry for help. Sincerely try to be their friend and seek to understand the root cause or causes of their distress. Find something to like about them and show appreciation for their friendship. Some you will be able to help. However, there are some people you are never really going to get along with. That is why the Apostle Paul said, "If possible, so far as it depends upon you, be at peace with all men." (Romans 12:18) You have to know that some people have problems, hidden sins and demons they love so much they may not yet be ready to give up. Do the best you can to get along with them but it is okay if it never turns out to be the best relationship in the world. Some people aren't at peace with themselves so because of that, they can't be at peace with anyone else. However, you can still be a ray of sunshine in their life.

Another important part of being a people person is learning how to handle criticism. No matter what you do, you can count on it, you are going to be criticized. Somebody isn't going to like it first of all just because you have upset the status quo. If you did it good, you did it too good. If you did it bad, you should have done it better or you should have done it their way. Just settle it in your heart that you are not going to let criticism bother you. Of course we must not only be willing to hear the critiques of others but I believe we should also write them down and put them in a file. Some criticism is beneficial and writing it down gives us a much better opportunity to study these comments and pray over them to see if there isn't something there that we should really be changing. We all live in a natural body and our mind doesn't really want to hear it. I think it is called stubbornness. We must also fight off the natural inclination to think that we are always right. Oftentimes we need to change and improve. So we should consider criticism a blessing and receive the good from it as well.

Realize that there are few things we'll find in our journey better than life-long friendships. Settle it in your mind, you will never be even a good leader if you don't like people and enjoy being around them. It is not so much what they can do for you but what you can do for them that is important. Never miss an opportunity to be a blessing. We should see our friendship with everyone as an opportunity to help and encourage them. It is important to see everyone we meet as a lifelong friend. We only go around once so help everyone you can. Who knows, tomorrow we might actually be the one needing a little help from our friends.

What it means to have the character trait of **BEING A PEOPLE PERSON:**

- Truly liking and enjoying interaction with other people
- Truly seeing the good in others and appreciating their talents and abilities
- Having the joy of encouraging others in their gifts and talents
- Appreciating the opportunity we have to learn from, serve and help others

- The ability to be comfortable in our own skin around other people while, at the same time, being open to improving our personality
- Having the grace not to interfere with the peculiar enjoyments of others
- Enjoying the challenge of difficult people and learning how to help them in life

ERSEVERENCE—   **Study start date:** _____ **Finish date:** _____

The life we all have inherited as human beings is not a race for success, a race for prosperity or a race for greatness, but a race of faith. Oh, it's fine to be a success, to prosper and even be great in the eyes of the Lord but faith is the only thing given to man that will truly please God. (Hebrews 11:6) It is how we bring Heaven to earth and get all our needs met by God. We have also been promised in the Word that, in this life, we will have tribulation. Sure, we all have many good days but trouble will come and usually come when we least expect it.

Life, we find, is not a sprint but an endurance race. In this race we meet with many unforeseen obstacles, opponents and oppressors. That is exactly why Paul told us in the book of Hebrews to "run with patience the race that is set before us." (Hebrews 21:1) The path is not only hard but long so we must be ready to "endure hardship as a good soldier of Jesus Christ" (II Timothy 2:3) if we expect to make it to the finish line.

In this country we have the Indy 500, the Daytona 500 and the Talladega 500, all of which are endurance races. The greatest obstacles are not the courses themselves, the speed of the courses or the number of competitors. The greatest obstacle is the length of the course. It brings with it, the possibility of exhaustion and mistakes brought on by fatigue. The other problem is that these long distance runs cause mechanical failures with machines, tires and equipment. These races are tests of both men and machines.

Because our race is so long and arduous as human beings, the Master gave us some very important advice in the book of Hebrews. He said, we need to look directly "to Jesus, the author and finisher of our faith, who for the joy that was set before Him endured the cross, despising the shame and has sat down as the right hand of the throne of God." (Hebrews 12:2) He was rejected, falsely accused, ridiculed, scourged, beaten, mocked, deserted and hung on a cross as an evil doer. Though He deserved none of this, He endured it all because he looked to the end of the race and the great joy of triumph in the salvation of many souls. . The writer went on to say to "consider Him who endures such hostility from sinners against Himself, lest (we) become weary and discouraged in (our) souls." If He was met with such hostility, can we expect any less? Then he asked if we had forgotten the exhortation that speaks to us as true sons: "My son, do not despise the chastening of the Lord, nor be discouraged when you are rebuked by Him; for whom the Lord loves He chastens, and scourges every son whom He receives." (Hebrews 12:5.6)

He reminded us how important it was that we endure this chastening because God was dealing with us as sons and not as illegitimates. This is what all true earthly fathers do to their sons. He continued saying, we all had earthly fathers who had to correct us and yet, we still respected them. How much more should we submit ourselves to the Father of Spirits and be blessed to find life that is truly life. We all endured chastening from them as they thought best for a short time so God does all this for the express purpose that we may receive the great blessing of His divine nature. Though chastening never feels good at moment, it will later yield the fruit of peace and righteousness to those who have allowed themselves to be trained thereby. (Hebrews 12:11) So Paul says we are to strengthen our hands for the work and pursue peace and holiness with all men because without it none of us are going to see the Lord.

Several other admonitions were given specifically for our race in this life.. In chapter six of Hebrews he cautioned us not to "become sluggish but (to) imitate those who through faith and patience inherit the promises." (Hebrews 6:12) At the same time, we are to lay "aside every weight and the sin which so easily ensnares us" (Hebrews 21:1) because it only comes to "steal, kill and destroy" (John 10:10) So get rid of it! Compromise will kill us as a Christian so get rid of all earthly entanglements. Paul also commanded us to "come out from among (the world) and be separate … touch not the unclean thing and (our God) will receive you." (II Corinthians 6:17)

The best example of this I know is the late Floyd Parker, a friend of mine. He was born just a few miles from my house on a large tract of rocky land where his family had a little cabin. Floyd was one of eight children and they had a very abusive father. The family always thought that Floyd and his brother, Robert, were a bit slow.so these two younger boys caught a lot of flack from the older kids as they were growing up. They were truck (vegetable and producer) and dairy farmers but they were extremely poor working this subpar land. Everyone had to work all the time. The little cabin the family lived in only had two room so as all the kids came along they added a small lean-to alongside of it to accommodate the increase. It was so poorly built that there were spaces between the slats that made up the floor. During the winters when it snowed, it would blow up under the little house making the spaces between the slats look like white lines when you looked down at the floor. They certainly couldn't afford much heat so they all had to sleep under a whole pile of blankets at night. The blankets were so heavy they felt like lead weights.

One day Floyd's uncle and father were visiting in the kitchen of their little cabin as they often did. Floyd, in the next room of course, overheard his uncle say, "You know, Floyd will probably never go into the Army and he will probably have to be taken care of by his brothers and sisters all his life." Hearing that, Floyd said to himself right then and there, "Oh, no they won't." Floyd was faithful in his younger years to go to church and was greatly blessed to find the Lord. He finished high school the best he could but still really couldn't read or write very well. He immediately tried to enlist in the Army and much to his surprise, they took him. After several years, he finished his tour, did our country a good job as a soldier, and received an honorable discharge.

When he came home from the Army, he continued to attend church and met a beautiful, little girl who was valedictorian of her high school class. They soon fell in love and got married. She got a job which paid very little in a five and dime store and he took a job driving a route truck for Mathis Dairy. The couple didn't make much but were always thankful for everything. They always tithed and kept the Lord foremost in their family and personal lives. God gave them wisdom with their finances and they began to save their money. Somehow his job with Mathis Dairy ended so he felt led to apply for a job at a glass store in Decatur, Georgia. They granted him an interview but quickly gave him the brush off.

As he was walking down the street toward their little apartment after the interview, Floyd was praying and felt leading him to start his own glass business. He figured if this other company didn't need him, God would help him start his own. When he got home, he told his wife of his plans and she agreed. He took the $3,000 they had in savings, rented a little commercial storefront in downtown Decatur and put in an order for a lot of glass. In order to get the low, wholesale price they had to order over $2,000 worth at a time. The delivery truck promply came out and, conveniently, there happened to be a big tree behind the store, fully equipped with a heavy rope and a block and tackle. They hoisted the glass up into the air, secured it with the rope and tied off on the tree. Floyd handed the driver his check for payment and just as the truck left the property, the rope broke and all the glass crashed to the ground, breaking into a million pieces. It looked like their little enterprise had surely come to an early and abrupt end. They were now out of money. Floyd told his wife about it and said, "I'm going to borrow the money and order more glass but we're going on." He wasn't about to quit because there was no quit in him.

They did go on. He went out on the road and did the selling to all the builders in Atlanta and made deliveries while she kept the books and operated the store. Their small glass company soon began to prosper. I happened to be one of his customers as a builder back before I knew him personally. The company prospered so much that they were having to hire new people all the time.

A few years later the Atlanta Journal started publishing a list in their newspaper of the 100 biggest builders in Atlanta. He sat down with the paper and wondered how many he knew. He actually knew every one of them and what surprised them both was that his company was supplying fully ninety percent of them their glass and window screens and others besides. Soon Floyd was doing so well that he started driving a Mercedes Benz. He also bought himself an airplane that he used primarily to fly evangelists around the southeast to preach the Gospel. Several of his brothers and sisters started coming to him for help and he helped them because that spirit was in him. He even took care of his brother, Robert, until the day he died. However, no matter how much God blessed him, he continued to tithe and give to the Lord's work. In fact, he never paid himself more in any of the years he was in business than he gave to the Lord. Floyd passed away a few years ago but left this world a mighty blessed man—who knew a thing or two about perseverance. He yet remains today an icon of the Lord's faithfulness to all those who refuse to give up.

What it means to have the character trait of **PERSERVERANCE:**

- To remain steadfast in painful trials
- To stay with a task, mission or enterprise despite the odds, counter influences, attacks, fatigue and blows until the victory is won
- To never become discouraged
- The mental and intestinal fortitude to refuse to give up regardless of the current facts or the situation
- Continuing in an endeavor or venture long past what most think is reasonable or even what your own mind tells you is reasonable
- To continue resolutely in spite of ill treatment, lagging polls, the odds, the pain or interference
- To retain one's position fixed and unchanged in society or with one's immediate company or work associates regardless of contrary influences or being either in the minority or the odd-man-out.
- Staying with a matter or course until the desired results are obtained regardless of the cost in time, effort, treasure or political capital

ERSISTENCE—See PERSERVERANCE

PERSUASIVENESS— **Study start date: _____ Finish date: _____**

Normally, for anyone to be able to persuade others to a particular point of view, they must either be a great salesman or be fully convinced about the truth of a matter, point of view or the value of a product. The Apostle Paul was, without a doubt, the greatest of all the apostles and a prime example of the fruitfulness of a life of persuasiveness. To accomplish what he did, raising up all the churches in Asia, it took great skill, charisma, enthusiasm and persuasiveness. God, no doubt, gave him many gifts and talents but he, none the less, had to be fully convinced of an entirely new belief system. This was not easily accomplished in the life of one so zealous, raised up in Judaism. His was a dramatic conversion which included the loss of his sight for three days (with no assurance during this time that he would ever get it back) and a direct confrontation with Christ, Himself. Paul was so completely affected by it all he said, "I am persuaded that neither death nor life, nor angels nor principalities, nor powers, nor things present nor things to come, nor height nor depth, nor any other created thing, shall be able to separate us from the love of God which is in Christ Jesus our Lord." Romans 8:38

He was so persuaded, in fact, that he was not only willing to do the work necessary to build the Kingdom on earth but was also willing to suffer whatever came his way in order to fulfill his purpose. What things? Here are a few: "From the Jews five times (he) received forty stripes minus one. Three times (he) was beaten with rods; once (he) was shipwrecked; a night and a day (he had) been in the deep; in journeys often, in perils of water, in perils of robbers, in perils of my own countrymen, in perils of the Gentiles, in perils in the city, in perils in the wilderness, in perils in the sea, in perils among false brethren; in weariness and toil, in sleeplessness often, in hunger and thirst, in fastings often, in cold and nakedness" and more. (II Corinthians 11:24–27) Nevertheless, he said, "I know whom I have believed and am persuaded that He is able to keep what I have committed to Him until that day." (I Timothy 1:12) He committed his life unto death looking to that day. What day? The Day of Recompense, the day we receive our reward from God in Heaven. Paul was also "fully persuaded that what (God) had promised He was also able to perform" (Romans 4:21) For one who was so zealous to destroy the church and kill its members, to come to these conclusions with such conviction, was no less than the work of God in Paul's life.

Precious little will ever be accomplished in life without the ability to persuade others to one's point of view. It is a trait that can and must be learned. To persuade anyone to do or believe anything, one must first begin from a positive standpoint. For someone to even listen to us, they must feel that, first, we are credible and trustworthy and, secondly, we are sincere and have their best interest at heart. There must be good will flowing between the parties. Finally, your arguments must be sound, easily understood and convincing.

There is no doubt as to Paul's persuasiveness, I invite you to read just one of the books he wrote in the New Testament. A whole book? Yes, but it won't take long because it is only one page—a total of thirteen sentences. It is the letter Paul wrote to a slave owner named Philemon. What he attempted to do in those thirteen sentences was to persuade Philemon to completely exonerate one of his run-away slaves who had become converted under Paul's ministry and was, at that moment, actually working for him fulltime. Well, it's not really even thirteen sentences because one was the salutation and last three were devoted to greetings from fellow Christians there with Paul whom Philemon probably knew, along with Paul's concluding blessing and closing remarks. If my math is correct, he had to get all this done in just nine sentences! Certainly this would be difficult for anyone to accomplish in a letter first of all and especially one so short. To make it happen, Paul had to be a master of persuasion and the greatest, self-taught psychologist on earth. He also had to show Philemon how it was in his own best interest to do what he was asking, knowing this fugitive slave he had good money invested in, might have deserved serious punishment if not a death. Although he was confident that he had the authority in Christ to command him to forgive Onesimus, he didn't. He chose rather to appeal to him as a brother in Christ and left it up to his own free will. He further said if this slave had wronged him or owed him anything, to charge it to his (Paul's) account and that Paul would repay it himself (not to mention the fact that Philemon who was also Paul's convert, owed him his own life as well). Then he gave Philemon a good name to live up to and said he had every confidence that he would do everything he asked and even more. Every point he made was full of faith, mercy, integrity, grace and compassion.

In life there are only two kinds of power: The power of position and the power of influence or persuasion. Those with the power of position in life have only so much latitude within which to operate and, therefore, have pretty limited options. Those with the power of influence such as wives, constituents who really know how to make a godly appeal to authority, donors and lobbyists, for example, in most cases, have tremendous power behind the scenes. This is why the law requires full disclosure when relatives, lobbyists or donors are involved in any phase of government or its decision making processes. The ability to persuade is powerful.

It is also well to remember the old axiom: Never argue with a fool because the bystanders may not be able to tell which one of you is the fool. So there are some people who are so whacko you had best not argue with them at all. Even with the best of people, we need to realize that arguments can get pretty testy and irrational at times and they can also get there pretty quickly. If you must debate an issue, here are 15 ways to win with persuasion:

1. Realize that you can never win an argument so refuse to argue. Agree only to **reason together** with them about the issue (in a civil tone).
2. Always begin in a friendly manner.
3. Show genuine respect for the other person and his opinions. Never say the other person is wrong. Let the facts you present speak for themselves.
4. If you find that you happen to be wrong about even a small part of the entire debate, admit it emphatically (we must be on the side of truth). This will cause other person to respect you even more and be more willing to admit being wrong himself.
5. Let the other person do a great deal of the talking. (Take notes. You will need them.)
6. Try your best to see things from the other person's view.
8. Try to find common ground
9. Remind them of the benefits in your proposal that will accrue to them.
10. Get the other person to start saying "Yes" immediately by appealing to generally accepted truths, laws of equity and nature
11. Dramatize your points, being sure to present your arguments in a manner that can be easily understood.
12. Show that you expect the best and believing the best of them in the situation (give them a good reputation to live up to).
13. If possible, show that you are sympathetic with the other person's points, ideas and desires.
14. Use some of the other person's points so they will feel the idea was really theirs to begin with.
15. Appeal by giving them the challenge of a higher and nobler motive to live up to.

What it means to have the character trait of **PERSUASIVENESS:**

- The ability to convince others by entreaty, postulation, facts and reason
- The ability to change opinions, beliefs and belief systems
- The ability to plead with and urge others to a particular positive end or result
- Having built a foundation of faithfulness and credibility to begin to deliver one's arguments
- The ability to show the other person how our idea or product will benefit him or her personally
- The ability to come up with convincing arguments and deliver them without creating offense

PIETY—   **Study start date:** _____ **Finish date:** _____

W e hear little of piety today but it is a very important part of a person's life. I'm afraid the term conjures up visions of a choir boy in a white robe quietly lighting candles in a cathedral but that is not anywhere within ten million light years of what the term really means.

You see, man was put here on earth primarily to find God who is, Himself, constantly drawing us by His Spirit. Establishing a relationship with God is critically important because it effects everything while we are here and all of eternity besides. Without Him, this earthly life is most miserable and empty. Without Him the only remaining option during our short stay here is to try to please ourselves, which is futile. The eye will never be satisfied with seeing, the ear with hearing, the stomach with food, no matter what we may try. Nothing will satisfy. Highly paid sports stars, movie stars, Wall Street bankers, real estate tycoons and politicians have all tried spending millions on themselves only to be all the more miserable. Truth is you can't eat enough steaks to make you happy, neither can you make enough money, take enough drugs, look at enough porn, have enough illicit relationships or eat enough ice cream to make you happy.

Indulgence will, sooner or later, cause us enormous grief, ill health, depression and heartache because the world just will not satisfy. "For we know that the whole creation groans and labors with birth pangs together until now," (Romans 8:22) Paul said. "For the earnest expectation of the creation eagerly waits for the revealing of the sons of God." (Romans 8:19) The heart and soul of man is locked in the prison of its own self-centeredness and despair because the whole earth and all that is in it is without hope. There are no answers in this life apart from God but we humans are easily deceived by the things of this world. We think they are real and lasting but they are not. God knows we are all going to set our affection on something so Paul encourages us to "Set (our) affection on things above, not on things on the earth." (Colossians 3:2) If we seek things like righteousness and love, amazingly, we will find "life, prosperity and honor." Proverbs 21:21 NIV

Another problem finding success and security on earth is that everything here is dying. Every blade of grass coming up out of the ground has already begun to die. Every child born of a woman is born to die. Every company, we know, has based its success on either a product or service. All products are quickly becoming obsolete in this technological age and will soon be replaced by a superior invention coming right down the pike. Services are also improved very quickly today by science, technology or a sharing of information on the internet or a combination of all three in a highly computerized world. Information and ideas travel with lightning speed today. Another problem is our bodies are decaying on the outside, having only a certain, very limited life span. Besides all this, there is nothing new under the sun and the wisest man in the world, Solomon, said, "All is vanity." (Ecclesiastes 1:2) The Apostle Paul agreed stating that, "The creation was made subject to vanity, not willingly but by reason of Him who hath subjected the same in hope." (Romans 8:20) All that has been done must be done again in this circle of life. No matter how many patents, products or companies we may own, they won't last or satisfy. The only answer is piety because "without holiness no one will see the Lord." Hebrews 12:14

As this is on my mind, I remember just yesterday driving through a small mill town near where we live on our way to give Thanksgiving turkeys to the needy and people who help them in our food ministry year-round. The streets were lined with little, shotgun houses. Now I'm not down on little houses. I've lived in a few and shelter is good no matter what size or shape it is. I lived in a mobile home once and I still hate having to give up the comfort and security of the pitter-patter of the raindrops on its tin roof on a rainy night. Had to, very reluctantly, leave that behind when I built my first home. Back to the ranch though, these little duplexes are actually a hundred years old or more and they go on in the vicinity seemingly forever. No telling how many people have lived in each one over time. Lots of mom's and dad's and little kids. Yet they, for the most part, have all come and gone, leaving no sign of their existence. There is not a single name tacked to a tree. No plaque on the side of any of the little houses stating who has lived there, what they contributed or what they had accomplished. Nothing. Nada. They came, they saw, they paid by the sweat of their brow in the cotton mill to get their rent ticket and allotments in the company store—and, next thing you know, they are gone. However, most did have kids so now the cycle starts all over again in a little shotgun houses down the street or around the corner. It is amazing. Vanity just like the preacher said. "Vanity of vanities … Vanity of vanities, all is vanity." (Ecclesiastes 1:2) The story is unchanged if you go by the houses on the wealthy side of town. The people too, come and go and are soon forgotten. The only difference is more people attend the funerals of the rich. Furthermore, what people build here on earth can and usually will soon be destroyed by rust, the moth, fire, thieves, obsolescence, war or many other detrimental forces loosed on purpose as Paul said, in the worldly realm.

Piety is certainly nothing we can lay claim to as something we did or accomplished. It is simply the product of a life of loving God, His free grace and the work of His Spirit in us. By the work of sanctification (being set apart by God) we are getting better but we never have any of our own piety. Jesus Christ is all our righteousness. We still, however, need to walk in some increasing degree of righteousness because without it, all that we accomplish here on earth can quickly be wiped away. In the last two weeks, five generals in the U. S. military, were under investigation for corruption. All had led tremendous lives of sacrifice and accomplishment as intrepid defenders of our country. However, a lack of character in their personal life and the way they conducted business when no one was watching (piety) caused them great shame and disgrace. Many of them face loss of rank, fines and forced retirement. Living for God certainly has its benefits here on earth. It will carry us to the finish line and on to a greater world beyond when this short life is over.

Piety has to do with being good but not completely because we can never, on our own, be good enough to please God. We are all imperfect and have all fallen short. It is ours to simply commit ourselves to doing His will and He adds the grace (ability) to make it possible. He gets all the credit for whatever success we have in the obedience realm. He is able; we are not. He can take anything and fix it. He can take our mess and make a miracle.

Piety has everything to do with one's relationship with God. Some people go through life trying to prove that there is no God when, in fact, He is "Father of all, who is above all, and through all, and in (us) all." (Ephesians 4:6) One need go no further in their search for Him than the first sentence in the Bible to suddenly possess tremendous revelation about the Master and Maker of the universe. It says, as we know, "In the beginning God created the heavens and the earth." (Genesis 1:1) Just believe it. No one can explain the miracle of birth, the origin of the universe or the sun's ability to maintain the exact same temperature for thousands of years (at least) without any new infusions of fuel that we are aware of. God is our creator and the maker of heaven and earth—plain and simple. His plan for man is to redeem us from our fallen nature and restore us to a wonderful relationship with Him.

To accomplish this, we know that "(He) so loved the world (the people in it) that He gave His only begotten Son, that whoever believes in Him should not perish but have everlasting life." (John 3:16) This is as simple as a person stopping at some point and asking God to forgive him of his sins, come into his heart and be his Savior and Lord. That's it. Understanding and accepting this, is our purpose on earth. We are here to find Him, know Him, serve Him, love Him, enjoy Him and bring Him glory in this one, short life. We will never find true life or a fulfilled life any other place. For indeed, "in Him we live and move and have our being …" (Acts 17:28) To live in this world and miss God entirely would be the greatest loss any man could ever suffer for eternity. In light of eternity, this life is nothing, not even a speck. We are just here to find Him, know Him, enjoy Him and prepare to live with, love and enjoy Him for eternity.

A person's relationship with God is not a ritual, a list of daily liturgical religious duties to be carried out methodically each day or a religious strait jacket God expects us to wear so we can sit still and be perfect. I, for one, have always liked a bit of excitement in life, always have and I guess I always will. I liked flying planes and jumping out of them, leading men in battle, building houses, building companies, riding horses, water skiing and a thousand other things. However, I can tell you that my life has never been more exciting than it has been since I accepted the Lord on a summer day in 1977. There is just nothing like preaching the Word and seeing the Holy Spirit work on the hearts of men bringing them to a saving knowledge of Jesus Christ. He knows how to use every one of us. He gave everyone gifts and talents and knows how and where to fit them into His universe most productively. When we have accepted Christ and His sacrifice for our sins, we enter into a vibrant, spiritual life and a natural Father—son or daughter relationship. We are here "To love Him with all (our) heart, with all (our) understanding and with all (our) strength …" Mark 12:33

When we set our affections upon Him and seek Him with all our might, happily we also find that He is "a rewarder of the diligent seeker." (Hebrews 11:6) Not a rewarder of everyone but only—the diligent seekers. When we truly seek Him and serve Him with all our hearts, He leads us to life that is truly life. Not only the abundant life but fulfilled, contented, productive, meaningful and purposeful life. We have hope that we can fulfill our divine purpose in this life and have great assurance of rewards in the one to come. Walking in His ways keeps us from evil, failure, depression, torment and an early grave. Life is not dull, boring or limited. It is all about love, freedom, compassion, abundance and the unlimited opportunity to walk hand-in-hand with the God of the Universe in victory. There is no better way to live.

What it means to have the character trait of **PIETY**:

- Fidelity
- Virtuous
- Being devout
- In covenant
- Devotion to spiritual worship and reverence for God
- Faithfulness to religious duties but also to our natural obligations to parents, children, employers and the government
- In prayer, fasting, tithing, daily Bible meditation, obedience and service to the church and our fellow man
- Visiting widows, orphans, prisoners and those in distress

POISE— **Study start date:** _____ **Finish date:** _____

As young people growing up, we are all easily intimidated by many things, not the least of which is performing or speaking before large groups of people. Thus the need for recitals, Toastmasters, group and individual sports, etc. We all need practice doing these things and seeing ourselves performing successfully so we can develop poise, which is the ability to operate with excellence under pressure. This is what a quarterback needs to stay in the pocket and find a receiver, knowing he is about to get hit by a 325 pound lineman moving at about 30 m.p.h.

When trouble comes, many out in the world shake like the leaves of a tree in high wind. They are easily intimidated and overcome in their minds by circumstances as well as being hugely effected by pain. They lack poise. The apostle Paul puts all these worrisome, agonizing, painful things in one little box. He then labeled it just "momentary," "light afflictions" and all of them, he said, were just "common to man." Nothing to be moved by or overly concerned with but things to simply deal with and be taken in stride.

The three Hebrew children showed great poise when they were hauled in before the king and threatened with execution by being thrown in the firey furnace if they refused to bow down to a false image. They just said, "O Nebuchadnezzar, we have no need to answer you in this matter. If that is the case, our God whom we serve is able to deliver us from the burning fiery furnace, and He will deliver us from your hand, O King. But, if not, let it be known to you, O king, that we do not serve your gods, nor will we worship the gold image which you have set up." You know the rest of the story.

What it means to have the character trait of **POISE**:

- Having a stable, calm, composed and balanced state of equilibrium regardless of the circumstances
- Not becoming irritable in a debate, a learning process or even in the heat of battle
- Being calm and collected in battle even when confronted with constant attempts on your life
- Not being irritated by the course personality of a froward, perverse or harsh supervisor or to be visibly moved by their comments
- Being calm and collected when speaking before dignitaries, magistrates or large groups of people
- Showing graciousness and tact in difficult situations and circumstances
- Having a meek and quiet spirit of submission to genuine, lawful authority
- Able to bear up under evil speaking and treatment while yet rendering blessing to your enemies for it all
- Maintaining a tranquil, pleasant state in the presence of angry outbursts

POSITIVE PHILOSOPHY, A —   Study start date: _____ Finish date: _____

Having a positive philosophy about life is crucial for not only success and even survival in this world. The word "philosophy" simply means the sum total of all a person has learned and from that what they believe is workable, wise and beneficial. Some people have a positive outlook on life, in general, because of their philosophy but, then, others couldn't possibly be more negative. However, no matter how positive a person is momentarily, it cannot be sustained over a lifetime without having the true, positive philosophy of the Kingdom of God coupled with the continuous encouragement of God's Word. Positive parental instruction and a positive education are helpful but they cannot sustain, as I said, a person over a lifetime. There are just simply too many negative influences and the trials of life are far too great.

Another huge problem is that stinking thinking is part of our fallen nature. It is fear-driven, only designed for survival and must be renewed day by day. To succeed over the long term, we must devote time every day to the crucial business of developing a **fitness program for our mind.** Few today realize that they will never become a success in life by education and neither will the mind, by itself, make you successful. Programming is what makes a person successful. We all live out the programming we have received from our parents, schooling, reading, the church and those we associate with. Hopefully, we have been blessed with Godly influences and the continual re-programming of daily reading and meditating the Word of God. We will, in fact, become what we think about all day long. That is just how it is.

About finding success in difficult times, God made Joshua some incredibly powerful promises. Among other things He said we must re-program ourselves every day with the Word of God. If he would just do this, meditate the Word daily, God made him some incredible promises. Since He is not a respecter of persons, He will do the same for us. He said,: "No man shall be able to stand before you all the days of your life (in any battle), as (He) was with Moses, so (He) will be with you. (He) will not leave you nor forsake you." (Joshua 1:5) How great is that? Then He command him to " … be strong and very courageous, that you may observe to do according to all the law which Moses My servant commanded you (and Joshua just had the Pentateuch, only the first five books of the Bible); do not turn from it to the right hand or to the left, that you may prosper wherever you go." (v.7) All these remarkable promises were predicated on one command: "This Book of the Law shall not depart from your mouth, but you shall meditate on it day and night that you may observe to do according to all that is written in it. For then you will make your way prosperous and then you will have good success." (v.8) Even that wasn't all of it, He gave him another incredible promise in verse 9 saying: "Have I not commanded you? Be strong and of good courage; do not be afraid, nor be dismayed for the Lord your God is with you wherever you go." What incredible promises! And, they are yours!

The word philosophy actually comes from the Greek word "philosophia" which means the love of wisdom. Since philosophy is the love and pursuit of wisdom, we must realize that true wisdom comes only from God and is, in fact, positive. Amazingly, in the secular world, philosophy is their attempt to find solutions to creation and all the problems of man apart from God. Their solutions are mostly speculative (rather than from observed from tests and scientific studies). The world, over time, has fabricated its own counterfeit of wisdom which is actually not wisdom at all and is, therefore, a hindrance to those who practice it. Proverbs 14:12 tells us "There is a way that seems right to man, but its end is the way of death." Some of their by-lines are:

- "Get all you can and can all you get."

- "Do unto others before they have a chance to do unto you."
- "What people don't know won't hurt them."
- "Always look out for number one."
- "You only go around once in life so get all the gusto you can get."
- "All's fair in love and war."
- "Whatever feels good, do it."

James, the brother of Jesus, penned these words and telling us clearly where true wisdom can be found: "Wisdom from above is first pure, then peace loving, considerate, submissive, full of mercy and good fruit, impartial and sincere. (James 3:17) It is humble, not damaging to others and submits to all the ordinances of man.

Although the practical application of wisdom in one's life frequently results in success, it will also, in some instances, bring persecution. Persecution is not to be feared, however, because it is God's income tax for grace. Yes, many Christians are, sooner or later, persecuted for righteousness sake but this, too, is positive in the end. Praise God for it. It is an honor to suffer for the Name of Jesus.

What it means to have the character trait of **A POSITIVE PHILOSOPHY**:

- A positive overall attitude about life and its purpose
- All the learning and concepts a person has obtained leading them to a positive outlook on life in general
- One's pursuit of wisdom by education, observation and study of the Word of God, resulting in a positive view point
- The ability to see the good in things.
- The Christian belief that all things, sooner or later, will turn out for the best for them. Romans 8:28
- The belief that there are opportunities in up and down markets as well.
- Having the mind of Christ

RUDENCE —

Note to the reader: Certainly the goal of life is to obtain character which includes wisdom but past gaining some wisdom is our great need of prudence. It, like wisdom, is different from all other character traits in that all others stand alone with a singular definition. Wisdom and Prudence include multiple traits. Wisdom has seven and Prudence ten, distinctly different but very important aspects.`

The Bible tells us clearly and unequivocally that the most valuable thing in the world is wisdom. This is what the wisest man on earth, Solomon said about its incredible benefits: "Happy is the man who finds (it) and the man who gains understanding (along with it). For her proceeds are better than the profits of silver and her gain than fine gold. She is more precious than rubies and all the things you may desire cannot compare with her. Length of days is in her right hand, and in her left hand riches and honor. Her ways are ways of pleasantness, and all her paths are peace. She is a tree of life to those who take hold of her, and happy are all who retain her." (Proverbs 3:13) Now you couldn't get a much better recommendation than this from one qualified to know. It also happens to be what God used to found the earth and established the heavens. (v.19) This is all certainly well and good but continuing on it says that wisdom doesn't dwell alone. Wisdom "dwell(s) with prudence and find(s) out knowledge and discretion. The fear of the Lord is to hate evil, pride and arrogance and the evil way and the perverse mouth I hate. Counsel is mine, and sound wisdom; I am understanding, I have strength."

Proverbs 8:12 —
"I, wisdom, dwell with prudence and find out knowledge and discretion."

We also know that "By (wisdom and prudence) kings reign and rulers decree justice. By me princes rule, and nobles, all the judges of the earth. I love those who love me, and those who seek me diligently will find me." (Proverbs 8:15–17) Prudence is a spiritual gift that also pays rewards in this life because the writer goes on to say, "Riches and honor are with me, enduring riches and righteousness. My fruit is better than gold, yes, than fine gold, and my revenue than choice silver. I traverse the way of righteousness, in the midst of the paths of justice. That I may cause those who love me to inherit wealth, that I may fill their treasuries." (Proverbs 8:18–21) With prudence laden to the bursting point with all these benefits, you would think there would be back-to-back teachings about it in all the schools and shouted from every street corner. See for yourself how important it might be.

First, what is it really? Prudence is intelligent understanding about life, human nature and eternity. It is practical wisdom. In fact, those who become "wise in heart" Solomon said, "will be called prudent." (Proverbs 16:21) Prudence is having sense to be careful, cautious and circumspect in our daily affairs. It is, of course, as I mentioned, closely allied with wisdom. Prudence is the foundation of attitudes and disciplines that wisdom must be built upon to actually begin to work for us. Unlike other individual character traits, as I mentioned, it is multi-faceted. What follows here are the ten aspects of prudence we need to build our lives upon. Without it, wisdom will do us very little good.

- The wisdom and ability to obey authority
- The ability to discipline one's self.
- Skill in the management of resources
- Being careful, cautions and circumspect
- The ability to make decisions as God would
- The ability to heed correction
- Having discretion
- The desire to seek and be crowned with true knowledge
- Knowing when to be silent and keep knowledge to ourselves
- Seeking to be totally dependent upon God

OBEY AUTHORITY, THE WISDOM AND ABILITY TO
A trait of Prudence   Study start date: _____ Finish date: _____

None of us are born with a desire to obey authority because, simply stated, as children none of us liked other people telling us what to do. "We were born in sin" (John 9:34) and had sin and rebellion in our members. I, for one, was certainly no different. I learned to obey my parents because they would immediately apply the rod of wisdom to my seat of intellect and that was not a very pretty thing. However, I can remember not obeying in kindergarten and elementary school. That meant a ton of trouble too. Later on when I got into a military college and found out how much pain there was in disobedience, the change was more dramatic. But, it wasn't until I became a Christian that I learned the blessing in not just letting the Lord, who is infinitely wiser and sovereign over my life, tell me a few things to do but I found out that I needed Him to tell me everything to do.

It makes it much easier to submit to authority when we come to know that Romans 13:1 tells us that all authority is from God and the very next verse says "whoever resists will bring judgment on themselves." We are not only to obey but to obey as unto the Lord. (Colossians 3:23) We know "The wise in heart accept commands, but a chattering fool comes to ruin." (Proverbs 10:8 NIV) When we resist authority, we are actually resisting God but, remember this, when we submit to authority, we are gaining power. He "resists the proud (rebellious) but gives grace to the humble." (I Peter 5:5) Submission doesn't make us less as a person, it makes us more. If one submits himself under God's mighty hand, we already know what He plans to do—"exalt you in due time." (v.6) We can't have authority in this life unless we are under authority and certainly no one can make us submit to either God or man. We, individually, have that power. It is up to us. A prudent man defers to those in authority. In I Peter 5:5 the Apostle said, "… submit yourselves to your elders. Yes, all of you be submissive to one another, and be clothed with humility", for His "Spirit will not strive with man forever." Genesis 6:3

Solomon recorded these words for our benefit: "The wise in heart will receive commands, but a prating fool will fall." (Proverbs 10:8) And, "By pride comes nothing but strife, but with the well-advised (instructed) is wisdom" (Proverbs 13:10) "The way of a fool is right in his own eyes but he who heeds counsel is wise." (Proverbs 12:15) Before we take off in life and do something, start a new business, a new outreach or go to war, we should first do our research and seek wise counsel. Each person we counsel with is going to teach us something and help us not only reach the right decision but to also take the right approach. Before we go out on the battle field with ten thousand to challenge someone coming against us with twenty thousand, we had better know what we are doing. (Luke 14:31) Once the battle is joined, there will be no quarter.

These are very important concepts to grasp. We know "The wise in heart will be called prudent." Proverbs 16:21

What it means to have **THE WISDOM AND ABILITY TO OBEY AUTHORITY:**

• Having an excitement about the Lord's guidance and instruction
• Gladly deferring to authority and doing things their way
• Making God and those in authority sovereign over our lives
• Realizing all authority is from God

ISCIPLINE ONE'S SELF, THE ABILITY TO
A trait of Prudence   Study start date: _____ Finish date: _____

W e might as well admit it, we were all born pre-programmed to be lazy and self content, and furthermore, we will soon find that acquiring the ability to discipline one's self has always been a rare talent. Being aware of this common failing among men, God gave us the entire book of Proverbs. At the beginning of the very first chapter, He tells us the purpose of this great book is, "To know wisdom and instruction, to perceive the words of understanding, to receive the instruction of wisdom, justice, judgment and equity; to give prudence to the simple, to the young man knowledge and discretion." Proverbs 1:2–4

In life all of us have two choices. We can either choose to discipline ourselves and reap the pleasant fruit of it or we can choose not to manage ourselves, be disciplined by others and have the judgment of God and circumstances of life come down upon us. The world's discipline is progressive. It can begin with words of correction from our parents and then a switch, if need be, to the strap. That failing, the world continues to ratchet up the consequences with fines and fees until it might one day reach prison time or even execution.

Discipline starts with learning to obey our parents. We know "A fool despises his father's instruction, but he who receives correction is prudent." (Proverbs 15:5) In life we must either constantly discipline ourselves to get out of bed in the morning, do our homework, observe the speed limits and follow instructions at work or suffer the consequences.. If we don't get out of bed early enough to get to work on time, we will soon be looking for another job. And, if we don't observe the speed limit, we might find ourselves without a drivers' license

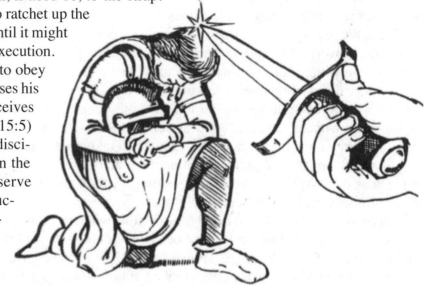

"Humble yourselves under the mighty hand of God that he may exalt you at the proper time." I Peter 5:6

and walking. If we can't do it on our own, we will find ourselves in prison where we will have everything decided for us. Someone will be telling us when to get up, what to wear and all of it down to the smallest details. Everybody has to learn to discipline themselves because we all have to share this planet, live together and be happy. Ignoring self-discipline, the Bible says, will cost us dearly. Proverbs 15:32 says, "He who disdains instruction despises his own soul, but he who heeds rebuke gets understanding." Then in Proverbs 13:18 we have these promises: "Poverty and shame shall be to him that refuses correction but he who regards a rebuke will be honored." You would think the writer is trying to get our attention. In Proverbs 21:1 we see these words recorded: "Whoever loves instruction (discipline) loves knowledge but he who hates correction is stupid." Proverbs 26:3 even tells us why some things were invented: "A whip is for the horse, a bridle for the donkey and a rod for the backs of fools." We are blessed as human beings to be able to open our eyes and actually see our abject poverty—apart from God and His wisdom.

We are blessed to find that we can't possibly make it without Him. We will fail at every turn. It took me thirty–two years to figure that out.

Another great human need is to have a disciplined tongue. We know "There is gold (and lots of it in the earth) and an abundance of rubies but lips that speak knowledge are a rare jewel." (Proverbs 20:15) James reminded us all what a terribly dangerous weapon we were born with and it is in our mouth. He said, "The tongue (without discipline) is a fire, a world of iniquity. The tongue is so set among our members that it defiles the whole body, and sets on fire the course of nature; and is itself set on fire by hell." (James 3:6) We must train our tongue to speak the truth with gentleness.

Another area where we will need to do some work is to discipline our hearts about what we set our affections on. Colossians 3:2 records these words: "Set your mind (heart) on things above, not on things on the earth." Things down here are corrupting constantly and quickly at that. Those things above will last and serve us well for eternity.

Yet another area we have all stumbled in at one time or another is the love of money. Proverbs 23:4 admonishes us: "Do not overwork to be rich; because of your own understanding, cease! Will you set your eyes on that which is not? For riches certainly make themselves wings; they fly away like an eagle toward heaven." Money certainly looks like it will make us happy. It looks like it will provide us security but it has invisible wings—and it will soon fly away. We need, therefore, to set our affections on spiritual things that will truly satisfy and last forever.

There are many areas in a person's life where prudence is a must, just a few are listed here. Appetite is another. Proverbs 23:21 says, "The drunkard and the glutton will come to poverty, and drowsiness will clothe a man with rags." Food and drink must be handled with moderation.

Another devastating enemy lurking out there to devour one's life is the prostitute. If we are not careful, we will be destroyed by her like the millions who came before us. Solomon, who had his own failings with women, tells us, "by means of a harlot a man is reduced to a crust of bread; and an adulteress will prey upon his precious life. Can a man take fire to his bosom, and his clothes not be burned? Can one walk on hot coals and his feet not be seared?" (Proverbs 6:26–28) The whole seventh chapter of the book of Proverbs is devoted to equipping a young man to identify and avoid the immense dangers of the prostitute and the adulteress.

Yet another pit-fall in life to avoid is associating with the wrong people. This is so dangerous, Solomon likens it to a man meeting "a bear robbed of her cubs." He said that would be preferable rather than walking with "a fool in his folly." (Proverbs 17:12) We would have a better chance being locked, weaponless, in a room with a she bear fresh robbed of her cubs (and there is absolutely no chance whatsoever) than to hang out with a fool. Why? Because a fool's life is full of pride, trouble, judgment and contagion. From these folds we are well-advised to keep our distance. Similarly, Proverbs 13:20 promises us, "He who walks with the wise will be wise, but the companion of fools will be destroyed."

Another enemy to be defeated in every man's life is laziness. It takes discipline to arise early and not waste our lives sleeping. Solomon asked, "How long will you slumber, O sluggard? When will you rise from your sleep? A little sleep, a little slumber, a little folding of the hands to sleep—So shall your poverty come on you like a prowler, and your need like an armed man." (Proverbs 6:9, 10) We can stay in bed until the crack of noon but a bandit called lack will quickly come upon us. Laziness can be overcome by seeing the benefits of arising early and having a good work ethic. Solomon said, "Go to the ant, you sluggard! Consider her ways and be wise, which, having no captain, overseer or ruler, provides her supplies in the summer and gathers her food in the harvest." (Proverbs 6:6–8) Mimic the ant. Like her, we need to learn to love our work and know that it is work that will bless us in life and not sleep. He went on to say in Ecclesiastes 3:13 that "every man should eat and drink and enjoy the good of his labor—it is the gift of God." The blessings of wealth, happiness and independence are found in loving our work and doing it well. Yes, there is a time to play and a time to sleep but when you work hard you can play hard and your sleep will be sweet.

We need to hang on to and learn to hold dear all these instructions. Solomon's advice was to "Take firm hold of instruction (here in Proverbs, throughout the Bible and wherever you are taught along life's path), do not let (it) go, keep her, for she is your life." (Proverbs 4:13) It will help us to gain a disciplined life so we can face difficult trials and provocation when they come. The man who can control his passions in adversity, is truly a rare gem. The person who has become disciplined, wise and prudent will receive a special blessing from God both in this life and the one to come.

What it means to have the character trait of **THE ABILITY TO DISCIPLINE ONE'S SELF:**

* The wisdom to seek moderation in all things
* Realizing our flesh is a major problem in life, needing constant correction and discipline to overcome
* Realizing that regarding correction leads to honor
* Realizing that the fear of the Lord is wisdom and a thing of beauty
* Having the grace to set our affections on the things above
* Knowing it is a grave responsibility we have to possess our bodies in honor and moderation

ANAGEMENT OF RESOURCES, SKILLED IN THE
A trait of Prudence   **Study start date:** _____ **Finish date:** _____

Most of us were not born into a family with trust funds or an abundance of wealth. We started the race of life with few to none in the area of resources and really wondered how we would ever make it coming out of the blocks with a zero in the assets column. Yet God still holds us each accountable to be found faithful with the resources He has provided us, however small. The good news is, having very little is actually no hindrance to Him opening the windows of Heaven and sending more our way. In the system He set up from the beginning of time for us to receive more from Him, all we have to do is be found faithful with the smallest things He gives us. We know He has also promised to move us into individual ownership in life if He sees that we have been found faithful with those things given into our care that belongs to others. ((Luke 16:12) He promises that there will be an accounting for each of us in a timely and fair manner. The Lord, who owns all things, is watching to see what we are doing with the smallest of things He has given us. He is a benevolent benefactor and you know God would never do us wrong.

Wise management is so important to Him that he gave us a special parable about a steward who had been found wasting his master's goods. The steward knew that his master was about to call him to give an account and knowing he was about to be put out, became fearful. He began to consider his options and knew he would likely not be able to find work. He was well aware that he was too lazy to dig ditches for a living and too prideful to beg. So, being lazy and dishonest, he tried to befriend his master's creditors by giving them substantial reductions on the balance sheets for what they owed. Now his master's creditors knew that he was a crook. Amazingly, God commended him for being shrewd but craftiness alone will never work over time. Besides, as I said, He is always watching to see if we will be faithful with that which belongs to others before He will give us that which is our own. He also said there is a pattern here and in the pattern there is a key. "He who is faithful in what is least is faithful also in much; and he who is unjust in what is least is unjust also in much." (Luke 16:10) What that means is there is nothing too small to start learning how to manage efficiently. Pennies and toothpicks are important in life. Don't waste anything or despise small matters.

In the Parable of the Minas, a nobleman was going to a foreign country for a while and gave ten minas (a mina being worth about $20.00) and told them to all see what they could gain by trading. Now we are only talking about ten minas or $200 here. Certainly a small sum. However, to the one who was faithful to double his by the time the master returned, he was not only determined capable of governing ten cities but was given them to govern. Now that was a major promotion for this wise manager—from ten minas to ten cities. Luke 16:17

Certainly, there is a gift of administration, but being a good manager of material things is also a discipline that can be learned. Since we are all going to be held accountable for our management skill or the lack thereof one day, we might want to learn all we can about it now.

One of the first lessons of management is—to just get started organizing. In this area, a little organization goes a long way. Use dispatch with your bill paying and filing. Make it your goal to touch a piece of paper only once and put it where it goes. Have a place for everything and let everything have a place. Have a notebook or file folder for your tax information and bills. File bills immediately and record it each time you pay a bill. At the end of the calendar year, you only have to do a little clean-up, checking and total some columns. You don't have to attack a whole pile of helter-skelter receipts that reached to the ceiling. Keep a note book on your rolling stock as to repairs with a separate page for each vehicle. This way you can easily see when you have a car that needs to be eliminated from your fleet. Having a small notebook in each of your vehicles showing the mileage, gas and oil consumption will also tell you when each one needs to go in for a tune-up, repairs or be traded. Even Solomon said we should "Be diligent to know the state of (our) flocks and attend to (our) herds." (Proverbs 27:23) However, today we keep most of our horses der the hood of our car. This means we need to check the oil and water every time we gas up. You never know when a stray rock might be slung up under your car and puncture the oil pan or cut a hole in a hose. Checking the transmission fluid, power steering and brake fluid regularly are things we need to know the condition of. It is important to get in the habit of checking all your vehicles for the proper anti-freeze level at the first cold snap each year. Waiting until the last moment to start checking the anti-freeze might catch you before you're ready and require and engine to be replaced because of a cracked block. Making the effort to keep all our vehicles in good working order pays dividends in many areas. It is important because we never know when we will need to rely on them unexpectedly. Also, maintaining them well certainly increases our ability to enjoy the use of them, be safe to operate and it makes them all the more valuable when it comes time to trade.

Animals were mentioned by Solomon here because they need special care and must be checked on a daily basis. They can't care for themselves in the least and must have a husbandman to care for their every need. If you don't care for them, they will, in fact, soon die. Having had a number of animals from dogs and cats to horses and everything in between, and I can tell you that I loved them all. However, every one of them, like most people, have bad habits as well as a few redeeming proclivities. The good points an animal has usually countervail the bad ones and we keep them. In the horse arena, for example, one will be a cribber (eats the stalls and fences), another will be a kicker, another will be mean as cat stuff and twice as nasty, some buck, others rear up and want to fall back down on top of you, on and on, ad infinitum. We just have to learn how to manage those things. Animals also have an uncanny ability to get into things they shouldn't. They cut themselves, contract diseases, come down with dysentery and a thousand other things. Study up as you may and you should, unless you become a veterinarian, you will probably never know everything about animal husbandry.

When you are responsible for a large organization, timely reports are necessary to ensure proper ongoing maintenance and performance. It is just not human nature to continue doing proper, systematic maintenance so there must be a regular reporting system and follow up, to be sure it is actually being done. As they say in the Army, "The men do well only what the boss checks." One would think that in wartime men on the front lines would clean and oil their rifles on a daily basis since their lives depended on them. Well, no. Laziness in some people is more powerful than the God-given instinct of self-pres-ervation. Now that's amazing! In Vietnam I always told the men it was my job to see to it that we won every one of our battles with the enemy and that I could send them all back home alive. And, if they didn't clean and oil their rifle every day, they would soon find themselves looking down the muzzle of a VC machine gun with nothing behind their trigger finger but a metallic click. Not the best feeling in the world. So I would require the platoon leaders to do a daily check and then do a random check myself.

General of the Army in World War II, George C. Marshall, said he was tough because "He believed men wanted to belong to a highly disciplined, hard-working, business-like organization they could be proud of and boast about. The stricter, the better within the prescribed hours."

He was such a good manager of his belongings, equipment, quarters and personal life, he was the only cadet ever to graduate from Virginia Military Institute never having received a single demerit. Because of his leadership and management skill, he quickly moved up the ranks to general officer. He was such an extraordinary manager, at the beginning of World War II, he was Chief of Staff of our Armed Forces and chief military advisor to President Franklin Delano Roosevelt. It was his job to contract for and super-vise the manufacture of all the tanks, ships, airplanes, munitions, uniforms, tents and mess kits for the

Army, Navy, Army Air Corps and Marines. He was also responsible for the training of all U.S. soldiers, sailors, airmen and marines. He did all this so well, with God's help, we won the war and he was called "the organizer of victory" by British Prime Minister Winston Churchill. However, our government was not through with him yet. They asked him to develop the plan (The Marshall Plan) to rebuild all of war-torn Europe. Of course, that was immensely successful as well. He was truly a man who knew how to manage resources.

Another important aspect of resource management is accounting. Primarily, we need to suspense our bills so we can not only pay them on time but conserve our capitol for cash flow. I realize there are problems in peoples' lives that make this impossible from time to time but this is always the goal. Our name and reputation in business is either won or lost in how we treat, appreciate and respect our creditors and pay our bills. You might want to write "Thanks" in the "Memo:" section of the check. This one word, I believe, lets people know two things: you appreciate their help supplying whatever it was and are happy with their prices and service. That is something they are really working for and few people ever seem to tell them. Paying on time or early also allows us to take the discounts some companies offer which in some businesses, like construction, can mount up to a pretty tidy sum over a year or a lifetime.

Dealing with physical items, learning to store materials for future use is also very important. Sometimes this may require having a little land to accomplish but this will pay great dividends in the long run. Knowing how to store materials and equipment out the rain, rot, and termites is essential. There is no sense storing something if it won't be usable when you need it in the future. An excellent bargain if you have a place to put them are used semi-trailers or metal connex boxes. Conex boxes are large, metal over-land and sea shipping containers. These and used trailers are fairly inexpensive and can store an abundance of material with the added benefit of being secure. They always appreciate some in value and can be sold later for, usually, more than they cost and you get all those years of free use in the middle. These large containers are almost like a commodity and there is always a market for them.

This is certainly far less than an exhaustive treatise on managing resources, but it is well to remember, a line I heard in a movie once which is only too true: "Fortune is infatuated with the efficient." Regardless of where you work, others are watching to see how you take care of business, how you take care of your car and your work space. If they find you faithful and neat, you are, mysteriously, going to be getting more and more responsibility. However, realizing early in life that we are only a steward of the things in our possession and that God is the true owner, helps tremendously in the area of being found faithful as a wise manager. One day soon we will all give an account to Him for our stewardship. Hopefully, He will say, "Well done, good and faithful servant. You have been faithful over a few things, I will make you ruler over many things. Enter into the joy of your Lord." Matthew 25:21

What it means to have the character trait of being **SKILLED IN THE MANAGMENT OF RESOURCES:**

- Has learned to waste not so we want not. (Example: turning lights off when not in the room or area)
- Being faithful in the smallest things
- Able to conserve resources
- Realizing we only have stewardship in this life, never ownership.
- Able to see value in things others consider refuse
- Being creative in the use of material things
- Able to save and store items for yet unknown future needs
- Taking the time and effort to become skilled in disciplines of building, welding, mechanics, printing, etc.

- Knowing the value of tools and having the ability to keep and maintain them.
- Keeping an inventory of things
- Knowing how to store materials cheaply
- Knowing how to purchase "seconds" in materials at a discount and use them effectively.

AREFUL, CAUTIOUS AND CIRCUMSPECT, BEING
A trait of Prudence   Study start date: _____ Finish date: _____

As a young man, regrettably, I did just about everything wrong a person possibly could. Because of that, life got pretty difficult from time-to-time. I was not careful about things. On the contrary we are admonished that "the prudent (man) considers well his steps." (Proverbs 14:15) And, Proverbs 14:8 also tells us, "The wisdom of the prudent is to understand his way but the folly of fools is deceit (lies)." The prudent man has studied well what he is doing, has sought wise counsel and considered all the advantages and disadvantages of a matter before proceeding. "A wise man (also) fears and departs form evil but a fool rages (into things) and is self-confident." (Proverbs 14:16) It takes a lifetime to gain character, to gain a good reputation and to build an estate. However, incredibly, it only takes a few minutes of foolishness to lose it all. Just one bad decision in response to temptation or provocation can devastate one's entire life. This can also happen by just one unwise decision, for example, to trust an unscrupulous person with your assets. Sometimes, people have lost their life's savings all in a moment. A friend of mine trusted an unscrupulous lawyer as her financial advisor after her husband died and it cost her the totality of her estate.

Another part of prudence is to be alert and ever at the ready, wyllie, you might say, as a

Coyote. Our enemy is insidious, constantly seeking, constantly probing and testing his prey. The apostle Peter said, "Be sober, be vigilant, because your adversary the devil walks about like a

roaring lion, seeking whom he may devour." (I Peter 5:8) Remember how God chose Gideon's army. He sent them all down to the creek to get a drink, seemingly a small task—but revealing. The ones who got down on all fours and lapped it up like a dog, taking no thought, momentarily, about their surroundings, he said to send home. They weren't cautious enough. The ones who took a knee and got some water cupped in their hands while keeping a constant watch all around them, he said, "Keep." Why? Because the devil always attacks at the same time: The time you think not. That's why we need to live ever at the ready. We need to be watchful, we need to be discerning. We have to be looking and listening.

Another significant part of prudence is the ability to recognize danger and hate it. Some people don't see the danger in drugs or illicit sex for example. Proverbs 27:12 tells us, "The prudent man foresees evil (danger) and hides himself; (while) the simple pass on and are punished." But, "The fear of the Lord is to hate evil, pride and arrogance and the evil way, and the perverse mouth (do) I, (prudence) hate." (Proverbs 8:13) Many of the things the world offers, although possibly pleasurable for a moment, will end in sorrow, pain and great loss. Proverbs 16:13 tells us, "The highway of the upright is to depart from evil; He who keeps his way preserves his soul."

A prudent man also understands time and judgment. The law of the harvest tells us you can't sow and reap in the same season. Everything takes time. God has an accounting set for everyone on planet earth in time. The prudent man understands that everything we do, think or say is a seed planted that will—in time–produce a crop. Whether a good or bad seed, it matters not, it will produce after its own kind. It is going to grow and produce fruit. Once the prudent man sees danger, he avoids it if at all possible. Wars and battles others bring to us can't be avoided..

The prudent also avoid hasty vows and commitments. Proverbs 20:25 declares, "It is a snare (trap) to devote (make a vow) rashly something as holy and afterward to reconsider (one's) vows." Pray and seek counsel about things first. Another part of this is to be careful to avoid debt because this definitely consists of making promises, taking on a new master and presuming upon the future. Romans 13:8 wisely says, "Owe no man anything but to love him." The borrower becomes the lender's slave and a pawn of the changing vicissitudes of life. The economy can take turns that will cause enormous trouble for those who have gotten themselves deeply entangled in debt. A prudent man avoids it like the plague. "He who hates being surety (refuses to strike hands in pledge, to cosign or guarantee a loan for others and) is (kept) safe." Proverbs 11:15

Another critical part of prudence is the ability to discern the arm of the flesh and avoid it as well. Jeremiah 17:5 says, "Cursed is the man who trusts in man and who makes flesh (the world and its systems) his strength." The world always gives us false hope—and is no help at all in times of trouble. It is likened to one building their house on sand. In this vein, it is also important, to wisely choose one's friends. Make no mistake, "Evil company corrupts good morals." (Proverbs 15:33) Make sure the friends you chose to fellowship with are growing Christians. Like a tree that is growing, people who are truly Christians are continually going to church, learning and growing in the things of God. However, if you travel with dogs, you can be sure, you are going to get fleas—or the mange or something worse.. In Proverbs 12:16 (NIV) Solomon said, "A righteous man is cautious in friendship but the way of the wicked (making unwise friendships) leads them astray." And, in Proverbs 13:20 we have this promise: "He who walks with the wise will be wise but the companion of fools will be destroyed."

Yet another critical part of prudence here is to put a careful watch over our tongue. We need to be careful what we say. Knowing that we have all said things we wish we hadn't—and, once spoken, we surely can't get them back. Proverbs 16:23 says, "The heart of the wise teaches his mouth, and adds learning (instruction) to his lips." A prudent man is also careful to seek God constantly for guidance into His perfect will. Our God is all about directing those who are His into the future. His plan for us may not make perfect sense at the moment but it will in time.

Proverbs 20:24 tells us, "A man's steps are (ordered) of the Lord; how then can a man understand his own way?" He can't. The prophet Jeremiah said, "I know the way of man is not within himself. It is not in man who walks to direct his own steps." We must seek God and ask Him to reveal His will to us. None of us know our right hand from our left or how to come in out of the rain and must have God's help to direct our lives.

What it means to have the character trait of **BEING CAREFUL, CAUTIOUS AND CIRCUMSPECT:**

- Realizing it takes only a moment, just one bad decision to lose one's reputation or a life estate.
- Knowing this, the prudent realize it is not a waste of time to seek wise counsel before stepping out in a new venture or battle.
- Realizing that we must be ever watchful and cautious because the enemy is prowling
- Realizing in everything there is time and judgment
- Realizing all of life is seed time and harvest
- Knowing it is wise to hate evil, sin and every wicked proposition
- The prudent man has identified the arm of the flesh and has decided to trust only in the Lord.
- Knowing the danger of being surety for the debts of others, hasty vows and entering into debt ourselves.
- Realizing the prudent man guards his tongue.

ECISIONS AS GOD WOULD, THE ABILITY TO MAKE
A trait of Prudence   Study start date: _____ Finish date: _____

Making wise decisions is so important because every decision we have made in life has brought us where we are today. Decisions will both make and mark our lives.

Bad decisions, we find soon enough, are just too painful and costly. The Bible tells us several things about bad decisions. In Genesis 13:7 we see the account about Abraham and Lot. They had been traveling with their herds and flocks comingled for a number of years. However, over time God had blessed them incredibly, such that their servants began to quarrel. Abraham decided it was time to part company. Whichever direction Lot chose, Abraham said he would go the other way. Of course, Lot chose the lush, low green valley. The easy path. The easy life. The path thousands of heathens had already taken and he chose to live among them. Immediately, Abraham struck out on the lonely path, choosing, to live on the rough side of the mountain with God. However, choosing the easy way soon led Lot and his family into spiritual decline and downward spiral of moral decadence. He was vexed daily by the things he saw and heard. In the end, his family had to flee and his wife was lost in the process.

Esau, another example, just because he was a bit famished one day, made the decision to sell his birth right for a bowl of porridge. Later he sought to regain it but could not find a place for repentance though he sought it with diligence and tears. A bad decision caused him the loss of his blessings. Hebrews 12:16, 17

A wrong decision, especially a decision to disobey the Lord, will also cause defeat. In Numbers 14:40 we have the account of the Hebrew children going up to fight the Amalekites and Canaanites who were dwelling there after Moses informed them that the Lord commanded them not to. Neither he nor the Ark of the Covenant left the camp during the attack and they were, in fact, defeated.

In I Samuel 15:4 we find the account of God giving Saul the victory over King Agag and the Amalekites. Against the Lord's explicit instructions to the contrary, Saul made the decision to keep some of the finer animals and King Agag as a war trophy. This caused him to be rejected as ruler of the people.

Rebellion, we know, will also cause apostasy. God told Solomon not to marry foreign wives because they would subtly bring division, pollute the true religion and cause him to bow down and worship those foreign gods himself. He did it anyway (I Kings 11:1) and died estranged from God. He was also told not to multiply his wives, gold or horses and did all three. Remember, there had to be a point at which Solomon knowingly crossed the line and knew full well he was being disobedient for God to judge him. He was not confused, unaware or taken by surprise; it was open and notorious rebellion.

Zedekiah came on the scene as the last king of Judah, after the Kingdom of Israel had long since been divided. Because of rebellion to God, the Northern Kingdom, Israel, had already been in captivity for 139 years. By this time, Nebuchadnezzar, king of Babylon, had already invaded Judah, conquered it, took all of the most skilled and able people off to exile. He left Zedekiah and the poorest people of the nation with him in the land. However, he made Zedekiah swear allegiance to him in the name of God. Zedekiah, however, continued to do evil against the Lord and despised God's prophets even after many warnings. He oppressed his people and committed adultery with his neighbors' wives. Then he rebelled against the king of Bablyon and broke his covenant. God then sent Jeremiah to him prophesying that He would soon send the king of Babylon against Judah, would completely destroy them and make them an object of scorn and horror. The whole country would become a desolate wasteland and they would serve the king of Babylon for seventy years. When Nebuchadnezzar laid siege upon Jerusalem, all the men fled like cowards in the night. Zedekiah fled with them but was captured and taken to the king at Riblah. There he was judged, bound with fetters and his eyes were put out. He was then taken away captive where he led a miserable existence as a blind slave in Babylon until his death. Bad decisions can have unthinkable consequences. II Chronicles 36, I Kings 24 and Jeremiah 24,25

They also cause division. In I Kings 12 we find King Rehoboam was facing a revolt from the people. He sought counsel and was told to speak kindly to them as one who was their servant. Instead he spoke harshly and arrogantly to them. This decision caused his kingdom to be permanently divided.

It would be so easy to simply say, we need to make right decisions the way God would but doing it is not so simple. The enemy can make sin and the way of compromise look so good. To be able to make wise decisions, the first step it to be granted the grace to see ourselves as destitute. We must see ourselves, as we truly are, hopeless apart from God and completely incapable of making right decisions. The Bible says we, on our own, don't know our right hand from our left. We don't know how to come in out of the rain. As a personal reference, I worked for thirty-two years out in the world and was pretty successful—I thought. The problem was that I hadn't yet been weighed in the balance. When that actually happened, I came up woefully lacking and great was the fall. I was wiped completely out. Why? My house was not built on the Rock. I hadn't been making right decisions. You see, it takes humility to follow the Lord. Prior to Jesus Christ entering our hearts, we think we can handle life quite well on our own and do things our way. Thank God for His grace to see our desperate need of His guidance.

Right decisions, on the other hand, are going to cause blessings to come and good things to start happening. First, by grace, they will cause faith to come. Hebrews 11:24 says Moses rose up one day and made a decision. Having lived in wealth and power for forty years, amazingly, he said, I am going to refuse "to be called the son of Pharaoh's daughter." He chose rather to suffer affliction with the children of God. He esteemed their reproach more valuable in the long run than the fleeting pleasures of sin which were so brief. He considered being reproached with God's people worth more in the end than all the treasures of Egypt put together—and by faith he forsook Egypt. Then things, though difficult for him for the moment, began to cause good things to happen. Over a long period of time, he gained the faith to go back to Egypt with a murder charge against him and, with no physical weapons, was able, with God's help, to deliver the Hebrew nation from Egyptian bondage.

Right decisions will also cause loyalty, a very precious thing, to spring forth. A few thousand years ago, Naomi, a Hebrew who had married a Moabite and had two sons who both later also married. At that time there happened to be a great famine in the land. Naomi's husband died and, amazingly, a little later both of her sons also passed away. She told her daughters-in-law to stay there in Moab where their relatives were but that she was going back to Israel. One of the daughters stayed but Ruth remained loyal to Naomi and returned with her to the land of her forefathers. That one good decision caused her to be blessed with a marriage to a man of great wealth (Ruth 1 & 2) and was also chosen by God to be in the blood line of Christ. (Matthew 1:5) Good decisions create great blessings. Deuteronomy 28:1–14 lists a number of blessings that follow when obeying God and following his commands. They are many and very great. However, Deuteronomy 28:15 and following declare the curses on those who make bad decisions. Being disobedient brings judgment.

Making right decisions is a learned process for everyone. A good method is to first state the question we are trying to answer very clearly and it is best to write it down. Then ask yourself how this decision will affect you on the Day of Recompense. Many times, however, people decide to do what is expedient and seems best for them at the moment. What is best for the moment is nowhere near as important as how this decision will affect us for eternity. What made Moses different from all the people in his time was that he "had respect unto the Day of Recompense." He wasn't concerned about his pay check on Friday or his popularity on any given day but how the decision would go for him for eternity—which is reality. That is the day you get what you will keep forever. Next we need to do our due-diligence and get all the facts that bear on the question. Study the subject. Read about it in books but first see what THE Book says about it. Write down the pertinent facts. The course we are considering should meet the James 3:17 test. It says that true wisdom from God is first of all "pure, then peaceable, gentle, willing to yield, full of mercy and good fruits, without partiality and without hypocrisy."

Next seek out wise counsel. Go to wise men who have been down the road with God, who have a proper testimony in life and have been found faithful. "For by wise counsel", Proverbs 24:6 tells us, "you will wage your own war and in a multitude of counselors there is safety." Then we need to proceed to the Law of the Kingdom test: "Whoever exalts himself will be humbled, and he who humbles himself will be exalted." Is the approach we are considering the humble path or is it born of pride? For we know that, "By humility and the fear of the Lord are riches and honor and life." (Proverbs 22:4) Then we need to lay it out before the Lord, pray and ask Him directly for wisdom and in James 1:5 and 6 we find that He will grant it to us liberally. He will tell you great and mighty things that you know not. (Jeremiah 33:3) We need to find His will because it is the Lord's will that will prevail. Certainly, "There are many plans in a man's heart, nevertheless, the Lord's counsel—that will stand." (Proverbs 19:21) Finally, we need to take out another sheet of paper and list all the advantages of a course of action and under the other column all the disadvantages. This will help immensely to make things clear and expose the proper path. We all have a million decisions to make in life. Don't take the easy path. Choose to go God's way.

What it means to have **THE ABILITY TO MAKE DECISIONS AS GOD WOULD:**

- First we must see ourselves as an abject failure apart from God and His will.
- Then ask God for wisdom on the subject and to show you His will.
- Search the Bible for all of His commands on the subject.
- Meditate on them for several days if you don't have to make an immediate decision.
- Find all your options and write down the advantages and disadvantages of each.
- The Holy Spirit will lead you to the truth in any situation.
- Decide not what is best for the moment but what will be best in light of eternity.
- Seek wise counsel.
- Obey God's commands.
- Decide to obey God's commands even though it may be difficult or sound impossible.

ORRECTION, THE ABILITY TO HEED—
A trait of Prudence   **Study start date: _____ Finish date: _____**

I t seems one of the most difficult things for human beings to handle is correction. We all want to think we are doing just fine. We all have to live with our inner self which is usually musing over several misconceptions we have about ourselves at the same time. The first lie we believe about ourselves is that we always know what is best. The second is that we can do any job well and probably as good as anybody else. The third lie is that everybody should like the job we did because we did our best. Finally, we believe that everyone should like us because we are who we are and God loves us.

Most who grow up in a home with a loving mother and father, unknowingly suffer under the illusion that everybody in the world is going to love them just like their parents. Oh what a rude awakening it is for those who leave home for the first time, join the military and step off the bus in the face of their kind-hearted and loving drill sergeant! (I'm being facetious of course) Here's this mountain of a guy with a huge chest and a small waist but with a voice loud enough to cause an earthquake any moment and he doesn't like you. I mean he really doesn't like you. Not the way you part your hair or anything. He doesn't even like it that you have hair and all-of-a-sudden you find out for the first time now that you have a tendency to slouch, your shoulders cave forward and you naturally droop your head like a buzzard. You thought you were pretty neat and now nothing, I mean nothing you do is right and he's got names for you that you never even heard of. Some of these names you wouldn't hang on a mangy, old, flee-bitten dog. Now, for the first time, you feel like you might be something a little lower than a pile of whale dung on the lowest part of the ocean.

It was no better for those whose parents dropped them off on the sidewalk at a military college with a few suit cases and a tooth brush. When those upperclassmen got hold of me, I thought I just ran into a tire shredder on steroids. They didn't like me or anything about me and it didn't look like that was ever going to change—at least any time during that century. Truth is there was a reason for their apparent dislike of this new, miserable piece of humanity the military was going to have to invest hundreds of thousands of dollars in to straighten out. Whether or not this was even possible was still in question at the time, by the way.

Although they would rarely come right out and say it, there was at least a couple reasons for all of this. First they wanted us to improve and God knows we all had plenty of room for that. And, just as important, another equally good reason was they wanted to see if we had the inner constitution to even be able to take correction. Could we handle somebody getting into our stuff—and I don't mean your foot locker or your duffle bag. I mean getting under your skin and down into where you live. Would we shrivel up like a violet or could we stand tall and take it? Would we flinch at the first strong rebuke, fold up our tent and go home to mamma or would we take the chastisement to heart, fix what we could as quickly as possible and keep our mouth shut in the process. Like they said, "You gotta' be able to take it before you can dish it out" and most importantly, although they never said it, "Humility comes before honor." (Proverbs 15:33) Though it certainly isn't easy for anyone to endure the process, I really believe America would be a better place if all our young men had to do two years in the military just like they do in Israel. It is good for everyone to learn that everybody in life is not going to like us.

Some correction is going to come our way in life and much of it will not be delivered in the gentlest fashion. Not only that but in the real world the devil and his demons are still around and they continue to do some terrible stuff. In addition, many of the people we meet out in the world don't like anybody very much; not even they themselves and we had better become accustomed to running into them on a fairly regular basis. Wherever we work we might as well know it is going to be the boss's way or the highway and he may not even care to hear about how you did it back in Maryland. If one doesn't grow some thick skin in a mighty big hurry, this new career is likely to come to naught in a hurry.

Correction must come in life because we live in a complicated, highly technical world operated almost totally by convention, i.e., the standard practices of society or a particular industry's way of doing things. Convention allows us to work together successfully as a society. Things like putting the return address in the top left hand corner of an envelope, the forwarding address in the lower middle with a zip code and the stamp on the top right corner is all convention. Do it any other way and your mail will likely be held up, thrown out or, at best, returned to you in a few weeks.

The problem is, just starting out, many young people have no idea what the world expects. We are all a blank sheet of paper and need someone to teach us. Some things are just plain hard to learn and even while we are learning, we will probably stand in need of some correction in the process. What we must come to realize is that correction is good and we can't live without it. We all need correction to perfect our technique, understanding and attitude. A wise man will listen intently to instruction, no matter who offers the correction. If it is our friends or coworkers, we need to realize they are actually taking a risk sharing their true feelings about our shortcomings. They could be risking their friendship with us just to share critically important, helpful information about our performance or lack thereof. Correction is a bit painful for all of us but we are compelled to receive it and make the necessary adjustments.

We are all humans and to make progress, we have to get past our feelings. Human nature does not like to admit that we could be wrong or in need of improvement. That's just the fallen human nature we were all born with. Everyone's mind naturally wants to reject the notion that we could be wrong or need improvement. I personally believe it is a good idea to write down the advice people give us, even if it doesn't seem spot on at the time, take it home and put it in a file. Ever so often open the file and review the critiques. Let the Holy Spirit speak to your spirit and then try wholeheartedly to receive it in a meaningful way. It was likely meant for your good and should be given the utmost consideration.

Corrections are so vitally important. A ship once set to sail from London to New York. Even before the captain gave the order to weigh anchor and shove off, he first sets the azimuth on his ship's compass to plot their course at sea. When they left the harbor, he made their first correction, based on his maps and the stars, and set a new azimuth. They followed that course for several hours and, once again, he made another correction, setting a new course. Time and again, the captain would make corrections until one day, they arrived safely at New York harbor. Obviously none of his azimuths were correct. Their course, effected by the weather, winds and ocean currents as well as the condition, number and trim of their sails, required constant correction to make his port. Actually, the captain never had the perfect azimuth but the sum total of all those corrections caused the successful result of reaching their destination safely for all aboard. Corrections were indispensable.

Each of us have fallen short in life and have found ourselves in need of correction from time to time. We all want happiness and Job told us where it could be found in life saying, "Behold, happy is the man whom God corrects; therefore do not despise the chastening of the Almighty. For He bruises, but He binds up; He wounds, but His hands make whole." (Job 5:17–18) Being made whole is what we, flawed, broken individuals truly need.

The entire book of Proverbs was written to give young people wisdom, which is the ability to live life skillfully and avoid the many pitfalls along the way. Incidentally, the youth department of a large church posted a sign that said, "Now is a good time to go out and make your million while you are still smarter than your parents." It is truly amazing that the older kids get, the smarter their parents become. In chapter three of Proverbs, the writer, Solomon, said, "My son, do not despise the chastening of the

Lord, nor detest His correction; for whom the Lord loves, He corrects, just as a father the son in whom he delights." (v.3:11, 12) So correction may be painful for a little while but life would, certainly, be far more painful without it. The Master is saying, "listen." In chapter one, verse 23 of Proverbs the writer says, "Turn at my reproof; surely I will pour out My Spirit on you; I will make My words known to you." If we would but listen, He would reveal His Word to us. The majority, however, will not. Solomon said only "A fool despises his father's instruction but he who receives correction is prudent." (v.15:5) Most children have a problem with all this because, "Foolishness is bound up in the heart of a child" but there is a solution to this, "the rod of correction will drive it far from him." (Proverbs 22:15) Yet some continue to stubbornly turn away. It is to these the Lord says, "They would have none of (My) counsel and despised My every rebuke. Therefore they shall eat the fruit of their own way, and be filled to the full with their own fancies. For the turning away of the simple will slay them, and the complacency of fools will destroy them; but whoever listens to Me will dwell safely, and will be secure, without fear of evil." (Proverbs 1:30–33) We are also given the promise that "He who keeps instruction is in the way of life, but he who refuses correction goes astray." (v.10:12) God's Word is clear, "He who hates correction is stupid" (v.12:1), and will come to "poverty and shame" (Proverbs 13:18) and "He who hates correction will die." (v.15:10) On the contrary, "He who heeds rebuke gets understanding" (15:32), is prudent (v.15:5) and shall be honored. (v. 13:18) So correction or "Reproofs of instruction are the way of life …" (Proverbs 6:23) As long as we occupy an earthly body, we are going to stand in need of correction. How we take correction will decide whether it will help or hurt us. If we really want to live life to the full, until it overflows, we must be teachable, quick to listen to correction from those around us and willing to take it to heart.

What it means to have the character trait of **THE ABILITY TO HEED CORRECTION:**

- Having the ability to listen, receive and harken to guidance, correction or critique
- Having the ability to accept suggestions, critique and rebuke to bring one into conformity with a set standard or level of competency
- Responding appropriately to reproofs of instruction
- Having the humility necessary to take advice, correction and reproof
- Having the desire to be freed from error
- Seeking rectification

ISCRETION, HAVING—
A trait of Prudence

Study start date: _____ **Finish date:** _____

King David was troubled when it occurred to him that he was living in a mansion and the Lord had no place at all for His house, so he took it upon himself to build a magnificent temple for Him. . His heart was right and the thought was right as well but the Lord told him that he had shed too much blood to build His temple. The honor to build it would fall, instead, to his son, Solomon, whom God would also give rest from his enemies. During this supernatural rest, the temple construction could go on and be completed. Knowing he was young and inexperienced, David said to his son, "Only the Lord give you wisdom and understanding (discretion), and give you charge over Israel, so that you may keep the law of the Lord your God. Then you shall prosper, if you are careful to observe the statutes and the ordinances which the Lord commanded Moses concerning Israel. Be strong and courageous, do not fear nor be dismayed." I Chronicles 22:12, 13

This young man, who had absolutely no construction or management experience, was amazingly given charge over building the most magnificent temple ever constructed. He had never dug a ditch or run any kind of a construction crew. Furthermore, he had never handled large sums of money. Solomon would have committed to his oversight: 100,000 talents of gold, 1,000,000 talents of silver, bronze and iron by weight unknown, etc. In addition to being in charge of the nation's military, as well as another large army of masons, stone cutters and craftsmen of every kind. It would also be his job to ensure quality and the correct architectural design. Having never started out at the entry level of a job in life and learning the intricacies of the various trades over time by experience, apprenticeship, application and study, Solomon was expected to do something very difficult: come into leadership from the top. He needed discretion, wisdom, discernment and humility to know how to seek out and select the wisest experts in these various fields He also needed wisdom to know when to rely on their advice and when to cast his own ideas aside. He would need diligence to constantly check every phase and detail to ensure quality.

Many young people are given special talents and skills, a handsome appearance and great responsibility at a young age. This can be due to many things: divine favor, the untimely passing of wealthy parents, actual demonstrated ability, education, an early meteoric rise to a high political position and many other possible events. All this will be for naught, however, without discretion. Some young women are granted the gift of beauty but are without discretion, such that their beauty is about as useless, out of place and obnoxious as a gold ring in a pig's snout. (Proverbs 11:22) Even with many advantages and preferments in life, discretion and discernment must be acquired for anyone to find success.

Not especially gifted, as a young lieutenant in the Army, having discretion became very important when I found myself an aide to a Major General. With 16,000 airborne soldiers under his command, he actually had two aides: a captain who stayed with him pretty much everywhere he went and a lieutenant, that would be me, who stayed at the office or field command post mostly as sort of a business manager, schedule keeper, letter writer, and a very occasional speech writer. I was the general's all around chief cook and bottle washer. (Although I never did any cooking.) Without question, I was the lowest ranking officer on Division Staff. Most were majors, lieutenant colonels, full colonels or generals. Don't guess I have to tell you that most of the time I felt like a long tail cat in a room full of rocking chairs. They had a saying the Army and it's true, that stuff rolls down hill. Good thing I learned much earlier atin the Corps at Texas A&M University when questioned as to why something was screwed up to always respond, "No excuse, Sir." Even if I didn't do it and regardless of who did, I would still accept responsibility for and say, "No excuse, Sir." Just one of the many, many lessons learned in the Corps was never to offer excuses or complaints even when falsely accused. The truth usually has a way of coming out in time and being able to bear a false accusation without complaint actually caused even more credit and favor to come in the final analysis. Don't worry though, I made more than my own share of mistakes too.

One time we flew a good part of the Division to South Korea in huge, C-141 jet transport planes to be involved in a field training exercise called Focus Retina and we all, of course, arrived on land by parachute. The purpose of the exercise was to let North Korea know that we could get there quickly and in large numbers if need be—some large scale saber rattling. Well, with that done, when we were flying back to North Carolina and refueled at an air base in Anchorage, Alaska. The commander there was friends with our general and came out to meet him during the short lay-over. As a greeting, the Base Commander gave our boss a bunch of frozen salmon to take home. Although it was freezing on the ground in Alaska, it was certainly not freezing at the time in the Carolinas so we decided to have the crew chief of our aircraft stow the salmon in the wheel well of the plane. Since we flew at 30,000 feet, the air was still freezing at that altitude and the wheel well, though not air conditioned, stayed at a freezing temperature all the time too. However, upon arrival at our destination, Pope A.F.B. in Fayetteville, North Carolina, we were so pre-occupied with getting staff cars lined up and everyone's baggage situated that both of us, the senior aide and I, forgot the salmon. Not only that but the plane had already taken off for Florida on its next mission when we discovered our mistake. It wasn't easy but we got the salmon back. The salmon fared well but our reputation for taking care of business certainly didn't. I discovered why aircraft crew chiefs kept written manifests of everything on board. Hmmmm!

Much of the credit for being able to navigate the sticky wickets in that job goes to a little poem one of my friends sharred with me at the time. It has been an invaluable help to me both then and over the years and is simply titled "If." Can't say I've always lived up to it but God knows I've tried. It is by Rudyard Kipling and is really all about discretion. Hope it blesses you as much as it has me.

"If you can keep your head when all about you
Are losing theirs and blaming it on you,
If you can trust yourself when all men doubt you,
But make allowance for their doubting too;
If you can wait and not be tired by waiting,
Or being lied about, don't deal in lies,
Or being hated don't give way to hating,
And yet don't look too good, nor talk too wise:
If you can dream—and not make dreams your master;
If you can think—and not make thoughts your aim,
If you can meet with triumph and disaster
And treat those two imposters just the same;
If you can bear to hear the truth you've spoken
Twisted by knaves to make a trap for fools,
Or watch the things you gave your life to, broken,
And stoop and build 'em up with worn-out tools:
If you can make one heap of all your winnings;
And risk it on one turn of pitch-and-toss,
And lose, and start again at your beginnings
And never breathe a word about your loss;
If you can force your heart and nerve and sinew

To serve your turn long after they are gone,
And so hold on when there is nothing in you
Except the Will which says to them: "Hold on."
If you can talk with crowds and keep your virtue,
Or walk with Kings—nor lose the common touch,
If neither foes nor loving friends can hurt you,
If all men count with you, but none too much;
If you can fill the unforgiving minute
With sixty seconds worth of distance run,
Yours is the Earth and everything that's in it
And—which is more—you'll be a Man, my son!

What it means to have the character trait of **DISCRETION**:

- Having the grace to avoid compromising people, places, publications, products and profane language
- Being cautious and careful in the choice of one's words so as not to unnecessarily offend
- Knowing when one should be silent
- The temperament to be slow to anger
- Moderation
- Understanding
- Being careful in the choice of one's clothes to avoid extremes or be provocative
- The freedom or latitude one has to decide things within certain legal, moral and spiritual bounds
- A level of demonstrated morality
- Knowing when to withhold privileged information in certain company
- The wisdom to (as far as it is possible) allow the other person to save face
- Being circumspect, careful and cautious in making decisions (but bold in execution)
- The ability to distinguish the wise and prudent course from the frivolous, the fads the the fool hardy

NOWLEDGE, THE DESIRE TO SEEK AND BE CROWNED WITH TRUE
A trait of Prudence   Study start date: _____ Finish date: _____

There are many kinds of knowledge in the world but all of them can be placed in two categories: worldly and spiritual. The worldly end of it includes all kinds of things—knowledge of mathematics, physics, how to farm and carpenter, fly airplanes, even street knowledge, and so on. Many go through life and never find that there is any other kind, but there is a superior knowledge. Worldly knowledge is sometimes deceptive and flawed but always useful only temporarily—in this present life. In fact, Colossians 2:8 tells us that we need to be very careful that we are not cheated by those out in the world by purveyors of this kind of knowledge. It says, "Beware lest anyone cheat you through philosophy and empty deceit, according to the traditions of men, according to the basic principles of the world and not according to Christ." Different renderings of this passage say to beware lest the world cheats you, steals from you or takes you captive. None are plausible options or outcomes.

On the contrary, spiritual knowledge is the pearl of great price. It is so much more valuable because we know the spirit rules over the natural in this world in the laws, power and even knowledge about life. Most importantly, it also has an eternal value. It is not just useful right now, it is good even into eternity and will never pass away.

Now about worldly knowledge the Bible warns that, "The way of the fool seems right to him, but a wise man listens to advice." (Proverbs 12:15) Then, Proverbs 14:12 tells us, "There is a way that seems right to a man (he is certain of it), but its end is the way of death." You see, after the fall in the Garden of Eden, the flesh and the mind were corrupted. So, if we make decisions in life with our minds, apart from God's counsel and the leading of His Spirit, our minds will, in fact, deceive us. In addition to this problem, people out in the world also happen to be a bit naïve. Proverbs 14:15 (NIV) tells us, "A simple man believes anything but a prudent man gives thought to his steps." We need to ponder our way. We need to be cautious and circumspect—looking also to the future consequences of our actions. We need to realize that all of us have the capacity and the natural inclination, being born with sin in our members, to make huge mistakes. Proverbs 14:6 tells us, "The mocker seeks wisdom and finds none, but knowledge comes easily to the discerning."

There will be troubling times ahead for all of us in life. Times of testing; times of provocation. Solomon told us, "He who gets wisdom loves his own soul; he who keeps (cherishes) understanding will find good." (Proverbs 19:8) We also know that God is the owner, steward, defender and distributor of all true knowledge. About this we find these words recorded in Proverbs 22:12: "The eyes of the Lord preserve knowledge but He overthrows (frustrates) the words of the faithless." The true knowledge of God is worth more than all the silver and gold in the world. Proverbs 18:15 tells us, "The heart of the prudent acquires knowledge, and the ear of the wise seeks knowledge." We must have it. It is our life. Proverbs 14:8 NIV says, "The wisdom of the prudent is to give thought to their ways, but the folly of fools is deception." God wants to give us so much wisdom that we will actually be crowned with it if only we will dedicate our lives to seeking it.

To find wisdom, the Bible says there are several things we must do: First of all, we need to give thought to our ways. (Proverbs 14:8) We need to look down the road of life and see what the consequences of our actions might bring. We must be very cautious. Secondly, if we are going to have wisdom, Proverbs 15:2 NIV says we need to commend it. "The tongue of the wise commends knowledge but the mouth of fools gushes folly." Then, once we have found it, we need to apply it in our lives. Proverbs

22:17 admonishes us to "Pay attention and listen to the sayings of the wise; and apply your heart to what I teach." Another unusual place we will find wisdom is from rebuke. Proverbs 19:25 NIV tells us, "Flog the mocker and the simple will learn prudence, rebuke a discerning man and he will gain knowledge (wisdom)." We also get it by obtaining the facts. The prudent study out the situations they are confronted with in life. They gather all the facts and refuse to go off half-cocked. Proverbs 13:16 says, "Every prudent man acts with knowledge but a fool lays open his folly." He waits until he has heard both sides of contested cases before making a decision.

Yet another way to get wisdom according to Psalm 1:2 is to meditate the Word day and night. King David took great delight in God's Word and studied it every day. This makes one both wise and prudent as well as causing whatever a person does to prosper. (v.3) Once acquired, we need to store it. Proverbs 18:15 says, "The heart of the prudent acquires knowledge, and the ear of the wise seeks knowledge." They take notes and keep it in a safe place so he can go back and review it or glean from it at a later date.

Once acquired, we also need to know what to do with it. Proverbs 15:7 NIV says, "The lips of the wise spreads knowledge, not so the hearts of fools." We need to share it with our friends—with those who love God. Ezra, the Bible tells us, set his heart to "seek the law of the Lord and to do it." His goal was not to just know it but to practice it in his daily life. Then, "To teach the nation." For this there is a promise and a reward. Solomon, the wisest man in the world, said, "Eat honey, my son, for it is good; honey from the comb is sweet to your taste. Know also that wisdom is sweet to your soul; if you find it, there is a future hope for you, and your hope will not be cut off." (Proverbs 24:13, 14) Your life won't be cut short and your vines will not cast their fruit before the proper time. God is making us all a promise here: if we will build our lives on wisdom and prudence, meditating on His Word, learning daily from the Lord, being discerning, careful and cautious, we will see the fruit of our doings. We will soon see what we do and build will prosper and endure the test of time. On the other hand, we all have known people who seemingly prosper out in the world for a time and then, suddenly, seemingly out of nowhere, trouble comes to them sufficient to wipe them out completely. All they have amassed and all they have done comes to nothing in a moment.

Yes, true knowledge and wisdom will come to us but we must seek it like a miner digging for silver and gold. It is going to take energy, sweat and considerable exertion. . We are going to have to get down and get dirty with this thing. But the Bible says, "If you seek her as silver, and search for her as for hidden treasures; then you will understand the fear of the Lord, and find the knowledge of God." (Proverbs 2:4, 5) We see the "if—then" principle here as we do throughout the Bible. **If** we will do what God says, **then** we are promised a certain result. As the world seeks the riches of silver and gold, we must, likewise, seek God's much more valuable and enduring spiritual riches. If we will do this, we will receive many blessings at the hand of God, Himself, both now and eternally.

What it means to have **THE DESIRE TO SEEK AND BE CROWNED WITH TRUE KNOWLEDGE.**

- Realizing that spiritual knowledge is the goal in life
- Realizing our mind is fallen and will lead us the wrong way apart from God's counsel.
- Knowing that Spiritual Knowledge will help us both now and in eternity.
- Realizing that to find it we must set our affections upon it and not worldly things.
- Realizing that we need to give careful thought to all our ways.
- Realizing that we need to think about the future consequences of our actions and decisions.
- Realizing True Knowledge is worth more than all the silver and gold in the world.
- Realizing that to have True Knowledge we must commend it.

- Realizing that True Knowledge can be found in correction and rebuke
- Realizing that True Knowledge can be found by meditating the Word day and night.
- Realizing that True Knowledge must be recorded and stored in a safe place.
- Realizing that True Knowledge, once acquired, must be protected and shared so it can multiply.

ILENT AND KEEP KNOWLEDGE TO OURSELVES, KNOWING WHEN TO BE
A trait of Prudence   Study start date: _____   Finish date: _____

One of the hardest things in the world for a man to do, according to the Book of James, is to tame the tongue. It may be the smallest member but it is capable of setting the world on fire. Psalm 141:3 records the prayer of King David where he said, "Set a guard, O Lord, over my mouth. Keep watch over the door of my lips." He was wise enough to know his mouth could get him in more trouble in a minute than he could get out of in a lifetime. We also know, "A prudent man keeps his knowledge to himself, but the heart of fools blurts out folly." (Proverbs 12:23) Why? Because "The tongue has the power of life and death, and those who love it will eat its fruit." (Proverbs 18:21) And, "From the fruit of his lips a man is filled with good things as surely as the work of his hands rewards him." (Proverbs 12:14) A prudent man will use words sparingly but also constructively. "A man of knowledge," according to Proverbs 17:27 "uses words with restraint, and a man of understanding is even-tempered." If we will guard our mouth, we are promised that our tongue will keep us from calamity. (Proverbs 21:23) Because, "When words are many, sin is not absent but he who holds his tongue is wise." Proverbs 10:19.

The sure sign of a fool is that he talks too much. This is not the best thing because "A fool's talk brings a rod to his back." On the contrary, "the lips of the wise protect them." (Proverbs 14:3) We are admonished in Proverbs 14:7 to "stay away from the foolish man for you will not find knowledge on his lips." In fact, "Though you grind a fool in a mortar, grinding him like grain with a pestle, you will not remove folly from him." (Proverbs 27:22) It goes deep.

Remember this, there is no lack of peevish, pernicious people in the world. The trials and provocations of life are such that one of the hardest things we must ever learn to do is to hold our tongue—especially when we are being chastised by a fool. Proverbs 27:3 says, "Stone is heavy and sand a burden, but provocation by a fool is heavier than both." "A man who lacks judgment derides his neighbor, but a man of understanding holds his tongue." (Proverbs 11:12) "Wise men store up knowledge" according to Proverbs 10:14 "but the mouth of a fool invites ruin."

There are also times we are specifically commanded by the Bible to remain silent. One is when we are in close proximity to the wicked. David said, "I will watch my ways and keep my tongue from sin; I will put a muzzle on my mouth as long as the wicked are in my presence." (Psalm 39:1) And the same is true being in the presence of a fool. In Proverbs 23:9 we find this admonition: "Do not speak to a fool for he will scorn the wisdom of your words. And, "Do not answer a fool according to his folly or you will be like him yourself." (Proverbs 26:4) In wicked times, when for example, the Lord had decided to judge Israel, the prophet Amos said, "the prudent (should) keep silent at that time; for it is an evil time." (Amos 5:13) We are also to keep silent about things spoken to us in confidence. Proverbs 11:13 says, "A talebearer revealeth secrets but he that is of a faithful spirit consealeth a matter." And, "If you argue your case with a neighbor, do not betray another man's confidence, or he who hears it may shame you and you will never lose your bad reputation." (Proverbs 25:9) Love also covers a multitude of wrong. "He who covers over an offense promotes love, but whoever repeats a matter separates close friends." (Proverbs 17:9) Neither does a prudent man tell all he knows. And finally, another time to remain silent is when we think we might have done well. Proverbs 27:2 advises that we are to, "Let another praise you and not your own mouth, someone else and not your own lips."

Then there are times, of course, when we must speak. Lord Chesterfield said in *Letters to His Son*, "Never seem more learned than the people you are with, wear your learning like a pocket watch and keep it hidden, do not pull it out to count the hours, but give the time when you are asked." We are also to guard against being purposefully short so as to distort the truth by the making of a half-truth. It, too, is a lie. Solomon said, "The lips of the righteous know what is fitting, but the mouth of the wicked what is perverse." (Proverbs 10:32) For "The mouth of the righteous is a fountain of life, but violence overwhelms the mouth of the wicked." (Proverbs 10:11) The words of the wise are powerful and are to be used only to build up, encourage, edify and bless.

What it means to **KNOWING WHEN TO BE SILENT AND KEEP KNOWLEDGE TO OURSELVES:**

- Knowing that our tongue will cause more trouble in life than anything else.
- Knowing that the tongue of wisdom can deliver us.
- Knowing that we should seek to make our words few.
- Knowing to keep silent around our enemies and the wicked.
- Knowing not to answer a fool according to his folly.
- Knowing to keep those things told us in confidence a secret.
- Knowing not to repeat the offenses of our neighbor.
- Knowing not to tell all we know about anything.
- Knowing to let another praise us and not our own lips.

EPENDENT UPON GOD, SEEKING TO BE TOTALLY
A trait of Prudence   **Study start date: _____ Finish date: _____**

A prudent man realizes, "The just shall live by faith" and that true humility is to have a goal of being totally dependent upon the Lord. He also knows that security, peace, provision, success, victory and fulfillment will only be found living a life of trust. It also happens to be the only place we will truly find the green pastures and still waters of life. Solomon's advice to his son was to "Trust in the Lord with all your heart, and lean not on your own understanding; in all your ways acknowledge Him and He will direct your paths." And where will they lead you? To the "green pastures and still waters." I grant you, some people out in the world are really smart and much smarter than most but it matters not. The important thing to remember is that none of us are smart enough to figure out our own lives and the paths we should take on our own. We will miss it every time. Jeremiah said, "… the way of man is not within himself, it is not in man who walks to direct his own steps." (Jeremiah 10:23) So there must be a time of seeking, serving and studying God in a person's life in order to set their moorings. We must all start, at some moment in time, at the same point- by throwing away all the world has taught us. Then we need to begin to build our life on the Rock, the solid rock of God's Word. We will soon find that the basis of all prudence must be faith. It is foolish and reckless to waste time on anything in life but learning to live by faith.

We all have two choices while here and only two: We can either be a tree planted by the streams of water or a bush on a salt wasteland out in the desert. In the latter case, we will actually be a tumble weed that has no roots, no purpose, produce no fruit and has no direction or meaning in life. They are blown by every wind of doctrine and are good only to be bundled up and thrown in the fire. In Jeremiah 17:5–8, the Lord, Himself, said, "Cursed is the man who trusts in man and who makes flesh (the world system and all its contrivances), (and) whose heart departs from the Lord. For he shall be like a shrub in the desert, and shall not see when good comes, but shall inhabit the parched places in the wilderness, in a salt land which is not inhabited," But He goes on to say, "Blessed is the man who trusts in the Lord, and whose hope (you might say—only hope) is the Lord. For he shall be like a tree planted by the waters, which spreads out its roots by the river and will not fear when heat comes; but its leaf will be green and will not be anxious in the year of drought, nor will cease from yielding fruit."

So, it is wise to stop at some point and ask God to show us areas in our lives where we are trusting in the arm of the flesh and free ourselves from them as quickly as possible. We find a word to the wise in Proverbs 22:17: "Incline (bow down) your ear and hear the words of the wise, and apply your heart to my knowledge; for it is a pleasant thing if you keep them within you; let them all be fixed upon your lips, so that your trust may be in the Lord; I have instructed you today, even you. Have I not written to you excellent things of counsels and knowledge, that I may make you know the certainty of the words of truth, that you may answer words of truth to those who send to you?" It is all in Him.

There are some things, however, we are told specifically not to trust in: "In our own way" (Hosea 16:3) because we don't know what way to go. Nor in riches because they are so "uncertain." (I Timothy 6:17) Solomon said, "Whoever trusts in his riches will fall, but the righteous will thrive like a green leaf." Proverbs 11:28 tells us we are not to trust in borrowed money but to "Owe no man anything …" (Romans 13:8) Jeremiah said. "do not trust in any brother." We are to keep our trust in the Lord. And we are admonished to "put not trust in princes." This would mean politicians today. Lastly, we are not to "trust in ourselves." There is only one place to put our trust and it goes on to say, "in God who raises the dead." I Corinthians 1:9

There are some things we are told specifically to trust in: The first is "in the name of the Lord." (Zephaniah 3:12) And, in the Lord, Himself because ultimately, "in Him shall the Gentiles trust." (Romans 15:2) "In the living God." (I Timothy 4:10) In God's way (Hebrews 3:10), God's Word (I Corinthians 3:10) and in His salvation (deliverance). (Psalm 78:22) These things are sure.

There are also some pretty important things trusting in the Lord promises to bring:

- You "shall be fed." Psalm 37:3
- You "shall be made fat." Proverbs 28:25
- You shall continue to "dwell in the land." Psalm 37:3
- You will "not be ashamed." Psalm 25:20
- The Lord will be your "shield and buckler." Psalm 9:4
- He will give you "the desires of your heart." Proverbs 37:4,5
- The Lord, Himself, will "Help (you)." Psalm 37:40
- He will "deliver you from the wicked." Psalm 37:40
- He will be your salvation. Psalm 37:40
- You will be "blessed." Psalm 40:4
- You will "possess the land." Isaiah 57:13
- You will be kept "safe." Proverbs 29:25
- You will "inherit (God's) Holy Mountain." Isaiah 57:13
- The Lord will defend you. Psalm 5:11
- He will show you his "marvelous lovingkindness." Psalm 17:7
- He will "save (you) by (His) right hand." Psalm 17:7
- You will "be as Mt. Zion, which cannot be removed, but abideth forever." Psalm 125:1
- You will also "hear (God's) lovingkindness in the morning." Psalm 143:8
- And, you will "know the way wherein (you) should walk." Psalm 143:8

How do we get there? Note the process in Isaiah 55:7 He said, "Let the wicked forsake his way, and the unrighteous man his thoughts; let him return to the Lord and He will have mercy on him; and to our God, for He will abundantly pardon." We were all wicked at one point. We were all stubborn and thought we knew how to conduct ourselves and do things in life. Even after salvation, the Bible says we need to forsake our thoughts. Why? Because He goes on to say, "'My thoughts are not your thoughts, nor are your ways My ways,' says the Lord. 'For as the heavens are higher than the earth, so are My ways higher than your ways, and My thoughts than your thoughts. For as the rain comes down and the snow from heaven, and do not return there, but water the earth and make it bring forth and bud, that it may give seed to the sower and bread to the eater. So shall My Word be that goes forth from My mouth; It shall not return to Me void, but it shall accomplish what I please and it shall prosper in the thing for which I sent it." (v. 8–11) If we will meditate the Word day and night, it will get in us and do its work. But, it is up to us, alone, to purpose to live by faith. We won't need to live a life of trust in Heaven. Now is the time and there is no better way to live on this planet than to live by faith. God created it, set it up and all of nature was created to respond to the man who lives by faith. Besides, the only way we can please God is by faith and this happens to be the way we are to get all our needs met as well.

What t means **TO SEEK TO BE TOTALLY DEPENDENT UPON GOD:**

- Realizing that it is wisdom and true humility to be totally dependent upon the Lord and that all else will fail us.
- Realizing everything we need and more will be found in a life of trust.
- Realizing we are not to be wise in our own eyes and to have confidence only in the Lord.
- Realizing we need to stop at some point and throw away all our worldly knowledge.
- Then we need to start building only on the solid rock of God's Word.
- Realizing that all prudence and security will be found in living by faith.
- Realizing that we are specifically commanded not to trust in princes, politicians, uncertain riches, our own way, in men or ourselves.
- Realizing we are commanded to trust in the Name of the Lord, in the Lord, Himself, in the Living God, the Word of God and His salvation.
  (Traits of Prudence end here)

PUNCTUALITY—   **Study start date: _____ Finish date: _____**

In the hedonistic society we live in today, being late to appointments or totally disregarding them is something no one likes but we all have to deal with. Yes, we have to deal with it but absolutely no one will ever learn to like it and it will only serve to diminish and will always inure to detriment of the one who is late. Certainly we have all been late at one time or another and probably all of us, myself included, have forgotten to look at our calendar and completely missed an appointment. This is terribly embarrassing and puts us in the unenviable position of having to call the offended party and apologize profusely. The problem, however, is not the occasional lapse every few years. It is continually not seeing the seriousness of this failure or understanding what it will do to a person's reputation and future. However, being on time shows great personal discipline and respect for the intrinsic value of the other person. It says, "You and your time are important to me." So important, in fact, that I would even be willing to possibly waste a little of my own time to be early enough so that I can be absolutely sure (as far as that is humanly possible) that I will never, ever be late.

Being late to an appointment causes us to lose easily half of our influence with the person we are to meet. They begin to wonder if they can trust us. If the appointment happens to be a first meeting, by being late, we have made a terrible first impression. Remember too now that you never get a second chance to make a good first impression. In an employment situation, as soon as we are late to work the first time, the boss automatically tosses our name in a box in his brain marked "Dud." This one, seemingly small, foolish oversight could actually destroy our potential for advancement and chances for a leadership position in the company. Think about it. We have just demonstrated to the leader that we can't even get our self to work on time. How in the world could we possibly think that they would trust us to get their whole department, unit or company to work or where they need to be on time? The quick answer is: We couldn't and they won't. They figure we could actually be counted on to dream up tons of excuses why nobody in this crazy world we live in should ever be expected to be anywhere on time.

The fact is, if you plan to just be on time, you are late—as a leader. Only if you are early, are you really on time. While reading a book during college about President Dwight Eisenhower I learned of his practice of always being ten minutes early for every appointment, regardless. That was a practice I accepted and practiced over the years. You see, being early for an appointment gives you several advantages: You then have time to get the "lay of the land" and will be at peace, alert, calm, ready and rested. You might even assist the leader who has the responsibility of setting things up for the entire crew. You are likely to get the opportunity to pick what detail you want t that day. If there is a flap in the overall plan, you will likely be asked to take care of it. If the boss has to leave on a moment's notice for an emergency elsewhere, guess who he is likely to put in charge in his absence? You got it. The one who already knows what the leader wants and what is going on that day. After a while, the boss will have it printed indelibly on his mind that you are always going to be early and you can be counted on to take care of business.

Planning to be "on time" is a myth and shows a terrible lack of good judgment. Over time there will, sooner or later, be the matter of a flat tire, a railroad crossing stop, a last minute emergency at home that needs attention or a million other things that could cause you to be late time and time again. So, if you are on time you are late. Why not plan to be ten minutes early so you won't ever have to worry about being late? If you are early, you are on time.

When we agree to meet someone or be somewhere at a particular time, it is a promise. Our very word is involved here. Always being early shows a sense of humility and respect for other people. It shows them that we consider them, the job and the task at hand, very important. Whatever you value as a person, others around, co-workers, employees and family members will also come to value as well.

What it means to have the character trait of **PUNCTUALITY**:

- Seeing appointments as an oath and a trust to be guarded and kept
- Being dependable to arrive at appointments set in a timely manner
- Characterized by regularly being on time
- Being ten minutes early to every appointment

URITY—   **Study start date: _____ Finish date: _____**

The characteristic of purity might sound about as exciting as counting the straws on a broom. However, in it we find the power to keep our lives and reputations from destruction as well as to put God in a position to deliver blessings and favor in this life as well as the one to come.

The absence of this character quality can destroy an entire career, family and life. No halfway, right thinking person would ever want to lose everything they spent a lifetime working for—but it, non-the-less, does happen. This phenomenon happens, actually, more frequently in the lives of people today than not.

For example, the Athletic Director for the University of Georgia, Damon Evans, had served very successfully in that position for a number of years, had a great education and scholastic record at UGA, had been a gifted wide receiver while in college there and was held in high esteem by Vince Dooly and the entire Bulldog Nation. He even had a great record for raising money for their athletic programs. However, five minutes after his DUI arrest, when the clock struck midnight, his new million dollar a year, five year contract with the University became official and was to go into effect. He had just been pulled over by the police in Atlanta, driving drunk, with a young woman other than his wife in the front seat of the car and had part of her personal lingerie in his hand. You can guess what happened to his contract and job as the Athletic Director very shortly thereafter. Then last week there was a news article about the four star commander of the U.S. Army African Command, General William "Kip" Ward who was just found guilty by the Inspector General of the Dept. of Defense for misappropriation of hundreds of thousands of dollars: by repeated misuse of military aircraft and vehicles by himself and his family members, accepting unauthorized gifts, using government funds to purchase gifts given to unauthorized personnel, making unauthorized expense reimbursements, etc. The final disposition of his case has not been decided by the Secretary of Defense at the time of this writing but it will likely end in a demotion and the end of an otherwise, stellar military career. You can be assured that neither of these men intended for the end of their stories to be anything like this.

We take no delight in the pain, disgrace and hardship moral failures have caused these two fine men and their families. If they had it all to do again, certainly they would have been more careful but there are very few "do over's" for those in occupying high positions in life. Notwithstanding being the President of the United States and knowing how to explain what "the definition of is is." Our only purpose is to learn from these examples and be warned. It can happen to anyone, even us. Like them, we might have a stellar record so far in life but we can't be foolish enough to think we have nothing to be concerned about. You just haven't been visited by the devil's best yet. Paul said, "be careful if you think you stand because you are about to fall." (I Corinthians 10:12) Pride in the form of misplaced confidence is our worst enemy. Remember, we have a worthy adversary who never quits, is constantly at work and the thing he would like best would be for us to become overconfident, even cavalier about the temptations of life. Thankfully, using all the defenses God has given us, we can certainly keep him at bay but, he will never give up. It is also well to remember that some of the strongest men and women in any field you can name, have indeed fallen and fallen hard. Please, don't be one of them.

As the world becomes progressively more wicked, institutions, families and individuals are caving to the dictates of the world system. We have a government laying down horrible laws and regulations about things previously unthinkable. People in the military must now accept and advance the sodomite lifestyle, doctors and health practitioners must assist in infanticide and birth control, etc. These two were just for openers. There are many more. God's standards for our life and conduct have never changed and never will. Solomon cautioned us to be on guard and always "Let (our) garments be white (pure) and let (our) head lack no oil (of gladness)." (Ecclesiastes 9:8) Paul likewise warned the Corinthians to be very careful "not to receive the grace of God in vain." (v. 6:1) Course talk, loose living and compromise can completely vitiate an otherwise productive life and record. Purity and truth must be the foundation of our lives in order to have and keep a proper testimony, live productively and, most importantly, receive a reward on the Day of Recompense. He went on to say we are to "give no offence in anything that our ministry may not be blamed. But in all things we commend ourselves as ministers of God: in much patience, in tribulations, in needs, in distresses, in stripes, in imprisonments, in tumults, in labors, in sleeplessness, in fastings; by purity, by knowledge, by longsuffering, by kindness, by the Holy Spirit, by sincere love, by the word of truth, by the power of God, by the armor of righteousness on the right hand and on the left, by honor and dishonor, by evil report and good report; as deceivers and yet true; as unknown and yet well known; as dying and behold we live; as chastened and yet not killed; as sorrowful, yet always rejoicing; as poor, yet making many rich; as having nothing and yet possessing all things." II Corinthians 6:3–10

To young Timothy, whom he was preparing for the battle as a minister, Paul said, "Let no one despise your youth, but be an example to the believers in word, in conduct, in love, in spirit, in faith, (and) in purity." (I Timothy 4:12) Make no mistake, as he also told the Corinthians, "a little leaven leavens the whole lump." (v.5:6) Just a little compromise, just a little deceit, just a little sin has incredible power in one's life to grow and ruin their entire life in due time but will destroy their testimony immediately.

They say there was once an auction in hell and the devil was the auctioneer. When the auction opened this particular, fateful day, he pulled certain tools of iniquity out of his black bag of tricks and placed them on the auction block for sale. In an effort to jack up the bidding on the front end, which all auctioneers are want to do, he first came out with a tool that his surrogates knew would work well: lies and deceit. The imps and demons were so excited, they started screaming & flailing their arms in a frenzy. The bidding opened at $15,000 and the devil took the bidders all the way to $23,550 before he slammed his gavel and delivered this prize to the highest, most heinous bidder. Then he picked and dug around in the bag a minute and deftly pulled out adultery and placed it on the block. His malefic troops went wild dreaming about who they had in mind back on earth to destroy with this little ditty. The bidding started at $19,000 and raced quickly to a closing bid of $29,300! The winning bidder couldn't wait for delivery of this tool so he pushed, shoved and clawed his way to the front, snatched it off the block and left like a dart for planet earth to perpetrate this evil on his target of choice. Now there appeared what looked like a rare little twinkle in the devil's normally dark, left eye as he searched feverishly in that dastardly black bag for a tool ever so small. Finally he found it and carefully placed this sharp, little, black iron wedge on his infamous auction block. As soon as it hit the block, though almost invisible, small as it was, his congregants knew exactly what it had to be. They began screaming to the top of their lungs, jumping, writhing and frothing at the mouth. They could hardly contain themselves. In fact, well, they couldn't. The bidding opened at a $1,300,000 before the devil could even get the "What am I bid?" out of his mouth. It shot up to three and four million in a heartbeat and was nowhere near the end—figuring by the cadence of the bids. They were coming forth like machinegun fire.

About that time and a bit confused, a bystander asked one of the demons, "What's the big deal about that little iron wedge. Why is it so valuable? What's all this hoopla over a little iron wedge?" He quipped, "Oh, you don't understand. That is the wedge of compromise. It is incredibly valuable because it's so small. We can slip it in a man's heart and he won't even know it's there. But with it, we can sell him anything we want immediately thereafter because he is totally defenseless. All we need is the least bit of a compromise and we can pull him and taunt him, playing cat and mouse to our heart's delight. It is the very license of Hell to totally destroy! Against that little wedge of compromise we can immediately ruin his testimony and cut his legs off spiritually. With it he will have no defense whatsoever from then on and we can take our good time to totally destroy him."

So many people having very productive lives are being destroyed every day. We just see the high profile ones recorded on the headlines of our newspapers. It is every day, some politician, high ranking government official, educator or preacher is caught in some nefarious act. Why is this so and what can be done about it? What can we do to protect ourselves from that little black wedge? There are several things we can and should do. Why live a good life with God's help and then let the enemy destroy us just before we receive our reward? Here are some things we can do:

- Realize how powerful and dangerous sin and compromise really are. Temptation and the enemy, come "only to steal, kill and destroy" (John 10:10) and for no other reason. We also know, when all sin is fully grown and formed, it always leads to and ends in death. James 1:15
- Do not underestimate the enemy. This is the biggest mistake most generals make in war. Remember, we each have our own spiritual war to fight and it isn't over until we die.
- We must see our great need of training in this critically vulnerable area of life on earth. We need practice just like an athlete preparing for the sports arena or a soldier for the field of battle. "By reason of use (we need to) have our senses exercised to discern both good and evil." Hebrews 5:14
- We need to ask God, Himself, for the gift of discernment. With this we will know supernaturally when someone is trying to deceive and entice us.
- We need to think only on the good things. Realize that all the battles of life are won or lost between our ears. The war is in our brains and we need to use Philippians 4:8 as a filter. These are the things we should think on: "Whatever things are true, whatever things are noble, whatever things are just, whatever things are pure, whatever things are lovely, whatever things are of good report, if there is any virtue and if there is anything praiseworthy—meditate on these things." Refuse to think about anything else.
- Pray the Lord's Prayer daily: Lord, "Lead (me) not into temptation but deliver (me) from evil." (Matthew 6:13) Pray and ask God for help daily and then confess you have it. You will have what you say.
- Make a covenant with your eyes, not to look lustfully upon a maid. (Job 31:1) David was also careful to "set no evil thing before (his) eyes." (Psalm 101:3) Today this would include smut magazines, corrupt movies, internet pornography, etc.
- Covenant with your body to "touch not the unclean thing." (II Corinthians 6:17) If we are going to keep from being deceived by the tricks of the enemy, it would be well to keep our hands and bodies from touching any of his tools, weapons, surrogates and implements. There is never a time that I need to touch a cigarette. I was actually dumb enough to be a three pack-a-day smoker and just a few minutes after I got on the plane coming home from a year in Vietnam, I quit—cold turkey and have never smoked another one since. Has it cost me anything? No. Did it kill me to quit smoking? No. Has it saved me anything? Yes. No telling how much money I have saved, including future medical bills and possibly shortening my life. I'm not proud of any of this but I certainly wasn't a choir boy coming up. I was 13th from the worst Air Force brat in the world. However bad you think I was, I was at least twice that bad. I used to buy my whiskey by the gallon and if that wasn't bad enough, I also bought it by the case from a wholesaler. I gave it up by the grace of God forty years ago and have never had a drink since. No. I am not afraid of it but I can think of no reason to touch the stuff ever again with any part of my body. Same with touching smut magazines and any woman, other than my wife. What a great protection this has been. And it doesn't cost you a dime. Imagine that. A security system on the market today that is totally free.

- Be a great lover and a great hater. King David loved the Lord and even was said to have a "heart after God." But, we are also to learn to hate sin and fear the Lord. Without this, we are defenseless. There is a price to pay for all iniquity, some here on earth and, remember, there is a Day of Recompense when we will all give an answer and receive our reward from God, Himself. It is the Lord we need to fear and not mere men.

- We need to ask God to give us the fear the Lord. A large part of it "is to hate evil, pride and arrogance and every wicked way." (Proverbs 8:13) There is no profit or benefit whatsoever in an evil proposition.

- Purpose to carefully and cautiously consider the matter before making promises and then make pledges only sparingly. We need to think before we commit because we must do what we promise. A man is only as good as his word and "none of (Samuel's) words (fell) to the ground." (I Samuel 3:19) We would do well to be like him.

- Refuse to be deceived by the tensile and fool's gold of the world. The things that we can see are passing away quickly and are not to be counted upon. Yes, we all have needs in this world but note what the Apostle John said. "Love not the world, neither the things that are in the world, if any man love the world, the love of the Father is not in him, for all that is in the world, the lust of the flesh, and the lust of the eyes and the pride of life, is not of the Father, but is of the world." (I John 2:15,16) Luke helped us determine what is truly important with these words: "what is highly esteemed among men is an abomination in the sight of God." (Luke 16:15) These things are fleeting. The real, invisible, spiritual things will last forever.

- Discipline yourself to make a written record of expenses and keep receipts for everything that costs more than ten cents. Keep copious records. It is not that hard to do. Buy a few inexpensive three-ring notebooks and get started. Notebooks are cheap. Tax fines, fees and the interest the government charges on unverifiable tax matters are anything but cheap. Don't give yourself room for sloppiness in business. Be honest in all things.

- Keep records and keep them forever. As one who has been around the block. Yes, I got here just after Noah landed his boat but let me tell you, don't believe the three, five or seven year stuff people tell you. The revenue agent man won't take your word for what you bought that stock for twenty-five years ago and they will take you to task for the withholding tax you paid them, as an employer, ten and twelve years ago. Even though you paid them, they won't have a record of it but you must. Remember, in tax matters, you are guilty until you can prove yourself innocent.

- Trust the discernment that God has given you to lead you in the right way. John wrote this so that those who would try to deceive us couldn't. "The anointing which you have received from Him abides in you, and you do not need that anyone teach you; but as the same anointing teaches you concerning all things, and is true, and is not a lie, and just as it has taught you, you will abide in Him." (I John 2:27) The truth, all truth, is in Him and that truth is in you so test the spirits to determine of what spirit they are of.

- Know this, you won't get away with it. In Numbers 32:23, we see these words recorded: "Be sure your sin will find you out." Furthermore, God is just and since time and memorial, "every transgression and disobedience (has) received a just recompense of reward."

- (Hebrews 2:2) Never forget that the consequences of sin may not come immediately, right along with the sin, but come they will. Thank God, however, we can confess our sins and find mercy.

It is my desire that all my friends will be blessed, "eat of the fat of the land," "prosper and be in good health," and "ride on the high places of the earth." None of us have seen our last temptation unless we are already in a fox hole two by two by you with a six foot lid of dirt on it. Remember, we will be delivered (in life) by the purity of (our) hands." Job 22:30

What it means to have the character trait of **PURITY**:

- The state of things having no contamination
- Ordered by the truth
- A homogeneous state
- Totally true
- No admixture
- Pristine
- Holiness
- Free from moral fault

PURPOSE—   **Study start date:** _____ **Finish date:** _____

Oftentimes people pass through their existence here gathering possessions and doing things fairly well but completely fail to fulfill their purpose in life. They might have acquired an abundance of things but not the right things. They certainly did things but not necessarily the right things. Many today think life and happiness is all about acquiring money, cars, boats, houses and giving vent to the flesh. Not so. All these things are in and of the world. God doesn't mind us having some things in the world. He owns everything. He just doesn't want us to set our hearts upon them and put them before our relationship with Him. Inspired by the Holy Spirit, the Apostle John said, "Beloved, I pray that you may prosper in all things and be in health, just as your soul prospers." (3 John 2) God loves for us to have things and be happy, but only as our soul prospers spiritually, sufficient to handle prosperity. Realize that there are a whole lot more people around who can handle poverty better than they can prosperity. Unfortunately, a multitude of possessions can cause one to have a whole set of even greater problems.

Actually, things we will find won't make us happy. As human beings, we can't even make ourselves happy. The most miserable people on earth are the rich who try to spend all they have on themselves—hoping to make themselves happy and, for it all, become all the more miserable. In every generation there are a world full of hedonistic people trying to make themselves happy this way but for all the expense, become perfect failures. Only when we dedicate ourselves to pleasing God and try our best to make Him happy, will He grant us the happiness we seek. He created each of us for a purpose. I believe every human being has a divine gift to do something or provide something very special for the world. There is nothing we could do or be better fitted for in this life than fulfilling our God-given purpose. God needs men and women to fill all the professions required in a well-balanced society. He wants us to prosper in those professions exactly as our souls are prospering spiritually.

Very few things in life are more pathetic than people who fall into major financial blessings but lack the character to manage this new-found prosperity. Oftentimes, sports stars fall into this malady. They come into multi-million dollar contracts immediately after college, spend lavishly on themselves and absent and fear of the Lord or financial wisdom, mismanage their fortunes. Within three years after retiring from their athletic careers, the majority have lost everything. How sad, but it is really worse than that. Many lose their fortunes and not only wreck their own lives but also the lives of many other people around them. A lack of character and spiritual depth has been the bane of many successful people in business, sports, politics or you name it.

We are here on earth for basically two reasons: First to obtain redemption ourselves and get our spirits ready for Heaven.so we will be happy there. The other reason is to win others to Christ and help them progress in their faith. (Philippians 1:25) Jesus said, "Follow me and I will make you fishers of men." (Matthew 4:19) He equips us by the power of the Holy Spirit to bear fruit as a Christian and thereby prove to be a disciple. Jesus said we all have a decision to make in our lives: either to abide in Him and bear much fruit or go it alone cut off from Him, bearing no fruit at all. The one who decides to be truly connected and bear fruit, God says, He will prune occasionally to bear even more fruit. Those who do not, He casts off as a branch that is withered and throws them in the fire to be burned. However, for those who live to please Him, He gives peace, joy, fruit, favor, blessings and the desires of our hearts.

One important thing I learned in college was to be very close attention when the professors tell you what is going to be on their tests and how it will be graded. How one's life will be graded by the Master is even more important. He said people will be "judged according to their works, by the things which were written in the books." (Revelation 20:12) Nothing is hidden and all things are being recorded. The questions will be, had they accepted Christ as Savior? This is their most important work. Secondly, did they fulfill their purpose? We all have a specific, God-given purpose. Nehemiah's purpose was to rebuild the wall surrounding Jerusalem. Noah had a purpose—to build the ark to the saving of his family and the whole human race. The Apostle Paul had a purpose—to proclaim the Gospel of Jesus Christ first to the Jews and then to the Gentiles. It was eve given to him to establish the first churches in Europe. He declared that those who knew him, "carefully followed (his) doctrine, manner of life, purpose, faith, longsuffering, love, perseverance, persecutions, (and) afflictions which happened to (him) at Antioch, at Iconium, at Lystra—which persecutions (he) endured. And out of them all the Lord delivered (him)." (II Timothy 3:11) Even through all the false accusations, beatings, imprisonments, work without ceasing day and night, long travels, starving from time-to-time and a thousand other things, when all the smoke and dust settled, everyone knew, very clearly, his purpose. It was patently obvious to all.

Our purpose might not be as dramatic, difficult or far reaching as Paul's, but we will never really know the totality of what God has for each of us until our lives are over. We might look at our little talent and few resources thinking, surely we couldn't do much but it is not up to us. It is Jesus who said, "Follow me and I will make you fishers of men." (Matthew 4:19) We just seek and follow the Lord and it is His job to "make" us and equip us to be fishers of men. It is all Him working through us and He does all things well.

There was not one person in the parable of the talents (Matthew 25) without at least one talent to fulfill their purpose. All had the same opportunity on different levels and God, being just, would have rewarded each equally for the same proportionate production. All had at least one talent and one is all we need. With God's help, we can do wonders with very little. Remember, little is much in the hands of God. We just need to step out in faith, be willing to accept some risks and get at it. And for this, the Master said we would each be rewarded with abundance.

Oh, to be sure, our lives are set about with many distractions. Some are burdened by sin conscientiousness—a troubling worry about the impending punishment for what we might have done wrong. Realizing there are sins of omission and commission in life. Then there are likewise some troubled by self-consciousness—a pre-occupation with self wants, self-gratification or a concern about what others might think about us. Both of these preoccupations hinder us from stepping out with the most ardent zeal and a full commitment to accomplishing our purpose in life. Daniel 11:23 tells us what life is really about and it is really just as simple as this: "People who know their God shall be strong and do exploits." Just knowing and spending time with God, meditating on His Word, fasting and praying makes one strong. When we are full grown in the faith, God, Himself, sends His soldiers out to do exploits.

We have many excellent tools and powerful weapons freely given to us to accomplish our purpose. We have "the Word of God which is living and powerful and sharper than any two-edged sword ..." It is constantly "piercing even to the dividing asunder of soul and spirit and the joints and marrow and is a discerner of the thoughts and intents of the heart." (Hebrews 4:12) We have scripture to deflect any fiery dart the enemy throws at us. We have the anointing of the Holy Spirit poured out upon us equal to or greater than any task God gives us. (Joel 2:28) We have the gift of faith that can move mountains. It can "Subdue kingdoms, work righteousness, obtain promises, stop the mouths of lions, quench the violence of fire, escape the edge of the sword, out of weakness make strong, become valiant in battle and turn to flight the armies of the aliens." (Hebrews 11:33, 34 paraphrased) Above all, we have love that "bears all things, believes all things, hopes all things (and) endures all things (because) love never fails. I Corinthians 13:7, 8

The problem is, most of the time, people don't take God's Word seriously. We look at our past, our weaknesses and all our failures. We want to see strength and power in ourselves on the basis of human merit to do things when, in fact, we should be looking at our weaknesses and rejoicing. It is in our weakness that the power of God is made strong. (II Corinthians 12:9–10) When we are weak, He is strong. Whatever He calls us to do, He will give us the anointing and power to accomplish it. Only you can accomplish your unique purpose. No one else can do what God created you to do. It is up to us to seek Him, know Him and serve Him; and then He will lead us to what we are to do. Keep asking Him, What would you have me to do Lord? You ask Him that about a thousand times with a sincere, sold-out heart and He will show you what your purpose is. Not only that but He will help you fulfill it. Nothing on earth could make you happier both now and in eternity.

What it means to have the character trait of **PURPOSE**:

- The intent and overall result and impact of one's life and work
- The God-given object of a person's whole life
- One's reason for occupying space and time on planet earth
- One's aim in life

UALITY, INSISTENT UPON—   **Study start date:** _____ **Finish date:** _____

Without high goals, great expectation and an insistence on quality, little of memorable note is ever found by we mere men who trod the earth. In our short time under the sun, if we expect to just get by, we probably won't. Second rate performers always get passed up, run over, shuffled to the side or fired. Mostly fired. For some reason, our performance always comes up somewhat shy of our goals in life. That's probably why they say, "Shoot at the stars and you might hit the moon." But remember this, all the world is attracted to quality and excellence in every field. Nobody wants a second or third rate friend, car, employee, horse or airplane.

Most children subconsciously set their expectations about performance in life based on the example set by their parents. My dad and mom set a high mark and for this I will be eternally grateful. Mom made straight A's in high school. Sorry, I never could get there; don't ever remember making an A. The only A's I got were for being Absent. She was also very helpful to my dad by volunteering her gift with flowers arranging for special events in the Air Force. Back in the late 50's, when the Shaw of Iran was a close friend of the United States, she decorated the Officer's Club for a huge reception and dinner party in his honor, hosted by General Curtis Le May, Commander of the Strategic Air Command. It was superb. You have never seen so many flower arrangements and carved ice statues, just for starters. She took on extra responsibilities like being the sponsor for the Teen Club (no small undertaking on such a large air base). My dad worked his way through college and then went through cadets in the Army Air Corps to become a pilot. As an officer in what was soon to become the Air Force, he, too, set a high mark to follow. They never said anything about all this, they just modeled courage and excellence before us boys every day. Ultimately dad served as a Squadron Commander of a large air refueling squadron at Dover A.F.B., Delaware. His unit won the Outstanding Air Refueling Squadron in the Air Force award and the Outstanding Aircraft Maintenance Unit Award every year he was the commander. They won everything. Even though they were a Strategic Air Command Squadron as a tenant on a Military Airlift Command base, they still won the Christmas display competition. For his service in that command, he was awarded the Air Force Commendation Medal. What a standard of excellence!

Quality work and quality performance come only from high goals and expectations. If one has high goals, it only follows logically and naturally, that he must then be willing to render a performance that would support this kind of expectation and lay down the energy deposits. Quality performance never happens by accident. It takes a whole lot of study, preparation, planning and a whole lot of hard work to bring it to fruition.

During college I read where those who served as administrative assistants to powerful people usually learned a lot and became fairly formidable in their own day. The problem is that most people are not interested in helping others, wanting so badly to be the big cheese themselves. Time spent as an administrative assistant is just as much a bona fide apprenticeship as that spent learning by people in any other business, trade or industry. The only difference is, in this case you are being taught by a master and you are able to see things few ever see.

My first assignment in the Army after Airborne and Ranger schools was as a platoon leader in the 82nd Airborne Division. My goal from day one, was to become an aide (or administrative assistant) to the Commanding General (CG) of that 16,000 man division. Truly, the chances of doing that were, as you might imagine, was slim to none. I was just another of probably a thousand young, butter-bar, 2nd Lieutenants in the bottom ranks of a huge airborne division. Now I didn't tell anyone. I wasn't a prideful person. Didn't tell my dad or mom or friends—just the Lord. I didn't even know how General's aides were selected. And, no, I certainly didn't think I was the smartest, strongest or the swiftest. Certainly not. Far from it. But, I did have faith and knew God would reward that if I would be willing to lay down the work. At the time, I was very familiar with the passage penned by the wisest man who ever lived with this promise: "Seest thou a man diligent in his business? He shall be before kings, he shall not stand before obscure men." (Proverbs 22:29) With the goal of being aide to the CG, I knew it would probably be necessary to demonstrate an exceptionally strong performance to be recommended as the outstanding platoon leader in my brigade and would then have to compete against the best the other two brigades had to offer as well. However, just having a goal like that gives you a special drive for excellence that most don't have. I knew my platoon had to be outstanding in company duties, unit morale, espirit de corps, keeping our barracks strak, performance on field exercises, physical training, having no weapons stolen, no A.W.O.L.'s, etc. We also had to do our best to support the goals of the company commander, etc.

Amazingly, long-story-short, I got the job as aide to the CG but amazingly, was given an Army Commendation Medal for that tour of duty in the Division as well. Was I perfect? Far from it. Nobody is. I got in trouble for lots of things: being too hard on the company jeeps, too exuberant on field training exercises and so on. But, you sure couldn't grade me down for loyalty or enthusiasm. My company commander, Captain Alex Hottel, himself, tenth in his class at West Point and a Rhodes Scholar, wrote in my efficiency report that "I have never seen nor am I likely to ever see again a lieutenant with so much enthusiasm." How much does it cost to be enthusiastic about your job and life in general? Nothing—but diligence to match it.

My next goal was to be a company commander as a lieutenant in Vietnam and I never heard of anyone doing that unless it was just for temporary field expediency if the commander was taken out by being wounded or killed in battle. Then, when a replacement captain could be located, that was the end to that temporary command. Well, even that happened. I was given a rifle company my first day in the field in Vietnam. In that job our mission was to close with and destroy the enemy and it was always my goal to accomplish every mission and win every battle assigned by my battalion commander. That was our job—to win every battle, defeat the enemy, win the war and defend our country. We were there to protect America's freedoms and I can tell you—freedom isn't free. No matter what other flowery things they might have said about me, I really wasn't too concerned, accomplishing every mission is what I worked for. My first battalion commander, Lt Colonel Bill Burkhardt, put this in my efficiency report: "He accomplished every task assigned him and achieved outstanding results in combat." His replacement, Lt. Colonel James Anderson, assumed command.and later stated in my efficiency report that " His company experienced difficult combat against NVA in bunkers, yet they always accomplished their missions. His company found more munitions (weapons and ammunition) and rice caches than any other company in (the) battalion." One of those base camps was so big that I later found that the battalion called it "The City." According to the official history of the 1st Battalion, 5th Cavalry in the Cambodian Invasion, our battalion accounted for 13% of all the rice, 26% of all the crew served weapons and 25% of all the enemy individual weapons captured by the entire First Cavlry Division.

I could go on and on through life about how these principles work but you get the picture. This is no testimonial about me. I was the one who nearly failed the first, second and the third grade. Even got put back in the ninth grade by my father for getting into so much trouble—even though I made fair grades. It is a testimonial to power of these spiritual principles! If God could do it for me, He can do it for anyone. Fact is, quality work, the fruit of true diligence, is appreciated everywhere you go—in or out the service. I am sure there were others who did better but I was just thankful to have had the opportunity to serve. Quality work though, mixed with diligence, loyalty and faith in God are an unbeatable combination. Ability, book knowledge, ancestry, intellect, strength and beauty all matter very little.

For there to be excellence in any organization, there must be servant leadership, diligence, determination and quality control. Good quality control is indispensable to the proper management of any organization, in production or in any manufacturing process. There will be no consistent quality without a consistent inspection process, conducted to attain it. For this to happen check lists must be developed to ensure both quality and performance. We were taught in the Army that the men did well only what the boss checks. The general I was aide to had his own way to see if a company commander really cared about his troops. He would check the restrooms for adequate toilet paper. Something as small as that? Yep. That, like good food in the mess hall, was a critically important item.

Faithfulness to demonstrate quality in the smallest things is necessary to be promotable anywhere in life. If anyone wants to keep a sloppy desk, work area or vehicle and dress like a slob, you can forget it. If you can't keep your own car in good repair and well maintained, what corporation is going to give you a fleet of fifty to look after? If you, personally, can't turn in an excellent report and get the job done on time with excellence, who wants someone who always has fantastic excuses? No. They are looking for a man who never needs excuses. All of this, like so many other things, goes back to the enduring truth of Luke 16:10: "He who is faithful in what is least is faithful also in much." And the Parable of the Talents where the Lord said to his servant, "you were faithful over a few things, I will make you ruler over many things. Enter into the joy of the Lord." (Matthew 25:21) The only proper goal in life is to be found faithful in our charge and faithful to our Lord and Master. We are all stewards of the Lord's earth; stewards of our company, ministry, family and possessions and this is not an optional rating we are to be seeking. The apostle Paul told us in I Corinthians 4:2: "It is required in stewards that one be found faithful." God, Himself said of "(His) servant Moses, he is faithful in all my house (meaning the whole nation)." (Numbers 12:7) In deed, in I Timothy 1:12 Paul thanked the Lord because "He counted (him) faithful." There can be no higher honor in this one, short life than to be counted faithful by the Lord Jesus Christ.

What it means to have the character trait of **BEING INSISTENCE UPON QUALITY:**

- Setting a high level of expectation
- Superior in kind
- No admixture or defect
- The highest rank of its kind
- Distinguished by excellence
- The highest grade
- The highest degree of excellence and workmanship

EADY, BEING—   **Study start date:** _____ **Finish date:** _____

Life comes at all of us one way usually: fast. Mamma said, "Opportunity only knocks once. So, be ready and don't let it pass you by." There is at least one thing we can count on in life. We can all know exactly when the enemy will attack. When? At a time you think not and least expect. That's always when the enemy comes at you. This means it is all the more important in this one, short life to learn to live at the ready. Some things happen so fast today that you can't even prepare for them. Automobile accidents and computer crashes are good examples but they are certainly not a lot of fun when we to have to deal with them. It is a fact, that after living through a war, one never loses the natural desire and intrinsic motivation to be ready at all times.

For the longest, I thought this old adage was true: "There are only two things for certain in life: death and taxes." No. When I got a little older, I found out there were three: death, taxes and change. It occurred to me that even things that didn't look like they could change many times did. But wait. I got a little older and realized something else that was just as constant—just as certain in life. There are four: death, taxes, change and trouble. If we aren't having trouble, don't worry it is just around the corner. Otherwise, the Master would have been wasting His breath telling us how important it was, while we are on this big blue marble, to build our lives on the Rock. He said the winds would blow, the rains would come and this was all alluding to tornados, hurricanes, recession, depressions, auto accidents, wars and plane crashes. There are thieves, false brethren, communists and terrorists. We can always look for more trouble.

For a thousand reasons we need to live at the ready and to be at the ready, we must prepare for our mission (or job) daily. As I have probably mentioned, at the military college I attended, Texas A&M University, they had discovered that in any large body of people, there would always be a few, what they called "Two Per-centers." There would always about 2% of the guys who didn't know what day of the week it was, what the uniform of the day was, what the drill was, where their equipment was or where they were supposed to be at any given moment in time. Not good. We certainly don't want to be found in that august group. All it takes is making an effort to be informed, think ahead and make a written note of our instructions. Remember, this little statement that has meant so much to me over a lifetime: "Things spoken speed away, those written endure." Getting into the habit of making a list of things to do and things to get ready is an indispensable habit to start.

Just for openers, there will always be a good many natural and man-made disasters a person needs to prepare for. We will likely be faced with hurricanes, tornadoes and earthquakes sooner or later. Even if they don't occur in our own neighborhood, the effects in one locale oftentimes cascade out over the entire country—creating shortages of many essentials. Just because you get hit by one really brutal hurricane, don't think that's it for a while. In New Orleans they had Katrina, Rita and Wilma! Bang! Almost back-to-back. Our northeastern coast was just recently hit by a thousand mile wide hurricane called Sandy that did about $50 billion in damage. That's right, billion with a "B." It had a totally devastating impact. Houses were washed and blown away, there were massive power outages and most service stations were either out of gas, couldn't get re-supplied or had no back-up generators to pump what gas they did have. Some lines of cars waiting for gas were three miles long. Then, a week later, here comes a nor- east-erner: high winds, tons of snow and freezing cold temperatures. And, don't ever expect the government to be there for you as an individual. They won't be. Politicians will tell you that they will be there for you and do it all but that's just what politicians do. They make empty, impossible promises and blow hot air. Frankly, the government is not set up for it, doesn't have the resources and never will be able to do for millions of people what they are going to need after a mega-wipe out. Besides, if that wasn't enough, our society is completely reliant on electrical power lines, technology, machines, appliances, electronic devices, automobiles and air planes, just to mention a few. These are all gone immediately in cataclysmic storms and hurricanes.

When these systems go down and no one can get gas or heating fuel, mass confusion, hysteria, thei-every, greed and anger set in. What's the point? Have some reserves. Keep a radio that can operate on batteries, several flash lights and a store of extra batteries. Have a diesel generator and the wiring of your house adapted to accommodate it for the short term. A wood-burning stove, a couple chain saws and a good size wood pile are also a necessity. Those who can, should have a well with a pitcher pump (hand pump) and a back-up generator for the house. It is always best to have some water stored in plastic containers to meet immediate needs as well. Having emergency food supplies on hand is critical and not all that expensive. Most importantly, when you have taken care of your own family, you will then be in a position to help others.

Another problem is that just about everything we deal with in life is made to disintegrate over time. Trees die and soon rot to the ground. Cars break down and require constant maintenance until they become so decrepit or obsolete they wind up in the junk yard. Computers, yes, I am sure you have already found, are a whole new set of problems with their hardware, software and constant program up-dates and glitches. Our bodies are breaking down along with all our equipment, houses, boats and airplanes. We live in a highly technical world. It is nothing like it was twenty years ago.

A few years ago, I took my youngest son in to the Verizon store to get him his first cell phone. The young salesman behind the counter had a laptop with an air card, a pager, a cell phone, a post-it note pad and a paper clip on the counter where he was working. It wasn't long before this Gen-Y sales clerk left to go to the back of the store to get my son's new phone. While he was gone I pointed to all his equipment there on the desk and asked my son how much of it he thought we had when I was his age. He didn't know so I told him, "The paper clip."

Everything today is computerized, hydraulic, pneumatic, mechanized, motorized and miniaturized. This just means there will always be a whole lot of break-downs and problems. Carrying a small Leatherman TM multi-tool and a small flash light today are indispensable. You never know when you will have to look down into the deep dark recesses of a carburetor, a computer or a closet or when you might need a set of pliers, or a Phillips-head screwdriver. And, whoever heard of walking out of the house without a pocket knife? You never know what's next but we need to be ready for anything. What should we do? Plan for the worst (get ready) and hope for the best. When opportunity or trouble arrives, it is too late to get ready.

The Parable of the Ten Virgins in Matthew 25 speaks to one thing: the importance of living at the ready. It is called a life and death parable as it demonstrates as well as promises eternal consequences and is all about being ready. More importantly, it is all about getting our soul ready to meet and give an account to the Master, who is the bridegroom. Doubtless, the most important business ever conducted by anyone on this planet is that of getting their soul ready to meet our Maker. You remember the story, there were five wise and five foolish virgins. The wise virgins had their lamps trimmed and paid the price to have plenty of extra oil on hand to endure the trials, disappointments and long waiting periods life was certain to have in store. Everything, we soon learn, always takes a whole lot longer to get done than we thought.

Why did the five who were foolish fail—at something so very important? Certainly procrastination, putting off the pain and hard work of preparation would rate right up there. They were thinking tomorrow is a much better day to get started because today it is perfect time to rest, recreate, eat, drink and be merry. Undoubtedly, laziness had to kick in there too. God knows we have all been lazy a bit here and there. The parable even says that "they all slumbered and slept." Where I come from all means all. So that means even the preachers need to be more diligent and keep a better watch on things. That means even Billy Sunday, Billy Graham and Smith Wigglesworth could have done better. Now I wouldn't put myself within ten million light years of this aforementioned, august group, but I better confess right here that I, too, could be a lot more diligent and diligence is about my only gift. But, I digress. Back to the ranch. I believe, far and away, the biggest reason for the failure here was this: their unwillingness to pay the price.

You see it costs you to be ready. It takes discipline to get ready. You have to get your lazy carcass up out of bed early every day and get at it. You have to be willing to work hard, sweat and eat a little dirt from time-to-time. You have to deny yourself. You have to take perfectly good seed that you could eat and enjoy or sell for a profit and set it aside in a dry, safe and secure place so you will have something to plant next season. Just think about what it takes to go into business as a farmer. You will need to buy a thousand acres of land, a couple John Deere tractors, a tiller, a bailer and a planter and build your barns and fences just for starters? The only thing this farmer, if he were like the five foolish virgins, left off was — (drum roll here) the seed. Or someone ostensibly going into a retail business. They rent a large commercial building in a dynamite location, buy and erect all the fixtures and shelving, pay for the signage and advertising, get all the utilities turned on, phone lines in, hire a staff and only leaving off one thing: the stock. Crazy. The stock in trace in this parable was the oil to light their way.

The whole point of this parable and life, itself, is being ready. You don't know when the bridegroom is coming. A month ago we had a young man in our church whose car broke down on the side of the road out in the country, in the middle of the night. He was walking along the side of the road to get help, gas or whatever and got run over by a car. The elderly lady driving said she didn't see him. He had no time to prepare, no time for death-bed repentance and didn't even know what, bless his heart, hit him. I certainly hope he was ready. However, the problem with the five foolish virgins in this parable was that they had no eternal diligence. They had oil enough to make a show — but no oil to persevere. The bridegroom came at midnight when no one was expecting him. Those who weren't ready had to go and do at the most inopportune time what they had previously found too difficult and refused to do earlier — go out and do the work necessary to buy oil. Only problem was it now happened to be time to go in to meet the bridegroom and celebrate. They, of course, found themselves embarrassingly, equitably and eternally locked out.

How do we buy oil? By seeking and serving the Lord. Loving God so much you want to serve Him, His church, the least, the lost and the unlovely. We have an outreach in our church called Manna Ministries which is set up to give food to the poor and what a blessing it is. Few people know what it is today to starve or be down and out. The young man that dispenses the food for us each week heard about a lady in town who was destitute, lonely and dying of cancer. He went by her house and knocked on the door. When she finally came to the door, of course, she looked pitiful with her hair was all gone. She was old and she was poor. He gave her some food in the name of the Lord (truly the Lord had given it to us in the first place) and it unbelievably thrilled her soul. When I heard about it, I said keep doing it every week. What was this young man doing? He was just doing what the love in his heart led him to do automatically — helping someone in need. He wasn't doing it to get points or be noticed. He just did it, like everything else he does, automatically. But in actuality, he was buying oil. Everyone taking their free time to preach to those in prison — are buying oil. Those who volunteer their time to work in the thrift stores — are just doing what they love and their hearts leads them to do but they are all buying oil. Those serving in the choir, working on the parking committee, mowing the grounds, street-reach, tithing and giving, serving on the elder board or prayer committee — are all buying oil. One day very soon, they will be glad they did.

Those who start businesses in life are the same ones who have the discipline not to spend their hard-earned money on partying or all that fancy wining and dining out. They are faithful to save a percentage of every dollar they make so they will, one day, have the investment capital they need when opportunity comes a'knocking. Instead of sleeping until the crack of noon, they have made a habit of getting up early, being read up, prayed up and already having shown up for a time alone with the Lord to get their marching orders for the day,

What it means to have the character trait of **BEING READY:**

- Having the proper equipment in a state of readiness and your troops (or staff) technically and tactically proficient to meet any contingency
- Prepared for immediate deployment or any attack
- Willingly mentally and physically disposed to maintain a state of alert
- Able to respond spontaneously
- Adroit
- Always takes the time to be informed, has looked at the daily weather report, knows the proper uniform and plans for the day.
- Always prepared, mentally, physically and spiritually
- Prepared for any eventuality, knowing trouble brings opportunity

RELATIONSHIPS, FAITHFUL IN— Study start date: _____ Finish date: _____

W hat is life about? Things or people? We all certainly need a few things and things can be tools to help make life easier, more enjoyable as well as our work more efficient but they also wear out, become obsolete and we get tired of even those things we use for enjoyment. People, on the other hand, are what life is really about. No man is an island. Hermits and loaners are never happy in this life. Just as well face it, we were all born selfish and self-centered but our worth in life will be determined by how much we can be devoted to others—to things, people and entities outside of ourselves. Only those who love people will ever be happy and experience life that is truly life.

We see in the life of David the importance of being faithful in relationships. When Samuel approached King Saul about failing to obey the Lord's command to take no spoil when he was sent out to annihilate the Amalekites, Saul defended his keeping King Agag as a war trophy and allowing the people to keep some of the best sheep to offer as sacrifices. Why? Because Saul thought 99 and a half would do with God—but it won't. Samuel's immediate response was because of his disobedience, God had rejected him as king over Israel. Subsequently, He told Samuel to anoint David as king, which he did, and the Spirit of the Lord came upon him from that day forward. Although he was anointed king by the prophet Samuel, David never challenged Saul but rather waited upon the Lord daily for deliverance and years to receive his crown.

After David was anointed, a distressing spirit began to trouble Saul and a search was made for someone to play the harp to sooth him. David was soon summoned to the King's court to play before the king when he became troubled and the distressing spirit would depart. Not long after this, the Armies of Israel were challenged for forty days by the Philistine champion, Goliath. When no one else would fight this giant, David, of course, did. He took him out with a stone from his sling shot. As soon as he killed Goliath, David was taken before King Saul by Abner, the commander of the army, with the giant's head in his hand. Saul had wanted to know whose son he was so Abner brought David to him. From that time on Saul, would not allow him to return to his father's house anymore. As soon as David finished speaking with Saul, his son Jonathan happened to be in the court and his soul was knit to David such that he loved him as himself. Jonathan and David also made a covenant between them and began a friendship like none they had ever had before. Jonathan took off his robe, armor, sword, belt and bow and gave it to David as a symbol of his devotion and the seriousness of this covenant. Both he and David had a heart to make covenant and a desire to knit their hearts together.

From this time on, wherever Saul sent David, he was over the Armies of Israel and behaved himself very wisely. However, after many successful battles, David happened to be returning to Jerusalem one day and the women came out for him singing with musical instruments and dancing in the streets. As they danced, they sang "Saul has slain his thousands, and David his ten thousands." This, of course caused Saul to be jealous of David from that time forward. Because Saul knew that the Lord was with David and that he behaved himself so wisely that he soon became afraid of him—but, on the other hand, all of Israel and Judah loved him as well. Because of this and the fact that Samuel had anointed him king, David began to experience the king's wrath as Saul tried his best to kill him.

One day in the court, King Saul told all his servants and his son, Jonathan, that he wanted them to kill David. Being a faithful friend, Jonathan told David about his father's plan to kill him and of his plan to intercede before his father on his behalf. He then told David to go into hiding immediately. However that appeal went, he intended to let David know. So Jonathan went before his father and asked that he not sin against David because he had not only done nothing against the king but he had also been extremely faithful in his service toward him. He also reminded Saul that David took his life in his own hands to kill the Philistine giant and brought about the great deliverance of Israel. He then boldly asked him, "Why then will you sin against innocent blood, to kill David without cause?" (I Samuel 19:5) So Saul listened to Jonathan and swore before the Lord not to kill him. Then Jonathan immediately went to David and told him all about this and then brought him before Saul to continue to minister in his presence as in the past. Jonathan took a great risk that day and proved he had a heart to be faithful in friendship even unto death.

After this there were many more battles with the Philistines in which David fought and struck many mighty blows causing them to flee before the armies of Israel. At one point the distressing spirit came against Saul as he was in his house. As David was playing music with his instrument, Saul took his spear and tried to pin him against the wall but, thankfully, he was agile enough to escape in the night. David finally had to go into hiding out in the desert and in and out of Philistia because Saul had three thousand of his best soldiers after him. Over the next few years, Saul tried to kill David twenty-seven times and David had the opportunity to take Saul out on two or three occasions but didn't. He left it all in God's able hands, knowing He would do what he had promised.

Time and again, Jonathan interceded for David and warned him about Saul's plans to kill him, because he loved him as his own soul. Things happened this way again and again until one day his father even threw a spear at Jonathan, trying to kill him too.

Finally, years later, both Saul and Jonathan were killed in a battle with the Philistines. When this happened, David wept greatly over their loss and told the people to teach the children of Judah to sing the Song of the Bow, recorded in II Samuel 1:19. After a time of great mourning, David inquired of the Lord as to where he should go in Judah. And the Lord said, "Go up." At that, David asked where he should go and the Lord said "To Hebron." II Samuel 2:1

So David then went up to Hebron, a city in the beautiful hill country about twenty miles south of Jerusalem, a land previously occupied by the Canaanites that was taken by Joshua and again by Caleb. It was the same place that had been the home of Abraham, Isaac and Jacob. It was here that David took his two wives, Ahinoam, the Jezreelitess, and Abagail, the widow of Nabal, the Carmelite. There David brought all the men that were with him and their families and they dwelt in the cities of Hebron. It was at Hebron that the men of Judah came and anointed David king over the house of Judah according to the word of the Lord by Samuel the prophet. It was also there that David sent messengers to the men of Jabesh Gilead, the men of Judah who had buried Saul, praising them for the kindness they had shown him in his day of distress. He promised to return that kindness to them himself and then spoke words of encouragement to them: He said, "Now therefore, let your hands be strengthened, and be valiant; for your master Saul is dead, and also the house of Judah has anointed me king over them." (II Samuel 2:7) It was there, in Hebron that David and his men spent seven years and a half years knitting their hearts together, learning to live in covenant.

In I John 3:16 we see these words written by John, the apostle, under the inspiration: "We have known and believed the love that God has for us, God is love and he who abides in love abides in God and God in him." Jesus was and is the measure of our covenant of love and the standard He gave us was to lay down our life for our friends. Jonathan met that measure and David was also willing to in battle time and time again for his friends and the whole nation. The last statement Jesus made on earth was his prayer in John 17:11 where he prayed, "Keep them through Your name those whom You have given Me, that they may be one as We are." He prayed that our hearts would be knit together in relationship as theirs. Then in verse 22 He prayed again that "the glory which You gave Me I have given them, that they may be one just as We are one;' Why? Because there is great strength in unity. We know Jesus went on to say, "If two of you agree on earth concerning anything that they ask, it will be done for them by My Father in heaven." (Matthew 18:19) This is so important because the power of God is multiplied in our lives in unity—hearts knit as one.

It was there in Hebron that David and his men knit their hearts together as a nation and people. It is also important to note that he picked and ranked his men not by family connections, wealth, smooth speaking or the depth of their theology but by:

1. Loyalty
2. Achievement

The result of this sound policy was a day-by-day increase and strengthening of his army and government. The same way our families, businesses and churches need to grow today. It is the will of God. Loyalty is so important because, obviously, it has to do with a person's ability to truly make covenant in the first place. The only alternative to loyalty is rebellion, selfish ambition, anarchy and sedition. Achievement is likewise important because as, we know, talk is cheap and many boast of a whole lot of things. However, in war, only one thing is important: that we get the victory. Failing that, nothing else matters. In business and management, results count, getting the job done—not talk, wishful thinking, empty visions of grandeur or the best excuses in the world.

What we see here in the lives of Jonathan and David is the importance, the power and the blessing inherent in being faithful in relationships. Making covenant and knitting one's heart to another is never accidental. No one can knit their heart to anyone unless they want to and make a conscious decision to do so in love—not for the benefits that might accrue to us but for what we can do for the other person. It also takes a heart capable of making covenant which, quite frankly, not all have. So many today never seem to be able to break through their life of selfishness. In this life we need to make a covenant to stand with the Lord, our mate, our friends, our boss and our pastor. This is what makes for life that is truly life. This is what makes relationships real. The ability to make covenant and knit our hearts to others is one of the greatest things that can ever happen to a person. The reward is great both in this life and the one hereafter.

It is such a joy to work for a boss and those around us, our friends and associates, for example, with the desire and joy in our heart solely to make them successful and even great in the eyes of the Lord. Knowing all the time that it is our great blessing to make them successful and this with no need of fanfare and no need of credit to us. All we need do is forget about ourselves, knit our heart to others around us quietly in our heart of hearts, help others especially in their times of great need and we will be successful beyond belief. "We (will) know that we have passed from death to life, because we love the brethren." (1 John 3:14) Nothing is sweeter than walking, living and working in love. David said his from Jonathan to him "was wonderful, surpassing the love of women." (II Samuel 1:26) When we are faithful in relationships, we will experience life that is truly life. Remember this too. If you don't love your coworkers, your friends and your boss, you don't have to worry about telling them. Whatever is in your heart has already been emanating from your choice of words, tone of voice, eyes, facial expressions, body language and mental telepathy. But, the contrary can also be true if you have love in your heart.

Being faithful in friendship means many things. The first thing is to choose your friends carefully. Because only "iron sharpens iron," choose only growing Christians. "He that walks with the wise will be wise but the companion of fools will be destroyed." (Proverbs 13:20) We are also admonished in Proverbs 22:24 not to ever make friends with an angry man. He has unresolved conflicts, issues and spirits than can spill over into your life.

The kind of friendship David and Jonathan had requires a deep kind of love that starts with respect and appreciation. We must appreciate our friend as a person and let them know we appreciate them. Love is the basis of friendship, giving and being there to help others and not being in it for some selfish motive. We know, "A friend loves at all times and a brother is born for adversity." (Proverbs 17:17) Not a sunshine or fair-weather friend but a rainy-day friend. Nothing will make us happier than being there for our friends. We should delight in being called upon in times of trouble.

A true friendship requires devotion. Being devoted to your friend's success and his or her goals in life. Always trying to help them get to the next level and receiving the desires of their hearts. Being willing to make investments in their lives. Jonathan gave his most cherished weapons. Several of David's mighty men, on one occasion, risked life and limb to go behind enemy lines and get him a drink of water from Jacob's well. Why? Because they knew he wanted it.

Another important ingredient in having friendships is showing ourselves friendly. If you look like you hate all of nature, the sun coming up in the morning and have been on a steady diet of lemons and peppers, no one will want to be around you. What is better? Showing yourself friendly and letting it spill over into your language.

A true friend will tell the truth and give honest counsel. Proverbs 27:9 tells us, "Ointment and perfume delight the heart and the sweetness of a man's friend gives delight by hearty counsel." Sometimes that counsel may be strong because "faithful are the wounds of a friend but the kisses of an enemy are deceitful." Proverbs 27:6

To engage in a true friendship, we must make ourselves vulnerable. Sure, the other person may betray us. They may let you down in some way but this just brings us to the indispensable importance of forgiveness. We all make mistakes. We all fail to some degree, albeit unintentionally hopefully, and this is where the only thing that will work to mend and retrieve the friendship at these times is forgiveness. Forgive them and love them anyway. Forgive them and trust them anyway. This is the only way you will ever have life-long friendships, the only kind that matter.

For a friendship to be meaningful we must also be thoughtful. Remember their birthday. Celebrate their triumphs and accomplishments. Commend them when they do well. Send them a note in the mail.

Pray for your friends and God will reveal ways you can be of help to them. Just praying for them is a mighty blessing—invoking God's favor, power and blessings in their life is tremendous. Being a friend and having friends is a lost art and treasure that only few find today. Truly that person is rich in this life who is rich in friendship and rich toward God.

What it means to have the character trait of being **FAITHFUL IN RELATIONSHIPS**:

- Firmly adhering to promises made to one another
- Keeping one's word regardless of what it costs us
- Making a practices knitting our heart to friends, family, co-workers and employers
- Being steadfast in one's affection for another
- Being dedicated to our friend's success
- Having a heart capable of making covenant
- Having brotherly love
- Being faithful in one's loyalty and devotion to others unto death
- Being faithful to others in their time of need or troubles

- Is into life-long friendships
- Making your friend, family or boss' friends your friends and their enemies your enemies
- Making real investments in the lives of our friends
- Never allowing yourself or others to put you in a position where your loyalty might be in question
- Being faithful to not only be at one's post but to fulfill our duty especially in times of danger

ELIABILITY / see FAITHFULNESS

ESILIENT—   **Study start date:** _____ **Finish date:** _____

In life, love, business and war, no one seems to get a steady, unending run of the breaks. Sooner or later it will be our turn in the barrel. Sooner or later we are granted admission by the Dean of Heaven to be inducted into the School of Hard Knocks. Life has a way of slipping up on us from the blind side and delivering unexpected, seemingly, low blows and heavy hits. Besides, we are all still fully capable of making mistakes, getting a little complacent and sometimes, in the wisdom of God, might need to be dealt with rather harshly with life's up's and down's. The important point is that some people take a lick and crumble to the ground, hitting the dust never to recover again. Others, however, take these poundings, get up, dust themselves off and keep right on trucking. That's right, they just get up and keep on going, but are even stronger for the lessons learned. Stronger, as they say, in the broken places. These folk have learned that the worst things that ever happen to us in life always turn out to be the best in the end – if we will let them. This is called the transcendent glory of God. We can experience it, that is, if we will be patient, thankful for the adversity and give God time. And, of course, this also presupposes that we have the Lord as our Savior, source and strength. Proverbs 1:23 gives some sage advice: "Turn at my rebuke; surely I will pour out my Spirit on you; I will make My words known to you." It is in these times of adversity that God wants to speak to us if we will be still in all the pain of our situation and listen.

When things go wrong, it is time to stop and see where we went wrong, being certain that, "Like a flitting sparrow, like a flying swallow, …a curse without cause shall not alight." (Proverbs 26:2) If we will stop and consider our ways and doings, if we will be honest, we will probably find there was some place we missed it. There is something we need to change. There is likely a flaw in our character that needs to be corrected. If we will do our part, "turn at the rebuke", pray and seek God's face in the matter, He will be faithful to do His part I promise and "make known (His) words to you." This is when the blessings start to flow. For "Many are the afflictions of the righteous but the Lord delivers him out of them all." (Psalm 34:19) Paul said we might be "struck down but not destroyed." (II Corinthians 4:9 NIV) King David also told us that "The steps of a good man are ordered by the Lord and He delights in his way. Though he fall, he shall not be utterly cast down; for the Lord upholds him with His hand." (Psalm 37:23, 24) God's mighty hand is an unbelievably powerful force and "an ever present help in time of trouble." (Psalm 46:1) "For the righteous man falls seven times …" But, he doesn't stay down for the ten count. He "rises again but the wicked …" are not so. They "are overthrown by calamity." Proverbs 24:16

As "the horse is prepared for the day of battle" (Proverbs 21:31) a man is to prepare for the day of trouble knowing every house (which is a man's life in the Bible) will be tried by fire. Trouble is most assuredly on the way and "If (we) faint in the day of adversity, (our) strength is small." (Proverbs 24:10) So get ready. Long ago, the prophet Micah put Israel's enemies on notice saying, "Do not rejoice over me, my enemy; when I fall, I will arise, when I sit in darkness. The Lord will be a light to me." (Micah 7:8) As "the horse is prepared for … battle" we will prepare, we will meditate the Word, we will fast and pray, as well as improve our skills and character. We will be faithful to do all we can but "victory is from the Lord." (Proverbs 21:31) This is true, that is, if our hope and trust is in Him.

Ben Franklin told us years ago, "Resolve to perform what you ought; perform without fail what you resolve." Stay at it, in other words, regardless of the cost, problems, a lack of resources, the changing tides of public opinion and the trials and tribulations of life. Never give up. If they knock you down, keep on getting up and go at it again. Keep on doing the right thing. In 1862 Abe Lincoln said in a White House interview with a reporter by the name of Frank Carpenter, "If I were to read, much less answer all the attacks made on me, this shop might well be closed for any other business. I do the very best I can; and I mean to keep doing so until the end. If the end brings me out all right, what is said against me won't amount to anything. If the end brings me out wrong, ten angels swearing I was right would make no difference."

This man had his failures but he took them in stride and gave God time to turn them into success. In 1832 he lost his job and was defeated for state legislature. However, he was elected captain of his company in the Illinois militia in the Black Hawk War. In 1833 he failed again in business but was appointed postmaster of New Salem, Illinois and deputy surveyor of Sangamon County. In 1834 he was elected to the Illinois state legislature but in 1835 his sweetheart died. In 1838 he had a nervous breakdown but was re-elected to the Illinois State Legislature and received his license to practice law before the state bar. In 1837 he led the Whig delegation in moving the Illinois state capital from Vandalia to Springfield and became a law partner with John Stuart. In 1838 he was defeated for Speaker but re-elected to the House, serving as Whig floor leader. In 1839 Abe was chosen as a presidential elector by the first Whig convention and was admitted to practice law in the U.S. Circuit Court. In 1840 he argued his first case before the Illinois Supreme Court and was re-elected to the Illinois state legislature. In 1841 he started a new law practice with Stephen Logan. In 1842 he was admitted to practice law in the U.S. District Court. In 1843 he was defeated for the nomination to represent his party to run for Congress. In 1844 he established a law practice with William Herndon and in 1846 was elected to Congress. In 1848 he lost the renomination by his party and chose not to run for Congress, abiding by the rule of rotation according to the Whig Party of which he was a member. In 1849 he was rejected for land officer but was admitted to practice law in the U.S. Supreme Court. That same year he declined an appointment as secretary and then as governor of the Oregon Territory. In 1864 he was elected to the Illinois state legislature but declined the seat to run for U.S. Senate but lost. In 1856 he was defeated for nomination as Vice President and in 1858 was again defeated in his bid for the U.S. Senate. In 1860, however, he was elected President of the United States.[22] Who was this man? Abe Lincoln.

What it means to have the character trait of **BEING RESILIENT:**

- Able to encounter blows, reversals and shocks without fracturing, deforming or losing one's zeal and momentum in life.
- The capacity to adjust quickly to changes, set-backs and the misfortunes and mistreatments in life.
- Not being deterred by failures, attacks or reversals

RESOURCEFULNESS—   **Study start date:** _____ **Finish date:** _____

In life very few of us ever start out with an abundance of resources. Unless our last name happens to be Rockefeller, most of us had to learn how to be faithful with that which is another man's before we ever had anything of our own. (Luke 16:12) Learning how to be a wise manager of resources is one of the most important lessons of life. This is simply how the process of resource allocation on this planet works. We must first be faithful in the very smallest things to gain the right to manage larger ventures. This is what Luke was speaking to when he penned these words: "He who is faithful in what is least is faithful also in much ..." (Luke 16:10a) Someone said, "Fortune is infatuated with the efficient," meaning good fortune and favor just happens to come upon those who are resourceful and efficient down to even the smallest details in life. We can't be derelict in the management of small resources and expect to be given authority to manage large organizations, high finance or enormous real estate projects. It just doesn't work that way.

Obviously, various people face the challenges and problems of life differently. Some look at life and think oh this is awful, so many problems, so many risks and so hard a climb, a whole lot of difficulty this life is sure to be. On the contrary, others think, Wow, what an opportunity! What a great challenge! How exciting to be put to the test. Then they get equipped the best they can, become very resourceful and tackle life with optimism, faith, going at it with all their might!

You see the real challenge in life is whether or not we can take little and make much. Certainly, we can all agree that, relatively speaking, life is short for everyone. Most of us also have limited talent and few resources to work with, so life gives us some very important questions we must answer: Can we manage to take care of ourselves and those we are responsible for? Can we learn to live within our means on less than we make and make ends meet? Can we go out and defeat a heathen hoard of 20,000 coming against us with only an army of 10,000? (Luke 14:31) Can we take something manufactured for one specific use and adapt it creatively to meet the present need? A whole TV series called "McIver" was produced around this idea and became quite popular back in the 80's. McIver was constantly getting into one bind after another as a detective, if I remember correctly. This guy could take a little wire, a strip or two of duct tape, a pocket knife and a pair of pliers and get out of any tight you could think of. He would always come up with some type of gadget or unique plan to save the day—and save the day he did—every time. With a little duct tape, wire and bubble gum he could fix anything from a broken heart to the crack of the break of day.

In life there is a constant need for new inventions because the times and our environment are constantly changing. We've heard it said, "If you can make a better mouse trap, the whole world will beat a path to your door." I always believed that but for about fifty years I thought the little spring loaded trap fastened to a small plank of wood we used to eliminate those little pests was so efficient, cheap and effective that nobody would probably ever improve upon it. Well, I was wrong. There have been several enterprising souls who have greatly improved, manufactured and put new mouse traps on the market just recently and they are selling like wildfire. What else out there needs improvement?

While serving in Vietnam a need arose that just being a little resourceful helped. Our infantry units there moved, carrying out our search and destroy mission, during the day while the enemy, to avoid detection by our reconnaissance aircraft, moved mostly under cover of darkness. Part of our search and destroy mission required that we also conduct a number of night ambushes along what was called the Ho Chi Minh Trail. This was the supply route from North Vietnam for the VC and NVA we were fighting there in the south. The manned ambushes we tried were very inefficient for a lot of reasons. The enemy could pick up on the smell of our G.I's smoking cigarettes (although they weren't to be smoke on an ambush but you know how that works) as well as their mosquito repellant, their coughing, talking, falling asleep and so on. Of course they were supposed to be the perfect soldiers but we didn't get a whole lot of those perfect models, myself included. Besides all the other problems with night ambushed, our men couldn't be expected to stay up all night on ambush and then fight the wait-a-minute vines in the hot jungle and be at their best fight gooks the next day. It occurred to me to take a PRC 10 radio battery, some wire, a spring, some claymore mines and some det (detonation) cord and make what I called an automatic ambush. We always tried to set up our NDP (Night Defensive Position) a short distance from at least one major trail and preferably a trail intersection. That would allow us to deploy about a dozen Claymore mines. These Claymores actually looked just like the old Polaroid cameras with a couple little bipod feet on the bottom to stand them up and aim them at a target. We would use three facing in each directions on a trail. Each automatic ambush system operated independent of the other and required its own battery, tripping device and electrical circuit.

The way it operated was by attaching a wire with a spring on it to a tree or stake on one side of a trail and then running it across the trail to a terminal on another specially rigged stake we drove into the ground for support to keep tension on the trip wire between the two points. When the wire was pulled taught across the trail the grounding point was suspended vertically by the spring in the middle of these two electrodes on this other specially rigged wooden stake. This stake had an electrically connected metal pin about the size of a nail that would pivot between two electrodes attached to the stake. If it touched the electrode on either side, it would complete the circuit sending an electrical charge to the blasting cap in the first Claymore and blow all six simultaneously. Once we had the trail wired and the Claymores all set and daisy chained (connected) together with det cord, we would roll the electrical wire for the circuit back to our NDP and the last thing we did was arm it by connecting the battery. If the bad guys walked through the trip wire, it would, of course, increase the tension on that wire and cause the metal pivot pin to ground out on the electrode on one side of the metal pin completing the circuit and setting off all the claymores. Now if, per chance, the enemy discovered the wire and cut it, the spring would pull that little metal ground pin to the electrode on the other side—completing the circuit to blow the Claymores as well. If they touched it, we had them either way. Each Claymore had about 200 quarter inch ball bearings packed on the inside of the front cover with C-4 explosive behind it and would spray all those ball bearings like they were shot from a cannon. A Claymore would easily mow down everything in its path. At night, except for those on sentinel or radio monitoring duty, we would all be tucked away, sleeping in our pup tents.

Several nights a week after we had gone to sleep, we'd hear a huge, earth shaking blast from one of the automatic ambushes going off and we'd simply go back to sleep. At first light we would send out a patrol to check the ambush, pick up all the weapons and ammunition, check the bodies for intel, and bring back the body count that had to be reported to battalion headquarters. This system allowed our men to get a good night's sleep so they could function at their best during the day. To my knowledge we never had our automatic ambushes compromised. The NVA and VC had very poor communications and they never even knew what hit them. The results were phenomenal. These ambushes were so effective, in fact, our battalion commander got our prototype info. to spread its use across the whole 1st Cavalry Division. Don't have any idea how far they got with that because we were too busy fighting the gooks every day ourselves. Best of all, only the VC and NVA got to have the privilege of giving their lives for their countries in these automatic ambushes and not one of ours were ever even wounded by them..

We have all heard the old axiom that "One man's trash is another man's treasure." So another secret in life is learning how to take what others see as worthless and turn it into something of value. One example of something like this that we can find in every community is old houses. Once they have become obsolete and a little run-down, the owners usually want to get rid of them so something new and useful can be built on the same property. At that point in their decision making process, they also know they are facing large expenses for demolition, removal and dump fees. A resourceful person can use their own labor to tear the building down and save a good deal of the lumber, plumbing fixtures, windows and doors, to build other structures. Young people, of course, have more time and energy than they do money so this system lets them use their time and excess energy to accumulate valuable building materials at very little cost. These ventures need to be well planned out so that you have a secure piece of property to store the material on and a building you are planning to use all the material in the construction of as soon as possible.

My granddad had my brother and I help him tear a building down when I was ten years old. We were getting paid big money back then — 50 cents an hour. My job was mostly pulling nails and hauling lumber. We used that material to build several additions on his own home and stored the rest of the lumber in the back of his feed store in town. He had enough lumber left over to do whatever he wanted for a long time thereafter. I determined with all the insight and wisdom my little ten year old mind could muster at the time that this was surely the hardest, hottest and dirtiest job you could ever find. I still believe I was right about that, by the way. Nobody said it would be easy so since then, I have followed my granddad's stellar example to tear down a number of these old houses and used them to build other buildings debt free — mostly for our church. It is an incredible joy!

Another way to be a bit resourceful and I am certainly not the repository of all wisdom on this subject, is to analyze a job you are about to have an outside company contract to perform. See if you can buy the equipment needed to do the job from a pawn shop or off Craig's List at 1/3 to ½ the cost of new equipment. Then get the material wholesale to do a job yourself or with in-house help that you supervise. If you can do it yourself, most of the time it can be done a whole lot cheaper. Why? Because you don't have to pay the other company's workman's comp. and health insurance, retirement contributions, holidays, truck, office rent and utility expenses, taxes to the I.R.S., profit and a few other small items like this. It would have cost you many times more to have hired it done but when the job is finished, you still own the equipment and will then, sure enough, possess the skill needed to do it again whenever the need arises.

Yet another way to multiply resources is learning to buy wholesale. There are many avenues available to accomplish this but few take advantage of them. If you have ever visited Israel you were probably, as I was, amazed at their ability to buy copper, gold, silver, diamonds, wood, alabaster and a million other things and with their skill, turn it into products. They then sell it right back to those who sold it to them in the first place. The Bible is all about faithfulness and resourcefulness. In every city in America there are wholesale dealers trading in just about every commodity under the sun so think "wholesale." Make friends with dealers. Just an example, there is a Farmers' Markets in every medium to large city in the country selling produce for a lot less than the grocery stores. They sell direct, eliminating the middle man and all the

overhead of the local grocery stores have to build into their prices. You can organize a neighborhood or church coop-group and rotate the duty of going to the market for everybody's produce each week. There can be a standard list of items that each family checks off and either faxes or emails it to the person having the shopping duty each week. Once the items are picked up by the person on duty that week, everyone stops by their house at a certain time on an agreed upon day, gets their produce and pays their bill. A whole lot can be saved on things like cantaloupes, watermelons, tomatoes, potatoes, beans, etc. It is fun, good fellowship and fairly easy to do.

Another area people can save considerably in is learning to buy cars wholesale. Since the average person will buy twelve cars over a lifetime, it is a process one certainly needs to devote a little time to become skilled at. Now if you are married and have four kids, the number of cars purchased shoots up to around 72 cars over a life time. Here are some things to consider. Since cars depreciate about 20% a years just after manufacture, it is best to buy cars that are at least two or three years old. Learning how to buy cars at auction is also a great way to multiply your buying power. Most cities have auto auctions that are open to the public and once you know how to buy through them, you can purchase cars usually at less than 25% of the actual cash value. Many prestige car dealerships like to get rid of their economy car trade-ins so they can sell more high dollar cars. Conversely, most economy car dealers like to "cash-out" of their land yacht trade-ins so they can use their capital to sell more small cars. Remember too, that some cars you find at auctions are, of course, junk so you need to know what to look for and how to check out the cars you are interested in bidding on before the auction starts. Actually, I have written a book on *How to Buy A Used Car* that tells you of the intricacies and trepidations of this process. For over ten years I was the licensed dealer for Cars For Christ ®, a dealership that sold used cars donated to our ministry and did very well. This one little book can save you a lot of money over a lifetime.

Here's just one tip. (Keep this a secret. Don't tell anyone I told you.) You can buy a car with a cloudy paint job or one in need of a small amount of body work that otherwise has a clean interior, a good body design as well as a good engine and running gear for next to nothing. Most people buy cars on the basis of "sparkle and shine" and they certainly don't want to fix someone else's problems. Take this ugly duckling you just bought for next to nothing to a paint shop and for about $300 have a new paint job put on it. A little body work if you need some is, of course, extra. Then you can either sell the car and double or triple your investment or drive it yourself and do it all on a shoe string. Before you attempt to buy a car at auction for the first time, always make it a point to go by just to be an observer to get the "lay of the land." Buy a bag of popcorn and a Coke and just be a spectator, a fly on the wall. Learn how to interpret what that fast-talking auctioneer is saying. Use this time to see what cars are going for in your market area and so on. You will find these auctions are a lot of fun. You never know what you are going to come away with. One time I went to a cattle auction to buy a couple calves and came home with two really good horses.

A number of years ago a salesman came by Cars For Christ and approached our sales manager about buying some advertising time on their mobile billboard trucks. We discussed it and I remembered a huge box truck with a diesel engine we had that had been donated to the ministry. It ran well but, as of that time, we hadn't found a good use for it. I said, "Let's have all the sides lettered with our Cars For Christ logo, suggesting people donate their old cars. Then, instead of paying a fee for only a few hours of ad time a day, we would have 100% of the ad time on our truck and it would be virtually free every time we sent it out to get some cars." It would be, in effect, a traveling billboard. Another good friend here in Atlanta, Ken Breier, who happens to be a terrific artist, made us a really cool Cars For Christ logo free.

Prior to all this, there was an old battery operated fork lift truck donated to the ministry and our research determined that replacing the batteries was more expensive that buying a whole new fork lift. The suggestion, at the time, was to sell it for scrap but I said, "No. Let's get our acetylene torch, cut it up and we will save the steel for something later instead of buying new, expensive steel at that time." We are forever building things. Well, since we decided to rig this truck to pick up donated cars, we figured that we could carry one inside the box truck and another on a tow dolly behind it, thus doubling the efficiency of the whole rig and would still get free advertising at the same time. We took the steel that had been saved from the old fork lift and made the head-ache bar behind the cab so the car we were carrying in the box couldn't break lose if ever there was a crash (worst case scenario) and slam into the driver inside the cab. We also took some of that old steel and made all the chain tie-downs and everything else that was needed. An old winch had been saved off of another donated vehicle was mounted on the back bumper of the box truck so the driver could pull non-running cars onto the tow dolly all by himself. Then we sent a man to a junk yard to find some aluminum to build the loading ramps and, as serendipity would have it, he found a perfect set of used set of fiberglass ramps to drive the running cars up into the box truck. They only wanted $125 for the ramps and they worked like a champ. What a deal! When we had the rig all painted up, and ready to go, I went with our driver on the "maiden voyage" to pick up the first two cars. The whole rig loaded with a car on the tow dolly was about half a city block long and I didn't want our driver to be nervous on his first trip. Well, we got both cars picked up without incident and two other people called about donating cars as a result of the signs on the side of the truck while we were out on the run. God is good and the whole rig cost us next to nothing. Praise the Lord!

What it means to have the character trait of **RESOURCEFULNESS**:

- Seeing value in things others consider refuse or of little worth
- The ability to take little and make much
- The ability to devise ways and means to overcome problems or meet needs in difficult situations
- Capable of surmounting daunting tasks
- The ability to use assets and equipment creatively to meet a need or provide a service
- The ability to take something made for one intended use and adapt it creatively for a present need

ESPECT FOR AUTHORITY & OTHERS — Study start date: ____ Finish date: _____

The other day I noticed a bumper sticker that said, "Challenge authority." In a world full of rebellion that has little respect for anybody or anything, that may seem like a reasonable, trendy approach. However, in God's hierarchal system of order, that kind of attitude will surely cut off one's blessings, extinguish all divine favor and will likely shorten your life.

When we look at nature, we probably won't even see it but God has set up this invisible, hierarchical system of government in the earth. He is the head of all things. the head of Christ and Christ is the head of the church. Furthermore, the man is head of the woman in the home just as Christ is the head of the church. Children, subsequently, are commanded to obey their parents and this is the first commandment with a promise. In so doing, God promises our children that they will enjoy long life. Everywhere we go, we will find someone is in authority. Every home, business and every little league baseball team has someone in charge. If we show them respect and obey their wishes, we will find favor, opportunity and blessings. If we oppose those in leadership, we will find rebuke and, more than likely, disaster in our relationships It is our decision. Whatever you want, it is there awaiting your response. Life is all about relationships. No man is an island unto himself. We do well if we learn to get along with and successfully interact with other people here on earth and especially those in authority. People who have no self-respect and those who have never been taught respect by their parents, usually have the greatest problem with this concept and, therefore, life in general. The Word of God promises us that faithfulness and obedience in the smallest things brings more opportunities and likely even some authority in due time. But you can't have authority unless you respect authority.

Romans 13:1 tells us that "every soul (must) be subject to the governing authorities. For there is no authority except from God, and the authorities that exist are appointed by God." So respecting authority is actually respecting God, His work and design in the earth. It continues, "whoever resists the authority resists the ordinance of God and those who resist will bring judgment on themselves." (v.2) Rulers and those in authority are usually not a problem unless we refuse to obey them. The writer also says they "are not a terror to good works but to evil." They are here to commend, bless and promote those who are obedient and do well. Then Paul said, "Do what is good and you will have the praise of the same. . For (they are) minister(s) to you for good. But if you do evil, be afraid, for (they do) not bear the sword in vain; for (they are) God's ministers … avengers(s) to execute wrath on (those) who practice evil." Make the decision to honor your boss by completing the tasks assigned as unto the Lord. (Colossians 3:23) Write down your assignments so you can't possibly make a mistake or, even worse, forget to do it. Work to make your supervisor's job easier. Think ahead and do things without being asked. Remember, you only have a job because your boss obviously has more than he or she can do. Think about it. If you had ten employees and nine of them consistently made things difficult for you, forgetting to do things occasionally, doing things their way or half way, wouldn't you let them go? On the other hand, if you had an employee who was capable and competent, showed attention to detail, always got the job done with excellence and showed respect for your authority, which one would you promote? Which one would you keep when times get tough and you have to let nine of them go?

We can choose to obey or disobey authority, but there is more than one reason to choose obedience. We should be subject to authority "not only because of wrath but also for conscience' sake." (v.5) It would be bad enough to go from judgment to rebuke, to loss and hardship day after day but there is still something even more important involved. One's conscience is in the balance as well. Without a clear conscience our faith won't operate and we will have no way to accomplish anything or please God because everything in the Kingdom is by faith. It is the only way to please God; not hard work, long hours, or even a Herculean effort will please Him. Only faith that operates by love. Hebrews 11:6

On occasion there may be a time to reject and come against authority. Certainly we are to defer to our leaders as long as what they are asking us to do is not illegal, immoral or unscriptural. Tyranny must be opposed but before attacking, the Bible admonishes us, in these rare circumstances, to seek a multitude of counsel first.

God's hierarchal system of authority on earth also includes having a healthy respect for our peers and fellow occupants as well. It is easy and somewhat natural for people to begin to look at others and judge them by their talents, abilities or even a seeming lack thereof. But, you see, respect isn't something we only give to others because they might have more abilities than we do. Respect is something we owe every human being, regardless of race, sex, creed, color, national origin, abilities or talents. Every person deserves our respect automatically just for being God's creation and being made in His image. They have been set here by His hand to function in cooperation with everyone else in society. It takes every person in the world to accomplish the mystery of God, to make society complete and offer all the services needed. It is prideful to think that we are more important than someone else just because we may have some superior ability, education or training. Whatever gave us the impression that our talent is more important than someone else's just because the world may be willing to pay more for our services for a short time? Every person deserves respect and should be honored. Paul said "… let nothing be done through selfish ambition or conceit but in lowliness of mind, esteem others better than yourselves." (Philippians 2:3) To think that we are better than anyone, our gifts and talents are more important than any other person's that people owe us something because we have achieved a little success here and there, is nothing but pride. We are admonished in scripture to give, what to us may appear to be the less honorable parts of the body, all the more honor.

If we want to succeed in life, the first step is to respect authority and the very next is to honor those who are our coworkers. Help them any way you can, asking for nothing. You see, streams have always received the waters of all the mountains surrounding them for the simple reason that they are below them. They are content to simply be a lowly conduit, serving the countryside in God's cycle of blessing. Because they stay below them, they will soon rain over all the mountains and valleys. So too, it is for the servant with a right spirit.

What it means to have the character trait of **RESPECT FOR AUTHORITY AND OTHERS**:

- Reverence for the person and/or position of others around us in life
- Esteem, credibility and respect afforded one's position or authority
- Deference shown to a superior
- Showing honor and obedience to those who are our leaders

ESPONSIBILITY, THE ABILITY TO ACCEPT — Study start date: _____ Finish date: _____

Many go through life trying their best to escape responsibility. Their hope is to avoid more work and the flack that always comes with doing anything productive out in the world. However, avoiding responsibility is pointless because both God and the world reward people for accepting responsibility, being productive and doing good work. Strange as it might be, there are millions of people who shudder at the thought of taking responsibility for anything, including themselves. They would rather live in a back-alley cardboard condo than get a job and have their own family and a home. Certainly there are those with debilitating mental and physical problems who can't take care of themselves. But for those who do have at least one talent (and everybody does), there is a world of potential totally wasted because of a mental attitude of escape or irresponsibility. It is truly incredible that some people would rather dumpster dive to find food than work, use their faith and, ultimately, eat of the fat of the land. Accepting responsibility and actually packing the lunch always leads to greater and greater positions of responsibility. Ultimately it allows one to have more resources and power to help more and more people. It also allows a person to move into the arena of getting paid to think, manage, direct and be creative instead of simply being charged with completing an assigned task.

You see, if you don't want any responsibility, don't worry—you won't have any. My momma said, "Responsibility comes to those who seek it." And, "Opportunity only knocks once. So you better be ready." The strangest thing, I found out she was right. Those who detest responsibility are certain, in their own minds that they would crumble under the weight of it. They evade it like the plague for many reasons, some real and some imagined. Fear of failure, fear of being criticized, a reluctance to being tied down to a schedule, having to be at work on time and stay not only the whole day but the whole week really bothers some people. To be accountable for the quantity and quality of the work is also a weight far too heavy for some to bear. Being responsible for the work and performance of others is also a problem for some. Leaders and producers in society are also responsible to choose daily between right and wrong, to decide who to hire and who to fire and what to buy or sell. They also make bold decisions about how to guide their enterprise, company, ministry or family into the future. Leaders must know how to navigate out in the world by faith without fear of failure or criticism.

I know I would much rather try and fail than to never try at all. One reason is that I love the thrill of finding new opportunities, taking risks, making decisions, trying things that have never been tried before and building new things. I don't think anyone with the right attitude in life every really fails at those things they give 110% to. I certainly have made my share of mistakes but if something doesn't work out so well the first time, we can go at it again from another angle with better resources and a bit more skill and wisdom acquired from our recent experience. It is a huge mistake to think we have to be right all the time. No one ever is. Certainly we want to plan, seek wise counsel and pray first but if we do make a mistake, admit it, learn from it and use that information to improve yourself and the situation. Life is full of all kind of opportunities and challenges. Every time we face one of these challenges and beat it, we go to the next with more experience, more knowledge and a greater expectation for victory. Accepting responsibility is thrilling. We should never fear failure. We should fear the foolishness and fearfulness of not trying and failing to even get in the game. That's far worse. One day we will have to give account for what we have done with the time and talents God has given us. (Matthew 25:14, Revelation 20:11) More responsibility is readily available to us by simply being faithful in the small things which have already been given to us. Take a look around. The world is full of unfulfilled needs and tasks undone. Find a need in your organization, take the initiative and fill it. What a joy, just to make the world a better place! Sure, you will probably be criticized no matter if it turns out well or otherwise. Critics never amount to much, never build anything and can't stop the positive things we are doing unless we let them.

When God made the heavens and the earth and all it contains, man was His final accomplishment, highest achievement and the crowning glory of all His creation. Being gracious, He even made man in His own image and gave him dominion over the whole earth. He created male and female, blessed them and commanded them to be fruitful, multiply, to fill the earth and subdue it. In a word, God gave man dominion. He certainly wouldn't have made this wonderful world and then leave it forsaken. It is man's to keep, rule, enjoy and be responsible for. having dominion over all the fish of the sea, the birds in the air, the cattle, every creeping thing, every fish in the sea and living thing that moves on the earth. We know He does all things well but this has never been more true than in creation. It is well because upon completion, He saw everything He had made and said "Indeed it was very good." (Genesis 1:31) Now if everyone on the planet was a shirker, think for a moment what the world would look like. This whole place would immediately be overrun with weeds, thorns, thistles, wild animals and thieves. Obviously, by the commandment of God, somebody has to step up on the wings of time and take charge. Someone has to accept responsibility, keep order, direct events and make things happen or nothing would ever get done.

Just to take up space and live on this planet, requires that we each accept at least, a modicum of responsibility. We are each accountable for the proper maintenance of our bodies and minds as well as giving God the maximum return on our time and talents while here. Beyond this, we are responsible for our every thought, word, action, attitude and secret motive. Once we have learned to manage ourselves fairly effectively, then we may be able to produce a family and fill the earth. Someone, specifically the father, is responsible for the whole family's protection, provision and training. What a joy and high honor it is to be blessed by God with a family. Before God one day, fathers will all give an account. For those who have accepted responsibility, experienced God's grace and know of His abundant help and mercy, it will be a great joy. For others who have squandered their time, talents and their opportunities in life, aside from missing out on seeing the bounty their labor, experiencing God's blessing and knowing the thrill of battle, the day of recompense will not be pretty.

The responsibility of privilege is another facet of this trait that we must consider. Those of us who have been blessed with sound bodies, minds and spirits along with a revelation, to some degree, of God's will, are truly blessed in this life. About this subject, Jesus said, "to whomsoever much is given, of him shall be much required: and to whom men have committed much, of him they will ask the more." (Luke 12:48) Speaking here to those who have much, the opportunities to help, bless and serve others will increase geometrically. To know to do good, to have the ability to do good and have the assets to do good and then not do it is a huge mistake. This is the responsibility of privilege. In America, compared to third world countries, all but the absolute poorest in this great country are rich and, therefore, able by comparison. For this privilege we will, one day, give account. Those who have been given much should be able to see the sorrow, lack and hardship others face and delight to relieve some of their misery in any way possible, giving the glory to God.

What it means to have the character trait of **THE ABILITY TO ACCEPT RESPONSIBILITY**

- The trust, fiduciary liability and accountability that accompanies a position of authority
- Duties, services and acts required by a job or the leader of a group
- Accepting the liability of being called to answer for an army, enterprise, political office or company
- Trustworthiness
- Reliability

- Accountability
- Resolve
- The willingness and capacity to be responsible
- Agreeing to be reliable, faithful, trustworthy and accountable
- The willingness to be accountable for the performance of others, your company and yourself
- Accepting physical, legal, moral, mental and/or spiritual accountability for others
- Gladly taking the heat for our own actions, inactions and mistakes as well as the mistakes of your subordinates

ESULTS ORIENTED / See MISSION ORIENTED

EVERENCE—   **Study start date:** _____ **Finish date:** _____

O nce, many years ago when I was in the commercial real estate business in Atlanta, I met a man who held a startling belief. He told me "The only way anyone could make it in business was to cheat." That was his belief and it would have been a grand waste of time for me to try to change it. However, after being in business myself for a number of years, I can tell you that I have been privileged to know and work with hundreds of honorable men and women who succeeded in their chosen fields and dishonesty, quite frankly, was something I never saw in them. They were honorable in all their dealings. Just as Paul told Titus, "To the pure all things are pure ..." They, out of a pure heart look for the best, expect the best and see the best in others. "But to those who are defiled and unbelieving nothing is pure; ... even their mind and conscience is defiled." (Titus 1:15) They have no self-respect so how could they possibly have respect or reverence for anything or anyone else around them.

True enough, over a lifetime, I have had the pleasure of rubbing shoulders with a vast array of people. From other ditch diggers on a pipe line in Texas, to men incarcerated when I was preaching in the jails and prisons for thirty years, construction workers in Canada, officers and enlisted men in the Army, every kind of person imaginable in the real estate business as well as all kinds of people as a pastor. Some people simply do not have any respect for anyone or anything but, thank God for one thing. At least they don't constitute the majority just yet. Those who haven't learned to respect anything or anybody in life will never have anything, do anything or make anything of themselves. There may be an occasional exception to this rule but even in those cases, their counterfeit success will be short-lived and their end is usually tragic.

According to Webster, the word 'revere' comes from the Latin: *reveri* which means to fear or respect, regarding as worthy of great honor. The word "respect" comes from the Latin: *respectus* which means looking back, to regard our previous estimate of something as having established value or worth. To revere.

There are several people, things, institutions and offices we are specifically commanded to respect and reverence:

God—Ethan, the Ezrahite, told us, "God is greatly to be feared in the assembly of the saints, and to be held in reverence by all those around Him." (Psalm 89:7) "Since we (have received) a kingdom which cannot be shaken," the writer of Hebrews said, "let us have grace, by which we may serve God acceptably with reverence and godly fear." (Hebrews 12:28) For "He sent redemption to His people; He has commanded His covenant forever: Holy and awesome is His name." Psalm 111:9

God's Sanctuary—The Lord, Himself, spoke to Moses saying, "You shall keep My Sabbaths and reverence My sanctuary: I am the Lord." Leviticus 19:30

Christ—In the parable of the wicked vinedressers, the landowner, who was a representation of God, sent several delegations to collect his portion of the fruit as rent. They were all disrespected, beaten, stoned and one was killed. Finally he sent His own son saying, "They will surely respect my son." (Matthew 21:37) However, they didn't, and in fact, killed Him too.

Parents—The fifth Commandment with promise says, "Honor your father and your mother, that your days may be long upon the land which the Lord your God is giving you." (Exodus 20:12) "We have had human fathers who corrected us, and we paid them respect" and so we should. Hebrews 12:9

Husbands—Paul said, "let the wife see that she respects her husband." Ephesians 5:33

Wives—Paul also told the church at Ephesis the importance of husbands loving their wives and to love her "as himself." That done properly must include respect.

Husbands—He went on to say, "Wives need to be loved and cherished but the husband needs respect.
Our leaders—We must also be careful to respect and "Obey those who rule over you and be submissive, for they watch out for your soul, as those who must give account. Let them do so with joy and not with grief, for that would be unprofitable for you." (Hebrews 13:17) Some leaders will be difficult to respect. In the Last Days we know there will be some who will "call evil good and good evil." In these rare cases the office they hold should be respected but we should never, ever condone sin. Tyranny, however, must be revolted against.
Our fellow man—We can't function correctly, succeed or fit correctly in to society unless we have a great deal of respect for our fellow man. Regardless of how many claim to be a self-made man, there is no such thing. We all had first grade teachers, someone taught us the shapes, colors & multiplication tables. Someone helped us by giving us our first job, etc. And few jobs are there where we can accomplish our part without the willing cooperation and assistance of others working with us. We will never have meaningful relationships with people until we do what Paul recommended in Philippians 2:3. He said to "consider others better than yourselves." Everyone, no matter, who they are, has gifts and talents. Their talents are just as needed in society as ours. They all know something we don't know, have been places we haven't been and can do something better than we can, so we need to respect them.
The lowly—God, Himself, sets the example here dealing with the likes of you and me and by inspiration, the Psalmist penned these words: "Though the Lord is on high, yet He regards the lowly ..." (Psalm 138:6) He also said to, "Be of the same mind toward one another." In other words, don't be a respecter of persons; treat all men equally. Be careful not to "set your mind on high things, but associate with the humble." Romans 12:16

There are some, of course, we are specifically told not to show favoritism or partiality to: those who come into our assembly with gold rings and fine clothing. (James 2:2, 3 & 9) And, "Blessed is the man who makes the Lord his trust and does not respect the proud ..." Psalm 40:4

It is sad but there are those who have no respect for anyone or anything in society today. Their pitiful attitude will, however, soon be their own just reward because, we must respect authority to ever have authority. All authority in the Kingdom is given and not taken. This is in exact accord with the Law of the Kingdom which says, "For whoever has (respects, appreciates and cherishes what he has), to him more will be given, and he will have abundance, but whoever does not have, even what he has will be taken away from him." Matthew 13:12

A good place to begin showing reverence in life is, of course, to the Lord, Himself. In this regard, the Psalmist said, "Make a joyful shout to the Lord, all ye lands: Serve the Lord with gladness; come before His presence with singing. Know that the Lord, He is good; it is He who has made us and not we ourselves; We are His people and the sheep of His pasture. Enter into His gates with thanksgiving and into His courts with praise. Be thankful to Him and bless His name. For the Lord is good; His mercy is everlasting and His truth endures to all generations." (Psalm 100:1–5) Next, with the Lord's help, we need to show reverence to our parents and elders.

What it means to have the character trait of **REVERENCE**:

- Deep respect for those in authority
- Veneration
- High esteem
- To hold in awe
- Respect for authority
- Paying respect to someone who is distinguished

- To adore
- Honor for others, institutions, those in authority and God
- The very state of being reverent
- Having genuine respect for police, soldiers, government officials and ministers
- Holding our elders and parents in high esteem

RIGHT SPIRIT, A —   **Study start date: _____ Finish date: _____**

Every government, company, religion and person has a spirit guiding them and we know that the prince of the power of the air owns everything on this earth outside of what has been dedicated to God. The governments of this world, the major corporations, the power generating companies and the armies of this world are not under the power and control of God. (Although He can always over-rule them at any time.) They operate by the rules of the prince of this world, contrary many times for sure to the Word of God. It is really not difficult to tell under whose control an entity might be. Jesus said, "If you love me, keep my commandments." (John 14:15) Oftentimes Christians are challenged to work for these entities and let their lights shine. We Christians are not of this world and it was not His prayer that we be taken out of the world but as the Father sent Him into the world, so He has also sent us saying, " … for their sakes I sanctify Myself, that they also may be sanctified by the truth." (John 17:19) Since He is the Truth, Paul said we, as believers, are to be "filled with the fruits of righteousness, which are by Jesus Christ, to the glory and praise of God." Philippians 1:11

Those who are saved and filled with the Holy Spirit (Acts 1:8) have something very unique about them. More than unique, it is power and a right spirit. They walk in God's righteousness, have a pure heart and have something you can see, His glory, shining on their faces. Are they always perfect? No, only Jesus is. But we know, "The statutes of the Lord are right, rejoicing the heart; (and) the commandment of the Lord is pure, enlightening the eyes." (Psalm 19:8) Their eyes are lights and their forehead is marked with peace. They have godliness and contentment and cannot be moved by the vicissitudes of the world system. (I Timothy 6:6) Their thoughts tend only to righteousness (Proverbs 12:5) and their conduct is pure and right. (Proverbs 21:8) They speak only the truth, walk in the armor of light (Ephesians 5:8) and we know God, Himself, "(leads) them forth by the right way." (Psalm 107:7) Those with a right spirit are not under their own power any longer but are moved by God's Law (Psalm 19:8), God's Word (Psalm 33:4), God's Way (Psalm 107:7) and the Holy Spirit. John 16:13

They also obey God no matter what the cost as did Peter and his companions, when commanded by a whole assembly of rulers and elders neither to speak nor teach in the name of Jesus ever again. This occurred immediately following the healing of the lame man at the gate called beautiful and him preaching the resurrection to the five thousand. Peter's response was, "Whether it is right in the sight of God to listen to you more than to God, you judge. For we cannot but speak the things which we have seen and heard." (Acts 4:19, 20) After they threatened Peter and the others further, amazingly, they let them go. Being let go, they went to the other disciples and gave them a report of all that the chief priests and elders had commanded them to do. When they heard it, they all raised their voices in prayer to God saying, "You are God, who made heaven and earth and the sea, and all that is in them, who by the mouth of Your servant David have said: 'Why did the nations rage, and the people plot vain things? The kings of the earth took their stand and the rulers were gathered together against the Lord and against His Christ.' For truly against Your holy Servant Jesus, whom You anointed, both Herod and Pontius Pilate, with the Gentiles and the people of Israel, were gathered together to do whatever Your hand and Your purpose determined before to be done. Now, Lord, look on their threats, and grant to Your servants that with all boldness they may speak Your word, by stretching out Your hand to heal, and that signs and wonders may be done through the name of Your holy Servant Jesus." (Acts 4:24–30) When they had prayed, the ground where they had assembled was shaken; they were filled afresh with the Holy Spirit and began to speak the word of God with boldness.

On another occasion while in Philippi, as Paul and Silas were praying, a slave girl who was possessed with a spirit of divination met with them. Her ability as a fortune-teller had brought her masters no small profit. By her ambiguous answers, she was able to confuse those using her services, making them think she was able to somehow meet their need to know the future. After this time of prayer, being actuated by an evil spirit, she continued to follow Paul and the group, crying out continually, "These men are the servants of the Most High God, who proclaim to us the way of salvation." (Acts 16:17) Ostensibly, her commendations might seem to the casual, momentary observer to be laudatory and even gracious. However, this kind of promotion was not sought, wanted or needed by men of God, since they got their praise and approval from God alone. She did this for many days until Paul got so annoyed he turned and commanded the spirit in the name of Jesus Christ to come out of her and at that very moment it did. However, when her owners found out that their hope for making money with her was now gone, they laid hands on Paul and Silas and brought them before the authorities in the marketplace. As is true most of the time in life, no good deed, even here, went unpunished.

These greedy opportunists then told the magistrates that Paul and Silas were Jews and were causing the city to be greatly troubled, teaching the Romans customs (actually a religion) which it was, according to them, not lawful for them as Romans to practice. When the crowd there rose up against these men of God, the magistrates tore their clothes and commanded that they be beaten with rods. After receiving many stripes, they were thrown into the inner prison and placed in stocks where escape was thought to be impossible. However, at midnight Paul and Silas were singing and praising God for the good fortune of being persecuted for the Name. Suddenly an earthquake shook the foundation of the prison so much that all the prison doors were opened and their chains were loosed. The head jailer, having drawn his sword, was about to kill himself for the loss of all his prisoners until Paul got to him. Trembling, the jailer asked what he must do to be saved and they said, "Believe on the Lord Jesus Christ, and you will be saved, you and your household." (Acts 16:31) Thereupon, they spoke the word of the Lord to them and all who were there were saved. Immediately, he and his whole family were baptized. They were fed when they went to the jailer's house and there was great rejoicing there as well. Paul, refusing to leave under cover of secrecy, stayed on in town. When morning came, amazingly, the magistrates sent word to let them go. However, he refused, being beaten as uncondemned Romans, preferring rather that they come and make them depart. When they heard they were Romans, the magistrates came pleading with them to go from the city. Then they went to the home of Lydia and after encouraging the brethren, they left the city.

Possessing a right spirit is the gift of God and cannot be obtained by any other means. On one occasion, having heard that the apostles had been to Samaria where the people had just received the word of God, Peter and John were sent to them to share the Holy Spirit baptism. A man called Simon the Sorcerer, being there and hearing of all the miracles the disciples were doing by the Spirit's power and believing he could profit from it, came offering to buy it. But Peter replied, "Your money perish with you, because you thought that the gift of God could be purchased with money! You have neither part nor portion in this matter, for your heart is not right in the sight of God. Repent therefore of this your wickedness, and pray God if perhaps the thought of your heart may be forgiven you. For I see that you are poisoned by bitterness and bound by iniquity. ." (Acts 8:20–23) At this, Simon asked that they pray that the Lord would forgive him and that none of these things would come upon him.

Jesus said in John 15:1 that He is the true vine and His Father is the vinedresser. He said it was imperative that every one of us be connected and committed to Him as a branch is connected by the resurrection power of the Holy Spirit to the true vine. This is so that we can bear much fruit. He also said, if we keep his commandments we will stay connected to Him. But, every branch that does not bear fruit would be good for nothing but to be cut off, bundled up and cast into the fire. But, if we abide in Him and His words abide in us, we will then be able to ask whatever we want according to His will and it will be done for us. "By this My Father is glorified that you bear much fruit; so you will (prove to) be my disciples." (John 15:8) A right spirit always produce much fruit.

What it means to have the character trait of **A RIGHT SPIRIT**:

- The Spirit of the Living God
- The Spirit of meekness, cooperation, truth, discernment, love, peace and joy
- The Holy Spirit
- The Salvation of the Lord

ECURITY, AN OVERWHELMING SENSE OF— Study start date: ____Finish date: ____

One of the greatest basic needs of the human heart is security: freedom from worry about what we did yesterday, losing what we have today or agonizing over where we will be and what might happen tomorrow. The fear of loss is paramount among men out in the world. So many things out there promise security but, in the final analysis, they will leave you woefully lacking. People are failing all around us in their professional, personal or family lives. What then, can a person build on? Where is the rock that can't be moved? Sometimes twenty, thirty, forty or fifty years of a person's life can be lost in a moment. Sometimes thousands and millions of dollars in investments, as well as all a person's toil and sweat is too much to lose in, seemingly, one fell swoop. No matter how smart, strong, rich, famous or how high up a person might be born in nobility, no one is protected from trouble on this planet. We all have need of security and a way to build our lives that will stand the test of time, trials, temptations and trouble.

A few weeks ago there was a front-page article in the Atlanta Journal-Constitution about the horrendous tornado that visited our little town, Conyers, exactly forty years ago. The article had a huge picture of a home that was located on Smyrna Road. It filled the top half of the front page from side to side. What made this enormous picture so striking was that the frame and foundation of this house were totally missing. It was a picture of a vacant lot except for a set of brick steps and the front porch stoop of the former home. The tornado picked up that enormous house and totally blew it all away. Thank God, for some reason, in His infinite mercy, the tornado sucked the entire family out of the home first and then blew it to pieces. Incredibly, all of them lived through the ordeal although many others in the same subdivision were not as fortunate. Then last week another tornado came to this area and struck a small town about twenty miles away. Eight more homes were completely destroyed. This proved, once again, the destructive power of tornados, however, they are but one of many insidious tools the enemy uses to destroy the lives of men and women on earth. There are so many more just as effective: embezzlement in business, drug addiction, slothfulness, false official statements, sickness, disease, accidents of all kinds, marital infidelity, hurricanes, tsunamis and a thousand other things. Any one of these has the capacity to destroy the whole life's work of a person momentarily.

God never promised we would be free from trouble. In fact, quite the opposite, He promised trouble was on the way. Every house (and a house is a life in the Bible), He promised will be tried by fire to see of what sort it is. (I Corinthians 3:13) Having built in my own life for thirty-two years at one point, and seeing what some might say was significant success out in the world, I saw it all blown away in an instant by an unfaithful marital partner. At the time, I couldn't believe it could happen but it did. The way it happened was a miracle because it allowed me to not only see but experience the transcendent glory of God. He showed me that the worst things in life only seem that way. They will, if we will be patient walking by faith and let God have His way, in the end, become the best things that ever happened to us. Losing a family, a son temporarily, the home I had built and even my job, was certainly enough for me to question the way I had been building. Great was the fall of my house. My decision, at the time, was to throw everything I knew about building and finding success in the trash and let God teach me His ways alone. You see, I had done some things my way and some God's way but the time for that foolishness had come to an abrupt, albeit, costly end. At the same time, I also had a divine encounter with God in my car while driving down the road. We discussed these things and I asked Him to save my soul. Oh, I already believed in God, Jesus, the Holy Spirit and the Bible. However, unknowingly, I had not yet been born again and Jesus was definitely not the Lord of my life. Everything changed that very day. I found peace and a new way to live, wori and build.

We find this new but ancient way of building given to us by the Master recorded in Matthew 7:24: "…whoever hears these sayings of Mine, and does them, I will liken him to a wise man who built his house on the rock and the rains descended, the floods came, and the winds blew and beat on that house; and it did not fall, for it was founded on the rock. But everyone who hears these sayings of Mine and does not do them, will be like a foolish man who built his house on the sand: and the rain descended, the floods came, and the winds blew and beat on that house; and it fell. And great was its fall." If we are wise, and build our lives on the rock of His Word, whatever we do will prevail and stand the test of time and tribulation. The Word of God and the love of Christ it speaks of are the only sure foundation for our life, love and practice.

This new way to build won't just jump on you, be at your fingertips and occupy all your thoughts overnight. It takes time, work and sweat to dig for it as a miner digs for precious metals in the earth. To those who are willing to take the time and pay the price, God gives many promises of supernatural security. In Joshua 1:3, at the death of Moses, God made these promises to Joshua, his aide: "Every place that the sole of your foot will tread upon I have given you." And in verse 5 He said, "No man shall be able to stand before you all the days of your life; as I was with Moses, so I will be with you, I will not leave you nor forsake you." Since God is not a respecter of persons, everything He promised to Joshua, He will do for any of us. Three times in the following few verses, He commanded him to be strong and courageous. The way He said that could be done was to "observe to do according to all the law which Moses (His) servant commanded you; do not turn from it to the right hand or to the left, that you may prosper wherever you go. This book of the Law shall not depart from your mouth, but you shall meditate in it day and night that you may observe to do according to all that is written in it. For then you will make your way prosperous and then you will have good success." Not only that but He also promised he would have no need to ever "be afraid or be dismayed for the Lord your God (will be) with you wherever you go." (v.9) What more could anyone ask?

In the New Testament, Paul warned us of the importance of this saying, "According to the grace of God which was given to me, as a wise master builder I have laid the foundation, and another builds on it. But let each one take heed how he builds on it. For no other foundation can anyone lay than that which is laid, which is Jesus Christ. Now if anyone builds on this foundation with gold, silver, precious stones, wood, hay or straw, each one's work will become clear; for the Day will declare it, because it will be revealed by fire; and the fire will test each one's work, of what sort it is." (I Corinthians 3:10–13) If we build with the world's cheapest materials: wood, hay and stray, the fires of life will quickly kindle against it and it will be up in smoke momentarily. If we take the time and pay the price to dig deep for the costly spiritual gold, silver and precious jewels, the same fires will try to kindle against it but it will not and cannot burn. And, "If anyone's work which he has built on it endures, he will receive a reward. If anyone's work is burned (who has accepted the blood of Christ and become a new creation), he will suffer loss; but he himself will be saved, yet so as through fire."

Regardless of what is going on around us, as believers, we can know that our life, our breath and all our ways are in God's hands. (Daniel 5:23) Even in combat, the Bible promises that "A thousand may fall at your side and ten thousand at your right hand; but it shall not come near you." (Psalm 91:7) We need to learn to be content in Him, as Paul was who said, "I know how to be abased, and I know how to abound. Everywhere and in all things I have learned both to be full and to be hungry, both to abound and to suffer need." But through it all, he still had the victory saying, "I can do all things through Christ who strengthens me." (Philippians 4:12, 13) In Him we are secure. The Master, in His infinite wisdom, gave us all freedom of choice. How we chose to build is our decision.

What it means to have the character trait of **SECURITY**:

- The state of being protected and secure
- Freedom from fear, intimidation, want or deprivation
- Guarded against loss

SELF-CONTROL —   **Study start date: _____ Finish date: _____**

In life God gave us a free will. We can either take the high road, choosing to walk after the Spirit or take the broad path, the low road, and live controlled by the lusts of the flesh—which, of course, will never be satisfied. Each choice is the gateway to a path that leads somewhere. One leads to excess, addiction, altercations, corruption, lasciviousness and sometimes prison but sooner or later always to death. The other to contentment, dominion, health, happiness, wealth, security and eternal life.

In Proverbs 25:29 we find this admonition: "Whoever has no rule over his own spirit is like a city broken down, without walls." Only a fool in a confrontation shows his annoyance and anger at once. On the other hand Solomon gave us an interesting insight into human nature with these words: "He who is slow to anger is better than the mighty, and he who rules his spirit than he who takes a city." (Proverbs 16:32) As valuable as an excellent general is in wartime (one who can take a city) of considerably greater worth is a man who has self-control. One able to take a city is practiced only in unleashing his basic self-preservation instincts to pound the enemy with every available military asset, from as many flanks as possible and that from land, sea and air if those assets happen to be available. On the contrary, a man who can control his spirit has the ability to reign in these baser propensities, hold his peace in difficult circumstances, remain calm in battle and endure provocation for the benefit of all concerned. The latter is a much more difficult prospect and a rare find among men, as I am sure we will all agree. This man will likely be capable of building consensus among angry people, de-escalating conflict between warring parties, allaying the fears of his neighbors, co-workers and employees, resolving thorny issues and making life-long friends out of enemies. Sure, we all get annoyed by the foolish fits of anger and asinine displays of stupidity we encounter on almost a daily basis but an old Chinese sage once said wisdom is to "always allow the other person to save face." (If at all possible.) Why? Because words are powerful and it is hard to make a friend out of someone when you have already cut his head verbally and handed it to him by exposing his folly.

We live in a world where most people are truly, totally out of control, constantly bursting into anger and raising their voice. They have no boundaries in their lives, no patience and just about anything will cause them to explode out of control. However, to manage anything of importance out in the world, we must first be able to manage ourselves. But, before we can manage our own bodies and lives, we must first be able to manage our thoughts because thoughts control everything we do. Thoughts breed emotions, emotions breed actions, actions repeated become our personality and our personality continued for a period of time becomes our character.

Life is just simply an A or B choice test and it is not something new. It was given to us by God, Himself, about three thousand years ago. Not only were these two choices brought to us but we have also been told, with assurance, where each of these two choices will lead. In Deuteronomy 30:15 God said: "I have set before you today life and good, death and evil, in that I command you today to love the Lord your God, to walk in His ways, and to keep His commandments, His statutes, and His judgments, that you may live and multiply; and the Lord your God will bless you in the land which you go to possess." That choice most assuredly brings long life, prosperity, the multiplication of our progeny and blessings in the land we will come to possess.

On the alternative, he said, " … if your heart turns away so that you do not hear, and are drawn away, and worship other gods and serve them, I announce to you today that you shall surely perish; you shall not prolong your days in the land which you … possess." (Deuteronomy 30:17, 18) This is certainly not the most delightful prospect I have ever heard. Now that we have these choices clearly laid out before us, He then, being the gracious benefactor that He is, and after giving us such a simple test, even gives us the right answer. He says, "Choose life, that both you and your descendants may live; that you may love the Lord your God, that you may obey His voice, and that you may cling to Him …" (v.19) All this for a very good reason: "for **He is your life** and the length of your days; and that you may dwell in the land which the Lord …" (v.20) has given you. Just so we don't get our eyes off of the ball and think that our life might consist of things like houses, lands, wives (or husbands), children, money in the bank, prestige, etc., He reminds us that simply knowing, loving and serving Him is life that is truly life. Living a life with power and self-control is far more real and valuable than anything man might dream up.

Self–control is certainly important not only in the area of making right personal choices but also in the arena of human relations. Happily we don't occupy this planet alone. It is a blessing to have other earthlings with which to share it but this also brings in another whole set of problems: human relations challenges. Self-control is the ability to set aside those things we know irritate those around us or cause them to stumble when we know they are not essential to our life, ministry or existence. It is the ability to hold one's peace in a heated exchange, knowing that hot words rarely result in good judgment and a positive result. Self-control is the ability to sometimes silently count to ten when irritated by the actions or words of an opponent, to give ourselves more time to cool off, think and take control of our emotions before responding. It is always saying less than we think. Self-control is the ability to respond to others in a different spirit than the one they are displaying coming at us. They may charge you in a rage of anger but you respond totally differently. Solomon in all his wisdom said, "a gentle tongue breaks a bone" (Proverbs 25:15) and "a soft answer turns away wrath." Proverbs 15:1

Certainly one of the most difficult areas, and there are many areas a person must master, is that of reigning in one's finances. Some people spend all they make before they even get a pay check and others spend more than they will make thirty years or more into the future. They reside in a daily deplorable state of lack and financial ruin —constantly chased by their creditors, they are the proud recipients of one cut-off notice after another, as well as many visits in the night by the "take-back-man." Having self-control in one's finances means always spending less than you make, paying the Lord His tithe first and then saving 10% for future capital requirements (so you can take advantage of the opportunities of life that God sends your way for being faithful to Him). Remember, just one small blessing of God's favor in a person's life can wipe out years of poverty and financial mismanagement.

Another area that requires great self-control is in our relations with the opposite sex. Indiscriminate relations with multiple sex partners (as we see happening out in the world today) can and surely will bring severe long-term consequences in the area of unwanted pregnancies, the contraction of sexually transmitted diseases, horrendous child support payments as well as broken lives and relationships. God gave us sex for a blessing. It was created to be pleasurable and habit forming but for the purpose of producing progeny and keeping a marriage together. It is only to be enjoyed in the state of holy matrimony. To protect ourselves, as men, in this area, we find there are several things we can do to avoid falling into temptation. First, we must realize that we are all human and will always be highly susceptible to temptation. The Bible warns us to "let him who thinks he stands take heed lest he fall." (I Corinthians 10:12) For those of us who haven't yet fallen to temptation as married men or women, we need to realize that we only stand by the grace of God. We haven't yet been tried by the devil's best or haven't been put in a hopeless state of mind in our marriage to be tempted to the max in this area. Among other things, we probably haven't been in a place, geographically, where the enemy could easily tempt us yet. We had better take all the precautions and protections God has given us. Here are some choices we might consider to keep us out of deadly trouble in this area:

1. Make a decision to "touch not the unclean thing." (II Corinthians 6:17) What would you miss out on in life if you refused to touch anything like drugs, pornographic magazines, or someone else's wife, etc.?
2. Make a covenant with your eyes as Job did "not to look lustfully upon a maid." (Job 31:1) This is exactly what sunk King David's boat with Bathsheba to wreak total havoc in his life, even though he had a heart after God.
3. Make the decision as King David did not to set any wicked thing before your eyes. (Ps 101:3) This would include certain things on TV, internet, movies, magazine, DVD's and CD's, etc. Again, what good things would this simple decision cause you to miss out on in life? Answer again: Not one thing.

Another area just about all of us can do better in is our eating habits. Self-control is the ability to eat the right things and stop eating before we are full.

What it means to have the character trait of **SELF-CONTROL:**

- Remaining calm in battle when the world is exploding all around you
- Letting the Spirit and the Word rule over our flesh about drink, drugs, porn, illicit sex and smoking
- Internal restraint one can exercise over their emotions, appetites, impulses and desires
- The determination and grace to walk in the Spirit and not according to the flesh
- The ability to do what we know we should and not what our base desires demand
- The grace to not only forgive but to also return good for evil

SELFLESSNESS— **Study start date:** _____ **Finish date:** _____

Today we have the me-first generation. Many today are all about I, me, my nobody else. They want to know what's in it for me? The only problem is they say, "A man who lives only for himself runs a very small business" and if we don't learn to master selfishness, it will soon defeat us.

Putting others ahead of ourselves is rare indeed, in today's society. A good example of this was an inmate on the front row at the jail service where I was preaching last night. He reached for the last free Bible in the carton but when he realized that he and two others all wanted it at the same time, he took it and in one motion turned and handed it to one of the others who also wanted it behind him. Everyone in the service was watching what was transpiring in front of them. This kind of selflessness is so rare in their environment that a huge round of applause immediately broke out for him. He was tested in this area and he passed the test. More than the public approval, the greatest joy was his for being selfless and kind.

Few people realize that with God as our Master, there is no need to worry about getting what we need. Notwithstanding a world full of robbery, stealing, embezzlement and greed, all that is required is to serve the Lord and put Him first. Just by doing this one thing, we won't ever need to fret, ever again, about food and clothing. Christ told us specifically not "to worry about what you will eat or what you will drink; nor about your body, what you will put on." Then He said, "Look at the birds of the air for they neither sow nor reap nor gather into barns; yet your heavenly Father feeds them. Are you not of more value than they?" (Matthew 7:25, 26) God knows we need these things. He said to, "Seek first the kingdom of God and His righteousness, and all these things shall be added to you." (Matthew 6:33) What things? All the things the Gentiles seek after: houses, lands, wives, husbands, children finances, clothes, etc. "For the grace of God that brings salvation has appeared to all men, teaching us that, denying ungodliness and worldly lusts, we should live soberly, righteously, and godly in (this) present age …" (Titus 2:11, 12) We just commit our way to the Lord and he adds the grace to follow and please Him. King David said, "I have been young, and now am old; yet I have not seen the righteous forsaken, nor his seed begging for bread." (Psalm 37:25) God takes good care of His own if we will seek Him and take care of His interests; He will take care of our interests.

In Romans 12:1 the Apostle Paul said, "I beseech you therefore brethren, by the mercies of God, that you present your bodies a living sacrifice, holy, acceptable to God, which is your reasonable service." Not something extra or special, just what is reasonably our duty. If we put ourselves first, we will never have enough in this life because the world just will not satisfy. If we put God and others first, and delight in serving them, we receive all we need. It is a great mystery. Peter told the Lord one day that he had left all to follow Him. Jesus replied, "Assuredly, I say to you, there is no one who has left house or parents or brothers or wife or children, for the sake of the kingdom of God, who shall not receive many times more in this present time, and in the age to come eternal life." (Luke 18:29, 30) This kind of living is rewarded by God, Himself.

An example of a great acts of selflessness in the Bible was demonstrated during one of the most severe famines that has ever occurred in the world. It happened in the days of Joseph and is recorded in the Book of Genesis. Joseph had already been sold as a slave and sent to Egypt by his brothers many years earlier. Hearing of food in Egypt, his father, Jacob, thinking Joseph had died many years before, sent his brothers to buy grain from the Egyptians. The brothers had all but forgotten about their younger brother and the last thing they expected was for him to be the Prime Minister of a foreign country.

Unknowingly his brothers came before Joseph to make their purchase. Testing his brothers and seeking an opportunity to reveal himself, Joseph had his own, silver cup planted in sack of grain Benjamin was to take back to his father's house in Canaan. When the cup was discovered in Benjamin's sack, the penalty was that person, the supposed thief, would become Joseph's slave and stay in Egypt for the rest of his life. But, then Judah interceded for Benjamin telling Joseph how dear he and another brother they thought had already died (being Joseph, himself) were to their father and that the loss of this, the younger brother, would be too much for their father to bear. So he pleaded with Joseph to let him take Benjamin's place and remain there as a slave. Because of this, Joseph could no longer restrain himself. He commanded that all his Egyptian advisors and guards leave the room so that no one remained but Joseph and his brothers. Weeping aloud, he made himself known saying, "I am Joseph; does my father still live?"

Joseph and his coat of many colors

(Genesis 45:3) His brothers were so startled at this, remembering their guilt of nearly killing him and then selling him as a slave years earlier, were so afraid they could not answer. Joseph then forgave them and told them not to grieve because of what they had done to him. It was God, he said, who caused them to sell him so that he could be sent there to Egypt before them to preserve life.

In Ephesus, the Apostle Paul he called the elders together to exhort them to the challenging task that lay before them. He reminded them that he had served the Lord with humility and tears, having endured many trials because of the Jews. He also reminded them that he had never compromised the Gospel. He said, "I kept back nothing that was helpful, but proclaimed it to you and taught you publicly and from house to house, testifying to the Jews and also to Greeks, repentance toward God and faith toward our Lord Jesus Christ. And, see, now I go bound in the spirit to Jerusalem, not knowing the things that will happen to me there, except that the Holy Spirit testifies in every city, saying that chains and tribulation await me. But none of these things move me; nor do I count my life dear to myself, so that I may finish my race with joy and the ministry which I received from the Lord Jesus, to testify of the gospel of the grace of God. And indeed, now I know that you all, among whom I have gone preaching the kingdom of God, will see my face no more." (Acts 20:21–25) He, like Christ and all the other apostles (except John) laid down his life for the Gospel. And, we know there is no greater love than this, that a man lay down his life for his friends. John 15:13

What it means to have the character trait of **SELFLESSNESS**:

- Possessing no concern for one's self
- The ability to forget self and be totally given to a mission
- The ability to put the interests of God, others above self.
- The willingness to risk life and limb to carry out a mission for God or country.
- Letting those under your charge be served first to be sure their needs are met before you partake.
- The willingness to leave a secure, high-paying job to answer a call to serve God.
- The grace to risk one's life and health to save and serve others.
- The willingness to devote your time, talent and treasure to help others to be great in the eyes of the Lord.
- Realizing that we are to seek first the Kingdom of God and His righteousness and He will reward us and give us whatever we need in His time.
- The power to give up position, preference, rights and one's life for the ministry, the mission or others.

ELF-MOTIVATED—   **Study start date:** _____ **Finish date:** _____

O ccasionally we found soldiers in the Army who were so lazy that they would have to drop their rifle just to carry their shadow. They wouldn't even clean their rifles every day without constant supervision even knowing that without cleaning in the steamy Vietnam jungles, when they made contact with the enemy they would likely have nothing behind their trigger finger but a metallic click. It was the only thing they had to save their own life and they still wouldn't do it. Most were fantastic, however. Of a truth, there are actually those in life who would stand around until hell froze over waiting for someone to come along and tell them what to do, almost to include when to take their next breath.

To really make it in life, one must have a powerful, over-arching goal to get out of bed and go at it every morning. Only self-motivated people can be placed in charge of the various businesses and entities out there in the world because they know where the start button is. Other folks can never find it. When left to themselves, they just sit and dream up a thousand reasons why right now is not a good time to get started. It is always too cold, too hot, we don't have enough material, it might rain, etc.

What it means to have the character trait of **BEING SELF-MOTIVATED:**

- Moved by inherent power
- A self-starter, fired up and motivated
- Having an inner drive to excel, produce, create, obtain and accomplish
- Having a desire to take in more territory for the Master
- Having a creative flare to invent and buck tradition to start new things
- One who doesn't wait for a command to do what they already know is both necessary and right
- One who is constantly finding out and searching for new and creative ideas
- Willing to venture well outside one's comfort zones for improvement and advancement
- Knows is one's heart the old adage is true: "No pain, no gain"
- Willing to study success and successful people in one's field
- Capable of starting initiatives without external motivation, direction or impetus
- Being goal oriented
- Those who have no need to hear the crack of the taskmaster's whip
- Impelled from within
- Able to make one's self do the mundane, difficult and distasteful things life is filled with first and in a timely manner
- One guided and impelled by a vision.

SENSITIVITY —   Study start date: _____ Finish date: _____

Sensitivity is a character quality closely akin to being alert but, more importantly, it is the ability to sense the feelings, wishes, hurts and desires of others. It is the ability to discern what others want without them having to say it either on paper or in so many words. It is a capacity we should try to improve upon. Then we can better fulfill the wishes of our leaders as well as meet the needs of those who are our followers and add value to their lives. Much can be learned from the voice inflections, facial expressions and body language of those around us. It is realizing that as much can be learned by what people don't say as by what they do. It is understanding that many times people have two reasons for what they have done. The real reason and one that sounds good. About this Solomon said, "The heart's real intentions are like deep water, but the person of discernment draws them out." Proverbs 20:5

The fact that every leader has "pet peeves," those things others do or fail to do that they dislike immensely, is simply a given. It is our responsibility, as a follower, to be alert to these proclivities and avoid them. Of course we are never to violate our own convictions but our mission as a follower is to please our superiors and be easy to lead.

It is well to note that before Nehemiah asked the heathen King in Babyong for permission to return to Jerusalem and rebuild the wall, he said, "If I have found favor in your sight …" Nehemiah understood his mission in life not to just get the job done but to do it in such a way that he would also find favor. He was not only to do the things the King required but sometimes even more than was required as well as things he knew he wanted but hadn't even asked for yet. Certainly we, as servants, are not to be apple polishers. We must always keep our integrity. However, we have all known people in life who are completely insensitive, even rude and reckless about the feelings of others around them. They people have taught us well that one can actually do the job, get it done on time and well and still manage to infuriate those they serve by not being sensitive to their desires and wishes. Of course this deals with an employment situation and is not to insinuate that a person should not stand up for what they truly believe as an individual—regardless of who is offended.

Sensitivity is also needful in the area of perceiving spiritual things. As we know, babes need milk. "But solid food belongs to those who are of full age, that is, those who by reason of use have their senses exercised to discern both good and evil." (Hebrews 5:12) We need to develop s high degree of sensitivity in following the Spirit so we can know what pleases the Lord. Remembering, of course, that every decision in life puts us on a path and will lead us someplace. We will soon arrive at a new destination. Good decisions can lead us to green pastures, still waters, peace and prosperity while, just as surely, bad decisions open us up to decline as well as more and more temptations, trials and ambushes set by the enemy. Where we find ourselves in life today is the direct result of all the decisions we have made thus far.

In this regard, a reporter was interviewing a highly successful industrial magnate to determine the secret to his phenomenal success at an early age. He asked, "How did you know to buy the right companies to begin with?" He replied, "Good decisions." "How then did you know which companies to add to achieve perfect vertical integration of all these companies?" He said, "Good decisions." Then he asked, "How did you know the right timing for these buy-outs?" Again he said, "Good decisions." Getting a bit frustrated, the reporter asked, "Well, how did you learn to make such good decisions?" He said, "Bad decisions." And, yes, we all have made some bad decisions. Those bad decisions, once made, can sometimes, thank God, be corrected. However, they are extremely valuable to us individually because through the pain they bring we learn to discern right from wrong and can start making good decisions. Those good decisions will soon start adding up and begin to multiply instead of the bad ones causing loses and throwing us into a downward spiral of decadence.

It is also important in today's environment to be alert to the needs, hardships and tragedies that those around us might have recently experienced. People working through the death of a family member, a job loss, a financial reversal or a divorce, need special consideration, space and, sometimes, help along with a great deal of understanding.

As we travel life's pathway we, as leaders, will meet two types of people, time and time again: givers and takers. We must be sensitive to each and know how to respond to them. Without divine intervention, it is almost impossible for people to switch between these two categories.

However, though it is very important, taken to the extreme, sensitivity can become hypersensitivity, working greatly to one's detriment. It can lay one open to being damaged emotionally as well as being easily hurt, irritated or offended by words spoken that were not even meant to be offensive. Sometimes wounded, hurting people can easily misconstrue words and situations unfolding around them. This will forever be happening. It is, no doubt, important to be sensitive to those around us but, again taken to extremes, having delicate feelings and being too sensitive will actually exclude one from leadership in an insensitive world.

What it means to have the character trait of **SENSITIVITY:**

- Capable of being excited, moved or stimulated by outside influences, information and the feelings of others
- Cognizant of one's environment
- Aware of the emotions and needs of others
- Highly alert and responsive to friends, co-workers and our supervisors
- Aware of the delicate feelings of others

S INCERITY —   Study start date: _____ Finish date: _____

S incerity we know is truth devoid of deceit, pretense or hypocrisy. Sadly, in America today, truth is little regarded in business, politics, personal relations and even many times, the church. Every day it is obvious that we live in an increasingly more hedonistic world. It's an I, me, my, me-first generation for the most part. America under Chicago street rules: The philosophy many go by is: Do it unto others before they get a chance to do it unto you. Look out for #1. Absolutely no weapons allowed for the good people so only the criminals have them. Politicians are willing to give the unions and the people whatever they want to stay in power even though they know it will mean utter bankruptcy for the municipality in due time. Then there are some who are willing to "tell the people what they want to hear to get their votes" and then do exactly the opposite. We have now had a demonstration of that on a national scale with the approval of Obamacare. They broke the law time and again to get it passed and said "the program is more important than procedure." (Just another way of stating that today the end justifies the means.) President Obama said, "If you like your doctor, you can keep him." "If you like your insurance policy, you can keep it." "We will drive down your healthcare cost by $2,500 per year." (When, in fact, it has already raised healthcare costs more than $3,500 — 15,000 per year) "Far more Americans will be insured," he said." When seventy million workers who formerly had insurance they were paying for it were booted out of the system. On and on, ad infinitum.

We have already been warned that in the last days these things will happen and a certain types of people will begin showing up. They will be "lovers of their own selves, covetous, boasters, proud, blasphemers, disobedient to parents, unthankful, unholy, without natural affection, truce breakers, false accusers, incontinent, fierce, despisers of those that are good, traitors, heady, high minded, lovers of pleasures more than lovers of God ..." II Timothy 3:2–4

In order to be happy and live successfully on this planet back in Joshua's day, he told us how to live saying, "Now therefore, fear the Lord, serve Him in sincerity and in truth ..." (Joshua 24:14) Paul exhorted all the younger men likewise to "be sober minded. In all things showing thyself a pattern of good works; in doctrine showing uncorruptness, gravity, sincerity (and) sound speech ..." (Titus 2:7 8 KJV) Our love must be sincere or it is not love at all.

Furthermore, all relationships and every sense of community involving mankind is based on truth and sincerity. Since cave man days, people have become increasingly specialized using their God-given gifts and talents such that we have come to rely on others in our community who are best equipped to provide the various goods and services we need. Some people are just more skilled, educated and prepared at certain tasks. It is also a given that in a complex, industrialized, computerized society, some must specialize to gain the requisite expertise and afford the specialized equipment necessary to perform certain tasks efficiently. We must rely on the heavy equipment operator, the pilot, the neurosurgeon, the CPA, and the auto mechanic for certain things. Having the skill, talent, education and equipment is not everything, however, they must also be trustworthy, contracting for their services. Without truth and sincerity in our relations, all contracts are immediately rendered worthless as good, trusting people are greatly damaged. These instruments or contracts are meant to be an exact representation of what the parties had agreed to but without truth and sincerity, they immediately become worth less than the paper they are written on. Furthermore, another huge building block of society is friendship. It means a lot in business and ministry. The value of a friendship is simply the trust and goodwill flowing between two people, the sincerity of their counsel and their understood willingness to stand with each other in their day of trouble.

For sincerity to be maintained in our relationships over the long term, it can only be accomplished with a servant's heart. Time, trouble, life's reversals and the fallen world system are too much for anyone to maintain this attitude in the power of the flesh. You just can't live on the basis of "what's in it for me?" At some point, we must ask God for the gift of a servant's heart, the ability to serve others as we would Him. Serving others with sincerity is what makes life both rewarding and meaningful. Those who just want to get in life, will never get enough but those who want to give, will be ever increasing their ability, resources and joy in doing so.

One of the greatest blessings in life are true, God-given, life-long friendships. To have and maintain these kind of friendships, investments of our own time and treasure are often required. Possibly the greatest friendships recorded in the Bible was that between David and Jonathan. It all started right after David, as a teenager, killed the giant, Goliath. Immediately after his demise and the subsequent rout of the Philistines it caused, Abner, the commander of the army, brought David before King Saul carrying the giant's head in his hand. Saul congratulated him profusely for this tremendous feat and conspicuous bravery. When he had congratulated David, immediately the soul of Jonathan was knit to the soul of David such that Jonathan loved David "as his own soul." (I Samuel 18:1) Saul was so impressed with young David that he immediately brought him on staff and would not even allow him go home to see his family any more. During this time, because of their great love, Jonathan and David also made covenant with each other. As a sign of this covenant, Jonathan took his robe and gave it to David, along with his armor, sword, bow and belt. After this, we know David went out on patrols wherever Saul sent him and behaved himself wisely. King Saul soon set him over his men of war and he was then accepted in the sight of the people as well as Saul's other servants. Years later when Jonathan was slain in battle, David remarked, "I am distressed for my brother Jonathan; you have been very pleasant to me; your love to me was wonderful, surpassing the love of women." (II Samuel 1:26) The friendship between Jonathan and David exemplifies true sincerity. What love. What sincerity between brothers. With the Holy Spirit today, we should have this same kind of love and sincerity or more for our brethren. Sincere love places integrity before all else and is genuine in every way. It is not only being what you appear to be but also doing what you say you will do.

As I write this, it occurred to me that people might not think there are friendships like this around today. Could anyone have a true friend like this anymore? I have truly been blessed with a number of good friends in life and what a tremendous blessing they are. One good friend, who has been a director of this ministry for over sixteen years also happens to own a heat and air company. He has been repairing and installing HVAC systems on people's homes and businesses for years and has been fixing those in our ministry properties free for almost as long as we have known each other. Coincidentally, the motor died in the air handler on one of our units the other day, so he sent one of his technicians by this morning to fix it. Upon completion, the serviceman called me over to sign the work order. Of course I am always willing to pay but when I signed the bill and asked what the charge would be, the service man said, "No charge." What kindness. What a friend. He has installed the heat and air in eight buildings the ministry has built by faith (debt free) to date. He said, "No charge." I mean the units, duct work, labor, materials, Freon and all. Besides all that he gave a large amount to the building fund and has given the ministry the benefit of his wise counsel on the board for all those years as well. He has also donated several huge, commercial refrigerators and then come back from time-to-time to keep them running for Manna Ministries, our food bank for the poor. Besides that he has been willing to take some of his Saturdays and evenings to go to battle along with me against the porn industry in our town. He has been willing to stand with me, personally, to either picket to close the Starship Porn Store here or in the subdivision in front of the owner's home. Knowing you can get attacked in those places he still does it. Now Gary Houser is a friend. Yes, his love is sincere and I am honored to be his friend. If I could be half the friend to him he has been to me, I'd be getting somewhere. Of course the best, most rewarding part of a friendship is not what a friend can do for us but the joy of being there to help them in their time of need. There is nothing better than being there to lift up a friend up when the world has them down for the count.

What it means to have the character trait of **SINCERITY:**

- To be true, free from hypocrisy
- Honesty of heart and mind
- Truly caring about the welfare of others
- Considering others first
- An absence of dissimulation and duplicity
- Pure, having no hidden agenda
- Always giving before asking others to
- The same on Monday as you are on Sunday
- Being a true believer in the cause, willing to risk all to see it through
- When questioned, answering all questions openly and honestly
- Willing to point out all of the pros as well as the cons of a venture or concept in advance
- Not willing to take advantage of anyone
- Living life as an open book
- Always the same when others are present or not
- Having a heart to be faithful in the small things
- Having your neighbor's best interest at heart
- Having a heart to serve others as unto the Lord
- Keeping your promises and making good your contracts no matter what the cost
- Aiming to please
- Able to love others as yourself
- Finishing well

TRAIGHTFORWARD/ see FRANKNESS: One who doesn't beat around the bush. Not a mealy-mouth Casper Milquetoast. One unafraid to take a position on matters of importance.

TATURE/ see BEARING

SUFFER, A HEART WILLING TO — Study start date: _____ Finish date: _____

In the world today, everybody wants to win the race, get the prize and have the million dollar business. The only problem is that precious few are willing to pay the price. The price, simply stated, in every field of endeavor is preparation and suffering … and those things don't come cheap. In a world full of couch potatoes, those willing to prepare for battle, practice for tournaments, suffer for a cause, sacrifice or go the extra mile to make customers happy are few and far between. Suffering may not be one of the most glamorous concepts but it may be one of the most important in obtaining success. You see, successful people are the ones who are willing to do the things unsuccessful people refuse to do. Success in business or any field, that is if your daddy doesn't own the company, comes from preparation, faithfulness, hard work and years of improving one's character. All of these things will come only one way and can be summed up in one word: suffering. No body, for example, wants to remain faithful when they feel like they have been slighted. Well, there is character trait that will solve this problem in an instant: forbearance. No matter where you work, things will never go your way all the time and your boss is never going to see everything just like you do. Just forgive them and let it roll off your back like so much water on a duck. Double down on your resolve, remain faithful and go back to work. Know that the boss will probably find the truth about it all later and get it corrected in time; Keep your head down and keep on producing. You'll be glad you did. We must be willing to surrender our personal rights on small matters, overlooking minor offences.

There was a fella in our town that went from one real estate company to the next every six months. He never could find one where things always went his way and just kept moving. All those seeds he was planting grew up to produce fruit for the companies he worked for but he was never there to benefit from it. Apparently no one ever told him that transplanting a tree across town causes it to go into shock and that it will take it four years to grow a sufficient root system to product fruit again.

Success in life is not some big secret. There are principles of success out there that work over and over for anyone who is willing to work them. You can pick them up very easily from supervisors, co-workers, books, magazines, newspaper articles and especially, dare I say it? The Bible. In fact, most success books are just reiterations of principles the author has taken from the Bible and since the authors have been dead for so long, they rarely even give them any credit. In our ministry, we operate The Shepherd's House and have a program to train men coming out of prison and off the streets to be successful. All of these men are freely given the same principles to incorporate in their lives and, hopefully, put them on the comeback-trail to success when they graduate. However, some will incorporate a few things into their lifestyle and work ethic but not that many are willing to pay the price to operate in all the things they learn. These success principles are what make the difference between winners and losers in the game of life. Everybody can say well, but all who say well are not, in fact, well.

Just one small case in point here. We tell these men when they start the program that they each have a choice in life to carry one of two things with them and I lift up two items, one in each hand. In the one, I have a common ballpoint pen and in the other a shovel. We say, "Which one do you want to carry?" Of course they all chose to carry the pen and then we tell them how critically important it is for a leader in today's world to **always** be equipped with a pen and a note pad. Today there is going to be an unending stream of numbers, names and facts coming at you. If you can't write them down, remember them and get things right — you are going to be passed over, shuffled to the side, run over or kicked to the curb. It is a highly competitive world out there. We are serious, in our ministry, about the business of building men, not warehousing failures. This little success principle is so important that residents get a demerit each time they are found without a pen. Five demerits total for any number of infractions, they bust it and are sent out the door. That being the case, they don't pass "Go" and certainly don't collect the "$200." Then again some, of course, make it all the way to graduation and come in to sign their final check from the ministry. As the check is passed to them to endorse, they start frisking their bodies all over like someone who just awoke from a deep sleep after laying on an ant bed. All this is, as you might imagine by now, in search of a pen—which is never to be found. Why? Because, although small, there is some pain and suffering involved in carrying a pen that may weigh all of a few ounces. If it weren't so, everybody would do it. Pens just get in the way, might come open in your pocket accidentally from time-to-time, and leak. It takes commitment and forethought to always have one on your person. They usually cost all of a dollar or so today which is a huge investment in success for those unwilling to invest in their future. There is sooooo much suffering involved in carrying a little pen and most people, even many who know it is impossible to be a success today without one, are not willing to pay the price.

They are just not willing to suffer—at all—for anything. Oh, they might bet on the lottery and hope to win—but suffer? Endure a little hardship or pain? Not only no but—unk-uh! You tell them that they have to get up early and quit "burning daylight" as John Wayne put it and they say, "Noooo! I'm not a morning person and I'm going to continue getting up until the crack of noon." Don't think I've ever really met anyone who liked getting up at 4:30 every day but many of us do it anyhow. It is a principle of success, far more difficult than carrying a pen. There are very few days in a year that my body and my mind want to get up that early but so what does that matter? I, by the grace of God, get up anyway. I work for God, have a purpose and simply must be efficient. To know to do well and do it not is sin to you." James 4:17

Sometimes on the job a person might be confronted with a boss they don't care for, respect or even like. Most are not willing to serve them as unto the Lord and wait for God's promotion process to kick in. They quit and immediately lose all the seed time and planting they invested there. Sometimes I call suffering eating dirt. To get anywhere in this crazy world, one must be humble and willing to eat a little dirt occasionally. You aren't going to always have it just like you want it everywhere you go in life. In addition, you have to pay your dues in most career fields. If you can't respect your boss, at least realize all authority comes from God so learn to respect their office. Forget who they are and what they are (within certain limits) and turn your work into them as unto the Lord. (Colossians 3:23) It sure makes working for them a whole lot easier. God will take care of them in His time—don't worry.

A good friend of mine, we'll call him Dave (Not his real name but this is a true story), went to work for a major corporation the day he graduated from college in an entry-level sales slot. Being a people person and one of the most efficient and capable people I have met, he killed the sales quotas they gave him and naturally made life-long friends both inside and outside the company. He never worked anywhere but this one company in all of his adult life. It was a good company that had good products but, like everywhere else, there were many problems. Despite being their best producer, he still faced personal challenges from those around him from time-to-time. They paid him well but he certainly earned it. Soon and most importantly, he accepted Christ. Otherwise, he might not have had the grace to stick it out.

After a number of years, the president retired and named a man to take the job who had several sons. All of them had good educations and their father gave most of them jobs in the company. All were about the same age as Dave. Problems kept cropping up. One of the territory managers got involved in an illicit sexual relationship with another staff member. Nepotism not only crept in, it came in like a tidal wave. About the various problems Dave was facing, one of the leaders of the company told him, "If it is not hurting the company financially, you need to just forget about it." Dave opined, "If we have to have that conversation, we don't need to have that conversation. If you allow that kind of stuff to go on, a whole lot of worse things are going to start happening." Instead of reacting to these people and having no direct control over them, he just refused to compromise his own position and started praying for them. Not for God to wipe them off the map but to arrest them, come into their lives and deliver them. Another time, one of the owner's sons started tapping his phone line and listening to his conversations and those with other officers of the company. Soon, the wiretapping equipment was discovered and verified by other leaders. All of this was reported to the president. He confronted his son, who promptly denied it. He then got back with Dave and said, "He told me he didn't do it and I have to believe him." Dave left all this with the Lord and continued to do an excellent job.

A few years later the president retired and because of Dave's production, organizational ability, character and exemplary record, incredibly, he made Dave president and CEO of the company. Dave worked for them for over forty years, starting out as a salesman and ended up CEO and the largest stock holder in the company. He sold their unprofitable manufacturing arm the first year he was president and doubled the company's overall profit. The company continued to grow and prosper unbelievably over the years. During his tenure, he was certainly blessed financially but he used his good fortune to bless a whole lot of people and ministries. Now tell me. How would this story have ended if he quit the first time things didn't go exactly his way?

Ever wonder why the grass always looks greener on the other side of the fence? Because you are looking at it from ground level, at a distance and it looks like there is grass everywhere. However, when you get over there and look down at it, you will find the same vacant, brown spots all over the place just like where you were before you jumped that fence.

What it means to have the character trait of **A HEART WILLING TO SUFFER**:

- The ability to give up certain rights and overlook some offences
- The ability to postpone gratification and endure hardships to obtain a future goal
- The ability to take criticism, punishment, death, pain or a loss in order to stay consistent with one's character or beliefs
- The ability to labor long, hard and even under duress in order to obtain
- The ability to pay the price for success and excellence to win a contest
- A willingness to pay the price to incorporate success principles and character in one's life

TEACHABLE, BEING —   Study start date: _____   Finish date: _____

There are many in this world who think they know everything. All of us have run into them from time to time. The problem is, that all the knowledge in the world is increasing daily at lightning speed so how is it that they see themselves as the embodiment of all knowledge? It is, of course, pride.

Let's think about this for a moment. It took thousands and thousands of years before the most basic inventions like the spear, wheel, bow and arrow and gun powder became common place in society. The invention of paper was such an incredible assist in the process of formulating language and the recording and transferring ideas and information. When Guttenberg invented the printing press in 1439, the printed page came of age and knowledge began to speed around the world. In 1844, Sam Morris invented the telegraph and information, for the first time, began to be transmitted electronically. About that time things really began to start popping. Then, like an explosion, we saw the invention of the light bulb, telephone, airplane, automobile, television, rockets, the computer and the internet. Incredibly, what man has learned in the hundred years after Sam invented the telegraph far outstripped all everyone had come to know up to that point–from the beginning of time!

Then knowledge began to double in ever increasingly, smaller berths of time, doubling at one point every eight years. Now, because of computers, if you can believe it, all knowledge doubles, according to some experts, every one or two years. The point being, of course, that it is nigh unto impossible for anyone to know everything and certainly none of us know enough. A teachable person understands, however, not only that there is very much to learn in the world, but they also believe that they possess so very little that they are willing to work diligently, on a daily basis, to gain more.

Some people will never be teachable for a number of reasons. Many are simply too stubborn and set in their ways to learn new things. Others are too lazy because learning is hard work and no one would pay the price unless they really see their desperate condition and truly love the pursuit of it. Many are too prideful to be taught by anybody about anything. Some think they already know enough. And still others, as aforementioned, think they already know everything. This is really a problem because it is almost impossible to tell someone who knows everything anything at all.

Another impediment to serious learning is that many who actually graduate from college think they are fully equipped and know all they will ever have need of learning. Remember, they graduated from the "University." Universe, being the word university is derived from according to Webster's Dictionary, means "the whole body of things." Most universities claim to have a corner on all the knowledge in the world but most don't even allow the knowledge of God to be taught on campus. Imagine that when the wisest man in the world said, "The fear of the Lord is the beginning of knowledge." (Proverbs 1:7) The knowledge of God and the fear of God is square one and they have excluded and demeaned all this. Graduating from college, however, is truly nothing more than a bit of a license to begin our study. Learning should be a life-long quest. The teachable should be learning from our environment, our leaders, our contemporaries, books, newspapers, magazines, our own mistakes, the mistakes of others, television, technology etc. A teachable person truly hungers and thirsts after knowledge. He is ever learning as part of a life-long pursuit to obtain something far more important than knowledge: wisdom from God. You can usually tell how much someone wants something by how hard they are willing to dig for it. The teachable person sees himself like the beggar Lazarus in Luke 16:20 desperately needing a crumb off of the rich man's table just to survive. We too should have such a desperate need of a crumb of wisdom from God's table every day just to make it, that we are willing to seek that crumb like a starving beggar.

Years ago I read somewhere that "ignorance is a consequence of being human, not knowing it is even more atrocious." (Anonymous) What a blessing it was to learn I was ignorant and that it was not only Ok to be ignorant but that this had to be square one for all of us in the realm of actually learning in life. This is so important if we want to be teachable for the rest of our short life on this planet! I gladly, and with literally no struggle at all, declared myself ignorant at that moment and set about to gain all the knowledge and wisdom I possibly could. Right, I know, it was my half of the class that always made the top half possible too. To his credit, a teachable person has prepared his heart and made himself available and open to be taught. A teachable person sees himself as destitute and totally intellectually bankrupt. He sees himself so needy and in so much danger that he is like a man drowning at the bottom of a lake. He, by the instinct of self-preservation, swims with all his might toward the surface, hoping against hope to gain a single, life giving, gasp of air. A teachable person sees opportunities to learn that others miss. The more he learns, instead of getting puffed up, the more he sees he doesn't know and the more he needs to learn. His focus is on obtaining more wisdom and knowledge and not on how much or how little he might possess at the time. Scripture reveals that "knowledge puffs up but love edifies. And if anyone thinks that he knows anything, he knows nothing yet as he ought to know." (I Corinthians 8:1, 2) Knowledge alone, in and of itself, can get us into serious trouble. Wisdom, though, is the gift of God that shows us how to use knowledge for ourselves and others in a constructive, profitable manner. The wise learner is ever comparing himself with God's Word and Jesus, and is trying to apply this knowledge to life's problems. He is ever finding deficiencies and lack. For this and other reasons, a teachable person is willing to go any distance, climb any mountain, swim any sea and pay any price to gain one, single ounce of wisdom, knowledge or prudence.

A part of being teachable is being open to correction. It is knowing that we all have blind spots in our life and walk. A teachable person not only accepts correction from others but welcomes it, counts it extremely valuable and takes it to heart. He understands that his flesh and mind naturally don't like to even think that he could need correction or improvement so he has learned to overcome that tendency by privately writing those corrections down and putting them in a file. Then he reviews them from time-to-time, asking the Holy Spirit to teach him on these issues. He realizes that how he perceive himself may, in fact, be far different from how others perceive him. A teachable person is so only too glad to make improvements. He shows his openness to receive instruction by his humility and eagerness to learn, change and be taught. To him, "open rebuke is better than secret love." (Proverbs 27:5) Such is the value of correction and we all need it.

A teachable person has come to know that "things spoken speed away but those written endure." If that is true and **it is**, knowledge needs to be retained in written form. Solomon told us to, "Take firm hold of instruction (knowledge), do not let go; keep her, for she is your life." (Proverbs 4:13) A teachable person has trained himself to take notes, cuts articles out of magazines and newspapers and save information alphabetically by topic in notebooks. He realizes, as Earl Nightingale said, "Ideas are like babies, everyone gets but a few and you had better take good care of every one you get." He realizes that just one good idea can be worth a million dollars. One good piece of advice may save a drowning man's life. A teachable person also realizes that even good ideas have their own good time for incubation, development, marketing and presentation. They realize that there is a time to gain knowledge and a time to put it to use and the two are, quite often, years apart. No amount of success will dampen a teachable person's quest for learning.

All learning, however, is not done inside the classroom and as we find from the incredible life of R.G. LeTourneau. He was born on November 30, 1888 in Richford, Vermont where at fourteen, with the blessing of his Christian parents (albeit also with concern), he left school as a 6th grade dropout. He moved first to Minnesota and later to Portland, Oregon where he became an apprentice as an ironmonger in the

East Portland Iron Works. There he learned the machinist and foundry trades while studying mechanics through a correspondence course. Later, wanderlust as a young man caused him to move to San Francisco where he worked for a power plant, learning welding and different applications of electricity. In 1909 he moved to Stockton, California where he worked at a number of trades including mining, farm labor, as a wood cutter and carpenter, acquiring a working knowledge of many trades that would prove valuable to him later in life.

In 1911 he took a job at the Superior Garage where he was able to learn auto mechanics and subsequently became half-owner. Because of neck injuries he sustained in a car-racing accident, he was not able to serve in the military during World War I but instead contributed to the war effort by working in the Mare Island Naval Shipyard as a maintenance assistant. There he was trained as an electrical machinist and was able to increase his welding skills. After the war, returning to Stockton, he found that his garage business had failed. In order to repay his part of the debts, he got a job repairing a crawler-tractor for Holt Manufacturing Company. Later he was employed by the tractor owner to grade and level about 40 acres of land using the tractor and a scraper in tow.

This kind of work was something LeTourneau especially liked, so in January of 1920 he purchased a used tractor and rented a scraper to start his own grading company. A couple years later he bought a tract of land in Stockton to start an engineering workshop where he designed and manufactured several new types of scrapers. His business kept expanding as he combined his contracting business and the equipment manufacturing to incorporate R.G, LeTourneau, Inc. In 1919 he felt a strong calling to the ministry and sought the counsel of his pastor, Rev. Bevol, about it, thinking to fulfill the Great Commission, he needed to be either a pastor or a missionary. However, his pastor told him "God needs businessmen too" so from that time on he considered his business to be a partnership with God.

During the 1920's and early 30's LeTourneau completed a number of large earthmoving projects. With the superior machines he designed, he was able to continually underbid his competition and get jobs. However, in 1933, in the middle of the Great Depression, he left contracting all-together to devote his attention and all the skills he had learned over a life-time to the manufacture of new and improved, large-scale earthmoving equipment. The company took off immediately. By 1935 he had built a manufacturing plant in Peoria, Illinois and then another in Toccoa, Georgia in 1938. He built another plant in Rydalmere, Australia in 1938, another in Vicksburg, Mississippi in 1942 and then yet another in Longview, Texas in 1945.

The name, LeTourneau, soon became synonymous with the giant earthmoving equipment worldwide. He was responsible for many inventions and 300 patents on many types of earth moving equipment, the concepts of which are still being used around the world today. He became one of the greatest inventors of all time. The equipment he built actually helped win the

War in both Europe and the Pacific Theaters. Many large landing strips needed to be built for our

Air Force during this time as well as huge equipment to move damaged bombers off runways as well as fighters on aircraft carriers. His companies grew to the point that they manufactured 70 percent of all the heavy, earth-moving equipment the Allied forces used in World War II.

His ingenuity and creative mind were responsible for the innovation of rubber tires in earthmoving equipment, electric wheel drive, mobile offshore drilling platforms and many improvements in large ground scrapers. In 1946 LeTourneau, always a believer in practical application combined with classroom instruction, purchased a vacant military hospital and the adjacent land in Longview, Texas where he established the Letourneau Technical Institute. It grew and in addition to technical training it began offering traditional college courses along with missionary training. All training there was based on a philosophy of combining a Christian testimony with education and a good work ethic. It grew into a college by 1961 and then attained university status. It is known today as LeTourneau University. This

L9419 R. G. LeTourneau Museum and Archives, The Margret Estes Library, LeTourneau University

"Crash Pusher"

private university has now expanded its offerings to include degrees in aeronautical sciences, engineering and liberal arts with a strong base of Christian influence as chapel attendance required three times a week for all students.

It was in 1953 that LeTourneau decided to sell his earth-moving equipment line to an outfit called the Westinghouse Air Brake Company. At that point, he began to apply all of his creative skills to the development of the electric wheel drive concept. In 1958 he re-entered the large earth-moving equipment manufacturing business using the electric wheel drive concept he had just invented. This, too, became very successful. At the age of 77, LeTourneau turned over the presidency of his corporation to his son Richard who continued in his dad's tradition of working daily to build more efficient and economical, giant earth-moving equipment.

The Lord prospered Mr. LeTourneau who began very early tithing to the Lord's work and continued to increase it over his life-time until he was giving 90% and keeping ten. His thought was never how much to give but how much he should keep. After giving $10 million to educational and religious ministries in 1959, the LeTourneau Foundation he did his giving through was still worth $40 million.

During his life he received countless awards for his accomplishments but in 1969, at the age of eighty, he suffered a stroke and went on to receive his true reward. With no formal education he became known as "The Dean of Earthmoving" His inventions elevated equipment from being rated in hundreds of horse power to thousands and from hundreds of tons of capacity to many thousands. More importantly, he was known as one who was teachable and the "Mover of Mountains and Men" who gave God the glory.[23]

What it means to have the character trait of **BEING TEACHABLE**:

- One who sees their lack and earnestly desires more wisdom and knowledge
- One capable of hearing instruction and being taught
- One who realizes that gaining knowledge increases their worth to God and others
- One acutely interested in learning more

EMPERANCE —   **Study start date:** _____ **Finish date:** _____

The world we live in is full of excess, provocations, temptations and false representations. People cut in front of us in traffic, we are falsely accused in the workplace, the dog eats one of our favorite shoes, the stock offering didn't come close to doing what the broker said, the horses get out of the pasture and we sometimes eat too much ice cream and cake at the birthday party. So what is needed when facing a life full of these temptations? Temperance. It is so easy to do what comes naturally a disagreement and go ballistic. We've all done it. But what does it get you? We get deeper in trouble and further in debt and to those around us whom we have so superbly offended, we must now apologize. To ever make much progress as a leader, we must first acquire the ability to discipline ourselves. We must develop the requisite self-control to master our own temper, passions, desires and sensual appetites. Otherwise, any progress we make will be quickly erased by our excesses and the enormous damage personally, socially, physically and financially they are sure to inflict. Truly, we must learn to govern ourselves before we can ever begin to lead others.

One of the most difficult situations we all face sooner or later in life is mistreatment and unfairness, usually by someone who is personally woefully lacking in many areas themselves. The ability to hold one's peace under this kind of treatment can ordinarily only be overcome by the power of the Holy Spirit and learning to look over the current trial by working as unto the Lord. Temperance is the ability to show restraint and not retaliate in kind. This is just one of the fruits of the Spirit catalogued in Galatians 5:22 & 23. The Apostle Paul said we are to give all diligence to "add to (our) faith virtue, to virtue knowledge, (and) to knowledge self-control …" (I Peter 1:5, 6) If we can keep on doing well, the truth will become known in time and our innocence will be rewarded. There will also be times that we will be blamed for things that we didn't do. In these instances, it is so important to hold our peace when being corrected or criticized and not answer back—even when we are not in the wrong.

Paul said, "everyone who competes for the prize (must be) temperate in all things. Now they do it to obtain a perishable crown, but we for an imperishable crown. Therefore, I run thus: not with uncertainty. Thus I fight: not as one who beats the air. But I discipline my body and bring it into subjection, lest, when I should have preached to others, I myself should become disqualified." (I Corinthians 9:25–27) Temperance is important in just about every area of life—in personal relationships as well as in eating, drinking and sex.

There will always be situations in life where lavish foods are set before us. This, of course, is a time to be restrained. We have this admonition in Proverbs 23:1-3: "When you sit down to eat with a ruler, consider carefully what is before you; and put a knife to your throat if you are a man given to appetite. Do not desire his delicacies, for they are deceptive food." Solomon said, " … found honey? Eat only as much as you need, lest you be filled with it and vomit." (Proverbs 25:16) Excessive sugar and fat intake are not the best things for your health. Enjoy a moderate amount and have the discipline to stop.

Moderation if not total restraint with alcohol is also both commendable and important. Regarding alcohol, the wisest man in the world asked these questions: "Who has woe? Who has sorrow? Who has contentions? Who has complaints? Who has wounds without cause? Who has redness of eyes?" His reply was, "Those who linger long at the wine, those who go in search of mixed wine." It is deceptive drink so be careful. "Do not look on the wine when it is red, when it sparkles in the (glass), when it swirls around smoothly; at the last it bites like a serpent, and stings like a viper. Your eyes will see strange things, and your heart will utter perverse things. Yes, you will be like one who lies down in the midst of the sea, or like one who lies at the top of the mast, saying: 'They struck me, but I was not hurt; they have beaten me, but I did not feel it. When shall I awake, that I may seek another drink?'" (Proverbs 23:29–35) Drinking in excess can cause the loss of your driver's license, job, marriage, and even your life. Is it worth it?

Another area in which temperance is necessary is with the opposite sex. We are commanded not to have sexual relations prior to marriage for many reasons: unwanted pregnancies, sexually transmitted diseases, the loss of a clear conscience, the loss of purity, our Christian witness, and the possibility of fooling oneself into thinking a person is in love—when they are not. Premarital sex can and has caused many people to marry a person they have no hope of ever getting along with. What a tragedy! God's plan for us is to find a companion we are attracted to just as friends to begin with. It should be someone with whom we have things in common, enjoy their company, respect their lifestyle and share the same belief system. In life, the harlot and the seductress are a great danger. Solomon warned us that "a harlot is a deep pit and a seductress is a narrow well. She also lies in wait as for a victim, and increases the unfaithful among men." (Proverbs 23:27, 28) There is absolutely nothing wrong with sex. However, God created it to be enjoyed as a blessing from Him only in the marriage bed. In the news, we just recently saw the fall of a four star general, David Petraeus, because of a tryst with his biographer. He had just recently been promoted to head the CIA but once his indiscretion was discovered, he had to resign in disgrace. He brought great pain and public humiliation to his family and completely destroyed an otherwise stellar career. What this tells us is a few minutes of intemperate behavior has the power to destroy a whole lifetime of good work.

Temperance is staying within reasonable limits and avoiding extremes, extravagance or excessiveness. Most of us have failed in many areas at some time in our lives. We have all fallen short of God's glory but, with His help, we can do better. Does this mean we will miss out on some enjoyments in life? Quite the contrary. God will cause us to "ride upon the high places of the land … feed you with the heritage of Jacob" (Isaiah 58:14), let you "eat the fat of the land" (Genesis 45:18) and "give you the desires of your heart" (Psalm 37:4) if we will delight ourselves in Him and exerciser temperance.

What it means to have the character trait of **TEMPERANCE**:

- Able to hold one's peace
- Moderation in consumption of food and drink
- Having control of one's sensual urges
- Moderation in one's thoughts, feelings and actions
- The absence of extravagance, railing or anger
- Having restraint
- The ability to control one's appetites and passions
- Not irritable, easily angered or provoked
- Abstinence from life controlling drugs or intoxicating drink

ENACITY—   **Study start date:** _____ **Finish date:** _____

L ife is a test. There are many hindrances, unexpected pot holes in the road, false promises, dead end streets, senseless times of waiting, avalanches and ambushes all along the way. It is also very much a marathon—and not a sprint. No matter what you decide to do in life, you can count on it taking longer than you expected and you can know that there will also be many unforeseen problems along the way. No one is exempt from trouble in this life. We must count on afflictions and be set mentally not only to endure them but to also make the best of them. All trials come to us with blessings in their hands but we can't have the blessings without endurance. Never be discouraged because there is one trait we can acquire that will cause us to overcome all of these: diligence practiced until it becomes tenacity. The world can stop just about anybody except the person with a made up mind and diligence—tenacity.

I guess war is a pretty good teacher. Few things motivate one to train more than the prospect of mortal combat. Having to face off with a well trained, equipped and experienced enemy on the battlefield is a prospect to behold. War is for real and there is no quarter. You can write it down in your book. In every encounter with the enemy, one side is going to win and the other is going to lose in a big way. Either we win and our side lives to fight another day or we die and the enemy will be triumphant and fight on. How would you have it? Beyond even the battles we fight each day, our country is also in a war. Either our country will win the war and we will continue to enjoy the liberties our forefathers fought and died for or we will be learning a new language as minions of a foreign, oppressive regime right here on our own soil. I much prefer the former. But winning doesn't always go to the strongest and swiftest but more often to the one who, just plain refuses to ever give up.

Did Paul have any difficulties in his ministry? Though more profitable in the ministry than any other apostle, he certainly wouldn't be counted among the rich and famous today. "In labors (he) was more abundant, in stripes above measure, in prisons more frequently, in deaths (both attempts and threats) often. From the Jews five times received forty stripes minus one. Three times was beaten with rods; once was stoned; three times was shipwrecked; a night and a day in the deep; in journeys often in perils of waters, in perils of robbers, in perils of my own countrymen, in perils of Gentiles, in perils in the city, in perils in the wilderness, in perils in the sea, in perils among false brethren; in weariness and toil, in sleepless-ness often, in hunger and thirst, in fastings often, in cold and nakedness—besides the other things, what (came) upon (him) daily; (was his) deep concern for all the churches." (II Corinthians 11:23–28) Certainly he didn't look for his reward here on earth.

Tenacity is the ability to continue to pursue a mission, staying loyal to our leaders when there is no hope, no pay check, a lack of food and little sleep but plenty of ridicule, false accusations and other extremely harsh conditions. It is the ability to see, embrace and hold on to the victory even when neg-ativity, defeat and hopelessness come crashing down all around you. It is the persistent application of one's self to a valued goal, mission or objective even amid provocation, temptation, a lack of proper appreciation, injustice and fatigue. It is truly the only quality that assures victory in life. Even faith fails to produce most of the time without tenacity. Amid all his failed experiments, Louis Pasteur made this summary of his success: "Let me tell you the secret that has led me to my goal. My strength lies solely in my tenacity."

In sales, it is the ability to endure a long string of "No's" with the sure knowledge that every one of them is getting you closer and closer to a "Yes." It is being tough skinned. A salesman who can't handle rejection, won't be a salesman long. The market has ups and downs, good days and bad, good customers and horrible customers, price fluctuations as well as government interference and red tape. There are good-paying customers and ones who planned to stiff you before they put the ink in their pen on your sales order. So what! It all comes with the territory. Keep going anyway! Start early and stay late. Wear the market out if need be and keep looking for customers not just to become buyers but, more importantly, to become your life-long friends. You will prevail. Weak sisters will soon fall away but you will still be there when the others have already hung up their spurs and quit.

Even God, Himself, we find is involved in many of the trials we face. He says, "As many as I love, I rebuke and chasten." (Revelations 3:16) "Every branch in Me that does not bear fruit He takes away; and every branch that bears fruit He prunes, that it may bear more fruit." (John 15:2) True. It is painful when the Lord comes around with those pruning shears but it is still, none-the-less, imperative if we are to grow and produce as we should. Trees and plants, left to themselves, produce far more branches and leaves than fruit. Since they all have only a finite root system with a limited capacity to supply the tree nutrients and water, to achieve maximum production, the husbandman must eliminate the unnecessary branches. This, of course, allows the tree to immediately devote more of its life-giving sap to fruit bearing. Christians, would get too fat, lazy and self-interested if there was no pruning going on in their lives. Without trials, we would produce precious little fruit. Most importantly we wouldn't need faith and neither would our faith grow and faith is the only thing that leases God.

Noah kept on building the ark for a hundred years even when the townspeople were laughing him to scorn for making such a huge misplaced investment in their community. It was quite laughable to them that he would build such a large boat so far from the nearest body of water. Joseph stayed faithful even though he was thrown in a pit, sold into slavery in Egypt, was falsely accused after doing a superb job for Potiphar and was forgotten by the men he had helped in prison. David stayed loyal to his country and countrymen even when Saul chased him for several years and tried twenty-seven times to kill him. All of these men kept the faith and stayed with it, regardless. They were still standing in the end to get God's prize for tenacity. Tenacity is that spirit in you that says in the face of all odds, "I will never give up."

What it means to have the character trait of **TENACITY**:

- Stick-to-it-iveness
- Dogged determination
- Not easily dissuaded or defeated
- The ability to adhere to the task
- Not allowing oneself to be deterred from a goal
- The ability to endure hardship in the face of tremendous adversity
- The habit of finishing what one starts regardless of the difficulty or how long it takes.
- The ability to stay obedient to your calling, duty and instructions.
- The ability to master things considered by others as untenable
- The resilience to bounce back even after many simultaneous, consecutive attacks of the enemy.

THANKFULNESS—   **Study start date:** _____ **Finish date:** _____

Being thankful sounds like about the easiest and most natural thing for a person to do because of all the blessings God showers us with daily. It is a fact, however that people are neither thankful naturally or by accident. Even though it is a command from God to "Enter His gates with thanksgiving, and into His courts with praise: (and to) be thankful unto Him and bless His name" (Psalm 100:4), it won't happen unless a person makes a conscious, firm decision to do it. One of the biggest problems mankind must overcome is being born into a body of fallen flesh, equipped with a sin nature and a corrupt, self-centered mind. As babies, we wanted everything and we wanted it immediately. We were only interested in our own needs and were hardly aware that there were other people with competing, plausible interests around us anywhere in the world. We aren't grateful for having sound bodies, good families, shoes on our feet, clothes on our backs or a roof over our heads. Every one of these things were the gift of divine providence. Truth is we take everything for granted and never really give a thought to how blessed we are to have been given these things by God's divine favor and goodness. It is usually later in life that we learn that no one has ever received anything that they didn't first receive from the Lord. (I Corinthians 4:7) We are created beings. Personhood and our very being is nothing less than the gift of God's grace. We are here at His pleasure. Any skill, talent, physical appearance, family heritage, character, employment, relationships, children, preferment's in life, etc. are, likewise, the gift of God. He owes us nothing and will be a debtor to no man. It wouldn't matter if you gave trillion dollars to the poor and gave your body to be burned, you can never overcome the price that was paid for you on the cross. Though it is our duty and great joy to serve, give and bless the Kingdom as we might, we will always be unprofitable servants.

We humans think only good things should come our way but the Bible says we are to be thankful **for** all things. (Ephesians 5:20) But what about the car accidents and all the bad stuff? Well, yes, the answer according to God is still yes. But, some might think we don't need to be thankful **in** all things. Well, yes again. Paul told the Philippians to be thankful in all things as well (Philippians 4:6) All things are in God's providence and though we may not see the good in them at the moment, we will eventually see the good in this life or the one to come. (Romans 8:28) The transcendent glory of God can even take our mistakes and messes and turn them into miracles. The most important thing to remember is that life in any form is a gift. It is our opportunity to find and know Him and, in some way, enlarge God's borders and bring glory to the Name.

Even when we get closer to God, if we are granted that great privilege, we still find, however, as many before us, that "the spirit is willing but the flesh is weak." (Mark 14:38) The flesh is always all about the flesh. It wants what it wants. It wants to be pampered every day and all the time. Only through a strong alliance of a person's spirit, mind and the Word of God, can it be overcome but it can be overcome, praise God.

In the Old Testament there were several thank offerings, sacrifices and feasts that were instituted for the simple purpose of helping the Israelites realize their need to be grateful for divine favor. Realizing, of course, that God is forever self-sufficient. He has need of nothing and certainly doesn't need man's sacrifices or gifts although He will receive them. They will, however, when given correctly and with the proper attitude, arise as a sweet smelling savor in His nostrils. Thankfulness is our duty, for which gratitude is the grace. Gratefulness is so foundational to having the proper relationship with God that Paul told the Romans it was because they were not thankful, that God could not bless them. (Romans 1:21) On the contrary, thankfulness is the very attitude that causes God to open the windows of Heaven to pour out our blessings. It is really pretty simple: Thankfulness brings more blessings and a lack of it dries them up.

A good example of how reticent we humans are to be thankful for benefits received is the account of Jesus healing the ten lepers in Luke 17:11. Because they were outcasts, forbidden to even get close to non-lepers in those days, they all cried out to Him in total desperation, at the top of their voices from a great distance. Parts of their face and fingers were rotting off from this terrible disease for which there was no known cure. In addition to their horrible appearance, the stench was all the more foreboding. We humans can and should be very sensitive, and understandably so, to the loss of part of our facial skin, ears and eye lids as is the case with those who have leprosy. Of course, Jesus healed them all but, amazingly, only one returned to give thanks. That's right. Only one soul had the presence of mind and heart after presenting himself to the priests as Jesus told them all to do and being healed, to make the journey back to Jesus and say, "Thank you." Incredible. What ingratitude! Well, this lone recipient of divine grace also got something else he didn't expect. He was not only healed but was also made "whole" by the Master. Thankfulness, we see then, brings even more and greater blessings because it shows we have a heart with room to receive more. It opens the floodgates of God's mercy and grace. If there were no other reason to be thankful, it also makes you joyful just to be in a continual state of thankfulness.

I don't think it was by accident only one returned in this biblical account. I believe thankfulness really happens to be that scarce in human nature. It is not what we own or have in our pockets that makes us thankful. It is what we have in our hearts. So God grant us grace to let thankfulness be one of our strongest points from this day forth.

What it means to have the character trait of **THANKFULNESS:**

- Showing appreciation, pleasure and satisfaction derived from a gift
- Gratefulness, realizing none of us deserve anything
- Realizing that apart from God's mercy we would all be in a very hot place
- Being appreciative of benefits received
- Being appreciative of the people, relationships and opportunities of life
- Heartfelt gratitude
- Acknowledging divine goodness or favor

HOROUGHNESS/see FOLLOW THROUGH or BEING A FINISHER:

THOUGHTFULNESS— Study start date: _____ Finish date: _____

One of the greatest joys of life is the gift of interaction with friends, family and associates. This thing is so real that it is evidenced by the simple fact that upon meeting old friends, sometimes many years later in life, our love for them is, amazingly, exactly the same as it was many years earlier. This was when our fellowship was, obviously, on a much more regular basis. Why? Because love never fails and it never diminishes. The passage of time doesn't effect it in the least.

Certainly one thing that can make our fellowship better is thoughtfulness about others; their needs, desires and wants. One's birthday is a good opportunity to take particular note of our special friends and fellow travelers here and now. They are all gifts from God both to us, individually, and the Body of Christ, as a whole. Every person we have been blessed to know is a gift to us directly from God. The question that yet remains, however, is how much of a blessing are we going to be to them? Just one way to do that is to remember their birthday and remind them how special, important and appreciated they are by us by sending them a card or an email. One day soon, they won't be here and neither will you. You will no longer have the opportunity to show your appreciation for them. If you have love or honor to bestow on a friend, do it now and not at their funeral.

One of the kindest, most thoughtful people I have ever known is my cousin, Willie Lee. She was born in a beautiful little town on the San Saba River called Menard, Texas and attended school there. Upon graduation from high school she first attended Tarleton State University, went on to Texas Women's College and then finished at Southwest Texas State University where she met her future husband. At the beginning of World War II she fell in love with this handsome young man who soon became an officer in the Army Air Corps. She and Lieutenant Allen Everett were married in Coral Gables, Florida. As a navigator, he flew bombers over the "hump" in the Himalayas during the war and was blessed to come home alive. After the war, he stayed in the Air Force Reserves and got a job at the Bevans State Bank in Menard where they made their home in town. Menard is a little town in West-Texas ranching country. They had two children, Carolyn and Pat. When they both of the kids were school age, Willie Lee started teaching school herself. All the kids she taught in school loved her. In addition to all her other activities, she was and always has been the heartbeat of our whole family for years and years. None of us ever have to remember our own birthday because she always calls and wishes us a happy one. That's a job too because my great grandparents met and married there on the banks of the San Saba River in 1888. They had eight kids who all got married, were pretty frisky and had a bunch of kids as did their kids on down the road. Today there are about 240 of us out of that one marriage.

It matters not what you do for Willie Lee—no matter what kind gesture you make, just wait; she will soon surpass you. Allen, her husband, retired as an officer with the bank, was a great friend and a gem in his own right. He died a few years later. Still, today you can call Willie Lee any time and she is always willing to stop and visit on the phone. When anyone in the family comes through town, they always stop by the house and visit with her. She will tell you all the latest (just the good stuff now) about everybody and will act like she never has anything else to do. She taught a Sunday school class at her church for years, was named the Chamber's person of the year, won the prestigious Pioneer Award and is just plain the greatest to all of us. Her next door neighbor died at 99 a few years ago and, just before passing, had one dying wish. She wondered if Willie Lee would continue to take care of her ten to twenty cats. Well, Willie Lee doesn't even like cats but you guessed it. Now half the cats in town come to her house every morning to get fed and she gladly does it. She promised.

She also helped me greatly for four years, writing a book about the family. We had a great time reminiscing about all the trials, troubles and exploits of our ancestors during the pioneer days. My wife and I like to take her out to eat at one of the local restaurants when we are in town but its not the easiest thing you ever did. Seems like every other person who walks in the place has to come by, hug her, tell her she is the greatest and how much they love her. Now if there ever was, in the history of the United States, a "Greatest Generation" and I believe there was, there must be a Greatest Gem of that Generation and she is, unquestionably, it. This was the generation that was case-hardened by living through the Great Depression. It made them tough, self-sufficient, determined and thankful for whatever small blessings came their way. They all wondered if they would make it but there is no guessing about it now. They made it—and were the better for it. However, without enduring all that hardship, it certainly would have been a whole lot harder for them to stand up to what they faced as a nation and individually in World War II. We just recently celebrated her 90th birthday at the Community Center there in Menard and it was packed with former students, friends, church members and family who came to honor her from all over the United States. Why is she so loved and respected? I believe it is because she is the most thoughtful person you will ever meet.

Proverbs 19:22 reminds us, "That which is desired in a man is kindness" and kind actions always come from kind thoughts. Being thoughtful and kind costs so little and means so much. We need to be very careful about what we think because that is what we will surely become. It is also important to be kind even to mean people because they usually need it more than anyone. And, there is no way we can be thoughtful without being observant. We need to be ever alert to see if there is a need others might have that we can accommodate. Do they need help finding a job? Finding a car? Finding a home? Keep your eyes wide open and be there for them in their time of need. Anybody can be a sunshine friend. What our friends really need is a rainy-day friend, someone who is there for them when they are temporarily down and out. Take them to lunch when you know they have lost their job or are struggling in some way. Be a listening ear.

Another way to be thoughtful of others is to remember their pet peeves. If you know something you do or like really bothers them, even though it is no problem to you or the Lord, have enough deference to discontinue it around them. Don't stop being yourself or believing or practicing the Truth but show a little patience with others. This is especially true with our bosses. It is up to us to find out what they like and don't like. It is our job to get along with them and not necessarily vice versa. Some people think they can do excellent work and that will be sufficient. We know you have the right to do whatever you want in life and you can do it all your way but if, in the process you alienate your supervisor, what have you gained? You will have lost everything in the end. Be thoughtful of those around you. Work in life to gain their favor, not just to get a promotion or a pay raise. If someone in your company is struggling with their job, quietly help them expecting nothing in return. Thoughtfulness is usually greatly appreciated.

Yet another way to be thoughtful is being aware of another person's means of being happy. If they like mustard on their dill pickles, just leave it alone. Just as long as you don't have to join them. Don't interfere with it. There is no percentage in disturbing an ant hill as long as it isn't in your own backyard.

In this world, it is a great blessing to be thoughtful and thankful for the things others do. Give them all the credit for jobs well done—even if you helped a good deal. Try to always meet the other person more than half way. It's true, our friends can either make us or break us in life but, more importantly, they are also one of our greatest sources of true happiness, comfort and enjoyment. Treat them well, forget yourself and you will find life to be a joy. Life is not all about us, it is about others.

In a marriage, it is the little things we do for our mate that lets them know how much we care and how special they are. A surprise invitation to meet somewhere for lunch. A surprise invitation to go out for breakfast. A surprise vacation to a place you know they would like. Of a truth, even your dog will leave and find a new home if you are not thoughtful of it and its needs for not only the basics, but for love, care and affection. Besides, far and away above everything else, the greatest joy in life is to give—not receive.

What it means to have the character trait of **THOUGHTFULNESS:**

- Being observant
- Being considerate
- Anticipating the needs of others
- Remembering others
- Being quick to give others praise as well as credit for a job well done

HRIFT —   **Study start date: _____ Finish date: _____**

Thrift and economics would, at first glance, seem to be very secular, mundane subjects, having little to do with a person's spirituality. Actually, the New Testament has more to say about finances than any other topic. Money has everything to do with our lives because it is what we exchange most of our life and our time on the job for—a pay check. More importantly, without great care, it can also become something we trust in and love more than God, Himself. Although it has its dangers, money is something God wants us all to learn to manage with excellence.

As we travel through life and our days come to an end, we, like every other human being who has come here before us, will have had only a certain, finite amount of money that was given into our stewardship. It comes to every one of us the same way. It can and will either be a great blessing in our life or a curse. Shrouded with many dark powers, it can change one's loyalties to both their duties, others around them and the truth. This is exactly why it is illegal to give jurists, governmental officials and pro athletes' bribes. Money is also hard to hang onto as well. It also has a strange, hidden powers to make us all want to "overwork to be rich" so we must be on our guard. The richest man in the world, Solomon, told us this arises out of our "own understanding …" He said, "cease! Will you set your eyes on that which is not? For riches certainly make themselves wings; they fly away like an eagle toward Heaven." (Proverbs 23:4, 5) Having great riches is a mirage and a false objective in life that can destroy a man's heart. Certainly everyone needs some money and we know from the Parable of the Talents (Matthew 25:14) that God is going to hold us accountable for the finances He gives us to determine if we have been good stewards. To obtain a favorable report in this life in hopes of the Master saying, "Well done thou good and faithful servant" we must have the proper attitude toward money, finances, stewardship and thrift as well as a good understanding of how all these things work.

Another danger of money is its tendency to engender pride and a false trust in it by those who may have an abundance. Paul told Timothy to "Command those who are rich in this present age not to be haughty, nor trust in uncertain riches but in the living God, who gives us richly all things to enjoy. Let them do good, that they be rich in good works, ready to give, willing to share, storing up for themselves a good foundation for the time to come, that they might lay hold of eternal life." (I Timothy 6:17–19) At the same time it is a great danger to the rich to hoard, it cam likewise provide them a great opportunity for good to bless others, make positive changes out in the world and help the poor.

Certainly the main issue is, as we have been told, that, "The love of money is the root of all evil." (I Timothy 6:10) It is always good to make a quick note here that the Bible didn't say money is the root of all evil but that the love of it is the problem. To keep this from happening, we must elevate ourselves above this by being rooted in something far better. Ephesians 3:17 commands us to be "rooted and grounded in love." It is also well to remember that, although important on earth, riches have no eternal value and will not help us in the day of God's wrath.

Yet another problem with seeking money is that we will all become like the thing we seek, think about and love the most—and money is deceitful. You think it is and then it is not. It vanishes away. We have all thought that it would provide security in life so much that Solomon said, "The rich man's wealth is his strong city, and a high wall in his own esteem." (Proverbs 18:11) They think their money will protect them from any problems in life. They think it will enable them to hire the best lawyers, doctors and advisors to get them out of any trouble that might come their way. But, it is, they find, a false hope. Only the Lord is a strong tower, our shield and the lifter of our heads.

Paul warned us not to be "conformed to this world." (Romans 12:2) We are to have different goals and objectives in life. We are to seek "to know Him (Christ) and the power of His resurrection, and the fellowship of His suffering, being conformed to His death." (Philippians 3:10) We will all live either by trusting in money or by believing all the promises of God. If we keep our eyes on Him, "Through faith and patience we inherit the promises." (Hebrews 6:12) We are here to become conformed to His image. David said, "As for me, I will behold thy face in righteousness. I shall be satisfied when I awake with thy likeness." (Psalm 17:15) And, as Paul promised, "… whom He did foreknow, He also did predestinate to be conformed to the image of his Son, that He might be the first born among many brethren." (Romans 8:29) He wants us to seek Him, humility and the wisdom that comes only from above. This is because He made us "to have dominion over the works of (our) hands (money and material things and) has put all things under His feet." (Psalm 8:6) Then in Proverbs 22:4 we find the secret to all this: "By humility and the fear of the Lord are riches, honor and life." So riches, honor and life are not goals but God's rewards, by-products of a life spent humbling ourselves and fearing Him. He wants us to seek wisdom, love and the Kingdom and the blessings of length of days, riches and honor must follow. His wisdom will actually enable us to be thrifty but not stingy; to be generous but not wasteful. Riches are only one of the by-products of wisdom. By seeking Christ and His wisdom, we receive all the by-products. Our objective in life should simply be to love Him and be found faithful.

So now we can see that it is obviously part of God's plan for man to have finances but it will take His wisdom for us to handle them skillfully and not waste or hoard them. According to the Bible, God uses finances as His school house of faith. We must learn to be faithful with the least, less significant things on earth (money), before we will ever be trusted with the great spiritual riches. Certainly we have all probably wasted many of the resources God has sent our way. This was accomplished very easily by spending it on frivolous activities and by buying exorbitantly expensive items like cars and houses, etc. A great assist in financial management is learning the distinction of buying on the basis of utility value rather than prestige value. All prestige items, be they houses, cars, watches, etc. are manufactured with more expensive materials and priced much higher so as to appeal to the pride of prestige buyers. Instead, we should be looking for utility value in our purchases. This alone will enable us to multiply the buying-power of our dollars, regardless of our income level.

Another common problem in finances is not realizing that we are not really the owners of the things God has sent our way but rather the stewards of them. Most people think their pay check is to be spent on finding the most pleasure possible for they themselves and they quickly set about to spend every. However, God's word says, "Moreover it is required in stewards that one be found faithful." (I Corinthians 4:2) This is not an option but a command. Only when we, as Christians, give up ownership of the things we have to God, can we assume the office of stewards. We then realize that for those finances to have the most usefulness to us and the Kingdom, we don't have to spend it all on ourselves.

Thrift is the discipline to limit ourselves to spend only what is truly necessary for reasonable goals and purposes. It is to live, as God commands, by percentages because He is a God of order and percentages. Saving money has always been very difficult for human beings. It is, however, not only possible but much easier if we learn to save and spend by percentages. We need to give a certain percentage of our income and save a percentage of our income. Thrift is learning to live on less than we make. It is also learning to shop for bargains and finding out how to buy wholesale to increase the buying power of our money. In any large city there are wholesale dealers of every kind. A wise man will find out who they are and benefit from these contacts. Another good thing to know is that in every manufacturing process there is waste. All manufacturers have seconds that they are willing to sell for a fraction of the retail price. Being thrifty is also learning to buy the machine necessary to get a job done in order to do it more economically and then to still have the machine or equipment on hand to do the job again the next time—even cheaper because the machine is already paid for. Thrift is also finding value in things others consider refuse (wrecking old houses for the material as an example) and finding alternate uses for items that were manufactured for some other use entirely.

Finally, a good part of thrift is understanding the compounding effect of money—how it multiplies when invested and increases on its own in a multiplied fashion. This has been called by some, the eighth wonder of the world.

One day, as in the Parable of the Talents, we will be called before the Master to give an account of what we have done with all the talents, gifts and possessions He gave us here on earth. God help us to be found faithful.

What it means to have the character trait of **THRIFT:**

- It is in and of itself prosperity
- Being careful and skillful in the management of resources placed in our charge
- Management practices that multiply resources and causes sound growth
- Knowing how to recycle
- Not being extravagant or wasteful
- Understanding the true cost of things

TIMING— **Study start date: _____ Finish date: _____**

It is important in life to do good and do all things as well as one possibly can but an equally critical element of success is having the right timing. Timing is everything. The farmer needs to plant at the proper time or season and to reap at the right time- not too early and, certainly, not too late. The Law of the Harvest is such that one must never try to plant and reap in the same season. Never try to pull the corn out before the ear is fully formed. The rancher needs to take his cattle to market at the most opportune time—as the market price for his animals may be about to peak as well.

Even a word of encouragement for a friend who has fallen on hard times must be shared at the proper moment. Proverbs 25:11 tells us, "A word fitly spoken is like apples of gold in a setting of silver." It refreshes the soul more than food and drink.

Timing is ever so important in war. The assembly area is point on the map designated for our friendlyforces to assemble and get ready to go into a battle. All our forces would be marshalled there, of course, to be in position to later march toward an objective, on line, side-by-side making a united front, all on the same azimuth (direction) to engage the enemy. The Infantry has a saying: "Hit the LD (Line of Departure) early or hit it late and you die." The LD is an imaginary, set, geographic line on the map in a commander's battle plan from which one's unit is to advance toward the enemy in unison, with your sister units on either side. If you hit it early, you will alert the enemy prematurely of the impending attack and lose the element of surprise. A unit starting out too soon, would probably be killed by the preparatory fire of our own artillery or the bombing runs of our Air Force. They might even be confused with the enemy being ahead of our other advancing troops and get shot up for that reason as well. If a unit hits it late, their troops may get confused and start firing on our sister elements ahead of them. Timing is everything in war. Hitting the LD late, will also cause a huge, gaping hole in the line or front of our forces that would allow the enemy to flank some of our friendly units, creating mayhem, confusion and a great many casualties.

Many battles in the Bible and many still today are planned to initiate in the early morning, just prior to first light. This is about the critical point of timing. Since our troops are already awake and advancing, having an attack planned at this moment, their eyes naturally have had time to adjust to the minimal light and are able to see almost as well as if it were daylight. The enemy, on the other hand, just awakening, can't see a thing, thus giving our troops a great advantage. Our troops are able to operate almost as if it were daylight with the enemy operating in the dark. This phenomenon is called BMNT or beginning morning nautical twilight.

Our fate as a country and possibly that of the world, unbeknownst to him at the time, rested on shoulders of a great general, Robert E. Lee, and the timing of just one major battle. Calling themselves the Confederate States of America, eleven southern states with a population (including their slaves) of half that of the North, asserted their right to succeed from the Union. Lee, who had a much smaller, poorly equipped army, was able, with his genius of planning, timing and strategy to wreak havoc on the much larger and, of course, better equipped Union forces. However, the most important battle of the entire Civil War was fought at a time and on a battle field not of his choosing.

Coming from another victory over the Federal Forces at Chancellorsville, the South was experiencing high morale while defeatism was spreading throughout the North. The Confederates had also defeated the Federals at Bull Run, Antietam and Fredericksburg. It was at this point that Lee made the bold decision to invade the North. Until this battle at Gettysburg, he had proved again and again his prowess as a field commander above all others. However, intel and communications not being what they are today, on July 1, 1863 the two armies actually collided into one another on ground not of Lee's choosing. The Army of North Virginia and the Army of the Potomac met and did what they always did. They fought. For two days they fought and the casualties on both sides were tremendous. Before the defenders could rally assistance, the Federal XI Corps was routed on the northern flank and forced to retreat. By the time more defenders could rally to their assistance, two Union corps had sustained better than fifty percent casualties. However, as providence would have it, General George Meade, the Union commander, was still in possession of the priceless military high ground at Cemetery Ridge, just south of a little town called Gettysburg.

Lee knew only too well at the time what most others did not. Timing in this war was such that for the Confederacy to win independence, they needed to strike a winning blow against the North and they needed to do it quickly. His objective at that moment was to engage the entire Union Army and destroy it. Everyone in the country knew that the North owned the military industrial complex of the country and had nearly all the manufacturing and munitions plants in those days. In the South, on the other hand, all Lee had was pretty much cotton and he knew his army, the Confederacy, was running low on everything an army needs: food, clothing, weapons, ammunition, mounts and troops. They had been lacking all this from the start but at this moment, they were critically short on everything except courage and the will to win.

To get diplomatic recognition and any kind of re-supply from England or France, Lee knew he had to show them that his Army had a good chance of winning. These countries needed to see that the South would be in a position to re-pay the loans for materiel this fledgling nation was seeking. President Abraham Lincoln had set up a very effective Union blockade on land and sea from day one of the war and had kept pulling the noose tighter and tighter as time marched on. On that fateful day, Lee sent Gen. George Pickett's division squarely into the middle of the Union Army, marching 1,400 feet over a mile-wide field and directly into the Yankee cannon fire that had not been halted by the hour-long pounding of the South's artillery. Because the Union troops held the high ground, most of their cannon fire had actually gone over the heads of the Yankees. Outnumbered to begin with that day, their ranks dwindled all the more as the Confederates were also taking heavy small arms fire climbing over fences. They finally made a gallant charge straight up a steep hill and over a stone fence right into the ranks of the Union Army. As a few of these brave Confederates fought right into the breach of union lines, unknowingly to them, that moment was the high point of the War for the South. Soon, however, these brave, seemingly victorious souls who yet remained alive, had to back-track their own steps down this blood-stained, body-littered, battlefield that concluded in a major defeat. This three day battle actually produced more casualties than any other in the Civil War, about 23,000 on both sides (killed, wounded, captured or missing). Due to their smaller size and the state of their supplies, this battle turned out to be far more detrimental to the South.

The question that will probably always be asked is what would history have written if another general who heard Lee's command to attack "if practicable" would have refused to allow the enemy the military high ground that day, made a swift flanking movement to give time to scout the enemy and attack again another day on ground and at a time of the Confederates' choosing?

Believing he could still be victorious, General Lee fought on with his fledgling, terribly out-numbered and ill-equipped but brave Army for nearly two more years. The war, however, was already over on the fateful third day of the battle of Gettysburg. Looking back now, for the South, it may have been the season but should certainly not been the time nor the place for them to mount their greatest offensive.[24, 25]

Over the entire war, 395,000 fell for the North 258,000 for the South. It was our country's first total war. More died in this bloody Civil War than in all the wars our country has fought put together both before and since. (This includes, of course, all wars, our own War of Independence from Britain, World War I, World War II, the Korean Conflict. Vietnam, both invasions of Iraq and Afghanistan). Though costly, it ended very beneficially in the preservation of our union and settled the fact for us as a nation that all men are indeed created equal and should, above all, be free. It was also the first war that was decided totally by the industrial might of the prevailing side. For the Confederates, timing, primarily, decided their fate. [26]

In life, the Scripture tell us, there is a time for everything. Solomon tells us, there is
"A time for every purpose under heaven:
A time to be born,
and a time to die;
A time to plant,
and a time to pluck what is planted;
A time to kill'
and a time to heal;
A time to break down,
and a time to build up;
A time to weep,
and a time to laugh;
A time to mourn,
and a time to dance;
A time to cast away stones,
and a time to gather stones;
A time to embrace,
and a time to refrain from embracing;
A time to gain,
and a time to lose;
A time to keep,
and a time to throw away;
A time to tear,
and a time to sew;
A time to keep silence,
and a time to speak;
A time to love,
and a time to hate;
A time of war;
and a time of peace." Ecclesiastes 3:1–8

Everything is truly beautiful in its own time. The prudent man will wait for the right time and the right season for everything. Some things, however, are in God's providence alone. We must wait upon Him but when He starts them, we must go.

In the workaday world, arriving at work early is being on time and getting there on time is actually being late. Always planning to make it in the door of the office at the bewitching hour forces the leaders of the company to wonder where you are and if you are actually going to make it each and every day. Our coworkers are already on the job, lining up the day's agenda, equipment, materiel and crews. Don't make everyone wonder. Being early is being wise.

What it means to have the character trait of **TIMING:**

- A prudent man waits for the right time and the right season
- The right timing is considerate of others as well as that which is already under way
- It is the ability to select the precise moment for maximum effect
- It is waiting until all things are ready
- Moving according to God's divine schedule
- Knowing how to wait upon the Lord
- Knowing the best timing for yourself and those around you

OLERANCE— This is a euphemism, a code word for compromise. Compromise is generally not acceptable. If something is wrong according to God's plan for man, it is wrong all the time and should never be tolerated. Men must not condone what God has condemned. If you are enticed by the world to do something wrong, it is obviously for some temporary personal gain. Jesus asked the better question: "What will it profit a man if he gains the whole world, and loses his own soul?" (Mark 8:36) G.K. Chesterton said, "Tolerance is a virtue for a man with no convictions."

RUE GRIT —   **Study start date:** _____ **Finish date:** _____

With the increased availability of more efficient, labor-saving devices; better communications; shorter working hours; higher pay, and more creature comforts, most people are also becoming more complacent. Anything that requires a little sweat, sacrifice or hard work is out of the question. Absent an easy task, soft words, a great many at-a-boys, lots of pats on the back and a silk pillow to sit on, when it comes to work, many today quickly retreat. This physical and mental softness is, in and of itself, the proximate cause of nations rarely lasting over 200 years. History just keeps on repeating itself. Although we got off to a great start here in 1776, we are where we are today because of lethargy, laziness and expecting everything to be given to us in a carry-out box. We have had freedom for so long that many think it is free and have forgotten what purchased it in the first place—things you don't hear much about today. Things like sweat, shed blood, sacrifice, hard work, dogged-determination and self-reliance.

Countries like ours don't just fall into oppression and the iron-fisted rule of an oppressive dictator overnight. It is a slow, insidious process over time. People are persecuted religiously, politically or by excessive regulation and taxation to the point they are finally willing to take up arms and deliver themselves, once again, at any cost. Nations go from tyranny to faith; from faith to courage; from courage to independence; from independence to self-reliance; from self-reliance to prosperity; from prosperity to complacency; from complacency to dependence on the government and from dependence on the government back to oppression. Where are we now in America? With so many having an entitlement attitude, it shouldn't be difficult to figure. We have more takers now than makers. As I am writing this, a socialist communist almost won the Democratic nomination for President of the United States. He actually had his honey moon in Russia! If this doesn't cause on pause in a free-enterprise, capitalist country, I don't know what will.

Another problem is so many don't know what a real day's work looks like. Just recently I heard a union boss on TV talking about how it was a safety risk for people to work more than forty hours a week. He claimed that people got weary working more hours than that, told how all kinds of safety issues would arise and how there would be far more accidents on the job. What about the farmers and ranchers of American who begin work before daylight and stay at it until way past dark—every day? What about our soldiers who battle in wars every day of the year with no holidays, weekends or days off? We have become a nation of wimps.

Back in the 1870's, my family started a ranching business in West Texas. My great grandfather, William Menzies, went there to challenge his destiny when he was twenty-one with nothing but a box of carpentry tools. However, after a short time he began breeding, breaking and selling horses and gentling mules. What he really needed in those days was a strong, virtuous, God-fearing wife. The woman he chose, Letha Ann Chastain, would prove, over time, to be one of the best decisions he ever made. She was everything he had hoped for and beautiful besides. Letha Ann was generous, godly and gracious.

She also blessed him with eight wonderful children and usually had to cook for at least ten people three times a day–on a wood-burning stove. There were, as you might imagine however, almost always more folk eating at their house every day because several of her brothers and their families also lived in the vicinity. One of her brothers, just across the river, had thirteen kids the same ages as hers and they were always over at various times to spend the night. Far and away, Letha Ann's most outstanding trait was her love for people. The Menzies home was always the meeting place for the ranching community east of town. In addition to their immediate relatives, Letha Ann's hospitality and giving spirit were known far and wide. Neighbors, relatives, their friends, the preacher on Sundays, travelers and even "down and outers" who came by were welcome. She had a "light bread" baking day and a laundry day once a week and made her own soap from lard in a huge black pot on an open fire. Do I even need to tell you it gets hot in Texas? I expect not.. "Lee," as she was lovingly known, also did all the mending and making of most of their clothes. The laundry was done with water heated in that same huge, black, iron pot sitting on the ground with a fire under it. She also had chickens, geese, guineas, hogs, ducks, turkeys, bees and her own herd of sheep. In addition to this, the family always had a twenty cow dairy so everyone got to milk cows twice a day—every day—no holidays, Saturdays or Sundays off. This meant they had to deal with about 150 gallons of milk a day at a time when there was no electricity, refrigeration, automobiles or trucks. The family also had an orchard with peach, pear, plum and fig trees.

In addition to everything else, they also had a vineyard as well as a 160 acre truck farm (vegetable)—but no truck of course. You probably know that a forty acre truck farm and a truck can kill a good family even today. They had only horse or mule-drawn wagons in their day. Even after a week full of churning butter and making buttermilk along with all her other duties, she would fill the back of the family wagon with all the produce the family didn't need for the week, get one of the kids to go with her and head off to town every Saturday morning. This meant a river crossing and an eight mile jog on cow-trails so rough they'd jar your eye teeth. There were no ranch or farm-to-market roads out in the country in those days. No motor graders and no gravel roads either. She would take her country produce and sell it to a number of steady customers on her route around town. With the profits, she would buy all the store-bought staples the family needed such as coffee, sugar, flour, etc. Because she bought all their furniture and the clothes she couldn't make, this allowed her husband, William, to invest his earnings for the cattle, sheep, horse and mule business in more land, animals and improvements. They served God, worked hard and the whole family flourished.

Now, if Letha Ann didn't already have enough to do at the time she already had six kids on the ground and one she was nursing in her arms, a lady not far down-river, died during childbirth. Since she was still nursing her seventh and thought she had enough milk for two babies, she offered to raise this new born too. The problem was her milk ran out shortly thereafter, in a day when there was no pabulum or other store-bought, milk substitutes available for infants. She gave it all she had but later had to give the little child up to be raised by an aunt in Alabama. This noble woman was at least willing to make room in her home and heart for this little, motherless baby.

During this time the men of the family were ranching eight thousand acres running cattle and sheep. Her husband, William, and their five boys were also managing 150 brood mares that were foaling every eleven months. That meant they were breaking, gentling and selling over 150 horses and mules a year in addition to managing the cattle, while helping with the dairy and farm. They also did custom harvesting for most of the other farmers in the valley with their sixteen horse and mule threshing machine. William and his boys were always building something and stringing fence on the ranch. He never stopped making improvements in his ranching operation.

Where my family settled is a hot, semi-arid, unforgiving land; no place for the faint of heart. The terrain also becomes more and more a land of scrub oaks, mesquite trees, cactus, rattlesnakes, jackrabbits, armadillos, and scorpions as you go West in Texas. In addition to all this, the early settlers had to deal with Indians, outlaws, droughts, floods, Bo weevils, screwworms and cholera just to mention a few of their problems. It has been said and rightly so that Texas was hard on men and dogs in those days but hell on women and horses. Regardless, Letha Ann was willing to do what was necessary to meet the dangers and difficulties of pioneer life head-on and subdue them. My dad told me she was always sharing a proverb, in season, about how to meet the perplexing challenges of life. She left a legacy to future generations of the joy of serving others from a humble heart. Letha Ann was faithful to God, her family and the community until the day she died. What she had only God knows.

The full account of her life is in my book, *The Spirit of Texas*.

What it means to have the character trait of **TRUE GRIT:**

- The "ability to endure hardness as a good soldier." II Timothy 2:3
- The ability to accomplish the mission even with long hours; deplorable, dirty conditions; little sleep; a lack of proper nourishment; enduring extreme temperatures; hard usage, harsh treatment; little or no pay and getting little or no appreciation.
- The ability to adapt to difficult circumstances, personalities and quickly changing requirements
- A firmness of spirit to endure to the end.
- Realizing we "can do all things through Christ who strengthens (us)." Philippians 4:13
- The courage when facing danger under extreme conditions, hardships and ordinarily overwhelming odds, to see and obtain the victory no matter what.
- The presence of mind to know your body will lie to you. It will tell you that you are finished when it can still go the same distance again.
- The intestinal fortitude to get up before daylight to meet with the Lord in His word so you live in the most productive part of each and every day enjoying divine guidance.
- It is to pray for a "mission impossible" that is important to God and then wait patiently sharpening your sword for His call to begin the exploit for Him. Daniel 11:32b

RUST—   **Study start date:** _____ **Finish date:** _____

It is sad to say but the world we live in today is filled with lies, half-truths and hypocrisy. It is hard to find anything or anyone to believe in. Wickedness is increasing geometrically, just as the Bible prophesied. (I Thessalonians 5:3) Having served on a county grand jury once and having heard all the cases the District Attorney wanted to try, I can tell you I don't know how today's judges do it. I honestly don't see how they can listen to a constant stream of the testimony of the horrible things people are doing today and not become cynical. It is no less than a tidal wave of corruption coming at them every day. Such is today's society. Certainly there are good people out there but they are normally not the ones coming before the court system.

This being so, trust is critically important in life. No one will ever accomplish anything significant without the ability to trust. Knowing how to find the right things to trust in is the key, so trust must begin within one's self. However, many people don't even like themselves because they know they don't keep their word or their agreements either. They then must judge everything and everybody from the perspective of their own wicked heart. God, Himself, even says, "The heart is deceitful above all things and desperately wicked" and asks, "who can know it?" (Jeremiah 17:9) You simply can't trust in a natural, unregenerate man. This is a terrible mistake. In Jeremiah 17:5 we find these words recorded: "Cursed is the man who trusts in man and makes flesh his strength, whose heart departs from the Lord." Every step a person takes toward trusting in man and his systems, tragically, his heart departs a little bit further from the Lord. Then he paints us a word picture of what this man's life will be like: "For he shall be like a shrub in the desert and shall not see when good comes, but shall inhabit the parched places in the wilderness, in a salt land which is not inhabited." (Jeremiah 17:6) He will be like a dried-up shrub, a tumbling tumbleweed, blown about by every wind of doctrine. Having no foundation or root system, no life in them, no meaning or purpose, no fruit, they are fit only to be cut down, bundled up and thrown in the fire. Certainly, nothing can live in a salt land where there is no trust in God.

We are entering a time now when wickedness and trouble will increase in the world like never before. Christians need to prepare themselves for this storm by building a consistent daily prayer life and time of meditating on God's Word. When these days arrive and become more and more frightful, there will also arise an army of God's people who have become more and more bold. These will be those who have learned to fearlessly trust in the name of the Lord.

David was such a man. He learned to call on the name of the Lord in every trial that came against him in life. He said, "In my distress I called upon the Lord, and cried to my God: and he did hear my voice out of His temple, and my cry did enter into His ears … He delivered me." (II Samuel 22:7, 18) It takes time and effort to prepare our hearts to live a life of trust and when he faced the greatest storm he had ever encountered, he was ready! He had already called upon that Name to help him defeat the lion and the bear. In times like these, he didn't have to look for a priest or someone else to lean on. He already had a song to sing through all the darkness and uncertainty saying, "The Lord is my rock, and my fortress and my deliverer; the God of my rock; in him will I trust: he is my shield, and the horn of my salvation, my high tower, and my refuge, my savior; thou savest me from violence. I will call on the Lord, who is worthy to be praised: so shall I be saved from mine enemies." II Samuel: 22:2- 4

Everyone trusts in something. However, there are some things in which we are warned, specifically, not to trust. First and foremost, we are not to trust in man (Jeremiah 17:5) and not in our bow or sword to be our salvation in battle. (Psalm 44:6) Should we be skilled with our bow and sword? Absolutely, but we are not to trust in them or the skill in our hand. We are not to trust in our wealth (Psalm 49:6), in princes (political leaders today) (Psalm 146:3), our own works (Jeremiah 48:7) or our own righteousness. Ezekiel 33:13

Where then are we to set our hearts to trust? We are to trust only in the Lord. Jeremiah gave us these words: "Blessed is the man who trusts in the Lord, and whose hope is in the Lord. For he shall be like a tree planted by the waters, which spreads out its roots by the river ... And (he) will not fear when heat comes; but its leaf will be green, and will not be anxious in the year of drought, nor will cease from yielding fruit." (v.8) We are not only to trust Him, but that trust must run deep. Solomon said "Trust in the Lord with all (your) heart, and lean not on (your) own understanding; in all (your) ways acknowledge Him, and He shall direct (your) paths." (Proverbs 3:5) Without trust in Him, we can never have faith and faith is the only thing that pleases God. (Hebrews 11:6) Faith is how we are to get our needs met as well as how we are to bring Heaven and earth together. We also must trust in His Holy Name (Psalm 33:21), His Word (Psalm 119:97–105) and in Christ the Lord. (Matthew 12:17–21) For we know it is "in His name (the) Gentiles will trust." v.21

What are some of the benefits of trusting in the Lord? The Psalmist David said, "let all those rejoice who put their trust in You; let them ever shout for joy, because You defend them; let those also who love Your name be joyful in You. For You, O Lord, will bless the righteous; with favor you will surround him as with a shield." (Psalm 5:11, 12) Not only is He our shield but the joy of the Lord is also our strength. Nehemiah 8:10

The Psalmist said, "Our fathers trusted in You; they trusted, and You delivered them. They cried to You, and were delivered; they trusted in You, and were not ashamed." (Psalm 22:4,5) In Him they found deliverance. "Oh, how great is Your goodness, which You have laid up for those who fear You, which you have prepared for those who trust in You ..." (Psalm 31:19) "Many sorrows shall be to the wicked but he who trusts in the Lord, mercy shall surround him." (Psalm 32:10) He is the source of all goodness and mercy and trusting in the Lord, the Psalmist promises us true safety: "Whenever I am afraid, I will trust in You, in God (I will praise His Word), in God I have put my trust; I will not fear. What can flesh do to me?" (Psalm 56:4) "In God I have put my trust; I will not be afraid. What can man do to me?" (Psalm 56:11) "Unto the upright there ariseth light in the darkness ... He shall not be afraid of evil tidings: his heart is fixed, trusting in the Lord, His heart shall be established, he shall not be afraid." (Psalm 112:4, 7, 8) This kind of trust, the prophet Isaiah promised would also lead us to our inheritance saying, "... he who puts his trust in (the Lord) shall possess the land, and shall inherit (His) Holy Mountain." (Isaiah 57:13) And, where will He guide us? To still waters and green pastures. (Psalm 23:2) We all need a guide because "the way of man is not in himself; it is not in man who walks to direct his own steps." Jeremiah 10:23

When we trust God, we will be led by His Spirit to know in whom and in what we can trust here on earth and where it is we are to go to find His plan for our lives. We will also know that our future is as bright as all the promises of God!

What it means to have the character trait of **TRUST:**

- To do or allow something without any fear or thought of misgivings
- Finding a place to repose confidence
- To have confidence in something or someone
- To rely on the truthfulness or accuracy of something
- To believe
- To depend on

TRUTH, A HEART COMMITTED TO THE — Study start date: _____ Finish date: _____

In America we love freedom and want everyone to be free. We know the only thing that will set us free is the truth. (John 8:32) The truth is a powerful, liberating thing. Bondage, disappointment and loss come from trusting people who do not love the truth enough to keep their promises. We know that there is but one source of truth who can give us the power to stand to it. Jesus said, "I am the way, the truth and the life." (John 14:6) Truth is determined by the nature and character of God. It is objective, universal, absolute and never changes. Truth is reality and agrees with reality. In a dark, deceptive world He made this startling promise: "If you abide in my Word, you are My disciples indeed. And you shall know the truth and the truth shall make you free." (John 8:31, 32) God's Word is truth because the Word and Jesus are one. ((John 1:1). Speaking the truth and living by the truth in all our dealings is what gives a person integrity. Although some people love the lie and continually practice deceit as their modus operandi, all of nature abhors a lie and will vomit it out in due time. So to succeed over the long term, have peace and be happy, one must be committed to the truth.

Insofar as life can have any real meaning, truth and living by the truth will definitely decide how much peace, prosperity and freedom we will enjoy here on earth. But when compared to its effect on reality, which is eternity, it is enormous. Eternity is so long and so much more important that it makes our time on this planet and what we may or may not enjoy here pale quickly by comparison. Whether or not we decide to live by the truth in this life will also determine our standing with God and where we will reside in eternity.

The Psalmist asks the question: "Lord, who may abide in Your tabernacle? Who may dwell in Your holy hill? (Psalm 15:1) The answer then comes: "He who walks uprightly and who works righteousness and speaks the truth in his heart; he who does not backbite with his tongue, nor does evil to his neighbor, nor does he take up a reproach against his friend; in whose eyes a vile person is despised, but he honors those who fear the Lord; he who swears to his own hurt and does not change; he who does not put out his money as usury, nor does he take a bribe against the innocent. He who does these things shall never be moved (even on this side of Heaven)." Psalm 15:2–5

Why is truth so important in society? Since the days of the cave man, people have tried to live in community so that each person could specialize and become much more proficient at providing certain tasks helpful to society. The way God made human beings, each has differing talents, strengths and proclivities. One person likely exceled at gathering and cracking muscles from the river bottom while another was skilled as a hunter using a spear or a bow and arrow. Still another learned to fashion knives, spears and arrows from flint and tree limbs to trade his expertise for muscles and deer meat. Even from cave man days, men sought a fair and equitable exchange of a certain amount of one item for a similar value in another commodity. This was the beginning of commerce as we know it. For it to work, however, their business dealings had to be based on truth so that each could make fair trades and keep commitments. Only then could pricing and expectations be relied upon when buying and selling. All contracts were, obviously, verbal to begin with but they still had to be founded on truth and honesty.

Truth is the bridge that ultimately joins hearts together for agreement in business and on it will pass every expression of life and love. Otherwise, when dishonest dealings occurred, our early predecessors had to get out the clubs out and use them on each other's heads—thus causing the immediate collapse of their primitive market. The first casualty in these market shake-ups was always, obviously, the truth and the second was a smooth round head, suddenly adorned with several knots of varying sizes, colors and shapes. From the earliest days, there was always an understood goal of fair trade and inherent equity in what was traded and received by each party. So, the basis of all trading and community was always truth. Without truth, there could be no trust. Every check written in society and received by another party today, requires a high degree of trust that those things specified on the face of it: the account number, the amount, the date, the credibility of the person who signed it, the bank, etc., are all true. And, most importantly, that the writer has at least the amount written on the check in the bank to draw upon. If any part of this turns out to be otherwise, trust is broken and commerce comes to an abrupt halt until truth and trust are, once again, restored.

It is also the case that the more a person's life is built on truth, the more life they will have and enjoy. On the contrary, the more a person's life is constructed on lies, the harder will be their way. Truth is the rock the whole kingdom of Heaven is built upon and it cannot be violated successfully. That is why the Bible says very broadly, "The way of the transgressor is hard." (Proverbs 13:15) God made the heavens and the earth and His laws of truth and equity are built right into everything He created. If we really want our lives, businesses, marriage and friendships to stand the test of time, we need to build on the solid rock of truth. No man can "live by bread (making money and eating bread) alone but by every word that proceeds out of the mouth of God." (Matthew 4:4) Nothing else will work, endure or satisfy. The Master showed us how to build and explained it this way: "Whoever hears these sayings of Mine, and does them, I will liken him to a wise man who built his house on the rock; and when the rain descended, the floods came and the winds blew and beat on that house; and it did not fall for it was founded on the rock." (Matthew 7:24, 25) So we can see from this that we can all expect the storms and troubles of life to beat vehemently against our house and a house in the Bible is a person's life. But it goes on to say, "Everyone who hears these sayings of Mine, and does not do them, will be like a foolish man who builds his house on the sand: and when the raid descended, the floods came, and the winds blew and beat on that house; and it fell. And great was its fall." (v.26, 27) Only two possible outcomes are here listed. The rock of truth or sand, success or failure, plain and simple.

In much the same way, a leader must be dedicated to the truth in order to have the moral authority to lead. People in legitimate businesses will not follow a corrupt leader. This is especially true in Christian businesses and organizations. Truth is the basis of the Christian kingdom on earth as well as Heaven. Paul told the Ephesians: to put "away lying. Let each one … speak the truth with his neighbor, for we are members of one another." (Ephesians 4:25) Friends, family, employees and business associates rely on the promises and commitments made by their associates, family members and fellow employees. And, rightly so.

As we have all seen, the truth has many enemies here on earth: expediency, pride, fear of loss, shame, self-preservation, greed and satan—just to name a few. Because of all these things, finding the truth among men can sometimes be difficult. This is especially true when dealing with hostile nations but truth for Christians is actually finding God's will for us in any given situation. There was a time when King Hezekiah was severely threatened by Sennacherib, king of Assyria. History had proven that he had just recently defeated all those nations round about and, at that moment in time, had his sights set on destroying Judah. The truth was that the armies of the king of Assyria had not only defeated all these other nations but had ground all these countries to powder. He had just sent an intimidating letter to Hezekiah saying that Jerusalem was next to fall into their hands. Certainly the people of Judah hadn't been perfect (no nation ever is). Was this a time for God's judgment against Judah or was Sennacherib's letter just a lie from the pits of hell. Hezekiah had to decide whether to sue for peace on any terms available or was the truth, in fact, that it was God would deliver them once again?

He took the letter to the House of God and laid it out before the Lord. Sometimes you can't go to books, actuary tables or industry experts to find the truth in certain situations. You can only get the truth directly from the Master. There, in the temple, he prayed mightily telling God who He was, that He was God alone over all the kingdoms of the earth. He told Him that He made both heaven and earth but that the king of Assyria had also laid waste to all the nations around them. After telling God who He was, he concluded his prayer saying, "Now therefore, O Lord our God, I pray, save us from his hand that all the kingdoms of the earth may know that You are the Lord God. You alone." (II Kings 19:19) Hezekiah must

have handled all this correctly because God immediately sent Isaiah the prophet to give him the word of the Lord. The God of Israel said, "Tell him 'Because you have prayed to Me against Sennacherib king of Assyria, I have heard'". In summary God said Sennacherib "shall not come into this city, nor shoot an arrow there, nor come before it with shield, nor build a siege mound against it. By the way that he came, by the same shall he return; and he shall not come into this city, says the Lord. For I will defend this city, to save it for my own sake and for My servant David's sake." (vv. 32–34) He also promised that the zeal of the Lord of hosts would do this. So it happened one night, soon thereafter, that the angel of the Lord went forth into the camp of the Assyrians and killed 185,000 of them. There were dead bodies everywhere. Dismayed and confused by this catastrophe, Sennacherib, king of Assyria, immediately returned to his home in Nineveh with what was left of his army and remained there. While he was worshiping in the temple of his god, his two sons struck him down with the sword and then escaped to the land of Arrarat. At this point, Esarhaddon, another one of his sons took the throne. Hezekiah sought God for the truth and the truth set the whole nation, which was in imminent danger, free.

There should come a day in all of our lives when we stop and drive our stakes down, deciding, once and for all, to hate evil and every wicked way. Realizing, of course that sin and wickedness never come to help and any imagined benefits are very short lived and much longer served by horrible consequences. The enemy, the master of deceit "comes (only) to steal, kill and destroy." (John 10:10) At that same moment one should, of course, decide to love the truth and dedicate their life to it—making the quality decision to always be on the side of truth. This is a decision to never bend it, twist it, color it grey or tell half of it and it is in that moment the Lord can add His blessing and favor in a person's life.

What it means to have the character trait of **A HEART COMMITTED TO THE TRUTH**.

- The state of something being framed accurately
- Something that is always the case and never changes
- Sincerity of action and character
- Words spoken that agree with actuality
- Fidelity to the original or a standard
- That which agrees with spiritual reality
- A body of accurate beliefs and propositions

- The properties of something being in accord with reality
- Actuality
- Conforming exactly with the facts
- Having no distortion
- Not just a half truth (because it can mislead and serve well to be a lie)

VIGILANCE— **Study start date:** _____ **Finish date:** _____

Edmund Burke said, for evil to triumph, to paraphrase, good men need only do nothing. Well, evil is triumphing in our world today mostly because men do nothing when they see it but they are also failing keeping watch over its insidious creep. The tenacity to stay alert begins to wane when the slog is long, resources dwindle, attrition mounts, the hours get long, friends depart and futility begins to set it. Because of this, regrettably, more battles in life are actually forfeited than lost. The enemy is allowed to sneak in and sets up a stronghold before being noticed. Many are also asleep today because they are indulging in drink, drugs and surfeiting. Others are asleep at the switch, just not minding their work and being careful to fulfill their duty. Others are spiritually just simply at ease in Zion. Because of these things, we need to remember when the enemy always going to come. Scripture tells us exactly when he's coming: At a time you think not. He is hoping to catch us all unaware.

Vigilance is an urgency to live "ever at the ready"—always wary of the enemy and his tactics. It is also realizing that we all live in a fallen body, good only for one thing: to be placed on the altar and crucified daily. Without constant awareness, our flesh is capable of going south in a moment. It is also realizing that the enemy is crouched at the door, ready to pounce upon the uninitiated and unsuspecting. Sin's desire is to rule over us. (Genesis 4:7) Those who have their head in a cloud, a haze, a mist or a fog are easy prey. The reward of vigilance, however, is freedom, peace and power.

What it means to have the character trait of **VIGILANCE**.

- Keeping constant watch
- Staying awake at one's post, committed to practice watchfulness with diligence
- Being careful to look past the fluff the representations of others and inspect the true character of the goods
- Never fully accepting a report until you have personally verified
- Careful to be found without spot and blameless
- Unrelenting watchfulness especially during times of fatigue
- Being careful, cautions and circumspect

VIRTUE—SEE PURITY

VISIONARY—   **Study start date: _____ Finish date: _____**

T here are really only two kinds of visionaries in the world. We have spiritual visionaries or prophets, and then there are the leaders who carry out exploits, ministries and missions who are not, necessarily, prophets. The world would certainly be a dull place without both. People too soon get bogged down in the drudgery of the day and the power of the past. The "We've always done it that way" and the "You just can't get there from here" syndromes start surfacing. Visionaries, on the other hand, cannot stand doing things the way they have always been done. They want to strike out into new territory, chart new waters and build a new and better mousetrap. These people have already been infected by the thrill of building something out of nothing by faith and have seen it work. They believe there is nothing under the sun, other than salvation, that can't be improved upon. They are the inventors, the imaginative, the innovators and the improvisers who have a creative flare in all they touch. There are, however, truthfully some words in the English language they detest and have absolutely no use for. Words like "no way" or "impossible." Actually, words like these just serve to energize and stoke the fires of creativity deep within them. The visionary would rather be free to be creative than rich, powerful, accepted, secure or admired.

They are always looking forward and never backward. Always looking to the future to innovate, improve and better meet the needs of people. They believe it is far better in life to see where you are going than to look back where you've been. After all, Lot's wife turned to salt for this one thing: looking back. Visionaries see things not as they are but as they can be and, most importantly, believe there is nothing impossible with God.

Visions are what visionaries are all about and are actually so important, they are also indispensable in God's plan for man on earth. They are simply objects and scenery that appear to men either in dreams, in a trance, in deep meditation, in prayer, sometimes with their eyes wide open or in the course of carrying out their duties, wide awake. Regardless, the images come clearly to mind and the visions always come to pass or are yet to come. A spiritual leader must be a visionary, able to set the world aside, spend time alone with the Lord in prayer, fasting and meditating on the Word, to get the vision from God and then to write it. It must be written to make it clear for others to grasp. The clarity and accuracy must remain to be faithful to the divine will. Just like John was told to "write" the vision of the New Jerusalem (Revelation 21:5), God also told the prophet Habakkuk to, "Write the vision, and make it plain upon tablets, that he may run that readeth it." (Habakkuk 2:2) Most visions are not for the moment but for a future time. Here God was saying " … the vision is yet for an appointed time, but at the end it shall speak, not lie: though it tarry, wait for it; because it will surely come, it will not tarry." (v.3) Some visions must be handed down from generation to generation. In other words, once you get the vision from God and have written it down, take it to heart. Regardless of the facts, difficulties, even impossible circumstances to the contrary, hang on. Drive your stakes down. Do not be moved by what you see, hear or feel. Though it takes longer than you expect, it will, in the end, come to pass and not lie. God, Himself, will do it and we know He cannot lie. He is faithful. There will always be those who doubt the vision and grow weary awaiting the plan to unfold. God warns us of the presence of doubters saying, "Behold, his soul which is lifted up is not upright in him: but the just shall live by his faith." (v.4) The vision will come only by faith, much hard work and patience. Be ready to wait for it.

Once the vision is written, the leader must be able share that vision for their organization, ministry or church and establish goals their people can understand and run with. An effective leader can formulate a plan to obtain what is needed and show others how to accomplish the next step as God unfolds His plan. The priorities of leaders are birthed out of their own individual values, beliefs, experience, faith and character.

Visions are so incredibly important that the Bible says, "Without a vision, the people perish." Proverbs 29:18) The way God made us humans, it is impossible for us to function without meaning and purpose in life. This is why people who retire with nothing to do will die, on the average, within two years. We need to be charged. We need to be fired up and motivated. We need to be purpose driven and goal oriented. We need a vision we attach our faith to so we can find fulfillment. We need to be on fire and burn for something greater than ourselves and the things of this present life.

God uses visions for many purposes. He used a vision to burn his plan and the Abrahamic Covenant into the heart of Abram saying, in part, "Do not be afraid, Abram, I am your shield, (and) your exceedingly great reward" as well as describing the number of his descendants (would be like the sand of the sea) and all the land He was about to give them (the nation Israel). (Genesis 15:1–21) Another time, He used a vision to speak to Jacob, commanding him to take his whole family to leave the Promised Land and take his whole family to Egypt because of the great famine about to come upon the land. (Genesis 46:3–5) God gave a vision to Isaiah to declare the fall of Babylon. (Isaiah 21:2–6) On another occasion Jehovah gave a vision to Samuel of impending judgment on the Prophet Eli's house for the iniquity he knew his sons were committing and he had done nothing about. (I Samuel 3:15–18) It was a vision and a dream that God used to give Daniel about the succession of worldly empires. (Daniel 7:1–8) Then He gave Daniel the vision of the four great beasts (four kings) that were to arise from out of the earth. (Daniel 7:15–19) Paul received a vision from God of His plan for man to repent, accept the death, burial and resurrection of Christ, turn their lives over to serving God and do works which were the fruit of repentance. This was the message he carried to Damascus and then to Jerusalem, all of Judea and finally to the Gentiles. Nothing less than a vision from God would have empowered him to accomplish all this in the face of such satanic and worldly opposition. (Acts 26:19 & 20) He also directed Paul to take his ministry to Macedonia when he had every intention of going to Asia. (Acts 16:9&10) Subsequently, He gave him much needed encouragement at Corinth when he was greatly persecuted saying, "Do not be afraid, but speak, and do not keep silent; for I am with you, and no one will attack you to hurt you: for I have many people in this city." (Acts 18:9&10) The mind and heart of man could not well endure these supernatural hardships, attacks and threats without a vision from God.

Another important point about visions not to be overlook is the fact that wherever God is, there you will also find the enemy. False prophets will try their best to imitate Him. About these false prophets He spoke these words to Jeremiah saying, "The prophets prophesy lies in My name. I have not sent them, commanded them, nor spoken to them; they prophesy to you a false vision, divination, a worthless thing, and the deceit in their heart. Therefore thus says the Lord concerning the prophets who prophesy in My name, whom I did not send, and who say, 'Sword and famine shall not be in this land'—'by sword and famine those prophets shall be consumed!" Jeremiah 14:14, 15

Since the Day of Pentecost, we have been in a dispensation of open visions. We have this promise of God's Spirit being poured out in Joel 2:28: "And it shall come to pass afterward that I will pour out My Spirit on all flesh; your sons and your daughters shall prophesy, your old men shall dream dreams, your young men shall see visions. And also on My menservants and on My maidservants I will pour out My spirit in those days."

Visions from God are critical for the advancement and direction of His Kingdom, as we have seen here. He has always been a great communicator, as the Creator it is certainly no problem for Him to put visions and dreams in our heads or speak into our hearts. He is God Almighty; Maker, Sustainer and Director of the Universe. Even so, when he gives a vision, there will always be the doubters. This happened in Israel during the days of Ezekiel because some of the prophecies being discredited which were for a future time and here is His answer: "Thus says the Lord God: 'None of My words will be postponed any more, but the word which I speak will be done.' says the Lord God.'" Ezekiel 12:28

What it means to have the character trait of **BEING A VISIONARY**.

- One who is able to imagine and dream
- One who is forward looking
- Someone capable of knowing the divine will and secrets of God
- One who is capable of receiving divine tasking and guidance
- One characterized by the ability to carry out visions though they may seem impossible

VOLUNTEER SPIRIT, A — **Study start date:** _____ **Finish date:** _____

The world is full of people refusing to work, afraid of work, allergic to work or trying their best to either get out of work or do as little as they can get by with and still get some semblance of a pay check. Still others are so paralyzed by fear of making a mistake and being criticized, they would never volunteer for anything. They are afraid of their own shadow.

On the other hand, this world is bursting with opportunity, just waiting for someone with a little initiative and a volunteer spirit. A million things that need fixed, things need to be changed, people need help, battles needing brave soldiers to come to the fore and frontiers needing fearless pioneers. There is no such thing as a company operating in perfection. For this reason, God appointed priests in the Jewish church to set in order the table and other articles in the Tabernacle of the tent of meeting. (Exodus 40:4) Everywhere you go there are many things that need the attention of dedicated, capable leadership. This was so even after Paul had ministered in Crete. You would think that the great Apostle would have gotten the job done but he didn't. No one ever does. It was "For this reason" Paul said he left Titus there that he "should set in order the things that (were) lacking and appoint elders in every city as (he had) commanded" him. (Titus 1:5) They had to be men who were blameless, of an even temper, not self-willed, stable in their marriages, men who could keep rank and men not given to loose living or insubordination.

Volunteerism, sadly, has been a rare commodity from the beginning of time. To be a volunteer, one must offer his services without coercion, most of the time free of charge. It is to lay yourself out for extra work, usually hard work and sometimes possibly having to accomplish it while being in harm's way. It is to take part in a transaction even though you have no legal standing or financial interest; just the heartfelt desire to serve others. Maybe just a desire to see the ultimate victory for your comrades—and usually with all the credit going to the team.

Volunteerism is an offer to one's supervisor to work late when needed, on Saturday without pay to help the company either solve a difficult problem or meet a pressing need. It is certainly a rare and distinguishing trait among employees working virtually anywhere in the world. Your competitors, remember, are all the while complaining about doing far, far too much during forty hours with too little pay. Still you are willing to do more than is required and can always marshal whatever help and resources that might be needed beyond that. Amazing how some always want to do less while others are willing to do more.

In the 1960's the Army introduced the All-Volunteer Army concept. That was great move on their part but God has had an All-Volunteer army from the beginning. He takes no one into His service who is not a volunteer. Oh, some can come in for a minute who are mamma called, daddy led and others who are profit motivated but they don't last long.

Early in Israel's history as a nation, young David, just a shepherd boy witnessed the reproach of the entire Israeli Army by a Philistine giant, named Goliath. Immediately he asked the soldiers in the vicinity how this uncircumcised Philistine could get away with challenging the armies of the Living God. His question was met only with blank, embarrassed, shameful stares. Seeing their cowardice, he then said, "Is there not a cause in Israel?" Meaning, can this challenge to our God, our army, to the defense of our nation, wives and children and our very honor not be enough to risk our lives to defeat this heathen on the battle field? He was certainly willing to take the challenge but was only a teenager. His own brother tried to belittle him and send him back home but it was no use. When all these things were reported to King Saul, David was told to report to him. Little David told the king, "Let no man's heart fail because of him; your servant will go and fight with this Philistine." (I Samuel 17:31) Saul, himself, tried his best to discourage him, his only volunteer but David would not be dissuaded. He soon ran to the giant on the battlefield with both armies watching intently. With the first smooth stone from his slingshot, he killed the giant singlehandedly. So there could be no doubt about the outcome of this encounter, he took the giant's sword and cut off his head, causing the entire Philistine army to flee in fear of their lives. This began a total rout by the Israelis as they started chasing them across the country, killing as many as they could as they went. David had a volunteer spirit that always came to the fore when trouble arose. In any family, company, church, army, business or war, God always has a man. Our own Ben Franklin reminded us "Those who give up liberty for temporary safety will have no liberty or safety."

In the year King Uzziah died, Isaiah saw a vision of the Lord sitting on a throne with His long robe filling the temple. (Isaiah 6:1) The Shekinah glory of the Lord was so great the door posts shook and smoke filled the whole temple. Presently, an angel took a hot coal from the altar and with long tongs touched Isaiah's lips to take away his sin. Then the voice of the Lord was heard saying, "Whom shall I send, and who will go for us?" (v.8b) In other words, who will go tell this prophesy to the people? To which Isaiah opined, "Here am I: Send me." Isaiah was a volunteer.

During another time, while exiled in Babylon, Nehemiah was a cup bearer in the King's court. All was well for him until the day one of his brethren arrived there from Jerusalem. He informed him that the walls of the city were torn down and the gates were burned with fire. All the people were discouraged, distressed and dis mayed.

Nehemiah returned to Jerusalem to rebuild the wall

At his report, Nehemiah just sat down and weep. He then began to fast and pray while confessing his sins and those of the nation, crying out to God. He reminded God of His covenant with Israel and asked Him to give him favor when he went before the king for permission to return to Jerusalem and rebuild the wall. Having been faithful servant, he had never been sorrowful in the king's presence—which was usually a capital offense. So the king asked why he was so sad since he wasn't sick. Then Nehemiah said it was because of the deplorable condition of the city of his father's sepulchers. Then the king asked what he wanted to do about it, so he prayed quickly once again and said, "If it pleases the king, and if your servant has found favor in your sight, I ask that you send me to Judah, to the city of my fathers' tombs that I may rebuild it." (Nehemiah 2:5) He basically said, 'Send me' and the king did. Nehemiah couldn't stand back when his God and his nation needed him. He was a volunteer.

Volunteerism is loyalty to the leader, the company, the cause and one's country. The leader will never forget those who volunteer in the time of great challenge.

It is interesting to note that volunteer work can, among all its other blessings, be good for one's health as well. So aside from being able to advance a cause one believes in greatly, it could actually, all the while, increase your lifespan. An article was published recently that cited a couple studies conducted by the University of Michigan and the Ontario Ministry of Health. In it the researchers reported that their research showed that volunteering has many benefits including an increase in self-esteem, protection against social isolation, lowering blood pressure, strengthening of the immune system and a reduction in the adverse effects of stress. What's more, these benefits could actually be achieved by volunteering as little as an hour a week. A Cornell University study indicated that volunteering boosts the levels of endorphins, chemicals in the brain known to be the cause of the "runner's high." These endorphins are also known for relieving one's stress and pain and can even play a role in lowering a person's blood pressure. Endorphins are also linked to helping promote positive self-esteem. The study also noted that 90 percent of adults 55 and older said they had 90 percent fewer colds and stomach aches during times they were volunteering at least once a week. Dr. Taylor Alexander, the author of *Volunteering and Healthy Aging,* was one of the very first to note in his study that people live longer because they volunteer.[27]

The benefits of volunteering seem to be endless. Aside from health benefits, volunteering broadens one's personal network and offers a time and place to form meaningful, life-long friendships. Many carry over into strong business relationships. It affords a person experience and builds their resume, as well as being both rewarding and fun. Many times giving yourself comes back over time like a boomerang to bless you again and again.

What it means to have the character trait of **A VOLUNTEER SPIRIT**.

- Offering one's self in the service of others of one's own free will
- Offering to give freely of one's time and talents to help others with no promise of financial reward
- Offering to take up arms for one's country without the compulsion of the draft
- A willingness to tackle a difficult problem for one's company or to serve on a difficult and dangerous mission for one's country.

WISDOM—   **Study start date:** _____ **Finish date:** _____

Note to the reader: As aforementioned in the introduction of Prudence, the goal of everyone's life should be to obtain character which certainly includes wisdom. But past gaining some wisdom is our great need of prudence. It, like wisdom, is different from all other character traits in that all others stand alone with a singular definition. Wisdom and Prudence include multiple traits. Wisdom has seven and Prudence ten, distinctly different but very important aspects.

The Bible tells us clearly and unequivocally that the most valuable thing in the world is wisdom. This is what the wisest man on earth, Solomon said about its incredible benefits: "Happy is the man who finds (it) and the man who gains understanding (along with it). For her proceeds are better than the profits of silver and her gain than fine gold. She is more precious than rubies and all the things you may desire cannot compare with her. Length of days is in her right hand, and in her left hand riches and honor. Her ways are ways of pleasantness, and all her paths are peace. She is a tree of life to those who take hold of her, and happy are all who retain her." (Proverbs 3:13) Now you couldn't get a much better recommendation than this from one qualified to know. It also happens to be what God used to found the earth and established the heavens. (v.19) All this is certainly well and good but continuing on it says that wisdom doesn't dwell

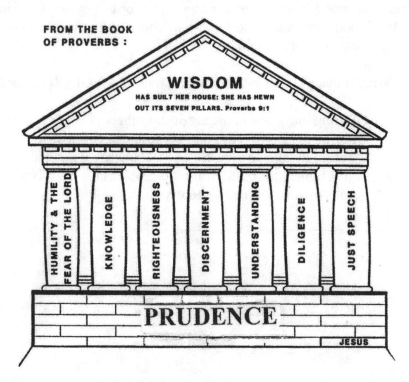

FROM THE BOOK OF PROVERBS :

WISDOM

HAS BUILT HER HOUSE; SHE HAS HEWN OUT ITS SEVEN PILLARS. Proverbs 9:1

HUMILITY & THE FEAR OF THE LORD | KNOWLEDGE | RIGHTEOUSNESS | DISCERNMENT | UNDERSTANDING | DILIGENCE | JUST SPEECH

PRUDENCE

JESUS

alone. Wisdom "dwell(s) with prudence and find(s) out knowledge and discretion.

We also know that "By (wisdom and prudence) kings reign and rulers decree justice. By me princes rule, and nobles, all the judges of the earth. I love those who love me, and those who seek me diligently will find me." (Proverbs 8:15–17) Prudence is a spiritual gift that also pays rewards in this life because the writer goes on to say, "Riches and honor are with me, enduring riches and righteousness. My fruit is better than gold, yes, than fine gold, and my revenue than choice silver. I traverse the way of righteousness, in the midst of the paths of justice. That I may cause those who love me to inherit wealth, that I may fill their treasuries." (Proverbs 8:18–21)

All one need do is pick up a newspaper any day of the week to see the number of lives devastated and strewn about the path of life. These are those who never answered wisdom's call, never grasped the fear of the Lord, going their own way; relying upon their own mind to make decisions. Two things on this planet they say are impossible for men to compute the value of: wisdom and the price of sin. Wisdom will take you farther than you could ever imagine and sin, to the contrary, lower to more pain than a man can bear (Hell). Wisdom is totally indispensable for a person to successfully navigate through this life with all its false promises, false brethren, fool's gold, fake allies and false objectives. Having experienced many of these things himself, Solomon said "Wisdom is the principal thing; therefore get wisdom" and along with it, "in all your getting …" use it to "get understanding." (Proverbs 4:7) The greatest cost of sin, on the other hand, among many other penalties is separation from God for eternity. .

Fools have little need of wisdom and this is probably because of their willingness to rush in where wise men refuse to go. Wisdom is so valuable that Solomon said the man is not only happy who finds it, "… her proceeds are better than the profit of silver and her gain than fine gold. She is more precious than rubies and all the things you may desire cannot compare with her." It not only works well in family and business affairs, but, "Length of days is in her right hand, in her left hand riches and honor. Her ways are ways of pleasantness and all her paths are peace. She is a tree of life to those who take hold of her and happy are all who retain her." Proverbs 3:13–18

On the contrary, a lack of wisdom will result in one making a whole host of bad decisions and taking the wrong paths in life. The results of these bad decisions are often very costly if not devastating but definitely painful. We have all gone down what we thought was the primrose path only to get a black eye at the end of it.

Wisdom is the ability to use and properly focus the knowledge we already have. Many, today, have plenty of knowledge but no idea how to apply it. Wisdom, therefore, is much like having a brush to apply knowledge where we need it in life. Many today have plenty of knowledge but little to no wisdom on how to apply it. Thus they render themselves unwise. It is the skill to judge in complicated, convoluted circumstances. It is the ability to make decisions the way God would. True wisdom is to be prudent, circumspect and cautious.

Wisdom is God's gift of supernatural answers to the perplexing problems of life. Having a little, temporary success in life and the world's applause means nothing. In Job 32:8 he said, "there is a spirit in (a) man, and the breath of the Almighty gives him understanding. Great men are not always wise, nor do the aged always understand justice." Anyone who compromises their convictions for the world's fleeting approval—in the face of truth and eternity—is not wise. Jeremiah warned us of man's blindness when he penning these words: " … a man's way is not in himself; nor is it in a man who walks to direct his steps." (Jeremiah 10:23) Left to himself, man is his own worst guide, so he must find a reliable source for direction and we know that wisdom only comes from God. In fact, "The fear of the Lord is the beginning of (it)" (Proverbs 9:10) and every treasure of wisdom and knowledge is hidden in Christ. (Colossians 2:3) Wisdom is realizing that this world will not satisfy and that its attainments are so very subject to rust, fire and thievery that we should set our hearts on gaining the gifts that can only come from above.

No matter what one intends to do in life, he must first stop and build a foundation. The greater part of that foundation is to gain a heart of wisdom and to seek it as a gift directly from God. To receive it one must first ask of Him and then receive it by faith. James said, "If any man lacks wisdom …" and there is a solution for this common malady—as we all lack wisdom. He says, "let him ask of God who gives to all liberally and without reproach, and it will be given to him." (James 1:5) One must also set his heart to have a high regard for wisdom and then proceed to seek it like a miner seeking silver and hidden treasure. (Proverbs 2:4) Silver, gold and diamonds in the Earth only yield themselves to the most persistent miners with a pick and shovel after much sweat and hard work. The wise man will, likewise, dedicate himself to the daily pursuit of it. We will find it in the Word, in prayer, being observant in our daily lives and learning from others as well as from our own trials in life. It falls on no man by chance.

It is important to note that there are also two kinds of wisdom: man's and God's. Man's comes from the head and the fallen nature. True wisdom comes from God's Spirit. James said: "The wisdom that is from above is first pure, then peaceable, gentle, willing to yield, full of mercy and good fruits, without partiality and without hypocrisy." (James 3:17) Whereas all the counsel of man, quite the contrary, is deceit.

Another way God gets His wisdom to us is through our trials and troubles. Therefore, we can prepare ourselves to receive it by doing something completely contrary to human nature, deciding that we will love these afflictions. It is in them that God is able to teach us His ways and laws. David said, "It is good for me that I have been afflicted, that I may learn your statutes." Psalm 119:71, 72

Still another part of the wisdom we need to attain in this life is to be like "the sons of Issachar who had understanding of the times, to know what Israel ought to do." (I Chronicles 12:32) To do this, we must study the Word, prophecy, current events and identify the harbingers of our time. As leaders, we must be alert and ever watchful to know what is happening in the world around us so that we can, with the wisdom God grants, guide our families, church and communities. Wisdom is something we should be asking God for as our main pursuit in life.

What it means to have the character trait of **WISDOM**:

- It is to number one's days and to spend one's time digging for it as with a pick and shovel
- It is to know what to do with knowledge
- It is not the ability to know what to do next week or next year but what to do next.
- It is having insight and understanding of the times
- It is having a good sense generally about human nature, cause and effect
- It is having common sense
- It is having the sense to avoid even the appearance of evil
- It is never becoming so foolish that you think we can't be tempted
- It is to always consider our self as weak so God can be mighty on our behalf
- It is the sense not to even tread on the devil's territory unless on a specific mission from God
- It is knowing that even Joseph ran from temptation
- It is to realize that true wisdom comes only from the inspiration of the Almighty. Job 32:8
- It is to realize that only by wisdom is a house (a life) built. Proverbs 24:3
- It is having a deep love for and a commitment to the will of God
- It is the sense to watch the eye gate, the ear gate and the food and drink intake of the body
- It is the sense to make a covenant with our eyes not to set any evil thing before them
- It is understanding how things relate
- It is knowing the inner qualities and propensities of things
- It is knowing one's inner and outer limits
- It is the ability to see life from God's perspective
- It is the ability to solve problems as God would
- It is to realize that one needs to seek a multitude of counsel before waging war or making major decisions in life like starting a business, getting married, etc.
- It is finding out what God is doing in our day and throwing our self into it wholeheartedly
- It is knowing that wisdom is a life-long pursuit

In broad categories, however, Wisdom is multi-faceted. It includes these seven very important pillars:

- Humility and the Fear of the Lord
- Knowledge
- Righteousness

- Discernment
- Understanding
- Diligence
- Just speech

HUMILITY AND THE FEAR OF THE LORD
A trait of wisdom   Study start date: _____ Finish date: _____

The fear of the Lord is truly a gift of God's grace. So many people out in the world love the lie, thievery, deceit and corruption. Not realizing that these things will eventually kill them, they follow on blindly led by their lust. It is so sad. They are really serving the enemy of their souls and don't know it. We know why he comes into their lives, and it is for nothing other than "to steal, kill and destroy." But our God comes, if they would only open their eyes, "that they may have life and that they may have it more abundantly." (John 10:10) The fear of the Lord and wisdom are tied together because when we humble ourselves, Psalm 34:11 says He "will teach you the fear of the Lord." We so dread His displeasure, knowing there are consequences for sin, and yet desire His favor so we cheerfully submit to His will and seek His face. We are so grateful of all his benefits and the forgiveness salvation brings that we worship Him in freedom, sincerity and truth. We gladly humble ourselves under His mighty hand because that is our rightful place and know it is His plan all along to exalt us in our humility in due time. (1 Peter 5:6) This humility is the beginning of everything with God. Proverbs 9:10 says, "The fear if the Lord is the beginning of wisdom." To man God Said, "the fear of the Lord that is wisdom" Job 28:28

The Fear of the Lord is commanded:

We find our duty in Deuteronomy 6:13: "You shall fear the Lord and serve Him, and shall take oaths in His name."

Because of his many benefits as our Lord and Master, "Therefore you shall keep the commandments of the Lord your God to walk in His ways and to fear Him." Deuteronomy 8:6

"…What does the Lord your God require of you, but to fear (Him), to walk in all His ways and to love Him, to serve the Lord your God with all your heart and with all your soul." Deuteronomy 10:12

Jesus said, :,,,Do not be afraid of those who kill the body, and after that have no more that they can do. But I will show you whom you should fear: Fear Him who, after He has killed, has power to cast into hell; yes I say to you, fear Him!" Luke 12:4, 5

Since we have received the gracious gift of "…a kingdom which cannot be moved, let us have grace, whereby we may serve God acceptably with reverence and godly fear." Hebrews 12:28

The Blessings of Fearing the Lord

It keeps us from sin as Moses said, "Do not fear (God's presence among you), for God has come to test you, and that His fear may be before you, so that you may not sin" Exodus 20:20

Moses told the people that God was giving them the Promised Land, a land flowing with milk and honey, but to take it you must "fear the Lord your God, … keep all His statutes and His commandments which

I command you, you and your sons and your grandson, all the days of your life, and that your days may be prolonged." Deuteronomy 6:2

Psalm 25:12-14 is laden with promises: The man that fears the Lord. "Him shall (God) teach in the way He chooses. He himself shall dwell in prosperity, and his descendants shall inherit the earth. The secret of the Lord is with those who fear Him, and He will show them His covenant."

"Behold, the eye of the Lord is upon them that fear Him, on those who hope in His mercy, to deliver their soul from death and to keep them alive in famine." Psalm 33:18, 19

"The angel of the Lord encamps all around those who fear Him and delivers them" Psalm 34:7

"Oh fear the Lord, you His saints! There is no want to those who fear Him." Psalm 34:8,9

What it means to have the character trait of **HUMILITY AND THE FEAR OF THE LORD**:

- Reverence and awe
- Trembling at the high price of disappointing Him
- Fearing the One with the power to cast the soul into Hell
- Realizing He, alone, is our savior and benevolent benefactor
- A deep desire and longing to please the Lord
- Obeying Him is our only hope to be free and find favor

NOWLEDGE, A HEART TO COLLECT AND RECORD –
A trait of wisdom   Study start date: ___ Finish date: ___

The word "know" in the Bible has a much broader meaning than our English word. The Bible word includes all the ordinary meanings of obtaining facts, sensing, perception and understanding. However, it goes on/ to include the deeper, more profound physical and spiritual experiences such as the knowledge of God, reality, the spiritual truth and the sexual experience. Apart from gaining knowledge, man is a simple sack of dust groveling blindly and hopelessly about the face of the earth. Only "the Lord gives wisdom, from His mouth come knowledge and understanding." (Proverbs 2:6) To His children "It is given to know the mysteries of the kingdom of Heaven but to (the heathen) it is not given." (Matthew 13:11) Even for those in the kingdom, it is gained initially by grace ant then incrementally by much effort, seeking and study.

Not having applied myself in high school, my grades were understandably not good, so when I went to college, I never had a problem thinking I was the sharpest knife in the drawer. After a year or so of college it dawned on me that as soon as I took the finals for my courses each semester, that I had another problem. I forgot everything I had learned. I knew why too. It was me again. I just wasn't as smart as all the other students. Surely they were remembering all that stuff. So I thought to myself, "This whole "going to college" thing is a huge waste of time, money and effort if I am going to forget everything at the end of every semester. So, my solution was to buy a 3-ring notebook with alphabetical dividers and start filing by topic everything I considered important: famous quotes, poems, philosophy, magazine and newspaper articles, etc. That one notebook has grown into volumes and volumes of notebooks over the years containing a lot of ideas and valuable information. Earl Nightingale once said, "Ideas are like babies. Nobody gets but a few so you better take good care of everyone you get." Then again, just one good idea can sometimes be worth more than a million dollars. How many great ideas have gotten by us and have fallen out of the cracks in our craniums over the years? There is an inscription at the Air Force Academy that reads, "Man's flight through life is powered by knowledge." The Bible even admonishes us to "Hold on to instruction (knowledge), do not let it go; guard it well, for it is your life." (Proverbs 4:13) While in our short stay on this planet, hard as we try, none of us will gain too much knowledge. However, while knowledge may have limits, ignorance knows no bounds.

About this same time in college I read somewhere that "Things spoken speed away but those written endure." I thought to myself, "Now that is truth if I've ever heard it." That means ninety-nine and ninety-nine one hundredths of everything we have ever heard in our lives has already been forgotten or soon will be. Our brains just aren't equipped to retain information for any length of time at all. For the same reason Confucius said, "A short pencil is better than a long memory." (I doubt if he really said that but it makes a lot of sense.) Hold on now because this next little bit of information is going to rock you. I also heard that "Ignorance was a consequence of being human but not knowing it was even more atrocious." How true! Think about it. There is so much knowledge in this world, so much to learn and know. Besides that, all knowledge doubles every 12 years now. No matter how much we learn and we should learn all we can, we are still hopelessly ignorant even after all the learning. It was then that I gladly and freely declared myself ignorant and still remain so to this day. However, I have tried to do something about it by learning all I can.

A few years ago I hosted a reunion of some of the officers who served in the First Cavalry Division in Vietnam. We met in conference room of my ministry building. This was about 40 years after the fact and the first time we had all gotten together. What an excellent group of leaders and warriors. We ate a lot of pizza, drank a lot of cokes and had lot of fun. Everyone told what they had done with their lives over the years. I just happened to sit next to a guy who also went to Texas A&M University, my alma mater, and we somehow got to talking about remembering what we had learned there. I asked him if he remembered all that information, thinking he was surely going to tell me yes or most of it or something. To my surprise he said, "I forgot every bit of it as soon as I took the finals." Same exact thing I had said 40 years earlier. The only difference in the two of us was that I saw myself as ignorant and declared myself so for all those years and have been collecting and recording information ever since. Forgetting just about everything, which I thought was a personal problem of mine, was actually a common malady among men. Mark Twain even said, "My memory is good but my forgetory is outstanding."

Interestingly, many years ago Aristotle Onassis, the Greek shipping magnate who married Jacqueline Kennedy, was talking with his son. On that occasion, he had just asked his dad to send him to college. Upon hearing the request Ari said, "Son, why do you want to go to college?" He opined, "Because I want to go in business and make a lot of money." His dad said, "Son, you don't need to go to college. Just get yourself a pen and a small note pad. Carry them with you at all times." He was teaching him how important it was in life and business to be observant, to be alert and take notes. Write down important information on price changes, know the players and the products in your chosen field, detect the trends and mega-trends, make a note of needs you find, etc. The oldest axiom in business is to "Find a need and fill it." What he might have been saying is that it is best in life not to walk around with one's head in a haze, a mist, a cloud or a fog expecting good fortune to fall on us like a rock. It probably won't. Be alert. Pay attention. Learn from everyone you meet. Write things down and keep a journal in your computer. Keep doing this and ideas and opportunities will surely come your way.

What it means to have the character trait of **A HEART TO COLLECT AND RECORD KNOWLEDGE:**

- Having an intrinsic, burning desire to gain knowledge and discretion
- Considering others smarter than yourself and taking notes every time you hear instruction so you can harvest the gems
- Filing your notes by topics (so you can easily find and reference them later)
- Counting knowledge more valuable than silver and gold
- Demonstrating that you count knowledge more valuable that silver and gold by keeping it in a safe place (having a good filing system)
- Learning to see value in things others consider worthless
- Noting market fluctuations
- Learning from your own mistakes and those making them around you
- Making a list of those things in life that are more dangerous than they appear to be
- Make a point of learning and recording the definitions of words
- Collecting ideas, philosophies, quotes, poems, statistics, newspaper and magazine articles, etc. You never know when they will be useful.
- Determining in your heart to love knowledge, instruction and correction
- Realizing that spiritual knowledge is more important than any other kind (I Corinthians 8:1b & 2)
- Remembering that a prudent man collects the facts before making decisions
- Knowing that writing down your leader's instructions every time will save you a lot of mistakes over a life time and earn you great favor as one who can not only "get the job done" but get it done right the first time.

RIGHTEOUSNESS– A trait of wisdom   Study start date: _____   Finish date: _____

No man can ever hope to be wise without the knowledge of the Holy One. When saved, the only righteousness we will ever have comes by faith in Christ. He is all our righteousness and it is all His alone. Even on our best day, the Bible says our righteousness is as filthy rags. (Isa 64:6) It does, however, include the state or quality, to some degree, of being free from sin and wrong doing as well as being just. God has only one robe for his saints, the robe of righteousness. He never alters His robe to fit a man, but a man to fit His robe.

The Old Testament definition signified a righteousness that conforms to the norm of God, Himself. It included ethical righteousness as well as equal justice for all as well as benevolences and salvation for those who were faithful to the Lord. The righteousness of the law was that obedience required by the Law required. Paul said, "We have previously charged both Jews and Greeks that they are all under sin. As it is written: 'There is none righteous, no, not one…" (Romans 3:10) However, the righteousness of faith is received by justification at salvation and is received totally by faith. (Romans 3:21-28) We take Christ's standing at that moment at His expense.. This perfect righteousness of Christ is imputed to us, as believers, when we accept Christ as our Savior. I Corinthians 1:30

In the New Testament, Paul gave it three meanings in his epistles: First, was the ethical conduct required by the commandments in the Law of Moses. The second, was a much higher standard on purity, holiness and uprightness expected of Christians and the third was the actual righteousness of God imparted to us by the gift of salvation through the blood of Jesus Christ.

God is the only true and righteous judge and as such, is the true and just distributor of all rewards and punishment. He has never made a mistake and it is impossible for Him to be wrong due to the fact that He is omniscient and needs nothing. He cannot be tempted..

THE BLESSINGS OF THE RIGHTEOUS

- You will abide in the tabernacle of God. Psalm 15:1
- God will sustain the righteous such that they shall never be moved. Psalm 55:2
- The Lord gives sound wisdom to the righteous. Proverbs 2:7
- He is a shield to them that walk uprightly. Proverbs 2:7
- His righteousness directs our way. Proverbs 11:5
- His righteousness will deliver us. Proverbs 11:6
- You will shine forth as the sun in the Kingdom of God. Matthew 13:43
- You will be visited with glory, honor and peace. Romans 2:10
- The Lord's eyes are upon you and His ears are attentive to your prayers. I Peter 3:12

What it means to have the character trait of **RIGHTEOUSNESS:**

- Being and doing right
- Being free from sin
- Purity in heart
- Living by the Truth
- Divine holiness
- The righteousness of God in Christ
- Equity in justice for all
- Benevolence to the poor

DISCERNMENT—A trait of wisdom   Study start date: _____ Finish date: _____

In order to avoid the consequences of their actions in life, some people will do their best to hide the truth with lies, half-truths, subterfuge and innuendo. In many cases these people are actually being led about, moved and motivated by demonic, deceiving spirits. A leader's ability to discern the truth in certain difficult situations may actually save a life, a cause, property a war, or prevent the convicting the wrong person in a court of law.

Having discernment is imperative for a leader. It is the ability to see the truth as well as the true condition in another person's life. Discernment is essential when you consider that "the whole world lies under the sway of the wicked one." (I John 4:19) As leaders, the welfare, whole lives and careers of people are often in our hands so we cannot afford to make mistakes or be led astray by the lies and craftiness of men. To avoid this, one must have several tools available and avail himself to all of them.

First of all, the prudent man doesn't listen only to the first person to present their side of an issue because they can easily frame the situation to reflect their positive points alone. Instead, he fully hears all sides. All the while he looks for motives, studies the history of the conflict between the parties, takes note of their body language, facial expressions, their voice inflections and tone of voice in order to discern the truth. He consults the Word.because it "is a discerner of the thoughts and intents of the heart(s)" of men. He researches the issue, studies relevant law, checks the pertinent regulations and gets all the facts before even seeking wise counsel and then goes to God in prayer to "discerns his way." (Proverbs 14:18) He can then ask God for the gift of wisdom (James 1:5) and "the discerning of spirits." I Corinthians 12:10

Another important area of having discernment is the ability to understanding what the wishes of a superior are regardless and in spite of what they actually may be telling us. Sometimes they may be testing our loyalty. Loyalty is everything in the kingdom of God. We see this ability to discern operating many times in the life of Elisha, the servant, successor and understudy of the great prophet Elijah. It was crucial in Elijah's selection process.

Having had a long and distinguished ministry as a prophet and having had his words confirmed by great miracles, Elijah prophesied a three and a half year drought on the land. In an agrarian economy where just about everyone's livelihood depended on livestock and crops, prophesying a drought was not a very popular or healthy thing to do before a wicked king like Ahab. He had also just recently perturbed his wife by calling all of her false prophets to a showdown on Mt. Carmel. Elijah gave her prophets first shot at showing that their god, Baal, was more powerful than his. They were to call on Baal to bring fire down from heaven and burn up a bull they were sacrificing. They called on Baal and they danced, they cried, they wailed and cut themselves with knives and spears until blood came out but ... of course nothing happened. Elijah began to mock them repeatedly asking if their god was meditating, on a journey, asleep or (one version of the Bible says) could it be that their god was busy relieving himself? He then prepared an altar with twelve smooth stones, had it loaded with wood and then had the bull placed on it. Next he had a ditch dug around it and had it drenched three separate times with four large water pots of water. Finally, he called upon the Lord God and fire immediately came down from Heaven and burned up not only the bull but the wood, the water, the twelve stones and the dust under all of it. This proved conclusively, of course, that Jezebel's prophets were false and Elijah's God, the true and living God, was both authentic, all-powerful and real.

At that moment Elijah commanded that the people seize Jezebel's 450 prophets and take them to the Brook Kishon. There Elijah personally saw to the execution of every one of them. (I Kings 18:20–40)

Later, he prophesied the end of that drought to Ahab. However, once Ahab had gone back and told Jezebel that Elijah had just killed all her prophets, she sent him a message promising to have him killed by the next day. Unable to deliver on her promise, Elijah escaped her cruel hand and then had a meeting with the Lord God. During that meeting, the Lord told him, among other things, to anoint Hazael King over Syria, Jehu King over Israel and Elisha as the prophet to succeed himself.

He then found Elisha plowing with not one but twelve yokes of oxen out in the field. (Elisha was not a slacker.) When he passed by, Elijah threw his mantle on him. Immediately, knowing what all this meant, he left his oxen and ran to Elijah saying, "Please let me kiss my father and my mother, and then I will follow you." (I Kings 19:19) Then Elijah said, "Go back again, for what have I done to you?" Basically he tested Elisha by telling him to go back to his parents if he thought that, in this situation, was appropriate but he was to settle all this for himself. But instead of bidding his parents farewell, Elisha imme-

diately turned back from him and showed his resolve by taking a yoke of oxen, killing them and cooking their flesh with the oxen's yoke and equipment for fuel and feeding the meat to the people standing by. (Burning the tools of his former livelihood was also a demonstration of his commitment to the ministry as well as burning a possible bridge for him to return to his old way of life.) Then he immediately arose to follow Elijah, to be his servant.

On another occasion, after the death of Ahab, Elijah rebuked his successor, King Ahaziah for inquiring of Baal-Zebub, the god of Ekron as to whether he would recover from an injury. Ahaziah immediately sent a captain and fifty men to lay hold of Elijah. They found him sitting on the top of a hill and the captain commanded him to come down. Elijah said, "If I am man of God, then let fire come down from heaven and consume you and your fifty men." It did. Then Ahaziah sent out another captain along with a company of fifty men and the exact same thing happened. When he commanded Elijah to come down, fire fell from Heaven and consumed them. Having discernment about the situation, the third captain of fifty Ahaziah sent was a bit more wise and discerning. He fell on his knees before Elijah and begged him to have mercy on him and his men. The angel of the Lord spoke to Elijah not to fear and to go with this captain to see the king so he did. Before the king, he boldly reiterated his prophecy that because he inquired of Baal-Zebub and believed there was no God in Israel, he would surely die and not come down off of his bed of sickness. So he died according to the word of Elijah. II Kings 1:1–17

After a period of time, many miracles and much ministry, it came time for the Lord to take Elijah up to Heaven so he went with Elisha from Gilgal. There Elijah tested his servant's discernment once again saying. "Stay here, please, for the Lord has sent me on to Bethl." (II Kings 2:2) But Elisha discerned that it was really not his master's will, so he declined the offer saying he would not stay there but go with him immediately. (Elijah had to have someone take his place in the ministry who would be loyal, who could discern spirits, the will of his master as well, and most importantly, the will of God.)

When they arrived at Bethl, the sons of the prophets came out to meet with Elisha and told him that it was likely that the Lord was about to take his master that day and was he aware of it? He then said, "Yes, but keep it to yourself."

Then Elijah came to his servant, Elisha, and said that the Lord was sending him on to Jericho that day and for him to tarry there, testing him once again. Elisha discerned his heart and declined the invitation, leaving immediately with him for Jericho.

Once there, the sons of the prophets at Jericho came to Elisha and, again, asked him if he was aware that the Lord God was going to take his master from over him that day? Again, he said he knew but asked them to keep it all to themselves. Then Elijah, said for him to please stay there because the Lord had commanded him to go on to the Jordan River. But he said, "As the Lord lives, and as your soul lives, I will not leave you!" (II Kings 2:6) So the two men left at once and went on to the Jordan.

Once arriving there, fifty men of the sons of the prophets came and stood observing them from a distance while the two prophets were at the edge of the Jordan. Elijah rolled up his mantle and struck the river dividing it in two so that the two men could cross over as on dry ground. Once they reached the other side, he told his servant Elisha that for being faithful in the ministry, he could ask whatever he wanted before he was taken up from him that day. Elisha said, "Please, let a double portion of your spirit be upon me." (II Kings 2:9) At that, the old prophet said that he had asked a very difficult thing but, nevertheless, if he would stay with him until he was taken up, it would be so for him and if not, it would not be. Then it was as they walked along and talked that a chariot and horses of fire came down from heaven, separated the two and God took Elijah up by a whirlwind into Heaven. When Elisha saw it, he cried, "My father, my father, the chariot of Israel and its horsemen!" (Meaning he considered Elijah, with God's power and anointing, the strength behind all Israel.) Then he tore his clothes in two, picked up his master's mantle and went back to the edge of the Jordan. There he struck the water with the mantle that had fallen to him and said, "Where is the Lord God of Elijah?" (II Kings 2:14) Immediately the water was divided just as before and he walked across the dry river bed to the other side.

The sons of the prophets at Jericho who witnessed all of this came to Elisha and said they now knew that the spirit of Elijah rested upon him. When they met him, they bowed down to the ground in front of him. Then they said there were fifty of them, strong servants of God, and would he send them to search for Elijah, his master because the Spirit of the Lord might have taken him to another mountain or valley. Then Elisha told them, very clearly, not to send anyone. But they kept on pleading with him until he grew weary of it and finally said, "Send them." (But it was not his will. None of these men discerned the will of their master, Elisha.) Thus they sent the fifty and searched for three days, of course, not finding him. When they returned to him at Jericho, he gently rebuked them saying, "Did I not say to you, 'Do not go'?" (II Kings 2:18) At that moment Elisha went forth in the ministry doing miracles by the power of the Spirit. Amazingly, the Bible records twenty miracles for Elijah and the best I know 39 for the ministry of Elisha.

From this we learn the importance of discerning the will of our superiors. People would do well to write down the commands of their superiors at the moment the instructions are given so they could not possibly become confused and go off doing what is in their own heart through pride, doubt, selfishness, forgetfulness or unbelief. Then all they would have to deal with would be discerning their leader's will. God has many rewards for those who are found obedient and faithful to their charge.

What it means to have the character trait of **DISCERNMENT:**

- The ability to comprehend the obscure
- The ability to know the true will and desires of our leader
- The ability to cut through the smoke screens and distractions to get to the truth
- Keen perception
- Sound judgment
- The ability to perceive the truth when given misinformation
- Insight
- Skill in listening and evaluating
- The ability to sift inadequate information mixed with misinformation and still connect the dots
- Keen intellectual insight
- The ability to penetrate the superficial to find the real substance of things

NDERSTANDING—A trait of wisdom Study start date: _____ Finish date: _____

U nderstanding the gift of God to all men if they will only receive it. We may not be able to see God but daily we can certainly see His power manifested. Paul told the Romans, " ... since the creation of the world His invisible attributes are clearly seen, being understood by the things that are made, even His eternal power and Godhead, so that they are without excuse." (Romans 1:20) David attested to the power of His Word as a gift to us as well saying, "Through Your precepts I get understanding; therefore I hate every false way." (Psalm 119:104) In the same Psalm he said, "The entrance of Your words gives light; it gives understanding to the simple." (v.130) Life is a matter of finding the Truth, the Son of the Living God, and then rejecting the false. John, the Apostle, penned these words: " ... we know that the Son of God has come and has given us an understanding, that we may know Him who is true; and we are in Him who is true, in His Son Jesus Christ. This is the true God and eternal life." I John 5:20

This is general revelation freely given to all believers but there is also specific revelation made known only to God's prophets. A good example of this was Daniel's revelation in the first year of Darius, the Mede, who ruled over the Chaldeans. "I, Daniel, understood by the books the number of the years specified by the word of the Lord through Jeremiah the prophet, that He would accomplish seventy years in the desolation of Jerusalem." (Daniel 9:2) This prophecy dealt with the total destruction of Jerusalem by Nebuchadnezzar and that the nation of Israel would go into captivity for a predetermined period of time. No man could imagine specific prophecies like these without a revelation from God.

To understand the world and how we fit in it, we must first know the Creator as well as His purpose for this world and us. When the Ephesians had come to faith in Christ from the worship of idols, Paul prayed "that the God of our Lord Jesus Christ, the Father of glory may give to (them) the spirit of wisdom and revelation in the knowledge of Him, the eyes of your understanding being enlightened; that (they) may know what is the hope of His calling, what are the riches of the glory of His inheritance in the saints, and what is the exceeding greatness of His power toward us who believe, according to the working of His mighty power which He worked in Christ ..." (Ephesians 1:17–19) It is not about political parties, the stock market and nations rising up against nations. These things are frail, miserable and minute in comparison to His power, eternal purpose, glory and majesty.

Certainly, in life we all need the benefit of reproof and rebuke from time to time. We have all taken many foolish mistakes. There are still some who refuse to listen to correction even though wisdom continues to pose the question: "How long, you simple ones, will you love simplicity? For scorners delight in their scorning, and fools hate knowledge. Turn (hear, harken and take heart) at my rebuke; surely I will pour out my spirit on you; I will make my words known to you." (Proverbs 1:22–23) Solomon also gave us a warning: "He who disdains instruction despises his own soul, but he who heeds rebuke gets understanding." (Proverbs 15:32) Correction and rebuke are beautiful gifts to the soul who delights in wisdom and truly wants to live a successful, God pleasing life.

The book of Proverbs talks about three things we find separately but must be inextricably woven together to be useful: wisdom, knowledge and understanding. Knowledge is finding, accumulating and knowing the facts. To have any understanding, one must possess a wide range of knowledge about both Biblical and secular things. Wisdom is knowing how and when to skillfully apply that knowledge to specific problems and issues of life. We are not referring here to man's wisdom but God's. The wisdom from above is distinctly different, It " ... is first pure, then peaceable, gentle, willing to yield, full of mercy and good fruits, without partiality and without hypocrisy." (James 3:17) It is a gift from the Almighty through prayer and meditation on His Word. We know, "… there is a spirit in (a) man, and the breath of the Almighty gives him understanding. Great men are not always wise, nor do the aged always understand justice." (Job 32:8, 9) People succeeding temporarily in business or high political office may appear to be wise and old men with grey hair may look like they ought to have gained some understanding over time but not necessarily. Time, temptation and tribulation will show all men for exactly who and what they are.

Understanding is knowing how best to use wisdom and knowledge to relate to life, problems and other people. Surely, many can go out and obtain a master's degree and a few doctorates while they are at it but they will only accumulate knowledge, the kind the Bible says "puffs up." This is why the wisest man in the world said, "Wisdom is the principal thing; therefore get wisdom. And in all your getting, get understanding." (Proverbs 4:7) It takes wisdom to ever get to the point of gaining understanding. And, "How much better to get wisdom than gold! And to get understanding is to be chosen rather than silver." (Proverbs 16:16) "To hate evil, pride and arrogance and the evil way and the perverse mouth I hate. Counsel is mine, and sound wisdom; I am understanding, I have strength." Proverbs 9:10

Understanding won't be found in secular books or the philosophy of man. This is where David said he found it: "Oh how I love Your law (the Word)! It is my meditation all the day. You, through Your commandments, make me wiser than my enemies; for they are ever with me. I have more understanding that all my teachers, for Your testimonies are my meditation. I understand more than the ancients, because I keep Your precepts." (Psalm 119:97–100) Gaining understanding with people is arriving at an inner knowing that there is a mutuality of interest between you to come to some common ground. It is achieved by trust, hope, respect and concern for one another that, though unwritten, is understood. Understanding between two people is a heart-felt belief that the other really cares and will do the right thing by you when you are not around. For this to occur, usually one must first be a good listener, show themselves to be friendly and take the time to know the other person's plight. The antithesis of this are people who are well known for being mean, captious and deceitful.

One night the Lord appeared to Solomon in a dream and said, "Ask! What shall I give you?" (I Kings 3:5) His father, David, being the greatest king, warrior and governor Israel ever had, young Solomon was feeling quite inadequate as successor to the crown. In part, he replied, "You have made Your servant king instead of my father David, but I am a little child; I do not know how to go out or come in. And Your servant is in the midst of Your people whom You have chosen, a great people, too numerous to be numbered or counted. Therefore, give to Your servant an understanding heart to judge Your people, that I may discern between good and evil. For who is able to judge this great people of Yours?" (I Kings 3:7–9) Since Solomon approached God with all humility, the request greatly pleased the Lord who said, "Because you have asked this thing, and have not asked long life for yourself, nor have asked riches for yourself, nor have asked the life of your enemies, but have asked for yourself understanding to discern justice, behold, I have done according to your words; see, I have given you a wise and understanding heart, so that there has not been anyone like you before you, nor shall any like you arise after you. And I have also given you what you have not asked for: both riches and honor, so that there shall not be anyone like you among the kings all your days. So, if you walk in My ways, to keep My statutes and My commandments, as your father David walked, then I will lengthen your days." (I Kings 3:11a-14) And the Lord exalted Solomon exceedingly in every way including vast economic and military power in addition to peace with the enemy nations around him.

In the heart of every human being, there is something they desire more than anything else. Many given this privilege would have chosen the beggarly things such as finances, long life or the life of their enemies to their own great detriment. However, we know from Solomon's life what pleases the Lord—for us to desire an understanding heart. Since everything in God's Kingdom is by faith, at some point, every human being should stop and pray asking God for this same treasure: wisdom and an understanding heart. Then we need to dedicate our lives to the pursuit of these things. That, we know, leads to every lasting blessing. Truly all the blessings of life are in the Spirit. In reality, the world has nothing for us. In Proverbs 24:3 we find these words recorded: "through wisdom a house is built, and by understanding it is established, by knowledge the rooms are filled with all precious and pleasant riches." There they are, all three, working together again: wisdom, knowledge and understanding. And, what will a lack of understanding get you? Solomon, goes on to say he "went by the field of the lazy man, and by the vineyard of the man devoid of understanding; and there it was, all overgrown with thorns; its surface was covered with nettles; its stone wall was broken down. When I saw it, I considered it well; I looked on it and received instruction: a little sleep, a little slumber, a little folding of the hands to rest; so shall your poverty come like a prowler and your need like an armed man." (Proverbs 24:30–34) Clearly, a lack of understanding will soon bring a person to abject poverty.

Among inanimate objects, understanding is also knowing how things work together and are inter-related—the reality of cause and effect. It is also the gift of God to have skill in the various arts, craftsmanship and mechanics. Just prior to building the tabernacle for God and crafting all the temple articles, Moses knew they had to be made with excellence. God spoke to him saying, "See, I have called by name Bezalel the son of Uri, the son of Hur, of the tribe of Judah. And I have filled him with the Spirit of God, in wisdom, in understanding, in knowledge, and in all manner of workmanship, to design artistic works, to work in gold, in silver, in bronze, in cutting jewels for setting, in crafting wood, and to work in all manner of workmanship." Exodus 31:2–5

Another important point about leadership is that the people who work for us in life need to understand at least three things about us as a leader. First, they must know that we truly care about them as a person. Second, that we have their best interest at heart and, finally, that we are able to equip, enhance and build them up in life. They need to know that you not only can but are sincerely interested in adding value to their life.

What it means to have the character trait of **UNDERSTANDING**.

- To have an intellectual grasp of the workings of something
- The ability to discern false pretenses
- Having knowledge of things in right relationship of cause and effect
- The ability to comprehend a concept, an enigma or a difficult to understand situation
- An attitude with people that communicates that you care about building a friendly relationship.
- The ability to coalesce the differences of various parties to agree on an agenda of truth.

ILIGENCE—A trait of wisdom   **Study start date:** _____ **Finish date:** _____

In the workplace, over time, we will see just about every type of person imaginable. Some are hard workers while others could actually be classified as professional shovel leaners. Surely you have seen county employees on "public works" jobs who can lean on their shovel handle with their feet spread apart and look so intently—like they are really doing something—as they watch others work in the ditch below them digging away, installing pipe or fixing a leak. Have you noticed how some government employees will slow up at a green light hoping to catch a red and then take forever to get their truck going after the light turns green. Neither will they make a left in the face of on-coming traffic unless there is about a mile long gap to the next on-coming car, nor fail to miss a stop at the doughnut shop or take the shortest route between two points. They intend to get done in a day only what they have to when somebody is watching and this only to keep their jobs and get a pay check. Some people you will find are obviously working for money and not as unto the Lord. They have yet to learn that their time is short on this planet and once wasted, they will never get it back. They haven't learned that it was only today that the Master gave us to be a blessing to others and have absolutely no assurance that we will we ever see a tomorrow Unfortunately, they haven't learned the joy of staying busy and trying to do more than is expected or required of them. Of course this is not to mean all government employees. God has some of his most excellent people in every arena of life—for which we should all be grateful.

Time is one of the most valuable assets a person will ever have on planet Earth. None of us has very much of it and it is so easy to waste. Many spend their time on totally unproductive activities. There is, however, a time to work and a time to play.

A man in prison called me one day and we had a good talk. During the conversation he said one thing that was quite revealing concerning his attitude about life that I never forgot. It was likely a great contributor to why he never really made it out in the world and the reason he found himself behind bars. He said, "Being on the outside is not much different than being in prison—you are just closer to your loved ones. If you get a job, you are just making someone else a profit." Wow! What he hated so bad about work was making his employer a profit. He certainly wanted the boss to make enough to pay him on Friday. Don't guess he ever studied economics enough to learn that his boss' company was only in business to provide a product or service to someone—and not lose money or break even doing it—but to make a profit. Out of the profit, he could pay his company's bills and his employees' wages so this guy would have a living, learn a trade, maybe start his own company someday and be blessed. His job was a God-given opportunity to learn the power of diligence and it should have been his springboard for advancement in life. Begrudging one's boss and company a profit from his labor, risk, long hours, skill and capital investments is totally a counterproductive philosophy—just plain, raw, unadulterated, common, old class envy. When we stop making our company more than we are costing them that is the day we will find a pink slip in our box. What this man was really afraid of and hated so badly, was the thought of being a profitable servant. This is one who always, gladly does more than is expected or required and causes their master to receive far more income than they are costing them.

Besides envy, this man really had a problem with a four letter word called work. You know I have pretty well been around the block by now but I have never seen the first person given a raise, a plaque or a letter of commendation for sleeping until the crack of noon every day, for taking the most exotic vacations or for going for the longest time on unemployment. No, people just get commended for their strong work ethic, their excellence, their loyalty to the company and for turning out a ton of (watch it, here comes that dreaded four letter word again) work. You see, work is our ticket to ride on the blue marble. It is what we give back to the world for our rite of passage. It is the dues we must all pay who want to live well, provide for our families and advance in society. If you hate work, you are just simply going to be at a whale of a disadvantage in life. No, you will be disqualified. On the contrary, if you love your work, the entire workforce and workplace will bless you. Furthermore, I have always said, if you love your work it will tell you its secrets. First thing you know you will be getting raises, commendations and promotions. You will be making inventions, starting businesses, making speeches and writing books. And for all this to happen, all you have to be is diligent.

To understand diligence, we must first understand work. Work is the gift God gave us to not only get our needs met but to be a blessing. Many other gifts will be given to us in life if we are faithful and learn to use this one well. Make your work a thing of beauty on the canvas of life God gives you time, talent and opportunity. Be diligent and do your 110% best at all times. You will be glad you did.

Diligence has only to do with work and is simply the ability to consistently stay busy and productive. It is one powerful force. It helps us redeem the time because we know the Bible says the days are evil. All the days you are allotted are short, few and full of trouble. The Bible also says our time here passes "swifter than a weaver's shuttle" and "as a cloud consumed and vanished away." Since this is true, we need to learn how to get a hold of our time and maximize it. One thing that really helps to get the most out of every day is to make a "To do list." Then we need to pray over it for wisdom to put it in the proper priority. People who don't have a list are at a huge disadvantage. They have to stop when they complete each task and go through all the mental gymnastics of balancing priorities and demands that have been placed upon them by everyone around them: their wife, their boss, their kids, their friends, the tax assessor, etc. After they have stewed for about fifteen minutes and have taken their third well deserved break and cup of coffee, they grudgingly plod half-heartedly into the next detail. On the contrary, people with a list have gotten up early, to hopefully seek the Lord in prayer, and have gotten His guidance, and have written it all down, clearly on paper. They have gotten their marching orders from Heaven, have ordered their priorities and are knocking them down one-by-one with lightning speed and with no wasted time wondering who is watching, what to do or what to do next. Moreover, they are executing each one with power, conviction, skill and have thrown all their heart, mind, strength and body into it with reckless abandon. The opposition had better get out of their way because you can actually see the obstructions and difficulties of life crumble in their wake. Sparks and dust will be flying about wherever they go. These people are going from one detail to the next in machinegun fashion and are packing more punch in their day than most people can imagine. You would think that they have learned the secret of how to put ten pounds of seeds in a five pound bag or something. Diligent people are usually working for the Master and they know He is "coming soon and (His) reward is with (Him) ... (He) will give to everyone according to what he has done." Rev. 22:12

If we really want to be blessed in this life, it is good to remember that the wisest man who ever lived said: "He who has a slack hand becomes poor, but the hand of the diligent makes rich." (Proverbs 10:4) "The soul of the lazy man desires and has nothing; but the soul of the diligent shall be made rich." (Proverbs 13:4) He went on to say, "A man's gift (or talent) makes room for him (opens doors) and brings him before great men." (Proverbs 18:16) He was so sure about its power to produce, he said, "See a man diligent in his business (or work)? (In due time) "He shall stand before kings; he shall not stand before obscure men." (Proverbs 22:29) Notice there were no caveats here as to age, I.Q., pedigree, education, etc. Incredible! Having diligence or a lack of it in a person's life will cause dramatically different results: King Solomon said," ... the slothful shall be put to forced labor" and "the hand of the diligent shall bear rule." (Proverbs 12:24)

Each of us are stewards of our own time and talents but not owners. Talents were given to us in trust to bless the Body of Christ, provide for our family and increase God's kingdom on earth. For them we will all someday give an account to the Master for how we used them. In this and all things we know "… it is required in stewards, that a man be found faithful." I Corinthians 4:2

What it means to have the character trait of **DILIGENCE:**

- The persevering application of one's self to a task assigned or what is at hand.
- The wisdom to stay busy and not waste valuable time.
- Refusing to waste valuable seconds because they make priceless minutes that, once wasted or spent wisely, can never be retrieved.
- If you run out of something to do, diligence it is the wisdom to quickly find something else to do
- Staying at something and making full use of all the time in a day.
- When the project at hand has been stalled momentarily for some reason, it is finding another small task for filler until the original task can be resumed
- It is arising early like the prophets, priests and patriarchs to redeem the time
- Unflagging attention to duty or the task at hand in the face of adversity, fatigue, attacks, a lack of appreciation or non-existent pay

UST SPEECH – A trait of wisdom   Study start date: _____ Finish date: _____

Speech is listed last in the series of the pillars of wisdom but it is certainly not least. You will need all the other aspects of wisdom operating in order to get to just speech, study it and then be able to use it effectively. Just speech is what we use our faith with to build and accomplish everything God has planned for us to do in our short time on earth. Faith is what God gave us to bring Heaven and Earth together as well as meet all our needs. In the Kingdom of God we receive **everything** by faith: salvation, the Holy Spirit, our daily bread, a mate, a business, a healing, you name it. And, we know that "Whatever is not of faith is sin." (Romans 14:23) Faith is the only thing that pleases God. You could have all the other character traits of wisdom and every character trait in this book working for you but failing to have just speech will cause you to fail totally and completely. So, without question, the most powerful and effective tool God has given us in our arsenal is the tongue (just speech). With it, we can heal the sick, raise the dead, cast out daemons and move mountains, as well as call those things that are not as though they were – until they come into being. With it we can build families, ministries and businesses or with it we can tear them all down. "Life and death are in the power of the tongue, and those who love it will eat its fruit." (Proverbs 18:21) And, we know, "A man will be satisfied with good by the fruit of his mouth." (Proverbs 12:14) Faith is certainly not only good but great! However, it is of little to no good apart from the tongue. In Mark 11:23 Jesus told us, "…whoever says (speaks) to this mountain (your need or problem in life), 'Be removed and be cast into the sea,' and does not doubt in his heart, but believes that those things he says will be done, he will have whatever he says."

Speech is basically that faculty given only to human beings to articulate words to express various thoughts and emotions. The Bible tells us of three categories of speech: one is wise or just speech whose ends or motives are good. Another is evil speech, whose motives and ends are malicious and detrimental. Finally, there is vain speech whose ends are foolish unproductive and empty. Trash talk and coarse language are ubiquitous in society today. Here we will look briefly at each category:

JUST SPEECH

Solomon said, "Wisdom is found on the lips of him who has understanding…" (Proverbs 10:13) As to value, he told us, "There is gold, and a multitude of rubies; but the lips of knowledge are a precious jewel." (Proverbs 20:15) And, "A word fitly spoken is like apples of gold in pictures of silver." (Proverbs 25:11) When in a heated argument, "A soft answer turns away wrath" (Proverbs 15:1b) and "A wholesome tongue is a tree of life." (Proverbs 15:4) Just speech is so powerful, Solomon said, "The mouth of the upright will deliver them." Proverbs 12:6

David said, "with my lips I have declared all the judgments of Your mouth." (Psalm 119:13) When I speak, he went to say, "I will speak of thy testimonies also before kings, and will not be ashamed." (Psalm 119:46) "My tongue shall speak of thy word: for all thy commandments are righteous." (Psalm 119:172)

We will all be known immediately by our speech. The Master said, "A good man out of the good treasure of his heart brings forth good; and an evil man out of the evil treasure of his heart brings forth evil. For out of the abundance of the heart his mouth speaks." (Luke 6:45) Paul admonished us, "Let no corrupt word proceed out of your mouth, but what is good for necessary edification, that it may impart grace to the hearers."(Ephesians 4:29) And, "Let your speech be always with grace, seasoned with salt, that you may know how you ought to answer each one." Colossians 4:6

EVIL SPEECH

Our speech can do damage in many ways. David exhorted us saying, "Keep your tongue from evil, and your lips from speaking deceit." (Psalm 34:13) Proud words and those intended to flatter are also troubling because he said, "The Lord shall cut off all flattering lips and the tongue that speaks proud things.." (Psalm 12:3)

Solomon said, "Put away from you a deceitful mouth, and put perverse lips far from you." (Proverbs 4:22) "An ungoldly man digs up evil and it is on his lips like a burning fire. A perverse man sows strife and a whisperer separates the best of friends."(Proverbs 16:27, 28) He also warned us that "He who has a deceitful heart finds no good and he who has a perverse tongue falls into evil." (Proverbs 17:20)

Paul warned about some saying, "Their throat is an open tomb; with their tongues they have practiced deceit; the poison of asps is under their lips; whose mouth is full of cursing and bitterness." (Romans 3:13, 14) He also said to be sure to "Let all bitterness, wrath, anger, clamor, and evil speaking be put away from you, with all malice." Ephesians 4:31

VAIN SPEECH

The Bible tells us that words are so powerful and important, we must not speak even one word foolishly, hastily or unnecessarily. Solomon said, "Wise men store up knowledge: but the mouth of the foolish is near destruction." (Proverbs 10:14) And, that "...the heart of fools proclaims foolishness." (Proverbs 12:23) A foolish person is always talking but Solomon shows us how dangerous this is, saying, "the prating fool will fall. (Proverbs 10:8b) When provoked, he admonished us not to "answer a fool according to his folly, lest you also be like him. Answer a fool according to his folly, lest he be wise in his own eyes." (Proverbs 26:4, 5) We should also study our responses by counting to ten in an argument to give ourselves time to respond wisely, because he went on to say, "Do you see a man hasty in his words? There is more hope for a fool than for him."

Paul told the Ephesians that some things are absolutely not fitting among saints, "neither filthiness, nor foolish talking, nor coarse jesting, which are not fitting, but rather giving of thanks." Ephesians 5:4

THE CONCLUSION

One of the greatest tools we have with which to build as a Christian, as I said, is the tongue, just speech. Whether or not we tame it will determine our status in life as either a builder or a wrecker. With our speech we will either "bless our God and Father, and with it we curse men, who have been made in the similitude of God." James goes on to say, "Out of the same mouth proceeds blessing and cursing. My brethren, these things ought not to be so. Does a spring send forth fresh water and bitter from the same opening? Can a fig tree, my brethren, bear olives, or a grapevine bear figs? Thus no spring yields both salt water and fresh." (James 3:9-12) The tongue may be our smallest member but note, in life, how a great forest fire it can kindle. We might be full of every kind of virtue but being lacking in this one area, of taming our tongue, can easily and quickly destroy all the good we ever hope to do.

"The tongue is a fire, a world of iniquity. The tongue is so set among our members that it defiles the whole body, and sets on fire the course of nature, and it is set on fire by hell. For every kind of beast and bird, or reptile and creature of the sea, is tamed and has been tamed by mankind. But no man can tame the tongue. It is an unruly evil, full of deadly poison." (James 3:6-8) Only with God's help can any man tame the tongue. We know "The mouth of the righteous speaks wisdom" (Psalm 37:30) To do this consistently, we need to ask the Master for help as David did saying, "Set a guard over my mouth. Keep watch over the door of my lips." (Psalm 1412:3) This is so important that the Master said, "That for every idle word men may speak, they will give account of it in the day of judgment." (Matthey 12:36) Therefore, we need to keep our speech silver and our silence golden.

What it means to have the character trait of **JUST SPEECH**:

- Saying and believing you have what you prayed for by faith but have yet to receive in the natural
- Blessing and cursing not
- Speaking the truth in love
- Sincere praise of good work
- Encouraging words
- Speaking the testimonies of God
- A timely, appropriate word
- Promotes health
- A soft answer in a heated argument
- A studied, wise response
- Words that impart grace
- Having a little love in your voice, coming from the love in your heart
- Speaking clearly and unequivocally, letting your 'Yes' be 'Yes' and your 'No', 'No.'
  (The traits of Wisdom end here)

ORKING AS UNTO THE LORD— Study start date: _____ Finish date: _____

There are billions of people at work on this planet every day and each one is working for something. Each one has a primary motivation. Some work to satisfy their stomach. The book of Ecclesiastes tells us when "A man's labor is for nothing more than to fill his stomach, his appetite is never satisfied." (6:7) Life that is truly life, however, is about more than this. Paul gave us the pattern on how to live, but "many walk, of whom I have told you often, and now tell you even weeping, that they are the enemies of the cross of Christ; whose end is destruction, whose god is their belly, and whose glory is in their shame—who set their mind on earthly things." (Philippians 3:18, 19) God has promised us all two things: food and raiment and with these things we need to learn to be content. (I Timothy 6:8) We can know "The righteous man (will eat) until he is satisfied but the stomach of the wicked is empty." Proverbs 13:25

Still others work to gain power in the world. More wars have been fought since the beginning of time because of the selfish ambitions of political leaders than anything else. These positions may look so very enticing with all their pomp, perks and privileges, but it has been said that every crown is lined with thorns. Candidates today must compromise their convictions to grab the brass ring. And, to what end? The public is so fickle, they will love you as a politician one day and, on the slightest whim or turn of events, will be ever too anxious to run you out of town on a rail the next. Besides, you can't please man and God. No one has ever done it and no one ever will because it is, indeed, impossible. There are still some political leaders, however, who practice their convictions, staying in office only as long as that remains possible.

Other people toil and slave for prestige—to have and to hold all the finer things. They want the most expensive cars, watches, diamonds, houses and sky boxes The problem is that these things will not satisfy and carry with them the requirement of a lot of maintenance, security and taxes. Some things, like jewelry, houses and automobiles, are also extremely vulnerable to thieves. The Master warned us about this and admonished us to be very careful where we placed our affections saying, "Do not lay up for yourselves treasures on earth, where moth and rust destroy and where thieves break in and steal; but lay up for yourselves treasure in heaven, where neither moth nor rust destroys and where thieves do not break in and steal. For where your treasure is, there your heart will be also." (Matthew 6:19–21) The things of this world will not satisfy. Certainly we all need some things as they make life easier for all of us. However, those who lust after things have told me that the coveting of them was more enjoyable than obtaining them. Sadly, their heart had been trained and corrupted by covetous practices. They have fallen prey to the traps of "the lust of the flesh, the lust of the eye and the pride of life." I John 2:16

Others work for the approval of men. Truthfully, most of us have worked, at some point in time, for the approval of those around us. Because that spirit was placed in us by God, we are to increase our skill and work hard to improve our lives. However, what we really need is acceptance by the God of the Universe. Once God accepts us into the Beloved, we no longer need man's approval. What freedom! God's approval is far better, satisfying completely. Just remember that the Lord is working in all things to bring you something much better if you are working as unto Him. Thank Him for the trials, be patient and let Him bless you. Romans 8:28

Another motivation is the love of money. Dollars will certainly buy some of the things we need and, will give us, to a very limited degree, a sense of security. So many go clamoring for it like a calf to a fresh flake of hay in the stall. Paul, the apostle warned us about this saying, " … the love of money is a root of all kinds of evil, for which some have strayed from the faith in their greediness and pierced themselves through with many sorrows." (I Timothy 6:10) "Those who desire to be rich fall into temptation and a snare and into many foolish and harmful lusts which drown men in destruction and perdition." (v.9) Men chase after it thinking it will meet their needs, make them happy and be a wall of protection against all of the worst things that might occur in life. About this tendency Solomon said, "The rich man's wealth is his strong city, and like a high wall in his own esteem (imagination)." (Proverbs 18:11) No, not necessarily and not in all cases. The Lord is provider, protector and avenger of all. Money can do some things for us and we all need some but it will not, in and of itself, make us happy or buy us protection. Money will not satisfy. Solomon wrote this in Ecclesiastes 5:10, "He who loves silver (money) will not be satisfied with silver; nor he who loves abundance, with increase. Those who love it will never get enough. This also is vanity." This, however, doesn't mean that God doesn't want to bless you abundantly as a reward for your faithfulness, hard work and seeking Him first. (Matthew 6:33) He wants to bless you in this life if He can trust you to be a blessing. Financial prosperity just cannot be our primary goal.

The solution to all this is learning to work as unto the Lord. Yes, we will, more than likely still be working in the natural for a physical company and a human being as our supervisor. However, when we enter the secret, invisible Kingdom of God, He enables us to work for our boss as unto the Lord. Paul gave Believers this command in Colossians 3:23: " . . whatever you do, do it heartily, as to the Lord and not unto men, knowing that from the Lord you will receive the reward of the inheritance; for you serve the Lord Christ." (Colossians 3:23) The key word here is "heartily" which means to give it all you've got. Be an all-outer! Give them 110%. We find a freedom and new energy in life when we give our work all our strength and all our might.

Regardless of whether you're earthly boss is generous and kind or a creep, work for him as unto the Lord. Serve him as if he were the Lord. Don't look for your boss's flaws as you will surely find some and start fixating on them. Look instead for his attributes and be thankful for them. Do your work and make your reports as if you were going to turn it all in to Christ and you, quite likely, won't have any problem with your boss being well pleased with your work. Working, on the contrary, for men causes people to consciously or subconsciously, ratchet their performance either up or down depending on their own evaluation of their boss as a human being and leader. This is a very dangerous practice if he is not a good leader because it lets you justify a poor performance. Turning in that kind of work, even temporarily, can get you fired so never let a boss's poor performance dictate yours. Paul's advice was: " … whatever you do in word or deed, do all in the name of the Lord Jesus giving thanks to God the Father through Him." (Colossians 3:17) Be thankful for every job as an opportunity to be of service. Every job is a stepping stone to greater responsibilities in the future. Don't let it be a stumbling block. Each job allows you to sow good seeds and have an opportunity to learn, improve your skills and increase your value to your company and current generation. Your work will also be observed by those around you and they, too, will likely recommend you for future opportunities. Even still, in a wicked world, your company or your boss might let you down but God is our source. Your good is not lost; He still has your reward in His hand. He can open up an unbelievable opportunity for you at any moment. He is faithful and tremendously able. Learning to work directly for Him will remove the fear of losing what you have invested in a job Working as unto Him will give you the freedom to be creative, to invest your best ideas and to give your employer your all. It is great to be free! God is our source and He promised those who live by faith, that "He is a rewarder of those who diligently seek Him." (Hebrews 11:6) The command the Master gave us in Matthew 6:33 is simple and so effective: "Seek first the kingdom of God and His righteousness and all these things will be added unto you." He said if we will but put His Kingdom first, He will take responsibility for adding whatever we might need. Since He owns everything and is all-powerful, no one could do this better. He also said, " … behold, I am coming quickly, and my reward is with Me, to give to every one according to his work." Revelation 22:12

Another advantage in working as unto the Lord and for His glory is that the circumstances of life can never defeat you, even temporarily, from accomplishing your goal. Those with financial goals can become terribly distraught in a down economy, when betrayed or by making a bad investment, etc. If, on the contrary, we have learned to be content in our current state and are working to bring glory to the Name, nothing can deter us. A bad economy just creates new opportunities in those down markets. God is still able to turn the messes we humans make into miracles. Jail time becomes an opportunity for ministry and writing. Paul, to me, the greatest Apostle, had the most joy, was the most thankful, the most accomplished and yet, was all the while, the most persecuted. For all of his faithfulness and success as a witness, a preacher and for starting all the churches in Europe, let's look for a moment at the pay check he got for his efforts. In comparison to the other disciples, he said he was "in labors more abundant, in stripes above measure, in prisons more frequently, in deaths often. From the Jews five times I received forty stripes minus one. Three times I was beaten with rods; once I was stoned; three times I was shipwrecked; a night and a day I have been in the deep; in journeys often, in perils of waters, in perils of my own countrymen, in perils of the Gentiles, in perils in the city, in perils in the wilderness, in perils in the sea, in perils among false brethren; in weariness and toil, in sleeplessness often, in hunger and thirst, in fastings often, in cold and nakedness—besides the other things, what comes upon me daily; my deep concern for all the churches." (II Corinthians 11:23–28) We see from his example that earthly circumstances do little to deter and much to advance the soldier of the Lord whose mind is focused solely on bringing glory to the Name.

Working as unto the Lord also includes practicing His presence at all times. David said, "I have set the Lord (ever) before me; because He is at my right hand I shall not be moved." (Psalm 16:8) Working for Him and having Him ever with us, makes us feel like David when he said, "… by You I can run through a troop, by my God I can leap over a wall." Psalm 18:29 AMPVER

What it means to have the character trait of **WORKING AS UNTO THE LORD:**

- Working in your heart, directly for the invisible Lord while on this planet.
- Expecting our reward from God instead of trusting in man.
- Receiving the joy of working for the God of the Universe and turning our work in to Him every day.
- Working in life to bring glory to the Name

ZEAL—

Study start date: _____ **Finish date:** _____

Zeal, though closely akin to enthusiasm, is actually something quite different. True zeal is mostly used to describe an intense desire for spiritual things and can be a tremendously beneficial and empowering force when properly directed. On the one hand, not correctly guided, it can be extremely detrimental. It can, in fact, be absolutely the worst thing to have a zeal for God without knowledge.

Certainly we will all agree, there are now and have always been many problems among men on this planet. It is also clear that, from the beginning of time, God had an answer to all the failings and problems of man on his drawing board, the remedy for which only His zeal could perform. Speaking through the prophet Isaiah, He said, "For unto us a Child is born, unto us a Son is given; and the government will be upon His shoulder, and His name will be called Wonderful, Counselor, Mighty God, Everlasting Father, Prince of Peace. Of the increase of His government and peace there will be no end. Upon the throne of David and over His kingdom, to order it and establish it with judgment and justice from that time forward, even forever, the zeal of the Lord of hosts will perform this." Isaiah 9:6, 7

His zeal, the gift of God's grace, is not only powerful but also glorious beyond description. Isaiah recorded these words: "Look down from heaven, and see from Your habitation, holy and glorious, where are Your zeal and Your strength ..." (Isaiah 63:15) His zeal alone is perfect. The zeal of God is its own great blessing and is available to some degree to all who seek it. Paul told Timothy, ". . in a great house there are not only vessels of gold and of silver, but also of wood and of earth; and some to honor, and some to dishonor." (II Timothy 2:20) To find it, the first thing we need to do is give up our sinful ways. Paul went on to say, "If a man therefore purge himself from these, (sins) he shall be a vessel unto honor, sanctified, and (fit) for the Master's use, and prepared unto every good work." (v.21) Next we must humble ourselves before God's mighty hand. He that humbles himself, God promises to exalt in due time. For God gives grace to the humble and His zeal by His own counsel. We don't know how much grace He has for each of us but the way to get all of it is simply to humble ourselves.

The zeal of some Christians has set such a vivid example that it served to stir up others in a positive way to do well also. The Apostle Paul commended the Corinthians saying, "Now concerning the ministering to the saints, it is superfluous for me to write to you; for I know your willingness, about which I boast of you to the Macedonians, that Achaia was ready a year ago; and your zeal has stirred up the majority." II Corinthians 9:1, 2

God is well able to use all things to His glory as even "godly sorrow produces repentance leading to salvation, not to be regretted; but the sorrow of the world produces death." (II Corinthians, 7:10) For those Paul was speaking to in Corinth at the time, their sorrow produced many good things, some of which were "vehement desire, . . zeal (and) vindication!" (v.11)

David loved God so much he said my "zeal for God's house has eaten me up ..." (Psalm 69:9) He loved God so supremely that he wanted to build Him a house and started gathered all the materials to do so. This was a huge amount of very costly things even in his day. However, God told him that he wouldn't be allowed to build it because his hands were bloody but that his son, Solomon, would. David's love for God was such that his highest prayer and most ardent desire was to "dwell in the house of the Lord forever." Psalm 23:6

When Jesus was clearing the money changers out of the temple with a whip and overturning their tables, his disciples remembered what was written about Him: "Zeal for Your house has eaten Me up." (John 2:17) Jesus came with zeal, like none other, to do the Father's will.

Above all Paul said, "Brethren, my heart's desire and prayer to God for Israel is that they may be saved. For I bear them witness that they have a zeal for God but not according to knowledge." (Romans 10:1, 2) The error of the Jews he was speaking of was their ignorance of God's righteousness. They were trying to establish a righteousness of their own when, in fact, accepting Christ was not only the end of the law but the only way to righteousness, peace and the Father. Although he was free from every kind of bondage, Paul had enough zeal to make himself the servant of all so that he might win more to Christ. About this zeal he said, "I have become all things to all men, that I might by all means save some." (I Corinthians 9:22) This he did for the sake of the gospel. God's grace in the form of zeal made Paul the spiritual giant he was and propelled him, even under the constant onslaught of the enemy, to establish all the churches in Asia. He was more than willing to suffer "the loss of all things, and count them as rubbish, that (he might) gain Christ and be found in Him …" (Philippians 3:8, 9) His goal was to fulfill his purpose as an evangelist and attain eternal life through the resurrection from the dead.

Zeal is good and certainly greatly to be desired as I mentioned but it must be properly directed according to the knowledge and counsel of God's Word. We see the proper kind of zeal in the life of Joshua when he made a covenant with the people of Israel at Shechem saying, "Now therefore, fear the Lord, serve Him in sincerity and in truth, and put away the gods which your fathers served on the other side of the River and in Egypt. Serve the Lord! And if it seems evil to you to serve the Lord, choose for yourselves this day whom you will serve, whether the gods which your fathers served that were on the other side of the river, or the gods of the Amorites, in whose land you dwell. But as for me and my house, we will serve the Lord." (Joshua 24:14, 15) Then the people responded saying that forsaking the Lord and serving other gods was now far from them. They recounted the fact that it was the Lord, alone, who had brought them up out of Egypt with great signs and wonders. It was the Lord who drove out the other nations in the Promised Land before them. Then Joshua warned them that turning from the Lord to serve foreign gods would bring His wrath upon them and consume them even after He had done them so much good. The people then said, "No, but we will serve the Lord!" v.21

Not all of those in the Bible used their zeal correctly. "Saul in his zeal for the people of Israel and Judah" we know, "had sought to slay the Gibeonites." (II Samuel 21:20) This was the nation that deceived Israel and caused them to make a reciprocal covenant of peace and protection with them by deceptively posing as foreigners. Because they took the claims of these people at face value and didn't check them out properly, they fell prey to this trap. The Gibeonites came to them in old worn out clothes, with moldy bread and worn out sandals feigning citizenship in a foreign country. Once the covenant was made, the Israelites couldn't break it. However, many years later, Saul in his ignorance did, causing God's wrath to fall on the nation. Keeping our promises and covenants is most important with God.

Another example from scripture of the power of zeal in a person's life was that found in Jehu, an obscure but intrepid Israeli cavalry commander. He, no doubt, had a tremendous zeal for God that allowed him to accomplish truly amazing things but his lack of knowledge caused it not to end as well for him as it could. Even so. his life stands, to this day, giving us great assurance that even in a wicked, treacherous world, God's power can deliver the most decadent nation amid the most dire circumstances. Jehu truly accomplished great things but as we will soon see, his life also brings a grave warning we can ill afford to miss about having the correct kind of zeal. His story also important to the church today because so much is said about the horrible deeds of Ahab and Jezebel but so little about their just end.

Prior to Jehu's arrival in the history of Israel, the nation was in total disarray spiritually, economically and militarily. Notwithstanding God's patience and innumerable demonstrations of grace and mercy toward them, as a final act of kindness He leveled a three and a half year drought on the country in hopes of getting their attention … but, to no avail. This was a huge blow to a country with a totally agrarian society. There being virtually no industry in those days, everyone depended on crops and animals for their livelihood. So, not only was the true religion decimated and the economy destroyed but the government had never been more corrupt. In addition to all this, the people continued to bring forth rotten, poisonous fruit and were in total despair.

The curtain opened on the stage of history in the life of Jehu during the reign of two of the most evil people who ever lived, the nominal King Ahab and his wife, the infamous, Jezebel. Ahab is credited in the eyes of the Lord as having done more evil than any of the kings before him. That happend to be a pretty high bar to surpass since he was preceded by the likes of King Jereboam, Nadab, Baasha, Elah, Zimri and Omri.

Foundational in Ahab's progress abounding in iniquity, was his decision to marry one Jezebel, the daughter of Ethbaal, the King of Tyre and Sidon. Her father had formerly served as priest of Astarte before he violently overthrew his brother, Pelles, to take his throne. Upon becoming queen, Jezebel immediately seduced her husband to worship and serve Baal. Being a very weak-willed man and following her lead, he set up an altar in the temple of Baal he had built in Samaria. He made it complete with an Asherah pole and with all this provoked the Lord to anger more than all the kings before him. Jezebel's effect on Ahab and Israel were immediate, detrimental and far reaching. So wicked was she that even today, centuries later, her name is used to epitomize all that is synonymous with a treacherous, deceitful, rebellious, domineering woman. But wicked as she and Ahab were, it is patently obvious for the Scriptures how our merciful heavenly Father strove long and hard, time and again, to give them opportunity to repent and to work through them to meet the needs of His people. Things, by this time, had sunken so low in Israel that God sent a prophet to Ahab announcing several years of drought to hopefully, awaken and turn them from their idol worship. He even spoke to Ahab through another prophet saying that He would give him the victory over an enormous foreign army just to prove that he was the Lord (I Kings 20:13) This all came to pass. However, the coupe de grass was Jezebel having Naboth, a common citizen, murdered to steal his vineyard for her husband.

At one point Elijah ran forty days and nights to Mt. Horeb, the Mountain of God, for fear Jezebel would carry out her promise to kill him, just as she had all the other true prophets. Upon his arrival at Mt. Horeb, God asked him what he was doing there. To this he replied, "I have been very zealous for the Lord God of hosts; because the children of Israel have forsaken Your covenant, torn down Your altars and killed Your prophets with the sword. I alone am left; and they seek to take my life." (I Kings 19:14) God told him to go back to the desert of Damascus and anoint Hazael king over Syria. He was also to anoint Jehu, son of Nimshi king over Israel and Elisha as prophet in his place. He went on to say, "It shall be that whoever escapes the sword of Hazael, Jehu will kill; and whoever escapes the sword of Jehu, Elisha will kill. Yet I have reserved seven thousand in Israel, all whose knees have not bowed to Baal, and every mouth that has not kissed him." I Kings 19:18

Ahab and Jezebel continued in their rebellion to God until they had done so much evil, God finally sent Elijah on a personal errand to them to prophesy their eminent, certain demise. Elijah said, "…because you have sold yourself to do evil in the eyes of the Lord, I am going to bring disaster on you. I will consume your descendants and cut off from Ahab every last male in Israel—slave or free. I will make your house like the house of Jeroboam the son of Nebat, and like the house of Baasha the son of Ahijah, because of the provocation with which you have provoked Me to anger, and made Israel sin.' And concerning Jezebel the Lord says, 'The dogs will eat Jezebel by the wall of Jezreel. The dogs shall eat whoever belongs to Ahab and dies in the city and the birds of the air shall eat whoever dies in the field.' But there was no one like Ahab who sold himself to do wickedness in the sight of the Lord, because Jezebel his wife stirred him up." (I Kings 21:20–25)

A few years later Ahab confederated with Jehoshaphat, king of Judah, to war against Syria in an effort to retake the province of Ramoth Gilead. However, Jehoshaphat wisely advised him to inquire of the

Lord first. Instead he inquired of the prophets of Baal and was told to attack. When he went to Micah, God's prophet, his advice was that he would meet with disaster and never come back. Of course, Ahab ordered him to be put in jail and fed bread and water until he, hopefully, returned safely from the battle.

In an effort to defy the true prophet of God, Israel and Judah went to battle with Syria and Ramoth Gilead. Ahab decided to disguise himself from the enemy and asked Jehoshaphat to wear his royal robes. Mysteriously, the Syrian commander, about this time, ordered thirty-two chariot commanders not to fight with anyone in this battle but the king of Israel. (Of course this was at the hand of God.) When the Syrian troops thought they had Ahab cornered, Jehoshaphat cried out and the Syrians saw that it was not the king of Israel after all and turned back from their pursuit.

Presently, a Syrian soldier, drew his bow at random and let fly an arrow that just happened to strike the king of Israel between the joints of his armor. He slumped immediately in his chariot and asked his driver to take him out of the fighting to a vantage point nearby where he watched the battle rage all day. His blood continued to drip onto the floor of the chariot until he died that evening. Just as the sun was setting the Israelis called retreat and brought Ahab to Samaria where he was buried. Someone washed his chariot at the pool of Samaria (where prostitutes bathed) and the dogs licked up his blood just as the Word of the Lord had been spoken through Elijah, Micaiah and the un-named prophet.

After several years and the succession of several sons of Ahab, another of his sons, Joram, became king of Israel. Again, he joined forces with Jehoram who was then the king of Judah, to war, once again, with Syria at Ramoth Gilead. However, Joram was wounded by the Syrians and returned to Jezreel to heal where Ahaziah, the king of Judah went down to meet him. About this time, the prophet Elisha called one of the group's prophets and told him to take the flask of oil he gave him, go to Jehu the son of Jehoshaphat, the son of Nimshi, anoint him with oil and declare the word of the Lord says he is now king over Israel.

The prophet found Jehu sitting with several of the other army officers and asked him to come aside to give him a message. They went into a house nearby where the prophet anointed him king and prophesied over him saying, "This is what the Lord, God of Israel, says: 'I anoint you king over the Lord's people Israel. You are to destroy the house of Ahab your master, and I will avenge the blood of my servants the prophets and the blood of all the Lord's servants shed by Jezebel. The whole house of Ahab will perish. I will cut off from Ahab every last male in Israel–slave or free. I will make the house of Ahab like the house of Jeroboam son of Nebat and like the house of Baasha, son of Ahijah. As for Jezebel, dogs will devour her on the plot of ground at Jezreel and no one will bury her.'" (II Kings 9:6–10) When he had finished prophesying, he opened the door and ran.

Jehu then advised the officers who were there with him of the prophet's commands and began to plot the destruction of Joram, Ahab's son. He took a company of cavalry and rode to Jezreel where he knew Joram was recuperating and Ahaziah had come to visit him. As Jehu approached the city, a couple of messengers were sent out to him to discover his intentions. Both were quickly intimidated by Jehu, I capitulated and fell in behind him. When this was reported to Joram, he said that the second messenger was not coming back either and he thought it looked like Jehu, the son of Nimshi, because he drove like a madman. Then Joram and Ahaziah, King of Judah, rode out in their chariots to meet him. It just so happened that they met Jehu at the plot of ground that had belonged to Naboth the Jezreelite. When Joram saw it was indeed Jehu, he asked if he had come in peace. Ominously, Jehu replied, "How can there be peace, as long as all the idolatry and witchcraft of your mother Jezebel abound?" (II Kings 9:22) Joram turned his chariot immediately and fled shouting to his accomplice, "Treachery, Ahaziah!" Jehu drew back his bow with all his might and shot Joram between the shoulders. The arrow went out at his heart and he slumped down in his chariot. Then Jehu commanded Bidkar, his chariot captain, to "Pick him up and

He drives like a madman

throw him on the field that belonged to Naboth the Jezreelite" saying, "Remember how you and I were riding together in chariots behind Ahab his father when the Lord made this prophecy about him: 'Yesterday I saw the blood of Naboth and the blood of his sons, declares the Lord and I will surely make you pay for it on this plot of ground, declares the Lord.' Now then, pick him up and throw him on that plot, in accordance with the word of the Lord." II Kings 9:25, 26

Seeing all this, Ahaziah fled by way of the garden house, up the road to Beth Haggan. Jehu chased him and commanded his men to kill him too. They wounded him in his chariot on the way up to Gur near Ibleam. However, he escaped long enough to flee to Meggido where he died.

Jehu did all, we know, as a soldier with great zeal, the same way he drove his chariot, "like a madman." (II Kings 9:20) He killed Joram, Ahab's son, who was king at the time and next saw to the death of his mother, Jezebel, such that one of her servants threw her out of an upper story window in the streets of Jezreel where, according to prophecy, the dogs devoured her body.

Jehu then sent a couple messages to the palace administrators, the heads of the city and

Jezebel's demise

the guardians of Ahab's children and told them first to appoint someone king and come out against him in battle. However, they already knew that two other much stronger kings couldn't overcome him, so they, too, capitulated and agreed to take the heads of their master's sons and meet him in Jezreel by the same time the next day. When the elders got the second missive, they slaughtered all seventy of Ahab's sons and brought their heads in a basket to Jehu in Jezreel. It was there that Jehu ordered that they be placed in two stacks at the gate of the city. The next morning Jehu went out and standing before all the people he said, "You are innocent. It was I who conspired against my master and killed him, but who killed all these? Know then that not a word the Lord has spoken against the house of Ahab will fail. The Lord has done what he promised through his servant Elijah." (II Kings 10:9,10) So Jehu went on to kill everyone that remained of the house of Ahab in Jezreel, all of his officers, his relatives and priests until there was no one left.

After this Jehu left for Samaria. There, at the shearing house at Beth Eked, he met some of Ahaziah's (King of Judah) relatives and had all forty-two of them slaughtered by his men by the well at Beth Eked. Upon his departure, he came upon Johonadab, the son of Recab who was coming to meet him. As he approached, Jehu inquired if he was in accord with him and he answered in the affirmative. Then Jehu gave him a hand to help him into his chariot saying, "Come with me and see my zeal for the Lord." Jehu had him ride along with him in his chariot. When they came to Samaria, Jehu killed all that remained there of the house of Ahab until there was no one left according to the word of the Lord which He spoke through Elijah.

Now, having eliminated all the descendants and political rivals from Ahab's line, Jehu's next move was to rid the false religion from the land. He called all the people together and professed, ostensibly, to be a follower of Baal more than Ahab. He then summoned all the prophets of Baal, all his ministers and all his priests to a great sacrifice for Baal. He told them anyone who failed to attend would be killed. When they arrived at the temple, he had them go inside where they were all given red robes to wear for the ceremony. As they started making their sacrifices, he gave the order to kill everyone and destroy the sacred stone of Baal as well. Then they tore the temple down and used the site for a latrine up to the time the Biblical account was written.

In one orchestrated move, Jehu eliminated all the Baal worshippers and their priests from the land of Israel. Regrettably, however, because of a lack of knowledge, from the sins of Jeroboam and the worship of golden calves at Bethel and Dan, he did not turn away. The task he was given was difficult, dangerous and fraught with treachery. Although he erred in other ways, because he had done so well executing what was right against the family of Ahab, God promised that his sons would reign to the fourth generation. But he failed to keep the law of the Lord by worshipping the golden calves and caused the nation to sin, in this way, as well. At this time, the Lord began to judge Israel by reducing the size of her borders. Hazael was allowed to prevail over Israel in battle taking all the land east of the Jordan, this being the fulfillment of Leviticus 26:14–45 and Deuteronomy 26:15–68.

Up to this point, the kingdoms of Israel and Judah had continued to increase in wickedness, especially under Ahab. Amazingly, God gave Ahab victory over the Syrians twice to show His willingness to help the nation even under Ahab's wicked reign. Then He assisted the Israelites by defeating the Moabites and making the water appear as blood. In another war with Syria, God blinded the whole army at the hands of Elisha who led them captive to Samaria. Then He raised up Jehu to rid the land of Ahab, his family and the false religion of Baal. In all this, and regardless of the great sin of the people, God did not forsake them but neither was He able to get the people's attention with all these displays of power. The downward spiral of decadence had begun that would one day end in the captivity of the whole nation. Jehu had a zeal but he lacked the essential grounding in the knowledge of God's Word. Although he accomplished a great deal by defeating two wicked kings and destroying Baal worship, he was never able, in the end, to accomplish in his life what he could have for God. He later went into the same sins he judged Ahab for. Instead of accomplishing his mission for Gods glory alone, he did it for his own advancement and also managed to pursue some of his own resentments as well. He went forth with malice for the sinners but without any particular hatred for their sins. He also continued to worship the golden calves, refusing to follow God's laws.

The greatest blessing is this life is for God to grant us zeal for His heart, will and church—and that according to knowledge.

What it means to have the character trait of **ZEAL:**

- Ardent pursuit of things spiritual
- Passion for things in God's Kingdom
- Religious fervor
- A burning desire to know and please God
- A passion for God's House

Chapter Four
Epilogue

ere are a few cautions, suggestions and some of the many benefits of that will accrue to you from this character study.

DILIGENCE

For this study to work, one must be diligent to stay with it. The greatest enemy you will encounter while studying *The Character Trait Journal* is complacency in several forms. One is not to stay with a systematic, **three week schedule** because of emergencies and the press of other things. Time is of the essence here as in so many areas of life. Keep on track by updating a calendar showing the beginning and end of your three week study period for each trait. If you absolutely can't do a trait on the exact "start date," commit to do it the very next day so you can stay on schedule.

Complacency is the thief in your mind that will come to you after you have engrafted a number of traits saying, you are doing well enough in this area so you can suspend your study before completing all of them. Stay with it. The rewards to you, personally, are life transforming and will help you for the rest of your life. Each trait has its own reward waiting for you.

START WITH YOUR FAMILY'S STUDY EARLY

Children have no inhibitions and learn at a young age more rapidly than older folks. Once a child begins school in the first grade, they are an empty vessels in search of all the best things in life – even on their beginning level. The world will offer them a smorgasbord of all the very worst things. The first grade is a good time for the family to start teaching children the traits on the three week cycle. There are enough traits in this book to last (on a three week schedule) until they graduate from high school without repeating. This character trait study will fill them up with wisdom and godly character and will change their focus by giving them new, positive values.

SUCCESSFUL JOB INTERVIEWS

The Character Trait Journal will also help in preparing for successful job interviews. It help in securing a position just by mentioning to the interviewer that you will be bringing several invisible character traits with you that will no doubt help the company. You might say, if it is true or course, that you have made a long-time study of character in your personal development. You might want to mention just three to five such as honesty, loyalty, diligence, attention to detail and a positive attitude. Just mentioning these things will likely set you apart from the rest of the field and make you a very welcome, added blessing to their staff.

MATE SELECTION

One of the greatest concerns parents have, of course, is who their children will marry. For young people, this one decision will likely define their chances for happiness for the rest of their lives. To this point, I will share a true story. We had a beautiful young, sixteen year old girl in our church whom, against my advice, began dating a totally irresponsible, lazy, self-serving young man. (Believe it or not I'm being generous with my description here) He was a fast talker and nice looking but, honestly, older people could look at him and tell that he couldn't keep a job and was totally in-capable of being responsible for a wife and a family. His standard attire was blue jeans, no shoes and sometimes, on special occasions, a T-shirt. Well, you guessed it, he soon got her pregnant out of wedlock. After having that child, she tried to get rid of him but couldn't because she couldn't deny him visitation rights even though he gave the child no financial support. Well, she had another child by him. Finally, the only way she thought she could get him out of her life was to change her name and move out west—which she did. What this young lady lacked, bless her heart, was a blue print in her mind of what kind of character the young man of her dreams ought to have. With the proper blue print in her heart, she probably wouldn't have allowed him more than the first conversation. Some of the finest young men in the church often make the same, fatal mistake. They marry a beautiful girl devoid of character who later, among other things, betrays her vows.

Selecting the wrong mate is one of the biggest mistakes people can make in life. It is so easy for young people, especially, to be blinded by someone's appearance and personality. They allow themselves to become friends with the wrong people, then begin dating and ultimately find themselves falling in love with and marrying the wrong person. By having a blue print of proper character traits and the knowledge of their incredible value when engrafted in one's heart, a person will be empowered to reject even the most handsome suitor if they are devoid or seriously lacking in this area. This leaves them open to finally receiving God's best.

MAINTAINING FOCUS

A great assist in maintaining focus on a particular character trait in the family, class, church or business is to make several quick posters for the trait. With computers, this can be done very easily by typing the name of the trait as large as possible with bold print on an 8 1/2 X 11 sheet of paper with the page layout on landscape.

ENTHUSIASM

The benefits of engrafting character are truly endless. May God's character bless you, your family, life, health, work and ministry.

Bibliography

[1] Loehr, Jim, *The Only Way To Win*, Cover 2012.

[2] Ibid, p. 62

[3] Ibid, p. 63

[4] Ibid, p. 44

[5] Pear, Robert, "Medical Mistakes Are Killers." *The Atlanta Journal-Constitution*, November 30, 1999.

[6] King, Mike, "Study says 14% Harmed as Patients." *The Atlanta, Journal-Constitution*, February 7, 1991

[7] ANAM, *God's Little Devotional Book for Leaders*, p.27

[8] *Words To Live By*. by William Nichols

[9] *Wikipedia*, www.widpedia.org, Muhammad Ali, pp 1–17, September 11, 2015

[10] 24 Celebrities Who Served In the Military, *Celebrities, Culture,, Editor's Choice*, www.ijreview.com, 2014

[11] Professional Atheletes and Coaches Who Served in the Military, www.losangerles.cbs

local.com, 2014

[12] Blueberries, www.womenfitness.net- April 29, 2011 pp 1–4.

[13] Cinnamon, healthdiataries.com, 4/29/11, health benefits of cinnamon, p.1

[14] Wheat germ, www.suite101.com/content/omega-fatty-acids-a196184

[15] Honey, www.honey.com/nhb/benefits & nutritional facts

[16] Milk, The Encyclopedia Britannica, Vol. 15, © 1969, p. 456r

[17] Milk, Health benefits, www.gotmilk.com, April 29, 2011

[18] Coffee—www.eatingwell.com with permission from © 2010 Eating Well Inc. p.1

[19] Towers, Chip, "Coolest Nerd on Campus." *Atlanta Journal-Constitution*, September 26, 2012, p C-1

[20] Gamble, David, *The Teaching Home,*."Dad, Contra Mundum, Aug/Sept 1989, p 55.

[21] Compiled primarily by Captain Tommy Clack from multiple data bases and records obtained from the VA and the DOD as of May 7, 2015

[22] Adapted from a chart by history professor Lucas Morel, www.abrahamlincolnonline.org/lincoln/education/failures.htm, which was compiled from the Chronology in selected *Speeches and Writings/Lincoln* by Don E. Fehrenbacher, ed., 1992.

[23] Wikipedia, www.wickipedia.org, R.G. LeTourneau, April 30, 2013

[24] Huckaby, Darrell, "Remembering Battle of Gettysburg." *The Rockdale Citizen,* July 3, 2013;

[25] Wikpedia. Www.wikpedia.org. "Battle of Gettysburg," pp1–26

[26] Menzies, Winston *The Spirit of Texas,* 2011, pp 247,248

[27] *211 of South Central Georgia Monthly News Letter,* date unknown

Index

Of Character Traits

NOTE TO READER: The character traits marked "Prudence" and "Wisdom" below are not found in alphabetical order in the main body of this book but are found under the sections on PRUDENCE and WISDOM.

TRAIT:	PAGE NUMBER	READER'S ORDER OF STUDY
ACCEPTANCE, SELF	27	_____
ACCURACY	31	_____
ADVENTUROUS	33	_____
ADVERSITY, ABLE TO OVERCOME	36	_____
AGREEABLE IN NATURE	38	_____
ALERTNESS	40	_____
ALL-THE-WAY ATTITUDE	43	_____
APPRECIATION	46	_____
ATTENTION TO DETAIL	49	_____
ATTENTIVENESS/ See ALERTNESS,	52	
ATTENTION TO DETAIL & THOUGHTFULNESS		
ATTITUDE, A POSITIVE	53	_____
AUDACITY	57	_____
AUTHENTICITY	60	_____
AVAILABILITY	62	_____
BATTLE, LOVING THE	65	_____
BEARING	67	_____
BEAUTY, A SENSE OF	69	_____
BEING A ONE WOMAN MAN	71	_____
BENEVOLENCE	75	_____
BOLDNESS	78	_____
CAN-DO-ATTITUDE	80	_____
CAPABLE, BEING	82	_____
CAREFUL IN FRIENDSHIP	85	_____
CAREFUL, CAUTIOUS AND CIRCUMSPECT, BEING	400	_____
A trait of Prudence		
CAREFULNESS	88	_____
CAUTIOUSNESS	90	_____
CHANGE, THE ABILITY TO EMBRACE	92	_____

CHARISMA	96	_____
CHARITY	98	_____
COMMIT, THE ABILITY TO	103	_____
COMPASSION	107	_____
COMPETENCE	110	_____
CONFIDENCE	111	_____
CONGENIALITY	113	_____
CONSCIENTIOUS	116	_____
CONSIDERATE, BEING	119	_____
CONSISTENT	122	_____
CONTENTMENT	124	_____
CONVICTIONS	127	_____
COOPERATION	129	_____
CORRECTION, THE ABILITY TO HEED	405	_____
A trait of Prudence		
COURAGE	134	_____
COURTESY	141	_____
CREATIVITY	143	_____
DECISIONS AS GOD WOULD, THE ABILITY	402	_____
TO MAKE A trait of Prudence		
DECISIVENESS	149	_____
DEFERENCE	151	_____
DEPENDABILITY	154	_____
DEPENDENT UPON THE LORD, SEEKING	416	_____
TO BE TOTALLY A trait of Prudence		
DETERMINATION	156	_____
DEVOTION	158	_____
DILIGENDCE A trait of Wisdom	527	_____
DILIGENT SEEKER, A	162	_____
DISCERNMENT A trait of Wisdom	521	_____
DISCIPLINE	164	_____
DISCIPLINE ONE'S SELF, THE ABILITY TO	393	_____
A trait of Prudence		
DISCRETION A treat of Purdence	408	_____
DISPATCH	167	_____
DOMINION	168	_____
DREAMER, BEING A	172	_____
DUTY	176	_____
EARLY, RISING	179	_____
EFFICIENT TIME MANAGER	181	_____
EFFICIENT, BEING	184	_____
EMPATHY	187	_____
ENCOURAGEMENT	188	_____
ENDURANCE	190	_____
ENERGY	192	_____
ENTHUSIASM	197	_____

EXCELLENCE 199 _____
FAIR, BEING or FAIRNESS 201 _____
FAITH 203 _____
FEARLESS, BEING 205 _____
FINISHER, BEING A 210 _____
FLEXIBILITY 211 _____
FOCUS, THE ABILITY TO 213 _____
FOLLOW THROUGH 215 _____
FOLLOWERSHIP 217 _____
FORBEARANCE 219 _____
FORGIVENESS 222 _____
FOUNDATION BUILDER, A 224 _____
FRANKNESS 228 _____
FRIENDLINESS 229 _____
FRIEND, A RAINY DAY 231 _____
FRUGALITY 233 _____
GENEROSITY 236 _____
GENTLENESS 238 _____
GOAL ORIENTED, BEING 241 _____
GRACE 247 _____
GRATEFULNESS 250 _____
HAPPINESS 253 _____
HARD WORKING 255 _____
HEART 258 _____
HEART AFTER GOD, A 260 _____
HEART TO BE A BUILDER, A 264 _____
HEART TO HAVE INFLUENCE, A 266 _____
HEART TO HONOR, A 269 _____
HEART TO KEEP RANK, A 271 _____
HEART TO KNOW GOD, A 273 _____
HEART TO LISTEN, A 276 _____
HEART TO PREPARE FOR BATTLE, A 278 _____
HEART TO STAND ALONE, A 284 _____
HEART WILLING TO SUFFER, A 287 _____
HEART TO TAKE A STAND, A 289 _____
HEART TO WORK FOR FAVOR, A 291 _____
HELPFULNESS 295 _____
HONESTY 296 _____
HOPE 297 _____
HOSPITALITY 301 _____
HUMILITY AND THE FEAR OF THE LORD 516 _____
   A trait of Wisdom
INDUSTRY 306 _____
INITIATIVE, TAKING THE 308 _____
INNOVATIVE, BEING 311 _____
INSPIRING 315 _____

INSULT, THE ABILITY TO OVERLOOK AN	317	_____
INTEGRITY	320	_____
INTREPID	322	_____
JOY or JOYFULNESS	325	_____
JUST, JUSTICE or BEING JUST	327	_____
JUST SPEECH A trait of Wisdom	531	_____
KINDNESS	329	_____
KNOWLEDGE, A HEART TO COLLECT AND RECORD A trait of Wisdom	518	_____
KNOWLEDGE, THE DESIRE TO SEEK AND BE CROWNED WITH TRUE A trait of Prudence	411	_____
LEADERSHIP	330	_____
LIVING IN THE MOST PRODUCTIVE PART OF THE DAY	333	_____
LOVE /see CHARITY	334	_____
LOYALTY	335	_____
MANAGEMENT OF RESOURCES, SKILLED IN THE A trait of Prudence	396	_____
MEEKNESS	338	_____
MISSION ORIENTED, BEING	340	_____
MOTIVATION	342	_____
MOXIE	345	_____
NEATNESS	347	_____
NO, THE ABILITY TO SAY	349	_____
OBEDIENCE	351	_____
OBEY AUTHORITY, THE WISDOM AND ABILITY TO A trait of Prudence	392	_____
OBSERVANT	354	_____
OPTIMISM	357	_____
ORDERLINESS / see NEATNESS and	358	_____
ORGANIZATION	359	_____
PATIENCE	362	_____
PATRIOTIC	367	_____
PEACE	370	_____
PEACEMAKER, THE HEART OF A	372	_____
PEOPLE PERSON, BEING A	374	_____
PERSEVERNCE	378	_____
PERSISTENCE/ See PERSERVERABCE	380	_____
PERSUASIVENESS	381	_____
PIETY	384	_____
POISE	387	_____
POSITIVE PHILOSOPHY, A	388	_____
PRUDENCE — DEFINED	390	_____
PUNCTUALITY	419	_____
PURITY	421	_____
PURPOSE	426	_____

QUALITY, INSISTENT UPON 429

READY, BEING 432

RELATIONSHIP, FAITHFUL IN 426

RELIABILITY / see FAITHFULNESS 440

RESILIENT 441

RESOURCEFULNESS 443

RESPECT FOR AUTHORITY AND OTHERS 448

RESPONSIBILITY, THE ABILITY TO ACCEPT 450

RESULTS ORIENTED / See MISSION ORIENTED, BEING 452

REVERENCE 453

RIGHT SPIRIT, A 456

RIGHTEOUSNESS   A trait of Wisdom 520

SECURITY, AN OVERWHELMING SENSE OF 459

SELF CONTROL 461

SELFLESSNESS 464

SELF-MOTIVATED 467

SENSITIVITY 468

SILENT AND KEEP KNOWLEDGE TO OURSELVES, KNOWING WHEN TO BE   A trait of Purdence 414

SINCERITY 470

STRAIGHTFORWARDNESS / See FRANKNESS 472

STATURE / See BEARING 472

SUFFER, A HEART WILLING TO 473

TEACHABLE, BEING 476

TEMPERANCE 480

TENACITY 482

THANKFULNESS 484

THOROUGHNESS/ See FOLLOWTHROUGH or BEING A FINISHER 485

THOUGHTFULNESS 486

THRIFT 489

TIMING 492

TOLERANCE 494

TRUE GRIT 496

TRUST 499

TRUTH, A HEART COMMITTED TO THE 501

UNDERSTANDING   A trait of Wisdom 525

VIGILENCE 505

VIRTUE / see PURITY 505

VISIONARY 506

VOLUNTEER SPIRIT, A 509

WISDOM — DEFINED 512

WORKING AS UNTO THE LORD 534

ZEAL 537